The Unending Frontier

THE CALIFORNIA WORLD HISTORY LIBRARY

Edited by Edmund Burke III, Kenneth Pomeranz, and Patricia Seed

The Unending Frontier

*An Environmental History
of the Early Modern World*

John F. Richards

UNIVERSITY OF CALIFORNIA PRESS

Berkeley   Los Angeles   London

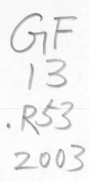

University of California Press
Berkeley and Los Angeles, California

University of California Press, Ltd.
London, England

© 2003 by the Regents of the University of California

Library of Congress Cataloging-in-Publication Data

Richards, John F.   The unending frontier : an environmental
history of the early modern world / John F. Richards.
     p.   cm.
   Includes bibliographical references and index.
   ISBN 0-520-23075-2 (cloth : alk. paper).
   1. Human ecology—History.   2. Nature—Effect of human beings
on—History.   I. Title.   II. Series.
GF13.R53   2001
304.2—dc21

                                        2001008658

Manufactured in the United States of America

12   11   10   09   08   07   06   05   04   03
10   9   8   7   6   5   4   3   2   1

The paper used in this publication is both acid-free and totally
chlorine-free (TCF). It meets the minimum requirements of
ANSI/NISO Z39.48–1992 (R 1997) (*Permanence of Paper*).

*The publisher gratefully acknowledges
the generous contribution to this book provided
by the General Endowment Fund
of the University of California Press Associates.*

To
Ann L. Richards

CONTENTS

MAPS

ix

TABLES

PREFACE

I am a firm believer in the value of world history. My preferred argument for doing world history is that history shapes identity and subsequent action. History writing and teaching shape social identity and human behavior. We desperately need a shared global identity that derives from knowledge and wisdom about a common human past. Hence my attempt in this book to write a world history, albeit one restricted to a few centuries and written from a single, somewhat narrow thematic perspective—that of environmental history. My original plan was to cover the entire period from 1500 to the present. This went by the wayside as I got involved in detailed synthesis and writing. I then decided to end the book at the outset of modernity in world history.

The Unending Frontier has evolved over years of teaching environmental history and world history. This has been an opportunistic, organic process. I did not set out with a master plan but worked up lectures and topics for my teaching based on books and articles that became available and that illustrated important environmental themes and questions. For example, the chapter on Japan originated in my reading of Conrad Totman's *Green Archipelago* when it first appeared about a decade ago. Similarly, I would never have attempted the chapter on Brazil if the late Warren Dean had not written *With Broadax and Firebrand,* his last and, to my mind, finest work. My interest in sugar landscapes grew out of lectures I drew from David Watts's historical geography, *The West Indies.*

Colleagues who have read and critiqued my entire manuscript at various stages include David Gilmartin, Richard Grove, John Headley, Martin Lewis, John McNeil, and Sanjay Subrahmaniam. Ken Pomeranz, editor of the series in which this book is placed, offered penetrating and helpful comments on the entire manuscript, as well as much encouragement. While writing this book, I adopted the practice of sending a draft version of each chapter to one or more experts in the field in question—usually those persons on whose work I relied most heavily. Nearly all responded generously with their comments and corrections. I wish to thank the late Jean Grove and Christian Pfister for comments on the climate chapter; Sucheta Mazumdar, Mark Elvin, and John Shepherd for assistance with China and Taiwan; Philip Brown for help with Tokugawa Japan; the late Jack Cell and Buchanan Sharpe for comments on the British Isles chapter; Jonathan Bone and David Moon for help with Russia and Siberia; Leonard Guelke for his comments on South Africa; Charlotte Kimber for reading the chapters on the West Indies; Peter Bakewell, Karl Butzer, Andrew Sluyter, and John TePaske for their comments on Mexico; Aline Helg for reading the chapter on Portuguese Brazil; Steven Buskirk, Denys Delage, Shepard Krech III, and Bruce Trigger for critiquing the North American fur trade chapter; Daniel Vickers for his assessment of the cod fisheries chapter; and Richard Ellis for reacting to the chapter on early modern whaling. I, of course, am responsible for any and all errors or omissions in the work.

A book of this sort, one that depends on access to and synthesis of published materials from many areas, could not have been written without Perkins Library at Duke University—one of the world's great research libraries. I thank my friends and colleagues on the Perkins staff, whose efforts I have always tried to support as a member of the Duke faculty and whose care and attention made my research on this book possible. Margaret Brill, Robert Byrd, Ashley Jackson, Deborah Jakubs, and Avinash Maheshwary, among others, have been especially helpful. We research scholars have good reason to be grateful to David Ferriero, University Librarian, and his predecessors, who champion the cause of Perkins Library both within and without the university. I also offer my thanks to Alan Tuttle, Director of the Library at the National Humanities Center, and his assistants Jean Houston and Eliza Robertson for their help in the last phase of my writing.

I have had the gift of time from various sources. The former chair of my department, Alex Roland, permitted me to adjust my teaching schedule so that I could have two semesters free of classroom requirements in order to write. One semester combined with a summer is equal to eight months of solid writing time. I am grateful to him for his support. I received a fellowship from the National Humanities Center that permitted me to complete the draft volume during the 2000–2001 academic year. This was a most welcome and timely respite funded by the MacArthur Foundation as part of its interest in environmental matters. Finally, my wife, Ann Richards, has encouraged me and cheerfully supported my writing for the past seven years. I dedicate this book to her.

Introduction

As the subtitle suggests, this book is an attempt to write environmental history on a global scale. The book's aim is to identify, describe, and reflect on the processes by which human beings intervened in the natural environment during the early modern period. From the late fifteenth century to the early nineteenth, the pace and magnitude of change increased in human societies in every part of the world. There were, moreover, shared processes of change of unprecedented intensity seen around the world.[1] Change in the early modern world forecast the direction of even greater changes to come during the nineteenth and twentieth centuries. Most dramatically, the total number of human beings nearly doubled, from 400 to 500 million in 1500 to 850 to 950 million in 1800.[2]

In this same period, human societies developed the largest, most complex, most efficient state and private organizations known since classical antiquity. The technology and organization of warfare became more effective and more devastating—especially with the use of firearms. During the early modern centuries, humans established new links—primarily by sea—around the entire world. In large measure because of maritime improvements, a new, truly global economy coalesced. Capital investment moved readily from one world region to another. Prices for commodities quoted in the urban centers of the new world economy sent signals to producers around the world. New commodities in increasing quantities and variety flowed to world markets. Monetary systems based on metallic forms of money—copper, gold, and silver—expanded and interlinked in new ways.

1. John F. Richards, "Early Modern India and World History," *Journal of World History* 8 (1997).
2. Ibid., 201.

Creation of a global system of transport and communication, begun in the early modern period, meant that human beings traveled long distances more readily than at any time in human history. Early modern land routes and connections became more passable. However, steady improvement in the safety, price, and capacity of sea travel was the primary accelerant to human mobility. A well-equipped and provisioned seagoing vessel manned by an experienced captain and crew could set out from virtually any port in the world and sail to any other port in the world, no matter how distant. Cultural mixing began the slow process of melding a genuine world culture (still in process at the turn of the second millennium). Aggressive trade, war, and settlement challenged and shocked isolated and insular local cultures and societies. A hesitantly emerging global consciousness was one of the most profound consequences of the speeded-up early modern circulation of peoples.

Verbal and written information passed between the world's regions and within regions at new levels of accuracy and quantity—aided by the rapid spread of printing. In addition to replication of prose, printing permitted replication of complex images in a boost to cartography and the natural sciences. Humans constructed a systematic, far more precise understanding of the shape, size, and complexity of the earth's surface and portrayed this understanding in ever more precise and widely read maps.[3] Identifying, naming, and classifying of the world's landforms, climates, minerals, human groups, animals, and plants proceeded at a dizzying pace. The natural sciences of today originated in the taxonomic impulses of enthusiastic observers who communicated their discoveries with great enthusiasm.

Societies in the early modern period still relied on human, animal, wind, and water power. Nevertheless, humans significantly altered the natural world before the industrial revolution. To be sure, the early modern period saw a number of important technological changes, but this was well before the widespread use of the steam engine as a new prime mover driven by fossil fuels. That invention, coupled with the scientific and technical revolutions that accompanied it, gave humans a previously undreamed-of capacity to manipulate the material world.[4] The industrial revolution marked a massive discontinuity in human history in ways that we are just now beginning to understand.

As the term *early modern* suggests, however, shared historical processes and long-term trends that accelerated in this period deeply influenced massive and growing human-induced environmental change during the nineteenth and twentieth centuries. There are profound continuities that link the environmental history of the early modern and modern worlds.

3. Jerry Brotton, *Trading Territories: Mapping the Early Modern World* (Ithaca, N.Y.: Cornell University Press, 1998).

4. Vaclav Smil, *Energy in World History* (Boulder, Colo.: Westview Press, 1994).

By means of illustrative case studies, this book offers a pan-global view of human impacts on the natural world—not the reverse. With the exception of the discussion of climatic change, each chapter describes anthropogenic change, or the effects of collective human action on the world's ecosystems. Using the relatively new approach called environmental history, the case studies measure material change to the extent that it can be determined. Every new historical approach creates its own sources simply by asking new questions of familiar documents. Practitioners in the new field also discover new sources ignored by more conventional historians in well-established fields. Therefore, for example, many travelers' accounts from this period offer up significant, but previously ignored, observations on environmental changes.

New insights also derive from modern scientific studies in biology, ecology, and environmental studies. These offer the environmental historian assistance in better defining the ecological implications of past human actions. Where possible, the book relies on detailed reconstruction of past environments done by historical geographers and historically minded ecologists. Where, unfortunately, these do not exist, discussion of environmental impacts becomes less precise and satisfactory. It is not easy to describe and assess environmental changes of the present, let alone those of the past.

Each chapter is a synthesis of scholarly and scientific materials written in or translated into English or French. In the best of all worlds, the author would be proficient in a half dozen more languages, but he is not. For better or for worse, English is today the most widely used language in global scholarly communication. Moreover, there exists an extensive historical literature in English for every world region in the early modern period. This literature usually includes English translations of important source materials.

Today, in a world with an increasingly shared world identity and world culture, it is important to begin writing world history. The results will be necessarily uneven and imperfect, skewed by those linguistic and cultural limitations invariably imposed on any single scholar. As in any other historical field, however, when multiple works appear, interpretations can be compared and critically assessed—and will be.

World history is not one grand narrative but rather must be written from multiple thematic, global perspectives that collectively illuminate humankind's common history. Environmental history is more than the sum of national environmental narratives. Instead, we must connect the issues and themes of environmental history with those of world history. If successful, this book will have made a contribution to world history as a genre as well as to environmental history. The long-term effects of human action are best seen in detail at the local level, but best understood in a holistic global perspective.

The book is made up of detailed case studies taken from nearly all parts of the world. These studies allow us to examine important shared processes of social and environmental change over the long term of three or more centuries. However, for some readers, the case studies examined in the book's chapters may take on a kaleidoscopic character. Each has juxtaposed details, colors, and shapes that form in unpredictable patterns. Each chapter relates a self-contained narrative with little direct connection or transition to the next. The criteria for inclusion, for choice of case study, may seem arbitrary, almost random. Interesting though the chapters may be, with insights and information not easily obtained, they are difficult to fit into a meaningful interpretation of environmental history and world history.

What, then, are the larger patterns and issues addressed in the book? What sorts of environmental impacts are we talking about? What is the global pattern? What shared historical processes do these case studies demonstrate? These historical processes are four in number: intensified human land use along settlement frontiers, biological invasions, intensified commercial hunting or the "world hunt," and energy and resource scarcities in core areas.

First and most important is the intensified human land use in every world region. Rising human numbers put increasing pressure on the land. Human settlement and sedentary cultivation expanded at the expense of forests, woodlands, wetlands, and savannas. Almost invariably such expansion caused a reduction in the quantity and diversity of vegetation or, to put it in other terms, a reduction in biomass and biodiversity. That is, sedentary cultivation depended on selection of one or a few favored plant species cultivated in plowed fields in place of a variety of grass, shrubs, and trees that had formerly occupied a newly cleared field. Agriculture was and continues to be the single most important means by which humans change the world's lands and its ecosystems.

The greater portion of new cultivation occurred in the ubiquitous frontiers of settlement.[5] In nearly every world region, technologically superior pioneer settlers invaded remote lands lightly occupied by shifting cultivators, hunter-gatherers, and pastoralists. Encouraged, directed, and subsidized by expansive states, surplus populations moved readily and easily to new areas promising employment or fertile land. In Africa, Eurasia, and the New World, they expelled, killed, or enslaved indigenous peoples enfeebled by low numbers, particularistic ethnicities and loyalties, susceptibility to new disease, and backward technology.

Expansive early modern states imposed new types of territoriality on frontier regions. Settlers and colonial regimes refused to recognize any existing

5. John F. Richards, "Only a World Perspective Is Significant: Settlement Frontiers and Property Rights in Early Modern World History," in *The Humanities and the Environment*, edited by Jill Conway, Kenneth Keniston, and Leo Marx (Cambridge: MIT Press, 1998).

property rights among indigenous peoples (or if they did so initially, these were soon abrogated). Instead, they viewed these lands as empty, to be claimed by the encroaching state. In turn, the colonizing state conferred property rights on its frontier settlers. These consisted of the usual bundle of rights common to settled societies in Eurasia: the rights to occupy, alienate, mortgage, and bequeath lands so owned. Often settlers were required to improve their lands by clearing and cultivation in order to retain them. Once property rights were guaranteed by state power, land markets emerged.[6] Cadastral surveying and mapping added new precision to notions of land ownership and aided nascent land markets.

As settlement frontiers advanced, human land use intensified and productivity per square kilometer rose. Simultaneously, biomass and biodiversity usually declined. Pioneers replaced forests, wetlands, grasslands, and other habitats with intensively cultivated fields and settlements. Rising market demand and declining transportation costs provided an outlet for timber and forest products such as potash, pitch and tar, meat and hides, medicinal plants, and waterfowl and other wild game that could either be hunted or grown by the new settlers. Rural industries such as iron smelting also made heavy use of abundant natural resources in newly opened regions of settlement.

Frontiers of settlement mark a significant change in the way humans use land and consume natural resources. In the Americas, in Africa, and in Eurasia, aggressive pioneers intruded on what they considered to be empty or waste lands so that they might occupy, settle, and cultivate the land by means of sedentary agriculture or commercial pastoralism. Numerous ethnic groups who practiced shifting cultivation, pastoralism, and hunting-gathering lost possession and ownership of their lands to new settlers. Many of these pioneers were Europeans sharing in the emerging maritime skills, military force, and state initiative that propelled European expansion around the world.

The terms *frontiersmen* and *pioneers* convey an image of lonely, intrepid, hardy venturers who fearlessly press deep into wildlands. These pioneers then tame the landscape and subdue its savage peoples. To a certain extent, this image, like all stereotypes, is accurate. Pioneer settlers were usually brave, often isolated, and often self-sufficient for lengthy periods. Frontier virtues such as self-reliance, independence, and resilience were manifest— so too were the frontier vices of cruelty, wastefulness, and ignorance.

Pioneer settlers changed the ecology of those regions they settled. Usually this took the form of obliterating older forms of cultivation and hunting and gathering in favor of more productive modes of sedentary agriculture and

6. Robert David Sack, *Human Territoriality: Its Theory and History* (Cambridge: Cambridge University Press, 1986).

livestock raising. In region after region, pioneers cleared land, drained wet-lands, irrigated dry lands, killed off wildlife, and expelled indigenous peoples in order to reduce biodiversity and biomass and thereby expand output.

Not generally recognized is the extent to which pioneer settlers on every frontier had to adapt to the specific ecological circumstances in which they found themselves. In every locality, there were peculiarities of moisture, soils, seasonality, temperature, flora, fauna, water tables, and dozens of other vari-ables to be learned. Some information came from the ecological knowledge of surviving indigenous peoples—but usually not enough. Often trial and er-ror produced solutions to problems of productivity and adaptation, but fre-quently these came only after difficulties and scarcities in the early years of settlement.

Stereotypes of settler frontiers are also misleading and distorted by the mythmaking propensities of collective memory. Every settler frontier in the early modern centuries depended heavily on linkages to a wider world. Every settler frontier required the active political, military, and fiscal en-gagement and support of an aggrandizing state. Every settler frontier rested on human energy and tools mobilized by means of capital investment and by market demand for frontier products. In the early modern world, virtu-ally all pioneer settlers funneled commodities obtained from cultivation, proto-industrial processing, hunting, and gathering to metropolitan mar-kets. All settlers were acutely aware of the larger forces that determined their success or failure.

Settler frontiers are transient episodes that leave evidence of their occur-rence. Physical changes such as the introduction, planned or accidental, of new species of plants, animals, insects, bacteria, and viruses can be recorded and mapped. Land cover and land use changes have direction and spatial ex-tent. The readily charted extension of new forms of human settlement can serve as a proxy indicator for manifold processes of change. Occurrences of cultural conflict and adjustment across the permeable membrane of the frontier can be recorded and mapped as well. Settlers learned from indige-nous peoples and from new ecosystems—often slowly and painfully. Indige-nous peoples rapidly learned more devastating lessons from encroaching settlers.

Determining just what constitutes frontier completion or maturity is of-ten difficult; frontiers of settlement signify a change from one form of hu-man exploitation of the natural world to another. Rarely do we find in the early modern period settlers moving into terrain wholly uninhabited by hu-man beings. Whether the earlier or the replacement form of land use was more exploitative or more sustainable is a vexed question. The Taino (Arawak) peoples of Hispaniola did not live in a pristine environment be-fore 1492. Their cumulative effect on the island ecosystems of the West In-dies was considerable. What is generally true, however, is that backward linkage of the frontier settler to the metropolis and the state was new. Insistent cultural signals and resource demands from a much larger society—an emergent world economy—got transmitted to the pioneer settlers and to those who survived among indigenous peoples.

Settler cultivation occasionally took the form of highly intensive industrial agriculture. Colonists cleared the rain forest landscapes of the West Indies, Atlantic Brazil, and the Canary Islands to grow and process cane sugar. Colonial planters imported African slaves to create a captive workforce. Plantation-grown cane sugar became one of the most valuable export products of the early modern world economy. Although limited in area, plantations obliterated complex ecosystems to create industrial platforms for the production of an export commodity.

Also associated with expanding cultivation was water control. Across Eurasia and the New World, early modern societies reclaimed tens of thousands of hectares of land either by draining wetlands or by bringing irrigation water to areas with scanty or unreliable rainfall. Successful wetlands drainage permitted new settlement of previously lightly inhabited lands, such as the fenlands of Britain's east coast. In China, state and local elites were continually engaged in water projects aimed at improving productivity of wet rice cultivation. Although significant, water control was not as important in large-scale environmental change as it later was to become, after introduction of the vast dams and perennial irrigation of the nineteenth and twentieth centuries.

The second major impact discussed is that of biological invasions tied to accelerating human mobility. During the early modern centuries, humans moved in greater numbers over longer distances and with greater frequency than ever before in human history. In various world regions, improved political conditions stimulated heavier overland traffic—especially on critically important routes such as the great highway to Edo in Tokugawa Japan—and modest improvements in bridges and road surfaces added speed and efficiency. However, the most significant leaps came in water transport. In Europe, China, Japan, Russia, and India, riverine transport grew to unprecedented volumes, sometimes aided by the growing number of artificial canals. In these same regions, coastal shipping rose exponentially as costs dropped and reliability and efficiency increased. The most spectacular advance lay in deepwater shipping, which by the end of the eighteenth century reliably tied human society in every inhabited world region with every other human society.

Human mobility encouraged world trade on a new scale and intensity. Traders moved commodities of all types faster, cheaper, and more reliably over longer distances than had occurred in the medieval centuries. Traders and merchants responding to market signals sought out, bought, packaged, and shipped both extracted natural resources and agricultural and industrial products from around the world. Even relatively low-priced, bulk commodities such as salt and timber could turn a profit in the growing world economy. As a result, humans gained access to and exploited natural resources—forests, marine mammals, fish, wildlife, and above all, fertile soils in favorable climates—that had been only lightly touched by human use, if at all.

When people traveled and migrated, so too did their associated animals, plants, insects, and viruses and other microorganisms. Intrusions into new ecosystems and landscapes by alien invaders became more common. Each human migrant or traveler carried with him or her a collection of associated animals, plants, and microbes in what Alfred W. Crosby has termed a "biological portmanteau."[7] The most notable effects resulted from the maritime link between the Americas and Eurasia and Africa. New animals and plants invaded the New World along with European and African human migrants, and many flourished in the absence of predators or other ecological checks to their reproduction. New World cultivars radically changed the diet and pharmacopoeia of the Old World. For example, as the chapter on early modern China points out, the adoption of maize in East Asia made it possible for pioneer settlers to better exploit marginal hill regions in East Asia. New World human populations previously unexposed to deadly microbes faced horrific pandemics. Returning migrants brought different diseases back to the Old World.

More than in any previous era, humans diffused exotic species of bacteria, insects, animals, and plants from their native habitats to new ecosystems scattered throughout the earth's land and waters. Some of these transfers and introductions were planned; far more were accidental. In its rising velocity of biological exchange, the early modern world forecast the bewildering speed of biological invasions recorded on a near-daily basis today.

During the early modern centuries, the numbers and range of Eurasian varieties of horses, cattle, sheep, goats, and pigs grew dramatically—especially in the New World. Colonial settlers seized upon the favorable ecological conditions for livestock raising that they found in the great grassland and savanna areas of mainland and island North and South America. By introducing domesticated ungulates, they intensified human use of ecosystems that were generally drier and less favorable to sedentary cultivation.

Ranchers (commercial pastoralists) built up herds of livestock and exported meat and hides to world markets. European colonists imported cattle, sheep, goats, and horses and dispersed them to graze and breed on grasslands and savannas previously inhabited only by wild animals. Commercial pastoralism became a worldwide industry that linked producing areas and markets on a global scale. Markets and prices for meat and hides were gen-

---

7. Alfred W. Crosby, *Ecological Imperialism: The Biological Expansion of Europe, 900–1900* (Cambridge: Cambridge University Press, 1986).

erally buoyant throughout the early modern period to 1800 and beyond. When new areas opened up for settlement, colonists adopted ranching as a satisfying and profitable way of life.

A third human-induced environmental impact was widespread depletion of larger animals, birds, and marine mammals. Early modern societies began the process of extirpation that was to culminate in the typical landscapes of the twenty-first century, from which virtually all large wild animals have vanished. Throughout the early modern world, for example, large predators that posed any conceivable threat to humans or their livestock died in unprecedented numbers. They lost habitat and prey to cultivated fields. Wolves, bears, tigers and other large cats, and other carnivores became the target of systematic hunting by pioneer settlers, who classed them as vermin to be killed in any way possible. Herbivores lost grazing areas to domesticated ungulates. Waterfowl lost habitat as marshes were drained. Other animals and birds whose fur, flesh, teeth, or feathers could be used by humans became prey for commercial hunters.

Increased human mobility encouraged the rapid growth of the "world hunt." In even the most remote regions on land and sea, hunters killed for the world market. Commercial hunters and gatherers killed off communities and species of wild fish, mammals, and birds, as well as trees and bushes, whose carcasses possessed value in the early modern world economy. Humans voraciously and systematically located, extracted, processed, packaged, shipped, priced, sold, and consumed wild animals in ever greater quantities over ever greater distances. Humans stripped wildlife from hitherto unexploited areas—a kind of windfall effect.

The rapidly growing world economy put traders in direct contact with indigenous peoples around the world who could cheaply extract timber, furs, and medicinal plants for commodity markets. Obsessive, market-driven modes of hunting and trapping were a new form of concentrated human intervention into complex ecosystems. Whereas previously humans in their hunting-and-gathering groups were but one of a number of predator species, commercial stimuli instilled in human hunters a new ruthlessness and ferocity. The most obvious effect of the world hunt was to extirpate target species of animals or birds from one region after another. However, the longer-term ecological consequences of market hunting for the world economy were complicated and probably more significant than we can reconstruct today. The effects on indigenous societies were also profound. Market hunting—when combined with political and military conquest—caused grave cultural, social, and ecological distortions that enfeebled those peoples caught in the new world economy.

The world hunt extended to the oceans. The world's northern oceans became hunting grounds exploited at a new scale and intensity. Early modern European seafaring proficiency and shipping provided access to greatly expanded ocean resources. For the first time, mariners outside the Mediterranean ventured beyond their coastal waters and voyaged long distances to hunt the fish, whales, seals, walruses, and other marine mammals of the world's oceans. The numbers of vessels and men employed, the capital invested, and the profits all rose steadily. In another resource windfall, fish and marine mammals became commodities in a steadily growing industry that brought cheap protein, oil, and other goods to landlocked consumers.

Building on experience, the sea hunters steadily accumulated greater knowledge and skill in their pursuit. Decade after decade, they deployed more cost-effective, more seaworthy vessels equipped with improved harpoons, nets, and processing tools. Distances traversed to reach good fishing grounds lengthened. When fish and mammal stocks were depleted in one region, hunters moved on to another, usually more remote, region. If one species was entirely depleted, hunters attacked another, less desirable species.

Other important concerns for environmental historians, such as the history of industrial pollution and urban environmental history, receive little attention in this book. Certainly, case studies of early modern industrial concentrations and their pollution and resource consumption could have been included, but are not. Similarly, comparative cases that illustrate sanitation, water supply, air pollution, and other environmental problems of early modern cities have been omitted. These processes, while manifestly important, are not as significant for world environmental history in this period as in the nineteenth and twentieth centuries. Most early modern cities had far smaller populations and areas with less extensive ecological footprints than modern cities have. Similarly, early modern industry was smaller in scale and had less impact on the environment than that seen today. Some industrial pollution associated with mining, as in the case of mercury used in the processing of New World silver mines, was significant and is discussed in this book.

In each chapter, there is a narrative of significant human impact on natural ecosystems. Around the early modern world, human populations consumed greater amounts of natural resources than ever before and often drastically changed natural habitats. They killed off some species of animals and birds and brought invading species to relatively undisturbed areas. They killed off, drove away, or enslaved weaker, less populous indigenous societies. Without question, this is a tragic story replete with brutality and waste. Ecologically rich regions suffered impoverishment and drastic change in a process that certainly can be termed degradation.

It is possible to tell this story simply as a tragedy that continues into the present day—a familiar story to all who hold deep concerns about the state of the world's natural environment. Many environmentalists and environmental historians view forest clearing as unfortunate and mourn the loss of wide expanses of forest cover. They deplore the killing off of large carnivores and other wildlife. They see sedentary cultivation and grazing as fundamentally negative activities that invariably lead to eroded soils and depauperate landscapes. Often they assume that catastrophic soil erosion must have followed the introduction of plow cultivation and large domesticated hooved livestock. For these environmentalists and historians, each case simply adds more proof of human callousness and greed and the dismaying ecological costs of these tendencies.

Such an approach, however resonant with our present-day fears and concerns, is distorting. It does not fully address the complexity of human interaction with the natural world in these centuries. Human action described in these chapters was usually purposeful in economic terms. For example, settlers who cleared forests did not do so for pleasure but aimed at supporting themselves by producing food and industrial crops for which there was a market demand. Hunters of whales did not embark on difficult and arduous voyages for sport. Instead, they hoped to bring scarce fats and a valuable industrial material (whalebone) to markets where these products were much in demand. Graziers and ranchers did not kill wolves or lions solely for pleasure. They were acting to defend their stock beset by a myriad of threats.

Our fourth and final theme reflects an early modern world of scarcity and uncertainty. From the relative comfort of the twenty-first century, we often ignore the deep-seated fears, insecurities, privations, and discomforts suffered by even the wealthiest and most powerful people in early modern societies. Food supplies were always precarious. Successive harvest failures meant malnutrition for many, even outright starvation amid the horrors of famines. Often war and the breakdown of public order made the effects of food scarcities more severe. Shipping surplus foods to regions stricken by dearth was not easy and often not even attempted.

Both individually and collectively, the drive to increase food production took on desperate urgency. Growing populations put intensifying demands on scarce natural resources—especially food and energy. By the eighteenth century, some societies in Eurasia clearly experienced growing scarcity and deprivation as they used up their resource endowments.

Two of the book's case studies examine the environmental impact of swelling populations in Japan and the British Isles—two of the most densely populated and productive core areas of Eurasia. The spiraling consumption of energy, food, and materials in these core regions began to collide with limited local and regional resources. Early modern cities and towns, stimulated by increased trade flows, added to their populations and converted neighboring rural tracts into urban settings. In the countryside, farmers cleared and plowed former grazing lands and other surplus areas. Often these were village lands managed by the village as a corporate entity under common property rules. As land became scarcer, villages felt pressure to privatize the commons.

Rising demands for energy put an enormous strain on local wood, peat, and other supplies of fuel. By the late eighteenth century, there were distinct signs of increasing materials and fuel scarcities. Both Japan and the British Isles suffered an energy crisis in common with other long-settled areas in Eurasia. Rising demand increased the scarcity of other natural resources too, such as wild game, freshwater fish, and wild plants. Diminished access to these virtually cost-free natural products hurt the living standards of peasants and other groups of rural inhabitants. Early modern Japan and Britain adopted very different methods to cope with energy and resource scarcity. Japan turned inward, toward conservation; Britain turned outward to seek new resources.

On the frontier, settlers found an unheard-of abundance of freshwater, nutritious pasture, fertile soil, forests and woods for the cutting, vast herds and flocks of edible wildlife that were easily hunted, and, frequently enough, valuable minerals. For the pioneer, natural gifts were to be had for the taking—along with natural hazards in the ill-understood new habitats. Nonetheless, the trope or theme of abundance resonated with the inhabitants of more densely settled regions, where resources were becoming scarce and expensive.

Moreover, when pioneer settlers brought new land under sedentary cultivation, they made landscapes more productive in economic terms. Each hectare of land put into row crops annually produced more food for more people than that same hectare had produced under the shifting cultivation of forest peoples. Each hectare of land used for livestock grazing generated more food for human use than it had provided before.

All depended on consistent, intelligent land managers.[8] Over several generations of farming and grazing, new settlers could by trial and error fine-tune their crops, fertilizers, methods, tools, and agricultural calendars to get acceptable yields year after year. With reasonably secure property rights, they could invest the energy and acquire the skill needed to reduce erosion and build up the quality of soils on their holdings. They could build terraces, drain wet areas, sustain woodlots, and carry out the hundreds of minute improvements that constitute good farming practice. They could continue to obtain part of their subsistence and their market products from hunting and gathering in remaining adjacent forests, jungles, savannas, or wetlands. The result was often a new, highly attractive, mixed countryside with great aesthetic appeal. Under appropriate, time-tested management, mixed landscapes can develop great resilience that permits them to continue to be productive and aesthetically appealing for centuries.

8. See Piers M. Blaikie and H. C. Brookfield, *Land Degradation and Society* (London: Methuen, 1987), 1–26.

It is easy to sympathize with the plight of those many indigenous peoples in the early modern world who suffered grievous losses. It is undeniable that, when these societies shattered, much that had been of great cultural and ecological value was lost. These are the peoples, quietly engaged in shifting cultivation with hoe and fire stick supplemented by hunting and gathering, who were expelled or killed by more powerful and technically advanced outsiders. It is clear that the resource needs of these indigenous peoples were less demanding of forests, jungles, savannas, and other ecosystems than those of the sedentary cultivators who succeeded them. It is reasonable to assume that these peoples lived in greater harmony with their natural environment and displayed greater sensitivity toward and knowledge of its vegetation and fauna.

Whether these many societies and cultures had developed sustainable practices that permitted continuing use of the land on a long-term basis is uncertain. We too-readily romanticize the relationship between such peoples and nature. Whether their demands on their habitats were really sustainable over centuries is a question that only painstaking research by archaeologists and linguists can find answers to. This book does not pretend to examine this question. Instead, several of its case studies describe and reflect on the responses of indigenous peoples to settler pressures and the stimuli of a new market demand for wildlife.

To summarize, fully nuanced environmental history should not present human-induced environmental change as an unrelieved tragedy of remorseless ecological degradation and accelerating damage. It is far too easy to see irreversible decline—to underestimate the resilience of ecosystems and to overestimate human-induced impacts as opposed to natural processes (e.g., in soil erosion). For example, conservationists and environmentalists have tended to regard the savannas of the Mediterranean world as forests degraded by overgrazing and tree cutting. In so doing they have extolled the virtues of the past undisturbed landscapes and mourned the depauperate state of Mediterranean "treed grasslands."[9] In their recent ecological history of Mediterranean Europe, A. T. Grove and Oliver Rackham take the opposite view:

> Conservationists are obsessed with what are (often wrongly) regarded as "undisturbed" ecosystems, and neglect the merits of cultural ecosystems. Savanna—whether natural or cultural—forms some of Europe's most beautiful landscapes, and supports many human activities. . . . Particularly important are savannas that have old grassland or ancient trees. The juxtaposition of abundant insect food, nectar from flowers, and nesting cavities in tree-holes

9. A. T. Grove and Oliver Rackham, *The Nature of Mediterranean Europe: An Ecological History* (New Haven: Yale University Press, 2001), 213.

sustains complex food chains. On the scale of conservation values savanna should come at least as high as forest.[10]

Browsing and grazing by livestock is crucial to the maintenance of savannas. If livestock are absent, Mediterranean savannas, depending on the mixture of soil and plants, infill with trees or with dense thickets of "tall, aggressive, very combustible grasses and undershrubs."[11]

Humans are part of nature, and they must act in order to survive. The benefits to human productivity and well-being that accrue from intervention in the natural environment and active management of the land and resources should also be assessed. Landscapes and ecosystems heavily affected by human action are not necessarily barren, unstable, or degraded. Over generations in many societies, land managers have devised ways to sustain productivity and retain desirable resources and aesthetic features on the land. Environmental history must be attentive to the dilemmas, the concerns, the motives, and the contexts of all historical actors, whether individuals or collectivities.

10. Ibid., 214.
11. Ibid., 215.

PART I

The Global Context

Chapter 1

The Early Modern World

THE ARGUMENT

During the early modern centuries, for the first time in human history, a truly global, interconnected society rapidly knit together. After 1500, a world economy took shape that stimulated economic productivity in every region. How and why did this new, interrelated world emerge at this time? The answer lies in a critical conjuncture between two developments: the expansive dynamism of European early modern capitalist societies, and the shared evolutionary progress in human organization that appears to have reached a critical threshold across Eurasia, if not the entire world.

In every world region, this conjuncture strengthened and fused early modern states (and quasi-state structures such as chartered trading companies) and markets and raised them to new levels of capacity and efficiency. These newly powerful institutions, acting in concert, intensified human impacts on the natural environment of nearly every region in the world.

Western Europe unquestionably played a disproportionately large role in shaping the early modern world and what may well be termed a world system. To state this is not to succumb to mindless Eurocentrism but simply to acknowledge an obvious fact. To what extent western Europe's dominance and its role as the site of the industrial revolution emerged from qualities peculiar to European history, genes, culture, and social institutions is a bitterly contested issue. The answer is unclear, to say the least, and not the concern of this book. What is manifest, however, is that the western European presence around the world, and western Europe's resource demands at home, caused important environmental effects in many world areas during the sixteenth century through the mid–nineteenth century.

Numerous long-term trends in western Europe joined to produce an explosive mixture of aggressive expansionism. In that region, strong central-izing states pressed eagerly for more resources, more production, and more territory. These states benefited from and encouraged technical progress—especially maritime and military—and fostered improved mechanisms for trade, production, and investment. Those groups concerned with profit, with capital accumulation, gained increasing influence over rulers and elites. Europe's maritime dominance over global sea routes lay at the heart of its political and economic strength. The dynamism of western Europe shaped a new world system.

Western Europe became primary beneficiary of the capitalist world econ-omy mainly by controlling interregional maritime trade. Markets centered in that region directed the exploitation of natural resources on a world scale. Europeans profited from wide-ranging commercial exploitation that made cheap resources flow into Western cities. Conversely, the demand for west-ern European goods soared with colonial expansion. As a result, large seg-ments of the European population enjoyed a higher standard of living than they would have otherwise. James Blaut concisely summarizes this argument:

> Before 1492, most of the preconditions that would be critical for the eventual rise of industrial capitalism were present not merely in parts of Europe but also in parts of Asia and Africa. After 1492, in the sixteenth and seventeenth cen-turies, Europe acquired three additional preconditions. One was the very con-siderable accumulation of wealth from the mines and plantations of America and from trade in Asia and Africa. The second, closely related to the first, was the huge enlargement of markets outside of western Europe for products either produced in western Europe or imported and then reexported; that is, a very great and almost constantly growing demand. Third, and most important of all, the social sectors involved with capitalism took political power on a wide scale in western Europe, something that had not happened elsewhere except on very small terrains. This, the bourgeois revolution, allowed the emerging capitalist class-community to mobilize state power toward its further rise.[1]

It is true that Patrick O'Brien has argued, in a formulation widely ac-cepted among early modern historians, that the quantitative dimensions of international trade with the rest of the world imply that external commerce was not that important for capital formation in western Europe. In addition, this European economic development in the early modern period was pri-marily due to internal economic forces. However, more recently, O'Brien, while maintaining his basic conclusion, has conceded that "without the dis-coveries and expansion of European power into Asia, Africa, and the Amer-icas, the European economy (in Victorian times) would have been poorer,

---

1. James M. Blaut, *The Colonizer's Model of the World: Geographical Diffusionism and Eurocentric History* (New York: Guilford Press, 1993), 201.

the composition of its output would have been more agricultural and less industrial in form[,] and lower proportions of its work force would have been employed in industry and resident in towns. Europe's potential for further and even more rapid advance—based upon indigenously generated science and technology—could have been restrained."[2]

Early modern western Europe took the lead in systematic understanding of the natural world. It was primarily European explorers, missionaries, merchants, whalers, seafarers, military officers, diplomats, scientists, and travelers who sent immense volumes of information pouring back to European capitals by letter, report, and word of mouth. Europeans at home received, processed, analyzed, synthesized, and recorded this torrent of data and eagerly sought more. The onset of movable-type printing and the growth of a publishing industry made wide dissemination of text and engraved images easy and, by comparison with hand-copied manuscripts, cheap. Intellectuals, whether associated with universities or not, voraciously consumed the information received. Rulers and trading companies sent out hundreds of exploring expeditions—usually accompanied by experts—aimed not at immediate profit but at gaining greater geographic information that would later return higher profits. Writers—some official, some unofficial; some commissioned, some acting independently—synthesized and popularized all forms of incoming data about the world.

Europeans were continuously engaged in a massive taxonomical exercise in which they named the parts and inhabitants of the world. European mapmakers identified, located, and named the world's seas and their wind patterns; its capes, headlands, bays, and harbors; its rivers and lakes; its mountain and hill ranges and passes, deserts, rain forests, fertile plains, and river deltas; its varied climate and seasonal regimes. Europeans engaged in a new global cartographic effort to lay out the surface of the entire world and to develop a system of universal coding by which every point on the globe was assigned a unique location according to determined latitude and longitude. They encountered and identified the distinctive physical appearance and cultural traits of thousands of distinctive ethnic groups of peoples in all the world's regions, and spatially located these peoples, no matter how isolated. They encountered, observed, classified, and named the world's trees, bushes, grasses, and flowers with due attention to possible economic uses. They encountered, observed, classified, and named the world's domestic and wild animals, birds, and fish and made a beginning at similar taxonomies of insects.

2. Patrick O'Brien, "European Economic Development: The Contribution of the Periphery," *Economic History Review,* 2d ser., 35 (1982): 39. See also O'Brien, "The Foundations of European Industrialization: From the Perspective of the World," in *Economic Effects of the European Expansion, 1492–1824,* edited by José Casas Pardo (Stuttgart: In Kommission bei F. Steiner, 1992), 463–502.

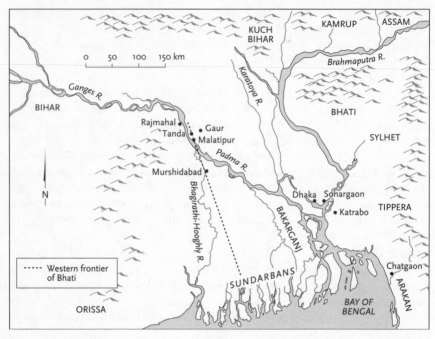

Map 1.1 Bengal in the Mughal age. Adapted from Richard Eaton, *The Rise of Islam and the Bengal Frontier, 1204–1760* (Berkeley and Los Angeles: University of California Press, 1993), map 4.

They found and wondered over fossils and geologic strata revealed to them in various regions of the world.

During this period, the new sciences of botany, zoology, and geology began to take shape. The older disciplines of history and geography became far more sophisticated. Methods of navigation on land and sea and systematic cartography became much more accurate and sophisticated. Systematic taxonomies of plants and animals that would become part of a new world culture emerged. By the eighteenth century, primarily because of systematic observation and recording of data, some intellectuals began to perceive the impact of human activity on the natural world.[3] Episodes of deforestation around the world triggered concerns about climate change and energy sources. Principles of forest management were debated and diffused among a far-flung intellectual constituency.

Knowledge of the natural world conferred power over previously unused natural resources across the globe. Rising human productivity in the six-

3. Richard Grove, *Green Imperialism: Colonial Expansion, Tropical Island Edens, and the Origins of Environmentalism, 1600–1860* (Cambridge: Cambridge University Press, 1995).

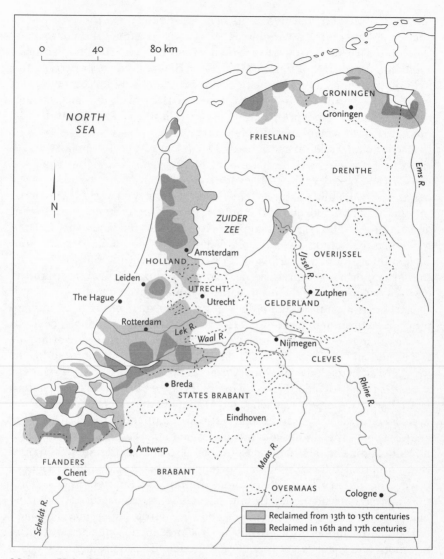

Map 1.2 United Provinces in the golden age, showing areas reclaimed from the sea, river estuaries, and lakes in medieval and early modern times. Adapted from Jonathan I. Israel, *The Dutch Republic: Its Rise, Greatness, and Fall, 1477–1806* (Oxford: Clarendon Press, 1995), maps 1 and 11.

teenth, seventeenth, and eighteenth centuries relied on improved access to abundant, low-cost natural resources. Resource extraction driven by the consolidating early modern world economy required intensified human management and control of the world's lands and, increasingly, its oceans. Human intervention caused dramatic changes in landscapes, ecosystems, and habitats around the world between 1500 and 1800. With demonstrated effectiveness came rising pride in human capabilities and a new, confident attitude toward the manipulation of nature.

Accumulating scientific insights and technical advances stimulated an appetite for intervention in the natural world. Advancing knowledge about the true size and nature of the globe made some humans more confident. They began to see unending natural abundance in an enlarged world as the source of wealth, profit, and material comfort. Proper organization, investment, and planning could convert wild places to domesticated landscapes suitable for human habitation. Even the sea could be diked off and the sea bottom turned into productive farmland. The ultimate civilizing mission became that of exploring, comprehending, and controlling the wild places of the earth in order to make them agreeable to human life and work.

European dynamism alone does not explain the full range of human-induced environmental change across the globe. Human-induced environmental change occurred in societies and regions where European impact was muted and indirect. Historians and other scholars rarely give sufficient weight to an extended evolutionary process in human history—a process of social learning, or adaptation.[4] This is the process by which individuals learned from experience and engaged in adaptation to meet their needs and wants in a satisfactory (rather than optimal) manner. By the early modern centuries, new social units and ideologies had emerged from individual innovation. Some adaptations were possible in some societies; some were not. By painful trial and error, human societies had become more proficient at organizing and managing the relations of humans with each other and human interaction with nature. Despite periods of regression, disaster, and loss of collective memory, humans managed to learn from experience. So-called traditional premodern society was never static. Small, often unnoticed innovations and changes slowly improved human life and productivity.

By the fifteenth century, human institutions had reached an evolutionary threshold—and were poised to attain a new level of complexity and capabil-

---

4. Stephen K. Sanderson, *Social Transformations: A General Theory of Historical Development* (Cambridge, Mass.: Blackwell, 1995). This theory of social evolution is based on the theoretical arguments of Stephen Sanderson. *Adaptation* is Sanderson's term; *social learning* is mine. Sanderson argues that the early modern transition to capitalism in Europe and Japan is an example of what he calls evolutionary materialism. This breakthrough rested on continuing, slow progress in world commercialization. I see slow progress in creating and operating complex, large-scale states and other organizations as equally important.

ity. The results of a recent symposium devoted to early modern comparative history across Eurasia support this argument. When the convener, Victor Lieberman, juxtaposed comparative data for Japan, Burma, Siam, Vietnam, France, and Russia, he detected a "little noted Eurasian pattern between c. 1450 and 1830 whereby localized societies in widely separated regions coalesced into larger units—politically, culturally, and commercially." Among these six disparate areas, he found several parallel developments. In each region, a political core engaged in territorial consolidation "of what had been fragmented, localized units." Each of these states "sought to strengthen their extractive, judicial, and military functions, and systems of provincial control." Each polity displayed growing political sophistication with a wider political vision, as well as "accumulating institutional expertise" in the structures and policies of the state.[5]

In each region, the state-building project involved imposing on central and provincial elites a "complex of linguistic, ritual, and stylistic practices" in a process of lateral cultural integration. At the same time, there occurred vertical penetration of elite culture and high tradition into popular culture, so that "the entire population of the country/kingdom became more distinct from people in adjacent countries." With more effective power and resources, each state sought greater power over religious organizations and doctrine and tighter monitoring and control over social behavior generally.[6]

These conclusions are consistent with those observed for other early modern states. Compare Vincent Cornell's conclusions about sixteenth-century Morocco:

> The 16th-century Sa'did dawla [state] was beginning to look remarkably like an absolutist state of 17th-century Europe—at least in terms of its ultimate developmental goals. The actual or projected acquisition by Sa'did Morocco of stable, "internationally" recognized boundaries, territorial contiguity, a common ideology and culture, state control of the means of force, control over geopolitical jurisdiction, control over the types and means of production, control over the circulation of currency, and control over taxation and expenditure—all of which, when added together, would signify the existence of a "nation."[7]

These essentially political successes occurred in a symbiotic relationship with dynamic economic growth. The latter rested on demographic increase, intensified international trade, and expanding literacy (with or without the aid of printing). Simultaneously, each state was deeply involved in building mil-

---

5. Victor Lieberman, "Transcending East-West Dichotomies: State and Culture Formation in Six Ostensibly Separate Areas," *Modern Asian Studies* 31 (1997): 468, 473, 474, 520.

6. Ibid., 479, 482.

7. Vincent J. Cornell, "Socioeconomic Dimensions of Reconquista and Jihad in Morocco: Portuguese Dukkala and the Sa'id Sus, 1450–1557," *International Journal of Middle East Studies* 22 (1990).

itary strength in the context of the new handgun and artillery technology. The soaring costs of new weapons, and the fortifications needed to withstand them, favored the largest and wealthiest polities. Military efforts stimulated both domestic production and external trade.

Around Eurasia and Africa, evolutionary progress improved and speeded trade, markets, and monetization and raised human productivity in industry and agriculture. In every world region, centralizing states building their military strength attained new territorial extent and new capabilities. They offered new levels of protection and reduced protection costs for merchants and traders in deepening and widening markets. Early modern states increased industrial production directly in state-owned enterprises. They offered subsidies and encouragement to preferred private industrial and trading enterprises. They created more reliable and useful monetary systems based on coinage minted with New World silver and gold. They converted more of their revenue systems from politically grounded tribute demands to taxation determined by productive capacity. State revenue demands on agriculture forced producers to market increasing shares of their harvests to obtain money to meet those tax assessments.

Stronger, more efficient early modern states and markets intensified and extended human impacts on the world's lands. States and markets encouraged voracious consumption of new, varied natural resources from even the most sparsely populated, seemingly marginal areas of the globe.

If we look at two other dissimilar early modern states—one an Asian land empire and one a European maritime state—we find additional support for the proposition that the more complex and capable large-scale human organizations exerted powerful pressures on the world's environment. During the seventeenth century, the Mughal Empire in India and the Dutch Republic in western Europe were among the most successful states in the world. The population and territory of the Mughal emperor were exceeded only by those of the Qing emperor of China. The complex institutions of the Mughal Empire were the product of a millennium of Indo-Muslim state building in South Asia. India's dense population powered a subcontinental economy of prodigious productivity. By contrast, the Dutch Republic's population and territories were but a tiny fraction of those of the Mughal emperor. However, the Dutch oligarchies presided over the richest, most active and aggressive maritime trading nation at that time. They also directed and nurtured what has been termed the world's first modern economy. Moreover, the Mughal Empire and the Dutch Republic were closely tied together in a symbiotic trading relationship mediated by the Dutch East India Company.[8]

8. John F. Richards, "Mughal State Finance and the Premodern World Economy," *Comparative Studies in Society and History* 23 (1981).

THE MUGHAL EMPIRE

For nearly a millennium, from the late seventh century onward, Muslim conquerors from the Islamic lands to the northwest of India gained dominant power over the Hindu-Buddhist social and cultural realm of the Indian subcontinent. Behind a slowly moving military frontier, successive Indo-Muslim rulers created states that were generally more centralized than the indigenous polities they conquered and assimilated. By the early thirteenth century, Indo-Muslim armies had traveled from Afghanistan to reach the central Indo-Gangetic plain and had established their capital at Delhi. The sultans of Delhi directed a series of long-distance military campaigns against non-Muslim kingdoms in the Deccan region and South India. So successful were their efforts that, by the end of the fourteenth century, Indo-Muslim rulers controlled most of the territory and populace of the subcontinent. Initially ruled from Delhi, the empire soon broke up into regional sultanates.

One of the foremost goals of these new states was to improve, expand, and intensify the existing land tax system by which the ruler demanded at every harvesttime a fixed share—increasingly paid in coin rather than produce—of the total agricultural produce of his realm. Indo-Muslim rulers also encouraged, by every means at their command, land settlement, forest clearing, and the extension of cultivation. Whenever possible, they encouraged cultivators to grow specialized cash crops. They founded and built markets and towns and provided the security necessary for these to flourish and for internal trade to develop. By the sixteenth century, the first Mughal rulers had inherited a vital, confident tradition of conquest, territorial assimilation, and state building, all resting on systematic expropriation of an agricultural surplus from the peasantry of India.[9]

The founding of the Mughal Empire dates from the victories of Babur, descendant of Timur and Chingiz Khan, over the Afghan Lodi Sultans of Delhi in 1526 and a confederacy of Hindu Rajput rulers in 1527. After Babur's death in 1530, his son and successor, Humayun, lost a series of campaigns against another powerful Afghan prince, was driven into exile in Persia, and returned to power in Delhi in 1555, just before his accidental death the next year. It was only during the half-century reign (1556–1605) of his son, Akbar, that the institutions and ethos of the mature Mughal Empire took shape. There emerged a distinctive Mughal cultural style and aesthetic based on sumptuous display and incalculable wealth that put its imprint on every region in the subcontinent.

9. John F. Richards, *The Mughal Empire*, vol. 1 of *The New Cambridge History of India* (Cambridge: Cambridge University Press, 1993). Unless otherwise noted, this section draws on material from *The Mughal Empire*.

Above all else, the Mughal Empire was a war state. Successive emperors remained preoccupied with war and needed little excuse to attack their neighbors. Throughout Akbar's reign and that of his three successors—Jahangir, Shah Jahan, and Aurangzeb—the Mughals were continually victorious against all challengers to their authority on the subcontinent. For a century and a half, Mughal armies continued to add new territories to the area directly ruled and administered by the emperor. Imperial warfare paid for itself. Tribute, plunder, and new revenues flowed into imperial coffers in amounts that offset the costs of conquest and expansion.

The Mughal Empire was a very large entity. By 1690, the twenty-one provinces of the Mughal Empire comprised some 3.2 million square kilometers—nearly all the lands of the Indian subcontinent save for the extreme southern tip.[10] At that date, the Mughal emperor was the acknowledged ruler of the approximately 100 million or more people living in those territories.

The Mughal Empire was a centralizing state. Members of the Timurid dynasty were extremely capable rulers who acted as their own chief executives. Men, money, information, and resources moved regularly and routinely throughout the empire by imperial order. The emperor commanded cadres of officials and military commanders of proven loyalty who carried out his orders in every province. Imperial officials served at the pleasure of the emperor and were available for transfer at a moment's notice to the most remote corner of the empire. The single imperial language was Persian, in which all official documents generated above the purely local level were written.

The Timurid rulers created a compelling image of grandeur, wealth, and supreme authority surrounding the person of the emperor. During daily public court audiences, as depicted in numerous Mughal book paintings, serried rows of imperial officers stood and bowed before the emperor on his throne. The emperor's contact with and authority over each of hundreds of high-ranking officers was a critical fulcrum of the empire. Each day the emperor awarded honorific garments sanctified by contact with his body to favored officers, religious figures, ambassadors, or local chiefs. Each day he awarded increases in ranks, new titles, choice assignments to favored officials and military commanders, and, less often, demotions and censure to those who displeased him. At each public audience, reports from the cadre of news writers deployed around the empire were read aloud and the emperor responded to them. The emperor also issued a stream of edicts, letters, and orders to provincial governors, army and fortress commanders, and city governors. Inserted in bamboo containers, these documents moved by relays of postal runners at the fastest possible pace from one end of the empire to another.

The Mughal Empire was an agrarian, not a maritime, empire. Territorial

10. Habib, *An Atlas of the Mughal Empire.*

expansion occurred by land, not by sea. The ruling Timurid dynasty based its wealth and power on the state's ability to tap directly into the enormous agrarian productivity of a greater and greater share of the lands of the Indian subcontinent. The emperor claimed a share of the harvest from each of his rural subjects. Indian peasant-farmers were extraordinarily skillful and productive. Despite the risks when the monsoons failed to materialize, they managed to produce two crops per year on a large proportion of their fields. For the regime, any measure that expanded sedentary plow cultivation— whether rice, wheat, or millet based—increased state revenues.

During the early period of Mughal rule, existing land-tax systems varied widely. Depending on a number of variables, the amount demanded could be relatively high or extremely low. It could resemble tribute exacted by negotiation or it could be a more systematic tax based on measured productive capacity. The tax could be paid in produce as a share of the harvest, or it could be paid in cash, in imperial coin. It could be paid by a chain of intermediaries between the producing village community and the state. Alternatively, it could be a direct transaction between individual villages and their officers and imperial officials.

The ultimate goal of the Mughals was to impose a uniform or regulation tax system, rather than a tribute system, throughout the empire. They aimed at fixing upon each cultivator and his fields a tax demand based on an evaluation of relative productivity. They wished to shunt aside and neutralize the position of rural aristocrats, to scrape away the hard, resistant shell of local warlord power in the countryside in order to deal directly with peasant communities. They wanted to collect not produce but money in imperial coin. Successive emperors made steady progress toward this objective from the mid–sixteenth century to the early eighteenth.

The Mughal Empire was highly monetized. Rather than collect food grains in kind to store and use as salary payments, as did the rulers of Tokugawa Japan, the Mughal emperors insisted on payments of taxes made in imperial coin. The regime relied on the operation of powerful, flexible market systems and a high-volume, high-quality coinage to make this policy work.

The Mughal emperors imposed a uniform trimetallic coinage system throughout the empire. Only imperial coin could be used to pay taxes, and the regime used only its own coin to pay its officials and soldiers. Minting was open and accessible to anyone possessing either bullion or foreign or anachronistic coins on payment of a mint fee. Imperial mints turned out tens of millions of coins in gold, silver, and copper. All coins issued were of high metallic purity and noteworthy design and manufacture. During the sixteenth century, the basic coin was the heavy copper dam used in great quantities for taxes, wages, commodity purchases, and other routine exchanges. By the early seventeenth century, as the value of copper climbed relative to silver, the silver rupee became a commonly used coin. Copious supplies of

New World gold and silver, and Japanese silver, flowed into Mughal mints for coining. Throughout the period of the centralized empire, until the 1720s, no debasement occurred in Mughal coin. Gold issues remained nearly pure and silver rupees never dropped below 96 percent purity.

Land revenue demands constituted about nine-tenths of regularly imposed Mughal taxes. The land tax acted like a giant pump that pulled food grains and other crops into the market system and made the surplus available for the state and for urban populations. Coin paid by grain dealers and traders for agricultural produce flowed into the countryside temporarily. Cash obtained by rural society rapidly flowed out, partly in the form of market purchases of salt, iron, and other commodities and as tax payments to imperial treasuries. State cash disbursements to several million persons drawing their salary and support from imperial and noble households and from military service sent a flow of payments for goods and services back into the economy.

The remaining one-tenth of revenues came from customs duties of between 2.5 and 5 percent of value imposed at major markets, seaports, and land frontier posts, from licenses and fees levied on groups of urban merchants and craftsmen, and from profits made by the prolific imperial mints, among other miscellaneous sources. Not so regular, but certainly of great importance, was a continuing flow of plunder and tribute into the imperial coffers. Ongoing territorial expansion meant that plundered royal hoards augmented the emperor's finances. Tribute payments imposed on subordinate principalities not yet conquered were another source of imperial income.

Under the regulation land revenue system (zabt) devised during Akbar's long reign (1556–1605), imperial officers carried out cadastral surveys to determine on a field-by-field basis the area under plow cultivation. Simultaneously, they gathered data on the crops grown, the average yields by quality of soil, and market prices paid for both the fall and spring harvests. They measured lands irrigated by wells or water diverted from rivers. With area, yield, and price data in hand, officials established tabular data from which to calculate a standard assessment for each field that could be summed to arrive at an annual revenue demand for the lands of each village community. The regime demanded about one-third of the harvest of food grains such as rice, wheat, and millet, and about one-fifth of the worth of more valuable salable crops such as tobacco, vegetables, poppy, sugar, and indigo. Imperial officers assessed fruit trees at so much per tree and domestic livestock at so much per animal. The state encouraged expansion by offering tax-free periods for those who brought new land into cultivation.

To collect the land tax, the Mughals had to deal with the locally entrenched rural aristocrats, known as zamindars. Most were Hindus who were chiefs and heads of lineages long subordinated by Muslim power. A minority were Muslims, some of them converts from Hinduism. Many zamindars descended from land-clearing pioneer settlers who drove off or enslaved in-digenous "tribal" non-Hindu groups. These rural aristocrats were dispersed throughout the Indian countryside in fortified residences that included ar-mories, treasuries, temples, or mosques as well as their living quarters. Of-ten zamindari headquarters were the impetus for the growth of small rural towns and markets. They deployed armed retainers in numbers ranging from a handful to several hundred or more. By coercion and the working of a complex web of kinship and caste ties, zamindars claimed a hereditary right to exact a share of the harvest from the peasant village communities that surrounded their headquarters. A zamindar's domain might be as tiny as a half dozen villages and as large as a hundred or more.

The regime's fixed goal was to reduce the power of these rural aristocrats by turning them into quasi officials socialized into the wider imperial cul-ture. The Mughals, like previous Indo-Muslim rulers, identified and recog-nized each zamindar by conferring a written patent of office in return for a written bond and monetary payments. Heirs to zamindari estates had to be confirmed anew when succession occurred. Zamindars thus favored were as-sured of imperial help in maintaining their power and position against ag-gressive lineage mates or invading neighbors. They received an allowance of 10 percent of the assessed land revenue, which they helped to collect, and were given tax-exempt homelands worked by tenant peasant cultivators. The state also fixed the boundaries of their holdings and intervened to prevent internecine warfare among the zamindars.

The Mughals divided the empire into primary territorial units called *par-ganas*. Each named *pargana* contained within its boundaries several small towns and market centers and from twenty to a hundred or more contiguous villages. Groups of *parganas* formed districts, and groups of districts formed provinces. The regime calculated and listed an assessed revenue valuation for each village, *pargana*, district, and province in the empire.

The *parganas*, usually the domains of several zamindars, formed the ad-ministrative unit through which the regime tried to gain access to the land revenue. The Mughal goal was to convert what had been miniature feudal kingdoms paying tribute into a petty administrative and fiscal unit defined by the emperor. The regime appointed a leading zamindar chief to be head of each *pargana* (called *chaudhuri* in the north and *deshumukh* in the south), whose primary responsibility was to ensure that the state's land tax was turned over as assessed. The regime also appointed a *pargana* account keeper from literate secretarial castes, usually Brahmin, to maintain revenue and land records for each village in the unit. These men received written documents of appointment for a fixed term and submitted signed bonds in return; they received tax-free lands and a 5 percent allowance on collections. The state also appointed a headman and accountant for each named village under similar terms.

By confirming local men in office, the state was able to extract revenues, information, and support from rural Indian society. The state also gradually subjected zamindars, local headmen, and accountants to a process of socialization by which they became quasi officials whose interests were identified with the empire. These local lords depended more heavily on the state to sustain their powers as, ironically, those powers were being constrained by the same state. In effect, the regime paid commissions to the local aristocracy in return for delivering up the assessed revenue. Zamindari rights even became salable by the seventeenth century, at prices that reflected the capitalized value of their allowances—not the value of the taxes they collected.

If, as sometimes occurred, zamindars attacked their neighbors, engaged in banditry, or resisted paying their taxes—the definition of rebellion—local military governors riding at the head of several hundred heavy cavalrymen soon attacked, defeated, killed or enslaved the rebels, and burnt their villages. More tractable zamindars then occupied the lands vacated by the insurgents. Such were not ordinary events, however. The mature Mughal land revenue system was a remarkable achievement. Year after year, imperial officials routinely collected a heavy tax demand drawn from tens of thousands of villages over a region the size of western Europe.

A complex bureaucracy managed finances. An imperial *diwan*, or finance minister, took responsibility for management of all revenues and expenditures, the treasury system, and the mints and currency. Four officials reported directly to him: the minister responsible for the imperial household, central treasuries, and mints; the minister of crown revenues; the minister of salaries and compensation of imperial officers; and the auditor-general, who deployed a body of fiscal examiners. Each had his own staff of subordinate, salaried officials. In every province of the empire, a provincial fiscal officer, the *diwan,* appointed by the imperial finance minister, controlled a similar set of officers to manage revenues, expenditures, and treasuries. Provincial *diwans* enjoyed powers independent of the provincial governors and did not report directly to them. Cadres of technically proficient clerks, mostly members of Hindu service castes who were literate in Persian, were the mainstay of the imperial fiscal system.

From one perspective, the Mughal fiscal system was tightly centralized and controlled. From another, it was radically decentralized. The latter aspect stems from the peculiar system by which the emperor appointed and paid imperial officers who could be deployed anywhere within the empire—or beyond, for that matter. Under the *mansabdari* system, each imperial officer had a mix of civil and military duties determined by the emperor. The emperor assigned to each of his servitors a *mansab,* or ranking expressed in dual decimal numbers: the first, or personal, rank *(zat)* measured relative status and salary; the second, or trooper, rank *(suwar)* denoted the numbers of armed and suitably mounted heavy cavalrymen the officer had to present for muster. Official documents routinely appended a two-part rank to each officer's titles when referring to an individual (e.g., Shitab Khan 3,000 *zat*/2,500 *suwar*). Each *mansabdar* received a salary appropriate to his personal rank and a fixed amount per trooper to pay his mounted contingent. Each imperial official was responsible for the recruitment, pay, equipment, horses, and discipline of his followers. These might range in number from a handful to several thousand, depending on the officer's rank.

Most imperial officers did not receive cash payments from the treasury. Instead, they obtained salary assignments *(jagirs)* that permitted them to collect the assessed land revenue from specified villages or even entire subdistricts. The salary assignment was not a fief bearing rights of occupancy and local power; instead, it awarded to the holder the tightly circumscribed right to demand the quarterly installments of the land revenue on the lands specified. The lands were not necessarily contiguous. A high-ranking nobleman might hold *jagir* rights to as many as two dozen separate blocks of land spread over several provinces. The financial ministry and provincial *diwans* exercised strict controls over the methods and levels of tax collection. Complaints of brutality and excess rapidly found their way to these officers by means of imperial news writers found in every major town or from petitions submitted by aggrieved landholders and peasants.

Overall, this was a flexible and efficient system that threw some of the largest administrative tasks into the hands of imperial officers. They were forced to become capable managers in their own self-interest. In order to get paid, they not only had to organize and maintain their military contingents to set imperial rules, but they also had to organize and maintain a secretariat that could send out agents to collect their share of the tax revenues. Their pay and perquisites, at least those of higher ranking officers, were sufficiently large that they could also pay for and enjoy huge households with many wives, concubines, and servants, as well as all the appurtenances of luxurious living—which was luxurious indeed in Mughal India. From this vantage point, the basic organizational form of the empire consisted of the staff, troops, and households of individual officers. These organizational clusters were arranged in a hierarchy determined by their rank and by the emperor's favor.

The emperor obtained most of his direct central revenues from his control over imperial crown lands, or *khalisa*. This was a pool of sequestered revenues from lands that were not available for *jagir* assignment. In effect, the emperor allocated himself a changing set of salary assignments. The imperial lands did not consist of specific areas long held by the ruler, such as those adjacent to the capital, but rather were tracts of the most productive lands in nearly every province. The proportion of lands placed in this status varied with the fiscal needs of the central treasury and the demands of the *mansabdar's* pay bill. Cadres of salaried revenue officials from the finance ministry under the direction of the minister for crown lands collected the emperor's revenues.

For two centuries, the rulers of Mughal India limited their policy aims to four interconnected goals: military victory, annexation of new territories, imposition of public order, and steadily growing land revenues. The complex, centralized imperial system of governance focused on these limited aims. Apart from operating a system of royal workshops that produced luxury goods and some weapons, the Mughal state maintained a largely hands-off approach to the economy and economic development. It relied on the private sector—on the powerful market institutions and responsiveness of the Indian economy—in every region to produce wealth while the state generated peace and security. Similarly, the Mughal state generally refrained from intrusive meddling in the intricate social system of India, with its cellular caste system and its self-regulating dynamics. Beyond substantial grants to religious institutions, the state did almost nothing for education, for technological development, or to further science.

Relatively little of what the Timurid rulers invested in public works had an environmental impact. To be sure, Shah Jahan's design and construction of Shahjahanabad Delhi (now Old Delhi) significantly changed the urban environment of that city. This project also required considerable water engineering and adjustment of the canal system that tapped the Yamuna River. Successive emperors also built caravanserais and planted trees along major highways. Beyond this, however, the state's primary environmental impact lay in its unremitting pressure to increase cultivation and its revenues from that cultivation. To do this, the state, as mentioned earlier, struggled with a long-term process of socialization directed at the rural aristocracy in the countryside. In sum, the Mughal Empire undertook only a few centrally important tasks, but it carried out these tasks successfully for a large population and an immense territory.

When Akbar assumed the throne in the mid–sixteenth century, even the broad Indo-Gangetic plain was far from fully settled and cultivated. Wide bands of forests bounded areas of dense settlement and cultivation. These jungly areas sheltered numerous wild animals, including tigers, lions, panthers, wolves, bears, and other large, dangerous predators, as well as wild boar, various species of deer, and other herbivores. Jungle zones also harbored indigenous tribal groups not assimilated into the caste system of Hindu society. These were usually seminomadic, shifting cultivators. Rebel zamindars, bandits, and others resisting the imperial regime fled to the jungles as well. Not surprisingly, imperial officials devised various measures to encourage forest clearing in every Mughal province.

A Mughal document describes imperial policies and practices in Bihar province, located in the eastern Gangetic plain, during the reign of Shah Jahan (1627–1658):

From the time of Shah Jahan it was customary that wood-cutters and plough-men used to accompany his troops, so that forests may be cleared and land cultivated. Ploughs used to be donated by the government. Short-term pattas [documents stating revenue demand] were given, [and these] fixed government demand at the rate of 1 anna per bigha [three-fifths of an acre] during the first year. Chaudhuris [*pargana* headmen] were appointed to keep the ri'aya [peasants] happy with their considerate behavior and to populate the country. They were to ensure that the pattas were issued in accordance with Imperial orders and that the pledged word was kept. There was a general order that whosoever cleared a forest and brought land under cultivation, such land would be his zamindari. . . . Ploughs should also be given on behalf of the State. The price of these ploughs should be realized from the zamindars in two to three years. Each hal mir (i.e., one who has four or five ploughs) should be found out and given a dastar [sash or turban, i.e., mark of honor] so that he may clear the forests and bring land into cultivation. In the manner, the people and the ri'aya would be attracted by good treatment to come from other regions and subas [provinces] to bring under cultivation wasteland and land under forests.[11]

As this document implies, imperial incentives regularly stimulated forest clearing and new cultivation from the mid–sixteenth century to the mid-eighteenth.

The most striking example of frontier expansion lay to the far northeast in the Bengal delta, in the area nearly coterminous with the boundaries of present-day Bangladesh. Despite appearances, the intensively cultivated wet rice landscape of the eastern Bengal delta, with its dense population of Muslim peasants, does not date from antiquity but is a recent product of the Mughal period. The eastern Bengal delta was the site of a well-defined agrarian frontier whose extended clearing and settlement took place only after Mughal conquest. Mughal officials directly encouraged forest clearing, water control, and wet rice cultivation by pioneering peasant cultivators coming from the west and north. Incessant, strenuous human effort transformed the wild wetlands and tropical forests of the delta into domesticated wetlands of paddies and palms.

To a considerable extent, a long-term eastward shift of the Ganges and its tributaries shaped this settlement frontier. From its origins high in the Himalayan Mountains, the perennial water flow of the Ganges continuously deposited silt at its mouth. This process of sedimentation, along with that of the Brahmaputra and its tributaries, steadily extended Bengal's alluvial lands south into the Bay of Bengal. The seasonal floods that occurred when Bengal's rivers overflowed their banks each year deposited fresh alluvium across

11. Passage quoted in Richard Eaton, *The Rise of Islam and the Bengal Frontier, 1204–1760* (Berkeley and Los Angeles: University of California Press, 1993), 228. This is a summarized translation supplied in Hasan, "Three Studies of Zamindari System."

the landscape that enriched the soil and increased the yields of rice and other wet crops. However, considerable portions of the great silt load carried by these rivers also deposited in the beds and formed embankments on the sides of these rivers. As the riverbeds rose in height, the river waters periodically burst through the banks and shifted the courses of the rivers. This natural process at times forced the complete abandonment of some tributaries and the creation of others. Because of this process, which accelerated in the sixteenth century, the path of the Ganges moved several hundred kilometers eastward to join with the Brahmaputra in a vast interlocking system pouring into the Bay of Bengal.

The net effect of this process was to leave the earlier settled regions of western Bengal with a much-constricted local river system that no longer carried the sediment needed to refertilize the soil. In this moribund delta region, river waters did not actively scour the marshes and streams as they had before. Crop yields declined. Malaria caused by stagnant, standing waters became much more dangerous and prevalent. By contrast, as the Ganges pushed eastward, the forested districts of eastern Bengal received more silt and fresh water and became more attractive to cultivation and settlement. Pioneers moved steadily into this young, active delta region.

Until the end of the sixteenth century, most of eastern Bengal was covered with thick rain forests and marshlands. Apart from more settled populations surrounding isolated towns on the rivers, its scanty population consisted of shifting cultivators and isolated communities of coastal and riverine fishers. Most of these inhabitants of eastern Bengal were adherents of forest goddesses such as Chandi or Manasa, whose worship and devotees were but lightly tied to the traditions and practices of Hindu Bengal. Imperial Mughal officers viewed the lands to the east as unpleasant wilderness in need of taming. They did not hesitate to offer written land grants to those entrepreneurs who undertook to clear the forests and settle communities of wet rice cultivators. In so doing they ignored any possible property rights regimes or claims of the indigenous peoples of the area. Imperial officials turned to Muslim Sufi leaders *(shaikhs)* to organize and lead communities of Muslim pioneers in the settlement of these new lands. Consequently, as the frontier advanced, a new, primarily Islamic, rural society grew up in eastern Bengal in direct contrast to the Hindu complexion of western Bengal.

The advancing settlement frontier was the direct result of more intrusive imperial power—far greater than that exercised by the preceding Afghan sultans of Bengal. When Sultan Daud, who had ascended to the throne in 1572, refused to acknowledge Mughal suzerainty as his father had done, the emperor Akbar sent twenty thousand veteran troops in boats down the Ganges River to invade Bengal. The Mughal forces brushed aside dispirited Afghan troops and triumphantly entered Tanda, the Afghan capital city in September 1574. The Mughals pursued the fleeing Afghans throughout western Bengal until they turned and were slaughtered in several bloody battles. Mughal consolidation, however, was hampered by a serious rebellion against Akbar by dissatisfied officials in the eastern provinces. The emperor lost control of Bengal completely for several years, until he finally crushed the rebellion in 1583.

By that date, western Bengal was largely pacified and open to the establishment of a standard imperial revenue system and administration. Eastern Bengal, or Bhati as the Mughals called it, remained turbulent. In the enormous area stretching eastward from Gaur—the old Bengali capital—and the Bhagirathi-Hooghly River to Sylhet, Tippera, and Arakan, resistance to the Mughals continued for the next three decades. Refusing to serve the Mughals, thousands of still-rebellious Afghans dispersed into the eastern Bengal hinterland. The rebels formed alliances with locally entrenched Hindu rajas and tribal chiefs. Isa Khan, a talented Bengali Muslim leader who ruled the town and hinterland of Katrabo deep in the eastern delta, emerged as the dominant resistance leader. Isa Khan brought the twelve leading Hindu rajas of the region together ("the twelve chieftains" who had been appointed governors of their territories by the sultans of Bengal) in an anti-Mughal coalition.

There followed a protracted, thirty-five-year war that fully tested imperial resolve and resources. In eastern Bengal's watery terrain, the Mughals could not rely on vast forces of mounted cavalry and huge cannons hauled by large teams of oxen. Instead, they had to recruit boatmen; build riverboats; arm them with cannons, musketeers, and archers; and fight naval battles with similarly equipped rebel war boats. The imperial flotillas were vulnerable to ambush as they moved through unfamiliar waters.

A turning point in the struggle occurred when Isa Khan died in 1599 (of natural causes) and the rebellion lost much of its momentum. In 1602, Raja Man Singh, one of Akbar's most trusted commanders, moved his headquarters from Rajmahal in the west to Dhaka near Sonargaon. Dhaka had a strategic location. It was connected to the Padma-Ganges river system at a point halfway between the Bay of Bengal and the older Indo-Muslim capitals in western Bengal. This was an important shift that permitted Man Singh, in a new show of imperial strength far to the east, to pursue and kill one of Isa Khan's sons and send another into flight. Man Singh set up a network of military posts and checkpoints in the region. The next Mughal governor, Islam Khan, sent by Akbar's successor, Jahangir (r. 1605–1627), completed the subjugation of the east.

In the now well-established Mughal style, Islam Khan engaged in continuous diplomatic negotiations with all the rebel leaders. Using a finely tuned combination of inducements and threats, he urged the rebels to submit to the Mughal emperor. If they did so, they would be enrolled in the corps of imperial officers as *mansabdars;* they would retain their ancestral lands now assigned to them as *jagirs,* or salary grants, in return for supplying fixed numbers of troops; and they would be employed on a wider stage to the extent their talents permitted. If they continued to resist, they would be captured and killed or imprisoned, they would lose their lands to direct imperial administration, and their dynasties would end in ignominy. Facing intense pressure, the rebel chiefs one by one capitulated or were killed. Even Musa Khan, son and successor of Isa Khan, surrendered his fleet of seven hundred war boats.

Newly imposed Mughal power created the stability and incentives necessary to settle eastern Bengal, but the state looked to private entrepreneurial energy to transform the jungle into revenue-paying rice lands. Bengali folk and Persian documentary sources refer to the key role of pioneering Muslim holy men. These *shaikhs* obtained grants of land either directly from Mughal imperial officials or from largely Hindu merchants and rural aristocrats who provided them with capital. The Muslim holy men used their charisma and organizational skills to mobilize their followers as they advanced into new lands. Their settlements were built around small rural mosques as the focal point. The *shaikhs* directed their followers as they cleared the forest, built embankments and other water control measures, and began settled wet rice cultivation. The Mughal state conferred tax-free status on the lands directly surrounding each mosque on condition that the revenues from the land go to support the staff and functions of the mosque. The peasant cultivators who settled under the aegis of the holy men began to pay regulation land revenue assessed after a five-year tax holiday granted those who cleared new lands.

For nearly fifty years, Muslim pioneers pressed steadily eastward under the umbrella of Mughal protection and encouragement. However, settlement of the rich, alluvial islands formed in the lower delta, the area known as the Sundarbans, proved impossible because of disruptive coastal raiding that made the area nearly uninhabitable. Flotillas of Assamese Magh and Portuguese raiders sailed from the fortified port of Chatgaon (Chittagong) in the Buddhist kingdom of Arakan on the eastern coast of the Bay of Bengal. These much-feared marauders sailed up the intricate waterways and plundered coastal and inland settlements along the entire Bengal delta. Their most profitable return came from taking slaves for the king of Arakan, which he used for forced labor or sold.

Finally, in 1665, the Mughal emperor Aurangzeb ordered Shaista Khan, governor of Bengal, to end this menace. Leaving Dhaka in December 1665, a land force of sixty-five hundred men hacked its way through thick forests for nearly two hundred kilometers accompanied by a fleet of 288 rowed and sailed war vessels that moved in tandem with the army. The Mughal army seized Chatgaon with little difficulty after a three-day siege and made the city the headquarters of a new Mughal district, but they left the defeated ruler of

Arakan the remainder of his kingdom. Immediately, a Mughal military governor and a district revenue officer began consolidating the new territory. The victors released many slaves of the former regime and in turn captured and enslaved the former raiders. The sizeable Portuguese community of Chatgaon, a special target for Mughal retribution, was transported in chains to the imperial court.

The annexation of Chatgaon ended coastal raiding and opened up the coastal Bengal delta regions for clearing and settlement. At Chatgaon itself, the Mughals found a port city supported largely by commerce and piracy, whose hinterland remained in dense jungle. Most of the Arakanese were still shifting cultivators who grew rice, cotton, indigo, chilies, and fruits using no more than iron hoes and dibble sticks on their burnt-over plots. The victors assumed the right to dispose of this "empty" land as they saw fit. Mughal troops in the expeditionary force received tax-free grants of land that they were free to clear and cultivate. The regime also dispensed hundreds of written orders *(sanads)* that awarded hereditary tax-free lands in the jungle to Muslim holy men and to the trustees of mosques and shrines of mystic orders.[12] These grantees in turn organized their followers to clear the forests and begin wet rice cultivation. For a century, until British conquest in the 1760s, imperial governors and those of the Bengal successor state fostered the transformation of the landscape of Arakan.

Bengal's dynamic early modern economy rested solidly on frontier-driven growth that continued until the mid– to late nineteenth century. Wild wetlands became domesticated wetlands as rice paddies replaced marshlands and deltaic forests. Mughal conquest and pacification in the eastern delta drove forest clearing and pioneer settlement that greatly increased Bengal's agricultural production. Between 1595 and 1659, assessed land revenues for eastern Bengal more than doubled, from 2.7 million rupees to 5.6 million rupees.[13] Bengal's revenues continued to increase over the next century as clearing and agricultural expansion steadily ate into the region's forests and wetlands.

By mid–seventeenth century, Mughal Bengal had become a vast granary that produced immense surpluses of cheap rice and ghee (clarified butter). Loaded on coasting vessels, Bengal's rice helped to feed deficit areas as far away as Gujarat on the west coast of India. Cheap, abundant foodstuffs also encouraged rising industrial output in the province. Bengal's cotton and silk

---

12. According to Eaton, "Between 1660 and 1760, a total of 288 known tax-free grants in jungle land were given to pioneers by Mughal authorities in Chittagong for the purpose of clearing forests and establishing permanent agricultural settlements" (*The Rise of Islam and the Bengal Frontier*, 239). Obviously many more grants were made for which documents did not survive.

13. Ibid., 199, table 4.

textiles found a ready and growing market in Asia and in Europe. The advance of the settlement frontier transformed the jungles and swamps of eastern Bengal into a new wet rice landscape.

THE DUTCH REPUBLIC

By comparison with the Mughal Empire, the Dutch Republic was infinitesimally small. In the mid–seventeenth century, the republic contained approximately 1.9 million persons living in an area of about forty-two thousand square kilometers. Probably a fifth of the land area was under water. Nonetheless, the citizens of this small state had a role in the world economy and an impact on the world's resources and natural environment far greater than their numbers would suggest.

The Dutch Republic emerged as a cohesive state during the late sixteenth century. The civil and military institutions of the republic were forged in the crucible of an eighty-year war for independence fought against the Hapsburg rulers of Spain. In part, the revolt emerged from the long-standing grievance that the Hapsburg rulers had excessively taxed the Low Countries to support their wars against France, in which the Netherlanders had little interest or concern. However, at its heart the revolt was a war of resistance waged by fervent Protestants against state-supported and enforced Catholicism. Protestant resentment at the executions of the Inquisition and the harsh policies of the duke of Alva, the Hapsburg governor of the Netherlands, finally burst out in violent rebellion in 1572.[14]

The initial armed resistance to the Hapsburgs was spontaneous and local. Throughout the northern Netherlands and to a lesser extent in the more Catholic south, Protestants seized control of the town councils and militias and expelled or subdued pro-Catholic and royalist sympathizers. As this occurred, iconoclastic mobs occupied Catholic churches; plundered and publicly destroyed images, icons, and paintings; and expelled priests and nuns from the towns. In August 1572, Prince William of Orange marched into the southern Netherlands with sixteen thousand troops and funds from neighboring German Protestant princes. The States, or Assembly of Towns, in Holland, the largest northern province, defied an order of the Spanish governor to meet, and instead met on their own at Dordrecht. Here, they recognized Prince William as stadtholder and captain-general, a position he had held under the Hapsburg crown, but also as "Protector" of the Netherlands as a whole, in repudiation of the duke of Alva. In their meeting, the States also agreed to fight to secure the ancient rights and privileges of the Netherlands and, more important, to bear most of the cost of this struggle. They also tried

14. The narrative of the Dutch Revolt that follows relies primarily on Jonathan I. Israel, *The Dutch Republic: Its Rise, Greatness, and Fall, 1477–1806* (Oxford: Clarendon Press, 1995).

to persuade other towns that had not yet committed to the revolt to declare themselves. From these elements—the town councils and militias, the States of Holland, and the aristocratic authority of the Prince of Orange—the nascent Dutch state formalized the institutions with which to fight a revolutionary war.

Brabant and Flanders, the southern provinces, revolted as well, but their patrician leaders were primarily interested in wringing political concessions from Philip II, not in repudiating Catholicism. The States General of the Hapsburg Netherlands met without being summoned by Philip II in Brussels and became the organizational center of the southern resistance. The more moderate nobles and patricians of the Catholic south still hoped for reconciliation with Philip II. Prince William, who remained at Brussels, tried to unify the north and south in their struggle against the Hapsburgs. Despite his best efforts, William was unable to persuade militants on both sides to agree to his formula for a religious peace that would permit open worship by both Catholics and Protestants. The division between the more moderate Catholic south and the militant Protestant north widened.

During the 1570s, Philip II, beset by war with the Ottoman Empire and a fiscal crisis, made little headway in suppressing the revolt. The demands of the continuing war encouraged Holland, the largest northern province, to devise new linkages between itself and the other Protestant northern provinces. In 1575, Holland formed a union between itself and Zeeland. The two Protestant provinces formed a single entity with a common administrative and tax structure, and a single military command with the Prince of Orange at its head.

However, the founding of the Dutch Republic is usually dated four years later, in January 1579, when the Treaty of Utrecht formalized the split between north and south. The provinces and cities that signed the Utrecht treaty agreed to form a new political and military union in perpetuity in order to better resist the Spaniards. The new union was named the United Provinces of the Netherlands, known in the international community as the States General. The first signatories included the provinces of Holland, Zeeland, Utrecht, Gelderland, and Zutphen (a part of Overijssel) followed by Overijssel, Friesland, and Groningen. In the south, the cities of Antwerp and Breda in Brabant, and Ghent, Brugge, and Ypres in Flanders, also signed. The treaty stipulated that each member would remain sovereign in its internal affairs, but that the union would act as one in foreign policy. Decisions on war, peace, and taxation were to be made unanimously. In May 1579, Prince William signed the Treaty of Utrecht and agreed to act as stadtholder.

The three decades after Utrecht saw the emergence of the ideological and institutional framework of the Dutch Republic in the north. During the 1580s, the revolutionary regime eventually turned away from monarchy toward a true republic. The States General thrice attempted to enlist foreign monarchical support by offering up the Netherlands as a protectorate. When in 1580 Philip II declared William of Orange an outlaw and called for his assassination, the States General responded by offering sovereignty over the Netherlands to the duke of Anjou, younger brother of Henri III of France. After Anjou agreed to constitutional safeguards and was installed, the States General passed the Act of Abjuration that repudiated the authority of Philip II of Spain and all his heirs in perpetuity. This sweeping measure removed Philip's name, titles, and coat of arms from coins, public buildings, and official documents. All public officials from lowest to highest had to take a new oath of loyalty to the States General in its struggle against the king of Spain.

Despite his French troops, Anjou failed to hold back a reinvigorated Spanish assault by fresh forces in the south. Frustrated by the successes of the duke of Parma, Anjou attempted a military coup in Brabant and Flanders. However, popular resistance in Antwerp and other cities forced Anjou to leave the Netherlands in 1583. Under increasing Spanish pressure, William of Orange removed north to Delft in Holland. The Spanish army in Flanders seized city after city in the south during 1583 and 1584. Thousands of frightened Protestant refugees made their way north. Holland increasingly was to supply the leadership and resources for the revolt. The refugees were joined by the States General, who transferred their gathering from Antwerp to finally settle in The Hague.

Other attempts at monarchy failed. Nascent republican resistance stopped a proposal to offer William the title of count and sovereignty over Holland and Zeeland—a measure that became moot with his assassination in July 1584 by a Catholic zealot. The States General then sent a Dutch embassy to offer sovereignty over the Netherlands to Henri III, king of France, in February 1585. Rebuffed by Henri, the States General then turned to England. In May 1585, the States General made the same offer to Elizabeth I. Instead of accepting the full proposal, Elizabeth offered to take the United Provinces under protection and send troops in return for a dominant voice in governance. Her commander, the earl of Leicester, was to be the political leader of the rebel state, with the title of governor-general. In this capacity he would head the Council of State, the executive committee of the States General, which would have two other English members appointed by Elizabeth.

As soon as Leicester and the English troops arrived, a struggle for dominance between him and Johan van Oldenbarnevelt, the Advocate (legal and executive secretary) of Holland, flared up. For example, the states of Holland and Zeeland, acting without approval from Elizabeth, appointed Maurits, second son of Prince William of Orange, as their stadtholder and forced Leicester to accept that they had the sovereign power to do so. However, the English intervention offered a rallying point for the smaller provinces jealous of Holland's power and for hard-line Calvinists irked by the relatively tolerant religious policies of Holland. Those who tried to curb Leicester's powers, however, became convinced that freedom for the United Provinces was best preserved by avoiding the protection of any monarch. Leicester, like Anjou, eventually tried a military coup that failed to mobilize adequate support; by late 1587, he returned to England in disgust. In 1588, Elizabeth, deeply concerned by the threat of the Spanish armada, ordered the remaining English emissaries to drop their opposition to Holland's hegemony in the hope of Dutch maritime aid.

Hereafter, the United Provinces were firmly committed to republicanism. At this critical juncture, Johan van Oldenbarnevelt emerged as the political leader whose skill and energy secured the unity, and improved the organizational capacity, of the Dutch state. Officially, Oldenbarnevelt—the Advocate of Holland, the representative of the Holland nobility, and Holland's main spokesman—enjoyed an unchallenged ascendance over the States General and its secretariat. He sharply undercut the independent power of the Council of State to make it instead the key administrative or executive arm of the States General. He brokered many shrewd political and administrative compromises to meet the demands of the lesser provinces for a share in power while enhancing Holland's dominance in the new federation.

The English intervention and its aftermath had been disastrous for the rebellion's military fortunes. By 1589, the Spanish had control over the entire southern Netherlands, and Spanish garrisons occupied the entire eastern side of the northern Netherlands, from Nijmegen to the Ems estuary. They were pressing hard from the south as well. At this juncture, however, the Dutch Republic could not have survived and flourished as it did, had it not built up, in a very short time, remarkable military strength. Within ten short years after Leicester's departure, the United Provinces became one of the most powerful military and naval powers in Europe.

In 1590, the Dutch "breakout" from Spanish encirclement began. Over the next seven years, the republic's military commanders, the stadtholders Prince Maurits and Willem Lodewijk, laid siege to and took forty-three strongly fortified and garrisoned towns (including some in adjacent German lands) and fifty-five Spanish forts. By 1597, the entire eastern half of the northern Netherlands was wholly in Dutch hands. The Dutch now controlled the Rhine, Waal, and IJssel Rivers and reopened them to commercial river traffic. These victories created a great defensive arc of strong frontier fortresses that shielded the republic on its southern and eastern landward borders. Under Oldenbarnevelt's direction, the States General imposed its own authority over the frontier fortresses. They became a federally controlled cordon administered and supplied by the Council of State.

In 1598, however, France and Spain concluded peace talks with the Treaty of Vervins, and an ailing and elderly Philip II set in motion talks with the Dutch for a settlement. Despite the prospect of the full weight of Spanish power being brought against the Dutch, Oldenbarnevelt and Maurits rejected various compromises and diplomatic overtures offered by the Spanish. They refused to permit Catholic worship or to acknowledge the authority of the Hapsburgs. Over the next decade, the Spanish and the Dutch were essentially stalemated. The republic survived a rash, overconfident invasion of Flanders by Maurits in 1600 that nearly ended in disaster on the beaches at the battle of Nieuwpoort. It fended off a Spanish counteroffensive during 1605–1606 that put part of the northeast under Spanish control again. Finally, both sides agreed to the Twelve Years' Truce in 1609 that froze the borders of the republic and offered a prolonged respite before the struggle resumed.

The Dutch military achievement rested on an interlocking set of organizational innovations. These were part of the extraordinary burst of state building that created the republic. Maurits, Lodewijk, and Oldenbarnevelt built a large professional standing army, reliably paid and strictly disciplined, that made near-optimal use of the most advanced firearms and fortification technology of the time. This was a large army, with fifty thousand men by 1607, which never disbanded. The Dutch army remained under civilian direction and retained the sympathy and support of the general population. The army fought a war for survival, for beliefs and principles shared by the majority of the republic's Protestant citizenry. Of course, the army could not have been so successful without the economic strength of the Dutch economy, which continued to flourish in spite of the war, and which supplied the tax revenues that paid for the military.

The list of Maurit's and Lodewijk's innovations is long. They may or may not constitute the leading edge of a military revolution—the point is debated—but they were certainly impressive.[15] In 1594, Lodewijk first proposed the notion of volley fire by sequential ranks of musketeers who, after firing, would countermarch—that is, retire to the rear of their ranks to take the two minutes required to reload, and then fire again in turn. The object was to keep up a steady, uninterrupted volley fire at the front. The musketeers stood in ten ranks, each of which came forward to fire a volley in turn and then marched to the rear to reload. Massed pikemen did not disappear, because they remained useful to protect the musketeers from enemy cavalry. The Dutch cavalry, equipped with wheel-lock pistols and short-barreled, matchlock harquebuses, developed a similar volley-firing maneuver during which they trotted toward enemy lines and fired their pistols in sequential ranks before retiring to reload.

15. See Jeremy Black, *A Military Revolution? Military Change and European Society, 1550–1800* (London: Macmillan, 1991); Geoffrey Parker, *The Military Revolution: Military Innovation and the Rise of the West, 1500–1800*, 2d ed. (Cambridge: Cambridge University Press, 1996).

To carry out these maneuvers successfully under battlefield conditions demanded a practiced rote response that could be imprinted only by constant drill and discipline. The counts of Nassau divided the army into smaller formations—companies of 120 men and 11 officers—and drilled them constantly. Maurits obtained funds from the States General to equip the army with weapons of the same size and caliber. He approved an illustrated drill manual that prescribed a complex set of numbered positions and operations for each of the firearms and the pike. All movements were to be executed on command.

The emphasis on continual drilling reinforced the orderliness and discipline of the Dutch army. For much of the year, the army remained in garrison, manning fortified towns and bastions. Tight military discipline that kept the troops busy was a protection for civil society. Recognizing the threat to civilians, the States General made sure to pay its army at frequent, regular intervals. The States General published a code of military conduct in 1590, which was read out to recruits and to all troops at the beginning of each campaigning season. Special military judicial officers enforced these rules in each garrison. There were severe penalties for theft, affrays, and assaults, but death by hanging was the penalty for abduction and rape. So effective were these measures that towns actually applied to have garrisons assigned them. These rules were applied equally strictly to armies on campaign or in siege camps.

By 1609, the republic's leaders employed their best military engineers to survey, plan, and construct a defensive ring of new, sophisticated fortifications along the eastern and southern borders of the republic. The Dutch fortifications built at this time followed the well-established *trace italienne* defense against siege guns. This consisted of relatively low, broad, fortified walls defended by a system of angled bastions with interlocking fields of fire. The two broad sides of the bastion came to a blunt arrowhead shape pointing outward from the wall and having narrow, notched side walls. The whole was usually protected by a wide moat and sometimes with outerworks beyond the moat. Because they had to modernize medieval fortifications in a short space of time, the Dutch engineers resorted to beaten earth rather than stone construction. They reduced the distance between bastions to two hundred meters or so to permit covering fire by muskets as well as cannons. A covered way permitted the garrison to man the outer edge of the moat, and outerworks such as diamond-shaped ravelins permitted concealed flanking fire.

Maurits and Lodewijk brought artillery and siege craft to a new level. From 1590 onward, the artillery was standardized. The state gun foundry cast cannons in three standard sizes: the 12-pounder field gun and the 24- and 48-pounder large siege guns. The Dutch also used mortars that could throw a 100-pound grenade up to 750 meters. Military engineers actively directed the investment in and construction of a complete siege line and the digging of approach trenches and redoubts, which lead to saps dug nearly up to the defending covered way. From these forward positions, soldiers tunneled their way under the defenses to undermine them either with explosives or simply by collapsing their tunnels. Throughout his thirty-seven-year career, Maurits was forced to take only one town by storm. The rest capitulated on terms that were generally humane and reasonable.

Impressive as they were, however, Maurits' military innovations would have been futile without a stable source of funds and direction from a cohesive state. Over the first thirty-seven years of the revolt, from 1572 to 1609, under the searing pressure of war, the institutional framework of the Dutch Republic assumed a definitive form that continued, basically unchanged, until 1795. Despite the apparent redundancy and inefficiency of the system by which each province retained great autonomy, the Dutch Republic proved capable of decisive, centralized action over an extended period. Its complex institutions successfully reached into province and town to mobilize opinion and resources. Occasionally, stalemates occurred, but these were not frequent or crippling.

The States General, in which Dutch sovereignty resided, became the primary instrument by which the seven provinces were united and coordinated in a confederal state.[16] The States General approved treaties, declared war and made peace, levied taxes, and raised armies and navies by a majority vote of its delegates. Each of the seven provinces could send as many representatives as it wished to the States General but could cast only one vote in a ranked sequence: first came Gelderland, as the only duchy, followed in turn by Holland, Zeeland, Utrecht, Friesland, Overijssel, and Groningen. By 1593, the Dutch States General had begun meeting in a permanent, unbroken, year-round session between sixteen to twenty-eight days a month. The delegates met in a small room in The Hague. The Assembly conducted its spoken proceedings, and recorded them, in Dutch.

The States General functioned through its committee system. The Council of State (Raad van State) became an administrative organ of the States General. Comprised of 12 provincial delegates (3 for Holland and 2 each for Friesland, Zeeland, and Gelderland, 1 for each of the remaining three provinces) and the 2 stadtholders ex officio, it administered the army, the fortresses, and those lands held by the States General outside the provinces. A general accounting office comprised 14 delegates—2 from each province—with a small permanent staff. This office computed revenue and expenses, drew up estimates, and supplied fiscal reports to the States General. The Mint Chamber regulated the values, weights, and content of coins minted by each of the provinces.

The most complex system involved the navy and customs. The admiralty

16. Israel, *The Dutch Republic,* 276–306.

colleges were named as follows: Amsterdam, South Holland, the North Quarter, Zeeland, and Friesland. These were spaced at port towns from south to north along the coast. These bodies of eleven or twelve delegates (with a majority from the province within which the admiralty college was located) administered each admiralty's warships, built warships, recruited seamen, and coordinated naval policy and action under the direction of the States General. Each admiralty also supervised customs collections, maintained guard boats on the rivers and harbors, and regulated shipping and fisheries in the territory under its jurisdiction.

The States General appointed the stadtholders, originally three under the Hapsburgs, who proved to be a potent weapon in the process of centralization and unification. Named stadtholder of Holland and Zeeland in 1584, Maurits, count of Nassau, added Utrecht, Gelderland, and Overijssel in 1590. He held these positions until his death in 1625. His cousin Willem Lodewijk, count of Nassau-Dillenberg, was stadtholder of Friesland and Groningen from 1584 until 1620. He could appear before the provincial assembly at any time and address it on any issue. He was also charged with appointing judges and overseeing the administration of justice in each province. Each stadtholder was also the captain-general or commander of the army and navy for each of his provinces. (Maurits was captain-general of the union as a whole, with Willem Lodewijk as his deputy.)

The stadtholder was the highest ranking dignitary in the union. Maurits, in particular, was the center of a courtly culture. At dinner in his living quarters in the Binnenhof in The Hague, Maurits entertained Dutch nobles and the French and German nobles who held commissions in the Dutch army. Non-nobles were subordinate. In practice, however, Maurits and Lodewijk worked harmoniously together with Oldenbarnevelt and other representatives from Holland to subordinate the provinces to the central union—at least until their final clash in 1619, which ended in Oldenbarnevelt's execution.

The States General annually fixed the overall levels for expenditure and taxation and assigned a quota for revenues to be raised by each province. The States General did have some revenues of its own, about one-fifth of the total, derived from customs revenues, stamp duties, and taxes levied in the extraprovincial lands administered directly by it. However, the remaining four-fifths of revenues were distributed crudely according to population and resources. In 1609, Holland paid 57.4 percent, Zeeland, 9.1 percent, and Friesland, 11.6 percent, with the remaining four provinces contributing from 5.75 percent to as little as 2.5 percent (contributed by Overijssel). Each province was free to determine its own mode of taxation. Generally, Holland and the more prosperous coastal provinces tended toward excise taxes on consumption, and the poorer, interior provinces relied on land taxes. Of the revenues raised by the center, nearly all went to pay for warfare and the military. As late as 1641, 86.2 percent of expenditures went to the army, navy, and fortifications, in a total budget of 23.7 million guilders.[17]

Each of the seven provinces retained the appearance of sovereignty within a federated state to which they gave up real powers. A representative assembly carried out both legislative and executive duties for each of the seven provinces. Although the representative units varied, the principle of true consultation and representation prevailed in each. Each province also developed a steering committee of experienced, prominent nobles and commoners who managed the affairs of the province under the direction of a permanent civil servant.

Holland took the lead in developing an effective form of provincial governance and heavily influenced the structure of the other provinces. By the 1590s, the States of Holland had assumed both legislative and executive power and met for more than two hundred days per year. Each of eighteen voting towns sent a permanent representative, who held one vote, to the States in The Hague. The nobility *(ritterschap)*, gradually shrinking in size since no new nobles were being created, had its own assembly in Holland that in turn sent to the States a representative with one vote. The nobility had precedence in speaking and voting, followed by representatives of the towns in order of rank.

The permanent head of the States of Holland was the Advocate, a position held by Oldenbarnevelt until his death. The Advocate headed a steering committee, the Gecommitteerde Raden, consisting of a representative of the nobility, a representative of each of the large towns, and a rota of members from small towns. The committee, bound by standing instructions issued by the States, oversaw the routine administration of the province.

The States could discuss and act on only those items included in an agenda circulated in advance to all the town governments by the Gecommitteerde Raden. This meant that the voting representatives were controlled by their respective town councils, and every issue of importance was debated at length in those councils. Similar procedures existed in the other voting provinces. The Dutch state relied on the informed consent and willing support of its citizenry to a degree that was probably unmatched throughout the early modern world.

As contemporary observers frequently noted, Dutch towns and cities displayed a notable degree of social discipline that could be seen in the cleanliness and order of those entities. These attributes depended in part on the social welfare institutions—orphanages, poor relief, and hospitals—maintained by each community. The self-regulating nature of Dutch society contributed directly to the success of the Dutch Republic. The most important

17. Marjolein C. 't. Hart, *The Making of a Bourgeois State: War, Politics, and Finance during the Dutch Revolt* (Manchester, Eng.: Manchester University Press, 1993), 62, table 2.7.

source of Dutch discipline and cohesion was the Dutch Reformed Church and the ascetic Calvinist discipline imposed on its members. Church discipline, imposed by the elders of each congregation, focused on correcting antisocial public behavior. In effect, Dutch Reformed Calvinism helped to bring about a "disciplinary revolution" in society and institutions that was a critical component of the new state under formation during the Dutch Revolt.[18]

The Dutch Republic's political and military institutions created a social and territorial space that encouraged expansive economic growth. The Dutch economy placed enormous resource demands on its own territory. The northern Netherlands became one of the most intensively managed landscapes to be found in the early modern world. However, Dutch economic power extended far beyond the borders of the republic. Dutch demands for fish, food grains, timber, salt, and other commodities directed a continuing inflow of those commodities for both consumption and reexport. Moreover, as several chapters in this book demonstrate, Dutch long-distance maritime trade had cascading effects on landscapes and peoples throughout the early modern world. The tiny population of the republic had an impact on the early modern world's natural environment far disproportionate to its size.

Within the confined and protected space of the republic, the buoyant Dutch economy in the seventeenth-century golden age rested on six synergistic developments. First, continuing immigration provided scarce labor, technical skills, and capital that nourished the economy. The population of the republic rose (within modern borders) from 1.2 to 1.3 million persons in 1550, to 1.4 to 1.5 million in 1600, and to 1.85 to 1.9 million in 1650. Much of this increase occurred in the cities, especially those in Holland and Zeeland, the prosperous maritime provinces.[19] The urbanization rate, already high, increased from 27 percent in 1525 to 42 percent by 1675.[20]

The republic attracted a steady inflow of immigrants from the southern Netherlands and from neighboring Protestant Germany. Without a constant flow of immigrants to counterbalance and exceed heavy urban mortality, the cities of the maritime coastal provinces could not have grown. There would have been a scarcity of labor. Instead, jobs at relatively high wages and offering relative social stability attracted thousands of unskilled and impoverished men and women each year to the Dutch coastal cities from Germany

18. Philip S. Gorski, "The Protestant Ethic Revisited: Disciplinary Revolution and State Formation in Holland and Prussia," *American Journal of Sociology* 99, no. 2 (1993).

19. Jan de Vries and A. M. van der Woude, *The First Modern Economy: Success, Failure, and Perseverance of the Dutch Economy, 1500–1815* (Cambridge: Cambridge University Press, 1997), 50, table 3.1.

20. Ibid., 61, table 3.9.

and from the poorer interior provinces. The republic also benefited from a significant infusion of affluent and highly skilled human capital. During the first forty years of the revolt, over one hundred thousand Protestant migrants moved from the southern Netherlands to the north. Most relocated to the cities of Holland and Zeeland. The southern migrants brought with them the fiscal and technical skills essential to the development of the most lucrative trades and industries formerly centered in the south. Other migrants were printers, artists, and skilled craftsmen who brought the techniques of diamond cutting, sugar refining, silk working, linen bleaching, and tile and pottery making.

Second, the republic encouraged mobilization of capital and entrepreneurial investment. From Antwerp, the émigrés brought a most sophisticated use of bills of exchange, which became "the nearly universal short-term credit instrument of international trade in the following 200 years."[21] Bills of exchange had emerged as a principal method to create credit, effect exchanges between currencies, and transfer payment at a distance. Usually these were drawn by the seller of the goods upon his customer or debtor. As codified by Amsterdam's municipal ordinances, these bills could be assigned by the drawer to others, who received the same rights; they had to be signed and endorsed; and they could be discounted for cash before the date of obligation. Short-term commercial credit was abundant and cheap in the republic. Merchants in other European cities, including London, regularly bought bills on the Amsterdam credit market for their business.

Transactions costs and costs of storage and security were also cheap. Low interest rates encouraged traders to store large quantities of goods in Amsterdam warehouses and other Dutch entrepôts. This, in turn, contributed to the republic's reputation as a place where all goods were continually available. Amsterdam also became a center for maritime insurance. Regulated by a municipal Chamber of Marine Insurance, brokers listed prices for at least twenty-one destinations throughout Europe, the Mediterranean, and the West Indies. Merchant banking houses emerged to offer speculative financing for long-distance trade by extending credit on bills. They also became involved in long-term lending to foreign governments with the encouragement of the States General.

In 1609, Amsterdam founded a municipal deposit and clearing bank on a Venetian model. The Bank of Amsterdam, or Wisselbank, took deposits, effected transfers between accounts, and accepted and paid bills of exchange. These services were fast, efficient, and safe, and they cost next to nothing. The Amsterdam Wisselbank "grew with the expansion of Amsterdam's commerce to become the clearinghouse of world trade, settling international

21. Ibid., 130.

debts and effecting transfers of capital."[22] Keeping a hefty 90 percent of deposits in coin and bullion in its vaults, the Wisselbank lent only to the States General and to the Dutch East India Company. Other municipal banks in Rotterdam and Utrecht followed on the same lines.

All of these trading functions came together at the highest level in the Amsterdam bourse *(Beurs)*, where merchants and brokers gathered in a single building of arcades around a central courtyard. Here, one could trade commodities, invest in new ventures, arrange for shipping and freight, and buy company shares, government bonds, and sea insurance. Into the Amsterdam bourse came a flood of information from markets around the world about creditworthiness of firms and states, and information about supply and demand for commodities in various markets. Newspapers began circulating with regular commercial news in print.

Third, the Dutch Republic came to dominate the shipping and commerce of the early modern world. By mid–seventeenth century, the republic's merchant fleet exceeded the combined size of those of England, Spain, and France. The estimated two thousand seagoing merchant ships of the time—from small coastal vessels of 80 tons shipping capacity to huge East Indiamen of 900 tons—had a combined capacity of 400,000 tons. Nearly fifty thousand men earned their living at sea. Dutch shipping and shipbuilding became the most technically advanced and largest in Europe. Dutch ships that required fewer crew members per unit of freight were cheaper and more efficient than those of their competitors.

Between 1570 and 1620, the number of long-distance markets serviced, and deepwater trading routes traveled, by Dutch traders exploded. They retained their dominance in the Baltic bulk trades that imported timber, naval stores, food grains, and copper for domestic use and reexport. However, rapid expansion came in the worldwide "rich trades"—the new commerce in sugar, furs, slaves, precious metals, diamonds, spices, and textiles.[23] Led by émigrés from the southern Netherlands, Dutch merchants developed new links with the Levant (Mediterranean), the Caribbean, Brazil, West Africa, Northern Russia, and the East Indies. The Dutch East India Company (Verenigde Oostindische Compagnie, or VOC), with its joint-stock format and monopoly of trade, became the primary conduit for Dutch trade with Japan, Southeast Asia, China, and India.[24]

From its inception, the VOC contributed mightily to the Dutch domestic economy. Those Asian goods that landed at the docks of the six cities and

22. Ibid., 131.

23. See Israel, *Dutch Primacy in World Trade.*

24. For a full discussion of the Dutch East India Company, the Verenigde Oostindische Compagnie, see chapter 3.

sold at auction brought in an average of around 8 to 9 million guilders per year by midcentury. The returning VOC fleet unloaded several million pounds of pepper, and somewhat lesser amounts of other spices, silk and cotton textiles, sugar, rhubarb and other "drugs," and various dyestuffs. All these sold for substantial profits at auction in Amsterdam. By the 1640s, the surplus of sales revenues over expenses ran to 2.3 million guilders per year. Dividends to shareholders were 6.5 percent per year.[25]

Dutch buyers of the VOC commodities reexported as much as three-quarters or more of their purchases to wider European and Mediterranean markets, making further profits from the Asian trade. Moreover, the VOC bought and paid for Dutch textiles, foodstuffs, and other goods to ship to Batavia as both supplies for consumption and trade goods—1.2 million guilders' worth per year in the 1660s. Every year, the VOC expended large sums to build and outfit large East Indiamen from Dutch shipyards. The VOC was the largest employer in the Dutch Republic and probably in the world; its number of employees at home and in Asia grew from 7,700 in 1625 to 21,900 in 1688.[26] In the 1660s, the VOC domestic payroll was 800,000 guilders per year; its employees abroad received 2.3 million guilders, most of which returned to Holland.[27]

Fourth, during the critical eighty years of the revolt, the Dutch greatly expanded the amount of protein and profits they took from the sea and from inland waterways. Dutch fisheries became more organized, specialized, market-oriented, and productive after the revolt.[28] The inland freshwater industry consisted of two areas of intensive commercial operations: first, the mouths of the major rivers and the Zeeland delta; and second, the Zuider Zee and Ij, along with watercourses that linked them to the lakes of North Holland. Around 1500, the inland fishery adopted a new, massive fishing vessel, the *waterschip*, as long as and broader than seagoing herring ships. By the early 1600s, some 130 of these great vessels used huge, tightly woven nets to sweep the fish into their holds. Catches of bream, roach, pike, perch, carp, and eel formed a major part of the urban diet until mid–seventeenth century. Intensive fishing of the rivers produced ample supplies of sturgeon, salmon, and eel for urban markets.

By 1650, however, the inland fisheries were in swift decline and ceased to be a major Dutch food source thereafter. Much of the decline seems to have been due to overfishing, but continual damming and draining of the interior lakes also hurt productivity. Rising sea levels turned the Zuider Zee into an increasingly saline lake.

25. De Vries and van der Woude, *The First Modern Economy*, 390–91, table 9.3.
26. Ibid., 432, table 10.3.
27. Ibid., 461, table 10.8B.
28. See ibid., 235–55, on the fisheries.

For the Dutch the "great fishery" was the deepwater herring fishery in the North Sea. By 1400, a technical breakthrough occurred that permitted long-distance fishing there. Dutch fishermen developed a technique of quickly gutting and salting herring while at sea. This permitted them to remain at sea for five to eight weeks at a time and to preserve the catch before returning. To make this workable, a second innovation was necessary: the purpose-built herring *buss,* a large vessel that carried a crew of eighteen to thirty men—essentially a floating factory.

By the late sixteenth century, as the revolt began, there were major shifts in the North Sea herring grounds. In addition to the long-known area off the Dogger Bank and the one near the English coast off East Anglia, new herring fishing grounds appeared in the northwestern portion of the North Sea between the Norwegian coast and the Shetland Islands. Simultaneously, formerly numerous herring shoals disappeared, after 1589, from off the Swedish coast. Dutch fishermen, long skilled and experienced in catching herring, moved with alacrity to tap these new grounds.

By the 1630s and 1640s, at the high point of the Dutch herring industry, some 500 herring *busses* sailed regularly into the North Sea. Around 1640, the annual average catch was about forty thousand metric tons of fish. Domestic consumption accounted for about one-fifth of the catch. The remaining portion of salted or pickled herring was reexported to the Baltic and Hamburg in the north and the region between the Rhine and the Seine in the south. After 1650, the herring fishery began a long, slow decline. Yields of herring per boat diminished, perhaps due to overfishing, perhaps due to shifts in herring movements. The Dutch also faced stiff competition from a revived Scandinavian fishery and a new Scottish herring fishery.

Unlike the herring industry, Dutch deepwater fishing for codfish—the so-called lesser fishery—grew in size and value throughout the seventeenth and most of the eighteenth century. From long-used grounds at Dogger Bank in the North Sea, Dutch fishing vessels sailed to new rich grounds off Iceland after 1650. Cod fishers used hooks and lines for the large fish, unlike the nets for the smaller herring, but they employed the same gutting and salting techniques. Strangely enough, the Dutch did not sail farther to take cod in New World waters, where the English and French caught great quantities of the fish.[29] Nevertheless, Icelandic cod were an important supplement to the declining herring fishery. Finally, Dutch whaling in northern waters began around 1600 and quickly developed into a major asset to the republic.[30]

Fifth, the republic wrung every possible return from its meager land base. Early modern Dutch cultivators steadily improved their productivity. Every year, farmers, either self-funded or capitalized by urban investors, increased

29. See chapter 15 for a full discussion of New World fisheries.
30. See chapter 16 on early modern whaling.

their inputs and upgraded crops on existing fields. Every year, investors funded drainage projects that brought reclaimed land under cultivation, either from the sea or from inland waters. Agricultural expansion profoundly changed the landscape and ecology of the northern Netherlands.

The low-lying lands of the republic divide geologically between expanses of primarily sandy soils—relatively infertile lands lying several meters above sea level—that pervade the interior (known as the "diluvial Netherlands") and the low-lying clays and peat soils deposited at sea level or even below by the Rhine, Maas, and other rivers flowing to the sea (the "alluvial Netherlands"). Although potentially fertile, the latter were marshy lands with a tangle of small streams, rivers, and ponds that required considerable effort to drain and cultivate.

Medieval farmers on the alluvial coastal lands steadily brought portions of these lands into cultivation by small-scale drainage projects protected by dikes that made grain production possible. Dutch nobles and monasteries organized and paid for larger reclamation projects. Relative to other parts of Europe, farmers in this region enjoyed well-defined rights to buy, sell, and mortgage their lands, strong security of tenure, and minimal feudal demands or obligations. Local associations of farmers maintained and guarded dikes to protect their fields from storms and tides.[31]

During the early sixteenth century, the rise of cities in the south, in Antwerp especially, had created new market demand for the products of livestock husbandry rather than grain farming. With the import of Baltic grains, the price of food grains also declined. Northern Dutch maritime farmers increasingly began producing butter and cheese and fattening cattle for city markets.

Throughout the late sixteenth century and the seventeenth century, shifts in technology and organization made possible large increases in output. Rising agricultural prices encouraged alluvial farmers to further improve soil quality. They rarely let fields stay fallow in the older three-field rotation of the medieval period. Instead, they liberally applied cattle manure, as well as boatloads of human and animal waste shipped from the growing cities. Nearly all of what farmers in Holland and Zeeland produced, they sold on the market for cash. They increased the scale of production for specialized crops that required heavy fertilization, such as hops, hemp (for ropes and sails), flax, and madder (a dyestuff). Dairying became a specialist industry with farms that concentrated on fresh milk production or cheese and butter.

Agricultural profits rose to the point that urban entrepreneurs saw investment possibilities in creating new land by drainage and pumping. One

31. Audrey M. Lambert, *The Making of the Dutch Landscape: An Historical Geography of the Netherlands* (London: Seminar Press, 1971).

approach was to drain shallow interior lakes by pumping their water into higher-level drainage canals that carried the surplus water to the ocean. Another alternative was to enclose tidal areas by dikes and pump out the water to create polders. The dike system, of course, had to be continually watched and maintained. Both methods uncovered new, fertile lands for cultivation.

New technical developments in windmills encouraged large-scale projects. The main limitation on the size and capacity of windmills was that the entire structure had to turn into the wind. In the 1560s, with a new design, only the top section, or cap, bearing the sails of the windmill rotated, not the entire structure. This innovation permitted much larger windmills with greater pumping capacity. Still, a single windmill could generate only enough power to move water up about one meter with its rotating wheel. To drain lakes deeper than this, engineers resorted to rows of windmills, each set at a higher level and acting in concert to push the water up as high as five meters. By 1630, Dutch engineers also began to increase pumping capacity by using Archimedean screws rather than wooden buckets to move water.

The most dramatic episode of lake drainage occurred in North Holland between 1610 and 1640. Leading Amsterdam merchants and other investors put 10 million guilders into draining a series of lakes using the new pumping techniques. These projects added fourteen thousand large farms covering a total of twenty-six thousand hectares to the cultivated area. By midcentury there were no more lakes in peninsular North Holland—these ecosystems with their fish, aquatic plants, and waterfowl had disappeared.[32]

Simultaneously, investors also looked to profit from creating polders in tidal areas. One hundred twenty-three prominent investors, including Johan van Oldenbarnevelt, raised 1.5 million guilders to drain and dike the North Holland Beemster polder. Begun in 1608, the project built forty-three of the newest and largest windmills to drain seven thousand hectares of land for cultivation. The neighboring Schermer polder scheme, begun in 1635, cost 1 million guilders. Investors funded similar projects, although on a smaller scale, in Friesland and Groningen.[33]

Overall, in the entire early modern period, between 1500 and 1815, the Dutch Republic reclaimed some 250,000 hectares of land.[34] This increased the cultivated land area of the alluvial zone by one-third. The ratio of cultivation to total area was extremely high in the maritime provinces (68 percent of Holland was under active cultivation). By the end of the period, the alluvial lands of the Dutch Republic were among the most intensively managed and exploited in the world.

Sixth and finally, the republic tapped into its extensive peat bogs for a

32. De Vries and van der Woude, *The First Modern Economy*, 29.
33. Israel, *The Dutch Republic*, 334.
34. De Vries and van der Woude, *The First Modern Economy*, 31.

cheap, abundant source of energy to meet the rapidly rising demand for industrial and domestic fuel. Peat extraction became a large-scale, capital-
intensive industry that had a significant environmental impact.[35] Energy-
intensive transforming industries—distilling, beer making, lime boiling,
brick and tile making, salt boiling, and iron working—all grew rapidly after
the revolt. Human numbers also rose, along with the accompanying need for
fuel for heating in the increasingly cold winters of the Little Ice Age. As early
as 1550, there was virtually no fuelwood to be cut in the Dutch lands. Wood
and charcoal were imported from Germany and Norway. Consumers turned
to peat, making it the principal energy source for the republic throughout
the seventeenth century.

In the alluvial regions, peat had for centuries been cut by farmers and
other rural dwellers, who needed little in the way of capital or tools to collect it. After compressing the peat into blocks and drying it, they either burnt
the blocks themselves or sold them on local markets. The aim was to cut peat
in the spring, from mid-March to mid-July, and have it thoroughly dried before winter began each year. Peat bogs in the alluvial districts were at or near
the water level, which permitted easy transport of peat turves by water to market. However, given the high water table, peat cutters could strip away only
the top layer from bogs that were actually several meters thick. Any deeper
cutting and they were flooded out. About 1530, peat diggers developed a new
tool, the *baggerbeugel,* which had a long wooden handle and a metal net basket.[36] Armed with this innovation, workers scraped the bog below the waterline and brought loose peat to the surface. They piled it on layers of reeds,
raked it, and mashed it to an even consistency. Then other workers, wearing
short planks on their feet, trod out excess water and compressed the peat
into slabs only 32 centimeters high. Once dried, it was cut into regularly
shaped turves, stored in ventilated barns, and then brought on barges to urban markets.

The new dredging technique resulted in deep, water-filled exhausted
peat bogs that formed lakes across the alluvial landscape. The peat that had
formerly held the water was gone, and the water table rose accordingly. Ironically, these areas probably were as great in extent as the drained interior
lakes combined. After 1650, declining agricultural prices meant that draining exhausted peat lands was not a viable economic proposition.

There were also ample peat bogs in the diluvial zone that had been little
exploited before the seventeenth century. These were in generally remote
and inaccessible areas in Groningen and other northern provinces. They lay

35. Richard W. Unger, "Energy Sources for the Dutch Golden Age: Peat, Wind, and Coal,"
Research in Economic History 9 (1984): 221–253.

36. Lambert, *The Making of the Dutch Landscape,* 210, fig. 60, offers a contemporary illustration of this process.

above the water table and could be cut more readily, but the cut peat could not be transported economically. However, rising demand and prices encouraged consortia of urban investors to pool their resources, buy large tracts of uninhabited diluvial peat bogs, dig extended canals into the bogs, and hire armies of laborers, mostly German temporary migrants, to cut the peat. Once exhausted, these lands could be converted to cultivable land if the surface soil were saved and then enriched by heavy manuring. For example, the capital city of Groningen subsidized the use of human manure to fertilize cultivation in former peat bogs. By 1800, some twenty-three thousand hectares of land in the province had been brought into cultivation in this way. The canals dug for peat conveyance remained in use and contributed to an invaluable transportation infrastructure.

Coal was the alternative energy source. Energy demands also stimulated coal imports from the southern Netherlands, Germany, England, and Scotland. Dutch industries, not homes, were the primary users of coal. Many industrial users preferred coal for forging and refining, since it gave about four times more thermal energy per unit of weight than peat. Storage and labor costs for using coal were much reduced. Coal imports are estimated to have averaged sixty-five thousand metric tons per year during the seventeenth century. These imports provided about two-fifths of the energy obtained from domestic peat supplies.[37] Peat production declined in the republic during the eighteenth century. Producing areas became increasingly distant from markets as active peat bogs were exhausted. Prices rose steadily, and as coal became more competitive, coal usage increased to roughly equal that of peat.

Taken together, however, peat and coal formed a low-cost energy supply that made possible an extraordinary level of comfort for the Dutch at home and an equally unusual concentration of energy-intensive industry. It is likely that the per capita energy supply doubled between 1560 and 1660 to reach 3 million kilocalories per person per year.

CONCLUSION

Across Eurasia and Africa (and perhaps the New World), human organizations were becoming larger, more complex, and more effective—especially states and quasi-state organizations. Having adapted and learned from continuing trial and error, rulers and elites in early modern states were more effective than their predecessors at providing basic public order within those territories they claimed. They mobilized and deployed larger armies and naval forces that were able to use the new gunpowder weaponry effectively. They did better than their predecessors at unifying fragmented polities un-

37. Unger, "Energy Sources for the Dutch Golden Age," 246.

der one system of authority. They did better at collecting taxes rather than tribute, which they assessed on some notion of public policy and relative productivity and with greater predictability and regularity. They were better than their predecessors at articulating ideologies and principles that legitimated their authority and appealed to their subjects.

Moreover, during the three and a half centuries of the early modern period, incremental improvements in all these areas characterized most states. That is, the process of learning and adaptation continued and accelerated in this period. Late-eighteenth-century states were more capable and effective than early-sixteenth-century states. Wartime conditions apart, the quality of public order was better for most people in Eurasia and Africa at the end of the early modern period than at its beginning.

These are large and—to some scholars—outrageous claims because they are very difficult to measure or to prove. There were numerous exceptions and episodes in which early modern states faltered and failed in these basic tasks. Any historian of the period can readily summon up many such examples. Nevertheless, the argument that states grew more effective is defensible and is supported by the case studies addressed in this book.

The examples of the Mughal Empire and the Dutch Republic illustrate, in very different contexts, the importance of the more capable early modern states. Each was the product of long processes of social evolution that culminated in critical episodes of contemporaneous state building: during the fifty-year reign of Akbar from 1556 to 1605, and during the first half of the Dutch Revolt from 1572 to 1609.

On the one hand, the Mughal Empire forcibly unified nearly the entire Indian subcontinent in one imperial system. This was a stunning achievement, one not seen since the days of the ancient pan-Indian rule of the Mauryas, if then. Within its growing territory, the empire offered stability and order but did not attempt radical intervention in either the society or the economy. The Mughal emperors won limited admiration, interest, respect, and obedience from most of their subjects most of the time, but asked for relatively little in the way of active support. Under the imperial umbrella, the already sophisticated regional economies of the subcontinent moved toward a new level of productivity and subcontinental integration. By and large, however, economic growth was not a product of technical innovation for either industry or agriculture but was more Smithian in form, responding to new market demands. Although not as yet fully studied, ongoing land clearing and land reclamation in every province proceeded well beyond medieval limits.

On the other hand, the Dutch Republic also offered stability and order in a far smaller territorial and social space. In many respects, the republic survived and flourished because it tapped into the compressed social energy, ideological fervor, technical skills, and organizational capacity of its citizens.

Society in the Dutch golden age was hospitable to technical, economic, and organizational innovation. To be an inhabitant of the republic during the golden age was to be an active participant, however humble, in a new enterprise, in the creation of a new society. However, to some extent, the territorial reach of the republic was far greater than that of the Mughal Empire, which did not show any serious interest in becoming a maritime power. During the seventeenth century, Dutch traders and their settlements were visible throughout the world. The same social energy and organizational innovation that created the republic at home brought the Dutch primacy in world trade abroad.

As these examples suggest, early modern states did supply public order—protected and defined physical and social space—in which individuals and groups could safely cultivate the land, buy and sell in ever more efficient markets, devise institutions that would permit them to live more or less comfortably in huge cities, and operate technically demanding industries. Moreover, in this period, the capacity of the state to exert power beyond its borders by war, trade, and ideological expression was greatly improved.

More effective early modern states with better public order improved the performance of markets and economic productivity generally. Certainly, markets continued to function, if less efficiently, during periods of state breakdown, and markets were also impeded by crude monopolistic political intervention. But overall, economies did better when states were more capable and effective. This is not to deny the destruction and economic loss caused by warfare, but only to point out that, in this period at least, such losses do not seem to have been totally crippling—as attested by the dazzling productivity of the Indian economy ruled by an empire that was perpetually at war and the Dutch Republic's stunning economic growth under wartime conditions.

If more capable and effective states sustained and encouraged economic production in the early modern world, this meant in turn that human impact on the natural environment would be felt at a level and at a global scale never seen before. And, indeed, this is what we see occurred around the globe as the demand for natural resources grew and new frontiers of settlement opened. The early modern world economy grew and strengthened because of the synergy between abundant, more accessible natural resources, strengthened states, and more productive and efficient markets.

Chapter 2

Climate and Early Modern World Environmental History

Although most historians have not addressed the issue, climatologists and climate historians have assembled increasingly robust evidence that the world's climate has changed significantly over the past millennium. They describe three phases: a change from a warm medieval era to a significantly cooler regime in the early modern centuries, followed by a considerably warmer trend in the twentieth century. This periodization raises significant questions about the environmental history of the early modern world.

Did this climatic change occur uniformly around the world in the early modern period, and what effects did it have on human societies? Presumably, for some periods in some places, cooler conditions made a significant difference to those who had to cope with more severe weather. What effects did this have on agricultural production, food security, mortality and fertility, and disease patterns? What were the cultural and social responses to greater stress? Human societies made significant advances in population and in productivity in the early modern centuries. Had the medieval warm period continued, would these advances have been even more extraordinary? Alternatively, did more difficult climatic conditions spur innovation and greater human productivity? Identifying and measuring these impacts involves a complex set of issues.

THE LITTLE ICE AGE

The early modern period in world history occurred during the most severe episode of what is often called the Little Ice Age, which lasted from the thirteenth century to the twentieth. The term implies that the early modern centuries saw a period of cooling by comparison with the late medieval and the modern warming epochs. According to Jean Grove, for geologists, geographers, and glacialists, "the term 'Little Ice Age' is widely used to describe the period of a few centuries between the Middle Ages and the warm period of the first half of the twentieth century, during which glaciers in many parts of the world expanded and fluctuated about more advanced positions than those they occupied in the centuries before or after this generally cooler interval." For climatologists, the Little Ice Age "was a period of lower temperature over most, if not all, the globe," with especially important consequences for sensitive areas such as high altitudes and high latitudes. The period divides into an early phase, followed by a more clement period in the fifteenth and early sixteenth centuries and culminates in a colder, more severe later phase between the mid–sixteenth and the late nineteenth or early twentieth centuries.[1]

The prospect of global warming and massive climate change forced by human-induced greenhouse gases has stimulated and encouraged scientific investigations into climate history generally and the Little Ice Age in particular. Climatologists have turned to proxy measurements instead of written documents to reconstruct past climates. Various "natural archives" that can be calibrated to annual or even seasonal resolution have been applied most extensively to temperate regions of the world.[2]

Dendrochronology, the study of annual growth rings in long-lived trees, relies on measurement and analysis of the width and other qualities of the annual growth ring. Systematic comparison of cores bored in the trunk permits the dendrochronologist to ascertain the temperature, precipitation, drought, and pressure patterns that determined the tree's growth for single and multiple years. For example, R. D. D'Arrigo and G. C. Jacoby used six dendroclimatic data series from white spruce (*Picea glauca* [Moench] Voss) and one series from northern white cedar (*Thuja occidentalis* L.) to reconstruct annual North American temperatures for the period 1601–1974. After careful calibration and checking, they concluded that "the main features are below average temperatures in the early 1600's, a cooling in the early 1700's, a relative warming in the later 1700's, an abrupt transition to cold temperatures in the early to mid-1800's part of the Little Ice Age, and the general warming trend over the past [i.e., twentieth] century."[3] When they

1. Jean M. Grove, *The Little Ice Age* (London: Methuen, 1988), 1–3.

2. Raymond S. Bradley and Philip D. Jones, *Climate since A.D. 1500*, rev. ed. (London: Routledge, 1995), 6–14.

3. R. D. D'Arrigo and G. C. Jacoby Jr., "Dendroclimatic Evidence from Northern North America," in *Climate since A.D. 1500*, edited by Raymond S. Bradley and Philip D. Jones, 296–311, rev. ed. (London: Routledge, 1995), 303–4. The authors used 1880–1974 as a calibration period from which to measure departures from the mean. This improves on an earlier reconstruction of annual temperature for the period 1671–1973. See G. C. Jacoby Jr. and R. D.

compared their series to earlier collations of tree-ring data for North America, the authors found broad similarities.

A comparable approach involves drilling cores into alpine and polar ice caps and ice sheets. When read, the ice cores, often several hundred meters in length, reveal annual strata of ice and snowfall accumulation that can be calibrated and dated. Scientists measure the annual snow accumulation for each layer of the core after adjustment for annual melting. Complex chemical isotopic analysis of the stratified core yields detailed information on temperature, precipitation, and atmospheric composition of annual weather variations.[4] For example, Russian scientists have extracted lengthy cores from the glaciated ice sheets covering the archipelagos and islands of the Arctic from the Barents to the Kara Sea. From the cores, they have reconstructed temperature changes for the past five hundred years that are consistent with other descriptions of Little Ice Age cooling.[5]

Two other methods yield promising results. Scientists take varved (annually laminated) sediments from coastal basins or lake beds and count them to assemble internal annual chronologies. They measure variations in thickness, changes in fossil pollen, and geochemical composition of each layer. Laminated sediments generate data about temperature, solar radiation, and precipitation (runoff).[6] Marine biologists study living scleractinian coral reefs two hundred to eight hundred years of age found in the shallow tropical oceans at ten to twenty meters. These reefs continuously deposit skeletal growth in coral colonies at rates that measure five to twenty millimeters each year. X rays show annual variations in density. Material incorporated into the coral skeleton shows environmental variations. For example, isotopic analysis of the coral bands offers data on temperature and precipitation variations.[7]

D'Arrigo, "Reconstructed Northern Hemisphere Annual Temperature since 1671 Based on High-Latitude Tree-Ring Data from North America," *Climatic Change* 14 (1989).

4. Alexander T. Wilson, "Isotope Evidence for Past Climatic and Environmental Change," in *Climate and History: Studies in Interdisciplinary History,* edited by Robert I. Rotberg and Theodore K. Rabb (Princeton, N.J.: Princeton University Press, 1981), 215–32.

5. A. Tarussov, "The Arctic from Svalbard to Severnaya Zemlya: Climatic Reconstructions from Ice Cores," in *Climate since A.D. 1500,* edited by Raymond S. Bradley and Philip D. Jones, rev. ed. (London: Routledge, 1995), 505–16. See fig. 26.7.

6. B. Zolitschka, "High Resolution Lacustrine Sediments and Their Potential for Palaeoclimatic Reconstruction," in *Climatic Variations and Forcing Mechanisms of the Last 2000 Years,* edited by Philip D. Jones, Raymond S. Bradley, Jean Jouzel, and the North Atlantic Treaty Organization, Scientific Affairs Division (Berlin: Springer, 1996); Jonathan T. Overpeck, "Varved Sediment Records of Recent Seasonal to Millennial-Scale Environmental Variability," in *Climatic Variations and Forcing Mechanisms of the Last 2000 Years,* edited by Philip D. Jones, Raymond S. Bradley, Jean Jouzel, and the North Atlantic Treaty Organization, Scientific Affairs Division (Berlin: Springer, 1996), 479–98.

7. J. M. Lough, D. J. Barnes, and R. B. Taylor, "The Potential of Massive Corals for the Study of High-Resolution Climate Variation in the Past Millennium," in *Climatic Variations and Forcing*

The results of extensive paleoclimate research published thus far corroborate and strengthen a consensus that there was indeed a significant, worldwide shift toward a cooler climate in the Northern Hemisphere during the early modern centuries. Leading climatologists have integrated long-term temperature data obtained from ice cores, sediments, tree rings, and other proxy data and combined it with long-term temperature data sets wrung from an array of human observations and notations found in written documents. They have meshed this with long-term direct instrumentation data that became increasingly available by the eighteenth century.

In a 1998 article, Michael E. Mann, Raymond S. Bradley, and Malcolm K. Hughes present annual mean temperature data for the Northern Hemisphere for the six centuries since 1400 C.E. Their data show "pronounced cold periods during the mid–sixteenth and late eighteenth centuries, and somewhat warmer intervals during the mid–sixteenth and late eighteenth centuries, with almost all years before the twentieth century well below the twentieth-century climatological mean."[8] These results confirm those reported earlier by Raymond S. Bradley and Philip D. Jones, who collated sixteen proxy databases from widely distributed regions to reconstruct global Northern Hemisphere summer temperatures. Bradley and Jones conclude that "in the Northern Hemisphere, the coldest intervals were from ~1570 to ~1730 and during most of the nineteenth century."[9]

A paleoclimatic record of circum-Arctic climatic change, published in 1997, also supports these general conclusions. A large group of scientists brought together twenty-nine databases derived from glaciers, tree rings, lake sediments, and marine sediments that pertain to the past four hundred years. For the twentieth century, they used instrumental records to calibrate the proxy data. This series shows generally colder conditions in the 1600s, warming in the 1700s, cooling in the first half of the 1800s, followed by "the peak warm conditions of the 20th century."[10]

HISTORIANS AND CLIMATE HISTORY

Historians doing research and writing about the early modern world now realize that this important climate shift occurred. Many are trying to calibrate their historical analyses to account for climate as a variable, not a constant.

Mechanisms of the Last 2000 Years, edited by Philip D. Jones, Raymond S. Bradley, Jean Jouzel, and the North Atlantic Treaty Organization, Scientific Affairs Division (Berlin: Springer, 1996).

8. Michael E. Mann, Raymond S. Bradley, and Malcolm K. Hughes, "Global-Scale Temperature Patterns and Climate Forcing over the Past Six Centuries," *Nature*, no. 392 (1998): 783.

9. Raymond S. Bradley and Philip D. Jones, " 'Little Ice Age' Summer Temperature Variations: Their Nature and Relevance to Recent Global Warming Trends," *Holocene* 3 (1993): 374.

10. J. Overpeck et al., "Arctic Environment Change of the Last Four Centuries," *Science* 278, no. 5341 (1997): 3.

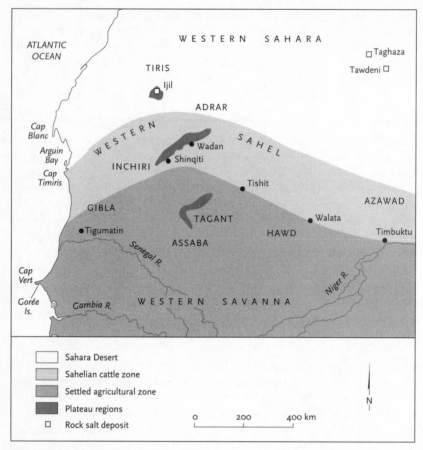

Map 2.1 Western Sahel, approximate location of ecological zones, c. 1600.
Adapted from James L. A. Webb, *Desert Frontier: Ecological and Economic Change
along the Western Sahel, 1600–1850* (Madison: University of Wisconsin Press,
1995), map 1.2, p. 10.

How to do this with precision is still a complicated issue. For historians of the
early modern period, there remain serious intellectual and practical obstacles to assimilating, understanding, and using climate data. For most historians, climate is an unacknowledged constant that has its own predictive
value. Nearly all historians engaged in the study of any region and society in
the early modern period have an intuitive, largely unexamined understanding of the climate of that region. They apply their personal experience of the
weather patterns of the locality or region they study to descriptions of seasonality and weather drawn from the sources they read. In some unstated

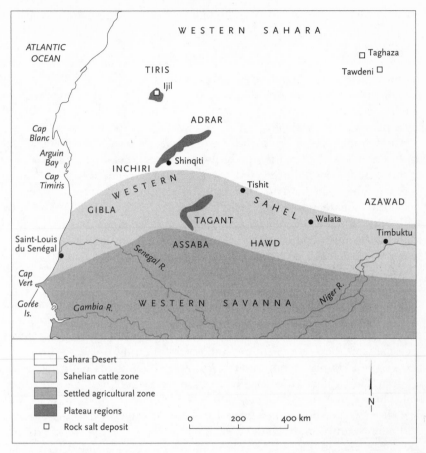

Map 2.2 Western Sahel, approximate location of ecological zones, c. 1850. Adapted from James L. A. Webb, *Desert Frontier: Ecological and Economic Change along the Western Sahel, 1600–1850* (Madison: University of Wisconsin Press, 1995), map 1.1, p. 6.

fashion, each historian then develops his or her own climate model. He or she applies this construct to better analyze the behavior of the people and groups studied.

For some time, historians have been vaguely aware that in the temperate zone, climate patterns were different from those that we experience today in those regions. However, few have directly addressed possible discrepancies between the climate and weather of today and the climate and weather that prevailed two to five centuries ago.

From written sources, it is possible to abstract reliable qualitative or anecdotal material about weather and climate. Far more than we do today, people living in the early modern centuries put enormous effort into shaping a shared model of local weather and climate—but without access to the kind of modern meteorological, statistical data common in the twenty-first century. Instead, steeped in shared experiences since early childhood, each person within a community participated actively in recall, interpretation, and if necessary, correction of a mental model of local climate. For most of these people, who lived and died by agriculture, this was second nature.

All inhabitants of a farmstead, hamlet, village, town, or city knew and avidly discussed what weather patterns should be expected for each season of the year. The model predicted norms of relative temperature, precipitation, humidity, wind, and hours of light and darkness as the year progressed. This local climate model anticipated severe weather-associated events such as floods, droughts, violent storms, raging fires, diseases, and plagues. In whatever form the history of the community was recorded—orally or written—so also the advance of weather each year was inscribed. Collective knowledge drawn from the model shaped seasonal rhythms of life, work, community, and household defenses against disaster.

Local climate models were continuously tested and refined. Religious and cultural rituals, cultivation, trade, industrial production, and movement of people and goods all relied on the predictability of climate at the local and regional scale. Severe aberrations and events often meant death for many people—not simply inconvenience or lowered standards of living. Early modern states, rulers, and their strategists inherited and improved on larger-scale climate models to collect revenues, encourage production, wage warfare, develop transport, and accomplish a host of other purposes.

If, however, historians concerned about the Little Ice Age are to extrapolate and formalize our understanding of these local-to-regional vernacular climate models, there must be a larger framework against which they may be assessed. We need consistent time-series data for each world region and its subregions and localities that reconstruct season-by-season and year-by-year weather back to the early medieval period. After uniform use of thermometers and other metrological instruments began in the late seventeenth century, more reliable long-term seasonal and annual data became available. For more than half the early modern period, however, these data have been acquired only by considerable effort and ingenuity in the use of disparate sources and statistical analysis.

Before the 1960s, most historians largely ignored a growing body of evidence from the physical sciences that climate in the recent past had varied considerably.[11] This indifference vanished when the prominent French his-

11. With the notable exception of Scandinavian historians who, early in the twentieth century, developed a theory of climate change to explain the demise of Norse populations in

torian Emmanuel Le Roy Ladurie published his widely read book *Times of Feast, Times of Famine: A History of Climate since the Year 1000* (the French original was published in 1967 and the English translation in 1971).[12] In 1972, the British meteorologist H. H. Lamb published *Climate: Present, Past, and Future*, in which he argues for a medieval warm period followed by cooling in the Little Ice Age of the early modern centuries.[13] In the same year, the historian Zhu Kezhen published (in Chinese) the first study of historic temperatures in China that took advantage of the rich, long-term documentation for that region.[14] In 1974, Gerard Manley compiled a record of monthly temperatures from 1659 to 1973 for central England, and in 1984, Christian Pfister published a similar compendium for Switzerland.[15] By the early 1980s, Ye. P. Borisenkov published (in Russian) data taken from chronicles to reconstruct Russian climate from the eleventh to the eighteenth centuries.[16] In 1980, Zhang De'er reconstructed nearly five centuries of winter temperatures in South China using data from local gazetteers.[17]

Over the past two decades, climate historians working in various world regions have refined and improved the methodologies discussed and have identified new documentary and proxy sources.[18] They have made substantial progress in compiling reliable annual and even seasonal weather data extending to 1400 C.E. and earlier. Often these methods necessitate close cooperation with physical and biological scientists. Written documents include diaries that often contain daily weather observations of relative temperature, humidity, wind, and precipitation. Diaries and other documents also record "weather-dependent natural phenomena"—floods, droughts, freezing, and

---

fourteenth-century Greenland. See Gustaf Utterstrom, "Climatic Fluctuations and Population Problems in Early Modern History," in *The Ends of the Earth*, edited by Donald Worster (Cambridge: Cambridge University Press, 1988).

12. Emmanuel Le Roy Ladurie, *Histoire du climat depuis l'an mil* (Paris: Flammarion, 1967).

13. H. H. Lamb, *Climate: Present, Past, and Future* (London: Methuen, 1972); Emmanuel Le Roy Ladurie, *Times of Feast, Times of Famine: A History of Climate since the Year 1000* (Garden City, N.Y.: Doubleday, 1971).

14. Cited in Robert B. Marks, " 'It Never Used to Snow': Climatic Variability and Harvest Yields in Late-Imperial South China, 1650–1850," in *Sediments of Time: Environment and Society in Chinese History*, edited by Mark Elvin and Liu Ts'ui-jung (Cambridge: Cambridge University Press, 1998), 414.

15. G. Manley, "Central England Temperatures: Monthly Means, 1659 to 1973," *Quarterly Journal of the Royal Meteorological Society* 100 (1974); Christian Pfister, *Das Klima der Schweiz von 1525–1860 und seine Bedeutung in der Geschichte von Bevölkerung und Landwirtschaft* (Bern: P. Haupt, 1984); Pfister, *Agrakonjunktur und Witterungsverlauf im westlichen Schweizer Mittelland* (Liebefeld: Lang Druck, 1975).

16. Ye. P. Borisenkov, "Documentary Evidence from the U.S.S.R.," in *Climate since A.D. 1500*, edited by Raymond S. Bradley and Philip D. Jones, rev. ed. (London: Routledge, 1995).

17. Cited in Marks, "It Never Used to Snow," 414.

18. In 1979, two nearly simultaneous scholarly meetings, one in Britain and one in the United States, brought climate history to a wider academic audience. The larger British meet-

break-up of lakes and rivers—and "weather-dependent biological phenomena," such as the arrival of migrant birds, flowering of trees and shrubs, and timing of the harvest. An array of written documents contains this type of information in scattered entries that must be searched and collated. Once obtained, careful content analysis is necessary for both individual and clustered records in order to arrive at numerical values for statistical analysis.[19]

Working together, scientists and historians have combined and analyzed individual data sets to construct long-term climate history data series for large regions. These syntheses generally confirm the trends inferred from glacial activity and from long-term individual and multiple proxy data sets.

Scientists and historians have also come together to test hypotheses about possible causes for the early modern cooling trend. For example, scientists have speculated on a possible connection between a low incidence of sunspots in the early modern Maunder Minimum (1645–1715) and global cooling. Between 1645 and 1715, an especially low number of sunspots implied lowered solar radiation and hence lowered temperature during one of the colder portions of the Little Ice Age.[20] The evidence is not conclusive, but two more recent studies argue that such a direct relationship is probable.

---

ing, the brainchild of Hubert H. Lamb, the pioneering climate historian, was grandly conceived. The British organizers, T. M. L. Wigley, M. J. Ingram, and G. Farmer, gathered more than 250 scholars and scientists from thirty countries to discuss approaches to studying past climate change over the five millennia of recorded human history throughout the world. In 1981, the organizers published selected papers in an edited volume, *Climate and History: Studies in Past Climates and Their Impact on Man* (Cambridge: Cambridge University Press), which continues to be read and cited today.

Also in 1979, two American historians, Robert Rotberg and Theodore Rabb, convened a "meeting of meteorologists, paleobotanists, astronomers, chemists, physicists and historians" sponsored by the Rockefeller Foundation. Questions and issues surrounding the Little Ice Age predominated in the meeting. The resulting essays—some methodological, some interpretive, and some containing programmatic suggestions for future research—appeared first in the *Journal of Interdisciplinary History* (spring 1980). Publication in book form the following year, under the title *Climate and History: Studies in Interdisciplinary History*, edited by Rotberg and Rabb, further stimulated interest, and encouraged expanded research, in a new and exciting field (Princeton, N.J.: Princeton University Press, 1981).

19. Roger Y. Anderson, "Long-Term Changes in the Frequency of Occurrence of El Niño Events," in *Climate since A.D. 1500,* edited by Raymond S. Bradley and Philip D. Jones, rev. ed. (London: Routledge, 1995), 6–7.

20. When specialists assembled and reported on the available evidence at a large conference in the early 1990s, they could not support the hypothesis. The editors of the conference volume concluded that "no general linkage between solar activity and terrestrial climate can be confirmed." Burkhard Frenzel et al., *Climatic Trends and Anomalies in Europe, 1675–1715: High Resolution Spatio-Temporal Reconstructions from Direct Meteorological Observations and Proxy Data: Methods and Results* (Stuttgart: G. Fischer, 1994), 1.

J. Luterbacher and his colleagues, after reconstructing sea-level air pressure and atmospheric circulation during the Late Maunder Minimum (1675–1715), argue that the more severe European weather during this period can be linked, in part, to lower solar radiation coupled with intense volcanic activity.[21] George C. Reid, using a modeling approach, also argues that solar irradiance may well have contributed to the cooler temperatures of this period.[22]

During the seventeenth century, years with extremely cool summers—1601, 1641–1643, 1659, 1666–1669, 1675, and 1698–1699—correlate with eight major volcanic eruptions.[23] All, save 1601 and 1641–1643, fall within the Maunder Minimum years. As the authors of a study of the 1600 eruption of Huaynaputina, Peru, comment, "It has long been established that gas and fine ash from large equatorial explosive eruptions can spread globally, and that the sulphuric acid that is consequently produced in the stratosphere can cause a small, but statistically significant, cooling of global temperatures."[24] The Huaynaputina eruption, one of the largest on record according to tree-ring and other proxy data, caused the summer of 1601 to be among the coolest in six hundred years in the Northern Hemisphere.[25]

After climate historians have reconstructed seasonal and annual weather data, another set of questions emerges. What were the effects of the Little Ice Age on human society, and how did humans adapt to these climate changes? Treating climate as a variable rather than a constant makes the historian's task more difficult. One difficulty is temporal. What period is to be considered? Long-term climate trends during the Little Ice Age were not smooth and uniform but instead became highly variable with more pronounced swings between cooler and warmer years. There were a number of irregularly occurring severe multiyear periods similar in seasonal temperature and precipitation. How does the historian interpret what appear to have been greater numbers of devastating windstorms or other extreme weather events that accompanied cooling temperatures?

Another difficulty is spatial. If we have reliable long-term weather data for

21. J. Luterbacher et al., "Monthly Mean Pressure Reconstruction for the Late Maunder Minimum Period (A.D. 1675–1715)," *International Journal of Climatology* 20, no. 10 (2000): 1049–66; J. Luterbacher, R. Rickli, E. Xoplaki, C. Tinguely, C. Beck, C. Pfister, and H. Wanner, "The Late Maunder Minimum (1675–1715): A Key Period for Studying Decadal Scale Climatic Change in Europe," *Climatic Change* 49 (June 2001): 441–62.

22. George C. Reid, "Solar Forcing of Global Climate Change since the Mid–Seventeenth Century," *Climatic Change* 37 (1997).

23. K. R. Briffa, P. D. Jones, F. H. Schweingruber, and T. J. Osborn, "Influence of Volcanic Eruptions on Northern Hemisphere Summer Temperature over the Past 600 Years," *Nature* 393 (1998).

24. Shanaka L. de Silva and Gregory A. Zielinski, "Global Influence of the A.D. 1600 Eruption of Huaynaputina, Peru," *Nature* 393 (June 4, 1998): 455.

25. Ibid., 457.

one relatively small region, can these same trends be applied to a wider area? Moreover, if so, should we assume the impact was the same on all human societies within that wider area? Can we make generalizations that extend to the major world regions such as Europe or Eurasia, or even to hemispheres or the globe itself?

Even a connection so seemingly straightforward as that between adverse temperature and precipitation and diminished or failed food-grain harvests in Europe or other temperate regions is not at all simple. For example, some economic historians studying the early modern centuries, such as Jan de Vries, have argued that evidence from the Netherlands suggests we cannot assume a direct causal connection between colder weather and economic distress.[26] Even if years with colder winters and/or wet summers are also those of reduced agricultural production, scarcities, and higher prices, there may well be a number of other socioeconomic or political variables that explain these economic phenomena equally well or even better. To isolate colder weather as a cause demands an analysis no less sophisticated than that required to identify any other causal factor.

In other world regions, the critical variable was not temperature but precipitation. For areas in tropical latitudes, the counterpart of cooling temperatures in Europe was diminution or even failure of rainfall and more frequent drought conditions. Obviously, when rains fail, rainfall-dependent agriculture fails as well. The causal connection between economic scarcity and human hunger is palpable. Even with more frequent droughts, however, the question of impact is complicated. Human societies can and do migrate, shift crops, irrigate, or take other corrective measures to reduce risks from drought.

Finally, we come to a bundle of questions about human adaptive behavior to perceived climate change. For example, did European cultivators shift their crop mixes and agricultural year calendars to adjust to harsher weather conditions during the Little Ice Age? Did they shift cultivation from less to more favorable climate zones? Such movement could be as limited as dropping from higher to lower elevations or as momentous as interregional or even intercontinental migration.

For illustration, we now turn to closer examination of three world regions: Europe, located wholly in the temperate zone; China, partly temperate and partly tropical; and West Africa, entirely in the tropics. For each of these regions, systematic research in climate history has generated interesting early modern climate histories and stimulated scholarly debates as to their linkage with human affairs.

---

26. Jan de Vries, "Measuring the Impact of Climate on History: The Search for Appropriate Methodologies," in *Climate and History: Studies in Interdisciplinary History,* edited by Robert I. Rotberg and Theodore K. Rabb (Princeton, N.J.: Princeton University Press, 1981).

EUROPE

Among the world regions, Europe has the best developed and most detailed climate history. A cadre of European climate historians has carried out organized, sustained research in this field for the past three decades or more. In 1999, Christian Pfister, Rudolf Bràzdil, and Rudiger Glaser edited and published in the journal *Climatic Change* twelve articles devoted to the climate history of sixteenth-century central Europe. This collection—the work of forty-five contributors—reveals the strength and depth of cross-disciplinary research under way on Europe's climate history of the early modern centuries.

The contributors drew on the resources of a climate database for central Europe systematically developed at the University of Bern. Pfister, a Swiss historian, has taken a leading role in organizing a cooperative effort to build a climate history database for Europe drawn from all possible documentary and proxy sources. Beginning with Switzerland and surrounding regions in central Europe, Pfister and his colleagues have developed systematic data for the period 1525–1979. From disparate sources—including 80,000 daily entries in weather diaries—these researchers have homogenized and coded the data to arrive at a temperature and wetness index for each month and each year over the four and a half centuries covered. The data are calibrated against a 1901–1960 reference period. Temperature and precipitation deviations from the 1901–1960 mean are calculated as eleven-year moving averages for each year as a whole and for each season.[27]

For sixteenth-century Switzerland alone, there are 7,350 weather observations, which reach nearly complete temporal coverage by the end of the century. For the first fifty years, weather observations exist for 228 months (38 percent) of the total 600 months. For the second fifty years, the total rises to 588 months or 98 percent.[28] Direct observations of weather and climate occur in written sources such as regional or town annals and chronicles; in church, university, hospital, and other institutional registers; and in personal records such as diaries. The explosive growth of printing and publishing generated a mass of documents far beyond that available for the medieval period. For example, printed almanacs, first published in the late fifteenth century, left spaces for weather observations by the owner.

27. Christian Pfister, "Monthly Temperature and Precipitation in Central Europe, 1525–1979: Quantifying Documentary Evidence on Weather and Its Effects," in *Climate since A.D. 1500*, edited by Raymond S. Bradley and Philip D. Jones, rev. ed. (London: Routledge, 1995).

28. Christian Pfister, Rudolf Bràzdil, Rudiger Glaser, Mariano Barriendos, Dario Camuffo, Mathias Deutsch, Petr Dobrovolnp, Silvia Enzi, Emanuela Guidoboni, Oldrich Kotyza, Stefan Militzer, Lajos Ràcz, and Fernando S. Rodrigo, "Documentary Evidence on Climate in Sixteenth-Century Europe," *Climatic Change* 43, no. 1 (1999): 62.

Some persons with a scientific bent maintained rigorous weather diaries. Among the most valuable of those surviving is the diary of Wolfgang Haller of Zurich, who entered 10,200 weather observations between 1545 and 1576. The astronomer Tycho Brahe and his assistants, at his observatory on the island of Hven in Denmark, made 4,962 weather observations for the period 1582–1597.[29] When compared with modern instrumentation data from the 1901–1960 reference period, the fine-grained detail in these diaries proved especially useful for setting up precipitation indices.

Other documents record indirect observations of changing biological phenomena or other data from which climate data can be inferred. Chroniclers and diarists recorded the freezing and thawing of lakes and rivers, floods and high water, severe storms, droughts, and dearth and failed harvests. Various records document the reduction of taxes and the incidence of weather-determined labor such as haymaking, work in vineyards, and ice cutting.

From diaries and an array of other documentary and proxy sources, the authors constructed a set of seasonal and annual indexes of temperature and precipitation for the sixteenth century. Data for the indices were weighted by area for the present-day territories of Germany, Switzerland, and the Czech Republic. The indices measure deviations from the means of temperature and precipitation for the same area in the period 1901–1960. According to the compilers, the indices show that temperatures in all seasons, but especially winter and spring, averaged one-half degree centigrade cooler than in the 1901–1960 reference period. All seasons, but especially winter (9.8 percent higher) and autumn (5.8 percent higher), had greater precipitation than the twentieth-century reference years. Despite the overall trend, there was considerable variation as "warmer phases alternated with colder ones and wetter phases with drier ones."[30]

These tendencies were becoming more severe toward the end of the 1500s, according to Rudiger Glaser and colleagues: "Altogether, an increasing decline of the temperature conditions is evident in central Europe during the second half of the century. In the course of the sixteenth century all seasons showed a significant cooling trend which was more and more accentuated."[31] The period 1586 to 1595 had an almost uninterrupted series

29. Christian Pfister, Rudolf Bràzdil, Rudiger Glaser, Anita Bokwa, Franz Holawe, Danuta Limanowka, Oldrich Kotyza, Jan Munzar, Laios Racz, Elisabeth Strommer, and Gabriela Schwarz-Zanetti, "Daily Weather Observations in Sixteenth-Century Europe," *Climatic Change* 43, no. 1 (1999): 116, table 1.

30. Rudiger Glaser, Rudolf Bràzdil, Christian Pfister, Petr Dobrovolnp, Mariano Barriendos Vallve, Anita Bokwa, Dario Camuffo, Oldrich Kotyza, Danuta Limanowka, Lajos Racz, and Fernando S. Rodrigo, "Seasonal Temperature and Precipitation Fluctuations in Selected Parts of Europe during the Sixteenth Century," *Climatic Change* 43, no. 1 (1999): 196.

31. Ibid.

of very cold winters in which the average temperature may have been minus two degrees centigrade below the 1901–1960 mean. Over the same period, summers were also unusually cool, with an "uninterrupted sequence of eight cool summers from 1591 to 1598 [that] may have been unique in the last 500 years."[32]

Long-term data from dendrochronological studies of long-lived trees in Fennoscandia in northern Europe and the Urals in western Siberia, as well as oak tree data from a transect across Europe, confirm this cooling trend. The tree-ring data are also consistent with the Russian ice-melt data from Svalbard in the Arctic Ocean. The authors of this synoptic study concluded "that there was a marked reduction in average summer, and probably annual, temperatures over much of Europe during the 16th century. In northern Europe and the Alps, this occurred abruptly at around 1570 and marked the start of a prolonged period of generally cool summers which lasted well into the next century."[33]

A restudy of the data on Swiss Alpine glaciers—especially that of the well-documented Great Aletsch, Lower Grindenwald, and Rhone glaciers—reached a similar conclusion. Toward the end of the sixteenth century, Alpine glaciers increased in size in an advance that did not end until the late nineteenth century. As they advanced, glaciers formed ice lakes by damming up rivers and streams that flowed along their sides. At irregular intervals, water broke through the ice dams to cause disastrous downstream flooding.[34]

Two of the articles in this collection directly tied colder and wetter weather in the second half of the sixteenth century with reduced output of wine and grains—two of the most important food crops of central Europe. Annual data on wine production for vineyards in Switzerland, lower Austria, Württemberg, and western Hungary show a pronounced slump beginning in 1587 that persisted as late as 1610. These declines correlate directly with the extended sequence of cold and wet summers at the end of the century. Since wine production was at its northern climatic margin in these regions, cold summers reduced output and cut sugar content in the grapes that were harvested. Consumers reacted to high prices for inferior wine by shifting to beer.[35]

32. Christian Pfister and Rudolf Bràzdil, "Climatic Variability in Sixteenth-Century Europe and Its Social Dimension: A Synthesis," *Climatic Change* 43, no. 1 (1999): 23–24.

33. K. R. Briffa, P. D. Jones, R. B. Vogel, F. H. Schweingruber, M. G. L. Baillie, and S. G. Shiyatov, "European Tree Rings and Climate in the Sixteenth Century," *Climatic Change* 43, no. 1 (1999): 165.

34. H. Holzhauser and H. J. Zumbuhl, "Glacier Fluctuations in the Western Swiss and French Alps in the Sixteenth Century," *Climatic Change* 43, no. 1 (September 1999): 223–37.

35. Erich Landsteiner, "The Crisis of Wine Production in Late Sixteenth-Century Central Europe: Climatic Causes and Economic Consequences," *Climatic Change* 43, no. 1 (September 1999): 323–34.

Similarly, the annual price series for rye in central Europe correlates directly with unfavorable seasonal temperatures and precipitation.[36] There is a robust correlation between price fluctuations and climatic-variable increases that is most noticeable in the last third of the century, 1565 to 1600. Pfister and Bràzdil argue "that in the last third of the sixteenth century[,] climate change became the most significant element affecting food prices."[37] This opinion challenges the more conventional view that increases in the money supply by New World precious metals or population levels determined food prices.

Finally, Wolfgang Behringer posits that there is a causal connection between worsening weather conditions reflected in dwindling harvests and the dramatic increase in burning of witches after 1560.[38] After enduring long, cold winters, followed by cold, wet springs and summers with curtailed harvests, fearful and anxious populations sought scapegoats throughout Europe. Behringer states, "Since everybody thought that the continuous crops failure was caused by witches of devilish hate, the whole country stood up for their eradication."[39] Witches were accused of weather making that brought severe thunderstorms, hailstorms, crop failures, floods, and cattle diseases. Under torture, accused witches confessed to planning to destroy grainfields and vineyards by altering the weather. In short, contemporaries recognized that their weather was changing for the worse.

For the longer early modern period, extending from circa 1500 to 1850, the central European database shows trends similar to those obtained from nondocumentary proxy sources. Beginning about 1560, seasonal and annual temperatures were consistently lower than the mean for 1901–1960. Several multiyear episodes of extreme cold stand out. During the 1690s, annual temperatures were nearly one degree centigrade lower than during the reference period. Annual temperatures did not reach these lows again for two hundred years. During the nineteenth century, "the coldest hundred year period since 1500," temperatures in the first decade of the nineteenth century and the 1880s were colder than those of the 1690s. Precipitation was consistently lower than that of the twentieth-century reference period. The only major exception to this profile is that summers in the late sixteenth cen-

36. Walter Bauerenfeind and Ulrich Woitek, "The Influence of Climatic Change on Price Fluctuations in Germany during the Sixteenth Century Price Revolution," *Climatic Change* 43, no. 1 (September 1999): 303–21.

37. Pfister and Bràzdil, "Climatic Variability in Sixteenth-Century Europe and Its Social Dimension," 42.

38. Wolfgang Behringer, "Climatic Change and Witch-Hunting: The Impact of the Little Ice Age on Mentalities," *Climatic Change* 43, no. 1 (September 1999): 335–51.

39. Ibid., 340–41, quoting from comments by Johannes Linden, canon at St. Simeon in Trier, in his description of the witch persecutions under Prince Archbishop Johannes VII von Schonenberg (r. 1581–1599).

tury were wetter than those in the reference period. In addition, summers through the 1700s were generally warmer and wetter than during the twentieth-century mean. Otherwise, the average temperature and precipitation fell below the 1901–1960 mean for each season, as well as for the year as a whole.[40]

The Swiss data are consistent with trends derived from climate data for other parts of Europe. For example, seasonal and annual temperature data for central England compiled for 1659 and after by Gerard Manley show "highly significant" statistical correlations with the Swiss temperatures.[41] An analysis of contemporary notations of severe winters for northern Italy between 1536 and 1855 shows that they coincide with the Swiss data almost exactly.[42] Seasonal mean temperatures for European Russia show pronounced winter weather from 1620 to 1890.[43] A detailed analysis of weather observations found in Jesuit correspondence from Castile between 1634 and 1648 reveals abnormally cold and wet winters; cold, but not abnormally rainy, springs; normal summers; and cold and wet autumns. According to F. S. Rodrigo, M. J. Esteban-Parra, and Y. Castro-Diez, "Among the principal meteorological phenomena detected in the period 1634–1648, we find intense rains and cold weather with heavy snowfalls."[44]

However, these long-term trends mask dramatic year-to-year oscillations. For example, in one of the earliest sets of instrumental observations, Louis Morin used a thermometer and barometer to record temperature and air pressure in his meteorological journal kept daily in central Paris between 1676 and 1713. Over the thirty-six years covered by the journal, winter temperatures for half (eighteen) of the years fell below the mean for 1901–1960. Four of these are among the most severe winters known for western Europe: 1684, 1695, 1697, and 1709. The other eighteen winters, however, had average temperatures above, and some well above (1683, 1686, 1702, 1707, 1708), the mean for the twentieth-century calibration period.[45]

Weather conditions in the eastern Mediterranean did not always coincide

40. Pfister, "Monthly Temperature and Precipitation in Central Europe," 136, fig. 6.4.

41. Ibid., 139, table 6.5.

42. D. Camuffo and S. Enzi, "Reconstructing the Climate of Northern Italy from Archives Sources," in *Climate since A.D. 1500*, edited by Raymond S. Bradley and Philip D. Jones, rev. ed. (London: Routledge, 1995), 150–51, table 7.1.

43. Borisenkov, "Documentary Evidence from the U.S.S.R.," 176, fig. 9.2.

44. F. S. Rodrigo, M. J. Esteban-Parra, and Y. Castro-Diez, "On the Use of the Jesuit Private Correspondence Records in Climate Reconstructions: A Case Study from Castile (Spain) for 1634–1648," *Climatic Change* 40 (1998): 639.

45. Christian Pfister and Walter Bareiss, "The Climate in Paris between 1675 and 1715 according to the Meteorological Journal of Louis Morin," in *Climatic Trends and Anomalies in Europe, 1675–1715: High Resolution Spatio-Temporal Reconstructions from Direct Meteorological Observations and Proxy Data: Methods and Results*, edited by Burkhard Frenzel, Christian Pfister, Birgit Gläser, and the European Science Foundation (Stuttgart: G. Fischer, 1994). Since central Paris

with those of southern Europe—although the general cooling trend is apparent. Venetian officials who ruled the island of Crete (Kriti) sent regular letters and reports to the doge, the head of the Venetian Republic, that contain dated references to weather and climate.[46] During the twentieth century, Crete normally had dry, hot summers and wet, mild winters. However, during the last century of Venetian rule, 1548 to 1648, Crete experienced twenty-one severe and very severe winters marked by "exceptional falls of snow, prolonged periods of abnormal cold, or rain so excessive as to prevent sowing of crops until late spring." Also unusual was the incidence of drought. In twenty-five years, the rains failed either in winter or spring or both.[47] By modern standards, these droughts were devastating: according to Jean Grove and Annalisa Conterio, "None of the twentieth century drought years have experienced such long rainless periods as those in the period 1547–1645, nor such a complete lack of winter rain."[48] Both severe wet winters and winter-spring drought had a serious impact on food-grain, grape, and olive harvests, as well as on animal herds. Clearly, adverse climate conditions placed an additional burden on the population of Crete in the early modern centuries.

In a 1988 article, Pfister develops evidence and strong arguments to show that severe Little Ice Age weather had an adverse economic effect on early modern European society.[49] He demonstrates that annual climate data for Switzerland correlate with annual price data for food grains. Years with unfavorable temperature and precipitation for cultivation were marked by abnormally high prices for the commodities that formed by far the greatest portion of the Swiss food budget.

Pfister devised a model to measure the effects of climate on agricultural production that assigns relative weights to seven types of unfavorable seasonal weather conditions. These include excessive rains in autumn, precocious onset of winter, excessive rains in winter, excessive rains in spring, low temperatures in spring, low temperatures in summer, and excessive rainfall during the harvest (July and August).[50] Using modern agronomic findings, he weighted most heavily the low temperatures in spring, especially the month of April, that delayed sowing and inhibited the fixing of nitrogen in the soil and thereby reduced the subsequent harvest. He weighted equally heavily the long periods of rain during the harvests, which encouraged mold

was an urban heat island even in the winter, it is likely that Morin's figures were slightly higher than those for the countryside.

46. Jean Grove and Annalisa Conterio, "The Climate of Crete in the Sixteenth and Seventeenth Centuries," *Climatic Change* 30 (1995).

47. Ibid., 224, table 1.

48. Ibid., 237. The last drought year for the hundred-year period was 1645.

49. Christian Pfister, "Fluctuations climatiques et prix céréaliers en Europe du XVIe au XXe siècle," *Annales, Economies, Sociétés, Civilization* 43, no. 1 (January–February 1988).

50. Ibid., 34–36.

and insect infestations and sharply reduced usable yields. He assigned lesser values to the other five conditions. When matched with monthly temperature and precipitation data, these weighted values resulted in a numerical value for the climate of each year to be matched with its food-grain prices.

Pfister developed his price series from several already published long-term series: monthly prices for purchasing grains for the public stores in Basel; prices paid each month for wheat, oats, and wheat-rye mixed flour by the municipal hospital in Lausanne; and monthly prices for grain negotiated by the peasants with the municipal government of Bern.[51]

He arranged these data in the form of running thirty-five-year averages and expressed their value as percentage of variance. The results of this calculation, when presented visually, reveal remarkable congruence between severe weather and high prices over three centuries, 1550 to 1850. Pfister points out that the two most highly weighted variables possess the greatest explanatory power. For example, price peaks in the years 1569–1574, 1586–1589, 1593–1597, 1626–1629, and 1688–1694 coincide with years of cold springs and wet summers. However, the periods of highest prices, such as in 1570–1571, were those in which cold springs and harvest rains persisted for two years in a row.[52] For those few episodes when high prices were not matched by adverse weather, war—with its scarcities and rising demand—offers a ready explanation for the divergence. It is only in the second half of the nineteenth century—when, after 1870, construction of a railway network permitted cheap, fast transport of bulk food supplies to the continental interior—that climate and prices began to diverge.

Drawing on his long-term Swiss data, Pfister makes a further argument that the Little Ice Age substantially lowered food production in Switzerland and central Europe. That is, from the 1560s until twentieth-century warming occurred, this part of Europe periodically suffered weather-caused food scarcities as harvest yields fluctuated.[53]

In other words, contrary to what Jan de Vries found for the Netherlands,

---

51. Ibid., 32–33.
52. Ibid., 37; 38–39, fig. 2.
53. Ibid., 47. Colder Little Ice Age weather, if associated with food scarcities, had negative demographic consequences. Patrick Galloway, a historical demographer, compared long-term annual variations in births, deaths, marriages, and grain prices with seasonal temperatures for England over the period 1545–1914; France, 1505–1914; Prussia, 1700–1914; and Sweden, 1735–1914. He found that annual fluctuations in food-grain prices, termed the "short-term positive check," had a direct impact for a few years on fertility and mortality. For all countries and all periods, short-term fertility and nuptiality declined, and mortality increased, as grain prices rose. Seasonal fluctuations in temperatures, termed "the short-term temperature mortality check," also had a direct effect on fertility and mortality. Mortality increased during and for a few years after cold winters and hot summers. However, there was only a weak association between temperature and fertility. "Secular Changes in the Short-Term Preventive, Positive, and Temperature Checks to Population Growth in Europe, 1460–1909," *Climatic Change* 26 (1994).

the Swiss data show that climate was a direct causal variable in central Europe that determined food prices. Unlike the Dutch, whose food markets received regular shipments of Baltic grain by sea to augment domestic production, the Swiss depended for subsistence almost entirely on their domestic production. Adverse climate in this period seems to have affected nearly all of western Europe.

It seems, however, that those European maritime and coastal countries with direct access to maritime trade were better able to offset harvest deficiencies by food imports. In other words, food imports had a strategic importance in excess of their nominal value. Countries like the Netherlands, England, Spain, and Portugal— whose foreign trade and colonial tribute surpluses enabled their populations to purchase New World codfish, West Indian sugar, or Baltic grain—were partially buffered against the effects of adverse climate.

CHINA

China's climate history conforms to the general Little Ice Age pattern. This history is more fully documented and can be reconstructed in greater detail than that of Europe or any other world region. Chinese historians and scientists have drawn on annual climate observations found in local gazetteers maintained by local gentry for centuries in nearly every local district or county. The earliest temperature series is the 1972 reconstruction by Zhu Kezhen, mentioned earlier, whose results have been reported in several Western language syntheses.[54] Zhu relied primarily on dates of lakes freezing in the lower Yangzi region to estimate the onset of cooler temperatures. More recently, the geographer Zheng Sizhong accepted Zhu's conclusions with some modifications. These two studies conclude that China's annual temperature dropped by approximately one degree centigrade in the period 1470 to 1850.[55] Within this lengthy period, the data point to five alternating cooler and warmer periods: cooler from 1470 to 1560, warmer from 1560 to 1620, cooler from 1620 to 1740, warmer from 1740 to 1830, and cooler from 1830 to 1850.[56]

54. Chia-cheng Chang, *The Reconstruction of Climate in China for Historical Times* (Beijing: Science Press, 1988).

55. Robert B. Marks, *Tigers, Rice, Silk, and Silt: Environment and Economy in Late Imperial South China* (Cambridge: Cambridge University Press, 1997), 491, fig. 1.5.

56. Ibid., 196, fig. 6.1. Dates in the text reflect Zheng Sizhong's periodization, not that of Zhu Kezhen as summarized by Marks in this figure. Tokugawa Japan appears to have diverged from this pattern. I. Maejima and Y. Tagima, deriving their temperature series from daily weather records kept at Hirosaki, find three distinct cold phases appearing in the two hundred years of the weather diary: 1611–1650, 1691–1720, and 1821–1850. "Climate of Little Ice Age in Japan," *Geographical Reports of Tokyo Metropolitan University* 18 (1983).

Bradley and Jones compared reconstructed summer temperature anomaly series for five regions: the East China, North China, lower Yellow River, Southeast China, and lower Yangzi regions in China for the period 1400 to 1950.[57] Each series, based on historical documentation, shows anomalies from the mean of summer temperatures for that region for the period 1860–1959. The overall pattern, according to Bradley and Jones, is as follows: "Temperatures declined from around 1500 to a pronounced minimum in the mid–seventeenth century. The 1650's were exceptionally cold throughout eastern China and Korea. Temperatures then rose, reaching levels comparable with those of the early twentieth century during brief periods in the eighteenth century. Cooler conditions again prevailed with low temperatures in the early to mid–nineteenth century."[58] When the records for the five regional series are averaged by decade and graphed, the patterns stand out in bold relief.[59] Especially dramatic is the plunge in Chinese temperatures to an average of minus four degrees centigrade in the 1650s. Chinese temperatures during the eighteenth century, unlike those in Europe, rarely climbed above the average for the 1860–1959 reference period. The combined Chinese temperature data are highly correlated with the composite Northern Hemisphere data for the period 1600 to 1959.[60] Clearly, Chinese temperatures were linked to cooling weather patterns common to all northern world regions in the early modern period.

China also has documentary sources from which extremely long-term annual precipitation data series can be extracted and analyzed. Chinese climatologists have compiled a historical atlas that plots a five-level relative wetness/dryness index for the period 1470–1998 for each of one hundred sites dispersed across China. The index levels range from Class 1 ("extremely wet, long-lasting/intense precipitation over large areas" causing significant flooding) to neutral Class 3 ("normal, good harvest, no record of flood or drought") to Class 5 ("extremely dry, long-lasting severe drought over large areas").[61] The index reflects conditions for the summer monsoon from May to September of each year that brings about 80 percent of China's rainfall.

57. The published data used by Bradley and Jones include Shaowu Wang and Risheng Wang, "Seasonal and Annual Temperature Variations since 1470 A.D. in East China," *Acta Meteorological Sinica* 4 (1990); Shaowu Wang, "Reconstruction of Temperature Series of North China from the 1380's to the 1980's," *Science in China*, ser. B, 34 (1991); Shaowu Wang, "Reconstruction of Palaeo-Temperature Series in China from the 1380's to the 1980's," *Warzburger Geographische Arbeiten* 80 (1991); Risheng Wang, Shaowu Wang, and K. Fraedrich, "An Approach to Reconstruction of Temperature on a Seasonal Basis Using Historical Documents from China," *International Journal of Climatology* 11 (1991).

58. Bradley and Jones, " 'Little Ice Age' Summer Temperature Variations," 370.

59. Ibid., 372, fig. 6 and table 1.

60. Ibid., fig. 6 and table 1.

61. Jie Song, "Changes in Dryness/Wetness in China during the Last 529 Years," *International Journal of Climatology* 20 (2000): 1006.

Somewhat surprisingly, precipitation was less variable and less extreme during the cooler early modern centuries than during the twentieth century. For the period 1470 to 1800, fifty-one-year moving average trends show that every year 40 to 50 of the 100 sites reported normal Class 3 precipitation—with a pronounced drop in the number of normal years during the mid–seventeenth century. After 1800, normal years dropped steadily from a high of fifty in 1800 to twenty-five in the early twentieth century.[62] Normal years became markedly less frequent throughout the nineteenth century, and their number reached a new low in the early twentieth century.

The indices for extreme wetness or extreme dryness show a different trajectory.[63] Heavy rainfall years with accompanying flooding were relatively high during the mid–sixteenth to the late seventeenth century, declined through much of the eighteenth century, started to rise in the nineteenth century, and then climbed to a new peak in the early twentieth century. Drought years were also relatively numerous in the seventeenth century and dwindled to low levels in the eighteenth and nineteenth centuries; they did not begin to increase in frequency until 1900.

In summary, in China during the Little Ice Age centuries, extreme rainfall conditions occurred at their highest intensity during the 1600s. The seventeenth century recorded numerous years with either excessive rainfall and flooding or sparse rainfall, drought, and dearth. However, the number of years with normal precipitation remained the same. The eighteenth century enjoyed more favorable precipitation conditions. After 1900, however, China's climate reached a new stage of both variability and stress from either too little or too much annual rainfall.

Prolonged adverse weather—drought and cold—accompanied and contributed to what has been termed a "seventeenth-century crisis in China."[64] For more than half a century, cataclysmic upheavals surrounded the rebellions leading to the fall of the Ming dynasty, the Manchu invasions, establishment of the Qing dynasty in 1644, and prolonged wars of Han Chinese resistance against the Manchus. China suffered a major demographic crisis as disease, famine, and war scourged the population.

62. Ibid., fig. 2. Trends from the 100-site and 25-site databases are in broad agreement.

63. Ibid., 1007, fig. 3. The number of sites reporting extreme wetness climbed to between 8 and 10 per year by the mid-1500s and remained at that level until the 1670s; the number declined to 6 per year during the 1700s, and it climbed steadily from 1800 to peak at 15 per year in the first decades of the twentieth century. The number of sites reporting extreme dryness leading to dearth dropped from a high in 1500 to less than 6 per year at midcentury, and climbed back to 9 per year in the 1620 to 1660 period. The number dropped to a new low of 4–6 reports per year during the 1700s and 1800s and climbed to an incidence of 12 per year in the twentieth century.

64. William Atwell, "A Seventeenth-Century 'General Crisis' in East Asia?" *Modern Asian Studies* 24, no. 4 (1990): 661–82.

Robert Marks reports the results of data assembled by Chinese historians for Lingan, a subtropical and tropical region formed by Guangxi and Guangdong provinces and located on China's southeast coast, that lend credence to a climatic impact. Lingan at midcentury was "in the depths of a mortality crisis, attended by, if not caused by, a subsistence crisis." For Guangdong province, between 1630 and 1690, local gazetteer writers in four of the six decades recorded severe cold with frost—even in such places as coastal Huilai county in 1636, where there was "snow, frost, and ice four or five inches deep on ponds. . . . They had never experienced anything like it before." The same period also saw numerous years with widespread drought and dearth, which peaked in the mid-1650s, judging from reports of dearth from nearly all Guangdong's counties. The people of Guangxi, Guangdong's neighboring province, endured the driest decades of any in the early modern centuries.[65]

During this period, local gazetteer writers reported numerous years with cold springs (with temperatures below fifteen degrees centigrade) that delayed rice transplanting. In some years with late springs, Guangdong and Guangxi farmers resorted to a single planting instead of their accustomed two crops of rice in a year. In some years, late spring freezes or snow killed the standing rice crop as well as fruit trees, fish in ponds, and even livestock. The gazetteer writers also recorded failure of the rains and subsequent harvests, scarcities, and rice prices that spiraled upward. Even in the warmer areas of southern China, cooler temperatures in the seventeenth century exacted a heavy price on agricultural production and human well-being.

WEST AFRICA

For West Africa, as for the tropics generally, "Little Ice Age" is a misnomer. The question of annual precipitation during the summer monsoon is the critical issue, not the cooling or warming of temperatures. Most of West Africa's annual precipitation comes in the summer months, when three great air masses meet at the intertropical convergence zone. The continental tropical air mass is a quasi-permanent, high-pressure cell, also known as the Sahara anticyclone, that remains high over the Sahara Desert throughout the year. This high, hot, dry air mass descends toward the earth, where it meets in the intertropical convergence zone with two moist, low-lying ocean air masses: the maritime tropical from the Indian Ocean and the maritime equatorial from the South Atlantic. In summer, the intertropical convergence zone moves northward when the high pressure of the tropical continental weakens as the sun reaches its highest point. This movement brings intense rainfall to the region as the moist tropical air reaches heated land surfaces.

65. Marks, *Tigers, Rice, Silk, and Silt*, 138; 141, fig. 4.2; 151; 200, fig. 6.3.

In the late 1970s, Sharon Nicholson, a historical meteorologist, published several articles reporting on her reconstruction of the climate history—long-term variations in precipitation—in the area of Africa that is north of ten degrees south of the equator.[66] To date, her work remains the standard. Nicholson used several long-term chronologies for river and lake levels from which relative wetness or dryness can be inferred. These include direct annual measurements made of the level of the Nile and of the levels of Lake Chad, Lake Turkana, and Lake Abhe, determined from lake sediments and pollen. She added long-term famine-drought chronologies for Senegambia and the Niger Bend developed from chronicles and other historical sources. She also assembled geographical descriptions and observations made by early European explorers.

From her synthesis of these disparate materials, Nicholson divided West Africa's climate history into wet and dry episodes. She concluded that the period from 700 to 1300 C.E. probably had wetter conditions throughout most of the region. The two centuries between 1300 and 1500 constituted a dry period. However, "climatic conditions wetter than those at present appear to have characterized the sixteenth and seventeenth centuries." After 1700, there began a slow drying process, although "a generally wetter character probably prevailed well into the eighteenth century."[67] In summary, between 1500 and 1800, roughly the dates of the Little Ice Age, rainfall in West Africa was more plentiful than in the preceding period or than occurs today.

The impact these shifts had on the natural environment and human society was profound. For the people, flora, and fauna of West Africa, annual rainfall levels marked by isohyets, or shifting west-east rainfall boundaries, are all-important. Moving from north to south, we find several rainfall regimes: First, the 100-millimeter-per-year isohyet marks the southern boundary of the Arab cultural domain in the Sahara Desert, where small groups of nomads sustain camels, sheep, and goats.[68] Second, the Sahelian cattle zone receives between 100 and 400 millimeters of rainfall from July to October each year. In the Sahel, Fula-speaking pastoralists graze cattle, sheep, and goats. In a pattern of transhumance, they move southward into

66. Sharon E. Nicholson, "Climatic Variations in the Sahel and Other African Regions during the Past Five Centuries," *Journal of Arid Environments* 1 (1978): 3–24; Nicholson, "The Methodology of Historical Climate Reconstruction and Its Application to Africa," *Journal of African History* 20 (1979): 31–49.

67. Nicholson, "Climatic Variations in the Sahel and Other African Regions during the Past Five Centuries," 44. However, George Brooks, in his classification, confines the wet period to 1500 to 1630, followed by an extended dry period until 1860. *Landlords and Strangers: Ecology, Society, and Trade in Western Africa, 1000–1630* (Boulder: Westview Press, 1993), 7. James C. McCann, in a 1999 survey, accepts Nicholson's periodization in preference to Brooks's. "Climate and Causation in African History," *International Journal of African Historical Studies* 32, nos. 2–3 (1999): 261–79.

68. Brooks, *Landlords and Strangers*, 11–12.

the moister savanna in the winter months. Since cattle herds must be watered daily, herders have to be located within a half-day's journey of wells or another water point.

At the third level, the 400-millimeter rainfall line separates the Sahel from the savanna. In the savanna, with rainfall measuring between 400 and 600 millimeters, African cultivators can grow drought-resistant sorghum and millets using long fallow or shifting cultivation techniques. Next, at the fourth level, above 600 millimeters, they can grow maize and a wider variety of rain-fed crops. At the fifth level, the 1,000-millimeter isohyet demarcates the more humid woodland savanna and the northern limit to the realm of the tsetse fly *(Glossina morsitans).* Finally, at the sixth level, precipitation measuring 1,500 millimeters or above can be found in the southwest and along the coast. This is where the tropical rainforest begins.[69]

During wetter periods, the isohyets advanced northward; during dryer periods, they retreated to the south. As precipitation increased during the sixteenth century, the northern limit of the Sahelian cattle zone extended well into the Adrar region, to about twenty-two degrees north latitude. The northern limit of human settlement and cultivation in the savanna (defined by the 400-millimeter isohyet) was marked by the towns of Tishit, Walata, and Timbuktu. During the sixteenth and seventeenth centuries, cultivators in the savanna grew maize, introduced by the Portuguese, which requires at least 600 millimeters of rain per year without irrigation.[70]

In the early eighteenth century, the region's climate became drier. The rainy season declined from six to three months as annual rainfall totals diminished. The rainfall boundaries began to move south. By 1850, the towns of Tishit, Walata, and Timbuktu defined the northern limit of the Sahelian cattle zone, not the agricultural savanna. Each zone had moved two hundred to three hundred kilometers to the south. Black African agriculturalists and cattle raisers retreated to the south; Arab camel nomads advanced. As the frontier of the Sahara pressed southward, so too did desert Arabs, who succeeded in imposing their patrilineal culture on Berbers and Black Africans to create a newly Arabized ethnic identity in the cattle-raising Sahel region.[71]

As in Europe and China, West Africa during the early modern centuries experienced a climate regime significantly different from that of the modern period. The people of West Africa, unlike the inhabitants of Europe and China, enjoyed wetter, favorable conditions in the sixteenth and seventeenth centuries that slowly became more arid and less auspicious in the eighteenth century. However, even the drier conditions during the 1700s

69. McCann, "Climate and Causation in African History," 265–67.

70. James L. A. Webb, *Desert Frontier: Ecological and Economic Change along the Western Sahel, 1600–1850* (Madison: University of Wisconsin Press, 1995). See p. 6, map 1.1.

71. Ibid., 10, map 1.2.

were better than the drought-prone years of the nineteenth and twentieth centuries. How, and to what extent, these trends in West Africa, and perhaps similar trends in other parts of the tropics, are linked to the climate history of the temperate regions in the early modern period are as-yet-unanswered questions.

GLOBAL CLIMATE CONNECTIONS

As scientific understanding of global climate patterns and forces continues to improve, it will help reconstruct past world climate histories. There is evidence that links severe weather years in the Little Ice Age with large-scale shifts in sea surface temperature and oceanic winds. For example, El Niño years seem to have been less frequent during the warm medieval centuries (1100 to 1300) and more frequent during the cooler early modern period (1500 to 1800).[72] Scientists have identified 59 El Niño–Southern Oscillation (ENSO) events that occurred between 1525 and 1800—an average of one every 4.6 years. These were divided approximately evenly between the sixteenth century (19); the seventeenth century (18); and the eighteenth century (22).[73]

The ENSO shift that has occurred every several years over the last five millennia "constitutes the single largest source of interannual climatic variability on a global scale" with "effects [that] are wide-ranging and severe."[74] A typical El Niño year begins between March and May and extends for twelve months or more, into the next calendar year. Ordinarily, the sea-surface air pressure on the eastern side of the Pacific is higher than that in the western Pacific along the equator. This differential drives east to west surface winds (easterlies) across the Pacific from the South American coast to Australia and Indonesia. When an El Niño year begins, the relationship reverses: eastern Pacific sea-surface air pressure drops and western Pacific sea-surface air pressure rises. This is referred to as the Southern Oscillation. No longer pushed by the air pressure, differential easterly winds that normally blow briskly from the South American coast across the equatorial Pacific weaken and retreat eastward. Tropical rainfall patterns move away from Australia and monsoon Asia, heading into the central and eastern Pacific.

ENSO climate effects on the tropics are substantial. Moist air above the

72. Anderson, "Long-Term Changes in the Frequency of Occurrence of El Niño Events," 194, fig. 9.1. Anderson's analysis rests on Quinn's use of the Nile flood data back to A.D. 622 and is still tentative.

73. W. H. Quinn and V. T. Neal, "The Historical Record of El Niño Events," in *Climate since A.D. 1500*, edited by Raymond S. Bradley and Philip D. Jones, rev. ed. (London: Routledge, 1995), 637, table 32.2.

74. Henry F. Diaz and Vera Markgraf, *El Niño: Historical and Paleoclimatic Aspects of the Southern Oscillation* (Cambridge: Cambridge University Press, 1992), 7.

eastern tropical Pacific warms, creates massive rain clouds, and releases heavy rainfall in Central and South America. The coastal plains of Ecuador and northern Peru often flood. On the western side of the Pacific, the easterlies virtually disappear in an El Niño year. This results in dry monsoon periods and drought—often catastrophic—for Australia, Indonesia, and other Southeast Asian countries; the Indian subcontinent; the highlands of Ethiopia; and southern Africa. Some of the most notable drought and famine episodes in India occurred during strong ENSO years.[75]

ENSO years create a global weather perturbation and thereby have an impact on temperate regions as well. For North America, El Niño winters tend to be mild over parts of the northern United States and western Canada and wet from Texas to Florida in the southern United States. What is not clear yet is whether ENSO years have a perceptible effect on climate in temperate Eurasia. That is, can we attribute any of the cooling and extreme weather years of the Little Ice Age to ENSO? Do anomalous weather years across Europe and Asia correlate with El Niño events?

Some correlations appear to exist. For example, the four hardest winters recorded by Morin in his Paris weather journal (see above)—1684, 1695, 1697, and 1709—have been identified as El Niño years.[76] Richard Grove has suggested a connection between the crop failures preceding the French Revolution and the ENSO events of 1789–1793 that also caused massive droughts and famine in India, Africa, and the New World. He argues that "an early precursor of the [ENSO] event may have been an unusually cold winter in western Europe in 1787–88, followed by a late and wet spring, and then a summer drought, resulting in the severe crop failures that preceded the French Revolution."[77] He posits a connection between the North Atlantic Oscillation of the previous January and the summer monsoon in India.

There could well be a link between the North Atlantic and Southern Oscillations. Normal regional atmospheric circulation in the North Atlantic is powered by westerly winds blowing between a low-pressure cell centered near Iceland and Greenland and a high-pressure cell centered near the Azores.[78] These intense westerlies bring cold continental air that is warmed by the ocean as it travels across to northern Europe. To the north and south

75. Ibid., 9; Henry F. Diaz and George N. Kiladis, "Atmospheric Teleconnections Associated with the Extreme Phases of the Southern Oscillation," in *El Niño: Historical and Paleoclimatic Aspects of the Southern Oscillation*, edited by Henry F. Diaz and Vera Markgraf (Cambridge: Cambridge University Press, 1992).

76. Quinn and Neal, "The Historical Record of El Niño Events," 629, table 32.1.

77. Richard H. Grove, "Global Impact of the 1789–93 El Niño," *Nature* 393 (May 28, 1998): 319.

78. Clara Dreser, "A Century of North Atlantic Data Indicates Interdecadal Change: Surface Temperature, Winds, and Ice in the North Atlantic," *Oceanus* 39 (1996): 11–14.

of the westerlies are bands of easterly winds. When the North Atlantic Oscillation occurs, a high-pressure cell builds up over northern Greenland, and the Azores cell shifts to low pressure. In this phase, the high-pressure system over northern Greenland pushes dry, cold polar air across northern Europe to cause cooler summers and more severe winters than normal. The normal westerlies are reversed, and easterlies bring polar air from northern Europe that is warmed over the ocean before it reaches North America.

CONCLUSION

Clearly, climate changes of the magnitude and extent described had an impact on human existence in a myriad of ways during the early modern centuries. For Eurasia and North America, the temperate zones of the northern hemisphere, there is ample evidence of prolonged adverse weather—colder, more variable, with less favorable precipitation—in all seasons. The societies exposed to this less clement weather suffered losses in comfort, productivity, and health, and even experienced increased mortality. The people of the time made incremental and at times dramatic changes in their lifestyles and modes of production to adapt to more severe weather. It is doubtful, however, that these climate conditions were sufficiently devastating to deflect or inhibit the evolutionary changes occurring in societies in the temperate regions.

We may argue that human societies were becoming more resilient and better able to cope with climate shocks. The populations of early modern China and Europe shared adverse weather conditions that inhibited agricultural production. As discussed in other chapters of this book, both societies, however, increased their food supplies by simultaneously intensifying land use and expanding cultivation into frontier regions. For China, the frontier regions, save for Taiwan, were contiguous to the Han Chinese heartland; for Europe, they incorporated vast expanses of New World lands. For Japan, on the other hand, adaptation took the form of conservation and efficient use of resources, not territorial expansion.

There is considerable evidence that human societies and institutions were growing more robust and capable over the three and a half centuries of the early modern period. Both states and markets became more efficient and extended their reach over wider territories. The rapidly growing worldwide capacity of maritime and freshwater fleets to move bulk commodities long distances in response to market signals was especially significant. States and societies could respond better to alleviate what earlier would have been disastrous harvest failures. In Europe, relief and welfare measures undertaken by states were more effective in the eighteenth century than in the fifteenth.

Much work remains for climate historians. In world regions where it is now possible to collect data, conventional historians need tabular, georeferenced, local monthly and seasonal data that will permit fine-grained analysis of climate-society linkages. These local data sets would reveal year-to-year and multiyear clusters of extreme climate conditions hidden in average figures and long-term generalizations. Simply calculating annual figures for frost-free summers by locality would be extremely helpful, for example. Similarly, local data on severe weather events—droughts, floods, hailstorms, blizzards, tidal surges, windstorms—and their presentation in a temporal and comparative spatial context could assist economic historians and others.

For temperate world regions other than Europe and East Asia, climate historians must carry out basic work to determine similarities and differences in regional climate sequences. For example, considerably more can be done to reconstruct the climate history of North America. At least for the temperate regions, we have a convincing, broadly accurate picture of early modern climate patterns and their consequences. For the tropics, we do not have even that. There, the issue is not temperature but precipitation. The West African example shows what can be done with often exiguous sources.

Simply working up systematic tabular data with a common metric for the lands of monsoon rainfall will be a massive but vital undertaking. Where do broadly coterminous failures of rains, droughts, and dearth occur, and when? These are empirical questions whose answers will greatly help our understanding of the forces that shaped human history in the early modern centuries.

PART II

Eurasia and Africa

Chapter 3

Pioneer Settlement on Taiwan

During the seventeenth century, a remarkable new organizational form—the chartered, joint-stock trading company—emerged from northern Europe. In England, France, the Netherlands, Sweden, and Denmark, merchants and investors formed joint-stock companies and obtained state charters that granted them monopoly powers to carry on long-distance trade with remote regions. The chartered trading companies proved to be more capable, efficient, and profitable than the state-run monopolies of Portugal and Spain that dominated trade between Europe and Asia and the New World in the sixteenth century. In part, the new companies reflected the entrepreneurial spirit of northern European societies. In part, they reflected the fast-expanding opportunities for long-distance trade that accompanied European maritime achievements in shipbuilding, mapmaking, navigation, and global exploration. And in part, they benefited from the fast-developing superiority of European firearms at sea and on land. By 1800, northern European trading companies had collectively mobilized and directed the flow of a large share of the natural resources and commodities extracted from the remainder of the globe and channeled it back to Europe.

The chartered trading company proved to have strength, resilience, and durability. Each chartered company mobilized large amounts of capital from numerous investors, who enjoyed limited liability. Each company was managed for profit by boards of directors, not royal officials. Each obtained and guarded jealously a monopoly on trade with a world region. Some were profitable; some not. However, most operated continuously for decades, and some even for centuries, in contrast to ephemeral, purely private enterprise.

Most important, however, each chartered company was an expression of the power and aggressiveness of the early modern European state that conceived it. Each company was vested with quasi-state powers to arm its ships and servants, build forts, negotiate with and make treaties with foreign rulers, and make war, if necessary, to protect its monopoly.

Of all the trading companies, the two most impressive in size, profitability, and longevity were competitors engaged in trade with Asia: the English East India Company, later to become the conqueror of India, and the Dutch East India Company, later ruler of the Indonesian archipelago. It was the Dutch East India Company that initiated—as an incidental aspect of its larger trading operations between Europe and Asia—a new settlement frontier on the previously isolated island of Taiwan off the China coast.

THE DUTCH EAST INDIA COMPANY

In the 1590s, Dutch merchants and traders became increasingly impatient with the royal Portuguese monopoly over imported Asian pepper and other spices. The Portuguese, united with the Spanish under the Hapsburg crown, sold their spices in northern Europe through an international syndicate that forced Dutch merchants to buy pepper and spices at high prices. Thanks to the inefficiency of the Portuguese in collecting and shipping enough pepper from its Asian sources to meet demand, the price of pepper remained high. The Dutch, then in rebellion against the Hapsburg monarchy and well aware of the weak control exerted by the Portuguese over their eastern empire, moved decisively to break their monopoly. By 1599, six competing Dutch merchant groups had invested in multivessel fleets sailing to Asia for pepper. Most returned with a salable cargo and initially made a profit, but the price of pepper began to drop quickly because of this new source of supply.[1]

Then, in 1600, the Advocate of Holland, Johan van Oldenbarnevelt, intervened to unify the competing merchant groups—each located in a different Dutch city—into a new, state-sponsored monopoly company. This was the Dutch East India Company (in Dutch, the Verenigde Oostindische Compagnie, commonly referred to as the VOC). The Dutch States General issued a formal charter, later renewed, that created a new company with an initial life of twenty-one years. The charter gave the VOC sole control over Dutch trade with Asia, and empowered it to build forts, maintain armies, and negotiate treaties with Asian rulers.

The States General charter provided for a single company divided into six chambers, one for each of the six cities from which merchants had organized Asian trading ventures. Amsterdam, the largest economic center, was limited to one-half total investment and returns; Zeeland, next largest, re-

---

1. Jan de Vries and A. M. van der Woude, *The First Modern Economy: Success, Failure, and Perseverance of the Dutch Economy, 1500–1815* (Cambridge: Cambridge University Press, 1997), 67–73; Jonathan I. Israel, *Dutch Primacy in World Trade, 1585–1740* (Oxford: Clarendon Press; New York: Oxford University Press, 1990).

ceived one-quarter share, and Rotterdam, Delft, Hoorn, and Enkhuizen each received one-sixteenth share. The charter granted investors from Amsterdam eight directors, and the five remaining chambers elected eight directors. An additional directorship circulated among the five smaller chambers, to make up a management board of seventeen directors. Each chamber operated its own warehouses and a wharf and sold its share of Asian goods when they arrived.

The initial capitalization was impressive. More than eighteen hundred investors contributed just over 6.4 million guilders to obtain shares in the new company. Of these, the largest investors, seventy-six in number, were full partners *(bewindhebbers)* who collectively possessed sole authority in the management of the VOC. The remaining investors became subordinate partners *(participanten)* with no management rights. Both classes of investors were liable only to the extent of their investment if the venture failed. The capital, once invested, could not be withdrawn for the life of the enterprise. If shareholders wanted to liquidate their investment, they could sell their shares to a buyer at the Amsterdam stock exchange. The full partners elected from among their number the seventeen directors (the Heeren XVII), who actually ran the company.

The newly organized VOC immediately sent out ships to purchase pepper, cloves, nutmeg, and mace at their production site in the Molucca Islands on the eastern Indonesian archipelago. The VOC directors aimed not just to buy spices but also to forcefully drive off the Portuguese and the English, who were also trading directly in this region, and create their own monopoly that would permit them to buy cheap and sell high in Europe. The Dutch built and manned four forts—Ternate, Tidore, Amboina, and Nassau—in the Spice Islands to clamp their hold on production. The States General supplied five armed warships for VOC use in Asian waters. By 1617, the Dutch had deployed forty fighting ships in their clashes with Portuguese, Spanish, and English traders in and near the Indonesian Archipelago.[2]

As they confronted the difficulties of controlling trading operations at such an extended distance, the VOC directors soon realized that they needed a permanent base in the region. Ideally, this should be a fortified port with full Dutch sovereignty. This would be the residence of a governor-general, who would direct purchases and command military operations to be undertaken against European competitors or uncooperative Asian rulers. In 1619, Jan Petersz. Coen founded Batavia, on western Java, which met these requirements and became the new VOC headquarters. Batavia retained its role as a Dutch capital throughout the colonial period.

Coen convinced the directors to send to Batavia more ships, supplies, and manpower than was necessary for direct spice shipments to the Dutch

---

2. Israel, *Dutch Primacy in World Trade,* 103.

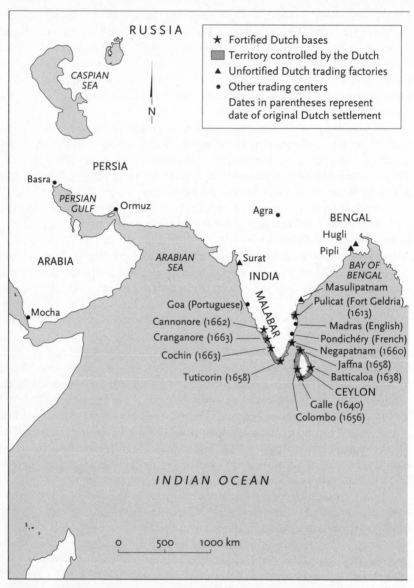

Map 3.1 Dutch empire in Asia, c. 1670. Adapted from Jonathan I. Israel, *Dutch Primacy in World Trade, 1585–1740* (Oxford: Clarendon Press; New York: Oxford University Press, 1990), map 5.4, pp. 182–83.

Peking •

JAPAN

Nagasaki

CHINA

PACIFIC
OCEAN

Amoy
(Spanish)
Canton •
Macao
(Portuguese)

TAIWAN
★
Fort Zeelandia
(1623–1661)

SIAM

PHILIPPINES
Manila • (Spanish)

Perak
Malacca (1641)
★

SUMATRA

CELEBES

Ternate (1605)

Tidore (1605)
★
Amboina
(1605)

BORNEO

Jambi ▲
Palembang ▲

★

★

Batavia
(1619)

JAVA

BANDA SEA

★

Macassar
(1666)

Solor

TIMOR

Fort
Nassau
(1609)

SULTANATE OF BANTAM
(under Dutch control from 1682)

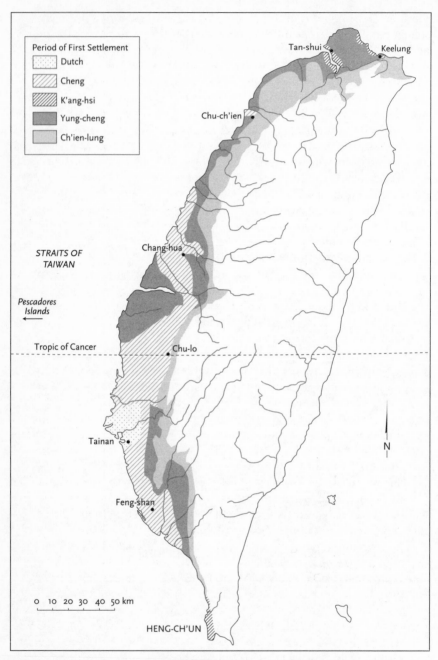

Map 3.2 Expansion of Han agricultural settlement. Adapted from John Robert Shepherd, *Statecraft and Political Economy on the Taiwan Frontier, 1600–1800* (Stanford, Calif.: Stanford University Press, 1993), map 6.4, p. 175.

Republic. He argued that the VOC could make large profits by buying and selling goods along maritime routes in Asia sufficient to pay for the pepper and spices sent home. The Dutch would no longer have to send out in its annual fleets either gold and silver or those relatively few European goods that found a market in Asia. The directors proved willing to invest heavily for this purpose. They committed funds to construct and equip a fleet of ships that would remain at Batavia and sail only in Asian waters. They funded the cost of setting up trading posts for VOC factors in a great arc across Asian waters. Dutch posts stretched from Mocha, at the entrance to the Red Sea, to Basra, at the head of the Persian Gulf, to Surat, on the west coast of India, to Galle and Batticaloa, on the coast of Ceylon (later known as Sri Lanka), to Pulicat, on the east coast of India, to Hugli, at the head of the Bay of Bengal, to Malacca, on the Malacca Straits, to Batavia, on the coast of Java, to Fort Zeelandia, on Taiwan, and to Nagasaki, in Japan.

Where local polities were weak, as in southern India, the Malayan Peninsula, and Taiwan, the Dutch built fortifications, asserted autonomous powers, and when feasible, even took on the role of colonial conqueror and ruler. After the Peace of Westphalia ended the Eighty Years' War between Spain and the Dutch Republic in 1648, the VOC hired thousands of decommissioned soldiers to serve on its ships and at its forts. The new troops made possible the final taking of Ceylon from the Portuguese. Where strong, confident regimes were in place, as in Safavid Persia, Mughal India, and Tokugawa Japan, VOC representatives became humble traders content to petition for whatever privileges they could obtain.

By mid–seventeenth century, Coen's arguments in favor of intra-Asian trade were vindicated. Large profits from the Asian trade paid for Batavia's running expenses and subsidized shipments of pepper and spices bound for Europe. The VOC, partly by dint of borrowed funds, endowed Batavia with a capital stock of money, European goods, and goods waiting shipment to Holland worth about 6.8 million guilders. The governor-general maintained absolute centralized control over the trading operations. All goods came first to Batavia before being reassigned and packaged for shipment to other trading stations as market opportunities dictated.

The governor-general commanded a fleet of vessels that he sent on regular trading voyages between Dutch trading stations in Asia. For example, VOC ships sailed from Batavia to the Dutch trading station and fort at Pulicat on India's east coast (or Coromandel Coast) and loaded Indian cotton textiles, plain and decorated, for transport to Batavia for profitable sale throughout the Southeast Asian world. They unloaded money or European trade goods for the VOC factors at Pulicat for further purchases. Alternatively, ships from Batavia carried Persian silk textiles for sale at Nagasaki in Japan. For the silk, VOC factors received payment in Japanese silver—then being mined in considerable quantities in that country.

The core of the VOC operation, however, remained the bilateral Asia-European exchange. Trading with Asia involved a minimum twenty-month turnaround time for the 13,500-nautical-mile (25,000-kilometer) voyage each way between the Dutch ports and Batavia. The commercial cycle was even longer, about thirty months: In the early spring of each year, the directors compiled a list of spices and other commodities in the amounts needed and sent it with that year's ships departing for Batavia. The list arrived nine to ten months later, at the end of that year. As the home fleet arrived, the return fleet set sail for Holland, arriving nine to ten months later (September to December), laden with the goods stipulated in the list that had arrived in Batavia twelve months earlier, not the recently received list. As the return fleet departed Batavia, VOC ships sailed for destinations throughout Asia to buy the goods requested in the current list. During the next twelve months, as the monsoons dictated, they arrived back at Batavia in time to assemble the next homeward bound cargo. The return fleet reached its home Dutch cities at the end of the year, closing the cycle two and a half years later.

Overcoming the complexities of long distances and prolonged trading periods, the VOC prospered and grew steadily. By the 1650s, the VOC sent annually an average of 20.5 ships with 10,095 tons capacity eastward. Each fleet carried supplies, money, trade goods, and an average of 4,020 persons (of whom only one in three ever returned).[3] Only half as many ships returned each year to Holland as departed. In the 1650s, an average of 10.2 returned East Indiamen tied up at the VOC docks. The remainder were lost, decommissioned, or put into intra-Asian service. Nevertheless, those 10 or so ships brought an enormously valuable cargo.

To get Asian goods, the Dutch, along with other Europeans, were forced to pay with gold and silver coin or bullion—not European manufactures or extracted products, which were not much in demand. The outward-bound fleets carried gold and silver coin and bullion in various forms, as well as limited quantities of Dutch woolen cloth and other goods that did find a limited market in Asia. The VOC traders also gained considerable quantities of specie by trading in Japan and Persia. In the 1650s, Batavia had at its disposal around 3.2 million guilders in specie each year: 1.2 million guilders sent from Holland, 1.3 million guilders from Japan, 600,000 guilders from Persia, and 249,000 guilders received on bills of exchange from its own employees. The latter, profiting from private trading and bribes, deposited specie with the VOC treasury in Batavia in return for bills to be paid in Holland.

Between 1600 and 1640, the VOC seized the bulk of the spice trade from the Portuguese, obtained a considerable share of the Indian textile market,

3. De Vries and van der Woude, *The First Modern Economy*, 438–39, table 10.4.

competed successfully with Asian traders in the Siamese and Japanese markets, and wrested the Chinese trade away from the Spanish in Manila and the Portuguese in Macao. Paul A. van Dyke suggests that there were three principal reasons for the VOC's success:

> First, the Company united Dutch political and economic ambitions under a single "national monopoly." The Dutch monopoly developed along secular lines with no ecclesiastical ties or obligations. Because they did not have to concern themselves with both a state and a religious hierarchy as was the case with the Iberians, the Dutch were able to focus more directly on the procurement of profits. Second, the VOC had a clear long-term objective that coincided with national ambitions. The spice monopsony was seen as the way by which the United Provinces could achieve economic prosperity and at the same time break the back of the Portuguese monopoly in Asia and Spain's political hold on the Netherlands. Third, the VOC created a communications and shipping network in Asia that was unsurpassed. Information about commodities and markets was quickly and effectively exchanged between the headquarters in Batavia and the outposts in Asia[,] enabling the Company to outmaneuvre its rivals.[4]

The VOC's increasingly valuable commercial interests in Asia soon had unexpected consequences for the people of the region, as the Dutch built their trading network protected, where possible, by fortified, autonomous trading enclaves.

In line with these strategic concerns, the VOC founded a trading colony on Taiwan in the 1620s.[5] Encountering little resistance from the indigenous peoples, the Dutch quickly became the dominant power on Taiwan's west coast. To improve productivity by introducing wet rice cultivation, the Dutch encouraged Chinese settlers to make the voyage across the Straits of Taiwan to settle on Taiwan. However, the Dutch presence was relatively brief. By the 1660s, defeated Ming Chinese fleeing the Manchu victors invaded Taiwan. They emphatically defeated and expelled the Dutch—an interesting exception to the usual European success in occupying and keeping fortified coastal enclaves across Asia. Two decades later, a Qing expeditionary force ousted the rebels and placed a provincial governor in charge of the island. Thereafter, Chinese settlement and intensification of land use continued in a pattern similar to that found at internal frontiers on the mainland.

4. Paul A. van Dyke, "How and Why the Dutch East India Company Became Competitive in Intra-Asian Trade in East Asia in the 1630's," *Itinerario* 21, no. 3 (1997): 41–56.

5. Hainan, the other large island off the Chinese mainland, has a history very similar to that of Taiwan. See Anne Allice Ceste, "A Frontier Minority in the Chinese World: The Li People of Hainan Island from the Han through the High Qing" (Ph.D. diss., State University of New York at Buffalo, 1995).

TAIWAN BEFORE DUTCH AND CHINESE SETTLEMENT

Before 1500, the island of Taiwan was relatively isolated from the mainland and from the trading routes on the South China Sea. Few opportunities for trade or lucrative conquest could be found on Taiwan. Although the island was situated only 160 kilometers offshore, the Straits of Taiwan made for a difficult sea passage as a result of strong currents characteristic of the shallow China sea. In summer, the straits were subject to severe typhoons, and in winter, heavy gales. In the absence of incentives, only Chinese fishermen, a few small-scale traders, and pirates who used the Pescadores Islands as a way station, bothered to make the sea crossing.

By the sixteenth century, Taiwan's isolation was ending, as maritime trade in the South China Sea linked it to the early modern world economy. The island became a refuge for Sino-Japanese smugglers and pirates seeking to evade Ming restrictions on maritime trade. Deerskins, taken by the indigenous peoples of the island, became a profitable export item to Japan and Southeast Asia. Europeans trying to break into the profitable trade of the South China Sea saw potential advantage in establishing bases on Taiwan.

Taiwan, also called Formosa by the Portuguese, is a sizeable island—thirty-six thousand square kilometers in area—that is both semitropical and tropical in its climate and vegetation. The Tropic of Cancer cuts through the middle of the island. Taiwan was covered with thick vegetation that varied by altitude from the seacoast plain to montane formations on mountains as high as three thousand meters.

Neolithic Austronesian settlers from southeastern China, who migrated to Taiwan as early as 4,000 B.C.E., introduced horticulture and the domesticated dog and pig to the island. By the beginning of our current era, the technologies of iron smelting and toolmaking had found their way across the straits. When the Dutch settled Taiwan, they discovered a sparse Taiwanese population of about a hundred thousand persons—fewer than three persons per square kilometer—divided into numerous groups on the western plain and some among the eastern hills. Not at all inclined to seafaring of any sort, the Taiwanese had minimal contact with the mainland and with other peoples in the Pacific.

Systems of basic production were broadly similar across the island. The natives of Taiwan lived in independent villages ranging in size from less than a hundred to a few thousand persons. Each village occupied a permanent site protected by dense circles of prickly bamboo and wooden palisades. Within the bounds of a Taiwanese village, each household provided shelter and space for cats, dogs, and chickens—the only domesticated animals. Coconut *(Cocos nucifera)* and fruit trees, betel palms *(Areca catechu)*, betel plants *(Piper betle)*, and vegetable gardens were attached to each homestead. Outside the village site, ample lands permitted regular abandonment of old fields and clearing and burning of new. The Taiwanese women and older men cultivated glutinous and nonglutinous rice *(Oriza sativa)*, foxtail millet *(Setaria italica)*, taro *(Colocasia esculenta)*, yams *(Dioscorea)*, and sugarcane *(Saccharum officinarum)* using digging sticks and hoes. The Taiwanese brewed fermented alcoholic drinks from rice, sugarcane, and millet to dispense freely in hospitality to guests and during celebrations and religious sacrifices.

Immediately circling the village were lands devoted to shifting cultivation under a common property regime. Every growing season, the men of the village marked off and did the first clearing of a new sector of land. Then, each domestic unit would intensively work and sow its own plot within this larger sector. Each domestic unit or kin group had exclusive use rights over its own plot, but only for the duration of the season. Only village members had access to these lands.

Beyond the zone of cultivation lay bounded tracts used exclusively by village members for hunting, fishing, and gathering. In some groups, these lands might be divided by lineage membership, but in most, they were common property available for use by all in the village. Any attempt by nonvillagers to enter and take wildlife or forest products in this zone was met by force. Beyond the two zones controlled by common property rules, where each village enforced territorial control, were interstitial lands where hunters were forced to share access to the resources and which served as buffers between potentially hostile settlements.[6]

Abundant game reduced pressure on cultivation. Men hunted predators such as leopards *(Leopardus)*, bears *(Ursus)*, and tigers *(Panthera tigris)* to protect their most prolific food source, the great deer herds of the island. A Chinese official who accompanied the Ming expedition of 1603 to the island commented:

> The mountains are most suited to deer. Walking and running, they are in herds of a thousand or a hundred. The men are skilled in using spears. These spears have bamboo shafts and iron points: they are five feet eight inches long, and very sharp. They always take them with them wherever they go. If they use them on deer the deer are killed, if they use them on tigers the tigers are killed. Ordinarily it is prohibited for an individual to hunt deer. In the winter, when the deer come out in herds, then some hundreds or tens of men will go after them, run them down until they are exhausted, and surround them. The spears find their marks and the catch is piled high as a hill; every village has its fill of deer meat. The meat that is left over is cut into strips, dried, and preserved; the deer tongue, deer penis, and deer sinew are also dried and preserved; the deer

6. John Robert Shepherd, *Statecraft and Political Economy on the Taiwan Frontier, 1600–1800* (Stanford, Calif.: Stanford University Press, 1993), 241–42.

skins and horns are piled high in the roof beams. The fawns are docile and they tame them and make pets of them.[7]

The deer were the only commercial crop available to the aborigines. Fish and shellfish were also plentiful. Women gathered and caught crabs, shrimp, and oysters. Men fished on the coast and along the rivers using spears, nets, and stupefying poison thrown in the water.

Despite many shared cultural traits, Taiwan's aborigines displayed formidable linguistic and cultural variety. Certainly, much interaction must have occurred over time, but the lack of political consolidation inhibited cultural uniformity. Forms of material culture—such as house types, weapons, and design motifs—associated with differing kinship patterns, fall into about six regional variants. Recent scholarship divides the Taiwanese into twenty distinct language groups, which do not necessarily coincide with cultural and social distinctions.[8] None of these languages included a writing system.

In early-seventeenth-century Taiwan, no overriding supravillage political authority existed. Temporary intervillage alliances occurred for defensive or aggressive purposes. Villages were governed by age-grade councils or similar mechanisms, not by strong chiefs. Internal stratification was limited to a division between more prestigious founder families and later-arriving commoner families within villages.

A generally warlike cultural bent, finding expression in decapitation of slain enemies and the display of skulls as trophies ("head-hunting"), was common to all Taiwanese. Continuing endemic, low-grade warfare was a preoccupation of adult males. The same Chinese official commented, "By nature they are brave and like to fight":

> If something causes a quarrel between neighboring villages, they mobilize their warriors, and at an agreed-upon date go to war. They kill and wound each other with the utmost of their strength, but the following day they make peace, and thereafter have the same relations as at first, without hating each other. Having cut off the heads, they strip the flesh from the skulls and hang them at their doors. Those who have many skeletons hanging at their doors are called braves.[9]

Division into feuding micropolities left the Taiwanese aborigines open to and largely defenseless against organized conquest, in spite of their ferocity as warriors.

---

7. Laurence G. Thompson, "The Earliest Chinese Eyewitness Accounts of the Formosan Aborigines," *Monumenta Serica: Journal of Oriental Studies of the Catholic University of Peking* 23 (1964): 175.

8. See J. R. Shepherd, *Statecraft and Political Economy on the Taiwan Frontier,* 30, map 2.1.

9. Thompson, "The Earliest Chinese Eyewitness Accounts of the Formosan Aborigines," 172.

During the 1500s, mainland contacts with Taiwan intensified as maritime trade increased generally in Asian waters. Chinese fishing grew more active off the Pescadores. Pirates and smugglers from China and Japan made use of the modest harbors and coves of the island with increasing frequency. Ming Chinese campaigns against piracy drove pirates, known as the *wako,* to take refuge on Taiwan. When the Ming court imposed a ban on direct trade with Japan in the 1590s, an indirect smuggling trade grew up between China and Japan via Taiwan. In 1603, the Ming emperor sent a war fleet to land at the pirate base on Tayouan Peninsula in an effort to end Japanese piracy and smuggling.[10]

By the early 1600s, a brisk trade had developed between Taiwan's indigenous aboriginal population and Chinese fishermen, smugglers, and pirates. The Taiwanese sold deerskins, dried venison, and deer horns in return for cloth; salt; and porcelain, brass, and copper goods. Cheap and durable, shorthaired deerskin hides were much in demand in China and even more so in Japan.[11] The Japanese used deerskin for leather armor, quivers, and saddle trimmings, among other military uses. Deerskin jackets, trousers, boots, and digitated socks *(tabi)* were widely used. Leather containers—pouches, boxes, and bags—were popular. The Japanese imported great numbers of deerskins from Thailand and Cambodia, from Luzon in the Philippines, and from Taiwan. The trade was profitable enough to encourage as many as fifteen hundred Chinese traders to take up residence in Taiwanese villages in order to organize the flow of deerskins to the major ports.

THE DUTCH REGIME

A powerful new entity entered the South China Sea in the early seventeenth century—the Dutch East India Company. The trading company intervened violently and aggressively in an attempt to monopolize the most profitable international trades in this region. As part of this strategy, the Dutch East India Company tried to break up the Portuguese Macao-Japan and Spanish Amoy-Manila trade monopolies. Success required a territorial foothold. When in 1622 a Dutch assault on Portuguese-held Macao failed, the Dutch fleet turned to Taiwan. In 1624, the Dutch East India Company strengthened

10. J. R. Shepherd, *Statecraft and Political Economy on the Taiwan Frontier,* 47. See also Liu Ts'ui-jung, "Han Migration and the Settlement of Taiwan," in *Sediments of Time: Environment and Society in Chinese History,* edited by Mark Elvin and Liu Ts'ui-jung (Cambridge: Cambridge University Press, 1998); and John E. Wills Jr., "The Seventeenth-Century Transformation: Taiwan under the Dutch and the Cheng Regime," in *Taiwan: A New History,* edited by Murray A. Rubinstein (Armonk, N.Y.: M. E. Sharpe, 1999).

11. Thomas O. Hollman, "Formosa and the Trade in Venison and Deer Skins," in *Emporia, Commodities, and Entrepreneurs in Asian Maritime Trade, c. 1400–1750,* edited by Roderich Ptak (Stuttgart: F. Steiner, 1991).

a bamboo stockade already built on Tayouan Peninsula, adjacent to Tainan, a harbor long used by Asian traders.[12] This became the Dutch headquarters, Fort Zeelandia. In 1625, the Dutch bought from the inhabitants of Hsin-kang village, located twelve kilometers inland, the right to build a town and entrepôt on the mainland side of Tainan harbor in return for fifteen pieces of handwoven cotton cloth from India.

Within twenty years, Fort Zeelandia had become the capital of a Dutch colony ruling most of Taiwan. The export trade in deerskins continued profitably, as did the transit trade to Japan and China. However, clashes with the neighboring Taiwanese, threats from the Spanish in the Philippines, the need for a reliable supply of cheap foodstuffs, pressure to find local revenues, and, not least, the Dutch Reformed Church's desire to proselytize the Taiwanese pressed the Dutch to move inland. In the mid-1630s, reinforced with additional company troops, they pacified the Taiwanese in the hinterland of Tayouan.

Dutch firelocks, warhorses, battle drums, and tactical discipline proved to be superior to the spears and bows of the Taiwanese. Company officials imposed short, separate treaties on twenty-eight villages within two days' march of Fort Zeelandia. In these documents, the Taiwanese promised to accept the authority of the States of Holland, not to turn their weapons against the Dutch, to help the Dutch against their enemies, not to molest the Chinese traders, and to appear before the company when requested.

In early February 1636, the Dutch governor called on each subject village to send a representative to a delegate's assembly at Tainan. Once they had assembled, the governor exhorted the delegates to refrain from internecine warfare. He gave each delegate his symbols of office: a black velvet robe, an orange flag, and a rattan staff headed by a silver insignia with the Dutch East India Company's coat of arms. Then the delegates feasted together in an unprecedented gathering of enemies. This was followed by a tour to each of the villages by Dutch officials. By the end of the year an additional twenty-nine villages had sent emissaries to the Dutch and placed themselves under company rule.[13] The Dutch governors held delegate assemblies every year thereafter until the end of their rule.[14]

By 1642, company troops had driven out a weakened Spanish garrison and settlement in the north at Keelung. The Dutch then turned to pacification of rebellious Taiwanese in the north. A large Dutch force moved south along the coast, crushing any aboriginal resistance and clearing out Chinese pirates and smugglers. By 1645, the Dutch were in control of the entire west-

12. J. R. Shepherd, *Statecraft and Political Economy on the Taiwan Frontier,* 51.

13. Ibid., 54–55.

14. Antonio Andrade, "Political Spectacle and Colonial Rule: The *Landdag* on Dutch Taiwan, 1629–1648," *Itinerario* 21, no. 3 (1997): 57–93.

ern coast of Taiwan. By midcentury, three hundred villages located on both the east coast and the west coast and a few in the mountains had formally submitted and accepted Dutch terms. This conquest was accomplished with no more than seven hundred trained company troops and with the assistance of varying numbers of Taiwanese auxiliaries.

The epicenter of Dutch power continued to be the southwest coast, around Zeelandia and Tainan. The Taiwanese aborigines in the southwest felt the heaviest impact from Dutch colonial policies. Strangely enough, however, one price for foreign occupation was not exacted from the Taiwanese aborigines: no record exists of abnormal outbreaks of disease or of heavy mortality. Apparently, the Taiwanese were sufficiently exposed to peoples from the mainland to share in the larger Eurasian disease pool, as were the people of the Philippines. Whatever else may have happened to them, the Taiwanese were spared the holocaust of disease.

Cultural assimilation by conversion of its aboriginal subjects to Christianity was one prominent Dutch East India Company policy on Taiwan. Two Dutch Reformed Church pastors sent out by the company became the effective civil administration in the southwestern core area. Ethnographers by necessity, these men learned the languages and customs of the region and acted as interpreters for the company. Backed by Dutch coercive power, the missionaries directly challenged the spiritual authority of Taiwanese female shamans and chastised (sometimes flogging) idol worshipers. The missionaries taught the precepts of Christianity to converts, who grew in number as Dutch power increased. Missionaries started village schools and trained catechists and lay preachers. They also served as judges and tax collectors as they made their rounds of the villages.

The company, as might be expected, made every effort to encourage the export of deerskins so that the pacified Taiwanese could pay taxes. By 1644, the company had imposed a system of village trade monopolies auctioned at competitive bidding to Chinese leaseholders. The auction winners bought venison and deerskins for export by the company and sold all trade goods needed in each village. Between 1635 and 1660, deerskins exported averaged 65,525 per year.[15] There is some evidence of depletion in deer populations during this period in the hunting grounds of the southwest core region.

The Dutch began also to try to change Taiwanese horticulture. The missionaries in particular were unimpressed by what they read as male sloth and female drudgery in cultivation. Coming from the Low Countries, one of the most intensively cultivated areas in the world at the time, they were also unimpressed by the yields of aboriginal shifting cultivation. The Taiwanese did not produce noticeable surpluses of food grains that could be used to

---

15. Data survive for eighteen of the total twenty-five years. J. R. Shepherd, *Statecraft and Political Economy on the Taiwan Frontier,* 79, n. 128.

feed the colonial settlement and garrison. By the 1640s, the Dutch had imported plows and draft oxen that they sold to the Taiwanese at cost. Some aborigines did adapt to cultivation by plow in the vicinity of Tainan, but the use of oxen to pull carts was a much more popular innovation in a land where humans had been the only beast of burden.

To reduce the expensive importation of rice from Japan and Thailand required to feed its garrison, the company turned to Chinese immigrants. The Chinese trading agents recruited peasant farmers from the densely populated areas of Fujian province just across the Straits of Taiwan. Later, the chief Chinese trader at Batavia and other wealthy Chinese traders associated with the Dutch put up funds to bring Chinese settlers to Taiwan to reclaim land and grow irrigated rice and sugarcane. The company financed irrigation works. It offered draft animals and seed at favorable terms to new settlers. It promised five- to ten-year tax holidays for pioneers who cleared, plowed, and irrigated land. If the company itself provided the capital for land clearing, Chinese settlers were offered tenancy rights. Chinese settlers apparently were free to occupy and reclaim village hunting lands without compensating the Taiwanese.[16] The Chinese settler population grew in pulses of immigration pushed by war and famine on the mainland to approximately thirty-five thousand persons by 1661. By that date, the sown area in sugarcane and rice under Chinese cultivation totaled 9,800 hectares.

Chinese settler migration to Taiwan had become a well-established alternative for peasants on the mainland. Families and kinship networks stretched from Taiwan's southwest core back to Fujian province. The economic benefits of Chinese land reclamation for the Dutch were undeniable. Fujianese intensive cultivation was far more productive and profitable per unit of area than indigenous systems were. The company was exporting sugar in sizable loads to Persia and Japan in a competitive world market. Before its loss, Taiwan was one of the company's most profitable territorial possessions in Asia.

However, the Chinese were less tractable than the island's aborigines. In September 1652, incensed by abuses committed by Dutch troops in collection of the monthly poll-tax payment, several thousand Chinese rural settlers in the southwest rebelled.[17] They assembled with harvesting sickles, sharpened bamboos, and a few firearms and swords to attack Fort Provintia in Sakam, with its small Dutch garrison. In response, the Dutch governor at Fort Zeelandia sent a force of 120 Dutch musketeers by boat across the bay. The Dutch musketry fire panicked the rebels, who broke and fled. Nearly 500 rebels were butchered in the sugarcane fields. Two days later, the company

16. Ibid., 86.
17. Johannes Huber, "Chinese Settlers against the Dutch East India Company: The Rebellion Led by Kuo Huai-i on Taiwan in 1652," in *Development and Decline of Fukien Province in the Seventeenth and Eighteenth Centuries*, edited by E. B. Vermeer (Leiden: Brill, 1990), 295–96.

forces, reinforced by Taiwanese Christian militia, fought a brief, pitched battle and again defeated the rebels. In the aftermath of these battles, some 3,000 rebels were caught and killed outright; others were dragged back to Zeelandia for torture and execution. Only eleven years later, Chinese settlers were quick to seize the moment and help drive the Dutch from Taiwan.

CHINESE DOMINATION

Defeat of the Dutch and their replacement by Chinese colonial rule signaled a new era of change for the land and people of Taiwan. In April 1661, the loyalist Ming general Cheng Ch'eng-kung, facing final defeat by the Manchus, brought a twenty-five-thousand-man army across the straits to Tayouan harbor. Welcomed by the Chinese settlers, Cheng's army rapidly gained control of the countryside, seized Fort Provintia, and laid siege to Fort Zeelandia. Outnumbered twenty to one, in February 1662 the Dutch garrison negotiated a surrender and sailed away from Taiwan in what was one of a very few such reversals imposed on them in Asia. Within days of Cheng's arrival, representatives of the Taiwanese villages in the plains had waited on Cheng, offered their submission and received honorific robes, caps, and boots in the Chinese tradition. Missionary authority in the villages collapsed completely as the Taiwanese repudiated the rites and symbols of Christianity and reverted to their ancestral practices.

In June 1662, Cheng died of natural causes. His eldest son, Cheng Chin, who still held fast to Amoy, the island city just off the mainland, returned with his troops to force his father's generals to accept him as the successor. Finally, in 1664, Manchu pressure forced Cheng Chin to leave Amoy and retreat to Taiwan with his 6,000 to 7,000 remaining troops. Here, he continued his father's policies of land reclamation and refugee settlement.

The last retreat of the Ming loyalists brought a large increase in the population of Taiwan. Nearly 40,000 Cheng soldiers and camp followers crossed the straits; another 30,000 war refugees are estimated to have arrived on Taiwan. When the Manchus forced the entire coastal population of Fujian to move several kilometers inland behind fortified walls, Cheng agents actively recruited migrants from this unhappy population. Some Chinese also moved back to China when political conditions improved. The Chinese population on Taiwan may have reached 120,000—an increase of 85,000 over the Dutch period.[18]

Before his death, Cheng established a Ming-style prefectural and county civil administration over Taiwan. The newly appointed magistrates immediately began registering land ownership by both Chinese and aboriginal holders so that they could collect food grains as taxes to feed Cheng's armies. In

18. J. R. Shepherd, *Statecraft and Political Economy on the Taiwan Frontier,* 96.

place of the Dutch commercially oriented system of tax leases or farms, the Cheng regime imposed fixed assessments based on crop and cultivated acreage. Cheng published regulations to ensure security of tenure on cultivated lands for both Chinese and aborigines.

To deal with a large, potentially troublesome, surplus population, Cheng looked to land reclamation and expansion of Chinese intensive agriculture on Taiwan. The regime encouraged wealthy officials to recruit refugees and invest their funds in opening up new lands. Cheng promised that those Chinese settlers who reclaimed "unused" lands by engaging in plow cultivation would be given legal ownership rights. Cheng also began military colonization in the extensive lands not immediately cultivated by the Taiwanese. He sent bodies of troops to clear and cultivate unopened aboriginal lands. Each colony received free plows and seed and orders to capture wild oxen left by the Dutch. They were promised a six-year exemption from land taxes. Under these incentives the registered taxable area primarily devoted to rice cultivation grew to be two and one-half times greater than it had been under the Dutch, to just over 29,150 hectares in lands primarily around Tainan.[19] Nevertheless, food shortages recurred, and the Cheng regime sent ships to Thailand and Luzon to buy rice to feed its army.

Predictably, the Taiwanese in the plains came under increasing pressure from the enlarged Chinese presence. Expanding rice cultivation nibbled at the tribal hunting reserves, and pressures to hunt continued. The head tax on plains aborigines was fixed by the state at 16,228 ounces of silver. The only way the tribals could pay the tax was to sell deerskins. The tax could be commuted to silver at .24 ounces per deerskin, which meant the plains aborigines had to deliver 67,617 hides in total each year.[20] The Cheng regime assumed control over the Dutch East India Company's monopoly on deerskin exports. These were maintained at the Dutch level of 50,000 to 100,000 skins per year sent to Japan. Cheng officials also resorted to impressing plains tribals into unpaid labor as porters and construction workers. Several bitter revolts expressed Taiwanese resentment against such harsh treatment.

By the early 1680s, after the death of Cheng, his son and successor presided over a fast-crumbling regime. In July 1683, the Qing admiral Shih Lang won a critical sea battle in the Pescadores that broke Cheng resistance. Shih Lang accepted the peaceful surrender of the Cheng forces on Taiwan in October 1683. After this victory the Qing emperor, who intended to abandon Taiwan, ordered the repatriation of some forty thousand rebel troops to the mainland. The emperor also decreed that any unmarried Chinese lacking a trade or property was to be returned to the mainland. Within a year, Shih Lang estimated that nearly half the Chinese population had left Taiwan.

19. Ibid., 99.
20. Ibid., 102.

Shih Lang contested this policy of abandonment. At a meeting of high officials in late 1683 at Fuzhou, he advanced a cogent set of strategic arguments for retaining Taiwan as a defensive base to protect the South China coastline. Shih's views prevailed with the emperor. In early 1684, Taiwan officially became a prefecture of Fujian province and the county-level Cheng administration was continued. A fresh ten-thousand-man land and marine force garrisoned the island. Official policy, however, was to minimize Taiwan's expenses and development by strictly regulating and limiting trade with and migration from the mainland. The regime did not wish to encourage Chinese settlement on Taiwan, for fear of political turbulence in a frontier province.

By imperial edict, only travelers with official permits could travel to Taiwan on the designated route between Amoy and Tainan. Only males could cross to Taiwan; they could not bring their wives and children with them. Chinese settlers already in Taiwan could not send for their families to join them. The imperial government continued its immigration policies throughout the eighteenth century. On three occasions, totaling only eleven years—1732–1740, 1746–1748, and 1760–61—did the regime relax prohibitions on family travel. When this occurred, Chinese migration soared and the regime closed the system again. For the first twenty to thirty years, the quarantine policy was reasonably successful. Settlement was curtailed. Male laborers crossed to Taiwan on a seasonal basis to work the harvest. Some remained, but others returned every year. Not until 1710 did the taxable lands cultivated by Chinese settlers return to their pre-1683 level on Taiwan.

By the early 1700s, demographic and economic forces began undercutting official policy. Illegal Chinese migration to Taiwan circumvented the quarantine policy, and Han settlement and land reclamation rose steadily. After the repatriation of the Cheng forces in 1684, the population of Taiwan, excluding the hill tribes, reached an estimated 130,000 (80,000 Chinese and 50,000 plains aborigines). In 1756, that total had reached 660,000 (the number of the plains aborigines remained constant at 50,000); by 1777, it had reached 839,000; and by 1824, 1.2 million.[21] Why these massive changes in the face of official Qing policy that had reversed Cheng prosettlement efforts?

The coastal prefectures of Fujian and Guangdong opposite Taiwan had become two of the most thickly populated, food-deficient areas in China. To the residents of these overcrowded regions, Taiwan's stretches of unreclaimed land offered a powerful incentive for migration. Despite official prohibitions, shipments of Taiwanese rice and sugar were smuggled to the mainland, where they fetched high prices. In a buoyant frontier economy, other economic niches could be found. Imperial coastal patrolling was

21. Ibid., 161, table 6.4.

largely ineffectual against illegal travel. Hundreds of illegal migrants sought out boat captains to ferry them across the straits for a fee—an amount often less than the cost of getting an official permit. The relatively short distance between the mainland and Taiwan meant that male migrants could follow a sojourning strategy and make one or more trips to Taiwan before committing themselves to permanent settlement and to bringing family members there with them.

Once arrived on Taiwan, illegal migrants were free to remain. Both legal and illegal migrants confronted no impediments to land ownership. Chinese settlers, new and old, were legally permitted to buy land and extend cultivation and settlement. Certainly, for tax purposes local officials were quick to register lands reclaimed by settlers. Land registered for taxation in 1684 amounted to 17,900 hectares; by 1762 (the last reliable figures until 1895), the total was 61,149 hectares and rising.[22] Migrants were not encouraged, however, to occupy or seize aboriginal lands.

Surprisingly, Taiwan's aborigines fared reasonably well by comparison with the indigenous peoples on the wrong side of other settler frontiers. Qing officials actively tried to prevent settler abuse of aborigines leading to violent conflict. One time-honored solution was to fix a boundary between civilization and savagery, between the cooked (civilized) population and raw (wild) aborigines. No Han settlers were permitted to pass the boundary line. In 1722, Man-Pao, the governor of Taiwan, fixed a north-south line stretching the length of the island along the western foothills to separate mountain from plain. In his 1736 memoir of Taiwan, Huang Shu-ching spelled out the problems the boundary was designed to correct:

> The raw aborigines in the mountains, whose wild nature is hard to tame, burn houses and kill people. In fact, most of the strife is due to the Chinese, who profit by crossing boundaries and encroaching on the land of raw . . . aborigines; they will not be satisfied until they have snatched it all. They are constantly forming gangs to enter the mountains and put up huts. They watch the aborigines hunt deer and often get killed trying to steal the game themselves. In other cases they go deep into the mountains to cut rattan and timber and meet with harm. In 1722 it was decided to set up stone stelae to mark a boundary ten or more *li* from raw aborigine settlements and to prohibit anyone from crossing it.[23]

Enforcement of this boundary line did protect the uncivilized (raw) mountain aborigines throughout the eighteenth century and beyond. The line was accurately surveyed in the 1750s, and earth-oxen boundaries were drawn. However, settlers and plains aborigines intruded beyond the line into the

22. Ibid., 169, table 6.5.
23. Quoted in ibid., 186.

foothills for illegal land clearing, for timber, and for control of irrigation water. In the 1780s, the Taiwan governor ordered a survey and redrew the line higher in the mountains.

The regime generally forced Chinese settlers to respect aboriginal land rights. Contrary to the general mandates of Chinese law, Taiwan prefects refused to consider uncultivated tribal hunting territories as wasteland to be claimed by the state. Ch'en Pin, Taiwan's prefect from 1710 to 1715, stated the matter clearly:

> Mainland subjects pay taxes on land and thereby acquire an ownership right that can be passed down through the generations; aboriginal tribes, since the present dynasty took control, also pay yearly tax quotas; therefore, the land of such tribes should be [recognized] as aborigine property. The tribes themselves should be allowed to decide whether to plant their land in seed, use it as pasture, or leave it as deer field. Moreover, every tribe has boundaries with its neighbors, and the aborigines do not allow these boundaries to be violated. How can Chinese coming from outside be allowed to occupy the land [and violate these boundaries]?[24]

Under this interpretation, which was generally followed, Chinese settlers were forced to negotiate with the tribals for land.

One early approach to gaining access to land was for the Chinese settler to agree to pay the commuted value of all or part of the head tax levied on the village. When this occurred and the proper papers were drawn up, the regime formally recognized the usufruct rights of the settler to clear land and sow crops in the village hunting areas. According to this arrangement, the settler was responsible for paying the land tax to the state as well. Under these terms, the advantage lay with the developer. He could subdivide his holdings and let them to individual peasant farmers, collect rent from them, and make a substantial profit. Nevertheless, the arrangement freed the aborigines from their tax burden.

Later, a switch occurred to standard tenancy agreements obtaining in Chinese land law. Under these agreements, the aborigines let land in perpetuity to Chinese settlers on payment of so many measures of paddy per unit of land per year. An imperial decree of 1724 explicitly permitted Chinese settlers to rent tribal lands according to this formula and stipulated that the tenants were to pay the land taxes due the state. This change reflects the increasing sophistication of the plains aborigines in dealing with a rising settler demand for land. As rent holders, they claimed a steady income stream from their former hunting areas.

The land rents were needed. By the mid-1700s, the material basis of plains aboriginal culture had been severely undercut. Overhunting and destruction

24. Ibid., 145.

of habitat by Chinese settlers steadily reduced the deer herds in the entire western plain. Taiwan's official gazetteer of 1740 commented that over-hunting had caused the disappearance of deer with more than seven growth rings on their antlers (i.e., deer more than seven years old). In succeeding decades, deer retreated to the foothills and the inner mountain ranges. When this occurred, the deerskin trade collapsed and the plains aborigines had to look for alternative livelihoods. If they could not trade deerskins, they could not obtain the various consumer goods they required.

One option for plains aborigines was to plow their fields, arrange for ir-rigation, and take up intensive rice and sugarcane cultivation for cash sale. Only a few seemed willing to accept the drudgery and concentration needed to grow a surplus for the market. Others simply lived off land rents and con-tinued to farm in their traditional manner. More appealing was a pastoral option. The Dutch had allowed cattle to run wild and recaptured them when they were needed. The aborigines enthusiastically built up herds of their own in great numbers. Two-wheeled oxcarts became a widely used method of transport. Many aborigines made a living trading oxen and hauling loads. Fi-nally, the physical endurance and bravery of the aborigines found them em-ployment by the Qing regime in various formations of militia. The regime re-lied on the aboriginals to supply loyal troops in times of settler rebellion—a critical factor in putting down the great rebellion of 1786–1788.

Qing officials generally believed that, if protected by the state, the plains aborigines would adopt civilized customs and behavior. In fact, the process of acculturation, of sinicization, was well under way by 1800. At varying tem-pos, plains aborigines became proficient in a Chinese language, adopted Chinese names, wore Chinese hair styles (the Manchu queue was made obligatory in 1758), used Chinese medicine, and worshiped in Chinese temples.

CONCLUSION

By the nineteenth century, the landscape of the western Taiwan plain re-sembled that of Fujian or Guangdong on the mainland. The vast deer herds of the early seventeenth century had been wiped out. The forest cover had been cleared. Han settlement prevailed, with its land clearance and intensi-fied rice and sugarcane cultivation. Irrigation works dotted the landscape. Taiwan regularly shipped surplus rice and sugar to the mainland and other markets in the South China Sea. Those indigenous peoples who had not been sinicized or assimilated were driven upward to the mountainous spine and to the less fertile eastern coast. Aboriginal income declined when export of deerskins ended with the depletion of the deer herds.

By 1824, the Han Chinese and plains aborigine population had increased, during a fifty-year period, to 1.2 million. By century's end, Taiwan's population topped 2.5 million.[25] By then, Han Chinese and assimilated Taiwanese were cultivating rice and sugarcane on six hundred thousand hectares of land as "the plains, the uplands, and the hillsides in the west and northeast of the island were almost all cultivated, and the opening up of the eastern longitudinal valley was already initiated."[26] The pioneer settlers had done their task, the frontier was ending.

The Dutch East India Company's founding of Zeelandia in 1624 was a catalyst for Chinese pioneer migration and settlement on Taiwan—a process of frontier expansion long under way on the mainland. However, unlike the Dutch colonial outpost on Java, where the Dutch steadily increased their power and influence at the expense of weak local polities, the outpost on Taiwan could not withstand the power of the centralized Chinese state. Even fleeing remnant forces of the defeated Ming empire readily expelled the Dutch. Thereafter, victorious Qing forces, after occupying and administering Taiwan, modulated and controlled, even if they could not really halt, Han frontier expansion on the island.

25. Ibid., 161, table 6.4. These figures do not include an estimate for the mountain, or "raw," aborigines.

26. Ts'ui-jung, "Han Migration and the Settlement of Taiwan," 196.

Chapter 4

Internal Frontiers and Intensified Land Use in China

Contrary to long-cherished Occidental notions of a static traditional Asian society, China in the early modern period was a dynamic and changing society. Under the Ming and Qing dynasties, China experienced impressive growth in population—similar to that of Europe in the same period. The accepted or conventional long-term scenario for human numbers in China proper is as follows: A generally agreed-on estimate for the early Ming dynasty in 1400 is 75 million.[1] Two hundred years later, around 1600, the human population had doubled, to 150 million. During the 1600s, heavy mortality associated with Ming dynastic breakup and Qing conquest pushed the total downward: at midcentury, it was about 130 million, with subsequent recovery to 150 million by 1700. Thereafter, the population spiraled rapidly upward in the eighteenth century to reach 320 million in 1800. By the second half of the eighteenth century, the implied annual rate of increase was .0079, or eight per thousand persons. This was a remarkable rate of growth for a preindustrial "mature agrarian society."[2] Growth slowed somewhat in

1. William Lavely and R. Bin Wong, "Revising the Malthusian Narrative: The Comparative Study of Population Dynamics in Late Imperial China," *Journal of Asian Studies* 57, no. 3 (1998): 717, table 1. Lavely and Wong accept the figures of Colin McEvedy and Richard Jones as a reasonable adjustment of various estimates. McEvedy and Jones show an estimate of 75 million (*Atlas of World Population History* [London: A. Lane, 1978], graph 4c). Dwight Perkins offers a range of 65 to 80 million (*Agricultural Development in China, 1368–1968*, 1st ed. [Chicago: Aldine, 1969], 16, table II.I). Martin Heidjra adjusts for underregistration by adding 25 million persons to the official total to arrive at a figure of 85 million ("The Socio-Economic Development of Rural China during the Ming," in *The Cambridge History of China*, edited by John King Fairbank and Denis Crispin Twitchett [Cambridge: Cambridge University Press, 1998], 437). These figures are for China proper, excluding Taiwan, Chinese Turkestan, Tibet, Manchuria, and Inner Mongolia.

2. Lavely and Wong, "Revising the Malthusian Narrative," 718.

the first half of the nineteenth century, to a .0054 annual rate, or an increase of five per thousand persons. China's population in 1850 was about 420 million. Over four and a half centuries, the population had risen more than five-fold, from 75 million to more than 400 million.[3]

During the early modern centuries, accelerating human demands for energy, food, clothing, housing, and industrial products put immense strains on land and natural resources in China. Agricultural production had to increase to keep pace with the growing population. Agricultural growth was both extensive and intensive. In response to demand, Chinese peasant farmers converted new lands to agriculture. Estimates adjusted from official sources put cultivated land in the early Ming at around 25 million hectares.[4] By mid–nineteenth century, land under sedentary cultivation had tripled to approximately 81 million hectares.[5] Nevertheless, expansion of cultivation did not equal growth in population. Even as the area of cultivation grew, Chinese farmers—especially those engaged in wet rice agriculture—devised more intensive methods of cultivation aimed at wringing higher yields from every *mou* of land.

Even though Europe saw a population increase of the same dimensions over the same period, the conventional interpretation casts China in the starkest of Malthusian terms, as a "demographic profligate" suffering from "rapid growth, periodic mortality crises, and [a] precarious balance of population and resources."[6] In this view, only mortality from famine, war, and pestilence—the Malthusian restraints—limited Chinese population growth. Unlike those in northwestern Europe, Chinese society marriage patterns did not offer strong preventive checks on fertility to regulate growth. As a result, China suffered from demographically driven poverty as it consumed its natural resources and moved into an environmental crisis.

Recently scholars have begun to revise this paradigm. They have shown that China's mortality rates do not appear to have exceeded those of Europe; that Chinese nutrition and living standards were equivalent, if not superior, to those of Europe; and that female infanticide served as a potent check on the birthrate.[7] If anything, China developed much more in accordance with

3. Ibid., 719, table 2. Ping-ti Ho lists 429 million for 1850 (*Studies on the Population of China, 1368–1953* [Cambridge: Harvard University Press, 1959]), 282, appendix I.

4. Perkins, *Agricultural Development in China*, 16. Or, 370 million *mou* plus or minus 70 million *mou*. Each *mou* was .067 hectare in the Qing period. Heidjra puts the registered land total at 429 million *mou* for the early Ming ("The Socio-Economic Development of Rural China during the Ming," 450, table 9.3).

5. Ibid. Or, 1,210 million *mou* plus or minus 50 million *mou*.

6. Lavely and Wong, "Revising the Malthusian Narrative," 714.

7. See especially Kenneth Pomeranz, *The Great Divergence: Europe, China, and the Making of the Modern World Economy* (Princeton, N.J.: Princeton University Press, 2000). See also Lavely and Wong, "Revising the Malthusian Narrative," 738–39.

the Boserup model, in which increasing population densities stimulate more productive agricultural techniques and greater labor inputs to meet demand.[8] This revisionist view is a powerful rebuttal to the Eurocentric notion of China living precipitously on the edge of a subsistence crisis because of its uncontrolled population growth. The evidence for comparable material living standards between the two societies is compelling and fascinating.

Powerful and pointed as it is, however, this body of criticism gives insufficient attention to the environmental history of China—especially in terms of land use—in this period. Historians of China have long known and documented the progress of internal colonization in the medieval and early modern periods. Conventional historical scholarship has understated the enormous importance of these expansive processes. In part, Chinese population growth was a response to recurring infusion of newly available land and natural resources. However, there is a companion environmental narrative.[9] Continuing internal colonization, followed by continuing agricultural intensification, dramatically transformed the Chinese landscape and the human relationship to nature. Widespread deforestation was only the most visible effect of these intensified land uses. The mid-Qing landscape of 1800 was a far more tamed and managed place than it had been in the early Ming of 1400.

Much of the dynamic economic growth and social change in early modern China resulted from expanding internal frontiers of settlement followed by intensified land use as the frontier ended. As mentioned above, cultivated land in China expanded by 50 to 60 million hectares in four centuries. A great number of these hectares derived from conversion of marginal lands adjacent to cultivated fields in already settled areas. However, tens of millions of hectares of new cultivation were added as Han Chinese settlers cleared internal frontier zones and converted them into fields under sedentary cultivation. Indigenous, non-Han ethnic groups, thinly settled shifting cultivators in more remote regions, gave way before the colonizing thrust of pioneering Chinese.

The fortuitous arrival and adoption of New World food crops—maize and sweet potato—proved to be a powerful aid in the work of cultivating hilly uplands without irrigation. Millions of Han Chinese migrants moved long distances in response to the inducements of internal settlement frontiers. Sometimes ahead of the state, sometimes responding to state initiatives, workers and settlers poured into thinly populated tracts and brought new land into

8. Ester Boserup, *Population and Technological Change: A Study of Long-Term Trends* (Chicago: University of Chicago Press, 1981).

9. The environmental history of China has recently been enriched by cooperative research between, and publication by, Chinese and Western scholars. For the English language publication, see Mark Elvin and Liu Tsui-jung, *Sediments of Time: Environment and Society in Chinese History* (Cambridge: Cambridge University Press, 1998).

production. Timbering, mining, and other extractive industries paced the expansion of dry farming. At the same time, the new resources tapped by these settlers helped to stimulate impressive commercialization, industrialization, and monetization in a unifying imperial economy.[10] Generally, the windfall effect of new resources and new crops improved, for a time at least, the material standards of both settlers and already settled populations. Early modern Chinese were by no means universally impoverished—quite the reverse. Material benefits accompanied expansion and intensification.

Expanded cultivation and intensified land use proceeded in early modern China in spite of adverse climatic conditions. Reconstruction of Chinese climate history during the Little Ice Age reveals that the Chinese people, in common with those in other temperate and subtropical world regions, experienced colder temperatures and suffered more extreme floods and droughts from the sixteenth to the nineteenth centuries.[11] On average, early modern Chinese farmers obtained scantier yields than they would have harvested under more favorable climate conditions. Such adversity probably encouraged farmers to migrate, reclaim new lands, and adopt new cultivars on a number of frontiers.

Continuing enlargement of settlement and sedentary cultivation under the Ming and Qing dynasties was ultimately self-limiting. Between 1800 and 1850, those regions in which further internal colonization was feasible and desirable dwindled in number. Apart from the mountainous terrain of Yunnan in the southwest, new frontiers lay only in Manchuria. The recurring infusion of new lands and new resources, no longer abundant, declined steadily, and Chinese society began to exhibit signs of resource and land scarcity. Energy, in the form of fuelwood, became expensive and hard to come by. For the latter part of the nineteenth century, but not for earlier centuries, the conventional view of a population pressing against resources in a growing environmental crisis is accurate.

This chapter first highlights the role of the imperial state in encouraging and enabling agricultural expansion and then describes how Chinese land use intensified in four regions: In Hunan province, intensified wet rice production and water management increased productivity in an already heavily settled region. In the Yangzi highlands, Han settlers, taking advantage of new food crops, expanded vertically into zones largely uninhabited by non-Han peoples. In Guizhou province, state-encouraged internal colonization and settlement pressed forward against desperate resistance by the Miao and other indigenous peoples of that region. In Manchuria, the Han dynasty's homeland, Han Chinese settlers burst through official barriers to begin

10. See, for example, Richard von Glahn, *Fountain of Fortune: Money and Monetary Policy in China, 1000–1700* (Berkeley and Los Angeles: University of California Press, 1996).
11. See chapter 2 for a full discussion of this issue.

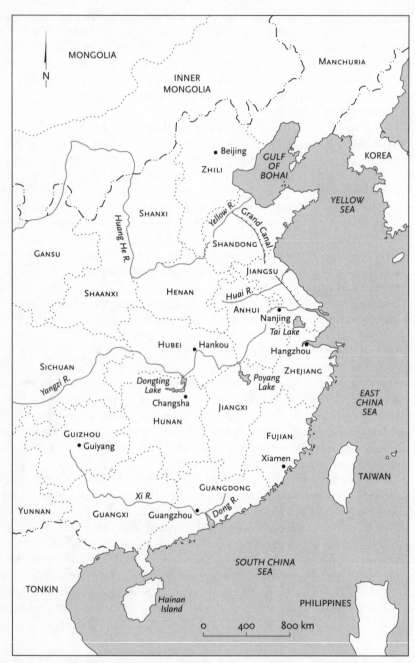

Map 4.1 Late imperial China under the Qing dynasty. Adapted from Sucheta Mazumdar, *Sugar and Society in China: Peasants, Technology, and the World Market* (Cambridge: Harvard University Asia Center, 1998), map 2, p. 16.

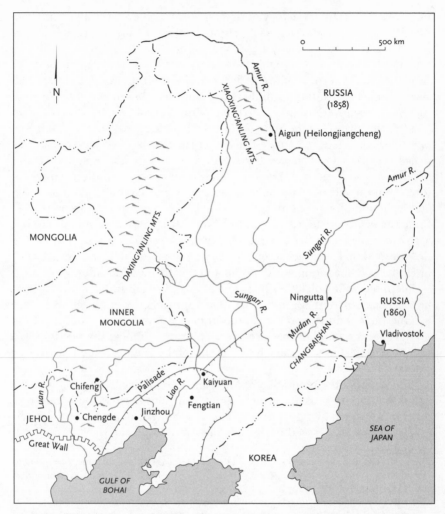

Map 4.2 Manchuria under the Qing dynasty. Adapted from James Reardon-Anderson, "Land Use and Society in Manchuria and Inner Mongolia during the Qing Dynasty," *Environmental History* 5, no. 4 (2000), map 1, p. 505.

cultivation in that region. The conclusion assesses the long-term implications of relentless clearance and deforestation for the Chinese environment.

LAND AND THE STATE

The Chinese state was vigorously involved in encouraging frontier settlement and in all aspects of increasing agricultural production in irrigated and in rain-fed tracts. The trajectory of demographic and environmental change was directly tied to the political fortunes of the state and correlates closely with dynastic rhythms. Under both the Ming and the Qing dynasties, the Chinese state stands out as arguably the strongest, most centralized, most stable of the early modern empires. When dynasties fell, political disorder had sharp impacts on human numbers and land use. When the state revived, these indices moved upward.[12] So did environmental pressures on the land.

After the turmoil of the Yuan decline during the 1300s, the early Ming emperors encouraged and funded resettlement and land reclamation of depopulated areas. Over the next two centuries, as many as 41 million hectares of land were cultivated.[13] When the Ming decline began in the 1630s, these totals plummeted because of heavy mortality and land abandonment. Recurring epidemics, drought, famine, desolation, and disorder accompanied both the widespread revolts against the Ming and the long-drawn-out Manchu invasion and conquest.[14] For example, official assessments at the time posited that "as much as one-quarter to one-third of the cultivated land" in Hubei and Shandong was depopulated during these decades.[15]

Recovery came quickly. Official Qing figures put cultivated land at 39 million hectares in 1661. By 1685, the total approached 50 million hectares.[16] For the next century and a half, the human numbers and cultivated land grew steadily: 82 million hectares were cultivated to meet the needs of 420 million people. Only the cataclysmic events of the Taiping Rebellion of 1857 reversed this trend.[17]

Generation after generation of Ming and Qing officials held firmly to the belief that aiding peasant farmers to intensify and expand food-grain production was their highest priority. The government depended on tax revenues from lands devoted to rice or wheat. Moreover, the social order itself

12. For an illustration of this sequence at the local level, see Hilary J. Beattie, *Land and Lineage in China: A Study of T'ung-ch'eng County, Anhwei, in the Ming and Ch'ing Dynasties* (Cambridge: Cambridge University Press, 1979).

13. Perkins's figure for 1600 is 500 million *mou* plus or minus 100 million (*Agricultural Development in China*, 16). Heidjra gives higher estimates ("The Socio-Economic Development of Rural China during the Ming," 451, table 9.4). His adjusted figure for the comprehensive Ming cadastral survey of 1580 is 733 million. In the same table, he also suggests that the figure for 1600 was 932 million *mou*, which seems improbable.

14. William Atwell, "The T'ai-ch'ang, T'ien-ch'i, and Ch'ung-chen Regimes," in *The Cambridge History of China*, edited by Denis Crispin Twitchett and John King Fairbank (Cambridge: Cambridge University Press, 1988), vol. 7, pt. 1, pp. 621–32.

15. Philip C. Huang, *The Peasant Economy and Social Change in North China* (Stanford, Calif.: Stanford University Press, 1985). See also the description of Hunan province below.

16. Eduard B. Vermeer, "Ch'ing Government Concerns with the Exploitation of New Farmland," in *Etudes thématiques*, edited by Léon Vandermeersch, vol. 3 (Paris: Ecole française d'Extrême-Orient, 1994). Perkins puts the cultivated area for 1685 at 740 million *mou* plus or minus 100 million (*Agricultural Development in China*, 16).

17. Perkins, *Agricultural Development in China*, 16.

depended on the rootedness and discipline of communities of peasant farmers subject to Confucian values and to government regulation. High-intensity cultivation of food grains left peasants little time and inclination for anything other than labor in the fields. To increase food-grain production was to increase the power and stability of the empire. These values were shared by the local Han gentry throughout the empire, who looked to land ownership and management as the foundation for their long-term security and prosperity.

Chang Ying, a mid-seventeenth-century Qing official, repudiated the readier profits of commerce and moneylending for the slower, but more satisfying, returns from land stewardship in his hortatory essay "Remarks on Real Estate":

> The merit of land is that . . . if you nourish the land generously then you will get a generous return. In some cases you may get three harvests in the four seasons or you may plant twice in one year. The central fields can be sown with rice or wheat and the side plots and banks can be planted with things like hemp, pulse and cotton for clothing. There will be some trifling income from every foot and inch of earth. That is why it is said that, "The earth does not grudge its riches," a very apposite remark. A man with land first supports his grandfather and father and then looks after his sons and grandsons. He has neither an air of self-satisfaction nor an appearance of weariness, nor any objection to enjoying pleasures and exerting loyalty to the full. When good things are renewed and increased every day and every month[,] he accepts them without shame and enjoys them without anxiety.[18]

The essay argues that success in examinations might lead to imperial office and eminence for some family members, and commercial opportunities might appear from time to time, but the true interests of the lineage rest on careful management of cultivated land in every generation.

Land reclamation was a task of the greatest urgency. When lands had fallen out of cultivation because of wars or natural disasters, officials acted to restore order, to offer start-up monies to returning refugee peasants, and to provide tax exemptions on newly cultivated lands. In 1658, the new Qing regime even set out annual quotas for areas of reclaimed land that district magistrates were expected to meet.[19] Local gentry shared these concerns. As landlords, they could increase their own wealth and security by reclaiming abandoned lands.

When population densities and market demands justified it, officials encouraged reclamation of marshes, newly created riverine islands, and other

18. Beattie, *Land and Lineage in China,* 144, appendix 3. This treatise is dated approximately 1697. Chang Ying's ancestral home was T'ung-Ch'eng county in Anhwei province, on the northern bank of the central Yangzi.

19. Vermeer, "Ch'ing Government Concerns with the Exploitation of New Farmland," 205–6.

wastelands by individual families, lineages, and even larger corporate structures. Official policy offered loans, security of tenure, and tax holidays on new lands.[20] At times, officials were remarkably shortsighted in their fixation on intensive grain production. They discouraged more flexible use of "wastelands" when peasants themselves saw their value as grazing lands, as fishing or waterfowl-hunting grounds, or as areas for raising reeds, fish, or fruit trees. Often village communities or lineages managed these less intensively used lands under common property regimes. Official rhetoric harshly condemned these practices. For example, a late Ming local official proclaimed:

> Stop the minor profit of the occupants of reedlands and grasslands! Registered wasteland is wasteland. Having reeds and grasses, still makes it wasteland. Yet some lazy people, without consideration for the land-term future, go after the minor profits of reeds and reject the great treasure of cultivation of crops. Not only do they not pursue land reclamation themselves, but they also hate others for doing so. When one investigates their purpose, it is to avoid taxation under the pretext of "wasteland." They cling to their minor profit and cherish their lazy life. Now the order that our farmland should gradually increase is written on stone tablets, the market places are more desolate every day, the government revenues fall short of the regular quota. How can we allow this under these circumstances! We should proclaim, that all reed- and grasslands and the like should be reclaimed and restored to cultivation.[21]

In practice, however, the authorities did in fact recognize the local common property lands used for pasture, fuelwood, and other purposes. Village chiefs and elites, powerful lineage groups, and local gentry defended these rights against official expropriation and pressure to cultivate.[22] District magistrates avoided serious conflict over these issues as much as possible. Nevertheless, as land became more valuable and scarce, individual households gradually encroached on common lands. Especially under the Qing dynasty, population increase, market demands, and potential profits put enormous pressures on local common property regimes in densely settled lowland areas.

LAND RECLAMATION FOR WET RICE PRODUCTION IN HUNAN PROVINCE

Hunan province, surrounded by hill ranges on the north, east, and west, is drained by the Xiang, one of the great rivers of China, which flows north-

---

20. This typology of land reclamation is set out in ibid., 203–4.
21. Quoted in ibid., 233.
22. Ibid., 238–39.

ward toward Dongting Lake, the largest inland body of water in China.[23] Navigable throughout its 811-kilometer length, the river served as the primary commercial route for Hunan. The Zi, Yuan, and Li Rivers also flow northward into Dongting Lake. Hunan's river valleys have soil, climate, and rainfall favorable to intensive rice cultivation. In the medieval centuries, Han Chinese migrants, moving south, settled the lowlands by draining swamp and marshlands and by building dikes and reservoirs for irrigated rice cultivation. Dense human and animal populations produced fertilizers to enrich soils already made fertile by river siltation.

In 1391, when the Ming dynasty assumed power in China, an empirewide household census revealed a modest population of between 1.8 and 2 million Han Chinese living in Hunan (exclusive of the indigenous Miao and other tribal non-Confucian peoples). Registered land, indicating sedentary cultivation, amounted to 732,000 hectares, or only 3 percent of the total land area of Hunan. Irrigated lands adjacent to Dongting Lake were the areas of densest settlement. Population and number of hectares cultivated were both considerably smaller than at the height of the Song and Yuan dynasties. This decline reflected the impact of political instability and warfare in the fourteenth century.

Although details are scarce, it is clear that Hunan went through a cycle of economic growth under the Ming as Han Chinese settlers from Jiangxi province in the west, already overcrowded, migrated to the province. Many notable Hunanese lineages still extant trace their arrival in the province to the Ming centuries.[24] As did all Chinese rulers, the Ming dynasty strongly favored and supported expanded cultivation. Newly cultivated lands were exempt from imperial taxes; areas of longer settlement were subject to ever increasing tax burdens.

Hunan's core area of densest population and highest rice production remained the land near Dongting Lake. The Ming emperors invested heavily in large dikes designed to protect against flooding and to secure land for cultivation at the northern end of the lake and along the Yangzi. Since Dongting Lake was the outlet for four major rivers flowing from the south and for the Yangzi flowing from the mountainous northeast, lake levels varied dramatically between summer highs and winter lows. Flooding in the spring and summer was a constant danger that the builders of the imperial dikes tried to protect against.

Another form of diking consisted of rectangular or round polders whose earthen walls enclosed farmland separated from the marshes and shores of

23. This section is based on the detailed study by Peter C. Perdue, *Exhausting the Earth: State and Peasant in Hunan, 1500–1850* (Cambridge: Council on East Asian Studies, Harvard University, distributed by Harvard University Press, 1987).

24. Ibid., 62.

the lake itself. The fields lay below the normal water level of the lake. Irrigating simply involved cutting small channels into the dikes to release water from the lake into the rice fields at the appropriate time. The costs of irrigation came in using animal and human power to pump water out of the sunken fields when it was no longer needed.[25]

Gentry landlords or lineage groups who mobilized the substantial capital needed to build and maintain Dongting dikes were well rewarded by abundant rice harvests and by exemption from taxes. The polders themselves set out the boundaries of farming communities bearing the names of the dikes that enclosed them. The silt-laden soils of the polder areas were remarkably fertile and productive when carefully irrigated and cultivated under a wet rice regime. Han settlers tended to move outward from Dongting Lake along the valleys of the Xiang, the Zi, the Yuan, and the Li Rivers. Aided by the state, they built embankments along the rivers to control seasonal flooding and protect low-lying paddy fields. Alluvial lands along the river bottoms proved to be nearly as fertile as those in Dongting Lake.[26]

By the early seventeenth century, Hunan was a rice-surplus area known for its bountiful production.[27] The last systematic land survey under the Ming, carried out in the period 1578–1582, shows a threefold increase in cultivated land to 1.9 million hectares, or 13.8 percent of the total area. Han population inferred from these numbers (in the absence of a household census) was probably between 5 and 6 million persons.[28] Nevertheless, most of Hunan remained a frontier inhabited by indigenous peoples, in some measure a result of Ming policies that sealed off "prohibited mountain regions" from settlement.[29]

Settlement and agricultural expansion came to an abrupt halt as the Ming empire began to break up under pressure from the Manchu invasion of 1629–1630. A series of internal rebellions began in the northwest and spread widely throughout the empire. The two major rebel leaders, Zhang Xianzhong and Li Zicheng, each campaigned briefly through Hunan in the 1640s and devastated several cities. However, other, smaller groups of rebels emerged to plunder and devastate Hunanese towns and cities. Hunan, as elsewhere, was beset by defiant tenant farmers and bondservants, who fought their masters and fled to join rebel bands. Tribal groups took advantage of

25. Ibid., 175.

26. For a description of similar kinds of land reclamation in the Pearl River delta, see Robert B. Marks, *Tigers, Rice, Silk, and Silt: Environment and Economy in Late Imperial South China* (Cambridge: Cambridge University Press, 1997).

27. Heidjra, "The Socio-Economic Development of Rural China during the Ming," 507, 546–48.

28. Perdue, *Exhausting the Earth*, 49.

29. Ibid., 60.

the confusion and government weakness to rebel and attack the Han settlers. Hunan degenerated under banditry and general lawlessness.

Even after the Manchus assumed formal power, instability continued.[30] In Hunan, rebellion and disorder reached its height in 1648, when Manchu forces moved into southern China. Rebels invaded every county in the province. A severe drought occurred in 1652, and alternating floods and droughts followed thereafter. The network of dikes along the rivers and Dongting Lake collapsed: "All those who could escape fled the lowlands and cities to seek shelter in the mountains. Groups of refugees gathered in mountain fortresses or caves that offered protection from armed attack. Those who could not escape were forced to adopt desperate survival strategies. Families sold themselves into bondage, and female infanticide became common among the poor."[31]

In a final disruption, the regime lost control of Hunan in 1674 to Wu San-gui, the most powerful of the "Three Feudatories" of South China, who revolted against the Manchus and proclaimed himself emperor of China in 1678. Several years of war left "empty markets, collapsed fences and wells, and fields occupied by wolves and thorns."[32]

Even after the new Manchu regime established political control, normality was slow to return to Hunan following the years of continuous warfare. Slowly, refugees filtered back to reclaim their land and homes. Successive governors found themselves fighting bandits in the hills, suppressing pirates who infested Dongting Lake and the Xiang River, and prosecuting innumerable cases of murder, as violence remained the norm in Hunan until the early years of the eighteenth century. Detailed figures from Changsha prefecture, one of the most devastated areas in the province, reveal that just over one-quarter of the lands registered as cultivated in 1582 were being worked in 1679.[33]

Qing officials tried a number of expedients to restore settlement and production. In the 1650s, the state declared all nontaxed and abandoned land the property of the state. The army collected surrendered rebels and refugees and settled them as military colonists on abandoned land with the promise of land ownership after three years. Unduly heavy taxes hampered this effort. And in the end, civilian landlords and their tenants were the agents of restoration. The regime offered a mix of tax exemptions on reclaimed fields, ownership rights for occupying peasants, and grants of seed, cattle, and tools.

30. These events are fully described in Atwell, "The T'ai-ch'ang, T'ien-ch'i, and Ch'ung-chen Regimes."

31. Perdue, *Exhausting the Earth*, 66.

32. Ibid.

33. Ibid., 72.

The Qing emperors, who faced little in the way of either external or internal military threats, were content to lightly tax the agrarian economy of China. Instead of adopting the Ming emphasis on land surveys and heavy taxation, the Qing emperors refused to order an empirewide cadastral survey for tax purposes. In its place, they used the last Ming figures from the 1582 land survey for normative land registration, deducting abandoned land and adding newly occupied lands, to arrive at the figure for taxable area. Landowners were asked to voluntarily report newly cleared and cultivated lands. This was a gigantic concession to local gentry and landlords in Hunan and throughout the empire. When reclaimed lands reached the 1582 totals, the gentry, tacitly permitted to do so by the regime, simply stopped reporting additional lands put under cultivation. In effect, gentry landlords received a permanent tax exemption on wastelands brought under the plow.

As confidence and stability returned, population increased and commercial market networks were reestablished. By the 1720s, registered land figures in Hunan had risen to the levels of the late Ming. In 1718, the regime took a renewed interest in water control in Hunan. The Kangxi emperor (r. 1661–1722), recognizing problems caused by flooding on the Yangzi and Dongting Lake that demanded expensive relief expenditures, made available large sums for dike building and repair. He also ordered local officials to encourage private investment in water control as well. These measures set off a new round of polder building on the lake and added to the rice harvests.

Under conditions of peace and order, Hunan's population grew steadily. By 1800, continuing immigration and natural increase had raised human numbers to 17 million—a threefold increase over the Ming figures. Immigrants from Jiangxi poured into Hunan, attracted by its revived economy. Merchants and traders seized the chance for profits in the fast-growing trade of the province: entrepreneurs who opened new tin, lead, iron, and coal mines in southern Hunan offered jobs to hundreds of thousands of migrant workers—at least until many mines were exhausted in the latter part of the eighteenth century. "Empty" land that could be occupied and cleared was by far the greatest inducement to migration. Established gentry landlords recruited migrants as tenants whose energies could be put to clearing and cultivating new, untaxed, and unreported lands.

Cultivable land became scarce in Hunan, and land prices rose steadily. Rising market demand encouraged wet rice farmers to alternate rice crops with other food crops such as buckwheat *(Fagopyrum)*, maize *(Zea maize)*, wheat, or beans in a form of double-cropping. Immigrants brought with them special early rice seed varieties. The new seeds enabled farmers to obtain an early rice crop harvested in the sixth lunar month, followed by a second sowing of a nonrice crop that matured in the tenth month. Planting wet rice early had the added advantage of insuring against years with excessive summer floodwaters that could ruin the unharvested rice. During the last years of the eighteenth century, the amount of cultivated land in Hunan rose to between 2.3 million hectares and 3.4 million hectares—or a threefold to fivefold increase over the late Ming totals.[34]

As pressure on the fertile valleys and lowland wet rice farming areas intensified, immigrants began clearing and occupying forested lands at increasingly higher elevations. Woodcutters, charcoal burners, miners, and bandits (loosely organized into small bands) also moved into the hills formerly occupied only sparsely by the Miao hill peoples (see below). Many of these immigrants simply occupied land as squatters or "shack people" with no legal rights to their holdings. Initially they practiced a form of slash-and-burn cultivation far more destructive of forest cover than practices by the indigenous non-Confucian peoples of the hills. Maize and sweet potato *(Ipomoea batatas),* introduced into Hunan by the eighteenth century, greatly improved the chances for successful rain-fed cultivation in the hills.

In the early eighteenth century, empirewide land-tax reforms reduced the demands made on poorer, marginal districts in Hunan and freed up capital for investment in the land. The regime made vigorous efforts to push hill farmers toward more intensive, more secure forms of cultivation that could include rice growing as well as the newer crops. Officials continually exhorted landlords to provide money and peasants to provide labor for dams, reservoirs, and pumping systems aimed at making maximum use of mountain rivers and streams. Dams made of large stone blocks filled reservoirs capable of irrigating thousands of *mou.* Smaller streams could be dammed to divert water to reservoirs, or channels could lead water directly to fields without damming. Water pumps powered by animals or humans lifted water from reservoirs to fields lying above them. Reservoirs or tanks in depressions collected and stored water for use during extended periods of scant rainfall. Proliferation of these irrigation works did make hill agriculture more secure and productive.

By mid–eighteenth century, many imperial officials became concerned about the environmental costs and dangers of forest clearance. They realized that, in general, water projects could help control erosion on newly cleared soils as well as improve production. An official memorial of 1776 commented that, after the forests were cut, "the earth was loose; when the big rains came, water rushed down from the highlands and mud and silt spread out below. Fertile areas near the mountains were repeatedly covered with sand and were abandoned."[35] Hunan's forest cover was rapidly disappearing in the face of the settler assault. Irrigation works stabilized both soil and rural populations.

34. Perkins, *Agricultural Development in China,* 234, table B.12; estimates are based on the official Qing totals for 1766. See also Perdue, *Exhausting the Earth,* 50, table 4.
35. Perdue, *Exhausting the Earth,* 88.

LAND RECLAMATION IN THE HILLS: THE YANGZI HIGHLANDS

The frontier of settlement pressed upward into the hills of central and South China. Prior to the late sixteenth century, there were many virtually uninhabited, forested hill tracts adjacent to areas of dense Han settlement and lowland wet rice cultivation. When there were no more lowland rice farming areas where farming could be intensified, and there were no more wetlands to reclaim, vertical land reclamation was the next step. Economic and demographic recovery under the early Qing emperors generated new demands for resources. Waves of Han Chinese settlers migrated from overcrowded landscapes to occupy and clear previously marginal uplands. Profits were to be made in extracting forest products and in growing cash crops in the hills for consumption in the lowlands.

The Portuguese had introduced maize, sweet potatoes, peanuts, and other New World domesticated plants into Fujian province on the southeast coast before the middle of the sixteenth century. Diffusion of the new cultivars inland took decades. However, by the late seventeenth century, maize and sweet potatoes, widely adopted by hill settlers, significantly raised the caloric output of dry farming in the hills. With this new technology, hill farmers could feed themselves and produce a surplus with far less risk than before. After 1700, forest clearing and human settlement proceeded at a remarkable pace in the uplands of central and southern China.

Until the early nineteenth century, the Qing emperors were favorably inclined toward this form of land clearing and settlement. The Qing emperors allowed free migration to many mountain areas that had been closed under the Ming.[36] They were aware of overcrowding in lowland areas and knew that many people were forced into migration to try and make a living. If these migrants could not find land and settle, they would turn to vagrancy and banditry. If new, previously unproductive lands could produce food, this was all to the good. Provincial and local officials were more ambivalent. They welcomed increased grain production in the hills but were uneasy about the mobility of the hill migrants, their propensity for violence, and their tendency to organize in heterodox groups such as secret societies. As clearing progressed, there were obvious problems of downstream erosion and flooding that threatened the productivity of lowland rice production. In response, provincial and local officials initiated water control and other irrigation works in the hills to reduce silting and runoff and improve output.

The Yangzi highlands, located in the economic core of central China, are one example of this type of land reclamation. The rugged highlands of the

36. For uplands frontier settlement in the Dabashan mountains in South Shaanxi, see Edward B. Vermeer, "The Mountain Frontier in Late Imperial China: Economic and Social Developments in the Dabashan," *T'oung Pao* 77 (1991).

Nan Shan mountain chain that lies just south of the middle and lower Yangzi River were not subject to Han settlement until very late.[37] Rather than move into the hills, peasant farmers along the Yangzi preferred to intensify their cultivation in the river lowlands. In this region survived the mixed deciduous and evergreen broadleaf forests of South China.[38] Unlike the mountainous regions farther south, the Yangzi highlands did not contain a non-Confucian, non-Han indigenous tribal population. These steep, forested hills were the home of wildlife (including tigers) and a few humans: hunters, plant gatherers, Daoist priests, and bandits.

The hill slopes did not lend themselves to wet rice cultivation without the exhausting labor of constructing terraces. Hidden valleys and plains where rice could have been cultivated were so remote that transporting grain to market would have been unprofitable. Slowly, however, land scarcity in settled provinces opened up a new frontier of settlement in the late Ming that accelerated during the Qing dynasty.

By the late Ming, Fujian and Guangdong provinces, and the lowland areas of Jiangxi province, in the southeast held dense populations. Increasing concentration of land ownership in a commercialized economy forced many peasants into precarious tenant or even landless status.[39] Uncertainty and turbulence accompanied the state's struggle against coastal piracy that relied on the drastic policy of forced removals of the entire coastal population, which was thought to be collaborating in the regions beset by piracy.[40] Later, the protracted violence as the southern Ming regime fought against the Manchus "contributed to a massive population shift in South China."[41] Some peasants took to the sea and migrated to Taiwan or Southeast Asia. Others moved inland, first to the hills of western Fujian and northwestern Guangdong, then across mountain passes to the Yangzi highlands in Kangxi and farther north. Jiangxi became a staging area for further migration to unpopulated uplands along the Yangzi.

The universal term for hill migrants was *pengmin*, or "shack people," in ref-

37. Stephen C. Averill, "The Shed People and the Opening of the Yangzi Highlands," *Modern China* 9 (1983); Anne Osborne, "Barren Mountains, Raging Rivers: The Ecological and Social Effects of Changing Landuse on the Lower Yangzi Periphery in Late Imperial China" (Ph.D. diss., Columbia University, 1989); Osborne, "Highlands and Lowlands: Economic and Ecological Interactions in the Lower Yangzi Region under the Qing," in *Sediments of Time: Environment and Society in Chinese History*, edited by Mark Elvin and Liu Ts'ui-jung (Cambridge: Cambridge University Press, 1998); Osborne, "The Local Politics of Land Reclamation in the Lower Yangzi Highlands," *Late Imperial China* 15 (1994): 1–46.

38. Nicholas K. Menzies, "Forestry," in *Science and Civilisation in China*, edited by Joseph Needham (Cambridge: University Press, 1996), vol. 6, pt. 3, sec. 423, pp. 553–54, table 21.

39. Averill, "The Shed People and the Opening of the Yangzi Highlands," 86–87; Heidjra, "The Socio-Economic Development of Rural China during the Ming," 544–52.

40. Osborne, "Barren Mountains, Raging Rivers," 68.

41. Averill, "The Shed People and the Opening of the Yangzi Highlands," 87.

erence to the temporary huts of brush or reeds they erected. This unflatter-
ing name reflects the hostility of the native lowland population who regarded
the newcomers with deep suspicion, fear, and contempt. According to Anne
Osborne, the term lumped together a number of diverse groups:

> It includes unattached men who entered the [uplands] border region only for
> the agricultural season, coming in the spring and departing in the autumn,
> who worked in the tea industry, on timber plantations, mined or grew sweet
> potatoes; slash-and-burn agriculturists who reclaimed mountain land on a
> share-cropping basis; groups of families engaged in commercial agriculture,
> and dependent for subsistence on purchased food; and proto-capitalist entre-
> preneurs who invested large sums of money to rent extensive mountain lands
> that they worked with hired labor. There were some who came to the moun-
> tains for a season, or for a few years, after bad harvests, but expected to return
> to their original districts, and did so voluntarily when conditions back home
> returned to normal. Others settled permanently, bought property, intermar-
> ried with the locals, and buried their dead in the local hills.[42]

As the above suggests, many locals depended on migrant labor and profited
by the migrants' presence but found the influx of strangers difficult to control. Migrants emboldened by the rigors of their experiences or embittered
by perceived lowland exploitation and contempt became defiant and at
times violent. Hill settlers bearing the same surname, even though they were
from different counties or provinces, created fictive lineages to give them
corporate strength. Strong migrant leaders emerged who attracted armed
men as followers; some of these formed the nuclei of secret societies. These
leaders became spokesmen in altercations with locals and officials. Given
provocation and opportunity, they turned to banditry and terrorism.

Most of the hill tracts were claimed and titled property, often tracts held
by lowland lineages as common property. If the land was truly remote and
unclaimed, migrants could occupy fields and eventually become owners by
right of possession and payment of taxes. More frequently, migrants paid
rents to obtain permission to clear and work land they occupied. Local landlords even sought out and sponsored migrants to use as labor for their extractive enterprises or tree farms or as tenant farmers.

Tenancy arrangements were largely the two-lords-per-field system often
associated with land reclamation. In this dual system, the landlords retained
subsurface ownership rights, and the tenants had surface or cultivation
rights. The landlord paid taxes to the state, and the tenant paid yearly rental
to the landlord. Each set of rights could be sold separately. The topsoil ten-

42. Osborne, "Barren Mountains, Raging Rivers," 144. See also Averill, "The Shed People
and the Opening of the Yangzi Highlands," for a similar analysis. Averill uses the term *shed people*
as a variant translation.

ants thereby received the rewards for any improvements they made to the land and had security of tenure.[43]

The two-lords-per-field system created powerful incentives for hill migrants to take up land, because they quickly obtained permanent rights of tenancy. The system also encouraged tension and violence between landlords and tenants when rapid shifts in ownership of topsoil rights occurred and the new occupiers resisted payment of rent.

The earliest phase of highland intrusion responded to commercial demand for scarce resources. Miners actively sought iron, lead, and tin ores that could be mined and processed on-site. Charcoal cutters and burners pushed deeper into the hills to find fuel. Paper mulberry and bamboo could be cleared and sold for papermaking. Entrepreneurs employed itinerant laborers to cut and float pine *(Pinus massoniana)* for fuelwood and *shan (Cunninghamia lanceolata)* for timber, both in much demand in the lowlands. Well-to-do local lineages or landlords who staked out property claims to the hillsides used labor bosses or intermediaries to recruit workers from crowded regions. After clearing and selling the existing forest cover, many timber merchants found it profitable to set up tree plantations in the hills. Cunninghamia was a favored plantation species. Whether planted or coppiced, this species would reach marketable size in as little as twenty years. Hill tree growers intercropped faster-growing, commercially valuable trees— such as the *thung* tree *(Aleurites fordii),* the lacquer tree *(Rhus verniciflua),* and the camphor tree *(Cinnamomum camphora)*—with the timber trees to generate revenues before the timber matured.[44]

The tree plantations offered work to hill migrants, who were needed to plant and protect the tree crops. Many forest workers stayed only seasonally in the hills and returned to their homes and families for the slack season. Some migrants became permanent settlers. They engaged in shifting cultivation on acidic yellow and red soils exposed after burning and clearing brush and tree cover. However, yields from traditional Chinese millets and other dry-farmed food crops were barely adequate to meet the caloric needs of the hill settlers, who lacked the long-developed specialized seeds and techniques of non-Han peoples living in similar situations.[45] Supplements from hunting, fishing, and gathering helped, but these activities demanded time and energy as well as skill.

43. Averill, "The Shed People and the Opening of the Yangzi Highlands," 115.

44. Osborne, "Barren Mountains, Raging Rivers," 72–73; Menzies, "Forestry," 629.

45. Whether and how successfully Han hill settlers cultivated millets is not at all clear in the literature. Especially in northern China, Han farmers had developed hundreds of varieties of both foxtail millet *(Setaria italica)* and broomcorn millet *(Panicum miliaceum)* with qualities aimed at almost any combination of soil and climate. Francesca Bray, "Agriculture," pt. 2 of *Biology and Biological Technology,* edited by Francesca Bray, vol. 6 of *Science and Civilisation in China,* edited by Joseph Needham (Cambridge: University Press, 1984), 434–38.

Most sixteenth-century and even seventeenth-century Han hill migrants remained tied to lowland subsidies, either by wages or proceeds from the sale of cash crops or forest products to lowland markets. They planted cash crops such as ramie *(Boehmeria nivea)*, edible tree fungus, fast-growing bamboo, and tea bushes in some hill areas with suitable soils.

Diffusion of New World food crops dramatically increased the food-producing potential of the Yangzi highlands. The sweet potato *(Ipomoiea batatas)* rapidly proved its superiority to the native Chinese aquatic taros and dry-farmed yams. The new tuber had a pleasant taste. Yields were phenomenally high. It was relatively immune to locusts and had far greater drought resistance. The new cultivar could be grown on relatively poor soil and thus did not compete with rice or other traditional food crops.[46]

The most widely adopted new cultivar was maize *(Zea mays)*. Settlers in the Yangzi highlands had learned the numerous benefits that maize offered over traditional dry-farmed grain crops: Overall, yields were appreciably higher than with millets. Maize did not have to be precisely timed; it could be planted from early to late in the season. Planting on slopes minimized the impact of frost (to which maize was susceptible) as the sun warmed the sites each day. Maize responded well to the deeper implantation of hoe cultivation characteristic of shifting cultivators. Maize had deep roots that helped anchor it on slopes and that resisted the effects of hard runoff or flooding. It was hardy under drought conditions and could be grown in soils in which millets would not be attempted. Labor requirements were much lighter, since growing maize required little weeding or attention in the field. Once ripened, maize grains protected by the husk were not as susceptible to damage in the field from wind, rain, or hailstorms. The whole crop could not easily be destroyed overnight by a hailstorm. A further advantage was that maize could be stored simply by hanging it on the rafters and walls in the husk without any special storage pits, jars, or other facilities.[47]

With maize at their disposal, the shack people stood a fair chance of feeding themselves and their families without any form of food subsidy from the lowlands. They could continue to labor for wages, or they could grow commercial crops like ramie or indigo for additional income. Streams of migrants cleared brush and trees, planted maize for several years, and, as fertility declined, shifted their fields. The result was massive deforestation in the highlands. The local history of Yushan, a hill county in Jiangxi province, written in 1784, eulogized the vanished landscape:

> The northwestern countryside produced firs in abundance. Those areas opened up near the mountains in the Yongzheng reign provided timber to

46. Ho, *Studies on the Population of China*, 186–87.

47. Perkins, *Agricultural Development in China*, 47–48; Bray, "Agriculture," 452–59; Osborne, "Barren Mountains, Raging Rivers," 158–70, 183–89.

Hangzhou. Recently as the population has multiplied and the fertility of the soil has been exhausted, they do not wait until those that [sic] are a handspan in diameter, and the axes ring ding! ding! Only old maples, which are useless, frequently enjoy longevity among the cliffs in the mountain areas, or together with pines and camphor trees provide shade for the towns. . . . Old farmers say that in the early Qianlong period, when the mountains of Huai and Yushan were opened up, the trees grew in profusion, bamboo groves were thick and dense, tailed deer grouped in herds and wandered or rested beside the paths. Ringed pheasants and hares could be caught everywhere in the mountains ready to hand. On the banks of Stone Drum Stream, mandarin ducks and egrets soared frequently. Men and animals were accustomed to one another and took no notice of each other. On the other hand, wild boar and a variety of bears and unfamiliar wild animals often did harm. Recently there has been expanded clearing of trees and bamboos, and the smoke of human habitation has become dense. The animals do not wait to be driven away, but have already withdrawn on their own.[48]

When fields of maize replaced hill forests, soil erosion followed. The migrants planted maize in spaced rows on steep slopes subject to hard rains. The unfertilized maize made heavy demands on the poor soil, yields fell off, and the hill farmers cleared new fields for planting. The silt load on the narrow mountain streams and rivers grew proportionately as exposed hills eroded. As these waterways silted up, downstream flooding grew in frequency and severity. Rivers rose to levels not seen before. Dikes and other water control projects in the lowlands were weakened, and fields with growing crops were destroyed.

By the end of the eighteenth century, officials and gentry commented on and analyzed the problems caused by highland reclamation. They called for stringent measures to expel hill settlers or at least to prevent them from growing maize, which contemporary opinion held was the primary cause of downstream flooding.[49] Despite these arguments, settlement in the Yangzi highlands was so massive and so established by this time that the Qing government could do little. The nineteenth-century emperors would have to muster more political will and resources than they seemingly possessed to reverse the frontier and restore the hill forests.

INDIGENOUS PEOPLES AND QING PRESSURE

Under the Qing, the moving frontier of Han settlement pressed against indigenous non-Confucian peoples south of the Yangzi. When necessary, the Qing state deployed ruthless military power to subdue resistance and protect

48. Osborne, "Barren Mountains, Raging Rivers," 92.
49. Ibid., 210–19.

settlers. This policy put acute pressures on indigenous peoples and their lands and natural resources. By mid–nineteenth century, Han settler expansion resulted in widespread deforestation throughout central and southern China. The consequences for energy supplies and timber, and the results of failure to control soil erosion, were severe.

In the hill areas shared between Guizhou and Hunan provinces, for example, the Miao people felt the full weight of Qing state power in the eighteenth century. Lying between the twenty-fifth and twenty-ninth parallels, Guizhou is a mountainous province, bordered on the east by Hunan and on the west by Yunnan. Difficult to reach, most of this rainy, semitropical land is between 600 and 1,000 meters elevation. The western portion of the province, on the Yunnan side, is a great massif that lies between 1,500 and 2,000 meters in elevation, with mountain peaks that reach as high as 3,000 meters. There is some reason to think that the Miao and other peoples in Guizhou were probably pushed into this less-fertile region in the medieval centuries under the Sung and Yuan dynasties as Han settlers occupied the more fertile lowlands of Hunan and other nearby regions.[50]

The early Ming emperors established a military presence in the region and fixed tributary ties with leading indigenous chiefs. Guizhou became a province distinct from Yunnan, with an imperial governor, in 1416. However, the forbidding nature of the area inhibited Chinese migration and settlement save in the form of military colonies. During the Ming period, imperial power in Guizhou took the form of about fifty walled cities and towns populated solely by Han Chinese military and civilians.[51]

Of the three most numerous indigenous peoples in Guizhou—the Miao, the Yao, and the Yi—the Miao, who were located in the eastern part of the province and whose lands spilled over into Hunan, were by virtue of their location most vulnerable to renewed state and settler expansion. Surviving Chinese accounts confirm that, by the end of the Ming period, the Miao exhibited a sophisticated, resilient society and robust economy well adapted to life in the highlands. The population was probably several hundred thousand. They spoke Miao-Yao, a Sino-Tibetan language, but were not literate. The Miao lived in hilltop villages fortified with wood palisades. They were organized by kinship into families and lineages dominated by aristocratic families. Village chiefs, originally charismatic warriors from founding village lineages, increasingly derived their authority from recognition by the Chinese

---

50. The following description is drawn almost exclusively from Claudine Lombard-Salmon, *Un exemple d'acculturation chinoise: La province du Gui Zhou au XVIIIe siècle* (Paris: École française d'Extrême-Orient, 1972). Alternative spellings of Guizhou include Ghi Zhou in French terminology and Kweichow in earlier scholarly works. The Miao are also known as the Hmong.

51. See the listing of these places in Lombard-Salmon, *Un exemple d'acculturation chinoise*, 255–56.

authorities and from their knowledge of the Chinese language. The chiefs accepted, allocated, and fulfilled Chinese demands for taxes in kind and corvée from their followers.

The Miao were a bellicose people. Young boys were socialized for the hunt and warfare. The Miao were armed with formidable muskets, crossbows, spears, and knives. They had developed a lethal poison that they employed on the tips of arrows. Villages and lineages often found themselves in various altercations marked by blood feuds and continuing low-level violence that was most disconcerting to the Han Chinese authorities.

In addition to hunting and gathering, the Miao farmed with a wide array of agricultural techniques ranging from shifting cultivation to intensive wet rice growing.[52] They slashed and burned new fields to grow maize on a three-year rotation. In common with most non-Confucian hill peoples, the Miao had taken enthusiastically to maize, which offered greater food security than the more traditional crops. Other dry-farmed crops included millets, sorghum, buckwheat, and wheat, as well as varieties of oilseeds, beans, and pulses. They grew cotton and hemp for fiber. When they found reasonably level plains and accessible mountain streams, they planted wet rice; at times, they constructed terraces on slopes for rice cultivation. The Miao raised buffaloes, horses, sheep, pigs, and poultry. Villages that had wetlands built fishponds and raised carp *(Cyprinus carpio)*, bream *(Abramis brama)*, and other food fish.

Miao artisanal skills were impressive. They used forges to work both silver, for ornamentation, and iron, for tools and weapons. In addition to hoes and machetes, they fashioned sharp steel knives, crossbows, lances, and firearms. Their muskets were reputed to be very accurate and lethal to a range of forty meters or more. Miao women wove cotton and other fibers into clothing and richly ornamented textiles used for presentation pieces. The women also brewed a potent form of rice wine that was consumed in lavish quantities at various celebrations and ceremonies.[53]

During the Ming, if not before, the Miao cut and sold choice timber to Chinese timber merchants, who floated it down the rivers to markets in Hunan. By the Qing period, the Miao regularly replanted cutover tracts with Cunninghamia and *Cryptomeria japonica*. First, for two or three years, they planted maize or wheat to work the soil, then they put in the seedlings. These were carefully culled and shaped as they grew. Fallen leaves were burnt to provide fertilizer around the young trees. By the twenty-year mark, a tree crop could be cut and sold profitably.[54]

---

52. Lombard-Salmon strangely omits any discussion of hunting, which must have contributed to Miao food budgets and been a considerable part of the training of young males.
53. Ibid., 129–30.
54. Ibid., 127–28.

At the beginning of the eighteenth century, after several decades of Qing rule, the Miao in Guizhou and Hunan faced an unpredictable, ominous future. After the Manchu takeover, substantial and increasing numbers of Han private traders moved freely into Miao territory to sell textiles, grains, and salt (often smuggled from the coast) and to buy in return timber, fuelwood, edible tree fungus, bamboo, wax, honey, tung oil (collected from the tree *Aleurites fordii*) and a pharmacopoeia of medicinal plants. These traders sold goods at high interest rates to Miao cultivators on credit, based on the security of the harvest. When crops failed or the prices were not high enough to repay the debt, traders in the border regions began taking over Miao lands and keeping the Miao on as sharecropping tenants. Alternatively, they seized the lands in question and brought in Han migrants to work them. Other Han settlers occupied Miao lands as illegal squatters. Violent clashes between Han and Miao occurred frequently. Between 1662 and 1711, eighteen revolts led by Miao chiefs were sufficiently serious to require imperial troops to subdue them.[55]

In part, more aggressive Qing policies aimed at engaging local chiefs more closely in Han culture had destabilized the system of indirect rule built up by the Ming dynasty. Under the Ming, local chiefs had paid tribute but were largely left autonomous within their domains as long as they maintained order and stability. In the 1680s, the Kangxi emperor decreed that succession to chieftainship should follow rules of strict patrilineal succession in the Han mode, rather than matrilineal succession as in the indigenous model. The emperor drove a wedge between the chiefly family and the chief's retainers by decreeing that any male heir less than fifteen years old would have to be guided by a male adult family retainer when he became chief. Moreover, all the male children of each native chief were to be enrolled in Chinese elementary schools to be established by Qing officials in each county. These rules, when combined with the continually more intrusive presence of Qing officials and Han settlers and traders, touched off internecine conflict between chiefs and rebellions against imperial rule that reached what imperial officials considered to be dangerous levels.[56]

Imperial officials engaged in a vigorous discussion about the most effective policy for administering Guizhou, Yunnan, and other remote lands in the southwest. The debate was grounded in sophisticated knowledge and understanding of the Miao. Generations of Qing officials posted to Guizhou and adjacent regions had recorded ethnographic observations of the Miao and other non-Han peoples. These observations included specific data on each named subgroup, their geographic location, and any specific informa-

55. Ibid., 174–75, 229–31.
56. John N. Herman, "Empire in the Southwest: Early Qing Reforms to the Native Chieftain System," *Journal of Asian Studies* 56, no. 1 (1997): 47–74.

tion that might be useful for conquest and administration. Gazetteer writers incorporated this ethnographic information, along with detailed wood-block illustrations of the indigenous peoples. The illustrations showed Miao dress, adornments, typical work, play, and ceremonies.[57]

One faction argued vehemently that the older form of indirect rule by tributary chiefs of the Miao and other non-Confucian groups must be reformed, because, apart from punitive action, the administration could exert little real control over the local chiefs. The hereditary chiefs in Guizhou should be removed from office and replaced by removable imperial officials. Despite arguments by opponents that such a policy would involve costly military action, the proponents argued that direct administration was a moral obligation for the empire.

Clearly, the Miao were seen as a depraved people and culture. Ordinary Miao were subject to the tyranny of the tributary chiefs and forced to pay excessive taxes, treated as virtual slaves, cruelly punished, and generally oppressed. Some renegade chiefs also captured and dealt in slaves, both indigenous and Han victims. The repulsive customs of these peoples included continual blood feuding and the ritual slaughter of buffaloes in annual religious rites. These were both disgusting and cruel and had to be abolished.

Only by direct administration could these bestial indigenous peoples be converted from their barbaric state and assimilated to Han civilization. The people should be registered, counted, and taxed by the imperial system. They should be encouraged to take up more intensive agriculture. Chinese Confucian schools for young boys in these regions could be established to begin the process of acculturation. Furthermore, under direct administration the rich forests and mineral resources of the region could be more efficiently developed for the benefit of the empire.[58]

The Yong Zheng emperor (r. 1723–1736) accepted the expansionist view. In 1726, he appointed Prince Ortai, an eminent Manchu administrator and advocate of a more aggressive southern policy, governor of Yunnan and Guizhou. Ortai organized a vastly more powerful military presence in Guizhou, strengthened existing fortified towns and cities, and constructed new redoubts. For the first four years of his governorship, he directed devastating military campaigns in the southern half of the province aimed at ending all Miao and Yao autonomy. Ortai's commanders fought numerous skirmishes with Miao guerilla forces. They won major battles with Miao armies numbering as many as ten thousand. They stormed fortified Miao villages, massacred the inhabitants, and burnt settlements. They captured and

57. Laura Hosttetler, "Qing Connections to the Early Modern World: Ethnography and Cartography in Eighteenth-Century China," *Modern Asian Studies* 34, no. 3 (2000): 623–62.

58. Lombard-Salmon summarizes the views of two prominent memorial writers of the period (*Un exemple d'acculturation chinoise*, 213–17).

executed rebel chiefs and their followers. They constructed and manned new military checkpoints as they advanced.

After conquest and pacification, Ortai initiated a series of measures aimed at transforming Miao society and culture. He displaced those chiefs who survived, confiscated all or part of their lands, and appointed local imperial officials. He assigned confiscated lands to soldiers who took up cultivation as military colonists. He banned private vendettas and confiscated crossbows and muskets by the thousand. He issued edicts that non-Han males must cut their hair and wear Han-style clothing. His officials instituted household responsibility and registration (the *bao jia*) and began a census and cadastral survey.

Within four years, the harsh military regime and its measures touched off a ferocious revolt centered at Tai Gong and Qing Jiang in the forested southeastern highlands in the heart of Miao territory. Miao rebels made sudden concerted attacks on Tai Gong and Qing Jiang, occupied them, and massacred many of the inhabitants. At Kai Li, they killed a thousand Han settlers and leveled the buildings. In response, the emperor ordered imperial troops from the provinces surrounding Guizhou into three relieving armies and sent them against the rebels.

The Miao pulled back from the Han towns and challenged the advancing armies, retreating into the forest after each clash. The Miao warriors fought desperately, even, by some accounts, killing their own wives and children so that the warriors would not surrender but fight to the death in battle. For a time, the situation looked so gloomy that the Yong Zheng emperor, just before his death, wondered whether to reverse these aggressive policies in the south.

When the Qianlong emperor (r. 1735–1795) ascended the throne in 1735, he replaced the failed military command in Guizhou. The new field commander devised a strategy aimed at conciliating assimilated Miao (the *shu,* or "cooked") in order to drive a wedge between them and the unassimilated, intransigent Miao rebels (the *sheng,* or "raw"). The new approach weakened the rebels, who were pushed back into the most remote highlands and detached from their supplies of grain. As various rebel groups emerged from hiding to attack imperial posts in search of food, they were systematically killed or taken prisoner.

By 1737, imperial armies had crushed the revolt. According to the official tally, 17,600 rebels died in battle and an additional 13,500 men were executed after they surrendered—half the 27,000 Miao taken prisoner. The victors seized 46,500 muskets, innumerable crossbows, and other weapons. They destroyed 1,224 Miao villages and spared 348 others.[59] The military

59. Ibid., 238.

seized lands belonging to the most culpable rebels and assigned them to nine military colonies.

Imperial victory and disarmament of the Miao put an end to further violent resistance in Guizhou. (A subsequent brief uprising in 1740 of Miao, Yao, Dong, and other indigenous peoples across the border in Hunan did not elicit any support or assistance from their compatriots in Guizhou.) The harsh lessons of the 1734–1737 uprising deterred further violent resistance until the great Miao war of 1795–1806 that engulfed both Guizhou and Hunan. By decisive, brutal action, the Qing state opened Guizhou's lands to unrestrained economic exploitation and its people to harsher forced cultural assimilation.

Protected by a strong military presence, Han settlers migrated in steadily increasing numbers. An official census put the population of Guizhou at just over 3 million in 1749, which increased to 5 million by the end of the century. As time passed, officials transferred desirable land worked by military colonists to the hands of private civilians. Cultivated acreage on the tax roles more than doubled.[60] The Han migrants invested heavily in dikes, noria, ditches, and other improvements to bring more water to their paddy fields. An innovative official brought in immigrants from Sichuan skilled in sericulture, who introduced silkworm larvae. This official and other entrepreneurs trained Miao villagers to spin and weave silk so successfully that it soon became a product exported from Guizhou.

Commercialization and resource extraction proceeded at a rapid pace. The previously feeble demand for money increased as copper cash replaced salt as the common medium of exchange. A new imperial mint opened in 1731. Han traders assembled in ever larger numbers in the fortified towns and moved confidently throughout the countryside. They transmitted a rising external demand for Guizhou's natural resources. Miao sold forest products, medicinal plants, and livestock. Timber merchants floated greater and greater volumes of timber down the rivers to outside markets after 1737. Guizhou's rich mineral deposits had long attracted attention. Tributary Miao chiefs had operated small-scale mines earlier, but pacification opened the entire province to Chinese miners. The first lead mine opened in 1724. The first copper mine in the province opened in 1741 and kept two thousand workers and twenty furnaces busy producing six hundred metric tons of copper per year.[61] A new phase in the assault on Guizhou's landscape had begun.

60. Ibid., 168, 172. Perkins rounds this figure to 3 million for the same year (*Agricultural Development in China*, 234).

61. Lombard-Salmon, *Un exemple d'acculturation chinoise*, 194. The figure given is 1 million *jin* at six hundred grams per *jin*.

THE NORTHERN FRONTIER

The remaining frontier lay to the north, beyond the Great Wall in Manchuria and eastern Inner Mongolia. In a process that accelerated with the population increases of the later Qing period, Chinese Han settlers moved north to clear forests or plow up grasslands for grain cultivation in regions that had been occupied for centuries by hunters, shifting cultivators, and pastoral nomads. To some extent, the Manchu regime succeeded in slowing this process by officially forbidding Chinese to migrate northward into Manchuria and even, after 1740, into Mongol territory, but pressures on both the people and the regime to open new lands were great. Once settlers had occupied and cleared land, plowed fields, and settled, they were rarely evicted but instead came under the protection of the imperial state. This was a vast underdeveloped region that offered copious fertile land, timber, and other valuable natural resources. According to Robert H. G. Lee, "Manchuria and eastern Inner Mongolia form a huge basin, surrounded by a horseshoe of mountains—the Changbaishan along the Korean and Russian borders in the east, the Xiaoxing'anling (Lesser Khingan) in the northeast, the Daxing'anling (Greater Khingan) in the west, and a complex block of ranges, known collectively as the Yanshan, in the southwest—with the bottom of the horseshoe opening into the Gulf of Bohai in the south."[62] The northern Chinese settlement frontier divides into Manchuria to the east and Mongol lands to the west. Manchuria further splits into southern, central, and northern Manchuria; the latter stretches as far north as the Russian border on the Amur River. Southern Manchuria is the area of recognized Chinese settlement that came to be surrounded by the fortified barrier called the Willow Palisade, a guarded line marked by trees and ditches punctuated by fortified gatehouses, which ran from the Great Wall north as far as Kaiyuan, crossed the Liao River, and then returned to the coast near the Korean border. The Mongol lands, directly north of Beijing and the Great Wall, were called Jehol. These divided into eastern Jehol in the Luan River valley and into the steep forested terrain of western Jehol. The frontier in each zone reveals a different dynamic and narrative.

First, in Manchuria proper, Han Chinese settlers during the Ming dynasty had moved north beyond the Great Wall into the valley of the Liao River. The swiftly moving Liao crosses the southern Manchurian plain before it empties into the Gulf of Bohai. This was a region of ample rainfall (more than five hundred millimeters per year) from a summer monsoon season, covered by a natural vegetation of mixed coniferous and broadleaf forest that permitted rain-fed cultivation. Although the growing season was short—100 to 150

---

62. Robert H. G. Lee, *The Manchurian Frontier in Ch'ing History* (Cambridge: Harvard University Press, 1970), 503.

frost-free days—conditions for wheat and millet farming were good, and Chinese settlers took full advantage of this on the lower Liao River. Beyond present-day Shenyang (Fengtian) at the forty-first parallel, however, Han Chinese settlers had not penetrated, and little land was under plow cultivation in Manchuria as a whole.[63] Instead, scattered communities of Manchus, Tungus, and other tribal peoples practiced limited, shifting cultivation, as well as fishing, hunting, and reindeer herding, throughout this vast expanse of potentially rich forests and grassy plains. The indigenous peoples of Manchuria had long exported three forest products valued highly by the Chinese: sable furs, ginseng, and pearls from river mollusks. Manchurian chieftains presented these commodities to the Ming court officials during tribute missions when they acknowledged their subordination to the emperor.

During the chaotic decades of the Qing conquest, Chinese settlements in the Liao River area suffered depopulation and devastation as the Han settlers either fled or were killed. In 1653, the new regime issued "Regulations on Recruitment and Reclamation in Liaodong," which offered free seed, draft animals, and a six-year tax moratorium on reclaimed land to Han peasants who would settle in the lower Liao River region.[64] Government agents moved through the northern provinces seeking recruits for the frontier. Land-hungry peasants responded readily to these appeals. The Qing government established a new administrative seat for Liaoyang prefecture *(fu)*—divided into two counties *(xian)*, Liaoyang and Haicheng—at the city of Fengtian east of the Liao River. Thereafter Fengtian became the center for Qing administration in Manchuria. In 1665, the administration created another prefecture at Jinzhou, west of the Liao River. By this date, resettlement had progressed to the point that there were ten counties demarcated in the Liao basin.

In 1668, however, the Kangxi emperor ended incentives and shifted to a policy of excluding Chinese migrants from Manchuria. The official reason given was that the emperor wanted to preserve his Manchu ancestral homeland from Chinese influences. He "wished to maintain the original horse-riding and hunting life-style and martial virtues of the Manchus and Mongols in their home territory, which should remain a recruiting ground for soldiers."[65] However, the regime also feared a repetition of the same alliance between Mongols, Manchus, and dissident Chinese in the north that had put the Qing dynasty into power.[66] If the government permitted migration into the area to continue, it was clear from the example of the Liao River mi-

63. James Reardon-Anderson, "Land Use and Society in Manchuria and Inner Mongolia during the Qing Dynasty," *Environmental History* 5, no. 4 (2000): 504.

64. Ibid., 507.

65. Vermeer, "Ch'ing Government Concerns with the Exploitation of New Farmland," 219.

66. Lee, *The Manchurian Frontier in Ch'ing History*, 20–21.

grants that there would be a flood of land-hungry Han Chinese moving into Manchuria.

After 1668, Qing emperors officially prohibited Chinese migration to Manchuria. The regime used an array of long-established methods to deter Han settlement. At permanent border stations, guards checked and stopped suspicious persons. Local officials investigated and registered new arrivals in Manchuria and sent back illegals. They destroyed homes and property of illegal settlers. Imperial regulations forbade contacts with the native population. Overall, however, enforcement of these harsh measures was at best sporadic and not effective.[67]

Despite this change in policy, the settlers continued to arrive in the Liao River valley. Between 1668 and 1681, an official census showed that the adult male population grew by 27,729 and the cultivated area increased by 11,724 hectares.[68] In 1681, the emperor ordered construction of the Willow Palisade. This Chinese Pale was supposed to bound the area of Han Chinese settlement in Manchuria.

As it turned out, however, preserving Manchuria from change was not possible. One problem was simply that the Manchus themselves who served in China proper invariably became more or less sinicized. This acculturation inevitably had an impact on the home territories. Another problem was the need to strengthen the defenses of Manchuria from the advance of Czarist Russia. Russian Cossacks had entered the Amur River valley by mid–seventeenth century. In response, the Qing emperor sent Manchu troops to the Amur and put military garrisons at Ningutta on the Mudan River in 1653 and Aigun (Heilongjiangcheng) on the Amur in 1683. To supply these forces, he established several agricultural colonies, including one each at Aigun and Ningutta, three on the Nonni River, and three on the Sungari River.[69] The emperor created "imperial estates," which he bestowed on Manchu noblemen to induce them to remain in the tribal homelands. Smaller land grants went to decommissioned Manchu soldiers (Bannermen) who agreed to return to Manchuria. The Sino-Russian Treaty of Nerchinsk, signed in 1689, relieved border tension between the two expansive empires. The Qing dynasty, however, maintained and strengthened its military presence in Manchuria, and the official Manchu settlements survived and prospered.

Invariably the agricultural colonies and Manchu landlords demanded Han Chinese peasant labor for their fields. The indigenous Manchus and

67. Vermeer, "Ch'ing Government Concerns with the Exploitation of New Farmland," 219–20.

68. Ibid., 508.

69. Reardon-Anderson, "Land Use and Society in Manchuria and Inner Mongolia during the Qing Dynasty," 508.

other peoples were not at all inclined to engage in intensive grain cultivation in the labor-intensive Chinese style. Manchu landlords wanted to live off rents from Chinese tenant smallholders. The regime permitted Chinese to cross the Willow Palisade or Great Wall as seasonal laborers. Some returned; many stayed on as tenants of Manchu landlords or as squatters on reclaimed land. Legally and illegally, thousands of Han migrants made their way along the chain of towns and courier stations to the north. Some were expelled, but far more were not. By the end of the seventeenth century, as much as two hundred thousand hectares of cultivated land had been plowed in Manchuria—most by Chinese settlers.[70]

Frontier settlement continued and intensified during the eighteenth century. In the area enclosed by the Willow Palisade along the Liao River, the population of the two prefectures of Fengtian province rose steadily, reaching 779,083 persons in 1781. The area of registered farmland paying taxes rose from only 3,717 hectares in 1661 to 35,420 hectares in 1724 and to 162,449 hectares in 1781. Considerably more land under the plow remained unregistered. Similar trends existed for the northern lands. The provinces of Jilin and Jeilongjiang together held a population of 172,000 in 1780. Cultivated lands attached to officially sponsored Manchu army or Banner lands (lands assigned for the upkeep of imperial Manchu Banner troops), noble estates, and courier stations reached 203,583 hectares in that year. Privately cultivated lands brought the total of plowed lands under sedentary cultivation in all of Manchuria to approximately 500,000 hectares.[71] This expansion was effected primarily by the Chinese. By this date, eight-tenths or more of the population of the Manchurian towns and garrisons were Chinese, not Manchu.

The Mongol lands, or Jehol, lying directly north of the Great Wall, were a region of heavily forested mountains, narrow ravines, and fast-flowing streams that occasionally opened into broad valleys. During the Ming period, settlers from the North China plain had moved into eastern Jehol along the Luan River valley. There, they formed an area of Chinese settlement and plow cultivation on the river's plain. Unusually, some lineages of two border Mongol tribes, the Kalaqins and the Tumets, settled in villages, plowed land, and began sedentary cultivation in this area as well. Both groups rented land to Chinese tenant farmers.

Shortly after the Manchu conquest of China, the new regime opened eastern Jehol to Manchu agricultural settlement. The Qing set up official and imperial farms outside the Great Wall and distributed land to Manchu soldiers. However, the regime made no attempt to forbid Chinese farmers from mi-

70. Ibid., 505.
71. Ibid., 506, 508.

grating into the region. Manchu landlords willingly rented their lands to Chinese tenant-farmers. Other Chinese settlers moved beyond the Manchu-owned land to occupy land illegally in more remote valleys and hills. Here, they terraced land and began cultivation on the slopes. By 1750, after nearly a century of expansion, a reported 136 official and imperial Manchu estates engaged in grain cultivation occupied an area of 39,040 hectares, and Chinese tenant farmers worked another 17,191 hectares as tenants. An indeterminate number of peasants lived as squatters beyond the enumerated colonies. For eastern Jehol, cultivated land probably totaled close to 100,000 hectares, and it was worked by up to two hundred thousand Chinese settlers.[72]

Western Jehol, at the center of Manchu ancestral lands, was an entirely different story. Here, there appears to have been almost no Chinese frontier settlement throughout the Ming period. In part, this may have been because its rainfall, at four hundred millimeters per year, put this area on the edge of possible rain-fed cultivation. In addition, the terrain was steep and forbidding, unlike the Luan and Liao River valleys. There were mixed broadleaf and coniferous forests with abundant wildlife, including tigers, bears, leopards, deer, wolves, boar, and wildcats. The area so impressed the Kangxi emperor when he visited the region in 1681 that he chose it as the site for an imperial hunting preserve and summer palace.

The resulting Imperial Hunting Enclosure, located near Chengde in present-day Hubei province, became the centerpiece of more than 100 designated imperial hunting preserves in the northeast. The 10,400-square-kilometer preserve straddled the zones of Han settled agricultural life and the pastoral steppe life of Central Asia. The terrain varied from flat steppe grasslands to the forested Ba Shan hills, which rose as high as seventeen hundred meters. The protected wildlife was plentiful and varied. Every year from the date of the preserve's establishment until 1820, the Manchu emperor, his court, and the Manchu Bannermen retired there during the summer months to reaffirm their origins as steppe horsemen, archers, and hunters. The rituals of the Autumn Hunt, as it was known, publicly reaffirmed the bonds of loyalty and obedience the emperor maintained with his princes, tributary rulers, and leaders of the empire.[73] The royal battue sent

72. Ibid., 510–12. This figure is calculated from the statement that there were "reportedly 42,924 Chinese tenant farmers in 103 colonies working 77,410 *mu* (4,722 ha) of farmland in Kalaqin Center Banner while additional Chinese tenants farmed 40,080 *mu* (2,445 ha) in Kalaqin Left Banner" (512). This calculation puts the land-person ratio at 9.1 per hectare of cultivated land. Total land listed in eastern Jehol also included 10,024 hectares farther north on the Daling River system in Tumet Right Banner. Adding all of the figures together, we arrive at 17,191 hectares under tenancy for the region, which works out to 156,438 persons.

73. Nicholas K. Menzies, *Forest and Land Management in Imperial China* (New York: St. Martin's Press, 1994), 55–64.

as many as twelve thousand soldiers into the mountains to surround and drive game toward the emperor at the killing grounds.

Between 1681 and 1820, when the annual royal sojourns were discontinued, strict controls and a system of guards prevented private hunting, clearing, or settlement in the imperial preserve itself. Throughout the eighteenth century, regular sightings of tigers suggest that the preserve's ecosystem remained relatively intact. After the Autumn Hunt was discontinued in 1820 and the court no longer came every year to the hunting enclosure, depredations against timber and wildlife in the preserve itself became almost impossible to control.

Ironically, however, the annual court visit stimulated both Manchu and Chinese settlement outside its boundaries in Chengde prefecture. Every summer, thousands of officials, retainers, servants, and soldiers descended on Chengde who had to be fed and maintained. To support this enterprise, the regime resettled thousands of craftsmen and cultivators and cleared land for official estates. The Kangxi and Qianlong emperors transformed the hamlet of Chengde into a summer retreat with a vast complex of palaces, gardens, and temples. Timber demands for this construction stripped the hills surrounding Chengde bare of tree cover. The population of Chengde prefecture swelled to 557,000 persons in 1778.

Late in the eighteenth century, the first cohorts of Chinese pioneers began to move north of Jehol and west of the Manchurian plain into the grasslands of the eastern end of the Mongolian steppe. Settlers moving into the broad basin of the Lahoa River and the area around the cities of Chifeng and Keshiketeng had a reported several thousand hectares under grain cultivation.[74] They rented land for plow cultivation from Mongol landlords.

By 1800, the area of sedentary cultivation beyond the Great Wall, while large in absolute terms, covered only a small portion of the possible frontier land to be reclaimed in this vast region. By the early nineteenth century, in the Manchurian provinces, the registered or legal Chinese population had reached only 2.5 million persons.[75] Nevertheless, during the seventeenth and eighteenth centuries, Chinese settler migration began to gather momentum; it would later explode. Manchuria and eastern Mongolia in the nineteenth century became the remaining frontier for land-hungry Chinese cultivators. By the 1860s, the Qing government reversed itself completely and began to encourage Han settlement as a defensive measure against Russian encroachment.[76]

74. Reardon-Anderson, "Land Use and Society in Manchuria and Inner Mongolia during the Qing Dynasty," 514.
75. Vermeer, "Ch'ing Government Concerns with the Exploitation of New Farmland," 220.
76. Ibid., 220.

CONCLUSION

When, by the early decades of the nineteenth century, Manchuria and Mongolia had become the only viable frontiers left, what were the implications for Chinese society? Continued frontier expansion had added essential lands to the agricultural base. Opening new lands ensured new supplies of charcoal, wood, and timber for the economy. However, energy supplies did not keep pace with human demands. During the course of the nineteenth century, it became more obvious that China's forests were unable to meet both industrial and domestic fuel requirements for the society.

China's natural environment was drastically altered from what it had been four centuries earlier. In every province, the more remote, peripheral areas of difficult terrain were no longer wild but instead were tamed and thickly settled. As Mark Elvin comments in a 1998 essay, "In late imperial times, economic, environmental, and social stress is evident everywhere."[77]

Late imperial China was a densely populated society whose inhabitants had to work the land harder and more intelligently than ever before to maintain their earnings and material comforts.[78] It was a society whose natural resources were becoming rapidly depleted and more expensive. It was a society whose landscape was stripped of forest cover and whose hills were subject to severe erosion never seen before. It was a society whose wildlife was fast disappearing and whose non-Han indigenous peoples were losing ground to Han migrants. It was a society subject to a growing energy crisis as fuelwood supplies diminished in region after region. Finally, it was a society that had not yet acquired new modes of industrial production using fossil fuels.

China in the late Qing faced an economy of growing scarcity—especially in supplies of wood, the principal source of energy. Deforestation was an invariable result of frontier expansion. Only in the northeast did the Qing attempt to preserve forested areas. Elsewhere, millions of hectares of formerly abundant forest cover were cleared and converted to cultivated fields.[79] Those forests that remained were steadily degraded as demands for wood and other forest products escalated. Food and fuel shortages became a common condition for many Chinese by 1800 and thereafter. Consider these

77. Mark Elvin, "The Environmental Policy of Imperial China," *China Quarterly*, no. 156 (1998): 737.

78. For a description of intensive Chinese cultivation practices, see George Macartney Macartney and J. L. Cramer-Byng, *An Embassy to China: Being the Journal Kept by Lord Macartney during His Embassy to the Emperor Chien-lung, 1793–1794* (Hamden, Conn.: Archon Books, 1963), 188.

79. Rhoads Murphey, "Deforestation in Modern China," in *Global Deforestation and the Nineteenth-Century World Economy*, edited by Richard P. Tucker and John F. Richards (Durham, N.C.: Duke University Press, 1983), 111.

verses from Jiang Tingyi, a poet living in the lower Yangzi region in the nineteenth century:

> The courtyard's full of fescues and of weeds,
> Pinetrees grow below the steps, as do numerous bamboos.
> We take fuel from them at dawn, to cook our morning meal,
> And at dusk we gather more to boil our evening gruel.
>
> It's easy to exhaust bamboos and pines,
> And weeds and grass never grow enough.
> One takes a hundred cash in hand at morning light,
> Comes home at nightfall with a purchased bundle.
> The wood will not burn well, if too full of damp,
> Nor the strained rice we're cooking be done satisfactorily.
> ·
> When we went walking in the hills during the past month
> The slopes were still covered—with trees—in abundance.
> Today we can see, as we pass along the frith,
> The hills, far off, sharp-edged and stripped.
>
> For cooking their food, the farmers have nothing.
> They even burn the axles of their water pumps.
> Farming thus grows ever worse afflicted.
> —Then they break up their houses and sell them in the city.
>
> By selling them off to the high-ranked and rich
> They can cook till tender their meat and fish.[80]

What was the Chinese response to deforestation? Village woodlots and forests managed as common property regimes became vitally important. As a study of Chinese forestry argues, agroforestry in village woodlands and tree plantations filled most domestic fuelwood and local construction needs in rural areas during the early modern centuries.[81] There is some evidence of restrained consumption and even deprivation occurring as fuel became more expensive and scarce.

For example, as he progressed along the Grand Canal in October 1793, Lord Macartney, the British emissary to the Qing emperor, wrote, "Wang and Chou [the two Chinese officials accompanying his mission] own that in the winter a great many poor people die in these provinces for want of sufficient clothing. It is chiefly their clothing that the Chinese trust to for a de-

---

80. Mark Elvin, "The *Bell of Poesy:* Thoughts on Poems as Information in Late-Imperial Environmental History," in *Studi in onore di Lionello Lanciotti,* edited by S. M. Carletti, M. Sacchetti, and P. Santagelo (Napoli: Istituto universitario orientale, 1996), 8–9. Elvin has translated selections from the *Qing Bell of Poesy* [Qing Shi duo], edited by Zhang Yingchang, a Qing official serving in the Grand Secretariat, and published in 1869.

81. Menzies, "Forestry," 666–67.

fense against cold weather. They have no fireplaces nor fixed stoves in their homes; they employ pans of charcoal for their culinary purposes and sometimes have braziers brought into their chambers, but these give only temporary heat.[82] The domestic demand for heating in North China may well have been considerably less than that of Europe: "Where interior space had to be warmed, the preference was for concentrated rather than diffused heat: heat in the kitchen stove and under the *k'ang* or hypocaust bed, rather than open fires in drawing-rooms, dining rooms, and even bedrooms as in the West."[83]

By the late nineteenth century, however, steadily rising demand seems to have outstripped agroforestry. Certainly, this is implied in a reminiscence of village life about fifty kilometers from Guangzhou in the Pearl River delta:

> In the 1880's, when I was young, we had a brick kiln in the village, and most of the houses were made of brick. We had to range rather far up into the hills to get wood to fire the kilns, and the older people in the village said that they remembered in their own youth there was more wood closer. They also said that the village used to keep a certain area protected as a wood lot so that they could have larger timbers for building. That was all gone by my time, and we would often be away all day and until after dark in our search for small twigs, brush, and other such things. The village also began to have trouble with bandits, and then with armies. Both of them cut into the few stands of trees the village kept behind the houses, and by the end of the dynasty there was nothing left. Wood for any purpose became so expensive, or so hard to get, that the brick kiln could no longer operate. Whatever we needed for building, or for coffins, we had to buy in the market, but most of us could not afford much.[84]

The extent to which various localities and regions in China responded to the scarcity of fuelwood by using coal instead is not well-defined. China since the Sung had used coal for various industrial purposes. In fact, Chinese technicians had long since used coal for iron making—a problem whose solution eluded European iron makers until the late eighteenth century. Throughout the early modern period, the inhabitants of Beijing obtained coal brought on camelback from the mines of the nearby Men-t'ou k'ou hills for cooking and heating.[85] Reasonably well-known deposits of coal were plentiful in northwestern China. Coal mining, used in an expanded iron industry, did expand somewhat under the Ming dynasty. It does not appear that

82. Macartney and Cramer-Byng, *An Embassy to China*, 165.

83. S. A. M. Adshead, *Material Culture in Europe and China, 1400–1800: The Rise of Consumerism* (New York: St. Martin's Press, 1997), 147. This work contains an extended comparison of the coal industry in England and China.

84. Murphey, "Deforestation in Modern China," 120.

85. T'o Teng, "Les mines de charbon de Men-t'ou k'ou," *Annales, Economies, Sociétés, Civilization* 22 (1967): 50–87.

coal production grew under the Qing. The Chinese did not widely adopt coal as a substitute for wood and charcoal prior to the twentieth century.[86]

It was only as industrialization gained momentum in the late nineteenth century that China began to shift to coal as a primary energy source. According to S. A. M. Adshead, as a direct result of early modern settlement frontiers and land reclamation, "China experienced a prolonged energy crisis, a shortage of energy at economical prices."[87]

86. Pomeranz, *The Great Divergence*, 62–65.

87. S. A. M. Adshead, "An Energy Crisis in Early Modern China," *Late Imperial China* 3 (1974): 20. Or, in another formulation, resource scarcity led early modern China into a "high-level equilibrium trap." Mark Elvin, *The Pattern of the Chinese Past* (Stanford, Calif.: Stanford University Press, 1973), 298 ff.

Chapter 5

Ecological Strategies in Tokugawa Japan

Beginning with the destruction of Kyoto in 1467, medieval Japan endured endemic civil war—swirling, violent conflict between dozens of autonomous barons (daimyo)—that did not fully end until 1615. These barons gave only nominal allegiance and obedience to the emperor or to the Muromachi *bakafu* (hegemonal baron) at Kyoto. After the warlord Oda Nobunaga (d. 1582) gained control of one-third of Japan, his brilliant successor, Toyotomi Hideyoshi (d. 1598), forced all daimyo to accept his dominance in a thirty-year process of war, political consolidation, and pacification. After Hideyoshi's death, Tokugawa Ieyasu (1543–1616), lord of Edo and the Kanto Plain, the largest domain in Japan, emerged victorious in a struggle for power. In 1603, acceding to Ieyasu's demands, the emperor Go-Yozei installed Ieyasu as shogun, or chief of the warrior estate, and conferred on him several other ceremonial court offices. By this action, the emperor legitimized Ieyasu's exercise of centralized authority over the Japanese islands. Two years later, Ieyasu arranged to have his titles transferred to his son Hidetada (r. 1605–1623).

Under the Tokugawa, Japan between 1615 and 1868 was freed of the affliction of virtually all warfare—internal and foreign. A militarized warrior elite determined to unify and stabilize the Japanese polity enforced this extraordinary achievement. The leaders of the Tokugawa house proved to be unusually determined and capable leaders who did not hesitate to impose their will on their barons or society. For two and a half centuries under the Tokugawa, the political culture of early modern Japan was one of "regulation and restraint that came to blanket the realm."[1] In part, the culture of re-

---

1. Conrad D. Totman, *Early Modern Japan* (Berkeley and Los Angeles: University of California Press, 1993), 30.

pression rested on edicts issued by the Bakafu central administration. However, its successful working depended even more on the assent and cooperation of dozens of daimyo, who implemented these policies within their holdings.

Those aspects of Tokugawa political culture that contributed to its stability also made it possible for the regime to confront, analyze, and act on a growing ecological crisis manifest by the late seventeenth century.[2] Tokugawa Japan devised and carried out many clever, ecologically sound strategies that increased production and reduced land degradation. Starting around 1670, the central Tokugawa shogun and his advisers, and the many daimyo and their elites, began to react to a growing scarcity of resources—especially forest resources. At the same time, local village elites began taking steps to assert tighter control over village lands and resources. The social discipline imposed by the Tokugawa regime at all levels made it possible to conserve forest and other resources and to regenerate resources. These measures were implemented despite an economy that failed to grow as rapidly as did the population in the eighteenth century.

Tokugawa Japan's political achievement is reasonably well-known, its ecological achievements less so. In direct contrast to the western European countries in this period, the Tokugawa elites confined their territorial expansion to the adjacent islands of Hokkaido and the Ryukyus. Beyond this limited sphere, they did not launch maritime ventures to seek out new lands for colonization and resource exploitation by the homeland. Instead, Japan deliberately turned inward and placed strict controls on its foreign relations. This decision forced the Japanese to consider their lands and natural resources as finite and limited. From this assumption, early modern Japanese society moved toward a minimalist, conservationist use of materials and the land.

JAPAN IN 1600

In 1600, Japan consisted primarily of the three islands of Honshu, Kyushu, and Shikoku, which together total 295,000 square kilometers in area. The island of Hokkaido remained a sparsely populated northern frontier area inhabited by the Ainus and other aboriginal peoples, with only a tiny Japanese population at its southern tip. The three islands extend fifteen hundred kilometers, from thirty-one degrees north latitude at the southern end of Kyushu to forty-two degrees at the northern extremity of Honshu. The climate is subtropical in the extreme south and becomes cold temperate in the north of Honshu. Annual average precipitation is 180 centimeters, with extremes

2. Conrad Totman, drawing on the insights of a group of Japanese historians, first articulated this ecological approach to early modern Japanese history in the English language literature.

ranging from 100 centimeters in the northeast to more than 400 in the southwest. A distinctive mountain spine covering 80 percent of the land area marks the archipelago. In this chain are some sixty active volcanoes. The sharply rising slopes and hill ranges tower over narrow valleys with swiftly running streams that open onto narrow alluvial plains on the ocean. The steep hillsides are covered with thin, coarse, immature soil subject to a high rate of natural erosion from heavy rains and the shocks of earthquakes and volcano eruptions.

Natural forest vegetation varies according to climate regimes from south to north. In the extreme south of Kyushu, tropical elements such as palms and banana trees survive. To the north, subtropical broadleaf evergreens are interspersed with oak and pine as well as the Japanese wax tree (*Rhus succedanea*) and the camphor tree (*Cinnamomum camphora*). On Honshu, from thirty-seven degrees north, are temperate mixed forests with some of the most valuable timber species: the hardwoods—including beech, chestnut, oak, and ash—and the conifers, including firs, pine, Japanese cedar, and Japanese cypress. At one-thousand-meter elevations on Honshu and on Hokkaido Island are boreal forests with dominant fir and pine. Earlier epochs, when Japan was an extension of the Eurasian mainland, permitted the dissemination of a rich diversity of plants on the archipelago.[3]

On the western coast, along the Sea of Japan, cold, snowy winters and cool, unpredictable summers have limited human settlement. To the east, the Chishima Current carries cold Arctic water past Hokkaido to the east coast of northern Honshu. Consequently, the hearth of Japanese civilization has been the fertile Kinai basin on the eastern coast sheltered by the Inland Sea. By 1600, this core region stretched eastward along the southern coast of Honshu to the Kobe Plain and then to Japan's largest plain, the Kanto. Climate favored dense settlement and intensive agriculture in the south. The Japan Current brought equatorial waters from east of the Philippines, north through the Ryukyus and then eastward along the coast south of the Kanto Plain and on into the Pacific. The warm water currents increased the ambient temperature and lengthened the growing season on the southeast coast. Both ocean currents supplied rich sources of fish, seaweed, and other marine products. The prevailing mountainous terrain meant that only about 12 percent of the total land surface of the main Japanese islands could be cultivated.

Japanese society in the late medieval and early modern periods displayed numerous features that surprised foreign observers and, for the most part, favorably impressed them. Japan's human population, dense by early modern standards, numbered about 12 million in 1600. By far the greater portion of this population was concentrated in the core regions of the eastern

3. Glenn Thomas Trewartha, *Japan, a Physical, Cultural, and Regional Geography* (Madison: University of Wisconsin, 1945).

coast. Cities were large and flourishing. Numerous fortified castle towns drew people and resources from the countryside as they provided both safety and economic opportunity during protracted warfare. Political elites, wealthy merchants, and others of higher status resided in cities, which were the repository of high culture and gracious living. Sophisticated wood-block printing, a standardized language, and relatively wide literacy throughout the country aided and encouraged a brisk exchange of information and ideas.

Travelers generally praised the cleanliness, order, and spaciousness of Japanese cities. Foreigners commented on the efficient sanitary methods adopted by the Japanese for disposal of human and other wastes. They marveled at the Japanese custom of relaxing in hot baths daily—a remarkable contrast to the personal hygiene of most of Eurasia. This custom probably had its origin in the early use of the many natural hot springs found throughout the islands. Every human settlement had its quota of public baths, where the inhabitants met and socialized daily.[4]

By comparison with other, similarly sized regions of Eurasia, such as the British Isles, the medieval Japanese were remarkably homogeneous. Save for the Ainus in the far north on Hokkaido, nearly all Japanese shared the same language, the same high culture, the same history and national identity, and the same two religious traditions. Other than the about-to-be extirpated Christian minority, nearly all Japanese worshiped at Shinto shrines or Buddhist temples and sometimes at both. These elements certainly did not guarantee either pan-Japanese solidarity or communication. Seemingly less-imposing cultural or social differences could readily be made a basis for conflict. Mutually unintelligible regional dialects marked off distinctive regional cultures. Sharp distinctions existed between aristocrats and commoners, although mobility for individuals and groups was possible. Nonetheless, despite these qualifications, Japanese society in 1600, possessing a level of cultural and social homogeneity exceptional for the early modern world, contained no vast cleavages to hinder Tokugawa unification.

Most Japanese lived in rural villages on permanent sites with permanent fields whose size varied with the productivity of the land. Depending on circumstances and local custom, farmers also engaged in burning and shifting cultivation in less fertile areas adjacent to their permanent fields. Hamlets in mountain valleys might have only two or three hundred people; large villages on the plains might contain two to three thousand.[5] Japanese families

4. Alan MacFarlane, *The Savage Wars of Peace: England, Japan, and the Malthusian Trap* (Oxford: Blackwell, 1997), 256–68. The Japanese did not use animal-fat-based soaps but rather rice bran powder encased in a sewn cloth, or other soaps from trees and bushes.

5. Tsuneo Sato, "Tokugawa Villages and Agriculture," in *Tokugawa Japan: The Social and Economic Antecedents of Modern Japan,* edited by Chie Nakane, Shinzabur Oishi, and Conrad D. Totman (Tokyo: University of Tokyo Press, 1990).

were generally patrilineal and patrilocal. Typically, peasants worked the land
as smallholders who had secure property rights to their own holdings or, in
many villages, rights to village lands periodically redistributed.[6] Each peasant possessed his own tools, residential plot, house, and gardens. Large rural
estates were confined to some held by temples and the nobility, but there
were few of these. Each village had a headman and a village assembly made
up of those peasant owners who were registered to pay the land tax. Often,
village elites were composed of rusticated, forcibly retired warriors (samurai), who had plied their trade by mobilizing peasant followers from their villages during the incessant pre-Tokugawa wars. Indentured servants and laborers formed an underclass in the village. At the bottom of village society
were the "outcastes" (*eta* or *burakumin*), who carried out the lowliest and most
polluted tasks in the community. Village officials, acting under the direction
of the assembly, apportioned shares in the village land tax burden on each
cultivator. Agents of the daimyo or shogun regularly collected payments of
rice to meet this obligation.

Throughout the medieval centuries, Japanese farmers had extended cultivation, invested in terraces and irrigation works, and increased their labor,
fertilizers, and other inputs as agriculture became more intensive and productive. Jorge Alvares, a Portuguese trader, left this impression of the rural
setting around Kagoshima in 1546:

> It is a beautiful and pleasing country, and has an abundance of trees, such as
> the pine, cedar, plum, cherry, peach, laurel, chestnut, walnut, oak (which
> yields many acorns) and elder. . . . There is also much fruit not to be found in
> our country; they grow the vegetables which we have in Portugal, except let-
> tuces, cabbages, dills, corianders, and even mint; all the rest they have. They
> also cultivate roses, carnations and many other scented flowers, as well as both
> sweet and bitter oranges, citrons (although I did not see any lemons), pome-
> granates and pears.
> The land is intensely cultivated and each year three crops are laid down in
> the following manner. In November they sow wheat, barley, turnips, radishes
> and other vegetables, such as beet, which they eat; in March they sow Indian
> corn, maize, mangos, chick-peas, beans, artichokes, cucumbers and melons; in
> July they sow rice, yams, garlic and onions. The land is fertilized each time with
> horse manure and dug with a spade, and then left fallow for a year. They use
> small, tough horses when working the land because they have but few cows,
> although in some places they use cows.
> There are no pigs, goats or sheep, and only a very few stringy hens. They
> hunt and eat deer, rabbits, pheasants, quails, doves and other birds. They hunt
> deer and rabbits with bows and arrows, and catch birds with nets. The nobles

6. Philip C. Brown, "State, Cultivator, Land: Determination of Land Tenures in Early Modern Japan Reconsidered," *Journal of Asian Studies* 56, no. 2 (1997): 421–44.

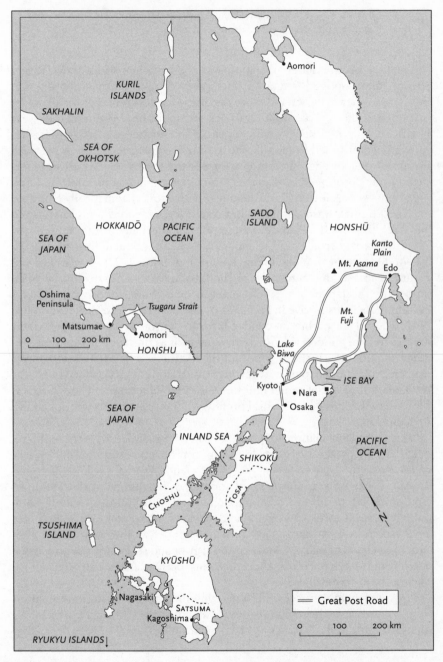

Map 5.1 Japan and Ezo. Adapted from Conrad Totman, *Early Modern Japan* (Berkeley and Los Angeles: University of California Press, 1993), map 2, p. xiv; map 3, p. xv.

employ splendid hawks and falcons[,] and I was told that they also hunted with royal eagles, but only the great lords were allowed to keep these birds for their amusement.[7]

Wet rice grown under irrigation was the principal food grain. River-, stream-, and pond-fed irrigation works were common. Wheat, barley, and millets were grown as rain-fed crops. Japanese farmers relied on small horses or cattle to pull iron plows and for pack transport, but in general they were not inclined to pastoralism. With few cattle and no sheep, goats, or pigs, they raised and consumed little milk, meat, or hides. Instead of raising livestock for meat, milk, or eggs like western European farmers, more efficient Japanese farmers produced food grains directly for human consumption. Lacking animal wastes for fertilizer, Japanese cultivators systematically collected and used human wastes as an all-important fertilizer for their crops. Dried and fresh fish and shellfish were an important alternate protein source.

As the passage from Alvares suggests, much of the land in the archipelago was under intense human management and control. Those areas of unmanaged forests that remained in the hills in 1600 were a resource to be tapped by the Japanese peasant. Since no indigenous aboriginal peoples lived in these forests (save in Hokkaido), Japanese rural dwellers could hunt boar, bears, deer, rabbits, and game birds for a protein supplement to their diet. Timber of all sorts was much in demand as a construction material. Virtually all buildings, including most of the fortified castles, were constructed primarily of wood. Japan had few workable stone quarries, little clay for brick making, and not much limestone for making cement. There also was a long-standing aesthetic cultural preference for wood, for its texture and visual appeal.

Rule-bound associations of peasant-owners, usually from several contiguous villages, managed large-scale common property resources such as irrigation works and shared forest- and pasturelands. Even at the level of the individual village, the simplest of pond-fed irrigation works required continuing cooperation for maintenance and distribution of water. Communally shared forest- and woodlands located adjacent to the village site were especially important. They provided timber and wood used for construction, charcoal making, and firewood; grass and rushes for sleeping mats; miscanthus thatch for roofs; and fruits, nuts, berries, and mushrooms for variety in the everyday diet.

Japan was notably successful in meeting the needs of a large population from its own agriculture and its domestic industries (rural and urban). Although it imported silk yarn and cloth, sugar, hides, and critical war-making

---

7. Quoted in Totman, *Early Modern Japan*, 8–9.

materials—such as lead, and saltpeter for gunpowder—the society of the archipelago could satisfy virtually all its requirements from its own resources. Successive hegemonic figures in the sixteenth century encouraged domestic trade by removing taxes, monopolistic markets, and restrictive guild privileges. New exploitation of Japanese mines encouraged the newly dominant Oda regime to begin a trimetallic—gold, silver, copper—coinage. Struck in large numbers, these high-quality coins increasingly helped to monetize the economy.[8] The land tax demand by the emerging Tokugawa state, figured and collected in rice, pulled that agricultural surplus into the towns and cities where urban markets in rice and other goods flourished. Traders carried out a brisk commerce in special products by each locality and region. As new technologies—New World crops and gunpowder weapons—found their way to Japan, the Japanese developed efficient means to adapt and use them.

STATE POWER

Effective political authority lay with the Tokugawa shogun, whose capital was Edo. Theoretically, supreme authority rested with the emperor at Kyoto, who conferred multiple offices and appointments on the shogun. The shogun's authority also rested on his position as patrimonial head of the Tokugawa house, the most powerful of warlord houses in Japan. The first Tokugawa to be appointed shogun, Ieyasu, posthumously became Toshugo, a Shinto deity with his own shrine. Toshugo was also regarded as an alternative manifestation of a bodhisattva in the Japanese Buddhist tradition. Legitimacy flowing from Neo-Confucian, Shinto, and Buddhist sources fused together with reverence for the emperor and long traditions of warrior rule.[9] The shogun maintained his headquarters at Edo, from which his own samurai officials directly administered about one-fourth of the land area of the archipelago.

Approximately 250 barons, or daimyo, ruling over the remaining area, swore personal fealty to the shogun as vassals and as warrior heads of patrimonial households. With a solemn blood oath, daimyo pledged loyalty, virtue, and obedience to all shogunal edicts. Their lord's approval was required before they could marry, make private alliances, or modify their castles. Investiture was heritable as a patrimony from daimyo to son, but the shogun could either accept or reject designated heirs. As in the Japanese kinship system, the daimyo role followed "stem succession"—that is, it was not divisible between heirs. Unseemly personal conduct—insolence, failure to re-

---

8. Asaho Naohiro, "The Sixteenth Century Unification," in *The Cambridge History of Japan*, edited by John Whitney Hall (Cambridge: Cambridge University Press, 1988), 4:61.

9. Mark Ravina, "State-Building and Political Economy in Early-Modern Japan," *Journal of Asian Studies* 54 (1995): 1003.

spond to orders, defiance—resulted in loss of position and, frequently in the early period, seizure of the domain by the shogun. Investiture by the shogun, with its privileges and rights, became part of the daimyo's family patrimony.

Each daimyo required his samurai and other retainers to swear a blood oath of personal fealty to him, not to the shogun. Within his domain, the daimyo retained formidable powers and autonomy. Each daimyo lived in a capital town dominated by a fortified castle. His domain "constituted a bastion of autonomous power complete with a legitimate authority figure, ideology of rule, government staff, administrative regulations, armed forces, tax base, producer populace and defined territories."[10] In return for substantial autonomy at home, the daimyo obediently trekked to Edo every other year on a strict timetable for their obligatory twelve-month residence at the capital. As stipulated by shogunal edict, they built mansions and left relatives and retainers in Edo as permanent hostages to their good behavior.

Seemingly contradictory in its opposed structures, the Tokugawa regime was a notably successful "compound state."[11] The shogunate fused together with the collection of domains into a strong, resilient, early modern state system. The regime wielded a monopoly of force and maintained stringent regulations for the domestic use of violence: The shogun restricted the troops, weapons, and fortifications available to each daimyo. No daimyo was permitted to attack another or engage in any kind of aggressive policies. First and foremost, daimyo were enjoined to maintain proper civil order within their domains. Failure to do so was reason for dismissal or transfer.

The early Tokugawa rulers made a critical structural change in Japanese society: they stripped away from rural society an entrenched warrior aristocracy.[12] As the civil wars wound down, masses of samurai and peasant soldiers were thrown out of work. Large numbers thronged to the cities, and others settled down in rural villages. To deal with this problem, Hideyoshi, in a 1588 edict, ordered all peasants to surrender bows, spears, swords, guns, and any other weapons they might possess.[13] The regime banned the manufacture and sale of firearms. Only hereditary warriors, the samurai, were to have access to weapons as the "sword became a badge of privilege for the warrior class."[14]

But the regime went further and forced samurai who had settled in rural villages as armed, dominant elites to leave the countryside and reside in the

10. Totman, *Early Modern Japan*, 119.

11. Ravina, "State-Building and Political Economy in Early-Modern Japan," 1017–19.

12. Toshio Furushima, "The Village and Agriculture during the Edo Period," in *The Cambridge History of Japan*, edited by John Whitney Hall (Cambridge: Cambridge University Press, 1988), 4:478–519.

13. Mary Elizabeth Berry, *Hideyoshi* (Cambridge: Harvard University Press, 1982), 102–6.

14. Ibid., 106.

castle towns. If samurai chose to remain in their village homes, their status became that of an upper peasant and they were disarmed along with everyone else. Shorn of both weapons and military elites, thousands of formerly armed and fortified villages lost the capacity for direct violent resistance. Hideyoshi's edicts forbade movement between the order of warriors and that of farmers. All types of soldiers were barred from reentering village society, and all farmers were barred from leaving full-time cultivation. Henceforth the military lost direct control over land.

Land surveying accompanied the process of disarmament. Hideyoshi issued edicts ordering a uniform process of land survey and registration using standardized measurements throughout the three islands. The survey records were to record the names of the actual cultivators of the land and to list their ownership rights. Under this system, annual inspections of crop yields and land valuations determined the tax to be paid by each proprietor-cultivator. Each village became a distinct administrative unit collectively responsible for the taxes imposed on its farmers. The surveyors entered the name of each farmer and his assessment, expressed in *koku* (approximately five bushels) of rice, in official cadastral registers. (The value of each daimyo's holding thereby came to be expressed in so many thousand *koku* of rice.) The annual land tax would be levied on whoever did the actual cultivation of the land, not on absentee or idle landlords.

Although startling in their direct language and in the horrific punishments promised for violations, Hideyoshi's edicts ratified and brought centralized state power in support of changes already under way in Japanese society. Pushing samurai off the land had already begun and was largely congenial to village elites. Daimyo recognized that Hideyoshi's policies actually strengthened their own internal power over their domains. Moreover, implementation of these edicts within each domain usually required time and effort to carry out. In some domains, actual cadastral surveys took place; elsewhere, other less formal inspection and measurement sufficed to set taxes and register ownership. Nonetheless, throughout the three islands even the most laggard domains gradually conformed to the spirit and, increasingly to the letter, of the uniform system.[15]

Hideyoshi further stipulated that peasants could not change occupations, and that they must remain in their ancestral villages. Hideyoshi and the Tokugawa shoguns that followed him ensured that the peasant smallholder, or self-cultivating farmer, would be the backbone of early modern Japanese agriculture and Japanese society. Hideyoshi, in keeping with popular Japa-

15. For a development of this argument, see Philip C. Brown, *Central Authority and Local Autonomy in the Formation of Early Modern Japan: The Case of Kaga Domain* (Stanford, Calif.: Stanford University Press, 1993).

nese sentiment, also disapproved of extreme forms of servitude. He prohibited slavery and slave trafficking with the Dutch and English East India Companies. In early modern Japan, the peasantry were strictly regulated and immobilized, but they were not serfs.

SECLUSION

The cultural, ideological, and political threat posed by the Christian Portuguese triggered a new isolationist orientation in Tokugawa Japan that has been termed *seclusion,* or *sakoku.* The three most significant aspects of this policy were the suppression of Christianity and expulsion of Europeans; the edicts forbidding foreign travel and maritime trade by Japanese; and the orders restricting foreign trade to Nagasaki port. One of the shogun's principal aims was to force individual daimyo away from foreign contacts and wealth-producing activities that might threaten centralized power. Only three domains retained any trading rights: Tsushima with Korea, Satsuma with the Ryukyu Islands, and Matsumae with Hokkaido Island.

From the 1540s onward, the Portuguese had been highly visible in Japan. Iberian ships offloaded the new firearms, spices, and Indian cotton textiles and carried away gold, silver, and copper produced from Japanese mines. Jesuit missionaries succeeded in converting several hundred thousand Japanese to Christianity, primarily on Kyushu Island. Several daimyo in Kyushu had become ardent converts to the new religion and supported Jesuit activities—so much so that, for nearly a decade, in the 1580s, the Society of Jesus ruled the port city of Nagasaki and its hinterland and acted as if they had full sovereignty.

Perceiving a threat, Hideyoshi, when he conquered Kyushu, quickly confiscated Nagasaki and placed it under his personal administration. He also issued an edict declaring Christianity to be a subversive religion.[16] The edict had a chilling effect on the public activities of the Jesuits but did not result in expulsions or a purge. By this proclamation, Hideyoshi took the initiative away from individual daimyo who had converted to Christianity.

In 1614, Tokugawa Ieyasu, the first shogun, issued an edict that prohibited Christianity in his own domains and ordered expulsion of all European missionaries. Thereafter, the shogunate, with active support from the daimyo, eradicated virtually all traces of Christianity throughout the islands. Vigorous surveillance and rewards to informers led to the denunciation of fugitive European missionaries and their Japanese followers. Capture meant torture that ended in either execution or apostasy. The regime forced all

16. Jurgis Elisonas, "Christianity and the Daimyo," in *The Cambridge History of Japan,* vol. 4, edited by John Whitney Hall (Cambridge: Cambridge University Press, 1988).

Japanese to register their affiliation with a local Buddhist temple as proof that they were not Christians.[17] By the 1630s, the Japanese inquisition had largely succeeded.

In 1635, the shogun issued an edict prohibiting foreign travel by any Japanese for any reason. The punishment for violation was execution. All Japanese living abroad were forbidden to return to their homeland. Japanese mariners were reduced to coastal traffic; foreign destinations were forbidden. In 1639, the shogun expelled all Portuguese from Japan and cut all diplomatic connections with Catholic countries. The next year, when the Portuguese sent a sixty-one-person delegation from Macao to reopen relations, the shogun ordered the entire delegation to be beheaded. Among the Europeans, only the resolutely anti-Catholic Dutch were permitted to occupy Deshima, a small islet in Nagasaki harbor to carry on trade. Chinese merchants were similarly confined in another enclave at Nagasaki.

From the 1630s, Tokugawa Japan turned inward in a search for stability and security. Not necessarily seclusion, this was primarily intended to be long-term maintenance of measured limits for Japanese society. Consistent with its techniques of repression and regulation in domestic affairs, the shogunate devised far-reaching measures to regulate Japan's external relations. Early modern Japan renounced any form of expansionism beyond its immediate sphere of influence. Its territorial ambitions were limited to gaining control over Hokkaido in the north and the Ryukyus in the south. Any thought of expansion on the mainland disappeared. Whereas Hideyoshi had invaded Korea and met disaster, no Japanese armies of invasion ever left the home islands under the Tokugawa. Henceforth, the shogunate presented a wary, bristling countenance to the external world that proved to be perhaps the most effective defensive weapon it possessed. In contrast to Java, Bengal, Taiwan, and other areas in Asia, the islands of Japan remained secure from foreign intervention throughout the Tokugawa centuries.

An essential part of the Tokugawa state's withdrawal was its strict regulation of maritime traffic between Japan and the rest of the world. For over two centuries, all Japanese subjects were confined to the archipelago unless explicitly permitted by state order to travel abroad. At a time when technical improvements in shipping and navigation encouraged long-distance, round-the-world sailing, and when Japanese mariners and merchants had been aggressively sailing as far as the Philippines and the Malay Peninsula, the Tokugawa regime restricted them to coastal and intra-island voyages. Japanese reaction to unexpected and unauthorized landings by foreign ships was swift and at times brutal. The shogunate constricted and controlled trade to an extent inconceivable for most other early modern regimes. The state prohib-

17. Ibid., 371.

ited trade in many goods—such as the export of firearms—enforced quotas for imports and exports, and specified only a few trading partners. As is well-known, Japan's seclusion was not total. The Tokugawa could not and did not wish to seal off the archipelago from all outside contact. Nevertheless, its diplomatic contacts were minimal and strictly regional. The shogunate maintained active diplomatic relations with only three neighboring regimes: Korea, a peer state; and two subordinate island polities, Ryukyu and Ezo (Hokkaido).[18] The shogunate entrusted routine diplomatic relations with these regimes to three border domains: Tsushima, Satsuma, and Matsumae. External trade, much of it controlled by the shogunate and aimed at securing Chinese silk and other commodities, followed these diplomatic relationships.

The shogunate devolved ordinary diplomacy and trade relations with Korea to the daimyo of the island of Tsushima—located midway between the Korean Peninsula and the Japanese archipelago. Tsushima established a permanent "Japan House" mission at Pusan, the nearest Korean port, with five hundred to six hundred resident Japanese diplomats and traders. A high-ranking Korean official acted as the Korean ruler's agent in dealing with the Japanese at Pusan. Direct communications between the shogun and Korean ruler occurred regularly. On the occasion of the accession of each shogun, the Korean rulers sent lavish state missions to Edo—twelve in all. However, Korean distrust of the Japanese barred them from reciprocal entry to the capital, Hansongbu, and restricted them to Pusan. Envoys from Tsushima traveled frequently to Pusan; Korean envoys went regularly to Tsushima. The Japanese in Pusan gathered information brought back from regular Korean embassies to Manchu China. Trade with Korea via Tsushima was the most important international exchange for early modern Japan. Supplementing the official trade of Chinese silk and Korean ginseng for Japanese silver and copper was a highly profitable private trade two to four times the volume and value of the official exchange.

The daimyo of Satsuma, the large domain located at the southern extremity of Kyushu Island, controlled interaction with the Ryukyu Islands. Satsuma forced the ruler of Ryukyu to accept Tokugawa supremacy by sending a naval force with three thousand troops to Ryukyu in 1609.[19] Until the 1680s, the shogunate, unable to trade directly with China, encouraged the import of Chinese silk and other goods from Ryukyu via Satsuma. After 1684, when the Chinese ban was relaxed, the shogun sharply limited the amount of silver that could be exported by Satsuma, a blow to the finances of that do-

18. Etsuko Hae-jin Kang, *Diplomacy and Ideology in Japanese-Korean Relations: From the Fifteenth to the Eighteenth Century* (Houndmills, Eng.: Macmillan; New York: St. Martin's Press, 1997).

19. Ronald P. Toby, *State and Diplomacy in Early Modern Japan: Asia in the Development of the Tokugawa Bakufu* (Princeton, N.J.: Princeton University Press, 1984), 45–46.

main.[20] Despite these policies, a brisk flow of goods from Ryukyu entered Japan in a smuggling trade carried out by Chinese traders who anchored off the coasts of Kyushu.

Formal relations between the shogunate and the Ainus of Ezo, "the barbarians of the north," were conducted through the agency of the Matsumae domain, based on the Oshima Peninsula on the southern tip of Hokkaido.[21] Since the twelfth century, armed Japanese merchants had made forays from northern Honshu to the southern shores of Hokkaido. By mid–fifteenth century, the progenitor of the Matsumae house, Takeda Nobuhira, was the leading figure among a dozen Japanese strongmen who had built forts on the Oshima Peninsula. In 1604, Hideyoshi confirmed the Matsumae daimyo in his holding and gave him and his heirs exclusive rights to trade with Ezo but no formal political authority over the people. The long struggle between the Ainus and the Japanese intruders ended in a decisive defeat for Ezo independence during Shakushain's War, 1669–1672. Shakushain, chief of the Hidaka Ainus of eastern Hokkaido, had attacked Matsumae in an attempt to regain control over trade with Honshu and to expel the Japanese from Hokkaido. With the aid of shogunate troops, Matsumae defeated Shakushain and his allies. The shogun formally divided Hokkaido into the Matsumae lands, from which Ainus were expelled and forbidden to enter, and the remainder of Hokkaido, which remained nominally under Ainu chiefs. Japanese traders could enter the Ainu territory only with Matsumae permission and only for limited periods. Thereafter, the Ainus were increasingly helpless before Japanese domination.[22]

In contrast to these relationships, the shogunate refused to enter into normal diplomatic relationships with Ming China despite intense interest in furthering direct Japan to China trade. In 1621, the shogun Hidetada flatly rejected an offer to open diplomatic relations and to cooperate on suppressing Japanese piracy. Henceforth, any diplomatic exchanges between China and Japan were to be conducted indirectly, by means of Korean agency.[23] Direct trade and informal exchanges, but no direct contact by embassies, continued with China. This estrangement resulted in part from the well-known Tokugawa sympathy for the Ming, and in part because the shogunate refused to accept the terms of submission and dependency demanded of lesser states by the Chinese emperors. At Nagasaki, Chinese traders, confined to a small area, were regulated by the Nagasaki magistrate.

20. Robert K. Sakai, "The Satsuma-Ryukyu Trade and the Tokugawa Seclusion Policy," *Journal of Asian Studies* 23 (1964).

21. Richard L. Edmonds, *Northern Frontiers of Qing China and Tokugawa Japan: A Comparative Study of Frontier Policy* (Chicago: University of Chicago Dept. of Geography, 1985).

22. David L. Howell, *Capitalism from Within: Economy, Society, and the State in a Japanese Fishery* (Berkeley and Los Angeles: University of California Press, 1995), 27–35.

23. Toby, *State and Diplomacy in Early Modern Japan*, 60–64.

Early in the eighteenth century, the shogunate further limited Chinese trade to that conducted by fewer than fifty vessels issued permits at Nagasaki for trade with China.[24]

Early attempts under Hideyoshi and his successors to devise satisfactory terms for diplomatic and trade relations with western Europeans eventually turned to rejection over the issue of Christianity. Neither the English nor the Spanish could overcome this growing barrier. For example, protracted negotiations to establish diplomatic and trade relations with the Spanish at Manila in the Philippines, initiated by Hideyoshi and after him the shoguns Ieyasu and Hidetada, ended in failure in the 1620s.[25] The Japanese simultaneously seem to have put aside any notion of expansion into the Philippines—a move that the weakly defended Spanish colonial ports like Manila could well have inspired.

Only one European nation—the Dutch Republic—retained limited rights to trade with Tokugawa Japan. The shogunate maintained a one-sided relationship with the Dutch East India Company to retain one primary conduit for trade with and information from the West. At Nagasaki, tightly controlled Dutch traders unloaded Chinese silk yarn and cloth, deerskins from Taiwan, ginseng, and other goods; they exported Japanese silver, gold, and copper. The Dutch "window" at Deshima Island in Nagasaki became a conduit for information from Europe during the early modern period.

POPULATION GROWTH IN THE SEVENTEENTH CENTURY

The Tokugawa regime's first hundred years, roughly coincidental with the seventeenth century, marks a period of sustained economic growth. Peace and political stability created the necessary backdrop for prolonged dynamic economic expansion. Simultaneously, land use and resource exploitation grew ever more intensive.

The secular change in gross population is striking. From an estimated 12 million in 1600, Japan's population more than doubled, to 24 to 30 million in 1721.[26] Japan's urban population grew much more rapidly than the aggregate numbers suggest. The Tokugawa concentration of power and wealth in Edo, the shogun's capital, including the practice of forced daimyo residence, brought migrants pouring into the city. From a population of about 30,000 in 1600, Edo went to a half million at midcentury and reached well

---

24. Ibid., 197–99.

25. W. Michael Mathes, "A Quarter Century of Trans-Pacific Diplomacy: New Spain and Japan, 1592–1617," *Journal of Asian History* 24 (1990).

26. Totman, *Early Modern Japan*, 140; Nakai Nobuhiko, "Commercial Change and Urban Growth in Early Modern Japan," in *The Cambridge History of Japan*, edited by John Whitney Hall (Cambridge: Cambridge University Press, 1988), 4:538. Both rely on the demographic research Hayami Akira did in the 1960s and 1970s.

over a million in 1720—with roughly half of these people holding samurai status.[27] By the latter date, Edo was probably the largest city in the world. Osaka, the busiest financial, commercial, and manufacturing center in Japan, reached 360,000 persons by 1700.[28] Dozens of daimyo castle towns became cities and commercial centers with populations of 100,000 or more. Throughout the countryside, numerous rural villages became commercial and industrial towns with 5,000 to 10,000 or more residents. Along the major post roads, formerly sleepy hamlets became post stations with several thousand inhabitants, offering food, drink, rest, and other services to travelers.

Seventeenth-century population growth in Japan is the reverse of the well-known and much-studied demographic trends in Europe for the same period. In early modern Europe, high death rates from pandemic disease slowed population growth until 1740, when the European population began to climb. Despite its dense population, Tokugawa Japan, unlike Europe and other regions of the early modern world, was only mildly afflicted by contagious diseases. A 1987 study suggests that "Japan's geography and her isolation from the major world trade routes provided a *cordon sanitaire* that prevented major diseases from penetrating Japan until the mid–nineteenth century."[29] Since Europeans were the major vectors for disease at this time, Japan's isolation was an asset in this regard. Smallpox, measles, influenza, and dysentery were the only contagious diseases implicated in epidemic outbreaks in Japan. Unlike New World populations, the Japanese had been long exposed to these diseases from the Chinese mainland, and mortality rates were those typical of exposed populations.[30]

THE SEVENTEENTH-CENTURY ECONOMY

The 1600s saw a stunning expansion in the volume of commerce and the scale and efficiency of markets in Tokugawa Japan. Partly, this can be attributed to official policies such as the minting of a uniform, stable trimetallic currency for the first time in Japanese history. Partly, it was a response to standardization of weights and measures across the archipelago. Partly, it was the abolition of toll and customs barriers between domains and cities. Systematic investment in public works by the shogun and by individual daimyo

27. Totman, *Early Modern Japan*, 153.

28. James L. McClain, "Space, Power, Wealth, and Status in Seventeenth-Century Osaka," in *Osaka: The Merchants' Capital of Early Modern Japan*, edited by James L. McClain and Osamu Wakita (Ithaca, N.Y.: Cornell University Press, 1999).

29. Ann Bowman Jannetta, *Epidemics and Mortality in Early Modern Japan* (Princeton, N.J.: Princeton University Press, 1987), 5.

30. Ibid., 65–71. Those few foreign travelers who did traverse Japan in this period commented on the absence of pandemic diseases.

aided commerce. Major roads were built and improved, such as the great post road between Edo and Kyoto that had some fifty post towns along the route. The shogun and daimyo operated efficient messenger services with post runners, and new private post services also sprang up. By 1700, runners could bring documents over the five hundred kilometers between Edo and Osaka in less than four days.[31]

Improvements in water transport facilitated trade in food grains and other commodities for mass consumption. Ports and harbors were dredged and protected with breakwaters. New charts of coastal waters, beacons, and lighthouses made it possible for goods to be shipped from any port on the archipelago to Edo and Osaka without off-loading for overland transport. A new western route ran along the edge of the Sea of Japan to the Shimonosei Strait to the Inland Sea and on to Osaka and Edo. The eastern circuit took shipping north on the Sea of Japan through Tsugaru Strait at the northern tip of Honshu and then south along the coast directly to Edo. Formerly it had been too dangerous to sail around Boso Peninsula, which protects Edo Bay.

International trade flourished despite restrictive controls imposed by the shogunate in the 1630s. Goods could not be carried by Japanese vessels, but Chinese junks and Dutch ships continued to call at Nagasaki, and trade continued via the Ryukyus, Korea, and Hokkaido. The most important imports were silk piece goods and silk yarn from China, followed by refined sugar from Taiwan and China; deerskins and other leather from Taiwan and Southeast Asia; and Chinese medicines, mercury, and other miscellaneous items not available in Japan. (The demand for saltpeter and other war-making materials dropped precipitously in the early seventeenth century.) Japan exported almost nothing but silver, gold, and refined copper. The import of Chinese silk yarn encouraged the growth of a domestic silk-weaving industry. The export of copper stimulated output and innovation in mining and refining. Foreign trade, relatively stable, "fluctuated between fifteen and twenty-five thousand *kanme* annually throughout the seventeenth century."[32] Three times Tokugawa foreign trade reached more than forty thousand *kanme:* in the mid-1630s, in the early 1660s, and in the mid-1690s.[33] The prices paid for imports at the port of entry probably doubled by the time of final sale to the consumer at markets in Osaka, Kyoto, Nara, and Edo. In the eastern domains, proceeds from foreign trade were substantial enough to

31. Constantine Nomikos Vaporis, *Breaking Barriers: Travel and the State in Early Modern Japan* (Cambridge: Council on East Asian Studies, Harvard University, 1994).

32. Robert L. Innes, "The Door Ajar: Japan's Foreign Trade in the Seventeenth Century" (Ph.D. diss., University of Michigan, 1980), 430. The *kanme* was a measure of silver weight (3.75 kg.) as well as a monetary unit. Between 1673 and 1711, imports, balanced by exports, averaged 19,294 *kanme* (72,353 kilograms) of silver yearly. Calculated from data given by Innes (416, table 23).

33. Ibid., 430.

partly offset the continuing drain of income and resources from the countryside to Edo, caused by the enormous costs of the alternate-year attendance requirement. Western domains were located too far from Edo to share in the economic prosperity this subsidy engendered, but they did benefit from the economic stimulus of commerce with foreign countries.[34]

Although indeed substantial in value, foreign goods brought into Japan were limited in overall amounts and in variety. By 1685, the shogunate imposed strict quotas on the numbers of boats and value of goods that the Chinese and Dutch traders could bring into Nagasaki. The leading import was high-quality silk cloth, but Indian-patterned and plain cotton piece goods, so much in demand elsewhere, formed only a small part of Dutch East India Company cargoes.[35] Shogunate restrictions on overall volume played a role in this. Engelbert Kaempfer, who lived in Japan for two years in the early 1690s, commented that piece goods or textiles were always popular and "return[ed] a fixed and reasonable profit." He went on to remark, "In view of Japan's large population, even a hundred times as much [imported textiles] would not satisfy the demand."[36]

Sugar brought from Taiwan, Ryukyu, southern China, and Southeast Asia rose to around 3.5 million *catties* (2.1 million kilograms) of sugar per year by the latter seventeenth century.[37] Most sugar was probably consumed by the voracious markets of the biggest cities. This meant that per capita consumption of imported sugar was only .08 kilograms per annum for a population of around 25 million. Other than small quantities of pepper, cinnamon, and other spices, no foodstuffs were imported.

Even though timber and lumber were becoming expensive, the Japanese confined their annual wood imports to about 160 metric tons of the red-dye wood known as *sappan* (brazilwood, *Caesalpinia sappan*) from Siam, a few metric tons of sandalwood *(Santalum album)* from Timor, and even tinier amounts of eagle-wood *(Aquilaria agallocha)*, an aromatic species from Southeast Asia.[38]

Hides and leather imports were modest, despite domestic sources limited to the few horses, oxen, and buffaloes used for riding and hauling. Japan imported wild buffalo skins and deerskins from Taiwan and Southeast Asia to

---

34. Ibid., 462.

35. Engelbert Kaempfer and Beatrice M. Bodart-Bailey, *Kaempfer's Japan: Tokugawa Culture Observed* (Honolulu: University of Hawaii Press, 1999), 209–10.

36. Ibid.

37. Innes, "The Door Ajar," 508. See also Sucheta Mazumdar, *Sugar and Society in China: Peasants, Technology, and the World Market* (Cambridge: Harvard University Asia Center, 1998), 78–83.

38. Peter Boomgaard, "The VOC Trade in Forest Products in the Seventeenth Century," in *Nature and the Orient: The Environmental History of South and Southeast Asia,* edited by Richard Grove, Vinita Damodaran, and Satpal Sangwan (Delhi: Oxford University Press, 1998).

be tanned and cut by *burakumin* leather workers. In the mid-1600s, the Dutch imported into Nagasaki an average of sixty-eight thousand deerskins per year, and Chinese traders also imported deerskins—probably a lesser number.[39] Matsumae domain on the southern tip of Hokkaido also shipped large numbers of deer pelts purchased from Ainu hunters. This relatively small inflow sufficed to meet limited demand in a society that used straw and clogs for ordinary footwear rather than leather, and wood and silk ropes for saddles and bridles. Deerskins supplied the raw material for military clothing and supplies, such as shooting gloves for archers.[40]

Considering the size and sophistication of Japan's population, and its limited resource base, there were surprising omissions in the list of imports. Under long-standing peaceful conditions, imports of weaponry, muskets, cannon, and other supplies understandably dwindled. Peace would also explain why horses were not a major import item as they were in other Asian countries. Why steel and iron did not figure more prominently in imports is not at all clear. Some luxury goods, such as Chinese porcelain ware, are also absent. Why Japan did not consume quantities of diamonds, rubies, emeralds, pearls, and other precious stones is something of a mystery—at least in view of the active demand for these items elsewhere.

The greatest stimulant to commercial activity, of course, was the steady increase in demand for goods and services generated by a growing population. The rural economy successfully met this challenge. According to Susan Hanley, "The new foods introduced during the late medieval period, rises in agricultural productivity during the Tokugawa period, improvements in transportation and a more varied diet for much of the population during the seventeenth and eighteenth centuries not only meant a lower incidence of disease and less fear of starvation but also an increase in longevity for many Japanese."[41]

Japanese peasants embraced the new markets, growing a wide range of crops for sale. Toward the end of the sixteenth century, Japanese farmers first learned how to grow cotton and began to produce it as a cash crop. Previously, only imported cotton was available, in limited amounts. Coarse hemp cloth was the usual fiber for ordinary clothing; luxury clothing was made of silk. Domestically produced cotton transformed clothing and bed-

39. Thomas O. Hollman, "Formosa and the Trade in Venison and Deer Skins," in *Emporia, Commodities, and Entrepreneurs in Asian Maritime Trade, c. 1400–1750*, edited by Roderich Ptak (Stuttgart: F. Steiner, 1991). Calculated from p. 273, table 2, for the period 1635–1659.

40. For a reference to "leather shooting glove attached," see Kaempfer and Bodart-Bailey, *Kaempfer's Japan*, 402; see 242–46 for a description of riding gear and traveling equipment.

41. Susan B. Hanley, "Tokugawa Society: Material Culture, Standard of Living, and Life Styles," in *The Cambridge History of Japan*, edited by John Whitney Hall (Cambridge: Cambridge University Press, 1988), 4:688.

ding for ordinary Japanese and in so doing dramatically increased the quality of life.[42]

Cottonseed also proved to have a valuable by-product. During the medieval centuries, the usual source of clean-burning oil for lamps was that made from the perilla plant *(Perilla frutescens)*, available only at high prices and in limited quantities. In the early 1600s, two Osaka merchants discovered how to press oil from cottonseed. Shortly thereafter, others devised techniques for pressing seeds from colza, or rape *(Brassica napus)*, for canola oil. In the area around Osaka, peasant farmers grew rapeseed as a second crop after harvesting cotton. Rapid growth in cotton and supplies of the seed made Osaka a center for lamp oil supplies.[43]

The most important new food crop was the sweet potato, introduced along with the white potato into Japan by the Portuguese in 1605. Originally used only for horse fodder, both kinds entered the human dietary within twenty years or so. Sweet potatoes were especially valuable as an upland dry-farmed crop that produced more calories per area cultivated than almost any other cultivar.[44]

Rice production climbed to meet a rising demand. Some portion of the increase came from more intensive agriculture on fields already cultivated. Assured of a market, Japanese farmers turned to better-yielding seeds from new varieties of rice. Often, larger farmers kept journals to record inputs and yields for every crop they harvested.

Japanese farmers continued to use human wastes efficiently to fertilize their fields—a resource in ample supply as the population doubled. At every home, at roadside toilets, and at communal toilets in the towns, feces and urine, carefully separated, were sold to collectors at steadily rising prices. Wastes from every town and city were transported by cart to the surrounding countryside, where they were stored for a time, fermenting, and then applied to the soil.[45] Japanese farmers also bought commercial fertilizers such as oil cakes made from the residue left after pressing cotton or rapeseeds for edible oil. Sardines caught by an increasingly efficient large-seine fishing industry were cheap enough to be ground up and used to enrich the soil. The most significant and costly form of intensification was conversion of rain-fed croplands into wet rice paddies on the alluvial plains. Among its other advantages, irrigation facilitated double-cropping with barley, wheat, or rapeseed after the wet rice harvest each year.

Ultimately, rising demand for foodstuffs could be met only by extending

42. Ibid., 4:689.
43. McClain, "Space, Power, Wealth, and Status in Seventeenth-Century Osaka," 68.
44. Hanley, "Tokugawa Society," 682.
45. MacFarlane, *The Savage Wars of Peace*, 154–69.

the area under cultivation. Japan's peasants responded eagerly. Between 1600 and 1720, cultivated land in Japan doubled, from 1.5 million hectares to 2.97 million hectares—or close to the increase in human numbers.[46] The greatest caloric return came from wet rice cultivation. To expand paddy fields demanded investment in new, reliable water control. The problem was not really lack of water but reliable placement of water in wet rice fields. During the medieval period, most irrigation projects were to be found along the upper reaches of the rivers where narrow valleys channeled the rivers and made it possible to water crops safely. Potentially fertile alluvial lands on the plains were subject to periodic flooding by the short, fast-flowing rivers spilling out of the north-south hill range, and consequently were not cultivated. Much of the alluvial land consisted of wetlands that required drainage as well.

CONTROLLING THE RIVERS

By mid–sixteenth century, Japanese technicians and engineers had begun to make significant advances in hydraulic engineering. They greatly improved their skills in building embankments *(tsutsumi)* that could withstand fast-moving water several meters in depth. They devised formulas for selecting embankment sites based on the type of soil and water pressure and volume. They encased stones in bamboo baskets or nets, stacked them as if they were large boulders, and used a web of wooden beams and posts to secure the baskets against water flow. They designed improved wooden water gates framed with iron nails and clamps and devised better techniques for siting and anchoring them. These improvements converged with more efficient methods for moving and using rock for walls and dams.[47]

Engineers devised new techniques to control river flooding. Rather than construct continuous dikes parallel to the river, they inserted discontinuous levees—reinforced by planted trees and bamboo—that projected into the river at angles designed to guide the river's flow. They did not try to straighten river meanders but instead left them untouched and broadened the riverbed whenever possible. They left levees and dikes high enough to moderate, but not to contain fully, overflows during flood stages. To handle the overflow, they often built double embankments or wide catchment basins. To divert water from valuable farmland or towns, they mobilized large

---

46. Sato, "Tokugawa Villages and Agriculture," 62.

47. Keiji Nagahara and Kozo Yamamura, "Shaping the Process of Unification: Technological Progress in Sixteenth- and Seventeenth-Century Japan," *Journal of Japanese Studies* 14 (1988): 84–85; Conrad D. Totman, "Preindustrial River Conservancy: Causes and Consequences," *Monumenta Nipponica* 47 (1992).

numbers of peasants to dig diversion channels to prevent flooding. These measures made it possible for peasants living along the mid and lower reaches of rivers on the plains to cultivate alluvial soils for the first time. With the rivers under control, the shogun and daimyo invested in long irrigation canals to bring river water directly to lands beyond the inundation plain and, in ditching, to provide drainage for potentially fertile wetlands.[48]

Scholars have identified thirty-three large river-control projects financed, planned, and completed by daimyo between 1596 and 1651 that opened up thousands of hectares of new wet rice fields.[49] More modest water control efforts also proliferated. By the close of the regime, there were several thousand new or expanded irrigation networks in operation throughout the archipelago.[50] Daimyo invested heavily in multivillage, multilevel irrigation projects in order to increase their tax revenues. Well-to-do peasants also took leadership in promoting and paying for irrigation efforts. Some irrigation works brought water to land already under the plow; others permitted expansion of settlement and wet rice cultivation to the full capacity of alluvial plains. In response to these opportunities, the rural settlement pattern in Tokugawa Japan shifted perceptibly from the hills to the plains.

New techniques also encouraged land reclamation from shallow tidal marshes surrounding river mouths at the ocean coastlines. Funded by daimyo and—increasingly in the later Tokugawa—by wealthy merchants engaged in land speculation, engineers enclosed marshy areas with dikes and pumped out the saline water to prepare the rich silty area for planting. Over several decades, beginning in 1685, merchants in Osaka invested in reclamation of the marshland near the delta of the Yodo River. Individual projects often surpassed one hundred hectares in size.[51]

Similarly, the Nobi Plain, an alluvial fan thirty to fifty miles in length along Ise Bay on the Pacific Coast of Honshu, was only "sparsely inhabited, a province of marshy grasses and water birds" at the beginning of the seventeenth century. Local peasants engaged in intensive ditching, diking, and diversion of floodwaters from the Kiso River to create polder lands for wet rice

48. Totman, "Preindustrial River Conservancy," 63–64.

49. John Whitney Hall, Keiji Nagahara, and Kozo Yamamura, *Japan before Tokugawa: Political Consolidation and Economic Growth, 1500–1650* (Princeton, N.J.: Princeton University Press, 1981), 330–34. Yamamura gives details of ten of these projects "designed to reclaim the sedimentary basins of Japan's largest rivers" (330).

50. William W. Kelly and Cornell University, China-Japan Program, *Water Control in Tokugawa Japan: Irrigation Organization in a Japanese River Basin, 1600–1870* (Ithaca, N.Y.: China-Japan Program, Cornell University, 1982), 14. For another case study of irrigation, see Luke Shepherd Roberts, *Mercantilism in a Japanese Domain: The Merchant Origins of Economic Nationalism in Eighteenth-Century Tosa* (Cambridge: Cambridge University Press, 1998), 74–75.

51. Furushima, "The Village and Agriculture during the Edo Period," 500.

cultivation. The heads of Ogaki domain gave rights to reclaimed land to heads of villages who would undertake this work. Today, the Nobi Plain is one of the most heavily cultivated areas in Japan.[52]

Another example, studied in detail, is the Shonai Plain (about 530 square kilometers) on the cold, sparsely populated northeastern coast along the Sea of Japan. The Aka River descends from the mountains to an alluvial fan at the southernmost portion of the Shonai Plain and then runs northward to the sea. Before 1600, the plain was a "poorly-drained marshland, with only scattered settlements on its perimeter and on natural levees of river courses throughout the otherwise undeveloped expanse of brush and reed vegetation."[53] The Aka River moved frequently among several channels that it had scoured across the plain. In 1605–1606, an official of the newly assigned two-thousand-square-kilometer Shonai domain, built, at the point the Aka River entered the plain, a short revetment of boulders and timber that redirected the flow of the river into a more central channel. This stabilized the river's flow and made it accessible to cultivators seeking water on either bank. Within fifteen years, village headmen had organized the digging of three main unlined canals along old river courses to tap into the Aka River in the foothills and then deliver gravity-fed water to undeveloped lands on the plain. By the early 1700s, local initiative created a dense network of subsidiary earth canals with intakes and spillways, gates and flumes, that brought reliable water supplies to ditches and then to bunded rice fields on the plain.

By the standards of the day, these were not sophisticated irrigation works. Village headmen and daimyo officials relied on their own judgment and local labor to build with readily available materials—earth, stone, straw matting, and timber. With minimal support from the daimyo, local officials assumed responsibility for operation of the main intake gates, for annual dredging, bank and gate repairs, and other maintenance for the main and branch canals. Guided by customary practice and negotiation, with little interference from the daimyo, they allocated water delivery to each branch canal and each village.

The expanding irrigation system stimulated large-scale settlement and land reclamation. In 1650, wet rice lands irrigated with Aka River water totaled about 5,000 hectares. By 1750, this figure had climbed to about 8,000 hectares, and by 1870, 9,600 hectares. In the latter year, some seventy-five thousand cultivating households from 250 villages drew water from the network. Cultivators in this system could rely on large volumes of water needed

---

52. Thomas C. Smith, Robert Y. Eng, and Robert T. Lundy, *Nakahara: Family Farming and Population in a Japanese Village, 1717–1830* (Stanford, Calif.: Stanford University Press, 1977), 33–34.

53. Kelly and Cornell University, China-Japan Program, *Water Control in Tokugawa Japan*, 1.

for the planting cycle from May to June, followed by lesser amounts of water alternately drained and applied as the plants grew in the summer. The intensively managed irrigation canals and bunded paddy fields of densely settled rice farmers replaced the scrub vegetation of the Shonai Plain—a significant ecological transformation repeated throughout Japan.

Japanese farmers also pressed aggressively upward onto the alluvial fans and even up hillsides to add capacity. As irrigation expanded on the plains, dry farming pushed into areas formerly considered marginal. Many peasant cultivators resorted to clearing and burning of woods and forests under a form of shifting cultivation that gave them an initial burst of nutrients in the soil. The lower forests came under an unprecedented assault by the peasantry.

FORESTS IN THE SEVENTEENTH CENTURY

From the period of pacification in the late 1500s until the late 1600s, Japanese forests were ruthlessly exploited to serve the buoyant early modern economy. The rural population put greater pressure on forests for construction timber, green fertilizer, and fuel for household and domestic consumption. More devastating was the insatiable demand for timber, charcoal, and other forest products from a soaring urban population and rising industrial production requiring fuel. By 1670, overcutting was beginning to reveal itself in the "bald" appearance of the mountains stripped of their tree cover. The thin, coarse, immature soil of the hillsides was eroding rapidly with the heavy spring and autumn rains and snow runoff.

During this century, Japanese ruling elites engaged in a vast construction boom that relied on wood from the archipelago's forests. The native architectural tradition was focused on wood instead of stone, brick, or pounded mud. Preference for wood can perhaps be attributed to the lack of horizontally layered sandstone that could be chiseled into building blocks. Stones were plentiful, but limestone deposits to be used for mortar and cement compounds were not. Japanese builders used clay and mud in tile roofs and plaster walls but continued to turn to wood as their primary building material. The Japanese maintained a strong cultural preference for the tactile and visual qualities of wood in their buildings and furnishings. Wood offered warmth that stone or brick did not possess. Forests and the wood they yielded were an essential element for the good life for all Japanese.

In the 1580s, Hideyoshi uprooted hundreds of thousands of samurai and their dependents from their rural villages and forced them to move to the approximately 250 castle towns being constructed by daimyo throughout the archipelago. Daimyo began to move from their hidden hilltop fortresses to build new castles in the middle of alluvial plains. These were multistoried wooden forts built on stone foundations, with larger and more elaborate walls, surrounded by immense moats. The samurai were given rice allowances to subsist on and confined to military and administrative duties. Responding to opportunities, hundreds of thousands of peasants, rural traders, and artisans followed the samurai into the new cities. As castle towns grew in size, new temples, shrines, homes, and shops required timber. Thousands of hectares of high forest had to be cleared to supply the materials for building a castle town.

Toyotomi Hideyoshi set the trend with his monumental buildings in Osaka and Kyoto. Hideyoshi demanded and got the highest quality timber from daimyo in all parts of the realm. To do so meant that loggers had to go into previously uncut high forests. When possible, Hideyoshi took major forests under his direct control. In 1586, he assumed direct administration of the Yoshino region south of Nara and required mountain villagers there to make tax payments in timber. Commands from the center spurred growth of a national lumber industry with identifiable brand marks for firms and with standardized processed products. Either at the felling place or at fixed points on the way to market, timber sawyers cut logs into usable segments. They cut standard logs, 3.6 to 5.4 meters in length; they squared pieces 10, 15, or 20 centimeters on a side; they split pieces designed for barrel making or shingles; and they fashioned flat pieces equivalent to boards or planking. They used the wood residue for charcoal making.[54]

Some of Hideyoshi's buildings were truly gargantuan. The Hokoji Temple he built in Kyoto had a Buddha hall 61 meters in height designed to house a 49-meter Buddha statue. Tokugawa Ieyasu, daimyo of the Tokai area, volunteered to provide the ridgepole. His loggers finally located a massive tree growing at the foot of Mount Fuji. They felled the tree, trimmed and cut it to form a timber eighty feet in length, carefully floated it downriver to the sea, from where it was taken by ship to Osaka and then up the Yodo River to Kyoto. The whole process took three months and fifty thousand man-days of corvée.[55]

Ieyasu followed Hideyoshi's example by building lavishly, bringing valuable high forestlands under his direct control, and demanding from daimyo large amounts of timber, shingles, and other wood products. Ieyasu also invested heavily in river improvement efforts aimed at clearing major rivers to make them passable for log rafts, and he encouraged lumbermen to build ships capable of navigating around dangerous headlands. Ieyasu's greatest

54. Conrad D. Totman, *The Lumber Industry in Early Modern Japan* (Honolulu: University of Hawaii Press, 1995), 57.

55. Conrad D. Totman, *The Green Archipelago: Forestry in Preindustrial Japan* (Berkeley and Los Angeles: University of California Press, 1989), 57.

monuments were his castles at Edo, Sunpu, and Nagoya. By one calculation, these three buildings alone consumed some 280,000 cubic meters of lumber, or the clear-cutting of at least 2,750 hectares of prime high forest.[56]

Periodic urban fires in these wooden cities caused fresh demands for timber for rebuilding. Edo averaged a substantial fire every 2.75 years between 1601 and 1866—a frequency that gave rise to the ironic term "the flowers of Edo" for its fires. Some of these were truly horrific conflagrations. The 1657 Meireki fire burnt for three days and consumed major buildings in Chiyoda castle, 500 daimyo mansions, 779 residences of lesser officials, 350 temples and shrines, and 400 blocks of commoner housing. Over one hundred thousand people died in the blaze. Reconstruction of the city required cutting at least ten thousand hectares of prime forestland—forests that were no longer either plentiful or easily accessible.[57] Other cities and castle towns repeatedly suffered the same scourge with the same results.

Relentless logging meant that nearly all the high-quality timber on Japan's three main islands was depleted. By the late 1600s, loggers were pressing into the southern tip of Hokkaido for first-quality timber. A well-known Tokugawa scholar complained in a widely quoted lament that "eight out of ten mountains of the realm have been denuded."[58] In the 1660s, the daimyo of Tugaru domain explicitly stated his obligation to sustain the forests as the third in the tasks of rulership:

> One's third consideration is the mountains. To elaborate, man is sustained by the five elements [*gogyo:* wood, fire, water, earth, and metal]. In our world today neither high nor low can survive for a moment if any one of the five is missing. . . . However, fire cannot sustain itself: it requires wood. Hence wood is central to a person's hearth and home [*kama*]. And wood comes from the mountains. Wood is fundamental to the hearth; the hearth is central to the person. Whether one be high or low, when one lacks wood, one lacks fire and cannot exist. One must take care that wood be abundant. To assure that wood not become scarce, one cherishes the mountains. And thus, because they are the foundation of the hearth, which nurtures the lives of all people, the mountains are to be treasured.

Rulers and ordinary folk alike began to see a growing timber scarcity for all purposes and to fear the ecological consequences of " bald" mountains for society.[59]

56. Ibid., 62.
57. Ibid., 68.
58. Ibid., 70 (quoting Kumazawa Banzan), 59.
59. Roberts describes forest depletion due to domainal policies in Tosa domain, the southern half of Shikoku (*Mercantilism in a Japanese Domain*).

DEMANDS ON THE RURAL ECONOMY

By the early years of the eighteenth century, Tokugawa Japan entered a period of growing resource and energy scarcity. Forest depletion was but one aspect of a larger problem. The doubling of an already dense population in the previous century had put a massive strain on the early modern economy. As Matsuo Hikotaro, a samurai writer, said of Tosa, his domain, in 1759, "It is astonishing to see the clear decline in our country's ability to produce wealth over the past fifty years. The agricultural tax has decreased annually, our forests have all been cut, the number of boats for commerce and fishing has dwindled."[60]

During the latter half of the Tokugawa period, Japanese cultivators seem to have hit an ecological ceiling beyond which they could not reliably extend land reclamation. In 1874, the first land use figures of the Meiji period revealed virtually no increase in the 1720 figure, with a total of 3.05 million hectares under cultivation.[61] At .1 hectares per capita under cultivation, and with almost no imports of foodstuffs, Japanese farmers continued to increase yields by more intensive inputs in a struggle to grow food and industrial crops in quantities sufficient to support a population of approximately 30 million. Long-standing shogunate attitudes ruled out aggressive territorial expansion beyond Japan's limited island domain.

Demand pressures expressed by the market and state forced the Tokugawa agrarian system to reorganize for greater production. Expanding the area of cultivation became increasingly expensive and unrewarding. Increased yields were the only solution to producing the foodstuffs and raw materials needed in the enlarged society. Prices for farm produce rose. For joint families, management of larger holdings grew more difficult and conflict ridden. Under these conditions, well-to-do owners found that their farms could be subdivided and leased profitably to tenant farmers holding tiny plots. There was a bifurcation of rural society.[62]

The later Tokugawa period displayed, on the one hand, a widespread population of wealthy landlords who occupied comfortable homes, cultivated diverse arts and letters, and engaged successfully in the life of the marketplace; on the other hand, it had a vastly greater population of smallholders and landless tenants and laborers. Ordinary Japanese responded to the threat of scarcity by working harder and more skillfully in a form of self-exploitation. Artisans and other urban workers were forced into more intensive production if they were not to fall by the wayside in the precarious economy. In the

60. Quoted in ibid., 56.
61. Ibid.
62. Totman, *Early Modern Japan,* 249.

countryside, tenant smallholders arduously and attentively cultivated their tiny plots. They evolved intricate daily and seasonal work rhythms designed to maximize the returns for each crop. Output per hectare of food crops, industrial crops—cotton, rapeseed, dyes, and sedge—and narcotics, such as tobacco, improved. Ubiquitous farm manuals promoted a cult of efficiency in every aspect of rural production. Even the tiniest savings, if they occurred daily, could help smallholders survive.

Under these conditions, significant numbers of peasants began to abandon their lands.[63] They gave up cultivating legally registered, taxed farmland. Many tenant farmers sought wage-paying jobs in nearby towns as an alternative to cultivating their unrewarding microplots. Often, they shifted their residences to the towns and departed the countryside. Sometimes entire families died out with no immediate heir, and no one stepped forward to take over their lands. This tendency was especially pronounced in northeastern Japan in the Kanto and Tohoku provinces. To a certain extent, this "flight from the countryside" was also a reaction to the maldistribution of an already crushing tax burden. Officials set taxes as a percentage of the total village output, so that high-yielding fields generally paid proportionately less than low-yielding fields. The process of internal distribution of the tax burden generally favored wealthier and more powerful farmers and overburdened poorer and weaker farmers.[64]

If returns on the rice tax are any indication, food production probably did not increase much in the eighteenth century. Both in the shogunate domains and across the *han*, or daimyo lands, rice tax collections leveled off and even declined in the second half of the eighteenth century. Administrative reforms that resulted in more rigorous methods of assessment and collection generated rising tax collections in the first six decades of the eighteenth century. In 1744, for example, the shogun's collections from his domains reached a record high for the regime: 1.8 million *koku* on lands whose total productive capacity was assessed at only 3.5 to 4 million *koku*.[65] Although this receded slightly, the shogun's rice tax remained between 1.65 and 1.7 million *koku* per year until 1764. The rice tax placed a heavy and increasing burden on all Japanese peasants. Growing peasant protests and unrest and crop failures pressed the total tax downward to around 1.5 million *koku* for the remainder of the century, with precipitous drops in famine years such as 1783 and 1786. Daimyo across Japan faced financial problems as their rice tax collections slowed over the same period.

63. Patricia Sippel, "Abandoned Fields: Negotiating Taxes in the Bakafu Domain," *Monumenta Nipponica* 53, no. 2 (1998).
64. Furushima, "The Village and Agriculture during the Edo Period," 498.
65. Ibid., 496.

Wet rice fields bore the heaviest tax burden, while rain-fed or dry-farmed crops, although frequently more valuable, were assessed at a lesser rate. According to Harold Bolitho, "Rice was the prestige cereal, credited with all sorts of benign properties, mystical, as when offered to the gods (for no other grain would do), and tonic, as when pressed on the sick as a preservative."[66] Most collections on wet rice lands were taken in kind, as sacks of rice, rather than in cash. These tax features in turn persuaded larger farmers to shift to less heavily taxed crops.

Steady commercialization in the economy encouraged farmers to take up new, intensively cultivated cash crops at the expense of rice. Profits to be made prompted them to engage in various forms of processing of these crops in agricultural byemployments or industries. For example, domestic sericulture produced a rising share of silk yarn for the Kyoto silk-weaving industry. By 1700, domestic yarns were equal to those imported, and their share rose steadily throughout the remainder of the century. In 1713, an official edict from the shogun called for Japanese weavers to use domestic as well as foreign yarn, echoing the sentiments in a report of the silk-weaving guild of the year before.[67] Sericulture and silk reeling became a major rural industry with growing demands for land, labor, and investment. The silk moths *(Bombyx mori)* consumed three hundred kilograms of mulberry leaves in order to spin cocoons sufficient to reel one kilogram of silk yarn. The average annual production of a twenty-year-old mulberry tree was about one hundred kilograms. Newly hatched larvae had to be fed shredded mulberry leaves three times a day during their monthlong molting period.[68]

Import substitution gave a similar impetus to sugar growing in Japan. Urbanization and the rapidly rising consumption of sweets inflated prices and the demand for sugar. Cultivators in the Ryukyus discovered profits in the Japanese market after 1650. Sugar cultivation and export through Satsuma became a major source of income for Ryukyu. By the 1700s, sugar growing had taken hold in Satsuma itself. The shogunate actively tried to encourage farmers to plant this crop in Satsuma (on Honshu's Pacific Coast), Shikoku, and Kyushu. These warm, humid areas had sandy soils suitable for sugarcane. By the 1830s, sugar flowing into Osaka for processing for the western market had risen to nearly 15,000 metric tons annually. Of this total, 10,000 tons came from domestic sources in Japan, more than 4,400 tons from Ryukyu, and the remaining 600 tons from Taiwan or China.[69] The supply of domestic sugar for Edo and the eastern market was probably as large, if not larger.

66. Harold Bolitho, "The *Han*," in *The Cambridge History of Japan*, edited by John Whitney Hall (Cambridge: Cambridge University Press, 1988), 4:214.
67. Innes, "The Door Ajar," 499–501.
68. Ibid., 480.
69. Ibid., 514–16.

Land devoted to sugarcane may have reached thirteen thousand hectares each year.[70]

Central government restraints on imports, combined with an increasing drive toward self-sufficiency, put Tokugawa food production uncomfortably close to annual consumption in the eighteenth century. After 1700, major famines—unknown in the previous century—demonstrated the growing precariousness of Tokugawa food supplies and had a perceptible demographic effect. Expanded cultivation pressed to the ecological margin meant that harvest failures increased in number and severity. Prolonged cold and rainy weather during the summer growing season led to crop failures. Highly intensive rice monoculture was vulnerable to insect plagues. In some domains such as Tosa, comprising the southern half of the island of Shikoku, famine conditions regularly occurred during the eighteenth century.[71] On three memorable occasions, the combination of circumstances was such that famine conditions occurred on a regional scale. The first major famine, known as the Kyoho famine, occurred in 1732. In northern Kyushu, a series of poor harvests culminated in disaster when wheat, barley, and rice crops failed nearly completely. As much as 20 percent of the population in that section of the island died.[72]

The Temmei famine of 1782–1785 was the most devastating. On August 4, 1783, a massive volcanic eruption from Mount Asama northwest of Edo killed two thousand people outright and destroyed their homes. Volcanic ash thrown up by the eruption darkened the skies for weeks afterward and deposited ash on fields fifty or more kilometers from the site. This followed the cold, wet weather that had prevailed throughout 1782, and which had reduced rice production. Continuing cold and wet weather in the spring of 1783 was followed by the cooling effects of volcanic dust that darkened the skies and by the deleterious effect of ashes covering fields. Early snows in October exacerbated volcanic effects. Widespread crop failures resulted. Deaths from the 1783–1784 catastrophe and its aftermath did significantly reduce the Tokugawa population. Famine-related mortality probably reached a million deaths.

The Tempo dearth of the 1830s in northeastern Japan was the third Tokugawa famine. In 1833, during a summer growing season abbreviated by late and early snow falls, only about a third of the expected crops grew. The next year, an abnormally wet summer in 1834 began a series of general crop fail-

70. Ibid. If total Japanese consumption were one kilogram per person, total consumption would be around 30,000 metric tons per year. If two-thirds of that amount were grown domestically, this would require at least thirteen thousand hectares of land (at 1.5 metric tons per hectare yield).

71. Roberts, *Mercantilism in a Japanese Domain*, 72–74. Famines occurred in this domain in 1682–1683, 1697–1708, 1732–1734, 1743–1749, 1766–1767, and 1784–1790.

72. MacFarlane, *The Savage Wars of Peace*, 71.

ures through 1836 that extended down the northeastern coast of Honshu to the middle of Japan.[73]

The famines served as emphatic warnings of a possible crisis to a society already attuned to scarcity of resources. Rather than reach outward beyond the limits of their self-imposed seclusion, the Japanese adopted a number of strategies that permitted dynamic economic growth within the resource limits of the home and Ryukyu Islands and their adjoining seas. These responses included frugality and simplicity of lifestyles, limits on population, intensified use of marine resources, forest regeneration, and intensified exploitation of Hokkaido's natural resources.

RESPONSES TO SCARCITY: SIMPLICITY AND AUSTERITY

One response lay in conservation and material simplicity. These tendencies were made explicit by official ideology. Successive shoguns promulgated and tried to enforce elaborate sumptuary legislation that tied consumption to status for samurai and commoners alike. Bigger houses, finer clothing, and other luxuries could be obtained only by possessing official rank. Even wealthy merchants and landlords were constrained in their lifestyles by these regulations. The regime's ideologues resorted to Confucian principles to argue that limiting consumption encouraged accumulation of stores and reserves to protect the country against disaster. By this rationing approach, the regime emphatically stated its preference for limited consumption and, to some extent, reinforced an existing tendency toward simple, almost severe, material culture.

The regime's sumptuary measures were not entirely arbitrary and imposed from above, but emerged from long-standing inclinations found in Japanese culture. A myriad of cultural choices favored simplicity and conservation of resources. By comparison with other contemporary societies, such as those of western Europe, the Japanese used less energy and fewer materials in their daily life without sacrificing essential aspects of comfort and pleasing design. For example, the unfitted, untailored Japanese kimono was "made from one long, rectangular length of cloth cut into eight pieces: the pattern [was] the same for everyone, male or female, child or adult. Every inch of cloth [was] used with no waste."[74]

During the eighteenth century, Tokugawa housing began to economize on the use of wood and adopted cheaper, renewable materials. The newer *shoin* style of light frame houses used timbers only for the posts and beams of the house and lighter sawn boards elsewhere. *Shoin* houses were parti-

73. Ibid., 73–74.
74. Hanley, "Tokugawa Society," 69.

tioned into separate rooms, with ceilings and sliding wall panels and doors that could be decorated easily. They used straw, rush, and reed for tatami and cushions, clay and plaster for walls. Since Japanese sat and slept on the floor, heavy, immovable chairs, large tables, and beds were not needed. Desks, decorative shelves, and storage areas were built into the fabric of the house.[75]

In the *shoin* style, entire rooms were readily opened up to verandas and to the garden, which became an extension of living space. To minimize the use of expensive heating fuel, the Japanese made maximum use of the sun in winter for heating by opening up the house. The open house was compatible with the Japanese approach to domestic heating: the principle was to heat each person's body rather than the air in the room. Charcoal, manufactured in steadily growing quantities, became the fuel of choice—partly because, unlike firewood, it could be controlled and regulated in small portable heaters. With devices such as the *kotatsu,* a small enclosed charcoal heater set under a table and enclosed by a quilt, the inhabitants of a house could be warmed on even the coldest days with little expenditure of fuel. Open hibachis, made of metal or, in later years, of ceramic, also served as portable heaters. Both styles could be moved around the house as the weather changed. Japanese charcoal makers developed refinements in burning to produce charcoal with a higher carbon content that burnt at a higher heat for a longer time. (Since Japanese houses were not airtight, there was little danger of asphyxiation.)[76]

In the warmer regions of Japan, householders gave up the traditional central open-hearth fireplace that warmed a number of people sitting around it while providing heat for cooking and drying food. Instead they adopted the *kamado*—or stove made of brick, stone, or earth—which had openings in the top for the insertion of pots called *kama.* The bottoms of the pots were in direct contact with the flames, rather than the top of the stove, and hence more fuel efficient. With the stove's multiple openings, cooks could prepare several dishes for the meal at once. Only in the mountainous areas and in the north, with their severe winters, did families retain the open-hearth fireplace as a heat source while adopting stoves for cooking.[77]

Perhaps the most important area of restraint lay in the Japanese diet. Rice, of course, was the mainstay of the diet, and rice had a higher yield-to-seed ratio than other food grains. Seafood and soybean and other food grains, rather than meat, supplied the greater amount of protein in the Tokugawa diet. A meat-based diet was probably not feasible in view of the eighteenth-century human-to-land ratio. Setting aside pasture and fodder for livestock

75. Ibid., 30–33.
76. Ibid., 61–62.
77. Ibid.

would not have been a reasonable option. Given a market choice, however, the early modern Japanese would probably have opted for meat. Most ate meat of any sort with gusto and appreciation despite the strictures of Buddhism. When the choice was available, they ate beef, chicken, and even pork raised in Satsuma. In the absence of a domestic livestock industry, the primary source of meat was wild game. Bears, wild boar, deer, rabbits, squirrels, pheasants, doves, ducks, badgers, and other animals sold readily in urban markets. However, steady losses of habitat meant that these supplies were declining by the latter half of the eighteenth century. It is unlikely that, at the time, the majority of Japanese ate meat regularly or commonly.[78]

RESPONSES TO SCARCITY: CONTROL OF HUMAN FERTILITY

The most remarkable response to resource constraints was the widely distributed control over human fertility.[79] Periodic censuses ordered by the shogun reveal a nearly stable population in the early eighteenth to the mid–nineteenth century. Population registers based on the village-level registers of religious faith form the basis for a long-term comparable data series for the commoner population. The 26.1 million total for commoners in 1721 remained stable through four additional censuses, until a drop during a disastrous famine pulled the total down to 24.9 million in 1792; the population reached 27.2 million by the census of 1828.[80] Some 2 million members of samurai households and their servants and retainers, whose higher income and consumption levels were stipulated by the state, did not show noticeable increases throughout the century. The contrast with the demography of the previous century is startling.

This stable population did not result from high mortality rates—on the contrary, early modern Japan's mortality was among the lowest known in the early modern world. Two of the three Malthusian checks on population were not that prominent in this period. Internal peace and relatively infrequent violent protests meant that violence did not claim many casualties. Having few of the most common Eurasian pandemic diseases, such as plague, malaria, typhoid, typhus, and diphtheria, the Japanese did not experience infectious disease as a major killer. Endemic smallpox exacted its toll on children when it struck; however, bouts of influenza and dysentery did not kill off large numbers of the population. Measles epidemics that occurred every twenty or thirty years had high morbidity but relatively low mortality. Com-

78. Ibid., 67.
79. Ibid., 32.
80. Ibid.; Totman, *Early Modern Japan,* 251.

pared to the populations of early modern Europe, Japanese society was relatively healthy.[81]

Zero population growth primarily resulted from decisions made by millions of fertile couples, who, wishing to avoid hard times, chose to raise fewer children. Demographic studies have shown a close, long-term correlation between fluctuations in the prices of rice and fertility. When rice prices shot up, live births went down, and the reverse. Late marriages, lengthened intervals between births by lengthened breast-feeding, contraception, abortions, and infanticide reduced fertility. Lowered frequency of intercourse due to labor migration by males seems to have played a role.[82] In addition to various modes of contraception and abortion, infanticide, although concealed and subject to official disapproval, was widely practiced. Despite its unpleasantness, poorer peasants seem to have employed this device as an effective way to limit children and to regulate the gender of their offspring.[83] Successful societal control of fertility served to limit suffering, starvation, and famine in early modern Japan.

Chronic malnutrition and hunger played a role in damping fertility in the countryside. Lacking income and entitlements, the poorest peasant families faced food scarcities when harvests were disappointing. Poorer women, often underfed and overworked, had sickly and weak babies. By 1700, many landholdings were divided into microholdings barely sufficient to support a family. Only through intensified labor inputs from all members of the family could these small units support the household. Increasingly poorer peasants turned to migratory seasonal labor to supplement household incomes.

RESPONSES TO SCARCITY: INTENSIFIED FISHING AND WHALING

In their search for new resources, early modern Japanese turned to the sea. Intensive fishing put new calories directly into the Japanese diet. New deepwater fishing tapped the abundant fish stocks generated by the southward-flowing arms of the cold Okhotsk Current.[84] Intensified coastal shipping led to the creation of small ports and coastal settlements. Numerous peasants found fishing more rewarding than tilling someone else's fields. Much of the catch went directly into markets and into the food supply, but large quantities of fish were ground into fish meal and sold for use as fertilizers. Any fish

81. Jannetta, *Epidemics and Mortality in Early Modern Japan.*

82. Laurel L. Cornell, "Infanticide in Early Modern Japan? Demography, Culture, and Population Growth," *Journal of Asian Studies* 55 (1996): 14.

83. Cornell argues that infanticide has been overly emphasized in its effects on fertility in Tokugawa Japan.

84. Arne Kalland, *Fishing Villages in Tokugawa Japan* (Honolulu: University of Hawaii Press, 1995).

was suitable for the latter purpose. This encouraged entrepreneurial fisher-men to acquire massive nets that required capstans and dozens of men to haul in entire schools of fish.

At each locality, fishermen developed and improved specialized tech-niques adapted to the immediate environment and to the observed behav-ior of the thirty or more species of fish caught and marketed. On sandy beaches with seafloors clear of rocks and other obstacles, fishermen de-ployed gigantic beach seines as long as 450 meters to pull in great quantities of sardines, sea bream, flying fish, and other species. Some of these seining methods employed secondary nets to frighten fish toward shore so that the beach seine could be run out behind them. In shallow water over rocky grounds, fishermen used boats for gillnetting, boat seining, diving, and spearing. These were also good areas for gathering seaweed and shellfish. For inshore waters from 15 to 40 meters deep, boat seines were the preferred tool. To gather sand lances, a single boat might let out a 190-meter seine in a semicircle, come back to its starting point, and then haul both ends of the net for the catch. Deepwater fishermen used longlines, hand lines, and en-circling nets and trolled.

Daimyo located on the coast claimed the sea as part of their fiefs, just as they did land within their boundaries. In effect, they created sea tenure as well as land tenure. Fishing villages could obtain access to the sea only by pay-ing their lord with products from the sea or with corvée. Coastal waters around Japan therefore became closed territories. There existed a general sense that fish stocks were limited and that they could be exhausted if indi-viduals had open access to beaches and the sea. Each fishing village obtained the right for its men to use a demarcated portion of the shoreline and the sea extending outward indefinitely from that territory. Neighboring domains demarcated coastline and sea territory between them just as they did their land boundaries. Defining sea tenure for individual villages was problematic in enclosed bays. In these situations, entire bays came to be viewed as the shared fishing territory of all villages lining the bay. Each village had a beach for launching boats that it considered its own.

Tokugawa fishermen aggressively pursued sea mammals—dolphins, sea otters, seals, and sea lions—for meat and oil on a scale not seen before. A new whaling industry emerged in the seventeenth century that brought in tons of whale meat for human consumption, whale oil for use as an insecticide, bone to be ground for fertilizer, and teeth and baleen to be carved for vari-ous objects. Whalers caught right and humpback whales when the animals migrated south from the Sea of Okhotsk to the Sea of Japan in December, and northward by the same route in April or May. By the end of the seven-teenth century, whalers were organizing large groups of people in boats to drive whales into large nets set in the open sea. Once a whale was entangled, fishermen killed it with harpoons. These operations required expensive equipment and boats, a large labor force of five hundred to a thousand persons, and careful planning. Entrepreneurs often formed syndicates of investors to finance whaling companies.[85]

Shellfish, sea cucumber, and kelp offered another significant source of food, fertilizer, and other useful products. Divers, most of them women, worked from shore or from boats, frequenting rocky, shallow waters all along the Japanese coast where highly valued abalone (from the family *Haliotidae,* the one-shelled snails) had anchored themselves. Collecting only in the warmer, summer months, the unprotected divers swam as deep as twelve to thirteen meters to reach their prey. The divers *(ama)* used a knife to separate the abalone from rocks and brought them to the surface. After the abalone's shell had been removed, its large muscular foot could be eaten. Traders bought fresh abalone, prized as a culinary delicacy, to sell to urban elites at high prices. They also dried abalone meat by means of ovens or the sun and sold this as a variant. By the end of the seventeenth century, large quantities of dried abalone meat from Japan were exported to the Chinese market. Dried abalone meat, cut in long thin strips *(noshi)*, also served as a decoration when affixed to religious offerings made at some Shinto shrines. Those domains with abalone fisheries also used *noshi* as an appropriate gift for the Tokugawa shogun.

REGENERATION OF FORESTS

Simply limiting births would not have been adequate to sustain such a dense population. By the late 1600s, human pressure on land and forest resources in the archipelago was heavy. In response, Tokugawa society adapted to growing scarcity, not by territorial expansion, but by systematic, sustainable use of renewable resources on land and sea.

Remarkably, Tokugawa Japan recognized the problem of forest depletion and the dangers of soil erosion in a mountainous narrow land in time to do something about it. From the shogun to the daimyo to village assemblies, those persons who held power in early modern Japan halted the predatory stripping of the forests and began the slow process of regrowth and regeneration.

Conservation and protection began with the shogun, who held one-quarter of the land area of the archipelago under his direct administration. The shogun placed responsibility for his own forests with a senior official in the finance ministry, who supervised a staff of officials and foresters. Virtually all the 250 daimyo followed this model and appointed senior officials known as forest or mountain magistrates to take charge of their domainal

85. Arne Kalland and Brian Moeran, *Japanese Whaling: End of an Era?* (London: Curzon Press, 1992), 65–71.

forests. The shogun and each daimyo organized and paid for forest surveys in each domain, using their own officials, to accurately bound the lord's forests and to mark off forests controlled by individual villages. Daimyo tended to claim hill forests endowed with valuable construction timber, whereas villages valued access to adjacent areas with bamboo and mixed broadleaf trees. Foresters, often local residents employed by the forestry officials, oversaw the management of each tract of official forest. State-controlled forests, or the "lord's forests," were scattered throughout the domain in tracts of varying sizes, some quite small. In the aggregate, however, official forests claimed by the shogun or his daimyo occupied the greater share of the archipelago's woodlands.[86]

The shogunate and each domain developed complex laws and administrative rules to protect and nurture state forests. Tokugawa forest laws fully recognized the principle of multiple-use, regulated forestry in which all forestlands "were to yield diverse goods, and they were to yield them to more than one recipient."[87] Occasionally, forestry officials banned entry and access to protect degraded forest stands, or they monopolized timber in specified tracts for state purposes. But forestry officials across the realm also were prepared to assign specific use rights to specific forest areas to individuals, communities, and institutions. These use rights were transferable, legitimate, and justifiable. Rural folk viewed the state forests in their vicinity as potential sources for grazing, green fodder, and other forest products if they were not that already. As the population grew and pressure on village forests rose, peasants everywhere agitated for access to state forest products.

Shogunate and daimyo forestry officials issued a stream of edicts to regulate usage. Depending on the state of the particular tract, recorded tree-by-tree in detailed registers, forest officials might license limited cutting, grazing, and other extraction by peasants. They prohibited cutting of cedar and oak, the most valuable timbers, to retain these for official timbering. Burning for shifting cultivation seems to have been universally prohibited on official lands. Inspections of timber and wood shipments carried out at a network of guard posts on highways and rivers helped officials enforce their edicts.

As the most valuable tree species dwindled, rulers throughout the realm issued sumptuary laws regulating woods used for building and other purposes. Generally, peasants were ordered not to use valuable cedar and oak in their dwellings. The amount of timber allowed for building purposes was regulated by the social status of the recipient. People of higher status could have larger dwellings and thus more timber. Samurai status and rank, carefully delineated by rice payments, limited the size and lavishness of their

86. Totman, *Green Archipelago*, 91–93.
87. Ibid., 88.

dwellings. Rulers prohibited the use of the most valuable woods for mundane purposes such as public signboards, small containers, or household utensils. In effect this constituted a system of public rationing that seems to have had some impact.

The remaining forests in Japan came under the control of village communities. Generally, the village headman and leading families in each village were tied together by shared descent from a common ancestor through the male line. Often the male head of the senior-most family in this patrilineage became headman as a hereditary right. Each village possessed a protective deity in its shrine, on whose behalf rites were performed during the year. In addition to collecting taxes and mustering corvée, the village headman, supported by the dominant families, managed the village woodlands and ponds. These were common property resources that were to yield multiple products to all members of the village. Early in the Tokugawa period, village elites began marking out and claiming village lands to protect them from encroachment by officials. Village territoriality ensured that "foreign" peasants were barred entry to these lands.

Each village developed its own rules to regulate access to fuelwood, fodder, green fertilizer, berries, and thatching grass. These rules constituted a system of rationing by limiting times of access or quantities to be harvested. Headmen and village councils often employed armed guards to ensure that the rules were obeyed. Together, rulers and village elites articulated and enforced complex rules and procedures for the archipelago's forests that were aimed at alleviating growing scarcity by slowing demand.

One solution was the discovery of an alternative fuel. Late in the seventeenth century, peasants near Kyushu began burning ground coal taken from coal seams in that locality.[88] Heavy fuel demands by salt makers, potteries, and sugar makers could be met by coal mined in Kyushu. Preferred fuel such as pine boughs for salt making became expensive and scarce, and more and more salt makers bought Kyushu coal. In the eyes of the Japanese, coal was a noxious substance that, when burnt, put ash and soot in the air which smelled bad and damaged crops. Farmers also protested against water pollution from coal mining around Kyushu. Local scarcity dictated that coal use continue and even expand, but there was no enthusiasm for this substitute fuel. Wood retained its aesthetic appeal as fuel.

Rationing and protection helped, but more was needed. Increasingly, Tokugawa Japanese engaged in regenerative forestry. At its most basic, this consisted in simply closing off cutover lands to human entry to encourage desired species to regrow. On a more sophisticated level, however, foresters in early modern Japan began to engage in systematic silviculture—purposeful tree planting based on a growing body of empirical knowledge. The tech-

88. Totman, *Early Modern Japan*, 271–72.

niques of obtaining seeds, preparing seedbeds, and transplanting them to permanent sites were perfected. Techniques of slip culture were also well understood. Japanese foresters took cuttings or shoots from young trees in winter and inserted them into either transplant beds or permanent sites. After the initial planting, foresters replaced losses with new seeds or cuttings for several years in order to ensure a full stand. Every year, foresters had to weed out grasses, annual weeds, brush, and vines and other competing vegetation that threatened their trees. As the trees grew, foresters periodically thinned stands for optimal returns and limbed larger trees to shape the most desirable timber. They also practiced coppicing by leaving live stumps for regrowth to obtain steady yields of wood.

Village intellectuals, itinerant scholars, and minor officials published a prolific technical literature consisting of farm manuals and journals devoted to increasing agricultural productivity. Aimed at the surprisingly large number of Japanese farmers who were literate, these manuals included detailed advice on obtaining sustained yields of timber, fuel, and green fodder from village woodlands.

In each domain, the daimyo requisitioned labor to plant trees and care for them under the forester's direction. Local elites assigned villagers to tree planting and nurturing on a regular basis in the village lands. The notion of plantation forestry—of trees grown as a slowly maturing crop—took hold. A forester from Tsugaru domain wrote, "The art of forestry is different from that of paddy or dry field. Though one may be spared flood, drought, frost, or snow, he still must give general care to the area for about ten years before withdrawing human effort. If this is done, the forests will be as though filled with a treasure whose virtue is so immense it will reach to one's children and grandchildren. Truly, one's prosperity will be eternal."[89] Following these principles, rural folk began planting trees on a regular basis using family or paid labor. Daimyo officials mustered labor to plant trees every spring.

Entrepreneurial foresters moved eagerly into a commercial mode by planting valuable trees on their own land or tracts leased from villagers in various profit-sharing arrangements. In central Japan, near the major urban centers, a market-oriented, commercial forestry industry appeared. Near Osaka, where there was good soil and a mild climate, unirrigated lands were used to grow high-quality cedar seedlings for sale. Brand-name plantation forest products were marketed. For example, the Yoshino plantations produced hundreds of thousands of four-inch barrel staves from high-quality cedar to meet the needs of the rice wine industry of Osaka. Here, foresters responded to a direct market link with brand-name products.

Widely accepted and applied, protective and regenerative forestry halted deforestation in Tokugawa Japan. Afforestation replaced exploitative over-

89. Totman, *Green Archipelago*, 124.

cutting. Early modern Japan retained its green hillsides, reduced soil erosion, and retained a supply of usable forest products.

THE NORTHERN FRONTIER: TOKUGAWA EXPLOITATION OF HOKKAIDO

Japan under the Tokugawa expanded its control north to the islands of Hokkaido and beyond to Sakhalin and the Kuril Islands in a trading and settlement frontier identical in its features to those of North America, Russia, and China. Japanese access to Matsumae domain from the main islands was strictly controlled and limited. In the seventeenth century, about twenty thousand Japanese resided within the domain. By the early nineteenth century, this had risen only to about thirty thousand persons. The settlers, known as *wajin*, did not engage in cultivation, even though millets and barley could have been grown. Instead the Matsumae rulers discouraged agriculture for both settlers and Ainus alike. Some settlers engaged in herring fisheries and others mined gold along the rivers. The primary economic base of the domain was trade with the Ainus. Matsumae extracted natural resources from the Ainus in an unequal exchange for Japanese implements and trade goods.

Annual, rigidly ritualized gift-giving ceremonies between Matsumae officials and Ezo chiefs ratified a brisk trade in commodities. Estate holders in the Matsumae domain set up trading posts on lands they held where Japanese merchants could come to trade with the Ainus. Japanese traders exchanged rice, tobacco, swords, sake, yeast, and other goods for deerskins, sea otter pelts, and other furs; salmon; kelp; and hawk and eagle feathers.[90] The Matsumae slowly extended their trading posts and guardhouses northward on both coasts deeper into Ezo territory, and the number of Japanese settlers increased. In the period 1799 to 1821, and again in 1854, the shogun assumed direct administrative control over Matsumae domain and the Ezo lands beyond.

The Ainus, a nonliterate Caucasoid people, formed the indigenous population of Hokkaido, Sakhalin, and the Kuril Islands. Relatively few, they may have numbered as many as forty thousand persons in the late 1600s.[91] By Japanese standards, they had a distinctively hirsute physical appearance, spoke a strange language with several dialects, held primitive animist religious beliefs, and possessed a relatively simple material culture. The Ainus

90. Brett L. Walker, "Reappraising the *Sakoku* Paradigm: The Ezo Trade and the Extension of Tokugawa Political Space into Hokkaido," *Journal of Asian History* 30 (1996).

91. Brett L. Walker, "Matsumae Domain and the Conquest of Ainu Lands: Ecology and Culture in Tokugawa Expansionism, 1593–1799" (Ph.D. diss., University of Oregon, 1997), 286–87. This is Walker's estimate for Hokkaido, Sakhalin, and the Kuril Islands combined.

were loosely organized into households, local settlement groups defined by patrilineal kinship ties, each with a headman, and an aggregate of all local settlements that lived along the same river valley.[92] Combinations of river valley groups were arrayed in chiefdoms headed by Ainu leaders.

Ainu subsistence depended on nearly year-round hunting of deer *(Cervus nippon)* and brown bears *(Ursus arctos)* in the upper reaches of the river valleys. They killed both animals with bows and arrows tipped with aconite poison and pursued them with dogs. They also relied on spring bows set on stumps or logs, designed to release a poison-tipped arrow when the prey tripped a cord strung along the trail. Ainu hunters were especially anxious to capture live bear cubs to rear for ritual killing in one of their most solemn religious ceremonies. The most abundant food source was salmon caught along the rivers as they made their spawning runs each year. The Ainus used an array of spears, platforms, nets, traps, and weirs to catch salmon. They had a repertoire of efficient, specialized techniques that varied with the progress of the salmon runs—even using torches for night fishing. The salmon season began in the summer with spawning runs of cherry salmon *(Oncorhynchus masou);* in fall were the dog salmon *(Oncorhynchus keta)* runs, lasting until December or January. The other major food items were nuts, berries, roots, and plants, which they dried and kept for winter consumption.[93] They also gathered plants for use as industrial materials.

During the sixteenth century, the Ainus maintained a high degree of political and economic independence. Ainu chiefs negotiated with and sometimes fought with Japanese intruders into Ezo. To the northeast, they traded and interacted freely with fellow Ainus on Sakhalin Island and in the Kurils. The Ainu chiefs built and maintained fleets of sailing vessels used to carry products of the hunt and fishery to trade for Chinese silks and other prestige goods and to obtain Russian-manufactured leather coats and hard liquor in the Kurils and Sakhalin. Ainu hunters killed sea otters for their pelts and obtained valuable goods from the Chinese traders they encountered. In the seventeenth century, the intensifying Tokugawa control over Ezo and the forced channeling of all Ainu trade through the Matsumae domain reduced the Ainus to middlemen who were compelled to continue the northeastern trade to satisfy Japanese desires for prestige Chinese goods.

Prior to 1615, trade between the Matsumae domain and Ainus occurred only once a year at a single port, Fukuyama, to which the Ainus traveled in a large coastal sailing vessel they built. Thereafter, the Matsumae ruler expanded trade relations by founding trading posts along the coastal rivers and

---

92. Hitoshi Watanabe, *The Ainu Ecosystem: Environment and Group Structure,* edited by the American Ethnological Society, rev. ed. (Seattle: University of Washington Press, 1973), 7–18.
93. Ibid., 19–31, 41, 81.

assigning monopoly trading rights for each post to one of his retainers.[94] The Matsumae traders offered large quantities of rice, salt, yeast, cloth and thread, iron pots and kettles, iron knives and tools, lacquerware, and other luxury goods. Two stimulants became increasingly important: rice wine (sake) and tobacco. The Ainus, in common with other peoples around the world at the same level of material development, found these products especially appealing.

Japanese in the Matsumae territories mobilized and directed the Ainus to hunt, fish, and gather for export. In return, the Ainus developed a variety of commodities for trade—especially the products of the hunt. In 1854, a Japanese observer wrote, "Ainu, when the winter fishing months end, journey into the mountain recesses to hunt deer, river otter, marten, eagles, (and other animals). They also hunt along the coast, where they take seal, sea lions, (and other marine mammals). This is their livelihood *(seigyo)*. At trading posts *(kaisho)* they trade (these commodities) for rice, sake, tobacco, cotton, needles, and thread. (The game that the Ainu bring to the trading posts) is called 'hunted commodities.'"[95]

Each year, tens of thousands of Ainu-supplied deerskins from Ezo competed with deerskins imported from Taiwan and Southeast Asia in the metropolitan markets. Traders snapped up bear furs and bear gallbladders for medicinal purposes. Smoked salmon from the Ainu fishery supplied markets in Osaka and Edo. Sea otter pelts brought high returns. Ainus gathered large quantities of dried sea cucumber, abalone, and kelp along the shore. In the late 1700s, a total of about three hundred Ainu boats worked the coastal waters for a sea cucumber catch that might yield 120,000 in a day. Several Ainu chiefs in eastern Ezo continued to manage a profitable trade exchanging Japanese coins and trade goods for sea otter pelts from the Kuril Islands. They then exchanged these pelts with Matsumae traders for rice and other commodities.[96]

During the Tokugawa centuries, Ainus hunted increasingly for trade and less for subsistence. They relied more and more on the trading posts for bales of rice to feed themselves. Most of them eagerly accepted various forms of seasonal credit from the Matsumae traders. Increasingly, Ainus hunted and fished to become "rich," to acquire trade goods, and to become great men in their society by display of lacquerware, fine clothing, swords, and ironware. Invariably, however, intensified hunting for the market meant exploitation beyond sustainable levels. A Japanese observer, echoing the views of other writers, commented in 1715 that "in recent years natural resources

---

94. Edmonds, "Northern Frontiers of Qing China and Tokugawa Japan," 85–112.
95. Quoted in Walker, "Matsumae Domain and the Conquest of Ainu Lands," 133.
96. Ibid., 140, 212.

throughout Ezo have become very scarce," and that deer pelts were in short supply. By the early nineteenth century, only three thousand deerskin pelts a year emerged from Ezo.[97]

The Matsumae domain encouraged and supported its own extractive activities within and beyond its domain, which were carried out, for the most part, by Japanese settlers themselves. These included an elaborate system for catching hawks for the burgeoning falconry market. Since the late medieval period, falconry had become deeply embedded in Japanese warrior culture as a symbol of power. The Matsumae domain was a principal source of hawks during the Tokugawa period, and the sale and presentation of hawks was an important part of its economy. By the late 1600s, Japanese hawk hunters *(takamachi)* had set up some three hundred sites from which to capture or purchase hawks. From these, they roamed freely throughout much of Ezo. The hawk hunters forced Ainus to act as porters and to supply dogs for food for the captive hawks they possessed. So offensive were these hawk hunters that they became a primary target during Shakushain's War of 1669. By the eighteenth century, hawks had become scarce, and fewer than two dozen birds per year were captured.[98]

The Matsumae domain steadily prospected for and engaged in hydraulic gold mining along many of Ezo's rivers. The Portuguese missionary Diego Carvalho described the industry:

> Their way of extracting gold from these mines is as follows. When they have decided on the mountain range in which, according to experts, there ought to be gold, friends and acquaintances get together and[,] united in a body[,] purchase from the [ruler] of Matsumae so many ells of the rivers which flow through the said range, for so many bars of gold, and they must needs pay these bars whether they find gold or not. And when a great number of such groups come to the river, they divert the flow of water along a different course and then dig into the sand which remains, until they reach the living stone and rock beneath the river bed. And in the sand lodged in the rents and fissures of the rock is found gold as fine as beach gravel.[99]

As might be expected, these mining practices disrupted spawning beds for salmon and reduced the annual Ainu catch on that river. Along with hawk hunting, this gold mining and the resultant salmon depletion were among the Ainu grievances that led to the 1669 war of resistance.

Over the two and a half centuries of growing dependency, the Ainus suffered the kinds of subjugation, humiliation, cultural despair, loss of eco-

97. Ibid., 155–56, 159.
98. Ibid., 60–91.
99. Quoted in ibid., 119–20.

nomic well-being, disease, and early death common to similar groups around the early modern world. Ainu intellectual, political, and economic horizons were constrained by Japanese pressure and control over their lives. The Ainus suffered the contempt and racial antipathy of contemporary Japanese. Official edicts prohibited Ainus from entering or settling within the Matsumae domain and strictly regulated Japanese movement into the remainder of Hokkaido. Moreover, the Matsumae domain went to great lengths to maintain a clear ethnic boundary between Ainus and Japanese by regulating language, clothing, and hairstyles.[100] That Ainus depended on Japanese traders for rice as a staple, rather than on deer and salmon, was especially damaging as these resources dwindled under intensified hunting and fishing. Episodes of starvation among Ainus recurred. Impoverished Ainus found work as laborers in the herring fisheries or in other capacities for the Japanese. Smallpox epidemics brought by the Japanese caused heavy mortality among the Ainus. Under these conditions, Ainu numbers thinned to as few as fifteen thousand persons in the mid–nineteenth century.[101]

CONCLUSION

Between 1700 and 1867, Tokugawa Japan avoided resorting to imports and so carefully managed its limited resources that it avoided catastrophic scarcities and social upheaval. In a truly remarkable societal response, early modern Japan responded to and overcame its ecological and economic crisis. The Tokugawa economy continued to flourish, showing manifold signs of economic prosperity and growth. Material comfort and ease rose for most of the society, but no Japanese evaded the resource constraints imposed by necessity. For the laborers and small tenant farmers in the countryside, the burden of resource scarcity was heavier. They worked long and hard to increase yields on smallholdings and, in times of scarcity, did not possess the entitlements required to purchase food and comfort in the marketplace.

We can only speculate as to why late Tokugawa Japan displayed such ingenuity and determination in coping with scarcity. Obviously, political stability and peace encouraged Japan's rulers to plan for the future and to impose policies that would be beneficial for the entire realm. Social stability in a society with minimal ethnic and religious differences seems to have been an advantage. As important was the cooperation and participation by dis-

100. David L. Howell, "Ainu Ethnicity and the Boundaries of the Early Modern Japanese State," *Past and Present*, no. 142 (1994): 86–87.

101. Walker, "Matsumae Domain and the Conquest of Ainu Lands," 287. The Japanese census figure for Ainus in 1854 was 15,171 persons.

armed local village elites in governance and in the techniques of production. Literacy was unquestionably a great asset to the dissemination of technical and moral information to the populace. Relative, self-imposed isolation also mattered. Japan under the Tokugawa was a bounded world with finite resources defined by islands in an archipelago.

Chapter 6

Landscape Change and Energy Transformation in the British Isles

Between 1500 and 1800, in common with other early modern societies, the British monarchy and its agencies and other private organizations developed new capability, efficiency, stability, and durability.[1] New, complex, large-scale organizations that enhanced human capacity for collective action mobilized and directed the rising flow of natural resources within and, increasingly, outside, the British Isles. These new organizations, whether monarchical or private, aggressively sought to increase their wealth and power by transforming the natural world. More and more persons found a path to power and wealth by working within government agencies and private companies that directly and indirectly exploited the natural resources of England, Wales, Scotland, Ireland, and the British colonies.

During the early modern centuries, the societies of the British Isles underwent other important changes. Human numbers swelled threefold, from around 5 million in 1500 to about 16 million in 1800, in spite of sustained out-migration to North America and the Caribbean.[2] Domestic warfare slowed and virtually ended as the London-based English regime imposed its power throughout the British Isles. Apart from continuing low-intensity pacification in Ireland, the mid–seventeenth century battles of the English Civil War and the Jacobite rebellions, Britain was at peace and rarely even threatened by internal revolt or external invasion. Domestic tranquility encouraged economic investment and spared society the costly, painful process of continually restoring destroyed material and social capital. Early modern

---

1. Michael J. Braddick, *State Formation in Early Modern England, c.1550–1700* (Cambridge: Cambridge University Press, 2000).
2. Colin McEvedy and Richard Jones, *Atlas of World Population History* (London: A. Lane, 1978), 49.

Britain shared with Tokugawa Japan the unusual benefit of internal peace and relative political stability.

Despite rising human numbers, food security in the British Isles actually improved. Better land management with enhanced capital investment intensified land use. This, in turn, pushed up agricultural productivity in nearly every region of the British Isles. Improved cultivation practices—planting better seeds, rotating crops, manuring, and other incremental changes—generated higher crop yields. Improved livestock breeding and pasture management raised meat and milk production. The cultivated area expanded as British peasants cleared, sowed, drained, and improved their fields. Vigorous market demand driven by rising populations, along with better roads and river and coastal-water transport, stimulated agricultural production. By mid–seventeenth century, famines were no longer an expected and unwelcome fact of life, in large measure because of spectacular increases in agricultural productivity but also because of cheap food imports.

England, largely by virtue of its maritime strength, became a world power with colonies and possessions and trading interests on a global scale. Colonial domination and world trading generated tribute and profits that translated into a favorable balance of trade. British consumers benefited from a growing influx of butter, meat, and staves from Ireland; silver and gold from the New World; saltpeter, spices, dyes, and textiles from the East Indies; copper and iron from Sweden; timber, potash, tar, and pitch from the Baltic lands and North America; furs and deerskins from North America and Siberia; coffee from Arabia; tea and porcelain from China; sugar from the Caribbean; and fish from Icelandic and North American waters. British producers benefited from the market created by transplanted compatriots—a quarter million strong by 1700—who offered a protected market for all manner of manufactured goods.[3] Power and trading efficiency conferred material prosperity and security.

Finally, the most remarkable transformation occurred in energy. Wood ceased to be the primary energy source, and coal became the fuel of choice for domestic and industrial purposes in the British Isles—well before the steam engine created a new, ravenous demand for coal. By mid–eighteenth century, the majority of Britons were buying and burning coal rather than wood to heat their houses, to cook their food, and to manufacture essential products. This changeover reflected wood's growing scarcity and soaring price, especially near larger towns and cities. Coal, on the other hand, was produced in abundance and sold at prices that rose slowly and moderately by comparison to fuelwood. Coal had been burned for limited purposes by

3. Nuala Zahedieh, "London and the Colonial Consumer in the Late Seventeenth Century," *Economic History Review* 47, no. 2 (1994).

other societies, but adoption of fossil fuels as an energy source in place of biomass fuels was unprecedented in human history.[4]

The presence of abundant, easily worked outcroppings of coal obviously made this innovation possible. Nevertheless, it was the combination of a state system inclined toward entrepreneurial activity, a society in which the wealthier landowners were accustomed to venturing into trade and production without loss of status, and the cumulative effect of a number of technical advances in industry, among other elements, that fostered the mining and consumption of coal.

GROWTH OF A POWERFUL CENTRALIZED STATE

During the sixteenth century, Henry VIII (r. 1509–1547) and later rulers of the Tudor dynasty built on earlier traditions to create a unified, powerful, monarchy. By century's end, Elizabeth I headed a strong, centralizing national state whose institutions were so robust that they were slowly developing a life of their own, independent of the whims of individual rulers.[5] A relatively efficient royal secretariat, working smoothly with the Privy Council, conducted the routine business of state. Ruthless, single-minded royal policies and actions inexorably demolished independent powers held by the nobility, by the church, by the chieftains of Ireland, and by local barons living along the Scottish borders and in other frontier regions. Tudor rulers also created channels for expression of political opinion and acceptable routes by which ambitious men could rise in royal service. Parliament retained its control over finance and thereby served as a check on the monarchy.

Strengthening the military arm of the state presented peculiar difficulties in England, since the monarchy could never pull together the resources necessary to create a large standing army and popular sentiment resisted that step. The primary concern of the Tudors was to disarm the great magnates whose armed retainers had supplied forces for royal wars in the past. As royal pressure caused these forces to dwindle, the monarchy relied on county militias headed by lord lieutenants. All able-bodied free men were liable for service and for providing their own arms on a scale determined by income. The latter were useful only for domestic purposes.[6] For foreign wars, the king turned to professional soldiers mobilized and paid for specific campaigns.

4. Brinley Thomas, "Escaping from Constraints: The Industrial Revolution in a Malthusian Context," *Journal of Interdisciplinary History* 15, no. 4 (1985); Thomas, "Was There an Energy Crisis in Great Britain in the Seventeenth Century?" *Explorations in Economic History* 23 (1986).

5. D. M. Loades, *Tudor Government: Structures of Authority in the Sixteenth Century* (Oxford: Blackwell, 1997).

6. John McGurk, *The Elizabethan Conquest of Ireland: The 1590s Crisis* (Manchester: Manchester University Press, 1997).

The most far-reaching step taken early in the dynasty was the establish-ment of a standing navy. Henry VIII, by 1547, had expanded his fleet to nearly sixty ships, varying in size from the behemoth flagship the *Henry Grace à Dieu*, which displaced fifteen hundred tons, to small rowbarges of twenty tons. The larger ships carried the most advanced guns of the time. Some he had commissioned and built in his own dockyards, some he had purchased, and some he had seized as prizes.[7] Annual costs for the fleet amounted to about five thousand pounds per year. By 1540, Henry had established a Council for Marine Causes consisting of three admirals, the clerk of the ships, treasurer, master of the ordnance, and others—all full-time, paid offi-cials.[8] Since his early conflict with France from 1511 to 1514, Henry had con-ceived of the navy as a military asset that should be continuously maintained. The navy served as the first line of defense of his kingdom and was used ag-gressively against French naval forces.

Away from London, in the core area of southern England, the Tudors bound local notables to the throne by requiring new, multifaceted services. In the new system, local justices of the peace became the key local officers of the Crown. The justices were organized into a thirty- to forty-member com-mission of the peace for each county. As they had earlier, the justices con-vened four times a year to receive indictments and hold trials at the quarter sessions. But the Tudor system added critically important administrative and police functions to the commission's judicial role: "The Justices of the Peace be those in whom at this time for the repressing of robbers, theeves, and vagabunds, of privie complots and conspiracies, for riotes and violences, and all other misdemeanours in the common wealth, the prince putteth his spe-cial trust."[9] Serving on such a commission became an honor much sought af-ter by the local gentry. By century's end, the justices were the most visible symbol of royal power in each county.

The Tudor state slowly but steadily extended its territorial reach from the fertile, intensively cultivated, tightly governed counties of southern England north to the outlying pastoral uplands of Wales and the Welsh borders and to Ireland. Nearly half the area of the British Isles consisted of sparsely set-tled lands, where the climate was harsher, the soils poorer, and the terrain rougher than in the rich, arable lowlands of southern England. The uplands were subject to political turbulence and insecurity that encouraged milita-rization. Strong kinship affiliations and powerful magnates with near royal autonomy and large, armed retinues fostered internecine violence among

---

7. D. M. Loades, *The Tudor Navy: An Administrative, Political, and Military History* (Aldershot, Eng.: Ashgate; Brookfield, Vt.: Scolar Press, 1992), 88.

8. J. R. Hill and Bryan Ranft, *The Oxford Illustrated History of the Royal Navy* (Oxford: Oxford University Press, 1995), 31–32.

9. Loades, *Tudor Government*, 125, quoting Thomas Smith, *De Republica Angelorum*, 104.

Map 6.1 Coalfields in the British Isles, c. 1700. Adapted from John Hatcher, *Before 1700: Towards the Age of Coal*, vol. 1 of *The History of the British Coal Industry* (Oxford: Clarendon Press, 1993), map 1.1, pp. 4–5.

pastoral peoples. Rather than plow tillage, people in these regions relied on transhumance within a kinship-based system of landownership and management. The English perceived extension of state power as a civilizing mission to restrain what they viewed as instability and irrational violence in the uplands. This was the only means by which the "cultural degeneracy" of the uncivilized and barbarous peoples who inhabited these wild fastnesses could be rectified.[10] Pastoralism was equated with barbarism—an attitude that colored British attitudes toward other pastoral peoples around the world as the British empire expanded.

Henry VIII intensified central power in each of these regions. Noble feuding in the marches of Wales brought royal intervention and a series of brutal pacification campaigns. Thereafter, the 1707 Act of Union imposed the same English law and administrative arrangements on Wales as obtained in southern England. A 1541 act proclaimed Henry king of Ireland. The act was intended "to provide for political unity of all the island's inhabitants in a single community of subjects under the unilateral jurisdiction of the crown."[11] All the troublesome Gaelic and Anglo-Norman nobles and chiefs whose territories previously had fallen outside English-controlled territory around Dublin were asked to acknowledge the sovereignty of the Tudor king. In return, they gained confirmation of their holdings and the rights of all freeborn English subjects. This was a first step in what was conceived as the civilizing of Ireland.

Scotland, however, was the great exception to this generalization. During the sixteenth century, the kingdom of Scotland was a well-governed early modern European state and a competing locus of power in the British Isles. As the London-centered English regime of the Tudors consolidated its power, various conventional scenarios for its relationship with Scotland were possible. These ranged from peaceful coexistence to continued warfare aimed at conquest. However, what actually developed during the course of the seventeenth century was unification between the two regimes. The British regime that emerged from this union gained immense strength from the willing cooperation, energy, and skills of the Scots who enlisted in its domestic and overseas enterprises. The Act of Union of 1707 offered a peaceful, positive solution to what might have become a debilitating series of wars, conquest, and bitter resistance in which either regime might have prevailed.

The movement toward union began with a dynastic accident. When Elizabeth I died in 1603, she left neither children nor surviving siblings. There-

10. Stephen G. Ellis, "Tudor State Formation and the Shaping of the British Isles," in *Conquest and Union: Fashioning a British State, 1485–1725*, edited by Stephen G. Ellis and Sarah Barber (London: Longman, 1995), 46.

11. Colm Lennon, *Sixteenth-Century Ireland: The Incomplete Conquest* (New York: St. Martin's Press, 1995), 154.

fore, under English law, her cousin King James VI, the Stuart king of Scotland, succeeded her as James I of England. James, the first of the Stuarts, was a dual monarch who wore two crowns: that of England and of Scotland. This Union of the Crowns did not create a unitary state, but James took the lead in formulating plans for the political integration of the two kingdoms by uniting their laws, parliaments, churches, councils, and economies. He failed in this initiative in the face of powerful opposition from both the English and the Scots. Nevertheless, the idea had been firmly planted.[12]

Under the early Stuart rulers, James I (r. 1603–1625) and Charles I (r. 1625–1649), the Tudor-built monarchy and centralizing state structure faltered and then split apart in civil war. Between 1639 and 1642, empty treasuries, refusals to pay new royal taxes, disorders in London and in the countryside, and defiance on the part of the county gentry were signs of state breakdown. Between 1642 and 1649, royalists and parliamentarians fought a bitter war that ended with the defeat and execution of Charles I.

In 1649, Oliver Cromwell, commander of the parliamentary forces, became Lord Protector of the English Commonwealth. The new regime was more intrusive, centralized, and militarized than anything that had come before it. Cromwell commanded a standing army of seventy thousand that was not disbanded after the civil war ended. Growth in the navy surpassed that of the army. By 1659, the Commonwealth had added 217 vessels to the original 35 ships whose masters and crews chose to support Parliament in 1648.[13] The navy played a critical role in preserving the Commonwealth by aggressive action against royalist fleets and privateers; in consolidating authority over Ireland, the Channel Islands, the West Indies, and Virginia; and in action against Portugal, Holland, France, Spain, and the Baltic powers.[14] The Navigation Act of 1651, touching off a purely naval war with the Dutch, gave notice of a new link between the navy and maritime trade.

During the English Civil War, the Scots sided with Charles I but were defeated at the Battle of Worcester by Oliver Cromwell. Cromwell's army occupied Scotland as a conquered country. In 1651, the English Parliament made an offer, a Tender of Union, to Scotland, which was accepted. This offer, never implemented, would have sent thirty Scottish representatives to the Westminster Parliament, abolished the Scottish Parliament, administered Scottish justice by both English and Scottish judges, and established

12. Brian P. Levack, *The Formation of the British State: England, Scotland, and the Union, 1603–1707* (Oxford: Clarendon Press; New York: Oxford University Press, 1987). See also Rosalind Mitchison, *Lordship to Patronage: Scotland, 1603–1745* (Edinburgh: Edinburgh University Press, 1990).

13. John Brewer, *The Sinews of Power: War, Money, and the English State, 1688–1783*, 1st Amer. ed. (New York: Knopf, 1989), 11.

14. B. S. Capp, *Cromwell's Navy: The Fleet and the English Revolution, 1648–1660* (Oxford: Clarendon Press; New York: Oxford University Press, 1989), 42–114.

complete free trade between the two countries. The proposed union died in 1659 when the Protectorate, Cromwell's government, failed.[15]

Throughout the Protectorate, sharp conflicts over the nature and direction of the state and society were never resolved. When the Protector died in 1658, holding kinglike powers and stature, his son Richard, unable to govern, left the office.[16] Under General George Monck's direction, a reassembled Parliament agreed on the restoration of the monarchy as the price of much-longed-for political stability.

Charles II, son of the executed king, arrived in London in 1660 to resume the throne on terms dictated by Parliament.[17] The older Tudor system that rested on an alliance between the monarchy and gentry, nobility, and church was refurbished. In a series of statutes, Parliament reestablished the Anglican Church under the supremacy of the king and passed a number of repressive measures to ensure conformity. As former Cromwellites were turned out, royalist gentry assumed their posts as justices of the peace and recovered at least some of their confiscated lands and estates.[18] Parliament, however, insisted on the restraints accepted by Charles I in 1641: the king could not set up his own courts and tribunals such as the Star Chamber; he could not tax without parliamentary approval; and Parliament must be called at least every three years.

Charles died in 1685 after a remarkably successful twenty-five-year reign, during which he gathered centralized powers into his own hands. His brother, James II, duke of York and an avowed Catholic, succeeded him. James's authoritarian measures and his attempts to improve conditions for English Catholics crystallized heavy resistance to the Stuarts. Prince William of Orange, stadtholder of the Netherlands and James's brother-in-law, landed an invasion force in England and called for a free Parliament to be formed. James II abandoned the throne and fled to France. A new Covenant Parliament offered the throne to William, who became William III of England.

Between 1689 and 1714, with a newly constrained monarch and a reinvigorated Parliament, and under the impetus of European war, the centralized British state acquired unprecedented resources, power, and capability. Immediately after William III's accession, the House of Commons voted to support their new monarch in a war against France. The war, welcomed by William as an extension of his earlier anti-Catholic, anti-French diplomacy,

15. Levack, *The Formation of the British State,* 9–11.

16. For a comparative overview of the English revolution and its causes, see Jack A. Goldstone, *Revolution and Rebellion in the Early Modern World* (Berkeley and Los Angeles: University of California Press, 1991), 63–169.

17. Geoffrey S. Holmes, *The Making of a Great Power: Late Stuart and Early Georgian Britain, 1660–1722* (London: Longman, 1993), 27–43.

18. Ibid., 35–37.

was prolonged, bloody, and expensive. The Nine Years' War proved to be only the prologue to more than a century of continuing warfare, with France as the principal enemy. The demands of war steeled the powers of the state. The rising complexity and scale of the British state can be seen in the central machinery of government, in tax collection and fiscal management, in the military and its resources, and in the extension of the state into colonial and quasi-colonial systems.

Union with Scotland remained a highly visible, public issue. At the Restoration in 1660, the Union of the Crowns was restored; it remained intact through the dynastic shift to the house of Hanover in 1688. Throughout this period of nearly a half century, the prospect of more meaningful political union between England and Scotland was the leading topic of public discourse in both countries. Proposal after proposal for union surfaced. Heated debates in both parliaments, equally vociferous pamphlets, public and private letters, and ongoing discussions among both elite and nonelite groups addressed the complex issues surrounding this question.[19]

By 1702, however, there was a serious possibility that Scotland would not accept the Hanoverian succession after Queen Anne, especially in view of Scottish unhappiness with the War of Spanish Succession. At this juncture, Queen Anne and her advisors, aided by Whig support in England and the Court Party in Scotland, permitted a successful union initiative in 1706. Commissioners appointed by the queen negotiated articles of union that were approved by both parliaments as a treaty on May 1, 1707.[20]

The new entity, the United Kingdom of Great Britain, consisted of a single crown, one indivisible monarchy, and one British Parliament. To this Parliament, the Scots sent forty-five members and eighteen elected peers. The treaty established free trade and granted Scotland the right to trade freely with the colonies. Scottish personal and criminal laws, the judiciary, and the church remained intact and separate. Scotland assumed the burden of paying taxes and customs at the English rate. Scots were now naturalized citizens of a larger, unitary state, that of Great Britain.[21]

This brought Scotland directly under the control of a newly capable and efficient regime. Under what was emerging as a limited parliamentary monarchy, William and his successors shared power and collective responsibility with a cabinet headed by a prime minister and with a parliament that now met annually. Circumscribed by limited financial resources, the king was forced to resort to Parliament for raising money—whether by taxation or borrowing. Parliamentary committees and boards regularly initiated in-

19. Levack, *The Formation of the British State*, 13–15.
20. Ibid., 12–13.
21. Ibid.

quiries about expenditures to obtain data from records and officials as fodder for debates. Increasingly, the fiscal operations of the state were transparent to a sizeable public.

The central administration grew in size and complexity. The Crown under the later Stuarts had already begun to shift from tax farming to taxes directly collected by officials, and from fee collecting to salaried officials. By the 1720s, there were approximately twelve thousand full-time civil servants in government employ.[22] Over half these men were engaged in collecting the excise tax on beer, spirits, and other items of everyday consumption, such as coal, leather, and candles. Excise men had to make regular rounds, carry out intricate measurements, and maintain scrupulous sets of books. New and old government departments—the Board of Trade, the Post Office, the Stamp Office, the Ordnance Office, the Navy Board—employed salaried and pensioned, full-time civil servants who worked long hours and developed expertise in their jobs. New methodical and rational procedures involved the use of arithmetical calculations and rudimentary statistics, audits and inspections, and systems of sanctions. Institutional loyalty was fostered by "an ethos of public duty and private probity."[23] These new practices often existed side-by-side with lavish sinecures and fee-paid posts in the older departments. However, the rewards for able men who began as clerks and worked their way up to serving as heads of offices like the Navy Board were considerable.

Between 1689 and 1714, the state "drastically remodeled" its fiscal operations and intensified the revenue burden on its subjects.[24] By the end of the War of Spanish Succession in 1713, there were approximately 135,000 men in the military (92,000 in the army and 43,000 in the navy). The average annual military expenditure was 7 million pounds, against total annual tax revenues of 5.4 million pounds.[25] The latter figure was three times the burden imposed by Cromwell under the Protectorate.

Financing the wars took extraordinary measures. First, the government sharply increased and expanded customs duties, expanded the excise tax, and contrived a new county-by-county tax on land rents. The latter, collected by local tax officers supervised by gentry commissioners in each county, brought in 2 million pounds each year. Second, in 1692–1693, the Treasury Commission floated a loan to the public for 1 million pounds that offered lifetime annuities, guaranteed by Parliament and funded through the yield of enhanced excise taxes. Successfully subscribed, this began a truly national, long-term debt, not monies owed to the monarch, in which loans were used to meet wartime expenses. Third, the Bank of England, chartered

22. Brewer, *The Sinews of Power,* 68.
23. Ibid., 69.
24. Holmes, *The Making of a Great Power,* 266.
25. Brewer, *The Sinews of Power,* 30, table 2.1.

as a private company in 1694, became the preferred channel to manage both short-term and long-term government loans. These measures helped to set up a market in London in government securities and to build a widespread group of investors who were beneficiaries of the regime.[26] By 1714, the national debt raised by these measures totaled 36.2 million pounds.

Britain's greatest investment was in the navy. Partly stimulated by the naval wars with the Dutch, the British fleet had grown spectacularly under Charles II. Between 1660 and 1688, the navy commissioned and built 107 warships. On average in this period, the navy consumed approximately a quarter of state expenditures.[27] In 1714, 225 vessels were in commission at a capital investment of 2.25 million pounds, or the equivalent of 4 percent of estimated national income.[28] To build and equip a first-rate, three-decker, ninety-six-gun battleship with a nine-hundred-man crew demanded a capital investment of between 33,000 and 39,000 pounds. To maintain and operate such a vessel in seaworthy fashion consumed as much as 26,000 pounds per year. These sums were far greater than the capital invested in any single industrial establishment in Britain at the time. By 1714, there were 20 of these monster, first-rate ships in the navy among 131 line-of-battle warships. To command and supply a fleet that often had forty thousand men at sea taxed the organizational capacities of the Admiralty Board, which commanded the fleet, and the Navy Board, its logistical arm.

Servicing the fleet necessitated secure home bases and naval dockyards, which became the largest industrial establishments of the age. Ship construction, repair, and supply demanded the highest order logistical planning and execution, as well as sophisticated financing and accounting. The Thames yards of Chatham, Deptford, and Woolwich were centers of naval supply and active shipbuilding. Plymouth, Portsmouth, and Sheerness maintained the operating fleet. The navy became the largest civilian employer in Britain, with a workforce of nearly seven thousand men in 1711.[29] Daniel Defoe's impression of Chatham dockyard at this time suggests the extraordinary nature of "this chief arsenal of the royal navy of Great Britain":

> The buildings here are indeed like the ships themselves, surprisingly large, and in their several kinds beautiful: The ware-houses, or rather streets of ware-houses, and store-houses for laying up the naval treasure are the largest in dimension, and the most in number that are anywhere to be seen in the world:

26. Ibid., 114–34.
27. D. C. Coleman, *Myth, History, and the Industrial Revolution* (London: Hambledon Press, 1992), 73.
28. Ibid., 34.
29. J. G. Coad and Royal Commission on Historical Monuments (England), *The Royal Dockyards, 1690–1850: Architecture and Engineering Works of the Sailing Navy* (Aldershot, Eng.: Ashgate; Brookfield, Vt.: Scolar Press, 1989), 3; Brewer, *The Sinews of Power,* 35–37; Philip MacDougall, *Royal Dockyards* (Newton Abbot: David and Charles, 1982).

The rope-walk for making cables, and the forges for anchors and other iron work, bear a proportion to the rest; as also the wet-dock for keeping masts, and yards of the greatest size, where they lye sunk in water to preserve them, the boat-yard, the anchor yard: all the whole, monstrously great and extensive, and not easily describ'd. . . .

The particular government of these yards, as they are call'd, is very remarkable, the commissioners, clerks, accomptants, &c. within doors, the storekeepers, yard-keepers, dock-keepers, watchmen, and all other officers without doors, with the subordination of all officers one to another respectively, as their degree and offices require is admirable. . . .

The building yards . . . and all the other yards and places . . . belonging to the navy, are like a well-ordered city; and tho' you see the whole place as it were in the utmost hurry, yet you see no confusion, every man knows his own business.[30]

The naval dockyards drew to their warehouses flows of material goods ranging from victuals to iron to timber. The Royal Navy was the leading purchaser of imported timber, tar, pitch, and other naval stores in the British Isles. Most of these were not produced domestically but were imported from the Baltic lands, the North American colonies, Ireland, and other sources. Britain's fleet generated a worldwide demand for resources.

In 1714, at the death of Queen Anne, Parliament successfully negotiated a tricky succession to another Stuart, George I, Elector of Hanover. A rebellion in Scotland by James Edward Stuart the following year was ill supported and easily put down. Thereafter, in contrast to the turbulence of the previous century, Britain enjoyed exceptional political stability under the Hanoverian dynasty.

Explanations for this achievement tend to stress several trends that coalesced by the early years of the century: First, quite simply, most Britons were unenthusiastic about reopening civil strife and cringed at the thought of possible regicide. They longed for stability. Second, a strong state contributed to stability. Cadres of professional civil servants had both a stake in stable government and professional expertise in administration. The government itself became a source of lucrative patronage for the governing classes. Third, the Whig Party dominated elections in what has been termed a system of "electoral oligarchy" in Parliament. Fourth, with a boom in trade and improvements in agriculture, the general living standards for most inhabitants of Britain (save the Irish), including the poorest classes, were rising. Finally, long-standing problems with the outlying regions moved toward resolu-

30. Daniel Defoe and G. D. H. Cole, *A Tour through the Whole Island of Great Britain* (London: Dent; New York: Dutton, 1962), 1:105–8.

tion.[31] The Act of Union with Scotland of 1707 held firm and reduced tension in that region. In Ireland, stability rested on firm colonial rule buttressed by the landowning protestant aristocracy. These circumstances permitted Robert Walpole, prime minister under George I, to craft a system of consensual politics in Parliament.

Stability and prosperity at home continued despite recurring, prolonged warfare throughout the century. For the most part, war did not touch British soil. Britain fought wars abroad for control of trade and colonies around the world in Europe, Asia, and the Americas. During this century, Britain became the dominant naval power in the world. The British fiscal state could project its military power virtually any place in the world's seas—this was a new imperial state of enormous reach. Controlled and directed trade brought vast quantities of goods and services into the home economy. The dynamic policies of this fiscal-military state, and its appetite for resources, left an indelible mark on the natural environment of England and many other areas in the world.

POPULATION, DISEASE, AND FOOD PRODUCTION

Long-term population and price trends in England conform to the European model. After 1470, the population of England and Wales grew rapidly to reach 3 million by 1550 and then 5.5 million by the 1650s. During the next half century, the population dropped slightly, hovering at around 5.2 million before rising again, to 5.7 million in the 1720s. After slow growth in the first decades of the eighteenth century, the population jumped to 8.8 million in 1800.[32] Over the same period, prices of consumables followed a three-phase trajectory similar to that of the demographic curve: a long steep rise followed by a plateau and then another period of extended increases.

During the first phase of strong population growth and price inflation before 1650, the English faced the possibility of massive food deficits. Unmistakable signs of scarcity appeared in the form of periodic mortality crises caused by food shortages. Widespread harvest failures spiked food prices and caused excess deaths due to malnutrition across England in 1500–1503, 1520–1521, 1527–1528, 1556, 1596–1598, and 1623. As the sixteenth century progressed, the crisis years worsened, going from periods of "dearth" to "famine." England shared with the rest of Europe the three-year sequence of wet, cold summers that ruined grain harvests in the mid-1590s. Detailed demographic research confirms the link between high grain prices and mor-

31. Holmes, *The Making of a Great Power,* 384–98.
32. Ibid., 403.

tality in a sampling of parishes across England at this time.[33] Despite the best efforts of the Tudor state to regulate the domestic grain trade to prevent hoarding, and to prohibit exports and encourage imports, England could not feed its entire population when successive harvests failed. Overall, agricultural output barely kept pace with the growth of population. Harvests in good years met the basic caloric demands of both rural and urban populations. In bad years, the poor and the weak starved.

Before 1650, the real cost of wages and manufactures lagged behind the soaring costs of food grains, meat, and fuelwood and the rental returns to landed property.[34] When these trends persisted throughout the sixteenth century and into the seventeenth, the rich got richer and the poor multiplied and got poorer. Rising inequality concentrated wealth and deprived the poor of even the most basic entitlements of food and shelter. As is well-known, widespread beggary and vagabondage resorted to by desperate homeless people made life less secure for all in this period.

How could this fast-increasing population be fed and supported by the country's agriculture? As anxieties mounted, English theorists, intellectuals, and practicing farmers debated, discussed, offered solutions, and generated an imposing printed and manuscript literature about farming techniques. This reappraisal was prompted by the insistent demand for food, which made itself felt in every quarter of the kingdom. For, as the population increased, not only were the towns obliged to seek larger supplies of food in the countryside, but every village too found itself supporting a larger number of families. Somehow the land in cultivation had to be made to grow more, the pastures had to be improved to support more stock, and the wastelands had to be put to better use. It is not surprising that writings on husbandry contemporary to the times are full of exhortations to improve yields and of examples of how this was done. People were convinced that everything could and should be employed and improved.

Responding to demand, British agriculture increased in efficiency and expanded its aggregate output during the sixteenth and seventeenth centuries and the first half of the eighteenth century. In retrospect, we can now see that, after the 1623 famine, Britain was no longer in serious jeopardy from subsistence crises. Scotland suffered a catastrophic famine between 1697 and 1699, but that was exceptional. This does not imply that every Briton was adequately fed—far from it—but only that, by comparison with other Euro-

33. Systematic analysis of several hundred Anglican church parish registers "reveal[s] a striking correspondence between grain prices and the level of baptisms, burials and marriages. Almost invariably, burials rose and both baptisms and marriages tumbled downward in years of high prices." Andrew B. Appleby, *Famine in Tudor and Stuart England* (Stanford, Calif.: Stanford University Press, 1978), 135.

34. D. H. Fischer, *The Great Wave: Price Revolutions and the Rhythm of History* (New York: Oxford University Press, 1996), 74, fig. 2.04.

peans, the British overall enjoyed far better food security in this period.[35] For example, France between 1700 and 1789 endured sixteen nationwide famines accompanied by high prices, food deprivation, disease, and accelerated mortality. It was only during the stress of the Napoleonic Wars that a famine condition revisited Britain, with failed harvests in 1794–1796 and 1799–1801.[36]

In some measure, of course, caloric supplements from the New World fisheries and from the sugar imported from the Caribbean helped, but these alone would not have resolved the growing food crisis.[37] Early modern England had reoriented its agricultural and pastoral economy to the point that it generated comfortable surpluses—especially in view of the changing demographic profile after 1650.[38] England was a special case among the early modern kingdoms of Europe. Regional specialization, growing national market integration, increased capital investment, intensified land use, and extension of arable lands all contributed to this increase.

The basic division of the country lay between the pastoral economy of the highland north and west and the mixed cereal and livestock farming of the lowland south and east.[39] Total output and yields per unit of land and worker rose steadily in both the cereal and pastoral regions. Increasing farm profits permitted capital investment and encouraged managerial innovation. The growing efficiency of early modern markets encouraged sales to the market and growing specialization.

As pastoral farmers in the uplands pressed toward the margin, the most unpromising terrain, soils, and vegetation in the kingdom yielded meat, hides, tallow, and wool in quantities not seen before even in the medieval period. The grass-growing counties of the north and west, with their wet, cool climate; poor, thin soils; and higher relief, proved to be cost-effective for cattle and sheep rearing. By the 1600s, numerous upland farmers were turning

35. Linda Colley, *Britons: Forging the Nation, 1707–1837* (New Haven: Yale University Press, 1992), 38–39.

36. Roger A. E. Wells, *Wretched Faces: Famine in Wartime England, 1793–1801* (New York: St. Martin's Press, 1988).

37. John Komlos, "The New World's Contribution to Food Consumption during the Industrial Revolution," *Journal of European Economic History* 27 (1998). Komlos estimates that, by 1816, sugar alone contributed 1 billion calories per day to the English diet (74).

38. Robert C. Allen, "Tracking the Agricultural Revolution in England," *Economic History Review* 52, no. 2 (1999); Mark Overton, "Re-establishing the English Agricultural Revolution," *Agricultural History Review* 44 (1996); Overton, *Agricultural Revolution in England: The Transformation of the Agrarian Economy, 1500–1850* (Cambridge: Cambridge University Press, 1996).

39. This description is taken from Joan Thirsk, ed., *The Agrarian History of England and Wales*, vol. 4: *1500–1640* (Cambridge: Cambridge University Press, 1967), 2–6. Thirsk "places the counties of Cornwall, Devon, Somerset, West Dorset, Gloucestershire, Herefordshire, Worcestershire, Shropshire, Staffordshire, Derbyshire, Cheshire, Lancashire, West Yorkshire, Durham, Northumberland, Cumberland and Westmorland in the pastoral zone."

to dairy farming as an alternative to stock raising. Young stock from these pastoral areas could be driven to lowland markets and profitably sold for subsequent fattening for the butcher. Greater care and selective breeding resulted in archaeological evidence that "points unmistakably towards an increase in the size of cattle and sheep between the fifteenth and seventeenth centuries."[40]

Until the 1590s, wool proved to be more profitable than grain for upland pastoralists and for large landlords in the mixed-farming region as well. Manorial lords and large farmers routinely ran flocks of a thousand sheep, and the largest sheep farmers had as many as fifteen thousand sheep.

The mixed-farming lowlands possessed richer, deeper soil, gentler topography, and drier, warmer climate that encouraged the growing of cereals, specialized industrial crops, and livestock, as well as dairying and horticulture. Excess cereals from the lowlands were shipped by coasting vessels to northern and western ports to help pay for livestock imports from the pastoral regions.

New evidence suggests that wheat yields increased in the sixteenth and early seventeenth centuries—especially in the south and west. More sophisticated techniques for reconstructing early modern yields per hectare from probate inventories have been developed that rely on records of estate valuations of stored and standing crops. Using these data, historians have argued that early modern English farmers began to exceed the average ten-bushels-per-acre figure of the medieval centuries. For example, in Oxfordshire, wheat went from 7.9 hectoliters per hectare in 1550 to an average of 11.1 in 1600, to 14.4 in 1650. In Norfolk County, similar calculations show wheat yields of 9.3 hectoliters per hectare in the last quarter of the fifteenth century, rising to 10.2 a hundred years later (1584–1599) and to as much as 15 for the period 1628–1640.[41] Although barley remained the principal crop in Norfolk, unlike in Oxfordshire, wheat's share of the cereal acreage rose to more than a quarter in the period 1584–1640.

Higher yields resulted from incremental advances in agricultural management and intensified capital investment in livestock, seeds, and fertilization, as well as from continuing improvement in the land itself. For example, in the south Midlands, farmers shifted from rye, barley, and oats to wheat and legumes—peas, beans, and vetches. The resulting increase in nitrogen in the soil from these nitrogen-fixing plants would have made a difference in yields, as would have a better selection of seeds. South Midlands farmers be-

40. Simon J. M. Davis and John V. Beckett, "Animal Husbandry and Agricultural Improvement: The Archaeological Evidence from Animal Bones and Teeth," *Rural History* 10, no. 1 (1999).
41. B. M. S. Campbell and M. Overton, "A New Perspective on Medieval and Early Modern Agriculture: Six Centuries of Norfolk Farming, c. 1250–c. 1850," *Past and Present* 141 (1993): 70, table 5.

gan to swap and sell better wheat seeds among themselves well before a trans-regional commercial market in seeds developed after 1660.[42]

For heavier clay soil districts that did not even support good pasture grasses and were too wet for good cereal crops, lowlands farmers turned to a new technology—subsurface drainage. They dug hollows in the furrows of their fields by plowing deeply and then digging with a spade a foot deeper. These drains were filled with stones, straw, sedges or other material that permitted water to flow and supported a roofing of dirt.[43]

One of the most important reasons for improved wheat yields lay in heavier capital investment in livestock—especially cattle and sheep in the lowlands. Stocking densities per hectare of arable land were higher than the medieval levels. There was an "apparent doubling in the stocking densities of virtually all classes of livestock between the Middle Ages and the early modern period."[44] More livestock meant more manure for fertilization and greater energy for traction in working the fields or for hauling loads. Farmers also improved the productivity of sheep by keeping them in enclosures and breeding selectively. To further improve their herds, farmers began to raise clover and turnips as winter feed for livestock—a measure that also raised output.

CAPITALIST FARMERS AND PEASANT FARMERS

As has long been recognized, early modern English agriculture improved by constructing a new capitalist, market-oriented set of institutions on the ruins of the medieval system of property rights and land management. The manorial system, with its reliance on servile estate labor, disintegrated in the labor shortages after the Black Death. Villeins fled more oppressive masters and negotiated better terms at manors anxious for labor. In the fifteenth and sixteenth centuries, evolving property rights in land encouraged capital investment, offered greater flexibility, and promised greater long-term security to those who would convert lands to more productive cropping and livestock rearing. Two different, and ultimately conflicting, paths opened up: one leading toward creation of a wealthy peasant class with substantial ownership rights to the land and well-defined rights of access to commons and wastelands; and another leading toward creation of large, compact, capitalist farms worked by wage laborers.

Both scenarios were part of a trend toward more flexible and powerful

42. Robert C. Allen, *Enclosure and the Yeoman* (Oxford: Clarendon Press; New York: Oxford University Press, 1992), 206; Allen, "Tracking the Agricultural Revolution in England."

43. Allen, *Enclosure and the Yeoman*, 119.

44. Campbell and Overton, "A New Perspective on Medieval and Early Modern Agriculture," 83.

forms of individual landownership at the expense of communal, collective modes of land tenure. The physical symbol of new expressions of territoriality lay in the process known as enclosure. Landowners claimed exclusive rights of ownership over formerly common lands by fencing or building hedgerows around that land.

In the first scenario, servile villeins formerly bound to the manor acquired free status as tenants at will and then obtained proprietary rights to the lands they farmed. The lord of the manor accepted tenants on his lands according to the custom of the manor by formal admission in the manorial court. So-called copyhold tenants were actually given copies of the manorial rolls to authenticate their holdings. Under copyholds of inheritance, the tenant paid a modest customary annual rent and a larger fine or fee when the property passed to his heir or was sold. Long-term security of tenure on payment of the rent was the most valuable proprietary benefit copyhold tenure conferred. Copyholds for lives were traditionally granted for the length of the lives of three people: the farmer, his wife, and his son. When the son married, he applied for and was given a new copyhold for lives. But there was no automatic right of renewal. Interventions by Tudor courts forced manorial lords to agree to sales and restrained them from arbitrarily evicting tenants and from raising customary rents or fees.

In the lowlands, many free peasants continued to farm in open field systems under common property regimes. In this system, observed across medieval Europe, both cultivable land and meadow were divided into elongated strips. Each cultivator held a number of these strips scattered among the village holdings. In the cultivated fields, village or manorial rules governed crop selection and fallowing at each season. Cultivated fields were open to grazing of the harvest stubble by all village-owned animals; grazing was also permitted when fields lay fallow. In the common pasture and village wastelands, village cultivators had rights to graze stock and gather fuelwood, peat, thatch, stone, mushrooms, berries, and other useful goods. The body of cultivators meeting in a manorial court or assembly enacted, enforced, and interpreted the rules for all.

The former monastic holding of Ombersley Manor in Worcestershire, a west Midlands county, part of the mixed-farming lowlands, offers one example of yeoman farmers who maintained their community and their common-property land rights until the early nineteenth century.[45] In 1605, a survey of Ombersley carried out by Samuel Sandys, who had acquired the manor in 1582, recorded 188 copyhold tenants, among whom was divided 1,821

45. P. Large, "Rural Society and Agricultural Change: Ombersley 1580–1700," in *English Rural Society, 1500–1800: Essays in Honor of Joan Thirsk*, edited by J. Thirsk, J. Chartres, and D. Hey (Cambridge: Cambridge University Press, 1990).

hectares of land, with a median of 6.1 hectares of land per farm. There were several freehold tenants with a total of 121.4 hectares, and the manorial, or demesne, lands, together with three extensive areas of common wasteland, totaled another 809.4 hectares. In addition to Ombersley village itself, there were sixteen hamlets within the manor. Each hamlet sent one representative ("homager or tythingman") to the manorial assembly. Each settlement had its own communal field system for cereal farming, as well as shared pastures and access to one of the three wastelands of the manor.

The light, sandy soil of the manor lent itself to a mixed-cereal and sheep-raising regime. The traditional crop rotation was rye, barley, and fallow. Ombersley's farmers obtained manure and direct income by breeding short-fleeced Ryland sheep to sell for wool and lambs for fattening. The average flock contained thirty-five sheep, and there was a customary limit of eighty head per farmer. Each farmer grazed his sheep on the extensive unfenced common wastelands during the day and folded them on the arable fields at night. The grazing was protected by strict rules laid down by the manorial assembly.

By the early 1600s, Ombersley farmers had begun to introduce pulses and oats on previously fallow land. In addition to adding nitrogen to the soil, these crops served as feed for horses and dairy cattle. By midcentury, Ombersley farmers had adopted clover as a crop and were planting clover seed on worn-out pastures and arable land. They also relied on temporary, partial enclosures worked out by mutual agreement that permitted controlled grazing on the clover-sown lands.

As the case of Ombersley manor implies, the seventeenth century was the high point of peasant agriculture before landlord-generated political pressures for higher rents destroyed the English peasantry in the eighteenth and early nineteenth centuries. For two centuries, the Ombersley manorial assembly, whose members were drawn from the most substantial copyhold tenants, remained the custodians of manorial customs and proved to be stout defenders of their rights against the lord of the manor. Over a struggle lasting nearly four decades, until 1627, the copyhold tenants readily raised funds and acquired legal representation in the royal Court of Exchequer to resist Sandys' attempts to raise annual rents and the fees for inheritance. Sandys did acquire the right to raise rents and fees but only within strictly circumscribed limits. He was also forced to recognize the strict customary rules of inheritance of the manor and approve transfers to heirs. After this early struggle, successive manorial lords at Ombersley were content with their modest rents and fees and refrained from direct challenges to the tenants' assembly and the customs of the manor.

In a second scenario, manorial lords and large farmers began to function as entrepreneurial capitalist landlords who consolidated larger holdings to grow crops and animals for market. Unconstrained by customary practice, they employed wage labor and sublet land to tenants, whom they charged full market rents. In the pastoral regions of the north and west, open grasslands could be demarcated and any residual rights bought up by manorial lords or landlords eager to expand their operations. They could muster capital, buy stock, and run cattle and sheep with the aid of hired labor.

But there were other forms of enclosure, in which occupying farmers within a village or a manor might agree among themselves to renounce common grazing and crop rotations within the village open fields or pasture. The proprietors consolidated their holdings by selling each other their interleaved strips of land held in open fields. When each possessed compact holdings, they bounded the new fields by ditches and hedges. Alternatively, groups of small farmers who could not agree might petition the authorities to have the common lands surveyed and apportioned by an objective commission.

Enclosures in the northern pastoral manor of Slaidburn, part of the holdings of the Duchy of Lancaster, in the region known as Bowland in the Yorkshire Pennines (today in Lancashire), illustrate this process. Bowland consisted of a dozen villages with a total area of twelve thousand hectares, mostly in meadow and pasture, with only 12 percent arable land. Between 1550 and 1630, the dominant copyhold tenant farmers of Bowland negotiated enclosure of about four thousand of the total sixty-five hundred hectares of common wasteland in the manor. After an initial phase of agreed-upon enclosures, disagreements prompted an appeal to the duchy. A commission of local gentry appointed by the chancellor of the Duchy of Lancaster held hearings, directed surveys, and then apportioned the land to copyhold tenant farmers. The latter thereby increased the size of their holdings and could by sale or exchange of dispersed tracts build up compact holdings.

Enclosure in this instance meant that village-controlled moorland and wooded wasteland was converted to individually owned, bounded, permanent pasture for cattle and sheep. Only the highest and most barren tracts of the wasteland in Bowland were left unenclosed. This change encouraged the spread of dispersed farmsteads away from nucleated villages. Those who lost out were undertenants, who were given small allotments determined by their landlords, and squatters, who received no allotments of land. All the lesser folk in the manor lost access to most of the highly productive common grazing land in the parish.[46]

This form of enclosure permitted greater freedom in agricultural practice for the encloser, but it weakened and destroyed the village common-property

46. John Porter, "Waste Land Reclamation in the Sixteenth and Seventeenth Centuries: The Case of South-Eastern Bowland, 1550–1630," *Transactions of the Historic Society of Lancashire and Cheshire for the Year 1977* 127 (1978).

regime.[47] Agreements for cropping and fallowing rotations dissolved. Communal pasture rights over village pastures also could be lost when individuals enclosed portions of that pasture. Even rights to graze livestock on harvest stubble in enclosed fields were denied the larger community. Unenclosed wastelands were essentially a reserve that could be brought into economic use as the population expanded. Village wastelands offered generally unrestricted access to supplementary resources such as game, honey, wax, fish, reeds, thatch, and medications that could be obtained by hunting, fishing, or gathering. Especially in the lowlands of the south and east, reserve lands or wastelands shrank and thereby reduced resources customarily afforded ordinary country folk. The village community suffered a loss that many times forced its poorer inhabitants into wage labor or migration.[48]

The rural population of early modern England exploited "natural resources and agricultural by-products" with an intensity far greater than had occurred in the medieval centuries and to a degree inconceivable today. Rural dwellers harvested seagull eggs or shore mussels or fished and hunted legally and often illegally to supplement their food supplies; dug and cut peat, fuelwood, gorse and furz (resinous flammable bushes), broom, sedge, and straw; gathered wattles, clay, sedge, and straw for house construction; collected slates and moss for roofs; cut wood and withes for clogs, dishes, utensils, furniture, and wicker and basket work; gathered down, feathers, and straw for bedding; collected meadow rushes for dipping in grease for illumination and broom for sweeping; and burnt wood and other vegetation to obtain potash for its alkalis used in soap making.[49] As the human-land ratio shrank and prices rose, these gathered products were more eagerly sought out.

Population pressures drove the expansion of arable land in Tudor and Stuart England. Woodlands, forests, moors, heaths, fens, and other lightly inhabited tracts were colonized, reclaimed, and settled. In a process of encroachment, increased numbers of land-hungry squatters occupied heaths, wastelands, and forestlands, built cottages, tilled a hectare or so of land, and grazed their livestock.[50] They did this illegally and, when discovered by the steward of the manor or forest officials, were generally permitted to stay as copyhold tenants on payment of a fine.[51] Some squatter hamlets provided

47. For a similar case of enclosure and its consequences in seventeenth-century Lancashire, see Graham Rogers, "Custom and Common Right: Waste Land Enclosure and Social Change in West Lancashire," *Agricultural History Review* 41 (1993).

48. Thirsk, ed., *The Agrarian History of England and Wales*, 4:200–201.

49. Donald Woodward, "Straw, Bracken, and the Wicklow Whale: The Exploitation of Natural Resources in England since 1500," *Past and Present*, no. 159 (1998).

50. Joan Thirsk, "Enclosure and Engrossing," in *The Agrarian History of England and Wales*, ed. Joan Thirsk (Cambridge: Cambridge University Press, 1967), 4:409–10.

51. Porter, "Waste Land Reclamation in the Sixteenth and Seventeenth Centuries," 8.

housing and partial sustenance to respectable rural day laborers, ironwork-ers, miners, and artisans such as broadcloth weavers.[52] Others sheltered dis-reputable settlements of vagabonds and bandits.

Ironically, the expanding cultivation steadily ate away the amount of nat-ural vegetation accessible to rural inhabitants in a continuing resource squeeze. In what was a shared worldwide process in the early modern world, population growth eroded rural access to gathered and hunted forest, wood-land, heathland, and grassland products. As this occurred, rural inhabitants were forced to buy substitutes on the market to meet their needs—or go without.

DRAINING THE FENLANDS

The most heavily capitalized early modern English effort to increase arable land occurred in the extensive coastal fens or marshes of East Anglia. The Crown and other manorial lords who controlled this region knew that large areas of unimproved common land in the fens provided them with but a minimal return. If dry, however, these lands promised to yield a lucrative rent when let out on market-determined rents. Livestock pressures on the grazing areas in the fens were also growing steadily.

In 1600, Parliament passed a General Draining Act for reclamation of "wastes, commons, marshes, and fenny grounds there subject to surrounding [flooding]" in the hope of "recovering many hundred thousand Acres of marshes."[53] By the terms of this act, the lords of manors and a majority of the holders of common-field rights might agree to give up a portion of the fen-lands for enclosure by investors in the drainage works. With this encourage-ment, groups of developers or "adventurers" invested large sums in projects aimed at diverting the flow of freshwater rivers directly to the sea in order to prevent seasonal flooding of the southeastern coastal marshes. With owner-ship rights assured, they could enclose dried-out tracts and plant oats, hemp, flax, rape and coleseed (both for oil pressing), and other profitable crops. These were bound to do well in the rich earth of the new lands. The devel-opers could also enclose additional rich pasture for sheep.

The early-seventeenth-century fenlands were scarcely an uninhabited morass or wilderness that justified reclaiming. At the sea face, they consisted of broad bands of fertile silt deposited afresh every year by alluvial action. Further inland was a belt of quaking peat bogs and occasional islands of higher land that were relatively dry. There was water aplenty in streams,

---

52. Buchanan Sharp, *In Contempt of All Authority: Rural Artisans and Riot in the West of England, 1586–1660* (Berkeley and Los Angeles: University of California Press, 1980), 156–74.

53. Quoted in H. C. Darby, *Draining of the Fens* (Cambridge: Cambridge University Press, 1940), 29.

lakes, and meres, and in winter nearly the whole region was flooded. These unpromising lands were inhabited by thousands of fen dwellers that for centuries had made good use of their watery terrain. They kept dry and mobile as they employed high wooden stilts to tend their herds, hunt, fish, and gather across the watery terrain. Despite an increasing population, the fens in the early seventeenth century still offered a secure and prosperous livelihood for its inhabitants.

Michael Drayton, an antidrainage pamphleteer, celebrated the fen way of life in verse:

> The toiling Fisher here is tewing [i.e., preparing] of his Net:
> The Fowler is employed his limed twigs to set.
> One underneath his Horse, to get a shoot doth stalk;
> Another over Dykes upon his Stilts doth walk;
> There other with their Spades, the Peats are squaring out,
> And others from their Carrs, are busily about,
> To draw out Sedge and Reed for Thatch and Stover fit,
> That whosoever would a Landskip [i.e., landscape] rightly hit,
> Beholding but my Fens, shall with more shapes be stored,
> Germany, or France, or Thuscan [sic] can afford.[54]

Fen villagers formed a close-knit society of nearly self-sufficient peasants who practiced an intricate seasonal husbandry. The fen dwellers cultivated arable plots on the edges and in islands of the fen that were protected by embankments and drained by ditches maintained by the community. They grazed cattle and sheep in summer on higher grasslands fertilized by winter flooding. In the driest tracts, the grazing season could last up to nine months. They grazed flocks of geese year round. They cut turves of peat and dried them for fuel essential in a largely treeless landscape. They fished for eels and other freshwater fish and caught wildfowl by the thousands every season. They took reeds for thatching, willows and alders for baskets and weirs. Fish and wildfowl from the fens, much-valued luxury items, fed discriminating London palates.[55]

Every drainage proposal met defiant criticism from opposed fen-dwellers, who feared, rightly, irretrievable loss to their way of life. Only the gentry stood to gain by drainage and enclosure. Division of the fen commons into portions for developers and for landlords to enclose left perhaps a third of the commons for allotments to tenants. Drainage also threatened access and resources that helped sustain the fen way of life. Not surprisingly, all the var-

---

54. Keith Lindley, *Fenland Riots and the English Revolution* (London: Heinemann Educational Books, 1982), 7. The quote is from M. Drayton, *The Second Part, or a Continuance of Polyobion* (n.p., 1622), 108.

55. See Darby, *The Medieval Fenland,* 21–85, for a full description of occupations in, and products of, the fens that continued until their drainage.

ied drainage projects generated vociferous and prolonged resistance. Local inhabitants forcefully protested enclosures by rioting, protesting in the streets, breaking dikes and sluices, and intimidating and injuring workmen. They found champions to write and publish pamphlets in a vigorous propaganda war against the improvers. They also pooled funds to sue for their rights in various legal venues.[56]

However, complicating this picture of idyllic life in the fens is another, rather more grim perspective. The low-lying coastal marshlands of southern England were the unhealthiest regions of the entire British Isles and were widely reputed to be so. Contemporaries believed that the slow-moving, dark, and stagnant waters of the region and the disagreeable smells they emitted were the cause of great unhealthiness. Inhabitants of the marshes were subject to endemic diseases collectively termed "marsh fever," "ague," "intermittent fever," "tertian fever," or "quartan fever."[57] Vicars rarely lived in their marshland parishes, so frightened were they of the agues and marsh fevers that afflicted their parishioners. These oozing, waterlogged marshlands sent forth such "noisome and stinking vapours, as are indeed prejudicial to the inhabitants' healths in general, but mostly to such as have been born and lived long in a better air, as the clergy can attest by sad experience."[58] Schoolmasters frequently died at their posts or resigned, with the result that there was little continuous schooling in the marshland and fen parishes.

Even though the inhabitants of the marshes were more resistant to endemic diseases than outsiders were, they suffered from chronic illness and heavy mortality. A range of anecdotal evidence suggests that outsiders viewed the marsh inhabitants as poor physical specimens, with their "pale and yellow visages, their feeble voices, their languishing eyes, [and] their bloated stomachs."[59] Crude death-rate data for Essex, Kent, and East Sussex for the 1670s show rates two to three times higher for marsh parishes below fifteen meters in height than for higher, nonmarsh parishes.[60] Burial-to-baptismal ratios show a similar divide in the 1670s, with marshland parishes having 132 burials for every hundred baptisms, and nonmarshland parishes having 83 burials to every hundred baptisms.[61] Despite the dangers, the marsh areas at-

<hr>

56. See Lindley, *Fenland Riots and the English Revolution*, 1–22, for a description of the public debate.

57. Mary J. Dobson, *Contours of Death and Disease in Early Modern England* (Cambridge: Cambridge University Press, 1997), 294–95.

58. From Thomas Cox's 1730 *History of Essex . . .* , quoted in Dobson, *Contours of Death and Disease in Early Modern England*, 295.

59. Dobson, *Contours of Death and Disease in Early Modern England*, 338.

60. Ibid., 153, table 3.23.

61. Ibid., 110, table 3.9. It is also possible that marsh or fen dwellers were less concerned with baptizing their children or had less opportunity to do so than those in nonmarsh parishes.

tracted a steady flow of migrants who came for seasonal harvesting or gathering, or to make a comfortable living smuggling goods through the braided waterways, or even to lure ships to the rocks by false signals ("wrecking") along the coast.

A 1997 study of southeastern England finds that "marsh fever" was in fact plasmodium malaria, which seems to have become especially virulent during the early modern centuries. The symptoms of marsh fever, with its alternating cold and hot episodes and periodicity, were typical of malaria. According to Thomas Sydenham, the famed late-seventeenth-century physician, who wrote of his experience with marsh fevers:

> All of them begin with a rigor and horror which is succeded by heat and that afterwards by a sweat. Dureing the cold and the hot fit[,] the patient is troubled for the most part with reaching to vomit and great sicknesse with thirst and dry tongue etc.[,] which symptoms goe off proportionably to the comeing on of the sweat[,] this seeming to be the solution of the fit. The patient remains well till the period wherein the fit comes about, which[,] in a quotidian is once in about twenty-four hours[,] in a tertian every other day[,] in a quartan every third day[,] reconing from the beginning of one to the beginning of the next.[62]

Other symptoms included enlargement of the spleen, malnutrition, weakening, and general debilitation from the recurring fevers, which lead to broken health among the sufferers. Moreover, since the mid–seventeenth century, doctors had known that fevers of this type could be cured by large doses of a Peruvian bark, called Jesuit bark, that contained the alkaloid quinine.[63] Unfortunately, few marsh dwellers could either afford or obtain ready amounts of Peruvian bark to use as a remedy.

Marsh fever, or malaria, was indeed confined to those low-lying, slightly saline coastal marshy regions in England and did not occur elsewhere. Of the five species of anopheles mosquito capable of carrying malaria parasites, only *Anopheles atroparvus* seems to have been the carrier of marsh fever in England. The spatial distribution of *Anopheles atroparvus*, with its limited flight range, coincides precisely with the distribution of marsh fevers and agues along estuarine marshes and areas open to coastal flooding. Of the four malaria parasites carried by the mosquito—*Plasmodium falciparum, Plasmodium vivax, Plasmodium ovale*, and *Plasmodium malariae*—it is likely that the more benign *vivax* and *malariae* were transmitted in England, rather than the tropical variety, *falciparum*, with its intermittent fevers and high fatality rate.[64]

62. Quoted in ibid., 312.
63. Ibid., 315.
64. Ibid., 320–27. Malaria was a disease contracted in summer. Warm summers increased the number of pools of standing water for breeding mosquitoes. Also, the summer temperatures had to be sufficiently warm. To ingest the parasite, the adult female mosquito must first bite a

Malaria contracted from *vivax* or *malariae* parasites did not kill outright so much as it afflicted the sufferer with a debilitating, long-term series of regularly recurring bouts of fever. Such repeated attacks resulted in a continuing state of ill-health and debility and, often, early demise—especially if new infections kept occurring. Weakened malaria sufferers were less able to resist other infectious diseases such as the whole battery of water-, air-, and insect-borne infectious diseases—dysentery, salmonella, plague, smallpox, typhus, tuberculosis, and influenza, among others—that assaulted the English in the early modern centuries.

In the propaganda wars, the manifest unhealthiness of the fens and marshes worked against those who resisted drainage. To most who did not live in the affected areas, schemes to drain the marshes were desirable. They promised an end to the disgusting effluvia of the wetlands and the disreputable, sickly societies sheltering therein.

The earliest successful large drainage project was in the north at Hatfield Chase marsh and the Isle of Axholme, lying between the counties of Yorkshire, Lincolnshire, and Nottinghamshire. This area included about twenty-eight thousand hectares of fenland held primarily under royal control. The money-strapped Charles I was lord of the largest manors located in the villages of Hatfield, Epworth, Crowle, and Misterton, as well as thirteen manors in other villages that divided fens commons rights in Lincolnshire. Charles was persuaded that he could increase his rents substantially by investing in drainage of this region.[65] Between 1626 and 1628, Cornelius Vermuyden, the well-known Dutch drainage engineer, drained Hatfield Chase, and the Crown began to take bids for leases from gentry who would cultivate the drained fenland. In the 1630s, there followed three more Crown-sponsored drainage projects in Lincolnshire.

Local copyholders and cottagers protested every one of these projects by rioting, damaging the dikes, and taking legal action aimed at reaffirming their ancient commoner rights. Even the commoners of Epworth Manor, who possessed a 1359 charter from the then manorial lord guaranteeing their commons rights from any further encroachment, lost three thousand hectares from the fifty-four-hundred-hectare Epworth common to the engi-

---

person or animal with malaria gametocytes in its bloodstream. Then, an average air temperature of sixteen degrees centigrade for at least sixteen days is necessary before the sexual cycle of *Plasmodium vivax* is complete and the mosquito is infective to human beings. In the marsh areas, there is a significant relationship between warm summer temperatures and higher mortality figures in the autumn and spring that follow. However, humans acted as infective reservoirs for *vivax* malaria for several years after infection. *Anopheles atroparvus* survived in a state of semihibernation in dwellings and cattle shelters over winters.

65. Lindley, *Fenland Riots and the English Revolution*, 23–33; Joan Thirsk, *English Peasant Farming: The Agrarian History of Lincolnshire from Tudor to Recent Times* (London: Routledge and Kegan Paul, 1957), 117–29.

neer Vermuyden and the Crown. The latter employed Star Chamber proceedings against rioting and King's Bench legal action to sweep aside lawsuits and obtain an award from the attorney general for division of the lands.[66]

In the south, increased silting at the mouths of the fenland rivers impelled a group of larger landlords in the area to approach Francis, earl of Bedford, himself a great fen landowner, with a grandiose plan to drain the entire southern fenlands. In 1631, the earl and thirteen other investors formed the Bedford Level Corporation and hired Vermuyden as project director. Their project, known as the Bedford Level, affected some 162,000 hectares of fenland in Lincolnshire, Northhamptonshire, Huntingdonshire, Norfolk, and Suffolk. Its chief drainage conduit diverted water from the river Ouse by a straight, 21-meter-wide and 24-kilometer-long channel right across the fens to Denver in Norfolk. Completed in 1637, this channel did drain large tracts, but considerable areas were still flooded. Vermuyden planned and began an additional eight separate channels, ranging in length from 3.2 to 16 kilometers.[67] However, fenland protests against drainage intensified and contributed to the atmosphere of unrest before the civil war. During the 1640s, the war brought an abrupt halt to all drainage work on the Bedford Level.

Generally, Crown sponsorship of drainage inclined most of the affected population to the Parliamentarian side. Many of the most prominent investors and nobles involved in drainage were Royalists. Roundhead armies obtained large numbers of recruits from this region. In Lincolnshire to the north, so intense was the hostility of the fen population to drainage that, in a series of riots, they broke down sluices and dikes to the point that the works no longer functioned and the waters were released.[68] Riots in the south also damaged some of the works but did not completely destroy them.

At the close of the war, during the interregnum, the question of fen drainage once again became a hotly debated issue in Parliament. The fen commoners organized a vigorous lobbying effort that prevented any parliamentary action to restore the abandoned works in Lincolnshire. The Bedford investors, however, did persuade Cromwell himself to support repair and continuance of the Bedford Level. In 1649, an act of Parliament recognized the legal right of the new earl of Bedford and the original investors to continue with their plans. Military units in the fenlands made it possible for Vermuyden to begin work in 1650. Upon completion in 1652, the original investors acquired ownership of 33,600 hectares of newly drained fenland

66. Lindley, *Fenland Riots and the English Revolution*, 26–32.
67. Darby, *The Medieval Fenland*, 41–42.
68. See Lindley, *Fenland Riots and the English Revolution*, 108–60, for a full description of these events.

that could be leased to tenant farmers. An additional 4,900 hectares of drained land went to the Crown.

Construction of the Bedford Level proved to be a decisive turning point in the history of the fens. Thereafter there was no turning back, as landlords and farmers continued to invest in maintaining and extending the area drained. Although many notable figures in the Commonwealth and Protectorate were investors in the project, the Bedford Level survived the Restoration. Clever advocacy on the part of the drainage company deflected attempts by drainage opponents to destroy the project and dissuaded Charles II from direct royal confiscation.[69] Royal yields from the newly drained fields in the southern fenlands brought lucrative rents to investors and bountiful crops to farmers who leased drained lands. The historian employed by the drainage investors, William Dugdale, reported of the town of Thorney "that the Fens now environing it are by the Adventurers draynings, more so drye, that there are of [sic] all sorts of corne and grasse, now growing thereon, the greatest plenty imaginable."[70]

Even serious long-term maintenance problems did not deter continuing development and improvement. The gradient, or fall, of the Bedford cuts, like the meandering rivers they replaced, was slight. Frequently during the year, North Sea high tides and heavy winds pressed against the silt-laden freshwater trying to pass through the sluice gates. The effect of silt buildup at the outlets was compounded by lowering of the interior peat zone as the bogs dried out. This subsidence slowly lowered the interior level in comparison to the coastal silt zone and further reduced the drainage flow. With each passing year, the level of the drainage channels rose relative to the fields on either side—a process that required continued embanking of the drainage channel with water-impervious soils.

By the 1700s, difficulties had reached the point that wind-driven pumps were put in place to lift water from minor channels and drains to the higher main channels and to move water over the seawalls into the ocean. The entire Bedford Level became a series of diked enclosures from which water from local streams was pumped upward to the main drainage channels.[71]

The direst predictions of the antidrainage pamphleteers did not immediately happen. Certainly, the rights of both copyhold tenants and cottagers were constrained in the south by major losses of common lands to the new

69. Francis Willmoth, "Dugdale's *History of Imbanking and Drayning:* A 'Royalist' Antiquarian in the Sixteen-Fifties," *Historical Research* 71, no. 176 (1998). Richard, Lord Gorges, commissioned William Dugdale to write a historical account of drainage that would firmly establish the legal basis for the drainer's activities and show the long-standing local efforts at drainage of the fens that began in the medieval period.

70. Quoted in Darby, *The Medieval Fenland*, 88.

71. Ibid., 120–21.

regime. However, large areas of undrained wetland remained. Fowling, thatching, and other activities continued to be profitable. In the north, it would be another hundred years, well into the second half of the eighteenth century, before substantial drainage works were once again planned and carried out. Over two centuries, however, the predrainage fen way of life was largely transformed as the area became the intensively cultivated fields seen today.

FOREST DEPLETION

During the sixteenth century and first half of the seventeenth, wood, the principal source of energy and primary building material for English society, became increasingly costly and less accessible. By the Tudor period, English forests, probably no more than 10 percent of land surface, were being rapidly depleted both by overcutting and by conversion to cultivation and pasture.[72] Energy demands from a population doubling in size and an energetic industrial sector strained the biomass resources of England. Between 1501 and 1601, the index of timber prices more than tripled, from a low of 89 (1450 = 100) to 323. Over the next half century, between 1601 and 1649, the price rose again, to 549.[73] Large-scale imports of Norway and Baltic softwood timber—fir *(Abies alba)*, pine *(Pinus sylvestris)*, and spruce *(Abies excelsa)* —soared as domestic hardwood supplies dwindled and prices rose.[74]

Regular supplies of fuelwood became ruinously expensive when secured from distant areas. The London price for fuelwood rose steeply from the late sixteenth century to the outbreak of the English Civil War in a trajectory far steeper than the general prices of commodities.[75]

Few tree-covered areas in England amounted to extensive forests; most were scattered, tree-covered tracts rarely more than a few square kilometers in size. Some of the more extensive ones were royal or noble lands managed as game reserves to promote deer hunting; some smaller tracts were kept as ornamental parks in estates. The majority of woodlands, however, were managed to produce a profit by growing timber and fuelwood under systematic forms of coppicing that could produce 2.5 metric tons of fuelwood from a hectare of land every twenty-five years.[76] Under these circumstances, forests and woodlands suffered:

72. John Hatcher, *Before 1700: Towards the Age of Coal,* vol. 1 of *The History of the British Coal Industry* (Oxford: Clarendon Press, 1993), 19.

73. Thirsk, ed., *The Agrarian History of England and Wales,* 846–50, table 6.

74. Ralph Davis, *The Rise of the English Shipping Industry in the Seventeenth and Eighteenth Centuries* (London: Macmillan; New York: St. Martin's Press, 1962), 19.

75. Hatcher, *Before 1700,* 37.

76. Ibid., 33.

The motives of those who grubbed up woodland in an age of rising population and impending food scarcity are not hard to comprehend. Woodland, as a general rule, was generally incapable of competing successfully with arable or even pasture farming for the use of the land in early modern times. Whatever the longer term returns from well-managed woodland might have been, when a thriving and profitable market existed for foodstuffs, as it did through most of the sixteenth and seventeenth centuries, the temptation to take a windfall gain by felling all the trees, selling the resultant timber and firewood, and then converting the land to crops or animals, was often too great for many landowners to resist. In this way much of the woodland was destroyed in the vicinity of towns, in just those locations where there was the heaviest demand for fuel.[77]

Squatting and colonization led to serious depletion of English forests. Often, popular demand for land led to a process of disafforestation—changing the legal definition of a piece of land from forest to wasteland and selling the land rights. Crown forests were administered by master foresters or chief stewards, local notables given hunting rights, who were charged with protecting forest cover and fostering deer herds for hunting. Colonization, tacitly encouraged by local manorial lords who charged rent to squatters in the royal forests adjoining their lands, led to a gradual transformation from wooded to arable lands. Anxious to obtain greater revenues, Crown officials were also willing to acquiesce in settlement and clearing and, on occasion, would agree to outright sale of land rights in the forests.

Once established, cottagers could obtain game and fuel from the surrounding forest, slowly expand their holdings, and provide a partible inheritance for their heirs. This was certainly the process at work in Bowland forest, adjacent to Lancashire Manor discussed above. Between 1500 and 1650, the royal forests of Bowland were entirely eradicated (virtually no tree cover remained), two deer parks were dismantled, and the lands were divided into small, enclosed farmsteads.[78]

A similar process of slow depletion hit the forests of Scotland. Since the Iron Age, Scotland had been but sparsely forested with patchy fir, pine, birch, and oak cover—even in the Highlands. In 1500, forests covered only 10 to 15 percent of the land surface.[79] Already by that date, all the largest mammals had disappeared, save the beaver and wolf, and both these species became extinct by the early 1600s. In large areas in the east of Scotland where the landscape was entirely destitute of trees, the inhabitants were forced to use peat or coal for fuel and to import Norwegian timber for construction. Increasingly, Scots throughout the region enclosed and managed their

77. Thirsk, "Enclosure and Engrossing," 4:409–10.

78. John Porter, "A Forest in Transition: Bowland, 1500–1650," *Transactions of the Historic Society of Lancashire and Cheshire for the Year 1974* 125 (1975).

79. T. C. Smout, *Nature Contested: Environmental History in Scotland and Northern England since 1600* (Edinburgh: Edinburgh University Press, 2000), 47.

woodlands by coppicing to obtain sustainable supplies of fuel for charcoal for gunpowder and iron making, and for tanbark and oak to split for basket weaving. Despite these conservation measures, the forests steadily gave way to agriculture and intensified grazing. The military surveys of the 1750s suggest that forest cover in Scotland had declined to 4 percent of the surface, and an estimate made in 1815 put the total at 3 percent of the land surface.[80] In summary, Scotland's forests were not the answer to Britain's energy needs.

In large measure because of timber shortages in England, Wales, and Scotland, Ireland suffered colonial exploitation of its forests during the seventeenth century. Firm colonial control freed proprietors to exploit Irish forests. The generally accepted estimate is that about one-eighth of Ireland was covered by forests and woods in 1600, and an additional amount was composed of land that was barren, boggy, or both. By 1700, the Irish woodlands had been reduced to about 2 percent of the total land area.[81] A flourishing seventeenth-century timber export trade died out in the early years of the eighteenth century, and Ireland became a timber-importing country.

The collapse of the Ulster rebellion led by Hugh O'Neill in 1603 marked the final stage in the Tudor conquest and opened up the island to more intensive colonization and economic exploitation. One of the inducements offered to English settlers was the profit to be made from cutting woodlands as part of their civilizing mission. Forests were the haunts of wolves and Irish rebels that were best cleared. Half-timbered houses in Londonderry and other new colonial settlements drew on cheap Irish oak supplies.

A newly expanded export timber trade sent roundwood, planks, and staves to European and, increasingly, to English and Scots markets. Staves were the principal export item. In the mid-1680s, Irish ports shipped over 20 million staves.[82] Irish coopers used native ash and oak to make curved staves and flat headpieces for barrels, hogsheads, and butts. These were shipped to be assembled with willow withes or bands at their destination.[83] The vigorous Irish export trade in provisions—butter, beef, tallow, and fish—also consumed large numbers of casks.

Other industries made inroads in the Irish woodlands. The export trade in tanned hides surged to over two hundred thousand hides per year in the mid-1660s after the Irish Cattle Acts banned the shipment of live cattle to England. Tanners, who preferred to strip bark off live oak trees to obtain the

---

80. Ibid., 46–47.
81. Eileen McCracken and Queen's University of Belfast, Institute of Irish Studies, *The Irish Woods since Tudor Times: Distribution and Exploitation* (Newton Abbot: David and Charles, 1971), 15. See also Eoin Neeson, *A History of Irish Forestry* (Dublin: Lilliput Press, 1991).
82. McCracken and Queen's University of Belfast, Institute of Irish Studies, *The Irish Woods since Tudor Times*, 109, table 8.
83. Ibid., 60.

most potent tanning agents, cooperated closely with timber merchants and cutters. Perhaps most voracious was the iron industry. English plantation owners imported English technicians and workers and invested considerable sums in ironworks aimed at taking advantage of Irish ores and cheap fuel. The price of timber was ten to twelve times cheaper in Ireland than in England.[84] Close to a hundred ironworks operating in the seventeenth century have been identified. The earliest works were on estates near the coast, but later works were opened in wooded valleys inland. Ore could be brought to the works on horseback, but charcoal was brittle and best made close by. In Ireland, in contrast to England, iron masters made no effort to set up coppicing systems to produce wood for charcoal on a more sustainable basis. Save for a handful of longer-term sites, most ironworks went out of production when local woods were depleted.[85]

Depletion of Irish woodlands invariably caused hardships to the general population. Peat, rather than wood or charcoal, necessarily became the cheapest and most accessible fuel.[86] Hazel growth, used extensively in rods for traditional wattling or siding of huts, declined precipitously by 1700. More and more, the rural Irish turned to sod and brushwood as construction materials for their huts.[87]

ROYAL NAVY AND ENGLISH OAK

The Royal Navy's increasingly difficult struggle throughout the early modern centuries to obtain homegrown timber for the repair and construction of its ships symbolizes the decline of British forests. Each newly built ship required prodigious amounts of timber. The rule of thumb for warships was that each rated ton consumed about 1.5 to 2 "loads" (2.1 to 2.8 cubic meters) of timber. Each merchantman commonly used 1 load (1.4 cubic meters) per shipping ton.[88] A great ship of the line, averaging 2,000 tons capacity, swallowed 4,200 to 5,600 cubic meters of timber—the timber of several thousand mature trees.[89] Constant repairs needed to keep the naval and mercantile fleet

84. Neeson, *A History of Irish Forestry*, 75.

85. Ibid., 90–96.

86. T. W. Moody, F. X. Martin, and F. J. Byrne, *A New History of Ireland* (Oxford: Clarendon Press, 1976).

87. Neeson, *A History of Irish Forestry*, 72.

88. Robert G. Albion, *Forests and Sea Power: The Timber Problem of the Royal Navy, 1652–1862* (Cambridge: Harvard University Press, 1926), 9, 116. A load was fifty cubic feet, or about six hundred board feet. A board foot was one inch by one inch by twelve inches.

89. John Evelyn and John Nisbet, *Sylva: A Discourse of Forest Trees and the Propagation of Timber in His Majesty's Dominions* (London: Doubleday and Company, 1908), 117. Evelyn extolled his brother's planting of oaks on his estate in Surrey, in which "one Tree with another [contained] by estimation three quarters of a *load* of *Timber* in each Tree, and in their *lops* three *Cord* of fire-wood." This works out to about one cubic meter of timber per oak tree.

operating added to the annual demand for shipping timber. Naval ship-builders, conservative to the core, would use only fir, elm, beech, and above all, oak for their vessels.

Both fir and Scotch pine *(Pinus sylvestris)* produced a superb, all-round timber that could be used to build an entire wooden ship. Because it was filled with resin rather than sap, fir could be dried or seasoned more quickly than oak, and it was much lighter. Generally, however, fir grew best in the short summers and colder winters of Scotland and the north. Supplies rapidly dwindled in the sixteenth century, and cheap imports of fir from the Baltic lands soon superseded domestic production.

Fir (or other suitable conifers), with its flexible strength and relatively light weight, was essential for the two dozen or more masts, yards, and spars in each large ship. The main masts of the largest first-rate, 120-gun battleship of the eighteenth century had to be 101.6 centimeters in diameter and 12.2 meters in height; even those of a light, 28-gun frigate were 50.8 centimeters in diameter and 8.2 meters in height. Fir trees had to grow for nearly a cen-tury to reach these dimensions, and few did so any longer in the British Isles. By mid–seventeenth century, mast timbers were nearly all either imported firs of the requisite size from the Baltic or white pine *(Pinus strobus)* from northern New England.

For the hull timbers, there were different requirements and prejudices. The "tough, cross-grained wood" of two species of English elm *(Ulmus campestris* and *Ulmus montana)* could be used in the ship's keel planking, where great strength was required. Beech planking, although not as strong as elm, was serviceable and used on occasion. However, English oak *(Quer-cus robur)* grown in England's moderate, humid climate—and especially those specimens that matured on the loamy and clayey soils of the south-east—was the ultimate shipbuilding timber. Oak was a strong and resilient wood that did not splinter easily when hit by a cannonball. If properly dried, or "seasoned," for two to three years, oak timber was resistant to dry rot fungi *(Xylostroma giganteum* and *Boletus hybridus),* which penetrated wood with "small white cottony fibres" and "gradually reduced it to powder."[90] Espe-cially critical were the large curved "compass timbers" taken from the largest oak trees. Shipbuilders looked for "knees," cut where large branches di-verged from the trunk, to use in attaching beams running the length of the ship to each of the ship's ribs. The beams in turn supported decking bear-ing the enormous weight and strain of actively fired cannons.

Rising demand for oak for building and for shipbuilding was manifest in rising prices by mid–sixteenth century. Before the civil war, royal forest poli-cies were concerned with revenue to be obtained from extraparliamentary sources rather than with conservation. Occasional attempts by Parliament to

90. Albion, *Forests and Sea Power,* 11–12.

implement timber conservation measures were not effective. Henry VIII's confiscation of church lands brought great tracts of oak forest in former monastery lands under his control. These his officials sold off for timbering before granting the land to new proprietors. Elizabeth I freely sold licenses to cut in the royal forests. Cutting reached the point that Lord Howard of Effingham, admiral of the fleet that defeated the Spanish Armada, protested that he was "grieved to think of the state her woods are now in, and what want there is for building and repairing her ships which are the jewels of her kingdom." Reports of rapid depletion were alarming. For example, the 92,232 oaks that foresters counted in Duffield Forest in 1560 had dropped to just 5,896 trees by 1587.[91]

James I, contemplating selling off part of the Crown forests, ordered foresters to survey the standing oaks on the royal domain. The returns showed 784,748 "Tymber Trees" and 682,058 "Decaying Trees" (i.e., overly mature), valued at nine hundred thousand pounds.[92] Despite expressed public concern, regular sales of the royal woodlands continued throughout his reign and increased under Charles I. In the 1620s, Charles sold two royal forests for funds to pay the fleet when it returned from its expedition to relieve the Huguenots in La Rochelle. In 1640, just before the rebellion, Charles granted the Forest of Dean to Sir John Wintour under the terms of a royal "Act for the Limitation of Forests," who then proceeded to clear wide tracts of timber over the seventeen years the forest was under his control.

The twenty-year interregnum resulted in massive forest clearing. The usual protections given royal wooded lands faltered during the war. Local populations freely cut and carried away firewood and timber from Crown lands. Private lands did not fare well either, as the new regime confiscated royalist estates and levied heavy fines. When that occurred, Parliament ordered timber felling and sales to pay the fines. After the Restoration, scores of royalist officers returned to find forests stripped from the estates they recovered. In 1644, the navy, given authorization to take whatever timber it needed from the royal forests, chases, and parks, cut heavily to meet its needs. Wartime needs and political instability had their usual effect on England's forests.

Continued depletion meant that, after 1660, the Royal Navy relied on a precarious supply of great oaks from royal lands and private estates. Immediately after the Restoration, the Navy Board appealed to the Royal Society for suggested methods to relieve the timber shortage. In response, John Evelyn wrote his great tract *Sylva: A Discourse of Forest Trees and the Propagation of Timber in His Majesty's Dominions*, appealing to the landowners of England to

91. Ibid., 123, 124.
92. Ibid., 125. This count did not include the Forest of Dean, which was considered the navy's reserve.

plant oaks and other trees to relieve "the impolitic diminution of our timber." His appeal and practical advice did encourage considerable numbers of landowners to plant trees as an investment for their estates.

Both Charles II and Parliament responded positively to Evelyn's appeal. A parliamentary act in 1668 called for the enclosure and planting of oaks on 4,452 hectares stripped of trees in the Forest of Dean—a policy that, surprisingly, was implemented. However, most of the great oaks needed for the Royal Navy came from the private lands of noble and gentry landowners. The most important of these was the Ashdown Forest in Sussex, with its 7,300 hectares of oak woodland. But this was an exception. Every year, agents of the Naval Board patiently searched out and contracted for small lots of oak timber from dozens of landowners.

Imported oak from the Baltic lands became a necessity even as the young oaks that had survived the civil war or were planted in the Restoration grew to maturity. After 1700, Britain relied increasingly on imported timber from the Baltic lands and North America for shipbuilding, construction, and other durable purposes. However, fuelwood was another matter. By 1775, the royal forests were nearly completely exhausted and private lands were not far behind. Nonetheless, even at this point, when supplies of American timber were sharply reduced, the navy successfully obtained supplies of Baltic timber. Even with timber difficult to obtain, Britain produced 181 naval ships (36 of them ships of the line) during the period of the American War.[93]

A NEW ENERGY SOURCE

Although well-known and usually mentioned in passing by historians, the British energy transformation from wood to coal demands greater consideration than it has received in the past. As John Nef argued nearly seventy years ago in his pathbreaking study of the British coal industry, "Between the accession of Elizabeth and the civil war, England, Wales, and Scotland faced an acute shortage of wood, which was common to most parts of the island rather than limited to special areas, and which we may describe as a national crisis without laying ourselves open to a charge of exaggeration."[94] The British response to this energy scarcity was to develop a new, more efficient fuel and to extract it in amounts sufficient to meet the needs of a dynamic and expanding society and economy.

93. R. J. B. Knight, "New England Forests and British Seapower: Albion Revisited," *American Neptune* 46, no. 4 (1986).

94. John Ulric Nef, *The Rise of the British Coal Industry* (London: G. Routledge, 1932), 1:161, as quoted in B. Thomas, "Was There an Energy Crisis in Great Britain in the Seventeenth Century?" Thomas summarizes the debate and concludes that Nef's arguments, put forward in his study of the British coal industry published in 1932, remain valid despite revisionist critiques. I share that view.

Why Britain made the astonishing changeover to coal, as did no other early modern society, is partly explained by its long-standing exploitation of numerous, easily worked outcroppings of coal found throughout England, Scotland, and Wales. Ready access to riverine and coastal transport made it feasible to ship coal over considerable distances. The medieval collieries of northeastern England near the Tyne River benefited from the economies of waterborne transport to London and other coastal and river ports. Tyneside collieries may have produced as much as 50,000 metric tons of coal per year in the late fourteenth century. In that same period, Newcastle exported around 7 tons per year to both British and continental markets. In general, this was a modest output and trade.

When coal consumption began to climb after 1550, the industry responded by steadily and rapidly increasing production. The dimensions of this change can be seen in the reasonably well-documented aggregate annual output figures for British coal mines: in the 1560s, coal produced for sale each year totaled approximately 227,000 metric tons; by 1700, this figure was 2.64 million tons—a twelvefold increase.[95] Throughout this period, supply easily met and often outran demand for coal. Nearly one thousand collieries distributed across fifteen major coalfields produced coal for the nation.

Systems of waterborne transport and distribution reached efficiencies and capacities that permitted coal to reach urban consumers at prices lower than for any competing fuel. The largest collieries were found in the northeast, in the Northumberland and Durham fields, which produced in the aggregate nearly half (1.25 million metric tons) of total output in 1700. A number of these collieries produced over 25,000 tons per year. In the remaining coalfields, however, smaller collieries were the norm. No more than a dozen collieries throughout England, Scotland, and Wales shipped as much as 20,000 tons a year per colliery. Another two dozen, regarded as exceptional by contemporaries, each shipped over 5,000 tons per year. The vast number of British collieries shipped from a few hundred to a few thousand metric tons of coal per year.

Early modern coal mining in the British Isles was primarily a matter of finding and following exposed coal outcroppings or seams. Cheapest, when feasible, was the open mining of near-surface seams, or the sinking of multiple shallow bell-pits no more than six meters deep. Where coal seams outcropped on the side of a hill, a tunnel, known as a day-hole or drift, could be driven horizontally into the hillside so that miners could simply walk or crawl directly into the hillside to reach the coalface.

The most productive mines were those in which a shaft was sunk vertically to reach a coal seam. When this difficult and often dangerous task was done,

95. Hatcher, *Before 1700.*

a more or less horizontal heading, or level, was then dug in a direction that could maximize output and permit water drainage. Levels were divided into sections, each worked by a single hewer, who left pillars of coal on both sides of him to support the roof. Alternatively, in long-wall working, the entire face of the seam was cleared out and the roof propped up by timber and stone pillars.

As miners exhausted the seam within reach, other shafts were sunk to follow out the coal deposits. Hewers used short-shafted picks, wedges, and hammers to slice coal from the face. Good hewers were able to cut the coal into the preferred larger chunks and thereby increase their pay based on an output system or piece rate. Haulers carried or dragged on sleds baskets of hewn coal weighing thirty-two to forty-five kilograms along the level to the shaft; from there, the baskets were brought to the surface by the same windlass mechanism that moved miners to and from the surface.

Drainage and air quality were the most intractable problems confronting early modern miners. Flooding was unpredictable and could ruin a mine and its owner. Ordinary seepage had to be removed continuously. Various pumping devices could be used that lifted water up the shaft by the windlass mechanism. Lifting water was heavy work, and the power choices limited to humans, horses, wind, and water. All were expensive, although windlasses became noticeably more efficient and powerful in the course of the seventeenth century. Chain pumps in various styles supplanted simple two-barrel or bucket systems.

Drainage was cheaper and more reliable, if feasible. From a surface point below the coal face, miners dug a channel, or adit, known as a sough, into a hillside where the coal seam was located so that gravity could drain off water at the coal face. Ordinary soughs might be more than one hundred meters; but deeper and larger collieries ran channels as long as three hundred meters with openings sunk along their length so that they could be kept clear and maintained.

Foul air could result simply from insufficient ventilation. However, this could be combined with chokedamp, which hindered breathing and was a long-term threat to the health of the miners. Chokedamp, or damp, was a mixture of carbon dioxide and nitrogen produced by the oxidation of carbonaceous deposits. Methods of improving ventilation advanced throughout the period. Sinking two or more shafts was one common approach to improving air flow. Soughs provided drafts as well as water drainage. Lamps were lit to warm the air and thus to bring in the colder, fresh air from the pithead.

Open candles and flames in the deeper pits also ran the risk of explosion when exposed to what was termed firedamp. When mixed with coal dust, the methane gases released when the coal was cut could burn when they reached 4 to 15 percent of the air in the level. The usual practice was to send a fire-

man down every morning to find and set off as safely as possible any concentrations of firedamp. As it was lighter than air, firedamp would gather in
globes near the roof of the level. Until the invention of the safety lamp, little
could be done beyond this, and fiery explosions in some mines were a regular occurrence.

Although encouraged and aided by state legislation and policy, the industry was essentially private, the product of gentry entrepreneurs responding to market forces. Even the monopoly over shipping of coal on the Tyne
River, held by royal charter since 1600 by the leading families of Newcastle
(the Company of Hostmen), did not stifle either competition or expansion.
Instead, the Hostmen used their favored position to acquire control over the
most productive collieries in the northeast. Coal from Newcastle still competed against that of Sunderland and numerous other coal-shipping ports.
Beyond the reach of the Newcastle oligarchy, anyone could develop a
coalmine. The monarchy, the wealthier aristocracy, and the Church were
content to remain rentiers who leased out their lands to others for mining.
Wherever accessible coal seams were found, entrepreneurial gentry developed collieries on their own land or leased the rights to land held by others.
Investment capital came largely from profits on farming or landholding.
Landowners could and did mortgage their lands to obtain funds for mining
ventures.

For example, gentry entrepreneurial drive on the part of the Lowther
family developed the small Cumberland coalfields located on the west coast
between Whitehaven and Maryport and northeast to Aspartia. Throughout
the sixteenth century, a sparse population, poor roads, and unnavigable
rivers constrained mining in this field. However, Christopher Lowther
(1611–1644) saw an opportunity to export local coal and salt to Ireland. By
the 1630s, Lowther was shipping twenty-four hundred metric tons of coal a
year from Whitehaven port to Dublin from two mines he had acquired. His
son, John Lowther (1642–1706), bought up promising coal properties along
the western slope of the St. Bees River, invested heavily in drainage levels,
and successfully worked three highly productive collieries. He also built a
network of cartways leading into Whitehaven and invested in deepening the
harbor and building a new pier. By the 1680s, his collieries were sending almost forty thousand tons of coal to Ireland each year.

Smaller collieries producing under a thousand metric tons of coal a year
could readily be managed by the owner himself with the aid of a reliable
banksman (a clerk-supervisor) and a workforce of less than a dozen men.
Larger workings, those that regularly produced above one thousand tons a
year and employed twenty to a hundred or more men, required a complex
industrial structure.[96]

96. Ibid., 282.

Well before the eighteenth century, the greater collieries possessed many of the characteristics commonly used to distinguish the classic new industrial enterprises of the industrial revolution from their predecessors. Production was concentrated on a single site (or a cluster of proximate sites), substantial amounts of capital were sunk into fixed assets, and the site was operated by a sizeable specialist, full-time workforce. Moreover, even collieries of more modest size were multidimensional enterprises, the efficient management of which necessitated a combination of detailed monitoring and creative policy making. The workforce had to be recruited, trained, controlled, and rewarded, output and sales monitored and recorded, and the fabric of the colliery and its machinery and equipment maintained. Production had to be geared to what was often a highly volatile market, dependent not only on the vagaries of the demand for coal within the hinterland but also on the cost and availability of transport and the presence of competition.

Moreover, the production process was not simply a matter of ensuring the efficient working of muscles or machines. The cutting of coal was rarely a matter of routine, and managers had to react to the geology of the seam as it revealed itself, and to the incidence of water or foul air. Finally, the assets of the colliery needed constant renewal, and continuous production demanded not only the undertaking of new sinkings and headings but also the provision of an ample flow of cash to pay for them.

Long-term profitability rested on how well owners and managers met these tests. Entrepreneurial skills had to be coupled with precise and orderly management. Well-defined work rules and routines; fair and equitable pay scales and output targets; accurate and consistent keeping of accounts; continuing maintenance of shafts, pillars, and drains—all were essential. Attracting and keeping a free workforce was not easy. Hauling coal from the face to the winding mechanism required only unskilled labor paid at the going rate for agricultural labor. However, skilled, reliable hewers who could cut a seam for maximum output and safety were well paid and could readily find work at other collieries. Reliable banksmen who could keep accounts were also essential to the colliery's success. Expert sinkers who could dig the vertical shafts and who could run horizontal drainage soughs to the lowest level of the coal to drain off water were much in demand.

There were also indirect costs associated with coal mining that became more obvious with expansion. Cultivation on the surface of the land and small-scale mining beneath it had coexisted without much difficulty in the medieval centuries. However, as aggressive entrepreneurs invested heavily to sink pits to reach productive coal seams, the environmental effects of that mining created new conflicts over land use.

In April 1620, Robert Cooper, attorney to the bishop of Durham, prepared a submission to the Chancery Court of the Palatinate of Durham on behalf of the copyhold tenants of Wickham Manor, located on the Tyne

River just east of Newcastle. In this submission, Cooper complained of pollution and devastation from coal mining on the holdings of the Wickham tenants.[97] Wickham Manor contained some of the most valuable and accessible coal seams in the British Isles. Cooper charged that the coal mine's owners and operators, known as the grand lessees, had in the past ten years sunk some 150 coal pits not just in the wastelands and commons but also in the grain fields of the manor, without the copyholder tenant's permission. The grand lessees were currently digging new pits. Of the existing pits, some 120 were now exhausted and left empty. These the grand lessees did not fence but left to fill up with water and to constitute a mortal hazard for humans and livestock—many of which had drowned in them. The miners simply left the "rubbishe and metall" or mine waste on the surrounding land so that the landowners could not cultivate.

Furthermore, in draining the mines with sluices and trenches underground, the miners had thereby drained and destroyed the manor's twenty springs and wells. Dwelling houses and even the parish church had been "undermyned" by the effects of subsidence and were "ruynated and falne downe." Miners indiscriminately opened new coalways through fields and meadows for the passage of coal wains (carts) to the river Tyne.

In response to the interrogatories of the court, the grand lessees argued that the charges were exaggerated and inaccurate. They were only acting within the provisions of the ninety-nine-year mining lease they held.[98] The grand lessees pointed out that they had tried to compensate the copyholders for trouble and damage in a reasonable way. Cooper, however, persisted and added to his complaint that over eighty hectares of good meadowland had been "quyte spoiled and cankered with the water that issueth out of the colewaists."[99] Presumably this was water contaminated with sulfur dioxide, nitrous oxide, lead, and other heavy metals.

When the matter came before the court, the copyhold tenants vehemently testified that, although one could quibble over the actual number of open pits, the pockmarked surface of the mining areas in the manor was plain to

97. David Levine and Keith Wrightson, *The Making of an Industrial Society: Whickham, 1560–1765* (Oxford: Clarendon Press; New York: Oxford University Press, 1991).

98. Ibid. On February 1, 1578, Elizabeth I extracted an unlimited mining lease from the bishop of Durham for a seventy-nine-year period at an annual rent of 117.15.8 pounds sterling. She conferred this lease and full lordship rights over Whickham Manor on Thomas Sutton, Master of Ordnance of the North, in return for a substantial payment. In 1582, the lease was extended to ninety-nine years. In 1583, the Hostmen of Newcastle bought the lease from Sutton for 12,000 pounds sterling. Finally, in 1599, the city of Newcastle, for whom the lease had been purchased, forced the lease owners to incorporate as a separate trading company with sole rights to trade coal in Newcastle. In return, the Hostmen assigned what was now called the "Grand Lease" to the mayor and burgesses of Newcastle, but they retained their personal shares in its revenues.

99. Ibid., 112.

see. The danger from these was well attested. Witnesses named five persons who had accidentally fallen into the open pits and drowned. Springs and wells were dried up. Moreover, coal dust spilling from the coal wains spoiled grain and hay growing in the fields. Meadows were sodden with "unwholesome" water that flowed from the drainage channels of the mines. Animals refused to drink the water or eat the grass affected by it. The tenants added that miners had stripped the manorial woodlands to obtain timber for their operations. They estimated that the lands "layed waste and spoiled" as being between one-quarter and one-third the total area of the manor.[100]

On September 6, 1621, Judge Sir Richard Hutton, chancellor of the County Palatine of Durham, found that "the sayd losse hurt and damage" to be "as is affirmed farr greater then was in former tymes by reason of the increase in pitts and workes of Collyerie" at Wickham. Hutton ordered the grand lessees to mitigate the grievances outlined in the complaint. They were to fill in and fence pits, to site coalways carefully, and to pay increased compensation for damages to the tenants. However, the chancellor also found that "the uttering and venting of coles from thence [from Wickham Manor] is become a matter of great necessitie and much concerninge the generall good of the kingdom." It was of "great benefitt and commoditie" to the king and many of his subjects that Wickham coal should be shipped to London and "to the most porte Townes and parts of this kingdom."[101] Valid though the complaints were, the national interest took priority. The grand lessees held full, unfettered rights to sink coal pits and to run coalways within any of the copyholder's lands and grounds for the duration of their lease.

Whatever the costs to agricultural land might be, the copyhold tenants of Wickham and other manors would have to live with intensive coal mining for the near future. Throughout the growing coal mining regions of the British Isles, the land would be marred by waste piles, empty pits, and subsidence. Water supplies would be contaminated by acidic and heavy metal deposits—the extent of which would be only partly visible to contemporaries.

MARKETS AND CONSUMPTION

During the medieval centuries, coal in England occupied two specialized market niches in iron and steel forging and in building. Smiths bought packets of coal by the hundredweight. In the forge, coal burnt slowly at relatively low temperatures and withstood frequent watering and blowing. Lime burners used a larger quantity of coal to produce high-quality mortar and plaster for great building projects. In areas where forests were depleted, coal came

100. Ibid., 113–15.
101. Ibid., 129–30.

into use as a heating fuel, especially for large institutions. For example, in the early 1300s at Durham and Northumberland near the coalfields in the northeast, the monks of Durham priory burnt some two hundred metric tons of coal per year for heating and cooking to supplement logs, kindling, and peat normally used.[102] Coal also offered more compact storage through the northern winter for priories, castles, and other institutional users.

The demographic consequences of the Black Death sharply curtailed overall energy demand in the fifteenth century and brought about considerable farm abandonment and forest regrowth. Cheap wood prices did not encourage coal consumption until demographic and economic recovery began in the early 1500s. By midcentury, long familiarity with coal, dwindling wood supplies, surging energy demands for domestic and industrial use, and favorable pricing all encouraged coal consumption despite a traditional preference for wood.

London dominated the growing national market for coal. Favorably placed to receive coastal shipments of coal from Newcastle, Londoners turned increasingly to coal for cooking and heating. In the mid–sixteenth century, when London and its suburbs probably had a population of 80,000 to 100,000, coal imports were about 20,000 metric tons or .2 to .25 tons per inhabitant. By 1610, the per capita import for a population of around 200,000 persons was .75 tons.[103] By 1700, London was taking up to 80 percent of Newcastle's coal. Toward the end of the seventeenth century, imports reached 400,000 to 450,000 tons for a population of 600,000, or roughly the same per capita consumption.

The changeover to coal was slow, expensive, and trying for Londoners. To burn at all, coal must be kept together in a compact unit so that enough heat can be attained. Coal requires a greater air flow, or draft, than wood. Coal smoke is denser and hangs heavier in the air than wood smoke. Through trial and error, London householders found they needed narrow hearths, shallow grates, and higher chimneys to deal with coal smoke in residential interiors. Even without these adjustments, ordinary folk burnt coal and put up with its smokiness and smell because it was cheaper. Coughing and breathing smoke were preferable to freezing. In view of the extraordinarily cold winters that recurred in the seventeenth century, coal was a much needed alternative fuel.

In London, wood and charcoal were fast becoming fuels for the well-to-do and, by the end of the seventeenth century, something of a luxury. This does not mean that coal was necessarily affordable by all, despite its low price relative to wood. In London during the seventeenth century, even at the higher wages prevalent in the capital, a common laborer had to work for ten to

102. Hatcher, *Before 1700*, 27.
103. Ibid., 41.

twelve days to buy a ton of coal, and a craftsman seven to eight days for the same amount.[104] In contrast to the tree cover during the medieval centuries, London's surrounding woodlands and copses either had disappeared or were jealously guarded by their owners to prevent illegal gathering of fuelwood.

For the poor, who more often than not had to choose between buying fuel and food, London's cold months were months of misery. Ironically, the seventeenth and eighteenth centuries were unusually cold for Europe. Between 1500 and 1550 occurred at least seventeen winters when the Thames froze completely. Domestic heating took on even greater urgency in the face of these unusually severe winters. If ample supplies of coal had not kept coming from Newcastle, mortality rates from cold and exposure would certainly have climbed to new heights in the severest of these cold winters. By the eighteenth century, London's dependence on coal was even more complete. In the severe winter of 1739–1740, coastal navigation virtually ended between December and February because of low temperatures, high winds, ice, and higher than normal tides. When coal shipments ceased, this proved to be a "social calamity" as "deaths from exposure and accident [sic] hypothermia multiplied in England through the winter months, the result of both the shortage of fuel and the inadequacies of the welfare system."[105]

The proliferating coal fires of the capital emitted streams of dense, sulfur-laden, smoke that gave London its well-known smoky gray atmosphere. By the mid-1600s, the capital's unremitting air pollution had reached the point of satire. John Evelyn, advocate for forest regeneration, wrote with only slight exaggeration "that London was enveloped in such a cloud of sea-coal, as if there be a resemblance of hell upon earth, it is in this volcano in a foggy day: this pestilent smoak, which corrodes the very yron [iron], and spoils all the moveables, leaving a soot on all things that it lights: and so fatally seizing on the lungs of the inhabitants, that cough and consumption spare no man."[106] Two years later, in his polemic *Fumifugium*, he detailed the deleterious effects of coal smoke by which clothes, hangings, and even washing put out to dry were dirtied, paintings tarnished, buildings corroded, water corrupted, and especially, human health threatened.[107]

This everyday menace persisted despite relatively favorable local climate conditions: London did not normally suffer from air inversions, in which air was trapped between high hill ranges in a bowl effect. When unusual climatic conditions did produce such inversions, the results were certainly harmful.

104. Ibid., 42.

105. John D. Post, *Food Shortage, Climatic Variability, and Epidemic Disease in Preindustrial Europe: The Mortality Peak in the Early 1740s* (Ithaca, N.Y.: Cornell University Press, 1985), 61.

106. John Evelyn, *A Character of England: as it was lately presented in a letter to a noble man of France* (London: Jo. Crooke, 1659), as quoted in Peter Brimblecombe, *The Big Smoke: A History of Air Pollution in London since Medieval Times* (London: Methuen, 1987), 47.

107. Brimblecombe, *The Big Smoke*, 49; John Evelyn, *Fumifugium* (Exeter: The Rota, 1976).

What were termed great stinking fogs did occur several times every year, and the mortality rates increased accordingly in the weeks following.[108]

A pioneer seventeenth-century demographer and epidemiologist, John Gaunt, analyzed London's bills of mortality and concluded that deaths from rickets, previously unnoticed, rose spectacularly to more than five hundred per year in the period after 1630. He and other observers commented that this new disease coincided with new unhealthy levels of air pollution in coal-using London. Certainly as a result of restricted access to sunlight, many inhabitants of London, already subject to a poor diet, may have absorbed much less vitamin D into their systems during the extended seventeenth-century winters.[109] Despite widely expressed unhappiness with air pollution, neither the city nor the monarchy seriously addressed abatement, apart from a few instances in which the Crown regulated especially noticeable industrial sources in the city.

The changeover to coal was not confined to the capital. Wherever reasonable access to coastal or riverine transport existed, as well as in the immediate hinterlands of collieries where land transport was at all feasible, consumers switched to coal. The London market did not claim entirely the roughly 700,000 metric tons of coal shipped along the coast from Newcastle and Sunderland each year. By the early 1680s, King's Lynn and Yarmouth were receiving 20 percent of the yearly shipments of coal from the northeast (compared to London's 60 percent). Rural and town folk alike throughout East Anglia routinely used cheap Tyneside coal. Hull and other ports in Yorkshire took 5 percent; Essex, just over 2 percent; and the south coast, 7 percent of the total.[110] Inland markets on the Tyne and Derwent Rivers obtained coal from the northeastern fields.

Elsewhere, another fourteen British coalfields each supplied their immediate hinterlands and fed export markets of varying size. Both Glasgow and Edinburgh were located adjacent to the main Scottish collieries. Scots sea shipments went to continental ports and to other regions in Scotland. Manchester lay directly within the Yorkshire fields; Sheffield and Nottingham within the Lancashire workings. The river Severn brought cheap coal to Worcester and Gloucester. The North Wales fields partly supplied that region. Inland towns not well served by rivers, such as Oxford, suffered higher prices and were slower to convert to coal. Dublin obtained its coal from the collieries across the Irish Sea in South Wales and later those in Cumberland. Most of the Irish, lacking coal seams, relied far more on wood and peat for fuel.

Remote areas in which the inhabitants had access to supplies of wood for

108. Brimblecombe, *The Big Smoke,* 59.
109. Ibid., 52–55.
110. Hatcher, *Before 1700,* 500, table 14.5.

fuel also lagged in the switchover to coal. For the rural poor, gathered fuels, no matter how inferior, were preferable to purchased fuel. Peat turves, when available nearby, were used extensively for domestic heating. For the many who could not afford either coal or wood, gathering was the only survival strategy. For the poorest, fuel consumption probably dropped and hardship increased.[111] However, everywhere in rural as well as urban homesteads, coal gained against other fuels.

Fuel-using industries comprised a large and growing segment of coal users in early modern Britain. By 1700, as much as a third of all coal produced was burnt in both old and new processing and manufacturing activities. Iron working, metal smelting, lime burning, salt making, brewing, and textile manufacturing consumed the most coal. Smiths, who in every village and town made and repaired horseshoes, iron implements, and utensils essential for daily life, actively sought out coal supplies in place of charcoal. Coal fires withstood the wind from the bellows when the smith heated the fire to work iron, and coals could be watered to make them bind and cake and, hence, last longer. In larger towns, centers of iron working had developed in which artisans turned out increasing quantities of cutlery, shovels, locks, bolts, scythes, plowshares, hinges, trivets, buckles, and especially, nails. Where coal was cheap, as in Sheffield and Nottingham, in or near the coalfields ironworkers flourished.[112]

Lime burners used heat to convert limestone (calcium carbonate) into lime (calcium oxide). Coal provided a slow, durable fire for limekilns. Builders used lime to make construction mortar and to color walls. Much of the housing stock of early modern Britain was improved or constructed anew to meet rising demands for privacy and comfort. In the sixteenth century, more farmers learned of the productivity gains that could be obtained by spreading lime over acidic soils. By 1700, lime was almost universally used in agriculture. It was not exceptional for farmers to haul in and spread several tons of lime per hectare. Where limestone quarries and coalfields converged, limekilns proliferated. So scattered and ubiquitous were limekilns that it is virtually impossible to determine either output or infer overall coal consumption.

English salt producers benefited in the late sixteenth century from French political turmoil that disrupted the flow of low-priced, imported salt from the Atlantic coast of France and Spain.[113] Suddenly the domestic industry boomed. When imports faltered, entrepreneurs hastened to set up salt pans to produce salt by boiling seawater, essential in view of the overcast English climate. Cheap, abundant fuel was crucial to success.

---

111. Woodward, "Straw, Bracken, and the Wicklow Whale," 53.
112. Hatcher, *Before 1700*, 423–25.
113. See ibid., 430–38, for a comprehensive discussion of salt making.

By the seventeenth century, salt boilers in Tyneside, located next to the coalfields and to low-cost water transport, dominated the market. Average annual shipments in the late seventeenth century were about 12,000 metric tons of salt per year. Since each ton of salt required between 6 and 8 metric tons of coal, this meant that the salt boilers consumed 80,000 to 100,000 tons of coal, or roughly 7 percent of the total output of the northeastern mines. Other prominent saltworks could be found in the Scottish coalfields along the Firth of Forth. Scots output normally varied between 6,000 and 8,000 tons of salt per year. Boiling to produce this amount required between 40,000 and 60,000 tons of coal. Other minor saltworks were scattered around the English coast wherever coalfields were located next to the sea, such as in the Dee estuary in Flint. By 1700, salt boiling consumed as much as 250,000 tons of coal, or 10 percent of total output.

Brewing beer and ale was another heavy fuel-using industry. In the sixteenth century, brewing by drinking-house proprietors largely replaced home brewing by women. In larger cities and towns, common brewers began supplying publicans with beer and ale. By the seventeenth century, brewing was becoming a highly organized, competitive, centralized, urban industry. The new practice of adding hops aided centralized production, since hops acted as a preservative. Beer traveled better and no longer had to be brewed where it was to be consumed. Consumption of beer and ale rose steadily as the number of public drinking houses rose to sixty thousand in England alone, or one for every eighty inhabitants in 1700. By that date, English brewers were producing annually an estimated 350 million gallons of beer, up from 250 million gallons a century earlier.

The brewing process demanded that large quantities of water be heated and cooled repeatedly. Malting also consumed fuel, since germinated barley was dried in a kiln over a moderate heat before being added to the mix. Wood fuel costs amounted to as much as 25 percent of production costs in the late sixteenth century and were rising fast. Brewers of beer, who competed hard on price, were quick to take advantage of cheap coal in place of wood.

Textile manufacture, especially that of woolens, which grew enormously in scale over the sixteenth and seventeenth centuries, was another heavy coal user. The industry needed fuel for kilns to dry yarn, to heat kettles to clean wool, and especially to boil cloth in dyeing. Also, alum, used as a mordant to fix dyes in textiles, had to be boiled to remove impurities. By mid–seventeenth century, some 8,000 metric tons of coal were being used annually in the alum pans.

Finally, to round out the list we can add new industries. By the late 1600s, as the use of soap for personal and domestic use spread, commercial soap boilers were burning large amounts of coal. By the end of the century, sugar refining in London had become another fuel-intensive industry. Glassmaking, stimulated by the demand for window glass in the rebuilding boom, pro-

vided another small but expanding market for coal. Brick making followed
a similar trajectory as wood prices soared and brick makers adapted to coal.
Only one significant industry resisted conversion to coal and remained
dependent on wood for its fuel. Metal smelting—reducing ore to pure iron,
tin, lead, and copper—soared between 1500 and 1700. Over the two centuries, English production of iron rose fivefold, to 25,000 metric tons per
year, of tin rose threefold, to 1,870 tons, and most dramatically, of lead rose
forty-six-fold, from 600 to 28,000 tons. Copper smelting, revived in England
on a small scale in the 1680s, also increased rapidly. Smelters burnt gigantic
amounts of charcoal. To produce a single ton of bar iron required cutting
and burning twelve cords of wood (43.5 cubic meters) for charcoal.

Ironmasters and other smelter operators were continually searching for
sources of charcoal. Many survived by systematic coppicing of neighboring
woodlands. Many smelting operations were located near coalfields. Nevertheless, severe technical constraints hindered ready conversion to coal. Burning coal gave off sulfur-ridden fumes that contaminated the metal. Attempts
to coke or preheat coal faltered because of the variability of coal supplies.

The other possible technical fix lay in furnace design. Reverberatory furnaces that separated burning coal from the ore by reflecting the heat from
the roof of the furnace to the ore section were the answer. Lower melting
points made it easier for nonferrous metals to be smelted in redesigned reverberatory furnaces. By the late 1600s, coal was a viable alternative to charcoal for lead and copper. It was only in the early eighteenth century that iron
smelting using coke proved successful. And it was not until 1784 that Henry
Cort's puddling and rolling process permitted the use of a reverberatory furnace to refine pig iron into bar iron.[114]

By 1700, coal had become the principal British energy source that was beginning to supplant wood as a fuel. Coal at the pithead had a value of around
five hundred thousand pounds in a national economy conventionally agreed
to be 50 million pounds. Coal at retail had a value each year of 1 to 2 million
pounds. Lacking coal as a fuel, British industry could not have grown as it
did. Lacking coal, the general population would have been distinctly more
uncomfortable in the winter and subject to a much-lowered standard of living as fuel prices soared. Lacking coal, the need to grow trees for fuel might
have superseded agriculture near the cities. Certainly, cheap, reliable supplies of coal stimulated the growth of cities in this period. Lacking coal, domestic wood production for fuel could not possibly have been an adequate
substitute.[115]

The best estimate of the extent of woodlands, plantations, hedgerows, and
incidental nonwoodland trees in late-seventeenth-century England is ap-

114. B. Thomas, "Escaping from Constraints," 730.
115. Ibid., 549.

preciably less than 1.2 million hectares. The annual yield of more than 1 acre of well-managed coppiced woodland was required to produce on a sustainable basis the heat energy of a ton of coal. On that basis, even if the total annual growth of England's woodland and hedgerow trees had been exclusively devoted to the production of firewood, this would have just about matched the calorific value of the 2 to 2.2 million metric tons of coal that English coal mines were yielding at this time. Since nearly half of all wood production was used as the all-purpose raw material in the early modern world, the energy shortfall would have been far greater. Even if we add in the possibility of exploiting the woodlands of Ireland, Scotland, and Wales, the same calculation applies. Wood was more expensive to transport than coal in terms of its energy yield.

After 1700, coal production and consumption continued to accelerate. In the first half of the eighteenth century, coal output rose from 2.7 to 5.2 million metric tons—nearly a doubling. By 1775, annual output had reached 8.9 million tons, and by 1800 the total was 15 million tons.[116] No new fields were found or developed. This impressive rise in production was the result of more intensive exploitation of those fields already known. A skilled body of technicians who were already masters of an impressive technology continued to make incremental improvements in the digging and transport of coal.[117] New technical innovations, such as the use of steam engines for lifting water up deeper and deeper shafts and adoption of improved ventilation systems, helped increase output. Artificial canals functioning as strategic links made it possible to move coal more efficiently to urban markets.

Domestic consumption of coal continued to soar as the population expanded. The coal transformation of the sixteenth and seventeenth centuries opened up a new, strategic resource to add to the influx of wealth gained by mercantile and colonial expansion.

CONCLUSION

Like Tokugawa Japan, the lands of the British Isles were among the most intensively managed of any society during the early modern period. Unlike Japan, however, Britain actively sought out and consumed new resources from new sources at home and abroad. It was a society that did not recognize limits to growth.

In Britain, improvements in human organization—especially in the state and other complex, large-scale organizations and in economic exchange—forced a steeply rising demand for natural resources. Agricultural intensifi-

116. Michael W. Flinn, with David Stoker. *1700–1830: The Industrial Revolution*, vol. 2 of *The History of the British Coal Industry* (Oxford: Clarendon Press, 1984),26, table 1.2.
117. Ibid., 3.

cation and expansion of cultivation fed a growing population and made significant changes in the landscape of the British Isles. Most remarkable, however, was the shift from wood and peat to domestically produced coal as the primary energy source for domestic and industrial use. Britain was the first society in the world to make that transition. The energy transformation resulting from coal is emblematic of a converging set of material and social changes that occurred in Britain over the three centuries of the early modern period. Burning coal appreciably added to the resources and wealth of that society. So also did the influx of resources resulting from aggressive worldwide trade and colonization in the New World—that is, tapping new domestic resources was synergistic with tapping new imported resources.

Chapter 7

Frontier Settlement in Russia

In the fourteenth century, Moscow was an obscure Slavic principality located on the eastern marches of European civilization. Ivan I (r. 1331–1340), Grand Prince of Moscow, claimed authority over several hundred thousand subjects and less than twenty thousand square kilometers of territory.[1] By the nineteenth century, Moscow had grown into the sprawling Russian empire—one of the largest and most powerful in the world. Tsar Nicholas II (r. 1894–1917) ruled over 125 million subjects in an empire stretching over 22 million square kilometers.[2] This extraordinary record of territorial growth against contiguous land borders is as impressive as the coterminous expansion of the British empire along the sea routes of the world. Dozens of kingdoms and principalities and hundreds of ethnic groups suffered defeat and assimilation by Russians. The language and culture and Eastern Orthodox Christian faith of the Russian heartland informed the imperial ethos of this vast empire.

Russians grew accustomed to the costs and the rewards—both material and psychic—of continuing expansion. Successful Russian domination of newly annexed lands depended on a continually expanding frontier of settlement. Year after year, decade after decade, a stream of pioneers flowed from the forested heartland of Russian civilization.

At midpoint in the sixteenth century, the eastern and southern boundaries of the Russian heartland marked interlinked ecological, economic, and

1. Robert O. Crummey, "Muscovy and the 'General Crisis of the Seventeenth Century,' " *Journal of Early Modern History* 2, no. 2 (1998): 36–39; for the territorial extent, see D. J. B. Shaw, *Russia in the Modern World: A New Geography* (Oxford: Blackwell, 1999), 2.

2. David Moon, "Peasant Migration and the Settlement of Russia's Frontiers, 1550–1897," *The Historical Journal* 40, no. 4 (1997): 859–60.

cultural-political boundaries. The densely forested landscape of the Russian heartland merged into the forest-steppe, with its black earth soils—a narrow transition zone leading to the true steppe grasslands. The peasant societies of Russia dissolved into Tatar pastoral nomadic societies. The Eastern Orthodox Christian culture and civilization of Russia abutted the Sunni Islamic faith and civilization of the Tatars and Turks. During the next century and a half, the Russian state burst past these bounds. Moscow, channeling the immense energies of the Russian people, seized control of and fostered Russian pioneer settlement of the central black earth region and middle portion of the river Volga in a process of intensive land reclamation and permanent agricultural settlement.[3]

DEFINING THE RUSSIAN HEARTLAND

Between 1462 and 1533, under the leadership of two strong rulers, Ivan III (r. 1462–1505) and Vasilii III (r. 1505–1533), Moscow became a major regional power and a coalescing nation-state. Ivan III completed Moscow's long struggle to impose centralized control over the twenty or more Russian principalities tributary to the Mongols in the fourteenth century. His greatest triumphs were the 1478 forcible annexation of the republic of Novgorod, with its control over the fur-rich northern regions, and the 1485 invasion and annexation of Tver—Moscow's two great rivals. As important was Ivan's public repudiation in 1476 of any further tribute payments to the Khan of the Golden Horde and the subsequent failure of a 1480 punitive expedition by the Mongols in a last attempt to enforce tribute payment. Vasilii III, continuing his father's protracted campaigns against the Grand Duchy of Lithuania to the west, in 1518 finally captured Smolensk. A negotiated treaty in 1522 confirmed Lithuania's loss of nearly one-third of its territories to Moscow. These and other successes brought all the Russian lands, both within the heartland and beyond, under Moscow's sovereignty.[4]

At his accession in 1533, Ivan IV ("Ivan the Terrible") ruled over 2.9 million square kilometers of land inhabited by between 6 and 6.5 million subjects.[5] Over half of Ivan IV's territories lay in the Novgorod Territory of the far north beyond St. Petersburg and Vologda, above sixty degrees north latitude, where the Russian forest gave way to the spruce and bogs of the hard-frozen taiga. Less than a half million persons lived in this vast region. A few Russian settlements were scattered among indigenous non-Russian peoples,

3. D. J. B. Shaw presents this conceptualization based on Donald Meinig's typology of Western imperial expansion (*Russia in the Modern World,* 4–9).

4. Robert O. Crummey, *The Formation of Muscovy, 1304–1613* (London: Longman, 1987), 84–93.

5. Ibid., 2.

whose hunting and gathering produced the furs so vital to Moscow's economy.[6]

Russian territorial expansion drew on the manpower and surpluses generated by peasant agriculture in the mixed-forest region of the northeast. This was the hearth, or heartland, of Russian civilization. In the late fifteenth century, the heartland stretched from Vologda in the north, 580 kilometers south to Tula; and from Smolensk in the west, 740 kilometers east to Novgorod.[7] These borders defined a region inhabited overwhelmingly by ethnic Russians who were adherents of the Eastern Orthodox Christian confession. Nine-tenths or more were peasant farmers engaged in plow cultivation of rye and other food grains on gray forest soils. Within the heartland could be found Moscow, Novgorod, and other urban centers of Russian civilization and life.

The agricultural surpluses available to Moscow's rulers were less abundant and less regular than those of their contemporaries in more favored regions of western Europe. The Russian heartland lay on the ecological margin of plowed, sedentary, food-grain cultivation in Europe. The continental climate was harsh, and winter the dominant season. Moscow, at 55° 45′ north, is only a few degrees south of the Arctic Circle. The mean temperature in January in the twentieth century is −10.3°C, and in July only 17.8°C. The region has an average of 141 frost-free days per year.[8] For much of the remainder of the year, snow covers the ground. Precipitation, on the other hand, at 575 millimeters, is adequate, although a summer maximum is less than optimal for ripening crops. In the early modern period, climate presumably was even less favorable than it is now.

Other natural conditions were more benign. The land was level—part of the grand Russian plain—less than two hundred meters above sea level at any point, and without steep hills or ravines to inhibit plow cultivation. Numerous streams and rivers that flowed across the plain supplied ready access to water and transportation. The soil, a gray podzol, was acidic and only adequately fertile but, given its loamy texture, easily tilled. Unless interrupted by human settlement, mixed coniferous and deciduous forests covered the land with a nearly continuous canopy.

Russian peasants cut their holdings from the forest. The conventional phrase denoting rural settlement in the medieval Russian lands was "Wherever the sokha [plow], scythe and axe have gone."[9] Essential tools included

---

6. Geoffrey Barraclough and Richard Overy, eds., *Hammond Atlas of World History*, 5th ed. (Maplewood, N.J.: Hammond, 1999), 161.

7. Moon, "Peasant Migration and the Settlement of Russia's Frontiers," 859; Shaw, *Russia in the Modern World*, 5, fig. 1.4.

8. Shaw, *Russia in the Modern World*, 13, table 1.1.

9. R. E. F. Smith, *Peasant Farming in Muscovy* (Cambridge: Cambridge University Press, 1977), 7.

a broad-bladed iron ax; the plow, or *sokha*, with two iron tines and wooden shafts and handles; and the short-handled scythe. Peasants employed and continued to use long-established slash-and-burn techniques. They partially cleared patches of forest with their axes, girdled large trees to kill them, and then fired the area. They sowed rye and other grains in the resulting clearings and relied on nutrients from the ashes to help fertilize their crops. They used the *sokha*, easily maneuverable around large stumps, to dig shallow furrows into the ash-covered, loose forest soil. After several years, the forest farmers opened up new forest clearings and left the old fields to be overgrown by birches and brush. Their short scythes cut hay grown up in the forest clearings and along water meadows.

By the fifteenth century, peasants in the heartland had started to adopt the more intensive European three-field system that produced more food from the same area of land. In this system, peasants planted one field with a spring crop, one with a winter crop, and left the third fallow. In the next year, they rotated the fields. The method demanded heavier plows and greater inputs of labor in clearing fields of stumps and in draining them. Livestock played a more important role in stump removal and in provision of manure for fertilizing the fields. Yields under the slash-and-burn system were high, but the total land area required was much larger than that under the three-field system.

Why this change? By mid–fifteenth century, the Russian population had recovered from the devastating losses in the fourteenth century caused by repeated wars and plague epidemics. As numbers increased, and as the state set limits on peasant mobility, pressures on the land increased.[10] In the 1470s, new landlords given conditional rights to estates *(pomest'e)* by Ivan III in return for military service assumed control over lands formerly owned by local landowners. These new *pomeschiki* demanded higher rents from tenants than the old landlords had. They stopped accepting furs as partial payment of rent and began demanding full payment in grain and other agricultural products. With their access to forestlands constrained, and with landlords making higher rental demands, peasants were forced to produce more on the lands they occupied—hence the three-field system.

Fifteenth-century Russian peasants worked individual farmsteads defined by occupancy rights, and they lived in household and work units defined by the nuclear family composed of a married couple with their children. The household might shelter additional dependents, kin or non-kin, but did not own slaves. Total farmstead area was typically between ten and seventeen hectares divided between the household area, arable land, and hayfields.[11]

10. Jane Martin, *Medieval Russia, 980–1584* (Cambridge: Cambridge University Press, 1995), 269.
11. Smith, *Peasant Farming in Muscovy,* 82–84, 87.

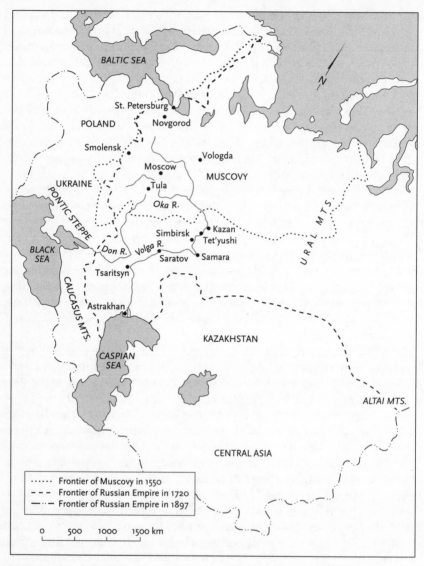

Map 7.1 Russia's political frontiers, 1550–1897. Adapted from David Moon, "Peasant Migration and the Settlement of Russia's Frontiers, 1550–1897," *The Historical Journal* 40, no. 4 (1997): 860.

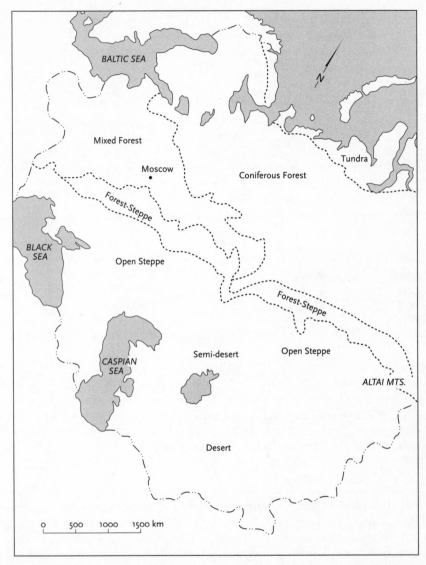

Map 7.2 Russia's environmental belts. Adapted from David Moon, "Peasant Migration and the Settlement of Russia's Frontiers, 1550–1897," *The Historical Journal* 40, no. 4 (1997): 875.

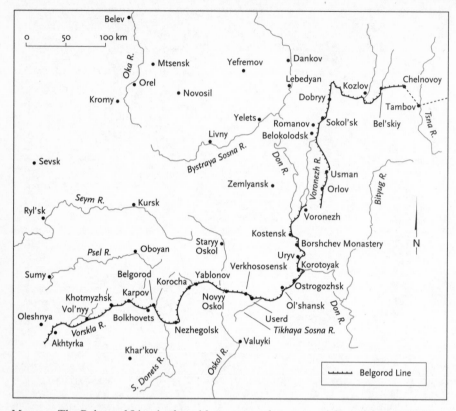

Map 7.3 The Belgorod Line in the mid–seventeenth century. Adapted from D. J. B. Shaw, "Southern Frontiers of Muscovy, 1550–1700," in *Studies in Russian Historical Geography*, ed. James H. Bater and R. A. French (London: Academic Press, 1983), fig. 6.3, p. 128.

Peasants had a limited number and variety of cultivars available to them. Their primary food grain was rye sown in either field or forest patch in the early winter and harvested the following midsummer. Other grains included buckwheat, sown with rye; small amounts of wheat, regarded as a luxury for cakes or communion bread; and oats, eaten by both humans and horses.[12] Russian peasants consumed grain in the form of bread, in dishes made with flour, in beer, and in a fermented drink called kvass. Turnips, the main vegetable crop, were sown on cut wheat fields or burnt forest clearings in June for harvesting in August. Peasants also grew small amounts of peas and lentils. They grew hemp for its fiber, used in cord and ropes, and for the oil

12. Ibid., 32–35.

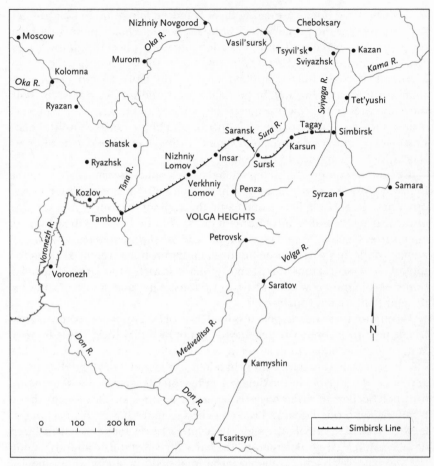

Map 7.4 The Simbirsk Line and settlement of the Volga Basin. Adapted from
D. J. B. Shaw, "Southern Frontiers of Muscovy, 1550–1700," in *Studies in Russian Historical Geography*, ed. James H. Bater and R. A. French (London: Academic Press, 1983), fig. 6.5, p. 133.

in its seeds. Flax, the main fiber plant, was grown by nearly every peasant in small areas set aside within the larger fields. Cabbages, beets, carrots, and onions were the customary garden produce.

Livestock were limited in number and nondescript in quality. A few chickens were kept to provide eggs, but these were rarely mentioned by sources contemporary to the times. Small, foraging pigs kept for meat were the most numerous domestic animal. Sheep gave up wool and meat and, most important, hides for warm winter coats—an essential item of clothing. Small-to medium-sized horses averaging three hundred kilograms in weight—and not oxen—were the primary work animals. A single horse pulling the standard plow, the usual work unit, was adequate for 4.4 hectares of sown area. Smaller farmsteads could get by with one horse; the larger ones needed two. Worn-out or excess horses supplied meat for the table. Peasants kept a few small cattle, whose live weight averaged two hundred kilograms, for both meat and milk. Each cow produced between two and two-and-a-half liters of milk a day—an important dietary contribution but a modest output.[13] Each horse or cow generated three to five metric tons of manure per year per animal, which was applied to the fields.

During the summer, both horses and cattle could graze and browse in the fields and forests and on the stubble in the fields after harvest. Winter was another matter. Feeding horses and cattle throughout the long winter was one of the Russian peasants' most difficult tasks. They had to keep their cattle in enclosures, "stalled," for 204 days of the year, according to the traditional almanac rendering. Each three-hundred-kilogram horse required .3 metric tons of oats, 1 to 1.2 tons of hay, and .3 tons of straw for the winter. Each two-hundred-kilogram cow needed 1.5 to 1.6 tons of hay and .5 tons of straw for the 200 or more days enclosed.[14]

Faced with these needs, peasants made use of every possible patch of grass to cut hay. In favored villages, hayfields might equal sown fields in area. Water meadows adjacent to rivers were especially productive. When the hay was ripe, peasants cut it with short-handled scythes, let it dry, and then raked and stacked it in ricks in the fields or in haylofts. A yield of about .7 metric tons per hectare of dried hay was regarded as normal. This meant that a farmstead with one horse and two cows had to make hay on 6.3 hectares of land to feed its animals through the winter. Leafy fodder such as birch branches and leaves supplemented the hay.[15] Straw produced after threshing rye and oats was readily available for animal bedding and a wide range of other domestic uses.

Under these conditions, most Russian peasant households produced enough to sustain themselves and their livestock in a normal year, but with a perilously slight surplus. Crop yields were poor by any standard. On average, rye and oats returned a low, three-to-one ratio of threshed grain to seed sown. Total output was low. Winter rye harvests averaged .36 metric tons of threshed grain per hectare sown. Oats yielded up to .48 tons per hectare sown. The net harvest after withholding one-third of the crop for next year's seed averaged .24 tons of rye and .32 tons of oats per hectare. In the three-

13. See ibid., 41–46, for domestic animals. Smith pegs production at 714 to 955 liters of milk per year (87).
14. Ibid., 92, table 9.
15. Ibid., 42–43.

field system, with one field always fallow, typical rye and oat plantings varied in area between 1 to 5 hectares.

Did these returns match the needs of humans and animals? The norm for subsistence can be determined from fifteenth-century legal documents that awarded each rural adult slightly over one-half kilogram of rye per day (.2 metric tons per year) and between one-quarter and one-third kilograms of oats per day (.1 tons per year). By this formula, a hectare of winter rye could feed one adult and a hectare of spring oats could feed three adults comfortably in a normal year. Cattle could subsist on hay, but horses required .7 to .8 tons of oats per animal per year. A single horse consumed the net yield of 2 hectares of spring oats.[16] By this standard, a household of four—husband, wife, and two children—with one horse to feed, could survive by harvesting 2.5 hectares of rye (allowing for each child one-half the adult consumption level) and 3 hectares of oats, if harvests were good.[17]

But what if harvests were not good—a not infrequent occurrence? What of the need, however modest, to enter the market and purchase iron, salt, or other consumption items? Most important, what of the demands of the landlord—whether monastery, nobleman, or serviceman—for rent, for a considerable share of the harvest either in grain or in cash? And what of the ruler's demands on the peasant commune for taxes, fees, and labor?[18] The answer lies in the forest—the peasants' shelter and sustenance beyond their fields. As in nearly all early modern peasant societies around the world, the invisible hectares of the forest substantially enlarged the peasants' holdings. Surrounding each farmstead and each settlement lay a capacious forest hinterland open to hunting, fishing, and gathering.

The early modern Russian peasants went into the forest to find fodder for their animals, fuel, and materials for clothing and shelter. Most peasants simply could not grow enough hay and grains to feed their livestock adequately. Gathering leafy fodder and hay from forest clearings was essential to keep the animals alive. Human survival absolutely depended on cutting immense quantities of firewood to burn throughout the year in rudimentary stoves. Peasants cut and stacked fuelwood in open-sided outbuildings. They gathered the dry spores of shelf fungi *(Fomes fomentarius* and *Fomes ignarius)* to catch the spark thrown by a struck flint and to bank a smoldering fire.

With these needs met, peasants cut and gathered wood to repair and build nearly all their tools and furnishings: yokes, plows, spades, harrows, shafts, tables, benches, chests, boxes, mortars and pestles, and bins, among others. They constructed various means of transport from wood: skis, snowshoes,

16. Ibid., 88 (the calculation is for 3 *chets* of rye at 65.5 kilograms per *chet* and 2–3 *chets* of rye at 43.7 kilograms per *chet*), 92, table 9.
17. This is Smith's model farmstead "B," with up to 16.5 hectares in total area. Ibid., 92 and 87, table 8.
18. Crummey, *The Formation of Muscovy,* 6–7; Martin, *Medieval Russia,* 268.

sledges, carts, wheels, rafts, and boats. They peeled birch bark to use as a writing material inscribed with a stylus. They cut and peeled the bark from oak, willow, and other trees to obtain tannin for working hides. They boiled pine roots to obtain pitch, tar, and resin. They even made footwear called "basket" shoes, woven from the bast of young lime tree shoots, which lasted only a month or so.[19] In some circumstances, peasants could produce surpluses of some of these forest products and sell them on the market to supplement their incomes.

Food from the forest was essential—especially in deficit harvest years. Gathered foods improved not just the caloric value but also the quality of food budgets. Honey from the forest was the only sweetener in the peasant diet. Peasants eagerly sought out wild bees' nests in the hollows of trees. They smoked out the bees and extracted the combs to strain out the honey and collect the wax. Often they cut hollows to encourage the bees to nest. Peasants marked trees with blazes to indicate ownership. Any estimate of returns is difficult to make, but the honey from even one or two trees could have been considerable.[20] Landlords often insisted on a share of the honey peasants collected from bee trees on their land. Surplus honey and beeswax in large quantities was a major item of export to the towns and cities.[21]

Peasants gathered hazelnuts, but the Russian forests do not seem to have offered the variety of edible nuts found in western Europe. Berries, however, were a different matter. Every peasant family picked hundreds of kilograms of barberries *(Berberis vulgaris)*, cowberries *(Vaccinium vitis idaea)*, bogberries *(Vaccinium oxycoccus)*, bilberries *(Vaccinium myrtillus)*, bog whortleberries *(Vaccinium uliginosum)*, dewberries *(Rubus caesius)*, stone bramble berries *(Rubus saxatilis)*, raspberries *(Rubus idaeus)*, cloudberries *(Rubus chamaemorus)*, wild strawberries *(Fragaria vesca)*, and white and black currants.[22] They picked hips of the dog rose *(Rosa canina)* and cinnamon rose *(Rosa cinnamomea)*, the fruits of the guelder rose *(Viburnum opulus)*, sorb-apples *(Sorbus)*, and bird-cherries *(Padus racemosa)*. Massed bushes of cowberries found in clearings in coniferous forests could yield .5 metric tons of berries per hectare. Other berries yielded .1 to .2 tons per hectare. Whether eaten fresh, combined with honey in preserves, or added to kvass as a flavoring element, berries in quantities such as these contributed significant amounts of vitamins and calories to the peasant diet.

Mushrooms added another easily gathered food to the diet. Russian peasants identified and picked several dozen edible mushrooms: *Boletus edulis*,

19. Smith, *Peasant Farming in Muscovy*, 51–55.

20. Ibid., 74–75; R. A. French, "Russians and the Forest," in *Studies in Russian Historical Geography*, edited by James H. Bater and R. A. French (London: Academic Press, 1983), 25.

21. French, "Russians and the Forest," 26.

22. Smith, *Peasant Farming in Muscovy*, 57.

Lactarius deliciosus, Russula vesca, and *Russula virescens,* among others. Fungi could readily be dried and stored. Fungi, containing up to 73 percent protein and 2 percent fat, supplemented a diet short on protein and fat. Yields were probably between six and fifty-two kilograms per hectare—but the number of hectares open to each peasant family was limited only by their willingness to trek longer distances in the forest.[23] Other miscellaneous edible plants included sorrel (*Rumex* sp.), nettles (*Urtica urens*), and blind nettles (*Lamium album*). A seventeenth-century dictionary compiled by an English visitor defines goutwort (*Aegopodium podagraria*) as "a herbe, which in the springe they gather out of the woods and eate much of it in pottage and with their meale."[24] He also listed ramson (*Allium ursinum*), or bear-garlic, used to make "a kinde of porridge or hodgpodg made of boild beets and onions" and the cold soup made with kvass and spring onions called *okroshka.*[25]

Fish from ponds and rivers were a significant source of protein and fat in the peasant diet. They could be eaten fresh or frozen or pickled in brine, sun dried, or smoked for future consumption. Food fish were likely larger and more numerous than they have been in the industrial era. In general, historians have overlooked freshwater fishing as a significant source of food for medieval and early modern populations.[26] Catches were large, and the ratio of caloric returns to human effort high. Fishing tools ranged from the simple to complex: fish spears, hooks and baited lines, wicker basket traps, large nets, trap nets, large seines, and fish weirs.[27] Emplaced or fixed traps and seines permitted peasant fishermen to continue to work in the fields and check on their devices at intervals. Fishing was also possible on ice in the frozen winter—another important advantage.

Those peasants who lived near the larger rivers caught large "noble" fish, which included several varieties of sturgeon. The sterlet (*Acipenser ruthunus*) was most widely distributed among the Russian rivers. The smallest of the sturgeon, at less than one meter in length, the sterlet was most likely to be taken by individual peasant fishermen.[28] For most peasants, smaller pond

23. Ibid., 59.
24. Quoted in ibid., 60.
25. Quoted in ibid.
26. Richard C. Hoffman, "Economic Development and Aquatic Ecosystems in Medieval Europe," *American Historical Review* 101, no. 3 (1996).
27. Smith, *Peasant Farming in Muscovy,* 64–65.
28. But each river contained abundant stocks of one or more other species: stellate sturgeon (*Acipenser stellatus*), Russian sturgeon (*Acipenser guldenstadti*), and sea sturgeon (*Acipenser sturio*). So large were these fish—at up to 3 meters in length and 225 kilograms in weight—and so palatable their flesh and roe, that royal officials tried to extract a share of any sturgeon caught. Other large, valuable fish included the Caspian inconnu (*Stenodus leucichthys* Guldenstadti) and the nelma (*Stenodus leucichthys nelma*). The English visitor called the inconnu "the white sammon [*sic*] of Volga" (ibid., 61). Salmon were common in the northern rivers but rare in the Russian heartland.

and river fish were probably more accessible and contributed more to their diet. Among these were several species of whitefish: the Volkhov whitefish *(Coregonus lavaretus baeri)*, the European or Neva whitefish *(Coregonus lavaretus)*, the omul *(Coregonus autumnalis)*, and the vendace *(Coregonus ablula)*. There were wild and pond carp *(Cyprinus carpio)*, bream *(Abramis brama)*, tench *(Tinca tinca)*, and cuttooth *(Rutilus frisii)*, among others. The smaller smelts *(Osmerus eperlanus)* could be caught in large batches.

Finally, the peasant resorted to the forest to hunt or trap birds or animals. Royal and noble prohibitions against peasant hunting of large game certainly inhibited, if it did not stop, peasants from pursuing with bow and spear the bear, red deer *(Cervus elaphus)*, roe deer *(Capreolus capreolus)*, boar *(Sus scrofa)*, and even the rare elk *(Alces alces)* in remote tracts. Rather than actively hunt, Russian peasants were more likely to dig pits or set snares or deadfalls to entrap beaver, white hare *(Lepus timidus)*, or even wild boar or deer. They also wove large nets to be raised suddenly in the path of flying waterfowl, which could take up to a hundred birds at a time. Wild game provided most of the meat that infrequently appeared on the peasant's table.[29]

Somewhat paradoxically, even as they relied on the forest for their survival, Russian peasants engaged in an ongoing assault on it. The peasantry's great task in the early modern centuries was to gradually clear the vast forested areas that surrounded isolated patches of human settlement. Throughout the Russian heartland, peasants were immersed in a dense, shadowed green-and-black forested landscape. A minority lived in small villages of 20 to 30 households; the majority lived in tiny hamlets with 2 to 4 households and their holdings. For example, twenty-one villages on a prosperous monastic estate near Moscow at the end of the fifteenth century each contained an average of only 27 households. Hamlets on the estate averaged 3.3 farmsteads clustered in glades cleared from the forest.[30] Few settlements had contiguous boundaries with one another. Between each isolated settlement lay wide bands of forest where "axe has not met with axe."

Slowly but steadily, peasants bit into the heartland's forest cover. Despite wide adoption of the three-field rotation, peasants persisted in slash-and-burn cultivation as well. They enlarged forest glades, and cut and burnt new patches in the surrounding forest, to grow crops supplementary to those in their primary fields. In times of trouble, they could resort to their outlying forest holdings and perhaps evade violence, plundering, or disease.

When their numbers increased, peasants engaged in an incremental process of internal colonization. Apparently, most young, newly married men did not remain in their parents' household but chose to clear a new patch of forest and build a house at a distance from their parental homestead. They

29. Ibid., 66–74.
30. Ibid., 122.

claimed their share of tools, livestock, and other goods in a system of partible inheritance. In moving away, they gained the nutrient benefit from initial clearing and burning for their first crops. They may have remained in slash-and-burn mode of cultivation for some time before attempting the more intensive three-field cultivation. The pioneer couple, who probably moved at most one or two kilometers from their natal homes, remained in close contact with their parents and other kin. Landlords and officials found it difficult to identify and track pioneer land reclamation at this level and at this scale.

Despite intensifying efforts by the state and landlord to immobilize them, Russian peasants remained mobile in this period. Peasants responded to ill treatment, to excessive rent or taxes, to epidemic disease, and to political unrest and violence by flight into new forestlands. Labor was scarce; land plentiful. Landlords, anxious to increase their revenues, welcomed migrating peasants and settled them on new lands within their estates. Beyond the Russian heartland, a new process of external migration and colonization began after 1500. Dissatisfied peasants could migrate to new lands on Moscow's frontiers to the east and south.

CONQUEST OF KAZAN AND ASTRAKHAN

During the 1550s, in a remarkable feat, Ivan IV seized vast new territories to the south and east of the Russian homeland. In 1552, Russian forces invaded the Tatar khanate of Kazan, took Kazan, its capital city, located on the upper portion of the river Volga, and annexed all the khanate's territories to Moscow. In 1556, Ivan deposed the khan of Astrakhan, occupied Astrakhan at the mouth of the Volga, and annexed the lands and peoples of that khanate to what had suddenly become a nascent Russian empire.[31] For Moscow and the Russian people, these triumphs suddenly opened new frontiers for settlement and new resources for exploitation. The entire basin of the river Volga, now ruled by Moscow, was open for settlement. The annexation of Kazan also encouraged Russian advances into the forest-steppe lands to the west, in the central black earth region south of the Oka River.

Ivan and his advisors left a senior general, Prince Alexander Gorbaty, as governor of the new regime. With Gorbaty remained a garrison of three thousand musketeers (streltsy) and fifteen hundred cavalrymen and officials. The latter, impoverished minor nobles, were hereditary military servicemen who received generous land grants to keep them in Kazan on a permanent basis. Gorbaty also deployed several units of mounted cossacks to be sent on patrol into the distant steppes.

31. Henry R. Huttenbach, "Muscovy's Conquest of Muslim Kazan and Astrakhan, 1552–56: The Conquest of the Volga: Prelude to Empire," in *Russian Colonial Expansion to 1917*, edited by Michael Rywkin (London: Mansell, 1988).

The tsar and the patriarch of Moscow moved rapidly to begin what proved to be a successful attempt to transform the Islamic realm of Kazan into a predominantly Eastern Orthodox Christian culture and society. The day after the tsar's triumphal march into Kazan, the patriarch of Moscow dedicated a former mosque to the construction of a great Eastern Orthodox Christian cathedral—the golden-cupolaed Pokrovskii Sobor, completed by 1557. Within a decade, the buildings and grounds of scores of churches and monastic orders studded the city and its hinterland. Thousands of freed Russian captives who remained in Kazan functioned as ready-made congregants and laborers for the churches. Thousands more residents of Kazan, including their erstwhile ruler, the last Kazan khan, converted to Christianity in the wake of the conquest. Yadagir, baptized as Simeon by the patriarch, became one of Ivan's military commanders. In 1555, Kazan became a separate archdiocese of the Eastern Orthodox Christian Church, whose head was especially charged with proselytizing for the faith among the Muslim population of the region.

Two years later, in 1554, Ivan sent an army south to occupy Astrakhan to consolidate his hold on the Volga. In 1555, the khan of the Crimea, reinforced with Ottoman troops, attacked the Russian garrison at Astrakhan but was driven off. Ivan then annexed Astrakhan, appointed a Russian governor, and began to fortify the city. The tsar applied the same procedures and goals of political assimilation and cultural reconstruction to Astrakhan that prevailed in Kazan. As a further security measure, the tsar tried to contain and coopt the suddenly unemployed Tatar soldiery. To siphon off potentially rebellious Tatar warriors from both Kazan and Astrakhan, Ivan recruited large contingents of steppe cavalrymen and sent them with generous pay and promises to join his armies massing to fight in the Livonian War, with its aim of access to the Baltic Sea.

Seizure of Kazan and Astrakhan opened a route on the river Volga to Russia's traders. After 1552, Russian traders and rivermen could sail freely along the Volga's entire length. They no longer had to pay heavy and sometimes capricious tolls, nor were they subject to expulsion for political reasons. Russia's exports could move along the Volga to link up with the intercontinental caravans that crossed Russia's lower reaches or connect with the Caspian sea routes that led to northern Iran.

Along with realizing his military successes, Ivan III had accelerated a process of centralized state building in Moscow. As his predecessors had begun to do before him, he presented himself as Grand Prince and tsar, and he cast himself as a divinely appointed, paternalistic protector of his subjects, his children. In public ceremony, frescos, literary texts, public decrees, and staged grand ceremonies, he articulated "a broader vision of princely intervention and control in the internal life of the realm."[32] He launched a new

32. Valerie Kivelson, "Merciful Father, Impersonal State: Russian Autocracy in Comparative Perspective," *Modern Asian Studies* 31 (1997).

building program in Moscow to create a physical setting in the capital suitable for this broader imperial vision. It was the tsar's duty to maintain "a godly, pious ordered society." The new rhetoric placed all in Russian society into a hierarchy of service and obligation to the tsar. Even the highest nobles termed themselves "slaves" of their master and embodied this relationship in rituals of abasement and submission.

To implement his vision, Ivan and his successors improved the military and civil institutions of the Moscow state. In order to provide armed, equipped cavalry without bankrupting his treasury, Ivan III created "the *pomeschiki* or gentry, a class of conditional landholders who supported their mandatory cavalry service by farming the parcels of land granted to them provisionally by the state."[33] To control this new military class, Ivan strengthened the already impressive civil administration. Hundreds of hereditary clerks kept lists and records of service by the gentry. They carried out censuses in an attempt to determine the wealth and location of the entire population. They kept an unending series of lists of taxpayers and taxes owed. The Muscovite state under Ivan was a documentary, bureaucratic state that supported the aspirations of the ruler. More capable central institutions permitted Ivan and his successors to mobilize the resources needed for further expansion.

Ivan's victories tilted the balance in the lands east of Moscow away from pastoral nomadism and toward the preferred Russian form of sedentary grain cultivation by densely settled peasant cultivators. Immediately after the conquest, Russian settlers—with the tacit approval of the regime—began moving spontaneously beyond the old Muscovite-Kazan frontier into the western Kazan lands bounded by an arc formed by the west bank of the river Volga as it flowed east to Kazan and then south past the confluence of the Kama River to Simbirsk and Samara.[34] This mid-Volga, or Volga Heights, region continued the forest-steppe east and south. Its black earth soil and forest-grasslands landscape powerfully attracted Russian settlers. Some Kazans had taken up cultivation, but the area remained largely uncultivated in the mid–sixteenth century.

Moscow readily granted lands to Russian colonists and proved willing to give the same privileges to non-Russian Tatars who had converted to Christianity and wished to take up plow cultivation. Many monasteries took up lands in the Volga river valley and attracted peasant cultivators.

After Kazan's fall, Russian colonization in the mid-Volga region remained slow and scattered. From their traditional grazing lands west and east of the

33. Ibid., 648.
34. Huttenbach, "Muscovy's Conquest of Muslim Kazan and Astrakhan," 63; D. J. B. Shaw, "Southern Frontiers of Muscovy, 1550–1700," in *Studies in Russian Historical Geography*, edited by James H. Bater and R. A. French (London: Academic Press, 1983), 133, fig. 6.5.

river Volga, the Nogay Tatars, aided on occasion by the Volga cossacks, the Kalmyks, and the Bashkirs, rode freely on annual raids into the former Kazan lands. The Tatars attacked Russian settlements and took hundreds of Russian captives for the slave trade. In response, the tsar ordered the building of fortified towns along the river Volga. On the lower Volga, below Kazan, these included Tet'yushi, founded in 1574; Samara, in 1586; Saratov, in 1590; and Tsaritsyn, in 1588. These measures helped but did not totally secure the lives and property of Russian peasant settlers in the region. Russian pioneer settlement in the mid-Volga forest-steppe region expanded hesitantly in tandem with that to the west, in the central black earth region south of the Oka River.

THE FOREST-STEPPE

Although Ivan III's successors claimed authority over the area south of the Oka River and east of the Dnieper River, throughout the sixteenth century and much of the seventeenth, the area was a contested and lightly inhabited frontier zone. The tsars of Moscow may have rejected tribute payments and formal submission to the Mongols, but their territories and subjects remained vulnerable to Tatar invasions. Moscow was perpetually on the defensive against repeated Crimean and Nogay Tatar assaults mounted from the steppe. By the middle of the seventeenth century, the terms of the encounter had changed. Moscow moved to the offensive and, by 1700, had extended its formal and effective authority to the limits of the forest-steppe.

The forest-steppe territories that the tsars acquired are classified today as the central black earth and mid-Volga regions of European Russia.[35] The forest-steppe is a 250- to 300-kilometer-wide transition zone beginning less than 200 kilometers south of Moscow that separates the northern forests and the grasslands of the true steppe. The forest-steppe stretches fully 3,000 kilometers from a point in Belarus level with Moscow southeastward in an arc that ends at the Altai Mountains.[36] Before Russian settlement, the dense forest cover of the Russian heartland gave way to more open country, in which grasslands alternated with forested areas. This was a mixed landscape marked by patches of broadleaf deciduous trees, mostly oak, with pine found on the sandy river terraces. Between forested areas lay treeless expanses with high grasses, thickets, and bushy flowering herbs. The density of forest cover declined on a north-to-south gradient as annual precipitation dropped.

35. Moon, "Peasant Migration and the Settlement of Russia's Frontiers," 864–65; I. Stebelsky, "Agriculture and Soil Erosion in the European Forest-Steppe," in *Studies in Russian Historical Geography*, edited by James H. Bater and R. A. French (London: Academic Press, 1983).

36. See Judith Pallot and Denis J. B. Shaw, *Landscape and Settlement in Romanov Russia, 1613–1917* (Oxford: Clarendon Press; New York: Oxford University Press, 1990), x, fig. 1.

Forest-steppe soils changed to *chernozem,* humus-rich black earth, far more fertile than the gray forest soils to the north. *Chernozem* constituted a dark upper soil band, often a meter thick, that was rich in organic matter derived from the dense grass cover and was low in acid content. Summer drought, with its high evaporation rates, reduced leaching from the upper soil layers. Winter frost slowed decomposition of organic matter. During the spring snowmelt, calcium compounds leached downward through the black earth layer, but were then drawn upward in the summer to concentrate in a lime-rich band beneath the black earth.

In the first half of the sixteenth century, the forest-steppe was sparsely populated by pastoralists, hunters, and other transients. By midcentury, a large number of Russians had begun settling in the region. Moscow recruited and sent some migrants to the frontier; the majority made their way on their own, often in flight. The forest-steppe's mix of open forests and grasslands, accessible river network, fertile soils, and prolific fish and wild game meant prosperity and abundance for those who could occupy the land. In the view of the ruler, aristocrats, and high-church officials, peasants could be settled and made productive on new fertile lands. For the aristocrat and commoner alike game, fish, waterfowl, and even wild honey, largely untouched, lay open to capture. To Russian peasants accustomed to the low fertility of the sandy, loamy, acidic gray soils of the northern forest, the southern black earth lands promised undreamed-of yields. Moving to the south, settlers experienced a somewhat less harsh winter climate and an extended number of frost-free days. In addition to material prosperity, the southern frontier held out a promise of freedom from oppression and repression, of a more fulfilling life.

TATARS

Desirable as they might be to Russian eyes, the southern frontier lands were not empty. In fact, their occupants, the Tatar nomads, were stronger militarily than the Russians. Although formally subordinate to the Ottoman sultan since 1478, the Giray khans of the Crimea presided over a powerful early modern Islamic state. They ruled with the advice and consent of the heads of the four dominant Tatar clans. The Ottomans administered the enclave surrounding the Black Sea port of Kaffa as an imperial province but did not otherwise interfere with Tatar autonomy. The Giray rulers mobilized the military power of their clan-based steppe warriors to extract regular tribute payments from Christian regimes, including Moscow, Poland, and the Danubian Principalities. When the Giray rulers assisted the Ottomans in campaigns against Christian states, a flow of booty returned to enrich the Islamic state and its capital. The leading industry and source of wealth for the Crimean khans and their subjects was slave trading. The Crimean Tatars were the leading suppliers of slaves to the entire Middle East through the markets at Kaffa. Nearly all those sold were Slavs taken as captives on annual raiding expeditions.[37]

Every year, bands of mounted Crimean or Nogay Tatars moved along well-established routes into Russian territory to plunder and take captives for the slave trade. Massive Tatar armies, mobile and lethal, periodically swept into the Russian lands, where they burnt, plundered, and seized Russians to sell. As Giles Fletcher, English ambassador to Moscow in the early 1580s, observed, the Crimean Tatars "that lieth south and southeastward from Russia . . . doth most annoy the country by often invasions, commonly once every year, sometimes entering very far within the inland parts."[38] On occasion, the Tatars reached Moscow, as they did in 1571. In that year, the Crimean khan Devlet Giray (r. 1551–1577), commanding a huge army, evaded the defending Russian army under the command of the tsar Ivan IV (r. 1533–1584) and occupied the outskirts of the capital. The Tatars fired the mass of wooden buildings outside the walls; the fire spread inside the city proper and drove the inhabitants out to be slaughtered by the invaders. The Tatars departed unscathed with thousands of Russian captives.[39]

The Tatars were fierce, highly mobile steppe cavalrymen. Each cavalryman trailed one, two, or even three spare horses in a practice that greatly increased their range. Clad in sheepskin but not armored (save for their commanders), each Tatar horseman deftly wielded composite steppe bows, swords, and short spears but rarely firearms. Fletcher commented that the Tatars were "very expert horsemen and use to shoot as readily backward as forward." Routine border incursions were "short and sudden," in which the Tatar horsemen moved "as wild geese fly, invading and retiring where they saw advantage." Their "chief booty" was a "store of captives, especially young boys and girls, whom they sell to the Turks or other of their neighbors."[40]

The Tatars were pastoralists who kept "great herds of kine [cattle] and flocks of black sheep rather for the skins and milk, which they carry with them in great bottles, than for the use of the flesh, though they sometimes eat of it." They raised so many horses that, despite their own prodigious use of horses for riding and for food, "there are brought yearly to the Moscow to be exchanged for other commodities thirty or forty thousand Tartar horse."[41]

The Tatars moved freely across the level grasslands of the steppe and forest-steppe landscape but did not cultivate crops or settle in one place.

---

37. Alan W. Fisher, *The Crimean Tatars: Studies of Nationalities in the USSR* (Stanford, Calif.: Hoover Institution Press, 1978), 8–36.

38. Giles Fletcher and Albert J. Schmidt, *Of the Rus Commonwealth* (Ithaca, N.Y.: Cornell University Press, for the Folger Shakespeare Library, Washington, D.C., 1966), 91.

39. Ibid.; Crummey, *The Formation of Muscovy*, 171; A. W. Fisher, *The Crimean Tatars*, 44.

40. Fletcher and Schmidt, *Of the Rus Commonwealth*, 95.

41. Ibid., 97.

They permitted "no private man to possess any lands but the whole country to be as a common." They had no fixed habitation but lived in "walking houses . . . built upon wheels like a shepherd's cottage. These they draw with them whithersoever they go, driving their cattle with them." The Tatars practiced seasonal migration timed to place their herds on newly ripening grass:

> They [the Tatars] begin to move their houses and cattle in the springtime from the south part of their country toward the north parts. And so, driving on till they have grazed all up to the farthest point northward, they return back again to their south country where they continue all the winter, by ten or twelve miles a stage; in the meanwhile the grass being sprung up again to serve for their cattle as they return. From the border of the Shchelkaly [a separate Tatar horde] toward the Caspian Sea to the Rus frontiers[,] they have a goodly country, especially on the south and southeast parts, but lost for lack of tillage.[42]

The strengths of the Tatars—their mobility and great herds—made them vulnerable to the slow encroachment of peasants and the Russian state. Peasant cultivators could occupy and hold plots of land, survive Tatar raids, and build fortified settlements without much, if any, state help. Nomad raiders passed through; they did not stay. The Russian state could found towns, build defenses, send troops, and formally bestow lands on state servicemen, who would further encourage peasant cultivation and settlement. In the long-term contest over the forest-steppe, the tenacious grip of the Russian cultivator prevailed.

FORTS AND COSSACKS

Slowly, the Moscow regime developed a set of frontier defenses against the Tatars. Although permeable by determined raiders, the strategies and fortifications evolved from bitter experience into a coherent system. The fortified towns and linked barriers that connected them served as a launching point for continuing Russian movement into the forest-steppe. Deepest and most exposed were the Severskiy cluster of *ukrainnyye* (literally, "frontier towns") located 600 kilometers southwest of Moscow in the region defined by the joining of the Desna and Seym Rivers. Slightly to the west of the regular Tatar raiding routes, the towns of Putivl, Ryl'sk, and Sevsk were protected by extensive forests and swamplands.

In the mid–sixteenth century, the effective boundary for Moscow, however, was much closer, less than 200 kilometers to the south. Two *zasekis*, or fortified lines built to stop or slow Tatar raiders, delineated the border zone. The *zaseki* closest to the capital ran 320 kilometers continuously from

42. Ibid., 98, 103.

Kozel'sk in the west, by way of Tula in the center, and ended at Ryazan in the east. The second line defended the eastern approaches to Moscow and ran from Ryazhsk to Shatsk and beyond. Each *zaseki* consisted of a continuous barrier formed by felled trees, earthen ramparts, trenches, and guard posts. Whenever possible, natural barriers such as swamps, deep forests, and streams were incorporated into the barrier. A network of guard posts stationed four to six days' journey south of the fortified line provided early warning of approaching Tatar raiders. The posts, placed at 10- to 12-kilometer intervals, were manned by six to ten mounted frontier guards.[43]

Moscow appointed state servicemen to guard the towns and fortifications along the lines. The garrisons received tax-free lands that they or their dependent peasants could cultivate in return for service. These permanent residents of the frontier rarely were subject to assignment to active campaigns elsewhere. Every summer when the Tatars were expected, large cavalries made up of state servitors sent from Moscow assembled in the south to reinforce the locally posted militias. Half patrolled the banks of the Oka River, and half guarded the *zaseki* to the south.[44] The frontier guards also were ordered to burn the steppe grass in great conflagrations every year in an effort to slow the Tatar armies.

Slowly and at great cost, the Russian state and Russian pioneer settlers managed to shift from a solely defensive posture to advance into the forest-steppe. This was a slow, incremental process achieved against stiff Tatar resistance. Establishing a dominant, if not unchallenged, presence in the forest-steppe south of the Tula defensive line required a century—from 1550 to 1650. This was an enterprise that required both official state and private initiatives and resources. State control and individual migration and settlement proceeded together, and each depended on the other.

Moscow played its part by building fortified towns in the forest-steppe beyond the Tula Line, garrisoning them with state servicemen and supplying them with food, weapons, and necessary supplies. Strategic frontier town building came in bursts of activity. The first occurred between 1585 and 1599, when Boris Godunov approved the founding and garrisoning of eight fortified towns: Livny, Voronezh, Yelets, Oskol, Kursk, Belgorod, Valuyki, and Tsarevborisov. All were sited to block or at least impede Tatar invasions.[45]

The original population of the new sixteenth-century frontier towns was primarily official. To each, Moscow sent complements of both contract and hereditary servicemen.[46] The former were musketeers and gunners, paid in

43. Shaw, "Southern Frontiers of Muscovy," 122–24.
44. Ibid.
45. Ibid., 125; Crummey, *The Formation of Muscovy,* 208.
46. Carol Belkin Stevens, *Soldiers on the Steppe: Army Reform and Social Change in Early Modern Russia* (DeKalb: Northern Illinois University Press, 1995), 17–18.

cash and kind, who manned the walls and fortifications of the towns. Many of these men turned to cultivation, handicrafts, or trade to supplement their pay. The higher-status servicemen were cavalrymen, who obtained tax-free grants of land located outside the walls of the town. On the far frontier, hereditary service grantees had only modest resources. Most seem to have cultivated their lands with their own labor and that of their families. Their smallholdings formed a hinterland of plowed and cultivated lands surrounding each town.

The new towns also attracted a heterogeneous mix of unofficial migrants. Discharged and unemployed or deserting servicemen, younger sons and other dependents of men already in frontier service in older areas, fleeing criminals, sedentarized steppe Tatars, and cossacks took up residence in or near the new centers. Decade after decade, however, peasants fleeing to the frontier made up the largest category of migrants. Most seem to have been attracted by the prospect of occupying cultivable land either as dependents on estates or as free peasants gathered in villages near the towns.

The more venturesome Russian migrants avoided the frontier towns and peasant villages in favor of life as cossacks (from the Turkic *kazak,* meaning "free man"). Since the 1400s, Russian and other Slavic migrants and fugitives had pressed into the forest-steppe and deeper into the true steppe to hunt, fish, gather honey, and raise livestock in imitation of the Tatars. Many found refuge from the Tatars and the Russians by settling far to the south in the heavily forested wetlands of the Dnieper, Don, and the other large rivers. Some cossacks took to the rivers in boats they built themselves, becoming fishermen, traders, and river pirates. Most were horsemen who developed their skills at moving and fighting on horseback to nearly equal those of the Tatars. They imitated the Tatars as well in raiding and plundering Russian settlements on the frontier.[47]

By the sixteenth century, most cossacks had coalesced into a half-dozen organized martial societies, or hosts. The largest and most powerful were the Zaporozhian host based along the lower reaches of the Dnieper River. Each host was a free society that prided itself on its autonomy. Each was organized democratically, with an assembly in which males had a vote. The assembly elected a headman *(ataman* or *hetman),* secretary-treasurer, and other officials to specified terms. Each host accepted applicants for membership regardless of ethnicity, religion, or language. The common language was Russian, with a strong Tatar infusion of terms and phrases. By the seventeenth century, cossack headmen were negotiating directly with Russian and Tatar officials as heads of state, which, in fact, they were.[48]

47. Shaw, "Southern Frontiers of Muscovy," 119–21.

48. Albert Seaton, *The Horsemen of the Steppes: The Story of the Cossacks* (New York: Hippocrene Books, 1985), 26–51.

Although the cossacks existed beyond any sort of formal control by the Russian state, they directly challenged the Tatar grip on the steppes merely by their presence. In effect, they served as an advance guard for Russian occupation and settlement. Gradually, the Russian state found that some cossacks could be enlisted to provide early warning of Tatar raids and invasions or even to serve as guards at its frontier posts. By and large, however, the cossacks were not ideal pioneers from the official Russian perspective. Cossacks disdained any sort of plow cultivation or lifestyle that smacked of the subservience of the Russian peasant. Apart from the greater pressures they placed on fish, wildlife, and forests, Cossack land-use patterns were similar to those of the Tatar pastoral nomads.

Through prosperity or dearth, political stability or turmoil, war or peace, the flow of fugitive peasants to the south remained a constant in Russian life. The state only occasionally acted to try to recover criminals or fleeing peasants, since it was generally in Moscow's interest to encourage its subjects to populate the frontier. Pioneers did not remain behind the defensive lines but ventured into the lands beyond. Recurring news of Tatar raids with their attendant atrocities may have slowed but did not halt this tendency.

In Moscow, the tsar and his officials were well aware of the extent of Tatar depredations. For example, the board in charge of frontier military affairs recorded 15,115 Russians either killed or taken captive in Kursk district alone from 1632 to 1646.[49] Protecting Russian settlers was a consistent goal of the Moscow state. Continued migration encouraged the state to invest in a more elaborate apparatus of frontier control and defense.

THE BELGOROD AND SIMBIRSK LINES

In 1635, after a three-and-a-half-decade pause, town building began again in a second surge, with the founding of the town of Kozlov. Over the next three decades, Moscow placed twenty-two new towns in a line that marked the effective limits of Russian authority over the central black earth region. At the same time, royal officials directed and paid for construction of 800 kilometers of stockades, earthen ramparts, trenches, and guard posts to link the new towns in a second *zaseki,* the Belgorod Line. Instead of its hundred-year practice of mustering its summer defensive forces along the Oka River and the Tula Line, by midcentury Moscow had begun sending them south to mass along the new defensive line.

The Belgorod Line defined Russia's mid-seventeenth-century claim on the forest-steppe. The new *zaseki* lay 400 kilometers south of the original line.

49. Brian Davies, "Village into Garrison: The Militarized Peasant Communities of Southern Muscovy," *Russian Review* 51 (October 1992): 481.

The Belgorod Line's western half ran eastward 350 kilometers, from Olesh-nya in the upper valley of the Vorskla River, through Belgorod to Ostro-gozhsk, just south of the Don River. This west-to-east segment placed a bar-rier directly across three of the four major Tatar invasion trails: the Muravsakaya to the west, aimed directly at Moscow; the Izumkaya in the in-terfluval area between the South Donets and Oskol Rivers; and the Kal'miusskaya, which paralleled the north-south course of the Don River. The middle section of the Belgorod Line turned north at Ostrogozhsk, fol-lowed the right bank of the Don River to Voronezh, and ended at Dobryy, 350 kilometers to the north. The last stretch of the line ran directly eastward again for 100 kilometers from Dobryy through Kozlov, ending at Chelnovoy. This final segment barred the Nogayaskaya invasion route followed by the Nogay Tatars from the east.[50]

Moscow's investment in the Belgorod Line coincided with a momentous turn in its social policy. The service cavalrymen had been agitating for greater control over their peasants. They claimed that they could not obtain sufficient labor to work the lands they had been granted by the state. Simul-taneously, the state bureaucracy pressed for more efficient tax collection and tighter control over taxpayers. In response, the state began a regimewide census aimed at fixing the location of taxpaying town residents and rural cul-tivators. In 1649, a comprehensive law code stipulated that peasants were bound to the land wherever they had been registered in the census. Peasants were now legally enserfed. The state undertook to capture fleeing peasants and to punish those who sheltered them. The frontier regions still offered some refuge to peasants fleeing serfdom, but state surveillance grew more effective over the years.[51]

Below the Belgorod Line, Ukrainian pioneer settlers from Polish territory poured into the region that became known as Slobodskaya Ukraina. Many were cossacks who were fleeing the Polish regime's efforts to enserf them and control their democratic institutions. They also reacted against harassment and persecution directed at Eastern Orthodox Christians. The Moscow gov-ernment welcomed the new settlers and offered them special privileges, in-cluding unregistered and unrestricted cultivation of unoccupied lands, trade free of duties, and free distillation of liquor.[52] Unlike cossacks on the steppe, most of these migrants settled down to sedentary grain cultivation.

The first Ukrainians in this wave settled at Chuguyev on the South Donets River in 1638. By the late 1670s, so many of their compatriots had settled in this region that the Moscow government began work on a new defensive

---

50. Shaw, "Southern Frontiers of Muscovy," 128, fig. 6.3.
51. Kivelson, "Merciful Father, Impersonal State," 649; Moon, *The Russian Peasantry,* 68–69.
52. Shaw, "Southern Frontiers of Muscovy," 130–31.

line. The Izyum Line outlined a triangular, or wedge-shaped, region, with its sharp point ending at the conjuncture of the South Donets and Oskol Rivers. With the extension of the Belgorod Line east to Simbirsk (see below), Russian defenses against the Tatars in the forest-steppe were complete and increasingly effective. By the early eighteenth century, settlers defended by these lines could plow the black earth soils with reasonable assurance that they and their property would not be burnt, plundered, or carried off to slavery by Tatar raiders. Moscow could begin to collect taxes and extract resources from its new domain.

By the turn of the eighteenth century, Russian and Ukrainian settlers had advanced across the forest-steppe, had reached the northern bounds of the true steppe, and were busily plowing up new lands. The Russian state claimed and exercised effective power over the entire central black earth region (286,000 square kilometers) and added six new provinces: Ryazan, Tula, Orel, Kursk, Voronezh, and Tambov. The recorded population of this region grew steadily from 850,000 adult males in 1678, to 1.5 million in 1719, to 2 million in 1762, and to 3.3 million in 1811.[53] Population density rose from as low as 10.5 persons per square kilometer to 14 per square kilometer to 23.5 per square kilometer over the same period. By 1762, one-quarter of all the tsar's subjects lived in the central black earth region.[54] Security against the Tatars encouraged migration. But as much as two-thirds of the increase came from improved fertility, as is generally the case with frontier populations who have access to new lands.[55]

The settlement of the mid-Volga region to the east followed a similar trajectory. However, it was not until the late 1640s that Moscow invested in defense of the region. Upon completion of the Belgorod Line, Moscow decided to build an extension that would thrust from Kozlov in the west 500 kilometers northeastward to end at Simbirsk on the river Volga. Between 1647 and 1654, the state founded a half dozen new towns along the route, fortified them, and staffed them with servicemen—Russians and Tatars.

The Simbirsk Line's fortified stockades, earthen ramparts, trenches, guard posts, and mobile patrols effectively secured the Volga forest-steppe regions for settlement and cultivation. Tatar raiders had to penetrate the line to reach the settlements and had to fight their way back if they succeeded in attacking settlements north of the line. Migration to the newly secure lands rose. Total rural male population in 1678 numbered only 221,000, slightly over one-quarter that of the central black earth region. By 1719, males num-

53. Moon, "Peasant Migration and the Settlement of Russia's Frontiers," 863, table 1; Stebelsky, "Agriculture and Soil Erosion in the European Forest-Steppe," 52, table 3.1.

54. Moon, "Peasant Migration and the Settlement of Russia's Frontiers," 864, table 2.

55. Ibid., 868–69.

bered 727,268, exactly half that of the central region, and continued to increase steadily, to 861,820 in 1762.[56]

POSTFRONTIER CONSOLIDATION

After the settlement frontier moved on, rural society in the central black earth region maintained a surprising level of material prosperity coupled with a deeply repressive agrarian order. About three-quarters of the estates in this region imposed labor services *(barschchina)* on their serfs instead of commuting these to annual dues levied in cash and kind *(obrok)*. Under the labor service regime, landlords set aside part of their estates as demesne land and handed over the rest to their serfs to cultivate for themselves. Landlords then required their serfs to work three days per week cultivating the demesne lands and left them the other three days to tend to their own plots.[57] In less fertile regions, where timber cutting or handicraft production was more lucrative, landlords demanded a share of serf production rather than relying on selling grain from their estates.

Throughout the black earth region, landlords profited and peasants lived relatively comfortably. There was no land shortage in this region. Instead, peasants, encouraged by estate managers, expanded their fields into unused land as population increased. Landlords had ample land at their disposal to give generous allotments for grain cultivation to their serfs and to retain for their own estate lands. The traditional three-field, strip method of grain cultivation still in place relied on leaving one-third of the land fallow each year. Despite landlord indifference to technical innovation and investment in agricultural inputs, the black soil continued to produce a relatively good seed-to-yield ratio for food grains—equivalent to those of western Europe. The peasants of this region had lost access to the forest resources enjoyed by their ancestors in the Moscow region, but they had gained soil of prodigious fertility.

Save in years of harvest failure, even serfs seem to have shared in a surprising degree of material prosperity, as evidenced by their diet, clothing, and disposable income. In addition to the harvests from their annually assigned grain strips, they kept their own domestic livestock and poultry and maintained produce gardens on their permanent household land. When harvests failed, serfs could look to their owners for minimal allotments of food grains to keep them from starving. Whether these benefits fully repaid them for the loss of personal freedom, subjection to frequent corporal punishment, or the serf owner's onerous control over their lives is questionable.

56. Ibid., 863, table 1.
57. Moon, *The Russian Peasantry*, 70.

These generalizations are supported by a case study of Petrovskoe estate, purchased in the early 1800s by the princely Gagarin family of Moscow. Petrovskoe consisted of six neighboring peasant settlements sited some 530 kilometers southeast of Moscow along the banks of the Vorona River in southern Tambov Province—directly in the black earth region.[58] The Gagarins were absentee owners who employed a bailiff and his staff to manage the estate. The land had been recently settled, and the estate counted just under eleven thousand hectares of arable land, with additional pasture, hayfields, woodlands, and uncultivated, long-fallow land. The Gagarins built up the total number of serfs to thirty-five hundred by bringing some in from their other estates. They added two hamlets to the original six settlements in the course of the century. Most of the grain grown on estate lands, apart from that rationed to household serfs and staff, moved directly to urban markets in return for cash payments.

Petrovskoe was highly profitable, with an average annual income of over sixty-one thousand rubles per year accruing to the owners by midcentury. Ultimately, the estate existed to supply that profit for absentee owners.[59] To that end, serfdom, even with the most enlightened ownership, was a coercive and brutalizing system—a remarkable shift from the freer conditions of the pioneer settlers of the region.

The Gagarin serfs were bound to the person of their lord, exchanging their labor for an allotment of plow land, a share in communal pastures and meadows, possession of a home with an adjacent garden, and limited rights to the estate woodlands. The estate allocated plow land not to households, which were multigenerational and large, but to work units (tiaglo) of husband-and-wife teams. The latter obtained plow land only as long as they met their labor obligations in the estate lands. Each household, however, owned the grain harvest and any sales from it in common. Generally, serfs worked half the time on their own fields and half on the estate lands. Each work team on the Gagarin estate routinely had access to between 9 and 9.6 hectares, including some long-fallow lands that were not part of the regular three-field rotation.[60] Over time, serfs quietly widened their strips at the expense of adjacent pasture and long-fallow lands.

On these parcels of land, allocated in strips by the peasant community, yields were high—higher than is commonly assumed for nineteenth-century Russian grain cultivation. The average yield for rye on estate lands for the period 1811 to 1860 was 12 hectoliters per hectare, or a seed-to-yield ratio of

58. Steven L. Hoch, *Serfdom and Social Control in Russia: Petrovskoe, a Village in Tambov* (Chicago: University of Chicago Press, 1986).

59. Ibid., 14.

60. Ibid., 26–27. Or, 6.2 to 6.3 *desiatinas*.

1:6.2.[61] This figure is similar to that of Germany in the same period. On average, a work team produced 35.3 hectoliters of rye, 22.8 hectoliters of oats, and 4.7 hectoliters of buckwheat or millet. After seed was set aside for the next year, and after losses in milling, flour returned to the household would be ample to sustain the husband-and-wife team for the year, along with 4 additional, nonworking persons in the household.[62] The oats fed draft horses and other livestock. Between 1810 and 1856, an average husband-and-wife work team at Petrovskoe supported itself and 2.6 to 3.5 additional persons. Households sold their excess grain and other produce to buy farm implements, draft animals, and household goods and to add to their savings. They paid their share of the taxes demanded by carrying the estate grain to market in winter, when they had much free time.

These data suggest that the serfs on Petrovskoe enjoyed a relatively good diet. They could keep cows, chickens, pigs, and other domestic livestock, as well as horses for plowing.[63] Each peasant homestead consisted, on average, of .85 hectares, which was more than adequate for a garden and fruit trees. With one milk cow for 4 to 5 persons, dairy products were readily available. It is likely that "the peasants of Petrovskoe were . . . better nourished than their French and Belgian counterparts at the turn of the nineteenth century."[64]

Other aspects of the serf's life on Petrovskoe were far less appealing. Housing tended to be exceedingly cramped, poorly ventilated, and badly constructed. On average, each hut, for households with a mean size of 8 to 9 persons, had between fifty and sixty square meters of space. This seems to be directly attributable to estate policies that rationed serf access to construction timber. The estate boasted a large forest reserve of 2,870 hectares, in which a large section of aspen, oak, and alder produced construction timber, and the remainder fuelwood. The serfs had only limited access to this resource. They obtained building logs, lumber, fuel, and torches for lighting

61. Ibid., 29, table 4. Oats had a yield of 1:4.9, with an average of 19.3 hectoliters per hectare; buckwheat 4.8 and 7.9, respectively. As Hoch points out, official figures drawn up by provincial governors at the time greatly underestimated average yields. Figures from special surveys, many unofficial, were similar to those for Petrovskoe.

62. Ibid., 40–41. The yield would be 25.3 hectoliters of rye flour, 3.7 of buckwheat, and 18.2 hectoliters of oats. Hoch assumes that 214 kilograms of milled grain would support one person at a bare subsistence level for a year.

63. A "topographical description of Tambov Province published by the General Staff of the army in 1851 noted that nearly all peasant households had from two to seven horses, one to five cows, and five to ten sheep along with an unspecified number of pigs and domestic poultry" (ibid., 47). On Petrovskoe estate, average per capita holdings of horses ranged from .47 to .57; cows and calves, .29 to .41; sheep, 1.06 to 1.89; pigs, .28 to .69; and beehives, .12 to .81. The trends slowly moved downward over a half century. Ibid., 46, table 10.

64. Ibid., 50.

their huts in return for eight extra days of labor per year per work team. They could not enter the forest and cut trees for firewood but were forced to use thatch instead.[65]

Petrovskoe, like other estates, embodied a system of involuntary servitude that immobilized the serfs. Estate managers relied on an ascending series of coercive practices and institutions. The linchpin of the disciplinary system, however, was regular floggings by birch rod (a mean of 37.4 strokes). Often these were accompanied by forcible shaving of half a male serf's hair and beard or by forcing him to wear an iron collar. Whipping was frequent. In the two years between 1826 and 1828, the bailiffs and elders flogged 79 percent of the adult males, 24 percent of them more than once.[66] Females were rarely flogged. Bailiffs also imposed fines that could extend to seizure of livestock, and they could remove overseers and other serf functionaries from office. Wrongdoing included a wide variety of offenses related to poorly performed corvée on estate lands or failure to provide it at all, theft, negligence on watch, domestic violence, and absence from the village.

Serfs disciplined themselves within patriarchal three-generation households rigidly controlled by the eldest male member. Men and women married early and received an additional allotment of land from the estate as a work team when they did so. Adult males rarely left their father's households to establish their own until his death, and by then they were at least thirty-five to forty-five years of age and grandparents themselves. Estate bailiffs forcibly prevented males from leaving their households before that time. In part, this was to ensure a higher standard of living for the group; but in reality, the policy reinforced the authority of the patriarch—especially over younger males.

Above the household, the peasant commune in each estate settlement distributed the lands annually, regulated its members, and paid taxes as a communal responsibility. The commune also cultivated some land to have emergency stores and help the needy. Commune elders adjudicated disputes and could carry out floggings and other punishments if approved by the bailiff. Serfs convicted of murder or other serious crimes were jailed or executed by state officials.

All coercion of the serfs ultimately rested on the hammer of state power. One reminder of this occurred when Moscow imposed conscription levies on the estate. The bailiff left peasant communes to decide which of their men aged between seventeen and thirty-five would be handed over to the authorities for a twenty-five-year military obligation. Male serfs saw this as a death sentence and often maimed themselves or even fled to avoid it. Commune elders had little trouble selecting men who had flouted their author-

---

65. Ibid., 57, 61, table 12.
66. Ibid., 162. There were 714 whippings for a workforce of 1,305 serfs in this period.

ity or were otherwise troublemakers. State officials would also, if requested, send serfs into exile in Siberia.

THE ENVIRONMENTAL IMPACT

The environmental impact of settlement is clear. This was a new, permanently settled human presence in the forest-steppe. Russian settlers actively intervened to change the habitat in ways that the pastoral nomads had not. They regularly burnt grasslands either to deny cover to Tatar raiders or to improve the land's fertility for grazing livestock. This eliminated coarse grass species and tall scrub. Settlers hunted, fished, and gathered at a new level of intensity. State servicemen rented from the state the rights to hunt, fish, and collect honey from lands well beyond the line of settled cultivation.[67]

Unlike previous human inhabitants of the forest-steppe, Russian and Ukrainian settlers plowed up a large portion of the grasslands to grow rye and other grains. Nearly all, save a small percentage of settlers, were cultivators who, as soon as they arrived, occupied and plowed new lands. The pioneers quickly discovered that they had to adapt their techniques to the new habitat. The root systems of the natural bunchgrass, fescue, bluegrass, and other turf grasses formed a dense, matted carapace over the black earth. The traditional single-horse-drawn light *sokha,* or plow, was useless. Instead, they developed a heavier iron plow, or *plug,* pulled by oxen that permitted them to cut the sod successfully.

As the region's population increased, so did the area of tilled land. By 1719, one-quarter of the land in the central black earth region had come under the plough. In that year, Orel and Tula, the earliest settled provinces, had 38 and 39 percent of land in tillage; Tambov and Voronezh, settled later, had only 18 and 11 percent. During the remainder of the eighteenth century, notable increases in cultivated land throughout the region evened out the disparities between provinces. The regionwide percentage of plowed land rose from 26 percent in 1719, to 34 percent in 1762, and to 47 percent in 1796.[68]

Plowing and sowing annual grain crops converted forest-steppe grasslands from wild to domesticated, from perennial to annual, and from mixed to single species grasses. Removal of the protective sod covering undoubtedly led to some soil erosion from wind and water. For example, tree-covered valley lands along rivers and streams, a favorite site for settlers, were vulnerable to erosion when they had been cut and plowed. Southern and eastern facing slopes were the first to thaw in the spring and were then vulnerable to the snowmelt runoff that cut rills and gullies as it flowed downhill.[69] On the other

---

67. Stebelsky, "Agriculture and Soil Erosion in the European Forest-Steppe," 53, 58.
68. Ibid., 54, table 3.2.
69. Ibid., 59.

hand, the one-third or more portion of the land devoted to hay and pasture was less subject to erosion. Hayfields bore a greater resemblance to the original grass cover of the region.

Burrowing animals, like the large marmot population that the settlers found in the forest-steppe, lost much of their habitat. The settlers themselves killed large numbers as vermin. Other species of small animals, birds, and insects were displaced by cultivation.

Grazing, trampling, and waste from large, domesticated livestock put new pressures on grasslands that undoubtedly changed species compositions over time. The settlers kept larger numbers of cattle than was the practice in the north. The need for double teams of draft oxen or stronger horses to pull heavier plows encouraged this development. However, ranching or commercial pastoralism did not emerge as a significant aspect of the frontier advance. Why more Russian settlers did not turn to cattle raising on the abundant, unoccupied grasslands is puzzling—especially in advance of the line of plow cultivation. Perhaps fears of Tatar and cossack raiding were the reason. Perhaps the mind-set and experience of Russian peasants prevented them from considering extensive pastoralism. Instead, on this frontier, plowing was the definitive act of possession.

The settlers cleared some forested lands for cultivation in fertile river and stream valleys but left much of the forest cover standing to serve as a defense against Tatar attack. However, those forested areas that were left did not survive unscathed. Coming as they did from a lavishly plentiful forest environment, the Russian pioneers in the black earth region turned naturally to the scattered forest stands for their fuel and material needs. As the settler population grew, pressures on the forests grew accordingly. When settler population densities approached those of the forested north, the biomass needs of each rural or town dweller had to be met from a woodland area grown smaller per capita. Continuing and intensifying lopping, cutting, and felling invariably degraded the region's forests and reduced them to much-depleted woodlots.[70]

CONCLUSION

By 1800, the black earth, forest-steppe settlement frontier had closed. By persistent, stubborn, generations-long military effort, the tsarist state had extended its fortified frontier lines to make new areas safe for pioneer settlement and cultivation. Those frontier lands that had earlier been under constant threat of Tatar violence were no longer threatened by raiding and destruction. Although Moscow did not involve itself overly much in local governance and rural society, the central state maintained public order, col-

70. Moon, *The Russian Peasantry*, 61–63.

lected taxes, conscripted soldiers, appointed local officials, and provided judicial and police services. A state-run militia suppressed local disturbances and caught runaway serfs and returned them to their owners. As a long-term policy, state encouragement of the settlement frontier had paid off in an expanding economy and growing state revenues.

What earlier had been an expansive frontier society with new lands to be cultivated was now a zone of orderly grain cultivation with clearly demarcated boundaries of ownership and occupancy. What had been a relatively mobile rural and free population was now immobilized and repressed in a pervasive system of serfdom imposed by state power. Ending the frontier ended the only possible means for peasants to escape the rigors of serfdom.

As Moscow lengthened its territorial reach, it successfully tapped the bounty of the fertile soils of the forest-steppe. An increasing agricultural surplus in the form of food grains and other products flowed from the new territories to town and city markets. Part of the surplus found its way into the coffers of the state as taxes; a larger portion went into the pockets of serf-owning landlords, many of whom actually lived in the cities. To preserve the fertility and productivity of the black earth region for the longer term, however, demanded a level of sophisticated land management that did not come easily to the absentee Russian landlords of the nineteenth century.

Chapter 8

Wildlife and Livestock
in South Africa

Between 1488 and 1652, Indian Ocean–bound vessels traveling down the coast of Africa to reach the winds of the "roaring forties" latitude frequently stopped at the welcoming shelter offered by the harbor at the Cape of Good Hope. First, Portuguese vessels sailing to Goa looked forward to obtaining freshwater and provisions and making repairs at the Cape. Later, after 1600, ships of the Dutch East India Company and the English East India Company did the same. The pastoralist Khoikhois who lived there were sometimes willing to trade freshly slaughtered cattle or sheep from their herds for pieces of iron or copper. Although sporadic and limited, this commerce between sailors and pastoralists proved beneficial to both parties.

In 1651, the directors of the Dutch East India Company decided to create a fortified settlement at Table Bay in order to provide fresh meat, fruits, vegetables, and other provisions to its ships sailing between Holland and Asian ports. The new way station was also to have a hospital, where invalids could be left; seamen who had recovered from illness would replace them. Many reports from seafarers who had put into Table Bay convinced the directors that a settlement there would, unlike the company's tropical possessions, be relatively healthy and could produce a surplus of food sufficient to meet the needs of its own and other vessels. To put this plan into effect, the directors readmitted into their service as governor Jan van Riebeeck, a private merchant also trained as a physician, who had been among those arguing that this was a viable undertaking.

As a junior merchant of the company, van Riebeeck had served in Batavia and on an extended mission to Tokugawa Japan. Discharged from the service for unapproved private trading in 1648, van Riebeeck sought out this assignment in order to resume his career with the company. On the return voyage from Japan, his ship had spent eighteen days anchored at the Cape loading survivors and goods from a wrecked Dutch East Indiaman. Van Riebeeck argued correctly that the indigenous peoples at the Cape were inoffensive and certainly not the ferocious cannibals some sailors' tales had made them out to be. The Khoikhois could be persuaded to barter their cattle and sheep to stock the herds of the new colony.

From the first, the company's modest investment in the Cape settlement paid off. The total number of Dutch ships, as well as those of other European countries, calling at the Cape grew steadily. During the busiest season, the first four months of the calendar year, as many as twenty to thirty ships might be in the harbor. Vessels that called at the Cape could rely on obtaining freshwater, fresh and corned meat, milk, citrus fruits, wine, and a wide variety of other supplies at reasonable prices fixed by company edict.

THE SETTING

From the foreshortened perspective of visitors to Cape Town, this southern tip of Africa was rich in resources and had copious winter rainfall, freshwater, grasslands, and even woodlands. Within the vicinity of the Cape, land could be cultivated for wheat, grapes, and other European crops. Even more welcome to visitors was the climate, which resembled that of southern Spain, with its sunshine and moderate temperatures year-round. The fact that the climate was reversed from that of the Northern Hemisphere—December to February were the summer months; June to August, the winter months—was a readily accepted anomaly. However, the abundant resources in the land adjacent to the cape's harbor were deceiving. Concealed, at first, was the arduous nature of the interior's physical terrain, its low annual rainfall totals, frequent droughts, lack of year-round freshwater sources, scanty vegetation, and dangerous wildlife. The Cape region was not a paradise but instead a harsh, dry region to which the nomadic pastoralism of the Khoikhois was nearly ideally suited.

The most distinctive physical feature of this large region was the division between the interior plateau, which ranged from nine hundred to thirty-five hundred meters elevation and featured many mountain and hill ranges and valleys, and the two- to three-hundred-kilometer-wide lowland coastal strip surrounding it. The boundary between the two areas was nearly everywhere dramatically marked by an abrupt, steep rise known as the Great Escarpment.[1] In the coastal region from Cape Town to Port Elizabeth, more than five hundred millimeters of rain fell annually, primarily in the winter monsoon months. The arid western two-thirds of the interior, both coastal low-

1. John H. Wellington, *Southern Africa: A Geographical Study* (Cambridge: Cambridge University Press, 1955), 35–36.

land and plateau, had rainfall totals as low as one hundred millimeters, with the bulk of the rains coming in the summer rather than the winter. In the eastern third of the country, where summer rainfall also prevailed, annual totals could climb to five hundred millimeters, and even higher along the Indian Ocean coast.[2]

There were several distinctive, regionally defined vegetation complexes: In the southwestern Cape, with its winter rainfall, a sclerophyll bush formation dominated. This consisted of several species of evergreen shrubs with hard, small, leathery leaves, but almost no trees. Many of the brownish or grayish colored bushes, some rising to five meters in height, contained oil or resin. Herbaceous vegetation consisted of leafless reedy plants (Rastioinacae) and some grasses. The transition to dryer desert conditions was marked by the rhinoceros bush *(Elytropappus rhinocerotis)*, a gray shrub standing .3 to 1 meter high, impregnated with wax and unpalatable to grazing animals.[3]

Desert conditions began in the Great Karoo and Little Karoo, where between 100 and 250 millimeters of rain fell annually and droughts were frequent. In this vast area flourished drought-resistant perennial desert shrubs with deep root systems and low rates of transpiration. These included the succulents, such as the low Kraalbos *(Galenia africana)* and the yellow milk bush *(Euphorbia mauritanica)*. Taller bushes, up to 1 meter high, included several other species of *Eurphorbia, Aloe, Cotyledon,* and *Portulacaria.* There were also numerous varieties of the psychoactive *Mesembryanthemum* (see below). Among the woody desert bushes were various species of *Pentzia,* the sweet resin bush *(Euryops multifadas),* the unpalatable "bitter Karoo" *(Chrysocoma tenuifolia),* and, in brackish soil, various *Salsola* species and the saltbush *(Atriplex capensis).* Annuals such as red grass *(Themada triandra),* spear grass *(Heteropogon contortus),* and many short grasses sprang up after the rains. Along the river courses of the Karoo, trees such as the sweet-thorn *(Acacia karoo)* were abundant.

Toward the east, at the four hundred millimeter isohyet, the plateau vegetation again became grassland and then, farther east, as rainfall increased, savanna. For herbivores, the most nutritious and digestible grass of the plateau grassland areas was red grass. Red grass was most nutritious in early summer. Because it became brown and tough in late summer and fall and developed a high proportion of lignin and cellulose, red grass was known as "sourveld grass."

To visitors to the Cape, one of the most remarkable aspects of the land was the variety and number of wildlife with exotic and intriguing colors, ap-

2. Whether the climate of the seventeenth century was appreciably different from that of today is yet to be established.

3. Wellington, *Southern Africa,* 275–76.

pearances, and habits. Many of these animals were large and aggressive enough to be dangerous to humans and their domesticated animals. Most were a source of usable flesh, skins, feathers, eggs, and, in the case of elephants, ivory. Certainly, the kaleidoscopic assortment of wild animals and birds deeply impressed Europeans, whose own wildlife was depleted and not even remotely as colorful in appearance. Throughout the seventeenth and eighteenth centuries, nearly every writer on the Cape region included descriptions of its exotic fauna.

Troops of up to a hundred grayish or dark brown chacma baboons *(Papio ursinus)* provided an entertaining sight and noisy welcome for newcomers to the Cape. They preyed on the fruits found in the vineyards, orchards, and gardens of the colonists. When discovered, those baboons on watch "gave a loud Cry; upon which the whole Troop *[sic]* to the Mountains, as if Destruction was close at their Heels; the Young ones jumping upon and posting away on the Old ones Backs in a Manner very diverting to see."[4]

Among the Cape's fauna was the black- to brown-and-white ostrich *(Struthio camelus)*, the huge flightless bird, up to 2.5 meters in height and 155 kilograms in weight for males, that grazed on the veld in flocks of five to fifty animals. With its elongated reddish to bluish neck, long naked legs, big brown eyes with thick lashes, and wide bill, the ostrich was a strange creature indeed. The early-eighteenth-century writer Peter Kolb comments, "Ostriches are so numerous in the Cape-Countries, that a Man can scarcely walk a Quarter of an Hour any Way in those Countries without seeing one or more of those Birds."[5] He notes, "These Birds are easily tam'd. And many tame ones are kept in the Cape-Fortress." One of the eggs "furnishes out a pretty good Meal for Three or Four Persons."[6]

Other herbivores grew to fantastic shapes and sizes, and some were formidably dangerous. African elephants *(Loxodonta africana)*, with their huge ears, long, flexible trunks, and ivory tusks, were enormous. Males towered 4 meters in height and weighed up to 6 metric tons.[7] Even stranger were the small groups of browsing giraffes *(Giraffa camelopardalis)*. These animals stood 3 meters at the shoulders and had great elongated necks and brown-and-black-patched coats on a yellow background. The generally solitary, hook-lipped, or black, rhinoceroses *(Diceros bicornis)* were grotesque in appearance, with their great, upwardly protruding horns, bare hides, ungainly foursquare short legs, and rounded 880-kilogram bodies. Herds of water-

4. Peter Kolb, *The Present State of the Cape of Good Hope* (New York: Johnson Reprint Corporation, 1968), 2:122.

5. Ibid., 2:146.

6. Ibid., 2:147.

7. My descriptions of land mammals rely on Reay H. N. Smithers and Clare Abbott, *Land Mammals of Southern Africa: A Field Guide*, 1st ed. (Braamfontein, Johannesburg: Macmillan South Africa, 1986).

loving hippopotamuses *(Hippopotamus amphibius)* inhabited stretches of rivers with sloping sandbanks and adjacent grazing areas for nightly feeding. Their naked, smooth, grayish black skin, massive heads, and barrel-shaped bodies gave them a distinctive appearance. They were twice the size of rhinos; males stood 1.5 meters at the shoulders and weighed 1.5 metric tons. Not so strange, but still fearsome, were the oxlike cape buffaloes *(Syncerus caffer)*, with their massive curving horns and heavily built bodies weighing up to 800 kilograms. These animals grazed in herds throughout the region.

The two wild pigs were smaller but as strange in appearance. Warthogs *(Phacochoerus aethiopicus)* gathered in small family groups around waterholes. These gray, rooting and grazing animals had coarse, bristly coats. Males weighed up to 100 kilograms. Their most distinctive features were their elongated heads with two pairs of sideways-growing canine teeth and two pairs of facial outgrowths of skin. There were also moisture-loving brown bushpigs *(Potamochoerus porcus)*, which were somewhat smaller than warthogs and moved in groups of up to twelve, dominated by a boar.

Ubiquitous were the grazing herds of various species of ungulates. Some, to visitors' eyes, were exotic. The cape mountain zebra *(Equus zebra)*, the Hartmann's mountain zebra *(Equus zebra hartmannae)*, and Burchell's zebra *(Equus burchelli)* grazed in small breeding bands across the grasslands of the Cape region. Distinctive with their celebrated black stripes on white bodies, the animals stood 115–160 centimeters at the shoulder and weighed 240–372 kilograms. Unique to the temperate Cape was the quagga *(Equus quagga)*, which has since become extinct. Its striping was confined to its head, neck, and forequarters, and it had a reddish brown back and white belly.

Nearly thirty species of antelope roamed the veld in the Cape region at this time. Probably most numerous were the black wildebeests *(Connochaetes gnou)* and blue wildebeests *(Connochaetes taurinus)* that grazed and browsed throughout the Cape interior in great herds of hundreds of thousands. Both species and both sexes had dramatic sweeping horns, heavy manes, and beards. The black males stood 1.2 meters at the shoulder and weighed 180 kilograms; blue males stood 1.5 meters and weighed 250 kilograms.

Looking much like a European or North American deer with its fawn-colored coat and small horns was the largest of the African antelopes, the eland *(Taurotragus oryx)*. Weighing up to 750 kilograms, eland were the favorite prey of Khoikhois and settler hunters. Unlike wildebeests, these were not an open grassland species; instead, they thrived in semiarid savanna and woodland areas. More widely distributed was the gemsbok *(Oryx gazella)*. These animals had black-and-white faces and distinctive pale fawn-gray coats with black bands; both sexes had rounded horns that stood straight up a half meter or more. Males weighed 240 kilograms. Other larger species included the kudu *(Tragelaphus strepsiceros)*, similar in size to the gemsbok, with curly, upwardly pointed horns. It roamed the savanna, not

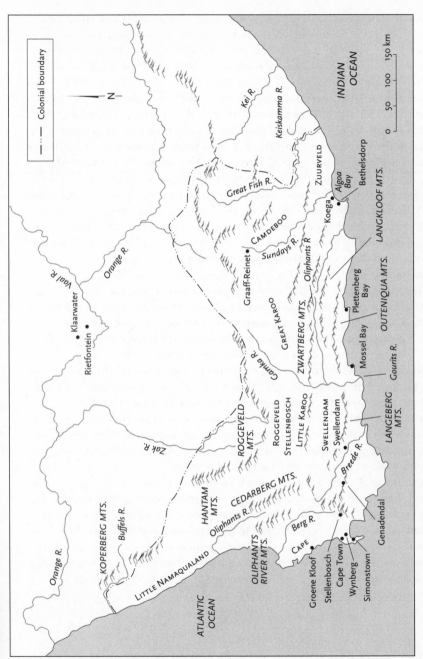

Map 8.1 South Africa in 1803. Adapted from William M. Freund, "The Cape under the Transitional Governments, 1795–1814," in *The Shaping of South African Society, 1652–1840*, ed. Richard Elphick and Hermann Giliomee (Middletown, Conn.: Wesleyan University Press, 1989), fig. 7.1, p. 326.

grassland. Additional antelope species ranged from the red hartebeest *(Alcelaphus buselaphus)* to the springbok *(Antidorcas marsupialis)*—the latter thrived in the more arid regions of the Cape—to tiny species such as the 10-kilogram grysbok *(Raphicerus melanotis)* found in thick scrub bush in the southern Cape.

Large predators were also very much in evidence. Seven species of cats stalked and killed ungulates and smaller prey. Among these were the African lion *(Panthera leo)*, which, at 240 kilograms for males, was the largest and most feared of the carnivores. Lions lived in well-defined home ranges, in prides of six to twelve animals. Spotted-coat cheetahs *(Acinonyx jubatus)* used their great speed in open country to hunt antelopes and other herding animals. Males weighed 54 kilograms. Spotted leopards *(Panthera pardus)*, although only 36 kilograms for males, were formidable nocturnal hunters that preyed on any warm-blooded prey, from mice to domestic cattle. The gray to reddish brown caracal *(Felis caracal)*, which had tasseled, black-backed upright ears, was a smaller (17 kilograms) version of the leopard and had similar nocturnal habits.

Other large carnivores included the spotted hyena *(Crocuta crocuta)*, a massively built animal with heavy forequarters (females, the larger gender, weighed 65 kilograms) and a formidable hunter of large ungulates, its main food. The smaller brown hyena *(Hyaena brunnea)* preyed on smaller game and scavenged, primarily at night. Both species had enormously powerful jaws and teeth. Other long-legged carnivores capable of running down fleet prey included the small, striped jackals *(Canis mesomelas; Canis adustus)*, which weighed less than 10 kilograms, and the Cape fox *(Vulpes chama)*. Especially noticeable to contemporary observers were the packs of wild dogs *(Lyacon pictus)* that ran down grazing ungulates and attacked domestic livestock. These dogs weighed up to 28 kilograms and had blotched black, yellow, and white coats, long legs, and rounded ears.

In addition to these large fauna, visitors noted the smaller animals, a wide variety of bird life that included edible partridges and waterfowl and many snakes and reptiles, several of them deadly poisonous. Few European visitors and settlers, however, were content to merely observe the rich wildlife. The danger that certain animals presented to humans, livestock, and crops; the demand for meat and hides; and male pleasure fueled a continuing assault on wildlife. After 1652, settlers' hunting led to wildlife depletion in an ever increasing arc outward from Cape Town.

KHOIKHOIS

The Khoikhois (the older, pejorative term is the Hottentots) were a herding people, who, along with a lower-status hunting people, the Sans, inhabited the African prairie, or veld, throughout what would eventually become the

Cape Colony of the Dutch East India Company (the Verenigde Oostindische Compagnie, or VOC). The Khoikhois spoke a distinctive unwritten click language that few Europeans ever succeeded in mastering. Probably pushed southward by more aggressive Bantu agriculturists from northern Botswana, Khoikhois eventually settled throughout the Cape region along the Atlantic Coast as far south as the ocean, as far east as the Indian Ocean, and as far north as the Great Fish River.

Numbering fifty thousand persons or even more in the first half of the seventeenth century, the Khoikhois were organized into patrilineal descent groups that were in turn loosely clustered into named groupings or tribes. The Khoikhois were transhumance pastoralists who lived off large herds of longhorn African cattle and fat-tailed sheep. Cattle and sheep were numerous in relation to people. A Dutch observer sent to buy cattle and sheep from a large Khoikhoi encampment reported that the group had fifteen thousand to sixteen thousand animals, "as numerous as the grass on the veld, and therefore the natives were obliged never to stay long at one place as the pasture was often quickly eaten bare."[8] Permanent supplies of freshwater were scarce, especially in the interior Cape. The Khoikhois migrated in groups "within their territories in complex patterns that involved the periodic dispersal and reunification of people and their livestock."[9] These were seasonal movements, but the Dutch could never predict just where the Khoikhois would go at any given time. By moving frequently, the Khoikhois gave the veld time to regenerate before it was grazed again.

Each Khoikhoi village, termed a kraal, consisted of a circle of huts facing inward surrounded by a brushwood fence. The huts were made of a light frame of poles covered with reed mats and animal skins. At night, people and animals were confined within the kraal for safety against attacks from lions, leopards, and other predators. Men of a single lineage claiming common ancestry occupied a single kraal. Clusters of lineages-kraals brought together several hundred to several thousand persons. Each lineage and each cluster of lineages had hereditary chiefs or leaders. Status was determined largely by seniority of lineage or distance from the male ancestor. Khoikhois were patrilocal and practiced lineage exogamy.

As with most pastoralists, an intimate relationship existed between the Khoikhois and their animals. The Khoikhois rode their cattle without saddles by fastening a bridle to a stick thrust through the animal's nose. When they moved the kraal, they put the huts and household possessions on the backs

8. Jan van Riebeeck and the Nederlandsche Oost-Indische Compagnie, *Journal* (Cape Town: A. A. Balkema, for the Van Riebeeck Society, 1952), 3:370.

9. Leonard Guelke and Robert Shell, "Landscape of Conquest: Frontier Water Alienation and Khoikhoi Strategies of Survival, 1652–1780," in *Agriculture, Resource Exploitation, and Environmental Change*, edited by Helen Wheatley (Aldershot, Eng.: Variorum, 1997).

of pack oxen. Oxen and bulls were trained for use as shields and barriers in warfare at their owner's command. They gelded young bulls and rams in special ceremonies each year. Khoikhois slaughtered cattle and sheep during fixed, recurring religious rituals. This was the only time they consumed meat. Milk was the staple food. The men drank cow's milk; women and children, ewe's milk. Women did all the milking and stored milk in cowhide sacks; over time, the milk became a form of butter. All Khoikhois relied on animal fat as a near-permanent body covering infrequently disturbed by bathing. A well-greased body was a sign of great prosperity. They had no tradition of weaving or textiles and, instead, used the skins of cattle, sheep, and wild animals for clothing. They slept on rush mats.

The most powerful of the Khoikhoi bands, the Attaqua, whose lands lay around present-day Oudtshoorn in the semidesert Little Karoo, controlled the supply of two species of narcotic plants, known as canna *(Mesembryanthemum expansum* and *Mesembryanthemum tortuosum).* Canna plants contain two psychoactive substances. From the oxalate in the root acting as a fermenting agent, the Khoikhois made alcohol by steeping the roots in honey and water. According to David Gordon, "When the alcohol-drenched root was chewed immediately after fermentation, it was a powerful intoxicant."[10] As the early-eighteenth-century observer Peter Kolb commented of the Khoikhois, "There is a root, gather'd in the Hottentot countries, called Khanna; which is in such esteem among the Hottentots for is *[sic]* great virtues that they adore it. What greatly inflames the value of this root is its scarcity, for 'tis rarely found."[11] The unfermented root also contains an alkaloid called mesembrine, a mild sedative that, in combination with the oxalic acid, has a moisturizing effect in the mouth. Khoikhois chewed the dried root to help alleviate their thirst. By the sixteenth century, the Khoikhois were also trading for *dagga,* or hashish, from Xhosa groups on the eastern coast.

The Khoikhois traded cattle and sheep with other Khoikhoi groups or with more distant Bantu to obtain copper, their most prized material possession, for use in ornaments. They also obtained iron with which to tip spears and arrows. Khoikhoi men actively hunted antelopes, eland, and other herbivores for meat. The Khoikhois also received game from their affiliated low-status clients, the Sans, who subsisted entirely by hunting and gathering. Each San band was tied directly by an exchange of goods and services to a particular Khoikhoi kraal. Smaller and physically different from their masters, the Sans apparently did not intermarry with the Khoikhois. They spoke

10. David Gordon, "From Rituals of Rapture to Rituals of Dependence: The Political Economy of Khoikhoi Narcotic Consumption, c. 1487–1870," *South African Historical Journal* 35 (1996): 69.
11. Quoted in ibid., 72.

the Khoikhoi language but retained their own language as well. Degraded, cattle-less Khoikhois also joined San hunting bands.

DUTCH SETTLEMENT

In early April 1652, Jan van Riebeeck landed at Table Bay with a small contingent of clerks, artisans, soldiers, farmers, and seamen, all employed by the Dutch East India Company. Over the ten years of his command, van Riebeeck succeeded admirably in his task. The tiny colony at the Cape of Good Hope survived and flourished because of the funds and organizational capacity of the VOC. However, the initial success and later expansion of the Cape Colony also depended on abundant natural resources on the site that were available for the taking.

Van Riebeeck's early journal entries often mention the numbers and variety of edible wild birds, animals, and fish. Fishing and gathering along the coast alone could have fed the settlement. The colonists regularly seined and salted thousands of Cape herring, gathered seabird eggs, killed penguins for their meat, and clubbed Cape fur seals for their oil, skin, and meat (reserved for slaves). Waterfowl were numerous, as were partridges and other edible land birds. Had the settlers decided to do so, they could have fed themselves well by hunting on the veld. Van Riebeeck notes, "Harts, hinds, small roe, eland, hares and other game are seen in large numbers every day now."[12]

Van Riebeeck discovered ample forests and woodlands near the colony. No more than one and a half Dutch miles from the settlement, on the reverse slopes of Table Mountain, he "found splendid forests with thousands of fine, thick, fairly tall and straight trees . . . of a kind almost like beech or ash, rather heavy and difficult to transport."[13] The governor kept parties of woodcutters busy in these forests daily to meet the construction needs of the colony. Nearer the fort, he encountered "thickets of short crooked trees" to be used for charcoal making and fuelwood.[14]

The most striking resource, however, was in the veld itself. According to van Riebeeck, "In this search for forests, we also found at several places the finest and richest arable and pasture land in the world, wide and level, through which many fine, indeed countless, fresh rivulets wind."[15] These broad, grassy, savanna lands cut by rivers and streams were the resource that nourished the massive herds of the Khoikhois and which in the end would

---

12. Van Riebeeck and the Nederlandsche Oost-Indische Compagnie, *Journal*, 1:61. However, the colonists found that neither their guns nor their dogs were all that effective in killing these animals—at least at first.
13. Ibid., 1:60.
14. Ibid.
15. Ibid.

prove irresistible to the colonists. Van Riebeeck's colonists bartered copper and tobacco for Khoikhoi cattle and sheep at every opportunity. Slowly they began building up the settlement's livestock herds while providing beef and mutton for visiting ships.

Wildlife abundance had its drawbacks in Africa. Lions, leopards, and even spotted hyenas were remarkably bold, aggressive predators against cattle and sheep and would maul and kill humans who got in the way. The Khoikhois had great difficulty with these large carnivores, as this journal entry suggests:

> To-day [June 12, 1655,] the Hottentots [Khoikhois] came to us with the request that a soldier or two might be sent to shoot a certain wild animal which was amongst their cattle and which they could neither trap nor kill. This was agreed to and we thereupon sent the sergeant with 3 or 4 soldiers, who found in the dunes, about a pederero [cannon] shot from the fort, all the Hottentots with branches and reeds around their heads looking like devils. They stood in a circle with assegais [spears] in their hands, having surrounded the animal in some bushes so that it dared not come out, neither dared they approach close to it. They threw their assegais into the bushes, hitting it, however, only once in the leg. Our sergeant, getting sight of the animal—it was a huge leopard— shot it in the neck with a firelock so that it fell dead. The Hottentots were greatly astonished to see such a wild animal killed so quickly.[16]

Imitating the Khoikhois, van Riebeeck's settlers put their cattle and sheep in a guarded, earthen-walled kraal at night and posted guards when the animals were grazing each day. In spite of these precautions, lions and leopards, during the settlement's early years, managed to enter the kraal and kill livestock and fowl.

Woodcutters traveling daily to the forests, and parties sent to find and barter with Khoikhois in the interior, discovered an even more perilous world. Humans who disturbed rhinoceroses and Cape buffaloes were in serious danger from their enraged charges. Large predators were even bolder in the interior. In late February 1658, sixteen company soldiers and two Khoikhois set off with two pack oxen to find a large Khoikhoi encampment. On the return journey, when the party had encamped for the night, "a large lion sprang upon one of our men as they were sitting in a circle round a small fire[,] . . . pinned him down and bit him in the right arm, seriously wounding him. The sergeant saw the beast[,] . . . seized a firelock and[,] placing the muzzle against the forehead of the animal, shot it."[17]

In response to these threats, on June 17, 1656, van Riebeeck, "in view of the heavy losses inflicted on the company's livestock by wild beasts," began to offer bounties of six Spanish reals for killing a lion and four for a leopard

16. Van Riebeeck and the Nederlandsche Oost-Indische Compagnie, *Journal*, 1:317.
17. Ibid., 2:249.

or wolf (hyena).[18] This was but the first of many such measures offering bounties for killing what were defined as dangerous vermin. Although only a tiny number of settlers or slaves were actually killed in predator attacks, many livestock were lost. It became clear that any attempt to move into the interior to farm or raise livestock would require a war against the larger wildlife. The conditions under which the Khoikhois survived could not and would not be tolerated by the better-armed company settlers.

In 1657, van Riebeeck began to give out land to company employees who wished to leave its service and settle as freemen.[19] These settlers were to sell grain and meat at fixed prices to the company vessels and thereby reduce dependence on the Khoikhois. In 1659, the nearby peninsular group of Khoikhois challenged the colony over access to excellent grazing areas and water sources on the Cape peninsula. The settlers claimed exclusive occupancy and use rights over these assets under terms of their grant from the company. Rising tensions over cattle stolen by the Khoikhois and beatings and abuses on the part of the Dutch colonists culminated in an armed clash, during which it became clear that the Khoikhois could not destroy or drive out the relatively few Dutch settlers equipped with firearms.[20]

The disparity between the bow-, arrow-, and spear-equipped Khoikhoi warrior and the mounted, arquebus-, pistol-, and saber-armed settler was overwhelming. Every settler household was heavily armed. The VOC actively encouraged the settlers to arm themselves and to shoot well. The settlers and free blacks were each organized into militia companies that demanded annual drills and shooting competitions. The settlers burnished their shooting skills by frequent hunting that also served to intimidate Khoikhois in the vicinity. As one VOC official, J. G. Grevenbroek, commented, "In the early days of the Colony the natives thought that our men who lived next to them could vomit fire. They stood by in amazement, while on the discharge of our guns they saw the largest wild animal, a lion, or an elephant, laid low by one leaden bullet as if struck by lightning. Our cavalry likewise they regarded as so many Centaurs, half horses, half men; at the sight of them they began to shake."[21]

During the postconflict negotiations, the Khoikhois argued with poignant clarity for just treatment from the Dutch.

18. Ibid., 2:41.

19. Leonard Guelke, "Freehold Farmers and Frontier Settlers, 1657–1780," in *The Shaping of South African Society, 1652–1840,* edited by Richard Elphick and Hermann Giliomee (Middletown, Conn.: Wesleyan University Press, 1989).

20. Leonard Guelke, "Ideology and Landscape of Settler Colonialism in Virginia and Dutch South Africa: A Comparative Analysis," in *Ideology and Landscape in Historical Perspective: Essays on the Meanings of Some Places in the Past,* edited by Alan R. H. Baker and Gideon Biger (Cambridge: Cambridge University Press, 1992), 138–39.

21. Quoted in Guelke and Shell, "Landscape of Conquest," 809.

April 5th and 6th. . . . At the fort to-day, peace was renewed with the chief [Gogosa] and overlord of the Kaapmans . . . and with all the principal men and chiefs. . . . They strongly insisted that we had been appropriating more and more of their land, which had been theirs all these centuries, and on which they had been accustomed to letting their cattle graze etc. They asked if they would be allowed to do such a thing supposing they went to Holland, and they added: *"It would be of little consequence if you people stayed here at the fort, but you come right into the interior and select the best land for yourselves, without even asking whether we mind or whether it will cause us any inconvenience."* They therefore strongly urged that they should again be given free access to this land for that purpose. At first we argued against this, saying there was not enough grass for their cattle as well as ours, to which they replied: *"Have we then no reason to prevent you from getting cattle, since if you have a large number, you will take up all our grazing grounds with them? As for the claim that the land is not big enough for us both, who should rather in justice give way, the rightful owner or the foreign intruder?"*

They thus remained adamant in their claim of old-established natural ownership. They said that they should at least be allowed to go and gather bitter almonds, which grow wild in abundance there, and to dig for roots as winter food. . . . When they persisted in their request, eventually they had to be told that they had now lost the land as the result of the war and had no alternative but to admit that it was no longer theirs, the more so because they could not be induced to restore the stolen cattle which they had unlawfully taken from us without any reason. Their land had thus fallen to us in a defensive war won by the sword as it were, and we intended to keep it.[22]

The Dutch answered the Khoikhoi appeal to natural law with the law of conquest.

Van Riebeeck initially tried to organize intensive mixed-grain and livestock farming on the Netherlands model in the vicinity of Cape Town. This effort failed against the appeal of more extensive farming and stock raising on the pastures of the veld, or savanna, outside Cape Town. Restless settlers soon began venturing beyond the confines of the tiny Dutch settlement to find fertile land and pasture for their steadily growing herds.

During the 1670s, in the second Khoikhoi-Dutch war, the company and the Khoikhois engaged in a series of violent encounters. What were in reality four punitive expeditions mounted by the Dutch humiliated the strongest and most anti-Dutch Khoikhoi leaders. At their close, the company began to exact a tribute in livestock from the Khoikhois adjacent to Cape Town. The company governor also claimed and exercised the right to appoint and, if necessary, to depose Khoikhoi leaders. The peninsular Khoikhois nearest Cape Town found their social structure breaking up as they lost herds and pas-

22. Van Riebeeck and the Nederlandsche Oost-Indische Compagnie, *Journal*, 3:195–96, emphasis supplied. Guelke, too, quotes this passage in "Ideology and Landscape of Settler Colonialism in Virginia and Dutch South Africa."

tures to the growing settlement. Many found employment with the company or residents of Cape Town in a trend that further weakened their society.

By 1679, the weakening of the peninsular Khoikhois encouraged the Dutch East India Company to begin a new policy of giving out land grants. Dutch and other white European settlers who undertook to farm beyond the immediate limits of the town in an area called Stellenbosch obtained property rights to tracts ranging from thirty-two to sixty-four hectares in size. When land in Stellenbosch filled up, the VOC judged that the colony should be expanded onto fertile land along the Berg River. This decision opened the door to more extensive agricultural practices.

Distinct areas of settlement grew up in an arc stretching from Hottentots-Holland, which lay 50 kilometers to the southeast of Cape Town; to Drakenstein, 50 kilometers east; to Paradeberg Plateau, 50 kilometers northeast; and to outliers in the northeast at Wagenmakers Valley as far as the land of Waveren, 100 kilometers distant from Cape Town. By 1717, some 2,000 settlers in Cape Town itself and its outlying farming districts inhabited 6,500 square kilometers of more or less continuous settlement. In theory, the 404 land freehold farmers holding formal titles farmed only 194 square kilometers, but in fact they occupied and managed a far greater area than these figures suggest.[23]

In assigning grants, the governor left large chunks of land unclaimed and open to rough grazing for the settler's livestock. The Dutch East India Company capitalized these grantees by providing free seeds and cattle in addition to free land. The company also granted credit to settlers to permit them to purchase slaves brought by company ships from Madagascar, East Africa, Malabar (southwest India), and Southeast Asia.[24] Neighboring Khoikhois could be employed in casual labor, although they were not supposed to be enslaved.

The settler population at the Cape divided into two groups: the townsfolk of Cape Town and grain and wine farmers in its immediate hinterland. The colonists were primarily Dutch, French Huguenot, and German skilled artisans, clerks, and soldiers who had left company service. Few migrated directly from Europe, and fewer still were of high social status. There was also an admixture of freed Malagasy, Indian, and Indonesian former slaves who made a living in and around Cape Town.

By the late eighteenth century, the total European population had risen to between forty thousand and fifty thousand persons; slaves, freed Asians and Africans, and Khoikhois probably numbered another fifty thousand per-

23. Guelke, "Freehold Farmers and Frontier Settlers," 77, table 2.1.

24. James C. Armstrong and Nigel A. Worden, "The Slaves, 1652–1834," in *The Shaping of South African Society, 1652–1840*, edited by Richard Elphick and Hermann Giliomee (Middletown, Conn.: Wesleyan University Press, 1989).

sons. Rural landholders divided into a few wealthy, large-estate owners and some well-to-do gentry who owned scores of slaves. Ordinary burghers used family labor and a few slaves to keep up a respectable standard of living. Poor, landless whites were relatively numerous. The most fortunate found work in supervisory roles for landowners. The white community, although stratified by landownership and wealth, was tightly knit and bound together by ties of patronage and debt.[25]

By this time, the colony had developed its own distinctive Boer culture with a shared history and identity. The Afrikaans dialect, consisting of seventeenth-century Dutch with a mixture of Portuguese, Malay, and Khoikhoi vocabulary, began to diverge from standard Dutch. Many, but not all, white settlers, or Boers, shared a fervent devotion to the Dutch Reformed Church. The Dutch East India Company actively financed and supported the Dutch Reformed Church as the official church of the colony. Most found congenial the Calvinist emphasis on the predestination of an elect. The Church was the main instrument of cultural continuity, education, and social cohesion for the Boer community. There was no great eagerness to convert either slaves or Khoikhois to the Dutch faith. Invariably, the settlers referred to themselves as Christians in distinction to other non-European groups in the colony.

Official and settler pressure on the Khoikhois increased steadily. Dutch East India Company agents and settlers offered goods to Khoikhois in payment for their livestock; often, if refused, they plundered cattle anyway. As the herds began to dwindle, the Khoikhois could not resort to a traditional method of recapitalization. The VOC prevented them from raiding other Khoikhois in the interior to obtain fresh cattle or sheep. As settlers dispersed beyond Cape Town, they closed vital water points and grazing areas that the Khoikhois in the southwestern Cape had long relied on. Settler violence forced the Khoikhois away from the Cape and into the more arid areas. Faced with loss of resources and future risk, more and more Khoikhois accepted jobs as full-time servants, herdsmen, and laborers for European farmers. Grevenbroek, who lived in Stellenbosch, observed:

> The natives . . . enthusiastically hire out their labour for a modest wage, and toil more submissively than Spartan helots. They are apt at applying their hands to unfamiliar tasks. Thus they readily acquire the veterinary skills to cure scab in sheep and they make faithful and efficient herd[er]s. They train oxen for use in ploughing. . . . Some of them are very accomplished riders and have learned to break horses and master them. . . . They chop wood, mind the fire, work in the kitchen, prune vines, gather grapes, or work the wine press industriously. . . . Their wives and daughters make reliable washerwomen and busy

25. Guelke, "Freehold Farmers and Frontier Settlers," 82.

chars. They wash plates and dishes, clean up dirt, gather sticks from the fields round-about, light the fires, cook well, and provide cheap labour for the Dutch.[26]

Finally, after more than a half century of European settlement, the Khoikhois were hit with a familiar catastrophe. In February 1713, visiting ships sent their linens ashore to be washed by the company slaves at Cape Town.[27] The laundry was infected with a smallpox virus that quickly spread to Europeans and slaves in Cape Town and killed hundreds of persons. From the peninsular Khoikhois in and around Cape Town, smallpox reached all the western Cape peoples. Estimates made in 1989 suggest that 30 percent of Khoikhois died in this pandemic.[28] This and two later episodes of smallpox damaged the social structure and pastoral economy of the surviving Khoikhois.

Since the founding of Cape Town, the company had treated the Khoikhois as legally free persons who were, however, under its jurisdiction. As dependents and servants of the white settlers, the Khoikhois drifted downward into a nebulous status that placed them near the bottom of colonial society, next to the African and Asian slaves they often labored beside. This increasingly close association with white settlers corroded the integrity of Khoikhoi culture by completing a process begun when they lost their lands and autonomous communities.

TREKBOERS

Farming of arable lands continued in the settled area next to Cape Town, but market demand for grain and wine remained limited. There were few incentives for greater production.[29] However, the demand for fresh meat was a different story. The crew and passengers of visiting ships bid for fresh meat above all else when they reached Cape Town. Some ships stayed as long as three or four weeks in port if they had a number of sick who were convalescing in the Cape hospital. Each ship bought over a hundred sheep and dozens of beeves for fresh meat and for preservation by corning.

26. Guelke and Shell, "Landscape of Conquest," 812.

27. Richard Elphick and V. C. Malherbe, "The Khoisan to 1828," in *The Shaping of South African Society, 1652–1840*, edited by Richard Elphick and Hermann Giliomee (Middletown, Conn.: Wesleyan University Press, 1989), 21; Russel S. Viljoen, "Disease and Society: VOC Cape Town, Its People, and the Smallpox Epidemics of 1713, 1755, and 1767," *Kleio* 27 (1995).

28. Elphick and Malherbe, "The Khoisan to 1828," 823, citing an unpublished paper by Robert Ross.

29. Robert Ross, "The Cape of Good Hope and the World Economy, 1652–1835," in *The Shaping of South African Society, 1652–1840*, edited by Richard Elphick and Hermann Giliomee (Middletown, Conn.: Wesleyan University Press, 1989), 243–80.

Although the Dutch East India Company made it illegal to do so, from the first the settlers in the vicinity of Cape Town began buying cattle and sheep from Khoikhois to augment their herds. The long-legged, fat-tailed Khoikhoi sheep did not produce usable wool. They were, however, excellent meat producers on the veld grasses that were not all that luxuriant by European standards. They were hardy and resistant to disease. Similarly, the African cattle were well suited to conditions on the veld and were good meat producers. The Dutch farmers bought Khoikhoi animals for what were probably very low prices. As conditions worsened for the Khoikhois, the farmers also began to hire them as low-wage herdsmen whose skills were extremely valuable.

When the Dutch settlers employed Khoikhoi herders, they also acquired the specialized techniques and practices necessary to raise livestock on the veld. Khoikhois had devised effective methods of training fighting oxen and pack oxen to serve their needs. Khoikhoi cattle were probably healthier and faster breeding than those of Europe. Each kraal possessed a "Cattle-Doctor" who "devotes the best part of his Time to the Study of the Disorders incident to Cattle," and who treated livestock disease and wounds, by close observation and immediate treatment with "the Lancet, the Cathartick or the Cordial."[30] Khoikhoi herders carefully nurtured infant calves and lambs in special huts at night and carried the young to their mothers to be suckled. To control the size of their herds, they gelded young rams and bulls and sold or traded off excess stock if their grazing lands were too crowded.

As the settlers' herds grew in size, they sent them under Khoikhoi herdsmen in a transhumance pattern to the upper veld in the dry summer months. Concerned about controlling the frontier, in 1692 Governor Simon van der Stel ordered farmers not to send their livestock more than one day's drive from their home farms. However, as livestock numbers rose, a shortage of good pastureland developed within the vicinity of the Cape. By 1701, Cape farmers owned 9,704 cattle (including oxen) and 53,126 sheep.[31]

As pressures on pastures built up, sons of established farmers and time-expired VOC servants and soldiers, who could never raise the capital necessary to buy a farm near Cape Town, all saw opportunities in the interior. With a much smaller investment, they could buy a wagon and oxen and could trade with the Khoikhois for cattle and sheep. They lived off the proceeds of hunting and set up homes with cattle and sheep pens on unoccupied but well-watered lands. Finally, in 1703, Governor Willem Adriaan van der Stel reversed his father's policy and issued free grazing permits to all applicants.

30. Kolb, *The Present State of the Cape of Good Hope,* 1:180.

31. Pieter van Duin and Robert Ross, *The Economy of the Cape Colony in the Eighteenth Century* (Leiden: Centre for the History of European Expansion, 1987), 150, appendix 9, table 1; P. J. Van der Merwe and Roger B. Beck, *The Migrant Farmer in the History of the Cape Colony, 1657–1842* (Athens: Ohio University Press, 1995), 40, has slightly different figures.

The permits granted them up to six months' grazing use of any lands they chose in the interior, as long as the center of the grazing area chosen was at least one hour's walk from that of another permit holder.[32] With this action, the VOC freely opened the frontier for settlement by migratory stock raisers, or *trekboers*.

These grants, which came to be known as "loan farms" *(leningplats)*, originally were merely revocable licenses to graze stock in a specified area. These were exclusive rights to graze, not common rights. When disputes occurred, the Cape government deputed local officials to adjudicate and fix boundaries. In 1713, the government conceded the right to farm grain on the tracts. Although not technically private ownership rights under the VOC, the loans were so secure that their possessors behaved as if they were indeed private owners of the land. In this fashion, a market in land began to emerge in which land was defined as a commodity. In the nineteenth century, these did indeed become private property rights under the British regime.

Over time, the mandatory one-hour walk separating loan farm centers dwindled to one-half hour. The common understanding among *trekboers* and officials was that "a loan farm lease gave him grazing rights on a circular 'farm' with the homestead at the center and a radius of a half hour's walk, about 3,000 paces." Therefore, each loan farmer had a minimum of 2,420 hectares that, in practice, gave him a much larger grazing area.

Commercial pastoralism on the veld was necessarily extensive. Water defined the pattern of settlement. The *trekboers* had to find reliable water points for their stock, either deep river pools, perennial springs, or wells. Their herds had to be watered daily, which meant that they could not graze more than a half day from a water source.

Many *trekboers* engaged in transhumance. In some areas, water supplies failed in the dry summer months, and they were forced into moving their animals to river valleys. Other settlers on the higher plateaus, where freezing conditions occurred in winter, such as on the Roggeveld, moved to the warmer plains in the winter for comfort and for the survival of their young livestock.

Growing numbers of family settlers moved into the interior as the eighteenth century progressed. With capital of one thousand guilders, a young *trekboer* could start with a horse, a wagon and oxen, twenty cattle, fifty sheep, a musket, and a few household goods. Those poorer young men who lacked any capital could become tenant farmers working on shares for those already holding loan farms. Or, as an alternative, they could band with a few others to hunt commercially for hippopotamuses and eland, or even elephants.

As they dispersed, the *trekboers* retained a sense of cohesion and mission

32. Guelke and Shell, "Landscape of Conquest," 77–78; Van der Merwe and Beck, *The Migrant Farmer in the History of the Cape Colony*, 38–39.

as a result of their shared identity as frontierspeople buoyed by the Old Testament teachings of the Dutch Reformed Church, with its stern images of pastoral peoples. Rural households held regular worship services, often daily, presided over by the patriarch of the family. Even the most remote settler families made occasional trips to take communion, baptize their children, and solemnize marriages at one of the Dutch churches established and paid for by the Cape government in the interior. Behind these shared cultural forms lay two fundamental, never-challenged beliefs: first, that the Boers were destined by God's will to be rulers over their slaves and the Khoikhois; and second, that the Boers were entitled to occupy and own all the lands they required.

The Cape settler frontier advanced at a deliberate pace for most of the eighteenth century. The terrain was difficult, and population reserves that could be drawn on were limited. The state did not encourage or fund town settlement within the interior, so there were few secondary centers to serve as markets or as jumping-off points for further advances. Instead, meat contractors and their agents traveled the interior buying up animals and driving them to the Cape. *Trekboers* and their families journeyed infrequently—sometimes yearly, sometimes not that often—to Cape Town to buy European provisions, commodities, tools, weapons, and other necessities.

Generally, *trekboers* avoided areas that had less than 250 millimeters of rainfall per year. This meant that most frontier settlement flowed toward the moister eastern Cape rather than north or northeast from Cape Town into areas where near-desert conditions prevailed. Those settlers who did venture north headed for the better-watered plateau areas. They reached the Cedarberg Mountains as early as 1710 but did not arrive at the arrowhead-shaped high plateau formed by the Hantsamsberg, Roggeveld, and Nieuweweld Mountains, 200 to 250 kilometers northeast of Cape Town, until the 1740s. By 1760, parties of settlers claimed lands in the Koperberg Mountains along the Buffels River, 450 kilometers north of Cape Town.[33]

The march to the east followed two distinct routes. In the first and earliest advance, *trekboers* occupied loan farms on the moister 60–100-kilometer-deep coastal strip running 700 kilometers from Cape Town all the way along the south coast to Algoa Bay. By the 1720s, they had traveled 200 kilometers to the east to reach the Swellendam region; by the 1750s, they had reached the Langkloof Mountains in the area north of Mossel Bay; and by 1770 they had reached Algoa Bay. By 1778, they occupied the Zuurveld (to the east of Algoa Bay) as far as the west bank of the Great Fish River. The second, and later, line of advance, some 100 to 125 kilometers inland, followed the wetter rainfall line formed over successive mountain ranges, and turned northeast at the Zwartberg Mountains. *Trekboers* reached the Camdebo region

33. Guelke, "Freehold Farmers and Frontier Settlers," 68, fig. 2.1.

along the Sundays River by 1767. By 1780, pioneer settlers were claiming loan farms along the west bank of the Great Fish River.

As the *trekboers* advanced north and east, they displaced Khoikhois from their favorite watering places and most verdant pastures. Some Khoikhois submitted quietly and withdrew their reduced herds to less favorable areas. Some became clients of the settlers who accepted pay and protection for labor while retaining some of their herds. Many even joined their masters in punitive expeditions against still-unreconciled Khoikhois. Other displaced Khoikhois, unwilling to submit, embittered, resentful, and frequently hungry, retaliated by raiding settlers' herds. They killed Khoikhoi shepherds and stole, and frequently slaughtered, the cattle. When pursued by angry *trekboers,* these resisting Khoikhois found refuge in more remote valleys and hill areas inhabited by San hunter-gatherer groups. The *trekboers* labeled these groups "Bushmen" *(bosjesmans)* or "Bushmen-Hottentots" *(bosjesmans-hottentoten).* Khoikhoi rebels and San hunters used poisoned arrows to great effect and, increasingly, possessed stolen firearms.[34]

The attacks began as early as 1701 in the Waveren region and continued throughout the century. By 1715, the raids forced the VOC to permit settlers to organize and launch punitive expeditions instead of using its own soldiers and officers as it had in the past. Continued resistance exploded in the first "Bushman War" of 1739. A wave of Bushmen raids on *trekboer* cattle in the Sandveld and Bokkeveld regions north of Cape Town in 1738 touched off the immediate formation of mounted militia units, or "commandos," among the settlers, which were raised and commanded by a *veldcorporaal.* In a savage war of reprisal, these commandos swept the entire area and attacked every Khoikhoi group found. They killed most of the men, made the women and children prisoners, and seized their herds. The reprisals were so violently successful that they cleared all Khoikhois from the Sandveld and Bokkeveld areas. A similar flurry of raiding followed by severe reprisals occurred in 1754–1755 in the Roggeveld. That brief war, too, ended with Khoikhoi defeat and expulsion.[35]

To the east, war came later, in the 1770s, when *trekboers* reached the Camdebo and Sneeuwberg regions in the northeast. The new arrivals met determined opposition when they tried to move north to make use of seasonal pastures. Bushmen, both Khoikhoi and San hunters from the Sneeuwberg region, attacked settler homesteads and herds. In response, in 1774, VOC authorities in Stellenbosch sent a combined force of three commandos totaling 100 European volunteers and 150 Khoikhoi dependents to aid the

34. Elphick and Malherbe, "The Khoisan to 1828," 22–28; Susan Newton-King, *Masters and Servants on the Cape Eastern Frontier, 1760–1803* (Cambridge: Cambridge University Press, 1999).

35. Newton-King, *Masters and Servants on the Cape Eastern Frontier,* 63–70.

beleaguered *trekboers*. In a series of fast-moving campaigns, these commandos killed or captured more than 700 men, women, and children and suffered only two or three casualties themselves. This bloody victory damped
but did not end continued resistance and raiding in this region, which were
met with periodic reprisals from local commandos. In the encounters, 2,000
to 3,000 Bushmen died. Another 2,000 to 3,000 that were taken captive became forced laborers for the victorious settlers. By the end of Dutch rule, the
trekboers had stamped out all resistance by Bushmen.[36] The western Khoikhois
had lost virtually all their herds, and the eastern Khoikhois who survived were
under enormous competitive pressure from the new pastoralists.

In 1795, some 10,000 *trekboers*, their families, and their servants were scattered over a vast area stretching from the Orange River in the north to the
Great Fish River in the east. Even in regions with good grass and water, *trekboers* were thinly settled. For example, in the Swellendam district along the
south central coast, in an area of about 11,500 square kilometers, there were
only 142 loan farms, which occupied less than a third of the area (3,436
square kilometers). In that district, in which there were an assumed 14 persons per household including *trekboer* families and servants, population density was only 1 person per 6 square kilometers.[37]

As late as 1806, after the British conquest, there were only 1,736 loan farms
in a territory that covered 388,500 square kilometers.[38] This implies that the
formal area granted under loan farms was about 42,000 square kilometers (at
2,420 hectares per farm), or only 10.8 percent of the total land area. That
minimum could reasonably be doubled to allow for untitled squatting, for
lands grazed beyond the formal limits, and for transhumance. This would
raise the share of land used for stock raising to about one-fifth. A then contemporary estimate for 1798 put total cattle under settler ownership at about
250,000 and sheep at 1.4 million.[39] On average, therefore, each loan farm
had 144 cattle and 749 sheep. The largest settlers counted herds of several
hundred cattle and several thousand sheep. Poor untitled and unsuccessful
frontiersmen might have had only a few cattle and a few dozen sheep. By
these figures, overall stocking densities would have averaged as many as 6 to
as few as 3 cattle and as many as 67 to as few as 33 sheep per square kilometer (depending on whether one uses the figure for formally granted areas or
doubles that figure). These densities seem low but actually could have been
high in their demands on water and the less well-watered veld vegetation.

36. Elphick and Malherbe, "The Khoisan to 1828," 27–28; Newton-King, *Masters and Servants
on the Cape Eastern Frontier,* 72–76.
37. Guelke, "Freehold Farmers and Frontier Settlers," 85–86.
38. A. J. Christopher, *Southern Africa* (Folkestone, Eng.: Dawson; Hamden, Conn.: Archon
Books, 1976), 50.
39. S. D. Neumark, *Economic Influences on the South African Frontier, 1652–1836* (Stanford,
Calif.: Stanford University Press, 1957), citing Barrow, p. 76.

TREKBOER AND NGUNI

Mingling with the remaining intact Khoikhoi tribes in the east was a Bantu people, the Nguni. This Xhosa-speaking people was advancing from the north into the valleys of the Fish, Keiskamm, and Buffels Rivers. The Nguni, like other Bantu, were also pastoralists who kept a distinctive breed of horn-less cattle. Unlike the Khoikhois, their women cultivated sorghum, from which they made bread. They had recently adopted maize obtained earlier from Portuguese traders in the north. The Nguni were shifting cultivators who burnt and pushed the borders of forest and bush back. They brewed a beer from millet and maize. Unlike the Khoikhois, they were a well-organized, aggressive warrior people who made capable use of their throwing spears in war and on the hunt.[40]

In 1635, a Portuguese ship, the *Nossa Senhora de Belem,* went aground at the mouth of the Xhora River on the southeast coast. The stranded crew spent six months there building themselves a boat. An extract from their journal offers a detailed word portrait of the Nguni:

> The men of this county are very lean and upright, tall of stature and handsome. They can endure great labour, hunger, and cold. . . . They are clothed in skins which hang over their shoulders to the knees; these are cow-hides, but they have the art of dressing them till they are as soft as velvet. There are rich and poor among them, but this is according to the number of their cattle. . . . Their arms are assagais [throwing spears] with broad, well-fashioned heads. Their shields are of elephant hide with handles like ours, but made like leathern tar-gets. . . . They all have dogs with ears and tails cropped, with which they hunt wild pigs and stags, as well as buffaloes, elephants, tigers, and lions.
>
> The kings have four, five, and seven wives. The women do all the work, planting and tilling the earth with sticks to prepare it for their grain, which is millet as large or larger than linseed. They have maize also, and plant large melons which are very good, and beans and gourds of many kinds, also sugar canes, though they brought us very few of these. Cows are what they chiefly value: these are very fine and the tamest cattle I have ever seen in any country. In the milk season they live chiefly upon it, making curds and turn [sic] it to sour, which was little to our taste.[41]

Like the *trekboers,* the Nguni were pioneer settlers moving southwest instead of northeast in search of good hunting and grazing land.

Beyond the Great Fish River, Nguni met Boer. Some cattle stealing and vi-olent clashes took place between white and black pastoralists. Trade also

---

40. Noël Mostert, *Frontiers: The Epic of South Africa's Creation and the Tragedy of the Xhosa People,* 1st Amer. ed. (New York: Knopf, distributed by Random House, 1992).

41. Monica Wilson and Leonard Monteath Thompson, *The Oxford History of South Africa* (Oxford: Clarendon Press, 1969) 1:82–83.

flourished. The Nguni wanted horses, knives, tobacco, and above all, muskets from the Boers. The Boers wanted elephant ivory and cattle from the Nguni. Boer missionaries made their way to the frontier to try and convert the Nguni to Christianity, with mixed success. Avid hunters trekked into the Nguni-held lands to kill the wild elephants that were plentiful there. Khoikhois who served settlers, traders, and missionaries acted as intermediaries and interpreters for both parties in these encounters.

After 1779, *trekboer* pressures intensified to the point that the British Cape government supported its frontiersmen in a series of nine distinct wars with the Nguni. The latter were more warlike, better organized, and more confident than the Khoikhois and had not been decimated by disease. The Dutch or Boers, who held the advantage in horses and firearms, prevailed only after much hard fighting. The Boers stopped the Nguni advance, pushed them back beyond the Great Fish River, and thereby opened up new lands for European pioneer settlement. Although defeated, the Nguni and other Bantu peoples did not suffer social destruction and retained a formidable capacity to resist European colonial pressure in the nineteenth century.

ENVIRONMENTAL IMPACT OF DUTCH SETTLEMENT

During Dutch rule at the Cape, from 1652 to 1795, a relatively small colonial population considerably altered the natural environment of the region. The most dramatic changes were to be seen in the pattern of urban and rural settlement within a one-hundred-kilometer radius of Cape Town. Here, settler plows turned up the veld grasses in a mode of cultivation unknown to the Khoikhois and planted wheat, vines, and other imported cultivars. The Cape immigrants brought the horse and the pig with them. However, the African longhorn cattle and fat-tailed sheep of the Khoikhois were already present and well adapted to the local environment.

One might assume, though, that little had changed beyond this settled region near the Cape. The nomadic pastoral Khoikhoi kraals were dispersed and their organization and culture broken. However, their successors, the *trekboers* and their Khoikhoi servants, managed flocks and herds similar to those of the Khoikhois. The *trekboers* had adapted to African-style, extensive pastoralism in this region. In order to obtain optimal pasture for their animals, early settlers imitated Khoikhoi seasonal transhumance movements and those observed in the larger wild herbivores.[42]

In the western Cape, *trekboers* settled at higher elevations on the Roggeveld, Bokkeveld, and Hantam Mountains carried out both summer and winter migrations. During the dry summers, they moved to use water and grass re-

42. Daniel P. Kruger, "Pastoral Strategies and Settlement Systems in Colonial South Africa," *Historical Geography* 24 (1995).

sources on a communal basis along the Zak and Orange Rivers. In the freezing winters, they brought their herds to lower elevations in the Thorn Karoo
and Namaqualand. Some loan farmers also followed the Khoikhoi practice of
moving sheep and cattle in summer from the western Cape east to the interior of the Great Karoo region, where summer rainfall began. Here, they
found that succulent Karoo shrubs flourished in the summer.

Trekboers in the southern Cape found themselves at the intersection of the
winter rainfall regime of the western Cape and the dominant summer rainfall regime of the moister east. Those loan farmers who were settled in the
higher Zwartberg and Outeniqua Mountains moved to the flat plains of the
Little and Great Karoo in the winter.

When trekboers approached the Gamtoos River, they reached the five-
hundred-millimeter isohyet, where the moist eastern Cape climate regime
began. Pastoralists learned to identify two types of grasses, sweetveld and
sourveld. Sweetveld grasses were nutritious all year long, even when dry.
Sourveld grasses were nutritious only during early growth, especially after
the onset of late-spring, early summer rains. After three months, the lignin
and cellulose content of these grasses, along with their protein and phosphorus content, declined and they became indigestible to livestock. According to Daniel P. Kruger, "In eastern South Africa, the pastoralist's best
strategy was to graze livestock on sweetveld grasses in the winter months, on
sourveld grasses in late spring and early summer, and on mixed veld during
the transition between this sweet-sourveld regime."[43] Moving to sourgrass in
the spring meant driving the herds toward the well-watered coast, where such
grasses were abundant.

Another of the Khoikhoi techniques the VOC settlers adopted was veld
burning to improve the growth of veld grasses. Kolb writes:

> The Kochaquas, as do the other Nations of the Hottentots, remove with their
> Cots and Cattle, from one part of their Territories for the Convenience of Pas-
> turage. When they find the Grass is too old and rank, they burn it on the
> Ground and depart, and return by the Time it comes up again, which is very
> soon; the Ashes of the Grass exceedingly enriching the Soil, which rarely wants
> Refreshments of Rain. The Grass grows very thick and high; and by this Prac-
> tice of burning it the Country is sometimes seen in a Blaze for several Miles
> about. In this, the Hottentots are imitated by the Europeans at the Cape.[44]

Carl Peter Thunberg, the Swedish botanist who traveled through the interior
veld during the 1770s, complained of the practice of veld burning that left
burnt, sooty bushes standing to the annoyance of travelers.[45] The benefits of

43. Ibid., 61.
44. Kolb, The Present State of the Cape of Good Hope, 1:62.
45. Carl Peter Thunberg and Vernon S. Forbes, Travels at the Cape of Good Hope, 1772–1775:
Based on the English Edition, London, 1793–1795 (Cape Town: Van Riebeeck Society, 1986),

burning must have been considerable. The settlers persisted in burning in spite of official bans enacted by the VOC at Cape Town in 1687 and again in 1741 with horrific penalties attached.[46] Veld burning, whether by Khoikhoi or settler, favored fire-resistant species of grasses and bushes.

Whether the herds of the *trekboers* actually grew to be greater in number than those of the Khoikhois they displaced is not easily established. Approximately fifty thousand Khoikhois inhabited the western and eastern Cape at the time of VOC settlement in 1652. The earliest Dutch observers reported large numbers of cattle and sheep—running into the thousands—herded by each Khoikhoi kraal, or encampment. The large numbers of animals estimated by the earliest Dutch observers imply that the Khoikhois conceivably could have grazed 250,000 cattle and 1.4 million sheep, the estimate for settler herds in 1798.

However, not all Khoikhois possessed an equal number of livestock. As Kolb is careful to point out, herd sizes varied with the resources available. Of the sixteen "nations" Kolb describes, the "Hessaquas are, perhaps[,] richer than any other Hottentot nation; that is[,] have more and better Cattle; for Wealth among the Hottentots is seen in no other kind. The Pastures here are, all of 'em, cover'd with Droves of Oxen and Flocks of Sheep."[47] On the other hand, "the Attaquas are possess'd of but a very indifferent Soil, and but ill provided with Water. For which reason they live in little Troops at a considerable Distance from one another, in Parts the most commodious. 'Tis owing to this too, they are not overstock'd with Cattle, having, for the most Part, only just so much as, with the Game they catch, is necessary to sustain 'em."[48] The latter description suggests that early impressions of Khoikhoi herds in the immediate vicinity of the Cape, with its abundant pasturage and water, should be adjusted to allow for smaller livestock numbers in less well-endowed areas. It may well be that the *trekboers* surpassed Khoikhoi livestock numbers by the end of the eighteenth century.

The *trekboers,* unlike the Khoikhois, were commercial pastoralists tied, however remotely, to the early modern world economy. They bred and grazed their animals for sale. They shipped their livestock to Cape Town's

---

83. "In many places I observed the land to have been set on fire for the purpose of clearing it. . . . Divers plains here, produce a very high sort of grass, which being of too coarse a nature, and unfit food for cattle, is not consumed, and thus prevents fresh verdure from springing up; not to mention that it harbours a great number of serpents and beasts of prey. Such a piece of land as this, therefore is set on fire, to the end that new grass may spring up from the roots. Now if any of these places were overgrown with bushes, these latter were burned quite black, and left standing in this sooty condition for a great length of time afterwards, to my great vexation, as that of other travelers, who were obliged to pass through them."

46. Ibid., 83, n. 225.
47. Kolb, *The Present State of the Cape of Good Hope,* 1:73.
48. Ibid., 1:71.

market to meet generally rising demand throughout the eighteenth century. Moreover, the *trekboers*, unlike the Khoikhois, settled in fixed locations, usually along the rivers or at other water points.[49] Control of water points also gave settlers access to ample game that converged on these watering places. Settler transhumance was far more predictable and fixed than that of Khoikhoi lineage groups that followed the rains each year.

The settlers' stocking densities and grazing practices pressed harder on the veld than did those of the Khoikhois. In his travel account of 1785, Anders Sparrman describes stock raising near Cape Town:

> In direct contradiction to the custom and example of the original inhabitants, the Hottentots [Khoikhois], the colonists turn their cattle out continually into the same fields, and that too in a much greater quantity than used to graze there in the time of the Hottentots; as they keep not only a number sufficient for their own use but likewise enough to supply the more plentiful tables . . . of Cape Town . . . as well as for the victualling of ships. . . .
>
> In consequence of the fields being thus continually grazed off[,] . . . grasses and herbs . . . are prevented . . . from thriving. . . . The rhinoceros bush which the cattle always pass by and leave untouched is suffered to take root.[50]

Rhinoceros bush was a commonly recognized sign of overgrazing.

As the *trekboers* moved eastward, so also did grazing pressures. Hendrik Swellengrebel, traveling to the east in 1776, recorded his impressions of farming on the extreme eastern edge of the *trekboer's* frontier. He reached the Camdebo region, "which in the language of the Hottentots means Green Hollow," located just south of the Sneeuwberg Mountains, where, unlike the Karooveld to the west, the terrain was "beautifully covered with grass," the best of which "is found under the thornbushes where it receives shade."[51] However, Swellengrebel warned that signs of degradation had already occurred within a few short years:

> In the Camdebo there are about 30 farms of which about 25 are inhabited. If they will not begin to conserve artificially the grazing for their cattle, it is to be feared that the luxuriance of the grass that has already started to deteriorate markedly, though settlement in the area only began 7 or 8 years ago, will not last long, and this veld will become deteriorated just like that which lies nearer the Cape. This has already gone so far that one, Jacobus Botha, has had to

49. Guelke and Shell, "Landscape of Conquest," 817.

50. Anders Sparrman and Vernon S. Forbes, *A Voyage to the Cape of Good Hope, towards the Antarctic Polar Circle, Round the World, and to the Country of the Hottentots and the Caffres, from the year 1772–1776, based on the English Editions of 1785–1786 Published by Robinson, London* (Cape Town: Van Riebeeck Society, 1975), 1:267–68.

51. Vernon S. Forbes, *Pioneer Travellers of South Africa: A Geographical Commentary upon Routes, Records, Observations, and Opinions of Travellers at the Cape, 1750–1800* (Cape Town: A. A. Balkema, 1965), 68.

move to the Great Fish River because he could find no pasture for his cattle here; and A. van den Berg spoke of wanting to trek elsewhere because he could not maintain himself on his own farm.[52]

Trekboer livestock grazing was probably more sustained and intense than that of the Khoikhoi cattle and sheep herds. Inappropriately heavy stocking ratios reduced some grazing areas to unusability in the first decades of settlement.

Vegetation degraded from what it had been before European settlement. Overgrazing caused reversion to xerophytic grasses with deeper root systems, such as *Eragrostis* species, *Cynodon* ("needle" grass) species, unpalatable shrubs such as the "bitter Karoo," and even rhinoceros bush.[53] Bushveld, or savanna, succeeded grasslands in the plateau and coastal areas of the eastern Cape. Abundant grasses were intermixed with acacias and aloe trees.

The European impact was heaviest on the Cape's array of large animals and birds. The settlers and their servants and slaves hunted incessantly. The hunt was the male settler's supreme pleasure and avocation. Firearms, including the lightly powered muskets of the period, proved lethal against even the biggest animals if used by skilled, determined hunters who were equipped with packs of hunting dogs.

As soon as they occupied their freehold lands, colonists in Stellenbosch, Drakenstein, Waveren, and other cultivated areas outside Cape Town used guns, dogs, traps, and snares in an unceasing hunt. To protect their herds, they, and their Khoikhoi workers and slaves hunted lions and leopards, often by using traps that consisted of loaded muskets that fired when the animal tripped a triggering device. They killed elephants to protect their crops; rhinoceroses and Cape buffaloes for meat and hides and to protect their persons; and eland, antelopes, hippopotamuses, and dozens of other animals and birds to supply meat. Settlers organized hunting parties to follow the rivers to shoot hippopotamuses for meat, fat, and hides. In the early eighteenth century, hippopotamus meat or fat sold for twelve to fifteen pence a pound at Cape Town and was much in demand.[54] Some venturesome colonists hunted elephants in the interior and sold their ivory to buyers in Cape Town, from whence it found its way into a world market.[55]

Hunting became a war of extinction. As the settler frontier expanded, wildlife retracted. To be sure, the Khoikhois had also been enthusiastic

---

52. Ibid. Passage translated from Swellengrebel's unpublished journals.
53. Wellington, *Southern Africa*, 287–88.
54. Kolb, *The Present State of the Cape of Good Hope*, 2:132.
55. Only fragmentary data for ivory exports have as yet been uncovered. For example, official figures reveal a five-year annual average of 645 kilograms of ivory exported from Cape Town between 1788 and 1793 (no data for 1791). As van Duin and Ross point out in a note, much more ivory was probably exported than is revealed by the official figures. Van Duin and Ross, *The Economy of the Cape Colony in the Eighteenth Century*, 132, appendix 5, table 9.

hunters, but they were far less deadly than the gun-wielding European colonists, since they did not extirpate any species. By the early eighteenth century, wild game was virtually nonexistent in the farming regions. Kolb comments of Hottentots-Holland, fifty kilometers southeast of Cape Town:

> This Quarter was formerly a great Haunt of Wild Beasts. The Lion, the Tiger, the Leopard, the Elephant, the Rhinoceros, the Elk, and every other Sort of Wild Beast, seen in the Cape-Countries, were to be met with here. But, by Powder and Ball, they were quickly destroy'd or frighten'd into remote Quarters. And now-a-days very rarely any Wild Beasts are seen here besides Deer, and Goats of several Kinds. When they are, they are quickly destroy'd or chac'd [sic] far away, and by the Fire and the Noise of Guns deterr'd from ever appearing there again.[56]

Only on the distant frontier regions was there still an abundance of game. Virtually cost-free meat from hunting fed company officials and soldiers at distant outposts. The VOC set up a network of military posts whose occupants engaged in trade with the Khoikhois or performed other functions. One such post, Oudepost I, was located 120 kilometers north of Cape Town, on the coast at the north point of Kraal Bay. There, a small group of VOC soldiers traded for cattle and other provisions with the Khoikhois and offered meat and other provisions to ships that were unable to reach the Cape due to bad weather. Between 1669 and 1732, Oudepost I was manned for this purpose. Despite their access to domesticated livestock, the soldiers at Oudepost I lived primarily off wild game. Faunal remains found at the site show that at least 74 percent were from wild animals as well as multiple species of fish, birds, and even sea turtles. Oudepost I "was not entirely the rural production and provisioning station of the archival record but was also a hunting camp deep in the heart of conquered land."[57]

Wild game similarly provisioned *trekboers*, their families, and their slaves. Thunberg, on his first journey outward from Cape Town in November 1772, arrived at Jacobus Botha's farm on the coast near Mossel Bay. At the Botha farm, Thunberg noted, "the fields hereabouts were full of wild buffaloes, so that it was not uncommon to see a hundred or two of them in a herd."[58] Botha fed his family and the fifty Khoikhois who labored for him with buffalo meat:

> The whole roof in the kitchen was hung with thick slices of buffalo's flesh, which being dried and smoked, they ate as hung-beef.
> Buffaloes were shot here by a Hottentot, who had been trained to this business by the farmer, and in this manner found the whole family in meat, with-

56. Kolb, *The Present State of the Cape of Good Hope*, 2:34.
57. Carmel Schrire, "Excavating Archives at Oudepost I, Cape," *Social Dynamics* 16, no. 1 (1990).
58. Thunberg and Forbes, *Travels at the Cape of Good Hope*, 93.

out having recourse to the [cattle]herd. The balls were counted out to him every time he went a shooting, and he was obliged to furnish the same number of buffaloes as he received of balls. Thus the many Hottentots that lived here were supported without expence, and without the decrease of the same cattle, which constitute the whole of the farmer's wealth. The greatest part of the flesh of the buffalo falls to the share of the Hottentots, but the hide to that of the master.[59]

During the 1770s and 1780s, travelers, enthusiastic natural scientists, and avid hunters toured these regions in search of plant and animal specimens and adventure. The journals of Sparrman, Thunberg, and Gordon describe a bloody, determined war of attrition carried out against African wildlife by *trekboers*—a war into which the sporting and scientific inclinations of visiting naturalists also fit comfortably.[60]

THE CAPE AS GLOBAL REST STATION

Cape Town more than fulfilled the Dutch East India Company's expectations. Between 1700 and 1793, just before the British conquest, 5,159 VOC East Indiamen and 3,234 other flag outward, or homeward bound, European vessels sailed into Cape Town's harbor. Of the average 89 vessels per year, 55 were VOC and 34 flew other flags.[61] If bound for Asia, they were 120 days or so out, with 70 days at sea left to reach Batavia on the nine- to ten-month voyage. If bound for Europe, the longer portion of the voyage lay ahead of them. Every year, thousands of sea-weary, battered, often ill and malnourished seamen, soldiers, officials, and traders found respite and refuge at Cape Town. The settlement helped to reduce the death rate from scurvy and other diseases that broke out on long, uninterrupted voyages.

At the Cape, the captains of these vessels took on freshwater, fresh flour, butter, cheese, bread, beer, wine, fruits, vegetables, and above all else, fresh or dried meat and livestock on the hoof. They refitted and repaired their ships and bought new sails and fittings and replaced lost or expended supplies. They exchanged news and information, passed on letters and orders, and enjoyed the climate and the delights of sociability on land. They landed their sick for treatment at the Cape hospital. Some of the invalids recovered in time to sail, many stayed longer. The VOC frequently deposited army units at the Cape for rest and convalescence before they resumed active duty

---

59. Ibid., 94.
60. Robert Jacob Gordon, P. E. Raper, and M. Boucher, *Robert Jacob Gordon: Cape Travels, 1777 to 1786* (Houghton, South Africa: Brenthurst Press, 1988).
61. Duin and Ross, *The Economy of the Cape Colony in the Eighteenth Century;* calculated from appendix 4. The centurylong average conceals a sharp rise in shipping traffic after 1770.

in Asia. Cape Town was truly a vital "refreshment station" in the world maritime trading network.

The Dutch East India Company made effective use of Cape Town's strategic location and natural resources. By a peculiarity of VOC bookkeeping that charged such items as the costs of regiments billeted and the supplies bought by VOC ships to the Cape treasury, Cape expenses exceeded its revenues by about two and a half times annually—a difference that required an annual subsidy.[62] However, this subsidy masked the true value of the goods and services produced at Cape Town made possible by access to the soil, vegetation, water, wildlife, and other natural resources of the Cape region.

The settler community produced enough food to feed the entire colony and its Khoikhoi dependents amply, with what were lavish food budgets by European standards. The settlers also met their needs for ordinary clothing and shelter by their own efforts. (Imports were largely low-bulk, high-value items such as Indian textiles, guns, lead, powder, coffee, tea, sugar, spices, paper, ink, and other items not grown or manufactured locally.) In the 1780s, Cape farmers were marketing 2.7 million liters of wine each year, most of which was consumed by settlers and visitors.[63]

In the eighteenth century, Cape farmers and pastoralists had to continually increase production simply to meet domestic demand. The total European and slave population of the colony, not counting Khoikhois, grew by nearly an order of magnitude, from 3,367 persons in 1704–1708 to 31,342 total in 1789–1793. The population of Cape Town comprised one-third the colony's total, growing to 10,400 persons by the latter period.[64]

The Cape Colony exported foodstuffs to Batavia as well. Cape farmers realized remarkably high wheat yield ratios—as high as 1:13 in the early eighteenth century. Even though yield ratios drifted steadily downward to 1:9 in the 1780s as soils were depleted, they were still among the best in the world.[65] Grain exports rose from an annual average of 3,571 hectoliters in 1706–1708 to 26,014 hectoliters for 1779–1782—the high point for the Dutch period.[66] Butter exports rose to 18,205 kilograms annually between 1791 and 1793. Only about 10 percent of the Cape wines were marketed, but these found a small, select market in Europe.

In addition, Cape Town mobilized large amounts of foodstuffs for visiting ships in the harbor. Each VOC and foreign ship bought an average of 40 hec-

62. Ben J. Heidjra and Anton D. Lowenberg, "Towards a Theory of Colonial Growth: The Case of the Dutch in Southern Africa," *Journal of Interdisciplinary Economics* 1 (1987): 257.

63. Duin and Ross, *The Economy of the Cape Colony in the Eighteenth Century*, 50, table 4.4.

64. Ibid., 126, appendix 3.

65. Ibid., 37, graph 3.5.

66. Ibid., 129, appendix 5, table 2.

toliters of wheat from Cape Town suppliers.[67] Farmers supplied butter, fruits, and vegetables as well, but the most important foodstuff from the viewpoint of both the colony and the ship's crews was meat. Butchers under contract to the VOC slaughtered and prepared beef and mutton for ships, and for consumption by VOC officials living in Cape Town, VOC slaves, and the inmates of the hospital. In the period 1725–1728, the contract butchers supplied the VOC with about 128,000 kilograms of meat per year; by 1779–1780, this figure had increased to 500,000 kilograms per year; and by 1790 the total had reached 600,000 kilograms.[68]

The contract butchers also sold beef and mutton at higher prices to foreign ships. Although a full data series is not available, 64 foreign vessels bought 540,000 kilograms of meat plus a number of live sheep at an average of 8.4 metric tons of meat per ship in 1779–1780. These purchases were price sensitive, and if the market price rose too high, ship captains would reduce their purchases. In the period after 1770, an average of 137 ships arrived at Cape Town each year.[69] If each took an average of 8,400 kilograms of meat, then the Cape was supplying 1.1 million kilograms (1,100 metric tons) of beef and mutton to seafarers each year. With an estimated 50 million kilograms live weight of livestock in the colony's herds, this represents 2.2 percent of the total herd slaughtered each year for the maritime trade.

Van Duin and Ross estimate that the overall meat production for the colony in 1781–1782 was about 2,375,000 kilograms, with just about two-thirds going to visiting ships.[70] With approximately 50 million kilograms of meat "on the hoof" in the colony, this suggests that 4.75 percent of the total herd was slaughtered each year. Cattle and sheep grazing in the remotest corners of the Cape veld had become a resource directly tied to the early modern world economy.

CONCLUSION

After 143 years of Dutch rule, a relatively small, but vigorous, European settler community lived well from the proceeds of farming and commercial pastoralism across this enormous region. The colony played a useful role in succoring the steadily rising maritime traffic between Europe and Asia. The

67. Ibid., 91, appendix 1. These amounts were in addition to any shipped as exports.

68. Ibid., 65. This figure includes twenty-five hundred sheep delivered live to the VOC to be placed on ships.

69. Thunberg and Forbes, *Travels at the Cape of Good Hope*, 93.

70. In the year from May 1781 to April 1782, the contract butchers slaughtered a total of 5,000 cattle and 34,000 sheep or the equivalent of 1,465,000 kilograms of meat. These supplies went to meet the needs of the VOC, crews of foreign ships, and a portion of the internal market in Cape Town. In addition, the butchers sold 5,000 sheep, or 100,000 kilograms of meat, to the visiting ships. One Dutch *pond* = 500 grams.

costs of this enterprise were met not by the settlers or the VOC but by the Khoikhois, who suffered loss of homes, lands, herds, and much of their cultural heritage. Despite attempts at resistance, surviving Khoikhois and Sans became clients of the European settlers.

By the end of the Dutch period, nearly all the larger fauna of the entire Cape region were depleted by unrelenting settler hunting made more lethal with firearms. Elephants, rhinoceroses, hippopotamuses, and other large, vulnerable animals had long since disappeared from longer settled regions nearer Cape Town. As the *trekboers* pushed their oxen and wagons into the interior, they relied on constant hunting to sustain them in both body and spirit. As the frontier expanded, wildlife diminished.

What was lost can be only dimly perceived from settler and traveler observations that survive. Some idea of the magnitude of the loss can be seen in the still-teeming wildlife of the "natural laboratory" formed by the protected Serengeti-Mara ecosystems on the East African interior plateau on the border of Tanzania and Kenya. Here, in grasslands and savannas of only twenty-five thousand square kilometers, estimates put the number of wildebeests at about 1.3 million, zebras at 200,000, and Thomson's gazelles at 440,000. Large predators abound, with 7,500 hyenas and 2,800 lions. The full list of large mammals living today in the Serengeti is similar to that of the Cape region in the seventeenth century.[71]

The large numbers and variety of migratory grazing animals in the Serengeti appear to improve rather than degrade the vegetation cover. According to S. J. McNaughton and F. F. Banyikwa:

> In the longer term, over periods of decades, grazers can affect plant community composition and soil properties in ways promoting higher nutritional status of available forages. . . . Forages in areas of high herbivore usage are characterized by higher fiber nutritional value, even during periods when there has been no grazing; this pattern carries across soil types. So, too, mineral properties are influenced by the intensity of herbivore use. Therefore, herbivores can create areas of nutritional sufficiency due to high usage even in the absence of intrinsic soil differences.
>
> Grazers have a strong promotive effect on biodiversity of the Serengeti grasslands. Fencing almost immediately results in a diversity decline as a few taller-growing species that invest heavily in stems overtop other species. Within a few years diversity plummets.[72]

71. A. R. E. Sinclair, "Serengeti Past and Present," in *Serengeti II: Dynamics, Management, and Conservation of an Ecosystem,* edited by A. R. E. Sinclair and Peter Arcese (Chicago: University of Chicago Press, 1995).

72. S. J. McNaughton and F. F. Banyikwa, "Plant Communities and Herbivory," in *Serengeti II: Dynamics, Management, and Conservation of an Ecosystem,* edited by A. R. E. Sinclair and Peter Arcese (Chicago: University of Chicago Press, 1995).

It seems reasonable to assume that the mid-seventeenth-century wildlife of the Cape—similar in density and composition to today's Serengeti—had similar effects on the grasslands and savannas of that region. If so, colonial extirpation and removal of wild grazers probably reduced both the nutritive value and biodiversity of the vegetation on the veld.

Further degradation came when *trekboer*-domesticated herds of cattle and sheep replaced the variety of wild ungulates and Khoikhoi herds that earlier had roamed the veld. Commercial pastoralism, less flexible than that of the nomadic grazing patterns of the Khoikhois, put new pressures on the grass cover of veld and savanna as settlers' stocking densities became too high. Unpalatable and non-nutritious deeper rooted bushes began to push out sweetveld and sourveld grasses.

A declining forage base, however, does not seem to have noticeably hindered commercial pastoralism at the Cape in the Dutch period. Settler herds and meat production continued without any noticeable problems throughout the eighteenth century. Whether this production was sustainable for the long term is not easily determined. It is possible that livestock production would have declined and perhaps even crashed in the nineteenth century without seeding, fertilization, and improved pastures.

What is unquestionable is the dramatic impact of Dutch colonial rule and the settlement frontier on the human society and natural environment of the Cape. In a century and a half, the Dutch East India Company's presence and policies radically changed the landscape and drastically altered the counterpoised interaction between humans and the fauna and vegetation of the region.

PART III

The Americas

Chapter 9

The Columbian Exchange

The West Indies

Christopher Columbus's voyages were the first systematic projection of state power to the Western Hemisphere. News of this feat inspired the imaginations of Renaissance statesmen and religious leaders. The monarchies of Europe, supported by rapidly growing organizational sophistication, economic resources, and military strength, saw the New World as a source of riches to be ruthlessly exploited. Gold and silver, human labor, timber, fertile lands, and new plants could all be put to the service of the state at home. The Church saw among the strange peoples of the New World a fertile source of new converts. Gold and the cross were the two motives for sending annual fleets to the New World. The pattern had long been set by the reconquest of Iberia from the Moors and then the stepping-stone conquest and occupation of the island of Madeira, the Azores, and the Canary Islands. The Spanish, along with the Portuguese, were the first European kingdoms to conquer and colonize vast areas of the American continent.

The first Spanish conquests after 1492 were in the islands of the Greater and Lesser Antilles in the Caribbean. Within three decades, between 1519 and 1540, the Spanish moved to the mainland and subjugated the densely populated heartlands of Mexico and Peru. By midcentury, Spain had claimed sovereignty over peoples occupying some 2 million square kilometers in the Americas. Only the area assigned to Portugal in Brazil was beyond its scope. Exploration and aggressive conquest continued, but the primary act of conquest had occurred.[1] To their Iberian conquerors, these were previously unknown and unimagined new lands and new societies. Even three

---

1. Leslie Bethell, *The Cambridge History of Latin America,* vol. 2 (Cambridge: Cambridge University Press, 1984).

earlier decades of experience in the Caribbean islands had not prepared them for the vast new territories acquired on the mainland.

State power and control found expression in the annual fleets of galleons that sailed virtually every year for three hundred years between Old World and New. The regularity of the *carrera de Indias* (annual fleets) is a measure of the determination of the early modern Spanish state and its rulers to hold fast to the glory and the profits of its New World empire. Had the voyages of these wooden sailing vessels faltered, the environmental effects of Spanish conquest and settlement in the New World might well have been considerably different. The annual transatlantic crossings formed a crucial link in the biological transfers characteristic of the early modern world.

Spain's Atlantic Coast ports were closer to the New World than any other European outlets. Andalusian Seville, even though located a hundred kilometers inland on the river Guadalquivir, became the primary port for the *carrera*. From the Gulf of Cadiz, prevailing northerly winds eased the departure of the fleet, often as many as forty or more vessels, for the Canary Islands. From this way station, the ships made use of the northeasterly trade winds to travel to Martinique, Dominica, or Guadeloupe in the Antilles for a stopover to load water and supplies. The next leg took ships to Havana and Veracruz. If all went well, the actual outward voyage could be as short as ten days to the Canaries, forty days to landfall in the West Indies, and another ten days to reach the mainland. Two months, however, was optimal, and most travelers reconciled themselves to six months or more in transit. On the return voyage, the fleets gathered at Havana, caught the Gulf Stream, and sailed north to reach the westerly trade winds for the passage across to the Azores.

By 1550, the square-rigged galleon of 400 to 600 or more tons capacity had become the preferred vessel for the *carrera*. If well maintained, each galleon could make as many as twenty Atlantic crossings. About a third of these vessels were constructed in northern Spanish shipyards, about a third in Dutch shipyards, and the remainder at Pacific and Atlantic Coast facilities in the Indies.

Considering the limited carrying capacity of even the largest galleons, the cumulative numbers of Spanish migrants is impressive. Perhaps 250,000 Spaniards traveled to the New World in the 1500s, and another 450,000 made the journey in the 1600s.[2] But the numbers dropped off sharply to about 50,000 in the 1700s, for a three-hundred-year total of 800,000 migrants.[3] Royal officials began early to regulate migration. Passage to the Indies re-

2. Murdo J. Macleod, "Spain and America: The Atlantic Trade, 1492–1720," in *The Cambridge History of Latin America*, edited by Leslie Bethell (Cambridge: Cambridge University Press, 1984), 4:356–57.

3. An estimate of only 53,000 for the eighteenth century is given in Nicholas Sanchez-Albornoz, "The Population of Colonial Spanish America," in *The Cambridge History of Latin America*, edited by Leslie Bethell (Cambridge: Cambridge University Press, 1984), 2:31.

quired official permission, which foreigners—Jews, Moors, and others—could not obtain. Most migrants were male, but the number of women migrants gradually rose to constitute one-fifth or more of the total in the sixteenth century; however, far fewer women than men migrated. Most migrants were young adults capable of work and procreation, not the very young or older populations. Officials, soldiers, missionaries, technicians, merchants, servants, and other Spaniards brought skills, values, biases, and hopes with them on the outward-bound journey. In the 1570s, migration and natural increase had brought the total Spanish population in the Indies to 150,000. Fifty years later, by 1620, this had tripled to 450,000 persons.[4] This recurring source of human energy fueled the Spanish colonization of the New World.

Each Atlantic crossing was a conduit for the discourse of power, ideology, and money between center and periphery, between metropolis and colony. From the Council of the Indies (founded in 1523) came voluminous written royal orders, patents of office, and letters. New cadres of officials filled vacant and newly created posts in the colonial state. Commanders, troops, weapons, and supplies of war sent on the ships of the *carrera* stiffened a continuing process of domination and pacification. The return flow of reports, petitions, accounts, and other documents provided vital data for the council and the king.

The *carrera* was also the arm of a mercantilist monopoly of trade managed by the Casa de la Contratación in Seville. The royal trading house organized the voyages, passengers, and cargo bound for the Indies. All American trade was channeled through Seville and monopolized by a guild of royally approved merchants. Grains, wine, olive oil, furniture, cloth, dishes, paintings, and other consumer objects met the need for replication of the home society and culture in the Indies. Each westward crossing brought with it the demands of the state for exotica (strange birds, animals, plants, people, artifacts, and stories), for coined and uncoined precious metals, for hides and sugar, and for any other commodities that could defray the expenses of empire and return a profit to the state.

Each ship sailing from Seville conveyed a varied biological cargo. Domesticated animals, vermin such as rats and insects, and useful cultivars and unwanted weeds made the trip. Likewise, new microorganisms, mostly harmful, traveled with people, animals, and insects as hosts. The sunlight, salt air, and enforced quarantine of a lengthy sea voyage hindered successful passage of some of the most potent germs but, in the end, did not prevent their transmission. On the return voyage, galleons setting sail from Havana or Acapulco carried with them a similar biological manifest of flora and fauna. Many of the most valuable cultivars planted in Eurasia today are New World

4. Ibid., 1:18.

plants such as maize and potatoes, which crossed the Atlantic in sixteenth-century galleons. The cord of the annual fleet tied the ecological worlds of Eurasia and the Americas with an unbreakable strand.

POPULATION AND DISEASE

The Columbian connection had a devastating effect on the indigenous human societies of the Americas. Although most scholars today concede methodological problems in reconstructing close population numbers with any certainty, they agree that the precontact New World populations were of much greater size than the estimated population of 6.5 million persons on the Iberian Peninsula in 1500, and were closer to the 81 million estimated total European population of that date.[5] The most systematic, region-by-region scholarly synthesis, compiled by William Denevan in the mid-1970s and revised in 1992, postulates a total New World population of 54 million (or a range of between 43 and 65 million, with a 20 percent margin of error) in 1492.[6] Continuing debate, examination of sources, and new perspectives suggest that these numbers are in the right order of magnitude.[7] The most populous regions included that of the Aztec civilization of central Mexico, with 14 million (±2.8 million), and of the Inca civilization of the central Andes, with 11.7 million (±2.3 million)—each double the size of Spain and Portugal put together.[8] More than four-fifths of these peoples became subjects of the Spanish king; the remainder fell under Portuguese rule in Brazil.[9]

There is growing agreement among scholars that, by the early seventeenth century, after a century of Spanish and Portuguese rule, the New

5. Colin McEvedy and Richard Jones, *Atlas of World Population History* (London: A. Lane, 1978), 18.

6. William M. Denevan, *The Native Population of the Americas in 1492*, 2d ed. (Madison: University of Wisconsin Press, 1992), xxviii–xxix, table 1. Denevan's single-number estimate is 53.9 million. See also W. George Lovell, " 'Heavy Shadows and Dark Night': Disease and Depopulation in Colonial Spanish America," *Annals of the Association of American Geographers* 82 (1992): 438.

7. David Henige, "On the Contact Population of Hispaniola: History as Higher Mathematics," *Hispanic American Historical Review* 58 (1978). In this book, Henige continues his assault on what he calls the "High Counters" who concoct high population figures for Central Mexico and the Andes with little justification. His writings have forced greater methodological clarity and admission of uncertainty on all concerned. My own view is that the Denevan figures are reasonable extrapolations based on several decades of research and controversy. His margins of error may well be too low, but overall, the populations of the New World were close to that of early modern Europe.

8. Denevan, *The Native Population of the Americas in 1492*, xxi–xxii, xxiv–xxv.

9. Denevan's revised figure for North America, including Florida and California, which came under Spanish control, is only 3.79 million. He estimates 5.66 million for Amazonia and 1.05 million for southern Brazil and Paraguay. Ibid., xxviii.

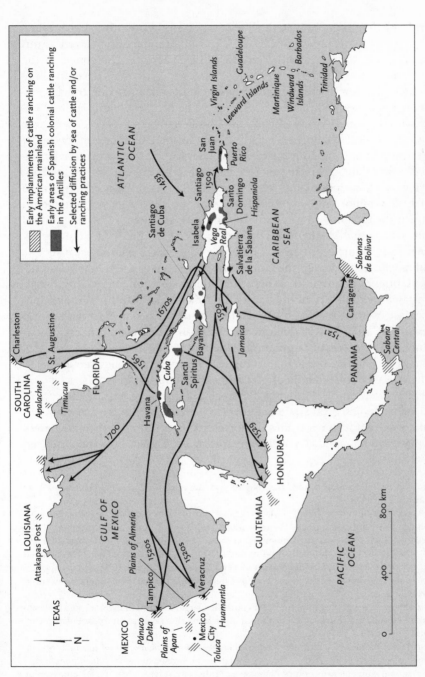

Map 9.1 Early cattle ranching in the West Indies. Adapted from Terry G. Jordan, *North American Cattle-Ranching Frontiers: Origins, Diffusion, and Differentiation* (Albuquerque: University of New Mexico Press, 1993), fig. 17, p. 66.

World Indian population had declined to 5 or 6 million. This was about one-tenth its estimated precontact size.[10] The Indian population stayed at this nadir during the seventeenth century. Only slowly over the course of the eighteenth century did gradual recovery occur, as survivors developed immunity to the new diseases. A growing mixed-race Spanish and Indian population, of course, complicates the picture. The continued migration of European whites and African blacks also swelled the numbers. After three centuries of Iberian rule, by the early 1800s, the total human numbers in the Americas had been restored to probably less than half the precontact number. By that date, Spanish America had a heterogeneous white, mestizo, black, and Indian population of approximately 13.5 million.[11] If we add to this the 4.4 million population of Portuguese Brazil in the early nineteenth century, the total was 17.9 million for the entire area under Iberian political control—colonial Mexico, the Caribbean, and South America.

Why this holocaust in such a relatively short time? New disease vectors suddenly introduced into the vulnerable populations of the New World began a sequence of horrific pandemics.[12] Rapidly spreading infectious disease devastated the indigenous peoples of the New World. It thinned their numbers, destroyed their institutions, and broke their resistance to Spanish aggression.[13] Certainly, well-documented Spanish brutality and maltreatment of successive American populations killed many Indians outright and contributed to lowered resistance to disease, but only repeated scourging by multiple waves of pandemic disease can explain this rapid falloff.

The sudden onset of diseases like smallpox that were outside the experience of any Indian group induced terror, avoidance, and even abandonment of the sick. Flight meant that all normal daily routines and work ended. Crops were not tended. The sick were not buried. The survivors experienced

10. Lovell, "Heavy Shadows and Dark Night," 438; Denevan, *The Native Population of the Americas in 1492*, xxix.

11. Sanchez-Albornoz, "The Population of Colonial Spanish America," 2:33–35. For colonial Brazil, the same long-term trend can be found, with an early-nineteenth-century total estimated to be 4.4 million persons. The white population was about 1.3 million; the black, 1.1 million. About 800,000 tribal Indians lived in the interior, and the remainder were assimilated Indians and mestizos. Maria Luiza Marcilio, "The Population of Colonial Brazil," in *The Cambridge History of Latin America*, vol. 2, edited by Leslie Bethell (Cambridge: Cambridge University Press, 1984).

12. The peoples of the Philippines, who possessed large numbers of livestock and had considerable contact with Eurasia, did not succumb to heavy disease mortality after Spanish conquest.

13. David E. Stannard illustrates just how a combination of heavy disease mortality and inhibited fertility could have reduced these populations by looking at the well-documented case of Hawaii in the nineteenth century. "Disease and Infertility: A New Look at the Demographic Collapse of Native Populations in the Wake of Western Contact," *Journal of American Studies* 24, no. 3 (1990): 510–28.

malnutrition, even starvation, when they returned. Demographic recovery after major pandemics was hindered by reduced fertility, stillbirths, and other physical effects, as well as by cultural depression, hopelessness, and malaise resulting from Spanish colonial domination.

The Spanish certainly did not set out to kill off New World populations by bringing new diseases. It is doubtful that this great tragedy worked to the long-term advantage of the Spanish. Surely, if given the choice, they would have opted for the survival of a large, docile subject population that could offer labor and goods as colonial tribute to their new masters. They had little or no understanding of the catastrophic forces they unwittingly carried across the Atlantic. Even had they understood the connection, there was little, if anything, they could do to end or even mitigate the suffering and death caused by these diseases. The Caribbean had become part of the Eurasian reservoir of infectious animal and human diseases not by human design but by the operation of biological processes.

THE WEST INDIES

The West Indies, which Columbus reached in 1492, forms a chain of islands stretching south from the mainland into the Caribbean Sea: the Greater Antilles, including Cuba, Puerto Rico, Hispaniola, and Jamaica; the Bahamas; and the clusters of smaller islands in the Lesser Antilles. These are tropical lands whose warm, humid climate is dominated by the sea. Steady northeastern trade winds blow across the islands year-round, punctuated only by occasional storms or hurricanes. In the late fifteenth century, the islands were luxuriant with vegetation. On the windward side of each island were thick canopies of double- and triple-story, true tropical rain forest. Lianas and epiphytes abounded. On the exposed sides, less verdant forests shaded off to scrub, bush, and grasslands. An impressive variety of tropical trees and other plants, reptiles, birds, and fish flourished. There were, however, no large herbivores and no large predators on any of the islands.[14]

In 1492, the West Indies supported a dense human population estimated by Denevan to be 3 million persons.[15] The indigenes were divided into more

14. David Watts, *The West Indies: Patterns of Development, Culture, and Environmental Change since 1492* (Cambridge: Cambridge University Press, 1987); for reproduction and translation of the most important original sources, see Robert G. Keith and J. H. Parry, *New Iberian World: A Documentary History of the Discovery and Settlement of Latin America to the Early Seventeenth Century*, 1st ed. (New York: Times Books, Hector and Rose, 1984), esp. vols. 1 and 2.

15. Denevan, *The Native Population of the Americas in 1492*. Denevan's estimate of 3 million persons for the West Indies includes a 20 percent margin of error (giving a range of 2.4 to 3.6 million). Denevan suggests a total population for the New World of 53.9 million in 1492, a range of 43–65 million (370). But as David Henige has pointed out, population estimates for the West Indies at the time of contact, as for the New World in general, cannot be substantiated and re-

numerous Tainos (Arawak), a smaller population of Guana-Hatabey hunter-gatherers in western Cuba, and Island Caribs in the Lesser Antilles, from Guadeloupe south.[16] Scholarly estimates of the 1492 population for Hispaniola alone—an island approximately the size of Portugal—are much contested. On the low end, scholars suggest the Taino population of Hispaniola at that time was 100,000 or even fewer persons. Most propose 500,000 to a million persons. High-end estimates range from 2 million to as much as 8 million.[17] In the absence of any direct quantitative evidence, narrowing the range of these estimates is difficult. Early Spanish observations did agree that this was a densely populated island. A midrange figure of 500,000 persons (6.5 persons per square kilometer) is certainly plausible.[18] Noble David Cook favors the figure 500,000, citing a guess made by Nikolaus Federmann, a German settler in Santo Domingo in the early 1530s: "Of five hundred thousand Indians or inhabitants of various nations and languages that existed on the island forty years ago, there remain fewer than twenty thousand living."[19]

From archeological evidence, it appears that the Tainos came to the Antilles from the mainland and settled there about the beginning of our present era. The Tainos, in common with the Island Caribs and the Guana-Hatabey peoples, were not literate, nor did they use metal or metal tools. They had no domesticated animals other than the dog. They consumed no alcohol or other narcotics, save tobacco, which they smoked as cigars. They had no currency or money for exchange, although some trade occurred. They had no sailing vessels, but they could skillfully traverse sea passages between islands in their paddle-driven dugout canoes. They had no centralized state or administration of governance beyond loosely organized chieftaincies.[20]

main informed guesses only (*Numbers from Nowhere*). In the late fifteenth century, the total population of the Iberian Peninsula was only about 7 to 8 million. Henige, "On the Contact Population of Hispaniola."

16. Irving Rouse, *The Tainos: Rise and Decline of the People Who Greeted Columbus* (New Haven: Yale University Press, 1992), 8–9, fig. 2. Rouse divides the Tainos into Western and Classic, who lived on Hispaniola, and Eastern Tainos, who lived on the Virgin and Leeward Islands. For Taino religious beliefs, see Ramón Pané and José Juan Arrom, *An Account of the Antiquities of the Indians: Chronicles of the New World Encounter* (Durham: Duke University Press, 1999).

17. Noble David Cook, *Born to Die: Disease and New World Conquest, 1492–1650* (Cambridge: Cambridge University Press, 1998), 23, table 1.1.

18. Hispaniola is 77,200 square kilometers in area. In his 1993 essay, Cook cites Frank Moya Pons's 1987 argument that a digging-stick horticulture supplemented with hunting and gathering could not support more than 20 to 30 persons per square kilometer. Moya Pons, *Después de Colón: Trabajo, sociedad y política en la economía del oro* (Madrid: Alianza, 1987), 184. Moya Pons himself arrived at an estimate of approximately 380,000, or 4.9 persons per square kilometer. Noble David Cook, "Disease and the Depopulation of Hispaniola, 1492–1518," *Colonial Latin American Review* 2 (1993): 213–46.

19. Cook, *Born to Die*, 22.

20. Watts, *The West Indies*, 5–25, 53–69. I use the term *Tainos* in preference to *Arawaks*, following Rouse.

In spite of these deficiencies—or perhaps because of them—the Tainos seem to have evolved an attractive lifestyle. They readily met their basic needs for food, shelter, and clothing. Famines, epidemics, and war were rare. Although Tainos were divided into a more privileged noble class and a majority of commoners, the harsh class distinctions typical of late medieval Europe were not in evidence. Commoners enjoyed personal dignity and freedom from arbitrary violence. The Spanish did not find any perceptible group of slaves or degraded persons in the society.

A chief, or *cacique*, who ruled each village could be either male or female. The *cacique* occupied the largest house facing the irregularly shaped plaza or village open space. Tainos lived in nucleated villages of up to two thousand persons in large, multifamily, dirt-floored structures made of timber and thatch. Baskets hung from the walls to store possessions; hammocks made of cordage were hung at night for sleeping. Groups of villages formed districts presided over by one of the village chiefs. Districts were grouped to form regions headed by the most notable district chief. In the late 1400s, there were five such regional chiefs discernible on Hispaniola. Conflict and violence was minimal. When armed clashes occurred, adult males were organized in bands under chiefs, but there was no distinct warrior caste. The primary threat came from aggression by the Caribs of the Lesser Antilles, who were active raiders.

Tainos grew cotton and wove it to make what little clothing, spreads, and other cloth was customary in this tropical climate. Taino adults were skilled carvers in stone, wood, shell, and bone; they were proficient potters. However, these skills were distributed widely rather than confined to a group of occupational specialists or artisans.

Land was held in common by members of each village. Surrounding each village were cultivated plots of land in which the Tainos grew manioc and sweet potatoes. This was horticulture *(conuco)* using digging sticks and hoes—not plows with draft animals. In this type of *conuco* horticulture, the Tainos first cleared forest areas by ringbarking and felling trees that were burnt at the end of the dry season. Burning infused phosphorus, calcium, and magnesium into the soil and permitted annual use of the plot until, after fifteen or twenty years, the soil began to lose fertility. Abandoned *conuco* lands were left fallow for about thirty years before they were cleared, burnt, and reused. The Tainos used their hoes to heap mounds of earth 1 to 2 meters high and 1.5 meters in circumference in orderly rows. In each mound, they inserted cuttings of manioc and sweet potato and seeds of squash and beans. The mounds made weeding and harvesting easier, improved drainage, and permitted longer-term storage of the tubers in the ground.

The *conuco* system provided phenomenal caloric returns. As the Spanish observer Friar Las Casas commented, "Twenty persons working six hours a day for one month will make a planting of such *conucos* that will provide bread for 300 people for two years."[21] Techniques for removing toxic cyanic acid from the bitter manioc permitted women to make unleavened bread and a food called cassava (cassava was later transmitted to Africa as a New World exchange product). Taino cultivators also grew maize, peanuts, calabashes, pepper, fruits, cotton, and tobacco in small garden plots.

Protein in the diet came from several sources. Taino men captured and penned green sea turtles *(Chelonia mydas)*, large air-breathing marine herbivores, until they were to be slaughtered for their meat. They speared manatees in the rivers and captured tree-climbing iguanas *(Iguana delicatissima)* for their meat. They pursued and ate hutias *(Plagiodontia* sp.), sizeable, furry indigenous rodents. They employed lines and hooks, nets, and poison to catch fresh- and saltwater fish.

The Tainos fed themselves well year-round by a combination of horticulture and hunting and gathering. Their resource base on the larger islands may have been sustainable even with a dense population. Multiple crop horticulture under the *conuco* system preserved soil fertility. Turtles, fish, and other prey were still abundant at the time of contact.

These people evidenced no vitamin deficiency diseases. Infectious diseases were few, and there seem to have been no viral diseases. They were subject to tuberculosis, leishmaniasis, amoebic dysentery, rickettsias, and three forms of treponematosis—yaws, pinta, and syphilis. Without large domestic animals as carriers, there apparently were no zoonoses of the type that infected Eurasian populations.[22] The general population was remarkably healthy by early modern European standards. Women bore three to five children, who seemed to live long lives. The overall condition of the Tainos and other Indian groups in the Caribbean strikingly contrasts with that of the ill-nourished, sickly ordinary folk of early modern Europe.

COLUMBIAN RULE IN HISPANIOLA

After much effort, Columbus obtained a royal patent and financing from Isabella and Ferdinand of Spain that authorized him to explore, discover, and claim for Spain any previously unknown (to Europeans) lands and islands surrounding the Atlantic. His three-ship fleet sailed from the southernmost of the Canary Islands on September 8, 1492, picked up the prevailing winds and made landfall in the Bahamas thirty-three days later, on October 12.

Columbus quickly determined from his first contacts with the natives of the West Indies that they were not the Asian peoples he had sought. Moreover, the indigenous peoples he encountered were not a military threat,

21. Quoted in ibid., 60.
22. Francisco Guerra, "The Earliest American Epidemic: The Influenza of 1493," *Social Science History* 12, no. 3 (1988); Cook, *Born to Die,* 17.

since they lacked even iron and steel weapons and were not warlike. Instead, these inhabitants of the Indies were hospitable, had readily given him food, and hence were likely to be willing servitors of Spain. Not only that, they wore beaten gold ornaments and had knowledge of active placer mining for gold.

After visiting several islands, including Cuba, Columbus landed on the northern coast of Hispaniola and established a small encampment at a place called Navidad. Columbus and his men began actively negotiating with the Indians for gold objects they possessed and for knowledge of the sources of that gold. One of his captains discovered gold placer mines 145 kilometers to the east in the hills named Cordillera Central by the Spanish. When, after several months, Columbus decided to return to Spain, thirty-nine Spaniards volunteered to remain behind at Navidad. In January 1493, Columbus loaded an exotic cargo of gold nuggets; several enslaved Taino men, women, and children; and some Taino crops, including maize, aboard his reprovisioned ships and set sail for home. On March 15, he made port in Spain.

Within six months, Columbus set out from Cadiz with seventeen ships and fifteen hundred male colonists: a mixed group of *fidalgos,* or aristocrats; soldiers; artisans; and a few priests. With them, they brought wheat, chickpea, and other seeds; fruit trees; grapevines; and sheep, goats, swine, and cattle. The fully armed colonists also brought the horses and dogs of war.[23] The royal orders commanded Columbus to establish a Spanish settlement, to convert the natives to Christianity, and to locate and mine gold. From Columbus down, all of the settlers feverishly anticipated riches from Taino gold. The Spanish monarchs urged Columbus to develop items of trade for export to Spain in order to develop the island's economy. Other than gold, the two most likely items were brazilwood trees, whose cores contained a valuable dye, and enslaved Tainos for sale in Spain.

Ferdinand and Isabella made one other portentous concession to Columbus. They completely ignored the existing structure of property rights under which the Tainos lived and cultivated in Hispaniola. These were to be abrogated. Regardless of previous ownership or occupancy, Columbus was authorized to grant or sell individual property rights in land to the colonists in Hispaniola under the terms of the *repartimiento* system. These rights could be secured by living on and cultivating the land for at least four years or by building a house, gristmill, or sugar mill on it. These were the principles applied to the redistribution of land after the reconquest of Granada. Lands not distributed under this system would become part of the royal domain. Any tracts with brazilwood or valuable mineral resources were to be retained under Crown ownership.

When he reached Navidad in November 1493, Columbus found that no

---

23. John Grier Varner and Jeannette Johnson Varner, *Dogs of the Conquest,* 1st ed. (Norman: University of Oklahoma Press, 1983); Cunningham, "The Biological Impacts of 1492."

Spaniards left behind had survived. They were dead either from fighting among themselves, exposure to syphilis (endemic and mild among the Tainos), or clashes with Tainos of the interior. Columbus moved his headquarters from Navidad up the coast to Isabella, much closer to the known placer gravels of the Cordillera.

Spanish brutality was much in evidence. All the Spaniards on Hispaniola suffered from paranoia. They continually suspected the Tainos of conspiring to surprise and, with their superior number, kill them. To a man, they were convinced that they must create awe and fear among the Tainos or they would be overcome. For this purpose, the dramatic punishments of late medieval Europe would have to be applied at any sign of defiance, betrayal, or disrespect. True exchanges for the gifts of food, which the Tainos showered on them, did not occur. Instead, when clothing "thefts" occurred, Columbus and his men publicly cut off the noses and ears of the suspected culprits. And they followed this by public decapitation of the *cacique* who tried to intervene.

Armed clashes followed, and several Spanish were killed by the angered Tainos in a surprise reprisal. Columbus hastened construction of a central fortification located in the center of the island and a network of intermediate forts. From this secure base, he sent out punitive expeditions against the nearest *caciques*. The Tainos could not offer effective resistance. As Las Casas commented, "How can a people who go about naked, have no weapons other than a bow and arrow and a kind of wooden lance, and no fortifications besides straw huts, attack or defend themselves against a people armed with steel weapons and firearms, horses, and lances who in two hours could pierce thousands and rip open as many bellies as they wished?"[24]

In 1495, Columbus decreed that all Tainos between the ages of fourteen and seventeen living in the gold-producing districts then directly controlled by the Spaniards were to pay a regular tribute in gold at three-month intervals. In areas that produced no gold, Columbus demanded tributes of cotton and spices. Rather then comply, Tainos in these regions abandoned their villages and fled in large numbers. Those Tainos who remained in the villages but could not pay the tribute were enslaved and put to forced labor in the gold-mining areas or were shipped to Europe.

Urged on by royal demands for profit, the colonists put brutal pressure on the Tainos to exploit all known sources of gold far more than had ever been the custom and to search relentlessly for new mines. Bands of armed Spaniards roamed central Hispaniola interrogating Tainos and looking for gold veins or placers. When new sources of gold were discovered, the Spanish compelled the Tainos to work them under horrendous conditions. At the same time, the Spanish demanded foodstuffs for themselves from the Tainos, who were forced to produce a surplus to meet the hearty appetites of their conquerors. This was an especially onerous burden, since *conuco* cultivation seems to have been nicely calibrated to produce sufficient food for each village but not a large surplus for export beyond the village. Spanish demands for food pushed the system to its limits.

These gold-seeking expeditions also were occasions for slave taking. Captive Taino men, women, and children were regularly shipped to Europe, which became one way to satisfy continuing royal demands that the new colony show a profit on the Crown's investment. Columbus aimed at sending four thousand captives a year to Europe to be sold to landowners in Iberia.

Deserted *conucos* rapidly grew weeds and secondary vegetation. Food shortages developed and led to famine conditions in the central part of the island. Mortality among the Tainos soared. Indices of cultural depression, such as increased suicide and decreased fertility, became manifest. It is very likely that the Tainos suffered from influenza compounded by malnutrition. In that year, Columbus added cassava to the list of acceptable tribute items to make up for food shortages among the colonists.

A rebellious dissident faction of settlers under Francisco Roldan, the mayor of Isabella (no longer the capital since the move to Santo Domingo on the south coast), forced an accommodation on Columbus that resulted in a significant shift in colonial policy. Roldan insisted on amending the allocations of land to Spanish settlers made under the *repartimiento* rules for distributing conquered territory. In addition to land rights, settlers should obtain property rights over Taino chieftains and their people located within or adjacent to their grants. The Tainos were to serve each grant holder by planting *conucos*, laboring in the mines, or providing personal service. This addition, which came to be known as the *encomienda*, became the basic means of inflicting servitude on Indians throughout Hispanic North and South America.

Between 1492 and 1542, just half a century, the Tainos on Hispaniola became nearly extinct. Scholars generally agree on the early-sixteenth-century numbers and their trend. The Taino population was estimated to be about 60,000 persons in 1508. In 1510, Diego Columbus counted 33,523 Tainos. Four years later, in 1514, the figure had dropped to 26,334. By 1518–1519, the Tainos had dwindled to 18,000 persons when the first smallpox epidemic hit.[25] Mortality from smallpox, added to other causes of death, brought the Hispaniolan Tainos to near extinction: there were about 2,000 persons in 1542. If the 1492 population had been around a half million persons, reduction to 18,000 in twenty-six years was a catastrophic decline.

Before the first well-documented onset of European-transmitted smallpox in 1518, there is little direct evidence of widespread Taino death from newly

25. Cook, *Born to Die,* 23–24; Cook, "Disease and the Depopulation of Hispaniola," 216.

transmitted European infectious diseases. Spanish violence and brutality caused deaths from malnutrition, overwork, injury, and cultural despair. Contemporary Spanish observers noted widespread sickness and mortality among the Spanish colonists but generally do not make similar observations about the Hispaniolans.

That twenty-six years could pass between Columbus's first voyage and the arrival of smallpox may seem strange. However, as Alfred W. Crosby points out, characteristics specific to the disease slowed its transmission across the Atlantic. Humans, not insects or animals, carry smallpox. This highly communicable virus is transmitted from person to person by secretions of the nose and throat and by secretions from its characteristic pustules. The disease runs its course—from incubation to high fever and vomiting, to skin eruptions, and to death or recovery—in less than a month. Any voyager infected with smallpox would be dead or recovered well before the ship arrived in the New World. Recovered smallpox victims were immune to recurrence and could not spread the disease when their pustules dried up. Heat and sunlight onboard ship tended to kill off the virus. Almost all voyagers were adults who probably had had smallpox earlier and were largely immune. The disease could be carried across only if several persons without immunity were on the same vessel, or if smallpox scabs in which the virus remained live were somehow carried in the bedding or clothes of a victim.[26] Therefore, the virus could be delayed, but would almost invariably arrive.

Some historians have argued inferentially that the Spanish colonists brought disease to the West Indies before 1518. Transmittal of other diseases, such as typhus carried by fleas, is not subject to the same barriers as smallpox. They posit that a mixture of new diseases may have killed many Indians in the first quarter century of contact. In the mid-1980s, a medical historian, Francisco Guerra, extrapolating from present-day epidemiological knowledge, argued that Columbus's ships on the second voyage carried an unseen lethal cargo.[27] The Spaniards were infected with a virulent strain of influenza from contact with pigs carrying swine fever virus. The probable suspects were eight sows taken aboard the fleet at the Canary Islands in early October 1493. Columbus himself fell sick December 10, 1493, one day after the illness manifested itself at Isabella, but he recovered. Mortality among the Spanish from disease with flulike symptoms was

26. Alfred W. Crosby, "Conquistador y Pestilencia: The First New World Pandemic and the Fall of the Great Indian Empires," *Hispanic American Historical Review* 47, no. 3 (1967): 326–27.

27. Guerra, "The Earliest American Epidemic"; Francisco Guerra, "The European-American Exchange," *History and Philosophy of the Life Sciences* 15, no. 3 (1993); and, following Guerra, Lovell, "Heavy Shadows and Dark Night." Guerra first advanced this thesis in the mid-1980s in Spanish publications; see Francisco Guerra, "La epidemia americana de influenza en 1493," *Revista de Indias* 45 (1985): 325–47; and Guerra, "El efecto demográfico de las epidemias tras el descubrimiento de America," *Revista de Indias* 46 (1986): 41–58.

heavy. Guerra argues that swine flue was acutely contagious, spread readily to the Taino population, and traveled with the Spanish as they voyaged to other islands.

Cook, while resisting Guerra's specific identification of influenza, has suggested that an assortment of diseases, possibly including typhus—all rampant in Spain at the time—undoubtedly assailed the Tainos just as the diseases infected the Spanish colonists.[28] This is a reasonable inference, but Cook can find only two direct statements about widespread disease among the Tainos to support his argument. That the Tainos were increasingly vulnerable to infection because of depression, stress, and maltreatment seems likely. That they were therefore susceptible to the infectious diseases brought by the Europeans is also likely. Human society in the West Indies now shared the Old World reservoir of infectious human and animal diseases.

SLAVES AND GOLD

Settler dissatisfaction, inadequate profits, and general bad management brought removal of Columbus and his family in disgrace in 1500. At Seville, the Crown formed a new ministry for administration of the Indies. This body sent out a royal judge as temporary governor, who administered the island until 1502. In that year, Frey Nicolas de Ovando arrived to begin a seven-year term as the royal governor of Hispaniola. With him came twenty-five hundred more Spanish settlers. This new influx included many skilled artisans, a number of priests, and, for the first time, a few Spanish women and children.

Contradictory, or at least ambivalent, royal orders to Ovando commanded him to encourage conversion of the Tainos to Christianity, to protect them from abuse, to punish those who harmed them, and to collect tribute from them based on the value of their lands. Simultaneously, he was to increase the revenues of the island. To do so, the new governor was permitted to force the Indians to labor in the gold mines, although they were not to be enslaved. They were to receive a just wage for their efforts. The new governor was to found new towns in which colonists and natives were segregated. The process of allocating land rights was to continue.

Ovando chose to stress revenues rather than the well-being of the Hispaniolans. Within two years, he had broken the power of the remaining *caciques* on the island to undercut any possible resistance to his policies. In a series of treacherous massacres and brutal battles, Ovando and his commanders killed hundreds of Taino chiefs and their families and effectively de-

28. Cook, *Born to Die*, 230. According to Cook, "Each subsequent ship and fleet brought from southern Spain new settlers, animals, plants, and obviously pathogens. To argue that illness was not transported is to assume the highly improbable."

stroyed indigenous leadership on Hispaniola. New Tainos chosen by the Spanish governor were appointed as chiefs and forced to mobilize their people for labor in the mines or for cultivation of cassava according to *encomienda* rules. The governor next altered the rules for land grants and Indian service to permit the transfer of Indian work groups wherever labor was needed on the island. The new rules specified that such transfers could not keep Tainos away from their home villages and cultivation more than six to eight months a year. The remaining months were to be reserved for food production.

Gold production soared under the new regime, helped by discoveries of new ore-bearing veins in the Cordillera in 1499 during Columbus's governorship. By 1502, Hispaniola was shipping a ton or more of gold back to Spain every year.[29] News of the gold attracted a steady flow of settlers from Spain and raised colonial numbers to between eight thousand and ten thousand by 1509, at the end of Ovando's governorship. Partly as a result of forced labor in the mines, Taino mortality continued to the point that an official count in 1508 found only sixty thousand indigenes left alive. The colonists began to import small numbers of black slaves from West Africa and the Canary Islands to work in the goldfields.

Just before he left Santo Domingo, Ovando obtained royal permission to raid "useless" islands without gold deposits, such as the Bahamas and Lesser Antilles, and to seize their inhabitants for additional gold-mine labor on Hispaniola. He also was authorized to send out official expeditions to Puerto Rico, Cuba, and Jamaica to find gold. When his successor, Diego Columbus, son of the admiral, landed at Santo Domingo in 1509 and assumed the royal governorship, a policy of aggressive expansion was already under way, one that he accepted enthusiastically.

Under Columbus, regular raids on the Bahamas continued steadily for five years. One observer estimated that some forty thousand Bahamians had been seized and taken to work in the gold mines. Las Casas stated that many of these unfortunate captives did not survive the sea crossing because of overcrowding and brutality. He claimed that Spanish ships could navigate between Hispaniola and the Bahamas "without compass or chart, merely by following for the distance between the Lucayan [Bahamian] Islands and Espanola, which is sixty or seventy leagues, the traces of those Indian corpses floating in the sea, corpses that had been cast overboard by earlier ships."[30] By 1514, the Bahama Islands were depopulated and would remain in that state for a century or more.

29. Kirkpatrick Sale, *The Conquest of Paradise: Christopher Columbus and the Columbian Legacy*, 1st ed. (New York: Knopf, distributed by Random House, 1990), 180–81.
30. Cited in Watts, *The West Indies*, 107.

Royal permits for slave raiding were quickly extended to include the islands of the Lesser Antilles as far as Curaçao, Aruba, Trinidad, and Tobago, off the Venezuelan coast. Even the ferocity of the Island Caribs did not spare them capture and transportation from their home islands. The Spaniards enslaved well over a hundred thousand Tainos and Caribs between 1509 and 1519. Remnant groups of Caribs retreated to the hilly interiors of their islands and resisted the slave raiders well enough to survive. Other islands, like Barbados, were completely stripped of their human populations.

In 1508, a small exploratory party under Juan Ponce de León landed in Puerto Rico and found gold placers in the less-populated western end of the island. A rush of Spanish miners from Hispaniola put the usual pressures on the Tainos of Puerto Rico. Within two years, the Tainos rebelled. They organized an uprising against the Spanish settlers in the west, which they coordinated with a raid on the eastern coast by Caribs from Saint Croix. Eighty Spanish settlers died in the attacks. Violent repression followed, in which great numbers of Tainos were worked to death in the gold mines, killed outright, or transported to Hispaniola, from which they did not return. As soon as the gold played out, the Spanish left a virtually depopulated island to feral swine and cattle.

Diego Columbus sent an expedition to occupy Jamaica in 1509. Active searching turned up little gold to be mined. Settlers obtained land grants with labor rights attached. In the absence of gold, the settlers forced the Tainos of Jamaica to work brutally hard to produce a surplus of manioc, cotton, and maize to export to Hispaniola and Cuba. As elsewhere, Spanish cattle, hogs, and horses were imported and allowed to graze freely without regard for protection of the *conuco* plots. Food scarcities, enslavement, and outright slaughter sharply reduced the Taino population on Jamaica. Within a decade, only isolated groups lived in retreat in the hills.

Cuba's turn came in 1511. An expedition under Diego Velasquez rapidly colonized the island. Within a year, the Spanish had established seven settlements, each located near a gold placer deposit adjacent to large Taino populations. Numerous Tainos from Cuba were enslaved and shipped out; the remainder were subject to the *encomienda* labor demands. Within seven or eight years, most of the Tainos were gone and replaced by herds of open-range livestock. Some survivors fleeing Spanish genocide found refuge in the Sierra Maestra.

On Hispaniola, the indigenous population plummeted under Diego Columbus's governorship. Most of the approximately eighteen thousand Tainos counted by a royal inspector in 1518 had been uprooted from their original homes by the forced labor system. At least a quarter were resident in Santo Domingo, and many were household servants of the Spanish settlers. With the death of Ferdinand and the accession of Charles V, a spirit of reform prevailed and the Spanish Crown began to acknowledge atrocities committed against the Tainos.[31] In 1518, a triumvirate of three Jeronymite missionaries replaced Diego Columbus as governor. These officials brought with them instructions to abolish forced labor, resettle the surviving Tainos in pueblos of four hundred to five hundred persons, and restore *conuco* horticulture for manioc.

Just as this program was going forward, the first smallpox cases arrived in Santo Domingo and spread rapidly through the susceptible Taino population of Hispaniola.[32] Writing on January 10, 1519, the friars reported to Charles V, "It has pleased Our Lord to bestow a pestilence, of small pox among the said Indians [of Hispaniola], and that it does not cease. From it have died and continue to die to the present almost a third of the said Indians."[33] Scarcely without a pause, the contagion leapt to Puerto Rico and the remaining islands of the West Indies. Shortly thereafter, yellow fever and malaria, presumably carried by African slaves, afflicted the indigenes as well. These assaults reduced the indigenous population of the larger islands to a residue of some hundreds of survivors.

In the face of the Taino die-off, Spanish officials tried to stabilize the settler population of Hispaniola and to devise for the colony an economic base more viable than gold mining. An entirely masculine body of settlers with little or no permanent attachment to the island was scarcely desirable. Officials encouraged Spanish women to migrate and marry settlers and, short of that, tried to induce male colonists to formally marry Taino women. In spite of these measures, nearly two-thirds of the colonists remained unmarried fortune seekers who likely would not find wealth on Hispaniola. Well before the departure of Diego Columbus, the gold mines of Hispaniola showed signs of exhaustion. By 1519, they were almost entirely worked out, and no viable new sources of gold were to be found.

As food production by the Tainos precipitously declined, the settlers themselves began to grow their own manioc in *conuco* plots. Numerous imported garden vegetables (cabbages, cauliflower, onions, lettuces, garlic, and eggplant) were successfully grown, as were oranges, limes, lemons, and citron. Bananas, grown on trees imported from the Canary Islands, flourished. African slaves, who were permitted to grow their own food crops, introduced African plants: yams and cashews, as well as medicinal plants such as cassia *(Cassia fistula)* and the castor oil plant.[34]

---

31. Patricia Seed, " 'Are These Also Not Men?': The Indians' Humanity and Capacity for Spanish Civilisation," *Journal of Latin American Studies*, 25, no. 3 (1993).

32. Crosby, "Conquistador y Pestilencia."

33. Quoted in Cook, *Born to Die*, 60.

34. See Watts, *The West Indies*, 116, table 3.1.

SUGAR PLANTING

For some years, the Dominican friars had been arguing for the development of commercial agriculture on Hispaniola so that valuable crops could replace gold. Despite earlier failures to grow commercially viable crops, the Dominicans argued that cane sugar was the best candidate. Moreover, the demand for sugar at home was rising. Europeans who could afford it were becoming addicted to the several forms of refined sugar grown in limited supplies around the Mediterranean and on the newly occupied Atlantic islands. Sugar, like coffee, tea, and spices, had a high market price relative to its bulk. Once heated, concentrated, and packed in granular form, it remained edible without spoiling for long periods of time. If protected from water damage, it could be shipped cheaply over long distances by water transport. Sugar was replacing honey as the main sweetener in northwestern Europe. Crystallized cane sugar was becoming a basic foodstuff, a commodity rather than an oddity, medicine, or decoration. In England, apples, plums, apricots, and pears were newly popular tree crops. These fruits were combined with cane sugar to make a wide variety of jams and jellies.[35]

Shoots from a hybrid variety (a combination of *Saccharum barberi* and *Saccharum officinarum*) long used in the Middle East, India, and Europe, traveled with Columbus on his second voyage from the Canary Islands to Hispaniola in 1493. Sugarcane flourished in the abundant water and heat of the West Indies. (Below an average annual temperature of 21°C, sugarcane's growth is severely reduced; between 11° and 13°C, its seeds will not germinate. The outer margin for sugarcane lies in the subtropics, where risk of frost is minimal.)[36]

New World Indian groups quickly determined that sugarcane was a much more powerful sweetener than anything they possessed in their dietary. Cane could be chewed, boiled in water to make a drink, and crushed with simple tools. Samples of cane passed readily from group to group on the mainland to the point that later European explorers assumed, erroneously, that the sugarcane grown by the Indians they encountered was native to the New World.[37]

In 1515, Gonzales Vellosa, a small landholder near Santo Domingo, encouraged by escalating sugar prices in Europe, obtained cane cuttings and imported an efficient sugar mill and technicians from the Canary Islands. Vellosa succeeded in growing and processing sugarcane for export. Follow-

35. Ibid., 177.
36. Ibid., 14.
37. J. H. Galloway, *The Sugar Cane Industry: An Historical Geography from Its Origins to 1914* (Cambridge: Cambridge University Press, 1989), 61–63.

ing Vellosa's example, other Spanish landowners on the southern coast invested in sugar to develop a zone of production with *estancias* (ranches) located in the coastal river valleys in an area of perhaps one hundred kilometers along the coast west from Santo Domingo.[38]

The estates were small, about one hundred hectares in size, of which half might be cultivated and the remainder left to woodlands. Planters devoted ten to twelve hectares to sugar, producing about 125 metric tons per year of brown, semirefined *muscavado* sugar. Lacking Indian labor, the proprietors imported black African slaves to work their holdings, with an average of two hundred slaves on each estate.[39] By the 1530s, there were thirty-four sugar mills operating on the island.

Sugarcane grew more or less continuously on plantation fields. The first planting of sugarcane took from twelve to eighteen months to reach harvest size. Subsequent crops from the same planting required less time, but still about twelve months. To maximize their investment in the crushing mill, animals, and slaves, the early Hispaniolan planters learned to stagger plantings of individual fields so that the crop would not ripen all at once. Instead, harvesting in some regions continued for as long as ten months of the cultivation year. After one crop was cut, several more crops regrew from the same stems and root systems before sugar yields declined.

Sugarcane has a long, cylindrical stalk, or stem, with narrow leaves attached. The thick green, yellow, or brownish red cane stems vary in diameter from two to five centimeters and grow to a height of four meters or even more. In cross section, each stem is crudely cylindrical. The stem has a rind enclosing and protecting a fleshy pith, where the sugar is stored. To get access to the sugar in the cane pith, the rind must be chewed or crushed.

Sugarcane reproduces asexually. The stem divides into joints from ten to thirty centimeters in length. Each joint is marked by a node revealed as a band or ring encircling the stalk. Each node contains a bud and root primordial. When severed and planted in soil, the node generates a new plant. One planting of seed cuttings or nodes gives several successive crops of cane. According to J. H. Galloway:

> After the harvest of the first crop, known as the plant cane, the roots and lower part of the stem remain in the ground. The short section of the stem which is left below the surface of the soil has its full complement of nodes, buds, and root primorida from which [to] develop new plants while the old root system rapidly decomposes providing nourishment for the new. Each of the crops suc-

38. Mervyn Ratekin, "The Early Sugar Industry in Espanola," *Hispanic American Historical Review* 34 (1954): 1–19. Also Huguette Chaunu, Pierre Chaunu, and Guy Arbellot, *Séville et l'Atlantique, 1504–1650* (Paris: A. Colin, 1955), 8:521–28.

39. Watts, *The West Indies*, 125.

ceeding the plant cane is a "ratoon" crop—the first ratoon, second ratoon, and so forth, the ultimate number depending on such factors as the local environmental conditions, the variety of cane, the yield of sugar, and the incidence of types of pests. The yield of sugar from ratoon crops usually is less than that from the plant cane and gradually declines until the ratoons are no longer profitable.[40]

When planting the first crop, slaves buried cane stems in rows in shallow furrows. They culled poor cane shoots at one month, followed by intensive weeding and attempts to kill off rats and other vermin. At harvesttime, slaves cut the stems about twelve to thirteen centimeters from the ground and left the plant in the field for ratooning. As soon as the cane was cut, it had to be crushed immediately to prevent fermentation. Thereafter, the juice was heated, filtered, and cooled to finally crystallize in loaves in a fixed sequence.

For the remainder of the century, Hispaniolan planters exported sugar to Seville regularly, until maritime traffic into Santo Domingo and other colonial markets fell off sharply in the 1590s. Spanish sugar growing on Hispaniola and other islands of the West Indies in the Caribbean failed to flourish or to compete with Brazilian sugar in the international markets. Limited shipments of sugar went primarily to colonial markets in the New World. Between 1568 and 1595, Hispaniolan planters shipped an average of 348 metric tons of sugar per year to Seville.[41] Santo Domingo was by far the largest exporter of sugar to Spain in the sixteenth century, as compared to Puerto Rico and Cuba.

CATTLE RANCHING

Other than sugar, the brightest prospects seemed to lie in exploitation of the herds of wild cattle that flourished under open grazing. Invading European livestock had dramatically altered human interaction with nature in the New World. Grass and pasture previously ignored by humans became a valuable resource. Cattle and swine flourished immediately in the humid climate of these islands. A few released Spanish hogs, which found abundant browse and no enemies in the island forests, became feral and prolific in their new ecological niche.

The marshes and savannas of the four Greater Antilles islands—Hispan-

---

40. J. H. Galloway, *The Sugar Cane Industry*, 13.

41. Chaunu, Chaunu, and Arbellot record a total of 4,526 metric tons (393,602 *arrobas*) of sugar sent from Hispaniola to Seville for thirteen years for which data exist, between 1568 and 1595, or an average of 348 metric tons per year (30,277 *arrobas*) recorded. *Séville et l'Atlantique*, 8:1004, 1008.

iola, Jamaica, Cuba, and Puerto Rico—became a base where the cattle-raising culture of Iberia found a new expression. About three to four hundred reddish brown or piebald Spanish longhorn cattle, or *criollos,* survived the voyage from the coastal cattle-breeding regions of Andalusia, or from the Canary Islands to the West Indies, between 1493 and 1512. These semiferal, uncastrated cattle came predominantly from Las Marismas, a marshy area of labor-extensive, open range commercial grazing on the coast of Andalusia. The immigrants reproduced at astonishingly rapid rates. The coastal marshes offered rich forage, as did the lowland grassland areas on each island. They had no grazing competitors, no menacing cattle diseases, and no predators in the early years. All the vast herds of *criollos* that later spread throughout Spanish colonial America were descended from this small band of migrants landed in the West Indies.[42]

Commercial cattle raising in the West Indies developed as an estate system of individual properties owned by a handful of Spanish colonists in an extension of the *repartimiento* system first articulated under Columbus in 1493. For the owners of larger estates, cattle ranching became a profitable and enviable way of life. They formed an island elite that had the means to live in town as absentee owners for much of the year but had the prestige of aristocratic horsemen.

Early on, cattle ownership carried with it the acknowledged right to graze on Crown lands. Gradually, a system of formal usufructary royal pastoral land grants evolved. Often circular in shape, with a two-league radius, these were huge tracts encompassing an area of 22,500 hectares or more. Generally, these large pastoral grants conveyed property rights over the most desirable, usually flatter, marshes and savannas on each island. Not all potential pasture was given out by the Crown. Some grazing lands remained in the Crown domain, especially in the hillier areas, and could be freely used by any cattle owners. Smaller ranchers and even men without lands could count on access to the less desirable domain lands to raise cattle.

The Andalusian term *hato,* originally the name for a herding encampment, came to designate lands devoted to cattle ranching. Mounted vaqueros used the Andalusian lance *(garrocha)* and the uncast lasso to gather the nearly wild cattle from the open range once a year for branding and earmarking in the dry season. Unlike in the Andalusian model, the cattle were not shifted seasonally but remained largely stationary. Since the primary product was the hide, they could be slaughtered right in the pasture if need be. The cowboys were black African slaves from West African cattle-herding societies, or free blacks brought from Andalusia, surviving Tainos, or even

42. Terry G. Jordan, *North American Cattle-Ranching Frontiers: Origins, Diffusion, and Differentiation* (Albuquerque: University of New Mexico Press, 1993), 67.

some young, unmarried Spanish settlers. A ranch boss employed by an absentee owner supervised them. On smaller ranches, the owner was resident and his male relatives, aided by a few slaves or servants, were the vaqueros.

This was entrepreneurial, profitable, large-scale commercial pastoralism. West Indian ranchers annually exported quantities of tanned hides (tanned with bark from the mangrove tree) to the Andalusian leather industry. At the period's height in the 1530s, Hispaniolan ranchers alone shipped 200,000 hides a year to Spain; by the latter half of the century, annual shipments had declined to just over a tenth of that figure.[43] In addition to land dedicated to cattle, the larger estates included ginger or sugar plantation areas; hog *corrales* in the forests; cassava, maize, and sweet potato fields; and vegetable gardens. Aside from hides, they exported sugar, ginger, dried meat, tallow, and lard to the Spanish mainland colonies. Island ranches sold thousands of live cattle as well to meet the demand for breeding herds on the mainland.

Beyond the reach of the rancher were numerous herds of completely feral cattle, horses, and pigs found in the hilly, forested areas of the islands. The wild cattle of the Antilles became the prey of market hunters who sold hides and tallow for export. Mounted on specially trained horses, these hide hunters pursued roaming cattle with packs of hunting dogs. They used a blade on the long Andalusian lance to thrust forward and cut the hamstrings of the fleeing animals. Dismounting, they used a knife on a shorter pole to kill the animal, stripped the hide and tallow, and left most of the meat for the dogs to eat. At times, the same techniques were used in pursuit of wild pigs.

THE ENVIRONMENTAL IMPACT

In the islands of the West Indies, dense human populations gave way to vast numbers of invading exotic grazing and rooting animals and new predators. Cattle and hogs flourished; so did horses and goats, although more slowly. These large animals put new pressures on the landscape as they consumed and trampled vegetation. The introduction of horses, cattle, pigs, and goats compacted the soil and increased runoff and soil erosion. David Watts comments, "In Espanola, there is some documentary evidence that the massive erosional gully forms, termed *barrancas* and *arroyos*, which are now so widespread on mountain land, postdate the advent of European grazing animals; and indeed there is no reason why gullies should have developed, even on steep slopes, under the environmentally conservative *conuco* system of pre-

---

43. Chaunu, Chaunu, and Arbellot, *Séville et l'Atlantique*, 8:1012–13, table 708. Hides shipped from Hispaniola averaged 26,387 per year between 1581 and 1607 (an eight-year sample).

Hispanic times."[44] Feral dogs—the larger European breeds—and cats, a new import, found ready prey in the indigenous hutias and iguanas, as well as in feral Spanish livestock.[45]

In the savannas, overgrazed by the introduced cattle, weeds replaced native grasses. No longer maintained by Tainos, the highly productive *conuco* system of land use virtually disappeared as abandoned plots reverted to fallow ground. Free-ranging pigs delighted in rooting up tubers from *conuco* mounds. As soon as weeding ended, a new vegetation cover of indigenous weeds and shrubs, including guava, acacias, shrub cottons, and later, palms, as well as introduced plants like various citrus species, quickly grew up.

By the beginning of the seventeenth century, the landscapes of Hispaniola and the other West Indies islands bore little resemblance to their preconquest state. The balanced *conuco* horticulture of the Tainos and Caribs no longer shaped the landscapes of the islands. Instead, Spanish ranchers and sugar planters were the land managers of the colonial regime. The hooves and teeth of the Spanish livestock allowed to roam in great numbers were the primary instruments of human impact on island ecosystems and vegetation.

CONCLUSION

When Columbus made landfall on an island in the Caribbean in 1492, this event established a new connection, a new conjuncture in world history. The newly created maritime connection between Old and New Worlds, between Eastern and Western Hemispheres, was of absolutely central importance for world environmental history. After 1492, interaction between humans and nature throughout the globe changed irrevocably. Post-Columbian regular maritime traffic from Europe supported a five-century process of expansion and control in the New World. Europeans restlessly explored new territory, conquered indigenous peoples, exploited newly discovered natural resources, settled colonies, cleared forests, expanded sedentary cultivation, and introduced new flora and fauna throughout the Western Hemisphere. With this new contact, biological exchanges began to occur on a global scale in a process that continues today.

The story of the earliest colonial venture in the New World—that of the Spanish on Hispaniola and the other West Indies islands—illustrates the immensity of the changes caused by the European invasion. Columbian discovery and colonial rule in the West Indies brought drastic changes to the

---

44. Watts, *The West Indies*, 119.

45. The Antilles hutia are divided into several families and species. The little-known Hispaniolan hutia has a long tail like the Cuban species and is apparently nocturnal.

people and natural environment of the Greater and Lesser Antilles. The environmental impact of Spanish colonial rule was more devastating in the Caribbean than in the remainder of the Americas. In many ways, this transformation reflects the vulnerability of island ecosystems to intrusive new species.

Chapter 10

Ranching, Mining, and Settlement Frontiers in Colonial Mexico

In 1519, just twenty-seven years after Columbus's first voyage, the Spanish landed in mainland North America in Mexico. With great audacity and luck, the Spanish defeated the powerful Aztecs and made themselves masters of central Mexico. Continued military success steadily increased their territory, and firm colonial rule prevented and discouraged rebellion. For the next three hundred years, Spanish colonial rule, Spanish settlers, Spanish cultural norms, and Spanish economic needs shaped and profoundly transformed the environment of Mexico.

To fully exploit their strange new empire, the Spanish had to control the labor of their subject populations, and they had to manage profitably, in ways satisfactory to European cultural norms, the extensive lands in their colonial domain. To accomplish these tasks meant that property rights in both labor and land had to be seized, redefined, reallocated, strengthened, and enforced for the benefit of the rulers. This was one of the great intellectual and operational projects, along with the dissemination of Christianity, that occupied the Spanish in the New World. Labor and land policies together drastically altered the relationship of humans to the environment in colonial America.

FIRST IMPRESSIONS

The most striking finding for the Spanish who ventured inland from Veracruz under Hernando Cortés in 1519 was the size and density of the society they encountered. The Indians of Mexico were as numerous and well organized as the societies of early modern Europe. As a corollary, although a religious and scholarly debate over the nature of the Indians continued, it was patently obvious that the indigenous peoples of the Americas were human beings, not beasts, not supernatural beings.[1] Despite certain technological disadvantages, the Indians were intelligent humans capable of communicating directly, and on largely equal intellectual terms, with their conquerors.[2]

Another, equally obvious determination by the Spanish intruders was that the mainland landscapes of cultivation and settlement in Mexico were aesthetically pleasing, intricately managed, and manifestly prosperous. The pre-conquest Indian inhabitants of Mexico had painstakingly constructed intensive, often irrigated, systems of productive horticulture tailored for each of the major ecological regions: the coastal lowlands, the piedmont, and the semiarid, broad, volcano-surrounded basins of the high plateau. So successful were these systems of cultivation that the inhabitants clearly produced abundant and even surplus food for themselves. When Cortés first landed on the gulf coast near what was to become Veracruz, he passed through the lands of the Totonac Indians. According to Thomas M. Whitmore and B. L. Turner:

> The area of the Spanish landfall was inhabited by the Totonac, who mastered the seasonal rhythm and environmental variation of the coastal plain and piedmont to produce crops for local subsistence as well as tribute, and possible commerce with the Aztec Empire. . . . The coastal plains and hills offered a complex mosaic of microenvironmental opportunities and constraints for agriculture. The cultivated landscapes encountered in this complex natural terrain consisted of a patchwork of different cultivation types interspersed with forests and scrub land. It is even likely that the forests were managed and may have sheltered orchards. The Totonac orchestrated their year-round cultivation with the spatial and temporal variations in soil-water conditions, working the well-drained lands during the rainy season, and the inundated lands in the dry season. . . . The landscape configured by these practices led Spaniards to describe the lowlands around Zempoala as "a garden with luxuriant vegetation."[3]

When Cortés reached the escarpment of the central Mexican Plateau, he found "a landscape of terraces" gradually changing to shifting cultivation on the steepest slopes.[4] Across the Sierra, in the Mesa Central in each basin, "clusters of villages and hamlets were scattered across the landscape."[5] Intensively cultivated gardens and orchards flourished. Throughout Mexico, the basic agricultural system "was anchored on maize, frijol beans and squash, emphasizing species of calabaza that yielded large seeds or delicate

---

1. Patricia Seed, " 'Are These Also Not Men?': The Indians' Humanity and Capacity for Spanish Civilisation," *Journal of Latin American Studies,* 25, no. 3 (1993).
2. Ibid.
3. Thomas M. Whitmore and B. L. Turner II, "Landscapes of Cultivation in Mesoamerica on the Eve of the Conquest," *Annals of the Association of American Geographers* 82 (1992): 406.
4. Ibid., 407.
5. Ibid., 408.

flowers used as potherbs."[6] At higher and cooler elevations, grain amaranths were important. Chili peppers and tomatoes were part of "a broader range of condiments." Vegetable oils came from the chia plant (*Salvia hispanica* L.).[7] Well-maintained weirs and check dams provided irrigation for crops sufficient to feed large, dense populations. Later Spanish observers in central Mexico corroborated these impressions. The New World may have been "savage" with "barbaric" peoples, but much of it certainly was not a wilderness—rather, it was a garden.

After climbing to the interior plateau and arriving at the Valley of Mexico, Cortés and his men confronted the amazing city of Tenochtitlan, later to become Mexico City. At that time, between 250,000 and 400,000 persons inhabited the Aztec capital.[8] Obviously, the city was a great political and imperial capital nourished by tribute. Its people relied on an intricate array of ecologically sophisticated agricultural and water control systems to produce food for the city and to manage the waters of its adjacent lakes. The soil, temperature, and moisture of the valley surrounding the city were "singularly appropriate for maize." High yields of maize from the valley's fields fed much of the city its basic food and provided supplies for winter storage. The noted artificial horticultural beds of the freshwater lakeshores or canals (the *chinampas*) fertilized by aquatic plants and other intensive inputs gave up rich harvests of produce for the city.[9]

The Spanish also noticed that interspersed between zones of denser human settlement and cultivation lay sparsely populated frontier regions in which different groups of hunters, gatherers, and shifting cultivators lived. For example, north of central Mexico, the Spanish encountered the Chichimecas and other groups whose relationship with the Aztecs had been one of tension, hostility, and negotiation. To the Spanish, these peoples occupied landscapes that were empty or were wastelands open to development if sufficient force were applied.

The climate was strange yet familiar—the reverse of the Mediterranean pattern of their homeland. Rain fell copiously in the summer months, from May through August, and was largely absent for the remainder of the year. Climate varied by altitude, with temperatures declining as one moved from the hot, wet coastal plains near Veracruz to the piedmont to the high interior plateau. Despite summer moisture, this was a semiarid land in which water sources and irrigation were of critical importance. The terrain and veg-

6. Karl W. Butzer, "The Americas before and after 1492: An Introduction to Current Geographical Research," *Annals of the Association of American Geographers* 82 (1992): 15–16.

7. Ibid.

8. Charles Gibson, *The Aztecs under Spanish Rule: A History of the Indians of the Valley of Mexico, 1519–1810* (Stanford, Calif.: Stanford University Press, 1964), 378. These are high estimates; some scholars suggest the population was no more than about sixty thousand.

9. Ibid., 300–21.

etation bore some resemblance to interior Spain and promised that some of the amenities of their homeland could be grown or implanted in the new lands.

For sixteenth-century Spanish, perhaps their most arresting discovery lay in the quantity of gold and silver possessed by the Aztecs. As had happened in the West Indies, the sight of such treasure so casually displayed aroused avarice surprising to the Indians. Cortés, in a well-known comment to the Aztec leader Montezuma said, "I and my companions suffer from a disease of the heart which can be cured only with gold."[10] In Mexico, unlike in Europe, gold, silver, and copper were not used for money. Copper and other alloys generally did not have utilitarian uses as tools, weapons, or utensils. Instead, in Mexico, "metallurgy was fundamentally a religious activity, wherein gold, copper and its alloys were used mainly for ornaments, worn and manipulated by priests in religious ceremonies and for the enhancement of political power and prestige by the elite."[11] The Spanish seized these artifacts— frequently copper-silver or silver-gold alloys—as loot, melted them down, and sent the refined metals back to Spain. In the Old World, unlike the Americas, gold and silver could be directly translated into coin that would buy weapons, human energy, and resources for ambitious rulers; it could be spent or stored by individuals thirsting for ease and security.

In the first two decades, up to 1540, the Spanish occupied themselves with the conqueror's task of plundering any and all supplies of gold found in Mexico and shipped much of this back to Spain. Thereafter, they turned themselves into prospectors, continually searching for sources of gold and silver. Discoveries of easily worked seams of silver in Mexico and Peru, and gold mines in central Chile and other sites, meant that the Spanish Crown, entitled to claim one-fifth of all treasure mined, could import ton after ton of silver and gold to a bullion-starved Europe. Coinage from the New World mines provided a solid financial base from which to strengthen the Spanish state.

DISEASE AND DEATH

The lethal impact of Old World diseases on previously unexposed populations is well documented for the Basin of Mexico and the Aztec capital of

10. Francisco López de Gómara and Lesley Byrd Simpson, *Cortés: The Life of the Conqueror, by His Secretary* (Berkeley and Los Angeles: University of California Press, 1964), 58; Peter J. Bakewell, *Silver Mining and Society in Colonial Mexico: Zacatecas, 1546–1700* (Cambridge: Cambridge University Press, 1971), 2:105.

11. Robert C. West, "Early Silver Mining in New Spain, 1531–1555," in *In Quest of Mineral Wealth: Aboriginal and Colonial Mining and Metallurgy in Spanish America*, edited by Alan K. Craig and Robert Cooper West, vol. 33 of *Geoscience and Man* (Baton Rouge: Geoscience Publications, Department of Geography and Anthropology, Louisiana State University, 1994), 52.

Tenochtitlan. The Spanish force that immediately followed Cortés in 1520 included at least one person infected with smallpox.[12] As noted earlier, this highly communicable virus is transmitted from person to person by secretions of the nose and throat and by secretions of its characteristic pustules. Smallpox scabs, even when discarded, can infect other humans on contact through shared use of clothing or bedding. While the Spaniards were negotiating with the Aztecs over a two-year period, a smallpox pandemic broke out in Tenochtitlan. An Aztec text describes the effects:

> While the Spaniards were in Tlaxcala, a great plague broke out here in Tenochtitlan. It began to spread during the thirteenth month [September 30 to October 19, 1520] and lasted for seventy days, striking everywhere in the city and killing a vast number of our people. Sores erupted on our faces, our breasts, our bellies; we were covered with agonizing sores from head to foot.
>
> The illness was so dreadful that no one could walk or move. The sick were so utterly helpless that they could only lie on their beds like corpses, unable to move their limbs or even their heads. They could not lie down or roll from one side to the other. If they did move their bodies they screamed with pain.
>
> A great many died from this plague, and many others died from hunger. They could not get up to search for food, and everyone else was too sick to care for them, so they starved to death in their beds.[13]

For an unexposed population, mortality from smallpox was likely to have been between 30 and 50 percent.[14] The turmoil associated with smallpox so weakened the Aztecs that the Spanish, aided by troops from the neighboring city-state of Tlaxcala, seized and occupied the Aztec capital on August 13, 1521.

After the smallpox plague of 1520–1521, the next eighty years of Spanish rule over central Mexico was punctuated by at least six episodes of pandemic disease: measles in 1531–1532, typhus in 1545–1548, mumps in 1550, measles in 1563–1564, typhus in 1576–1580, and measles in 1595.[15] Both Indian and Spanish sources attest to the severity of these outbreaks. Indian commentators frequently remarked that such diseases had been unknown before conquest and struggled to create new terms in their language to name these afflictions. All sources agree that the 1545–1548 typhus outbreak was more severe and had a higher death rate than the 1520–1521 smallpox

12. Hans J. Prem, "Disease Outbreaks in Central Mexico during the Sixteenth Century," in *Secret Judgments of God: Old World Disease in Colonial Spanish America,* edited by Noble David Cook and W. George Lovell (Norman: University of Oklahoma Press, 1991). This was the expedition sent by the governor of Cuba against Cortés, who was technically in rebellion.

13. Miguel León Portilla and Lysander Kemp, *The Broken Spears: The Aztec Account of the Conquest of Mexico* (Boston: Beacon Press, 1962), 92–93.

14. Hans J. Prem, "Spanish Colonization and Indian Property in Central Mexico, 1521–1620," *Annals of the Association of American Geographers* 82 (1992): 25.

15. Ibid., 47. Prem's identification of some of these diseases remains tentative.

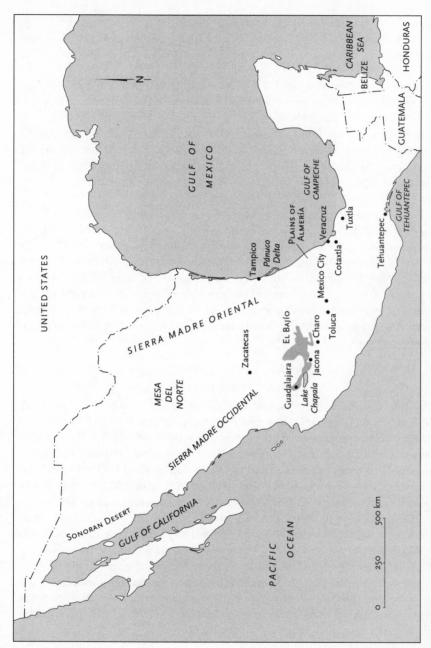

Map 10.1 Spanish colonial Mexico

pandemic. Several observers contemporary to the time estimated 60 to 90 percent mortality. The well-recorded outbreak of 1576–1580 revealed similar symptoms and similar mortality; one Spanish estimate at the end of the pandemic put the death toll at 2 million.[16]

Identifying these diseases is a difficult task. Although a single disease may be singled out, at least tentatively, the symptoms do not always correspond directly to contemporary symptoms for that disease. It is very likely that these were compound epidemics in which one disease acted as a trigger for the eruption of others already endemic. Certainly, gastrointestinal infections, testified to by frequent references to bloody stools, were always present. Some outbreaks also coincided with food shortages that increased their severity.

From this sad chronology, we can see how the Indian population of central Mexico plummeted in a series of abrupt drops. Indians dwindled from a precontact figure of 13.9 million to approximately 1 million by the early 1600s. Population loss on this scale emptied the landscape and made it possible for the Spanish to create a new society modeled after their homeland in central Mexico. The density of central Mexico's population enabled the spread of infectious disease and raised the death totals, but these outbreaks inevitably spread to even thinly populated parts of Spanish America and had the same results.

COLONIAL LAND USE

After the conquest, the Spanish recognized Indian property rights to the lands they occupied and cultivated in central Mexico.[17] If Indian lands remained occupied and cultivated, they were secure. Early on, the Spanish Crown established its claim to ownership of all unoccupied and uncultivated lands in New Spain. This assertion of ownership implied that the usual and customary rights of access to these royal domain lands which obtained in Spain were to function in the colony as well—especially grazing rights.

The Spanish were first interested in tribute and service, not land. As in Hispaniola, under *encomienda* terms granted by Cortés, individual colonists demanded produce and labor from specified Indian communities. But the Spanish Crown, aware of the disastrous record of *encomenderos* in the West Indies, restricted their demands on the Indians and discouraged award of these rights beyond the first wave of colonists. Thus constrained, *encomienda* rights did not prove to be as lucrative as hoped. Moreover, dwindling Indian num-

16. Ibid., 41.
17. Ibid.

bers steadily eroded the value of tribute rights over weakened Indian populations.

The most pressing goal of every colonist, beginning with Cortés himself, was to obtain grants to land that would convey private property rights to large estates. Despite at least one royal experiment aimed at creating smallholding farms among settlers, the thrust of Spanish landownership was toward large concentrations of land. Cortés had been authorized by the king in 1523 to award lands to those of his followers who would take up agriculture. He assumed control of large estates south of Mexico City and made numerous awards to his favored followers, who retained these lands. Thereafter, successive viceroys exercised their power to make grants of land for agricultural and grazing purposes—primarily to Spanish officials and military officers who had rendered noteworthy service to the colonial regime. Titles were also secured by religious institutions and by agents for powerful men who sought to increase their holdings. In central Mexico, sixteenth-century land grants conveyed title to smaller holdings for agricultural land *(caballerías)* of 43 hectares, to sheep ranches of 780 hectares, and to cattle ranches of 1756 hectares. Titles were first notarized and recorded, and subsequently examined and validated, by officials on payment of a fee.

Indians steadily lost lands to the Spanish. Sometimes colonists simply usurped lands by force, especially in the early decades of conquest. Sometimes Indians sold their lands to Spanish wishing to expand their estates. However, most important, dying Indian populations emptied lands formerly settled and cultivated. The surviving Indians did not have the energy or the capacity to farm all the lands thus opened up. Alienation of Indian landholdings accelerated after the population collapse in the aftermath of the pandemic that began in 1576. The practice of amalgamating surviving Indian families from broken villages into one settlement also freed up land for Spanish seizure.

Imposition of the new Spanish property rights regime, along with monetization, created a market in land rights—a European cultural phenomenon that had not been a prominent feature of Aztec society.[18] Aztec nobles held private landholdings that could be sold and inherited. A land market presumably existed but was truncated, since most Aztec land was managed by communities or institutions. Initially faltering, and not all that vital or active, land markets in colonial Mexico expanded in scale and the pace of transactions speeded up. Spanish owners of haciendas, or ranches, bought land from Indian communities or from their peers to expand their operations. Families sold off haciendas and ranches for a variety of reasons. As they acquired property rights, Indian communities and individuals and mestizos

18. C. Gibson, *The Aztecs under Spanish Rule,* 257–70.

bought and sold land. As pressures on the land grew greater in the 1700s, the pace of land exchanges picked up also (see below). Slowly, as demand and land prices rose, the market functioned to put land under its highest economic return. As the colonial population grew, intensification of land use followed, shaped largely by the market.

In an outcome that the Spanish colonial regime surely did not intend or plan for, plummeting Indian numbers meant that, after a hundred years of European occupation, human land use remained less intensive in Mexico than it was before the conquest. This also meant that, by inference at least, human impacts on the land were less intrusive than before 1519. Most important, since the conquest, human numbers in Mexico dropped precipitously from at least 10 million to 1.5 million.

Intensively cultivated lands declined from 250,000 square kilometers to 50,000 square kilometers (10,000 square kilometers cultivated and 40,000 square kilometers left fallow).[19] This was an 80 percent reduction in cultivated area caused by abandonment of land by Indians, for which the 10,000 square kilometers devoted to Spanish colonial agriculture did not compensate. Of the 200,000 square kilometers no longer under intensive Indian cultivation, Spanish pastoralists occupied about 125,000 square kilometers, leaving 75,000 square kilometers free to return to unmanaged vegetation. In short, the total area under human agropastoral use declined by 30 percent.[20]

Despite their much depleted numbers, during the first half of the seventeenth century, subjugated Indians still occupied and controlled 44 percent (220,000 square kilometers) of the 500,000-square-kilometer territory of New Spain. The Spanish termed these lands the *patrimonio primitivo*. Of this total, however, Indians actively cultivated only 40,000 square kilometers of land.[21] Another 30 percent (150,000 square kilometers) of the total land area of New Spain consisted of uncultivated desert or highlands technically owned by the Crown. The *tierras baldías* remained either uninhabited or sparsely occupied by unassimilated Indian groups. Spanish colonialists con-

19. The area under grants for cultivation was only four thousand square kilometers, but the authors estimate ten thousand square kilometers total to allow for hidden or illegal land occupation and cultivation. Karl W. Butzer and Elizabeth K. Butzer, "The Sixteenth-Century Environment of the Central Mexican Bajío: Archival Reconstruction from Colonial Land Grants and the Question of Spanish Ecological Impact," in *Culture, Form, and Place: Essays in Cultural and Historical Geography*, edited by Kent Mathewson (Baton Rouge: Geoscience Publications, Department of Geography and Anthropology, Louisiana State University, 1993), 175.

20. Ibid., 177.

21. Karl W. Butzer and Elizabeth K. Butzer, "Transfer of the Mediterranean Livestock Economy to New Spain: Adaptation and Ecological Consequences," in *Global Land Use Change: A Perspective from the Columbian Encounter*, edited by B. L. Turner (Madrid: Consejo Superior de Investigaciones Científicas, 1995).

trolled and managed the remaining 26 percent (130,000 square kilometers) of the total land area of Mexico.[22]

By the mid-1600s, a new colonial landscape had been created in New Spain, dominated by the colonial towns and mining settlements and by isolated estates. Spanish land use divided between settlement, agriculture, and commercial pastoralism as follows: Approximately nine thousand Spanish titleholders of *caballerías* occupied about 4,000 square kilometers. These landowners clustered in central Mexico, with nearly two-thirds near Mexico City and another fifth in the Bajío region in central Mexico. Conscripted Indian laborers or, increasingly, Indian wage laborers and black slaves did the actual work on these estates. Most of this sizeable area was plowed for wheat and other European crops to feed the colonial rulers. Numerous official permits for gristmills to grind flour reveal the extent of wheat cultivation.

Colonial land managers imposed a more extensive form of land use reminiscent of that found in their Iberian homeland. Reliance on draft animals inclined Spanish cultivation toward large fields on level or gently sloping lands with deep soil and good drainage. Wheat, sugarcane, and other new crops were rigorously monocropped—in contrast to precontact cultivation practices. Indian horticulture was admirably suited for steeper slopes, smaller fields, and shallower soils.[23] Maize, planted in rows with beans and other crops, did extremely well on these higher lands.

For example, in the Puebla Valley in central Mexico, the first Spanish settlers found to their surprise that the largely Nahuatl-speaking Indians living in the valley had left the low-lying valley and river bottomlands unsettled and uncultivated. Often these were no-man's-lands between separate political jurisdictions—partly because they were vulnerable to attack by hostile neighbors. The Spanish quickly began to occupy these lands, to plow large, flat fields in order to sow wheat, and to use the river waters for irrigation. Unlike the Indians, who relied solely on wooden digging sticks, the Spaniards used draft animals to pull plows that turned over the dense soils of the valley bottoms. Wheat was less vulnerable than maize to night frosts that hit the valley bottoms of central Mexico especially hard.[24]

EURASIAN INVADERS

The flora and fauna that invaded Mexico as part of the biological package carried by the intruders offered postconquest society significant advantages

22. Butzer, "The Americas before and after 1492," 352.
23. Ibid., 417.
24. Rik Hoekstra, *Two Worlds Merging: The Transformation of Society in the Valley of Puebla, 1570–1640* (Amsterdam: Cedla, 1993), 92–94.

in energy, nutrition, variety, and even aesthetic appeal often minimized or overlooked. Spanish horses and mules equipped for riding increased the speed, range, and comfort of human travel. Spanish oxen, horses, mules, and burros offered an alternative to human muscle for transporting goods. Burros became cheap enough for Indians to buy, breed, and use widely throughout New Spain. Draft animals permitted the use of wheeled vehicles and plow cultivation. Animals took over much drudgery formerly performed by human muscle and energy. Grazing livestock helped to fertilize fields and disperse seeds. Cattle, chickens, pigs, sheep, and goats supplied a new, plentiful, and cheap source of animal protein that augmented the semidomesticated native turkeys and wild game of the Indians. Wool from sheep and goats offered a new, warm, and durable textile for clothing.

Human diet and nutrition advanced significantly after the conquest. Introduced food plants "increased the repertoire of standard indigenous crop plants by roughly one-half, both in the temperate and tropical zones of Mexico."[25] Wheat, along with barley and rye, although rarely accepted by Indian cultivators, became a major food grain and alternative to maize and amaranth. Sugarcane, a new introduction, flourished and added a new sweetener to the New World diet. Spanish arboriculture introduced numerous fruit trees—citron, lemon, lime, sweet orange, sour orange, grapefruit, peach, quince, fig, banana, pear, apple, apricot, and pomegranate—that were enthusiastically grown by Indian as well as Spanish householders. These became new sources of vitamins, starches, and fructose. Spanish vegetables— lettuce, radish, cabbage, onion, melons, broad bean, chickpea, and bottle gourd—were widely grown, as were Spanish condiments such as garlic, mint, parsley, and coriander.

Introducing new plants and animals by filling "dietary and seasonal niches" significantly reduced the risks of drought and crop failure for human society in Mexico.[26] Meat animals converted previously unused grass and forage to protein and stored the resource in their bodies for use during drought periods. Nearly all the Mediterranean crops introduced were adapted to winter growth and were harvested as the indigenous crops were just beginning to grow.

By far the majority of Spanish-controlled lands were devoted to livestock rearing and grazing. In Mexico, as in the West Indies, heavy mortality among the Indians freed much land for grazing by European livestock.[27] Indian lands became available for occupation by Spanish colonialists only when

25. Karl W. Butzer, "Biological Transfer, Agricultural Change, and Environmental Implications of 1492," in *International Germ Plasm Transfer: Past and Present*, edited by R. R. Duncan (Madison, Wisc.: Crop Science Society of America, 1995), 18.

26. Ibid.

27. Lesley Byrd Simpson, *Exploitation of Land in Central Mexico in the Sixteenth Century* (Berkeley and Los Angeles: University of California Press, 1952), 18–19, table 1.

abandoned, not before. The needs of livestock producers did not expel Indians from their lands. Although many conflicts occurred when animals damaged Indian crops in their wanderings, royal officials did not knowingly award grazing titles over lands occupied and controlled by those Indians surviving disease.[28]

The fecundity of livestock was a commonplace observation among travelers. In the late 1580s, Father Alonso Ponce, who spent four years on tour throughout New Spain as an inspector for the Franciscan order, wrote:

> There are in that Province, . . . many valleys and wide and spacious savannas . . . where there are many pastures for cattle and sheep[,] . . . which have so multiplied that it seems they are native to the country, so full are the fields of them. They reproduce as in Castile, only more easily, because the land is temperate and there are no wolves or other animals to destroy them, as in Spain, [and they are bred] at less cost and with less labor. They have increased to such a degree that there are men who brand yearly 30,000 calves, not counting those that wander off and go wild. There is hardly an Indian town that does not have a slaughter house for the natives themselves in which infinite numbers of animals are killed . . . and it is all very cheap.[29]

Beef was indeed cheap and abundant for both the Spanish settlers and the Indians, who were developing a taste for it. By 1542, an *arrelde* of beef (1.84 kilograms) had dropped in price to only one-eighth of a silver real in Mexico City, whereas in Andalusia in the same year, the same weight of beef cost a full real.[30] Beef remained extraordinarily cheap by Old World standards throughout New Spain for the remainder of the century.

At the end of the first colonial century, the new commercial pastoralism was clearly triumphant. By 1620, some two thousand grantees held royal title to *estancias* designated for sheep grazing. Their rangelands extended over about 25,000 square kilometers in the central plateau. Approximately one thousand grantees held rights to *estancias* for winter pasture *(agostaderos)* over another 25,000 square kilometers of rangelands. In total, these ranchers grazed 6 to 8 million sheep over 50,000 square kilometers of grazing lands. Two thousand colonialists held royal titles permitting them to graze cattle at regulated stocking densities. Rangelands, comprising about 70,000 square kilometers, were mainly located in the western Bajío, the gulf lowlands, Toluca, and the Jalisco Lake district. Total herd size was somewhere between 1.5 and 2 million cattle in this period. Finally, two hundred grantees held

---

28. Butzer and Butzer, "The Sixteenth-Century Environment of the Central Mexican Bajio," 167–68.

29. Translated and quoted in Simpson, *Exploitation of Land in Central Mexico in the Sixteenth Century*, 2–3.

30. François Chevalier, *Land and Society in Colonial Mexico: The Great Hacienda* (Berkeley and Los Angeles: University of California Press, 1963), 92.

land grants to breed horses and mules in the Huasteca region. Perhaps 150,000 equines grazed on 5,000 square kilometers.[31]

To summarize, seventeenth-century Spanish ranchers maintained herds of 7 to 10 million animals that grazed over 125,000 square kilometers, or about a quarter of New Spain's territory. The spread of cattle, horses, and sheep, grazing on lands formerly cultivated by Indians or in savannas that had never known the teeth and hooves of large ungulates, marks a startling ecological transformation.

EARLY RANCHING AND SETTLEMENT FRONTIERS

Spanish settlement and livestock-rearing marched together. The hearth of cattle raising in New Spain was Mexico's gulf coast, where the habitat was similar to that found in coastal Andalusia. From three lowland coastal nuclei—Veracruz, the Plains of Almería, and Tampico at the delta of the Pánuco River—ranching began in the 1520s and spread throughout the coastal plain.[32] Before the conquest, the Nahua (Aztec) Indians along the coast managed intricate, intensive, and highly productive horticultural systems. In the vicinity of Veracruz, a quarter to a half million Nahuatl speakers grew maize on intensively cultivated coastal wetlands. By digging irrigation ditches and heaping the spoil on planting platforms, they regulated moisture in the planting platforms and kept a "nutrient sump" in the ditches. The ditches retained water during the dry season for a second crop.[33] After the conquest, grazing cattle dominated the landscape.

As the Indians rapidly died off, the Spanish immediately replaced their ecological system with one more to their own liking. Ranchers grazed cattle that flourished on the wet coastal savanna lands and employed a local transhumance pattern to support their cattle. During the wet summer season, cattle grazed the dry savanna lands of the interior piedmont while the coastlands were intermittently flooded. During the dry winter, ranchers burnt the piedmont pastures as they drove their herds down to the coastal savanna now dry enough to be grazed.[34]

31. Butzer and Butzer, "Transfer of the Mediterranean Livestock Economy to New Spain," 176, table 2.

32. Terry G. Jordan, *North American Cattle-Ranching Frontiers: Origins, Diffusion, and Differentiation* (Albuquerque: University of New Mexico Press, 1993), 86–97. Also Andrew Sluyter, "The Ecological Origins and Consequences of Cattle Ranching in Sixteenth Century Spain," *Geographical Review* 86 (1996).

33. Sluyter, "The Ecological Origins and Consequences of Cattle Ranching in Sixteenth Century Spain," 168; Sluyter, "The Making of the Myth in Postcolonial Development: Material Conceptual Landscape Transformation in Sixteenth-Century Veracruz," *Annals of the Association of American Geographers* 89, no. 3 (1999): 388.

34. Andrew Sluyter, "From Archive to Map to Pastoral Landscape: A Spatial Perspective on the Livestock Ecology of Sixteenth-Century New Spain," *Environmental History* 3, no. 4 (1998):

To the north, the Pánuco delta, closely resembling Guadalquivir in Andalusia, had luxuriant, seasonally flooded marshes with tall grass on the coast. Inland could be found wet, tallgrass savannas cleared from the rain forest by Indian burning, as well as extensive stretches of wooded grassland. Within a decade, by 1532, the Huastecan population of the Pánuco region, which had been afflicted by disease, enslavement for export, and starvation, had dwindled from a million persons to a few thousand survivors. West Indies cattle acquired in exchange for Huastecan slaves thrived in this environment.

Slowly, Spanish ranchers obtained legal title to *estancias,* defined as one-square-league plots (about 1,750 hectares), on the coast. For many, this was land that they had already settled and had begun grazing livestock on. Here, they replicated the Andalusian-Antillean specialized cattle-raising practice, with its extensive land use and minimal manpower invested in herd supervision. On these coastal ranches, mounted black African or mestizo vaqueros tended the cattle. They moved the animals to higher pasture during the dry season and managed annual roundups for branding and slaughter. Vaqueros also burnt their ranges at the end of the dry season to keep the grass new and tender and to prevent regrowth of the forest. Ranchers in the Pánuco delta specialized in horse raising to supply the needs of the entire coastal ranching industry.

Coastal ranchers sold hides for export to Seville and drove live cattle for sale for meat in adjacent highland urban markets. Generally, however, colonial Mexican ranches produced veal, rather than beef, as the primary meat product. Unlike in today's ranching, they did not castrate bulls to produce beef but slaughtered younger animals for meat. The ranches needed only a few bulls to service cows. They killed off excess bulls and older cows for hides and tallow. There was a strong domestic market for these products at the silver mines, which needed large quantities of ore bags and candles.

Along the eastern gulf coast, pioneer settlement and commercial pastoralism scarcely advanced at all in the sixteenth and seventeenth centuries. Fierce Indian resistance meant that the Pánuco delta remained the border between Spanish lands and those held by the Chichimecas. Great herds of feral cattle and horses had advanced beyond this line and flourished, but not Spanish colonization—possibly because no silver mines attracted pastoralists. It was not until the 1740s that José de Escandón founded several towns and large haciendas and brought in settlers north of Tampico. Cattle, sheep, and horse raising began to thrive in what became the province of Nuevo Santander (modern Tamaulipas). By 1795, nearly 112,000 cattle, 130,000 horses,

---

522; Sluyter, "Changes in the Landscape: Natives, Spaniards, and the Ecological Restructuration of Central Veracruz, Mexico, during the Sixteenth Century," Ph.D. diss., University of Texas at Austin (Ann Arbor: University Microfilms, 1995).

and large numbers of sheep reportedly grazed the rangelands of the northern Atlantic Coast and its interior.

The next center to attract settlers and develop ranching and Mediterranean-style agriculture lay in the Mesa Central, or Altiplano, of Mexico—the interior, temperate, high plateau. Along the road of conquest (the Camino Real) from the coast to Mexico City, ranching flourished by midcentury in three nuclei: the valley of Toluca, with sixty *estancias* and 150,000 cattle; the Llanos de Apan, centered on Tepeaplulco; and the Basin of Huamantla.[35] By the latter half of the century, specialized cattle raising in these areas had given way to diversified estates growing wheat, maize, sheep, goats, and pigs. Cattle raising remained significant in a far more labor-intensive regime than on the coast.

A Spanish-style stockbreeders' association, the *mesta*, regulated the seasonal transhumance of cattle and sheep, from higher summer pastures to more moist winter pastures lower down.[36] The livestock moved along rock-walled drove trails *(cañadas)* designed to protect crops as the animals passed. In 1551, the graziers obtained a royal patent extending the ancient Castilian right to graze their herds on harvest stubble from the maize fields of Indian farmers to all cropped areas.

Extensive cattle and sheep ranching next took hold in the Bajío, a large, well watered savanna covered with luxuriant, seasonal grasses and dotted with oak, acacia, mesquite, and cactus. The Bajío stretches westward 450 kilometers from Queretaro state to Guadalajara. It had not been a site for dense preconquest settlement and cultivation. Instead, this terrain was the abandoned home of hunter-gatherer Chichimecas, who had been forcibly driven out.

The Bajío remained a frontier region in which, for some time, ranches were fortified and defended by armed vaqueros against Chichimeca raids. Although the Bajío served as a staging area for further northward expansion of the ranching frontier, overgrazing by overly large herds of longhorns led to the introduction of sheep in great numbers. Simultaneously, the deep black soil of the prairie invited grain crops and diversification.[37]

By 1590, after fifty years of colonial settlement, the Bajío contained over 400 cattle *estancias,* with an estimated 800,000 head of cattle, and 350 sheep *estancias,* with approximately 1 million sheep. Despite these numbers, ecological damage was minimized because the cattle were allowed to roam freely to take advantage of pasturage in tracts unoccupied by either Indians or

35. Jordan, *North American Cattle-Ranching Frontiers,* 97–98.

36. William Howard Dusenberry, *The Mexican Mesta: The Administration of Ranching in Colonial Mexico* (Urbana: University of Illinois Press, 1963), 111–15.

37. Butzer and Butzer, "The Sixteenth-Century Environment of the Central Mexican Bajio." See also Butzer, "The Americas before and after 1492," 363; D. A. Brading, *Haciendas and Ranchos in the Mexican Bajio, Leon, 1700–1860* (Cambridge: Cambridge University Press, 1978).

Spaniards. Sheep raisers engaged in long-distance transhumance and thereby reduced pressure on dry-season pastures.

THE CORTÉS ESTATES

Ranching and Spanish settlement expanded quickly outward from the central Mexican Plateau. Surprisingly, the warmer tropical regions of southern Mexico were early sites for Spanish *estancias* and colonization. Despite relatively sparse numbers of Spanish colonists, livestock raising introduced by them had a considerable ecological and economic impact. The earliest and most aggressive colonist in the south was Hernando Cortés, conqueror of Mexico. Cortés, titled the Marques del Valle, claimed huge estates in southern Mexico that he and his descendants held for many generations. The estate—not simply a ranch but a large business enterprise—held sizeable lands to the south of Mexico City: in Charo, Toluca, and Cuernavaca, which lay just south of the capital; in Veracruz, Tuxtla, and Cotaxtla on the Atlantic gulf coast; in the Valle de Oaxaca to the southwest; and in Tehuantepec on the Pacific Coast. The Marquesado lands (as the estate came to be called) bracketed the Isthmus of Mexico between Cotaxtla and Tehuantepec.[38] A grant from Philip II gave Cortés labor and service rights over as many as 50,000 tributaries and access to thousands of hectares of potential grazing lands. Cortés and his successors raised cattle, sheep, goats, mules, and purebred horses on bounded haciendas scattered throughout the Marquesado lands. They sold live animals to markets in Mexico City and cattle hides for export to Seville.

One of the most productive and profitable regions in which Cortés acquired land was the highland Valle de Oaxaca occupied by Mixtec, Zapotec, and Nahua Indians to the southwest of Mexico City. Despite Oaxaca's warm, temperate, semiarid climate, its perennial rivers and a high water table encouraged intensive cultivation on its broad alluvial plain. During the sixteenth century, the Marquesado, and the lands of twenty or more other Spanish *estancia* owners, occupied unused grassy areas and grazed livestock in a transhumance system throughout the valley. By 1643, there were forty-one Spanish colonial estates or haciendas involved in mixed-livestock and grain farming within carefully stipulated territories.[39] When the Spanish exercised little control over their grazing cattle, the remaining Indian farmers complained to royal authorities. These complaints induced the Crown to enforce strict boundaries and restrictions on grazing livestock.

38. Lolita Gutiérrez Brockington, *The Leverage of Labor: Managing the Cortez Haciendas in Tehuantepec, 1588–1688* (Durham: Duke University Press, 1989). For spatial distribution of the estate holdings, see pp. 28–29, map 2.

39. William B. Taylor, *Landlord and Peasant in Colonial Oaxaca* (Stanford, Calif.: Stanford University Press, 1972), 121–22.

In this region, and across Mexico, Indian communities turned enthusiastically to raising sheep and goats. Among the Mixtecs in the late sixteenth
century, "nearly all communities, large and small, established sheep-goat *estancias* and began developing the herds that were to provide one of the primary sources of municipal revenues until the end of the colonial period."[40]

By the 1550s, estate administrators, discouraged by government restrictions and declining profits in Oaxaca, intensified or initiated new ranching
in Toluca, Charo, and Tuxtla, but especially in Tehuantepec.[41] Eleven years
after the founding of the Marquesado, in 1543, "the numbers of newly introduced livestock were impressive: 13,700 sheep; 700 cattle; 180 horses; and
1242 mules, donkeys and mares."[42]

Between the 1550s and 1630s, Spanish ranching steadily increased in
Tehuantepec. The "warm arid climate and the scrubby leguminous vegetation of the coastal plain were well suited to cattle, horses, mules, donkeys,
sheep, and goats."[43] A 1989 study by Zeitlin counts petitions by Spanish colonialists for 121 *estancias de ganado mayor* (horses, mules, donkeys, or cattle);
41 *estancias de ganado menor* (sheep and goats), and 43 *caballerías* for cultivation. The Dominicans held grants to 8 cattle and mule *estancias*. Zeitlin observes that, under the statutes prevailing, the private individuals obtaining
grants could have grazed as many as 60,500 cattle, horses, mules, and donkeys (at 500 head per title) and 82,000 sheep and goats (at 2,000 head per title). By 1609, a *mesta*, or stockbreeders' association, had formed at Tehuantepec City—the southernmost of eighteen *mestas* in New Spain.[44]

Calculated at the standard area, these secular and religious grants assigned more than 2,600 square kilometers to Spanish control. The Marquesado *estancias*, with properties added by purchase in the late sixteenth century, encompassed 1,300 square kilometers. The total, just under 4,000
square kilometers, occupied nearly all the surface area of the coastal plain
and piedmont in Tehuantepec.[45]

40. Ronald Spores, *The Mixtecs in Ancient and Colonial Times* (Norman: University of Oklahoma Press, 1984), 125.

41. Ibid., 37.

42. Judith Zeitlin, "Ranchers and Indians on the Southern Isthmus of Tehuantepec: Economic Change and Indigenous Survival in Colonial Mexico," *Hispanic American Historical Review*
69, no. 1 (1989): 36.

43. Ibid., 35.

44. Dusenberry, *The Mexican Mesta*, 50.

45. Simpson, *Exploitation of Land in Central Mexico in the Sixteenth Century*, 39. The numbers
may have been greater. In an earlier estimate for Tehuantepec, Simpson posited 83,000 sheep,
126,000 cattle, and 12,500 horses and mules grazed by Spanish ranchers by 1620. He added
63,000 head of sheep run by Indian grantees as well, for a total of 146,000 sheep. In Simpson's
calculation, the total area granted was 3,667 square kilometers, and, in his view, the total range
grazed was probably three times that amount, or 11,000 square kilometers.

THE VALLE DEL MEZQUITAL

Centered on the Tula River valley, the Valle del Mezquital comprises the lands directly to the north of the Valley of Mexico and Mexico City. The 10,139-square-kilometer Valle encompasses the catchment areas of the Tula and Moctezuma Rivers, actually a total of eight valleys, which range in elevation from seventeen hundred to twenty-two hundred meters and are bounded on three sides by high mountain ranges. The term *Valle del Mezquital*, meaning the valley where mesquite grows, emerged in the late 1600s to suggest the barrenness, aridity, and poverty of the area. The name continues to be symbolic of rural poverty today. The barrenness of the region has been accentuated by its position east of and adjacent to the Bajío which, after its livestock phase, became one of the richest grain-growing areas in New Spain.

At contact, the Valle was a densely settled region that served as a boundary between the Chichimeca hunters and gatherers and the agricultural folk of the Valley of Mexico. For at least four centuries, the Otomi Indians had lived in and shaped the landscape of these wide valleys. According to Elinor G. K. Melville, "[The Valle del Mezquital] was a fertile, densely populated, and complex agricultural mosaic composed of extensive croplands, woodlands, and native grasslands; of irrigation canals, dams, terraces, and limestone quarries. Oak and pine forests covered the hills, and springs and streams supplied the extensive irrigation systems."[46] Indian agriculture focused on production of maize, beans, and squash, together with cotton, chilies, and tomatoes. All depended on spring-fed irrigation that in turn relied on vegetative cover on the hills and dependable recharging of the water table.

The Valle del Mezquital still retained a sizeable Indian population when Spanish colonists began to introduce livestock into the existing agricultural system in the 1530s. Without legal authority, but simply acting as squatters, Spanish *encomenderos* holding tribute and labor rights over Indian settlements employed black slaves as herdsmen to set up corrals and huts adjacent to Indian villages and to graze the *encomenderos'* herds. From the colonists' viewpoint, this was perfectly justifiable. Putting grazing animals among agriculturists was a normal practice taken directly from their Iberian homeland.

Grass in Spain was a basic resource for raising livestock; grass in precontact Mexico had no immediate value to cultivators. In Castile, whenever land was not cultivated, it became common grazing land. This even applied to croplands outside of the planting-to-harvest cycle, so that crop stubble was a

---

46. Elinor G. K. Melville, *A Plague of Sheep: Environmental Consequences of the Conquest of Mexico* (Cambridge: Cambridge University Press, 1994), 31.

community resource. However, common grazing was strictly regulated by municipalities who set grazing periods and appointed municipal herders. This system worked to the advantage of both cultivator and stock raiser in the Spanish system.

Unfortunately for the Otomi Indians, who had no knowledge or experience in dealing with grazing animals, the intrusion was disastrous. Unused to fencing and unfamiliar with the rules surrounding Spanish common grazing lands, Indian farmers faced serious damage to their crops throughout the growing season. As the number of ungulates rose, violent clashes between Indian farmers and black herdsmen grew more frequent.

In an effort to protect Indian rights and food production, the viceroy Velasco in 1550 banned all cattle and horse raising in the area surrounding the Valley of Mexico, including the lands of the Valle del Mezquital. The viceroy did exempt sheep and goats, already numerous in the Valle, from this prohibition. Velasco also issued regulations to keep Spanish livestock out of Indian crops and communal lands by forbidding grazing within a one-league radius of each Indian settlement. Velasco continued to legitimate grazing by giving out grants for sheep *estancias* (formally set at 7.8 square kilometers) but assigned them in the unpopulated portions of the Valle.

Well-meaning as these policies were, they failed to protect a deteriorating Otomi population against a fast-moving surge in sheep raising. The tributary population of the region—that is, those adult Otomi Indians liable for tax and labor payments, who numbered between 226,000 and 452,000 individuals in 1519—dropped to an official head count of 76,946 by 1570 and, after the great pandemic of 1576–1581, to a mere remnant at 20,447 by 1600. The overall rate of decline for the century was more than 90 percent.[47] As sheep numbers soared upward, overshot capacity, and then dropped, Otomi numbers plummeted. A few high-ranking Otomi *caciques* or *principales* also obtained sheep-raising grants, but the majority of Indians suffered from the excesses of the herds.

In the fifty years between 1549 and 1599, the area converted to pastoralism in the Valle del Mezquital ballooned from a modest 2.6 percent to 61.4 percent, or nearly two-thirds of the total area. By the end of this period, most of these lands had been formally certified by royal grants and had entered the Spanish land tenure system. In the 1560s, prices for meat and wool began to rise in a seller's market that persisted until the end of the century. Responding to these price stimuli, Spanish growers brought the estimated numbers of sheep from 75,000 in the 1540s to an astronomical 4.4 million animals in the 1580s, a figure that dropped off to 2.9 million in the 1590s.[48] Density rose to a high rate of 436 animals per square kilometer of total area

---

47. Ibid., 43. The head count for tributaries was introduced in the 1550s and 1560s.
48. Ibid., 79, table 4.1.

in the 1580s and fell to 291 in the 1590s. Another measure of crowding is the stocking rate for each 7.8-square-kilometer sheep station. From 1,000 animals per station in the 1540s, this rose to a high of 10,000 animals per station in the 1570s, only to drop off to 3,700 per station in the 1590s.[49]

By the last decade of the sixteenth century, the more aggressive and better-funded Spanish landholders had moved toward consolidating their holdings into larger, extensively grazed haciendas. The latter combined sheep raising and agriculture in a system in which common access to pasture was no longer allowed. Instead, each sheep grower permitted only his animals to graze on the newly emptied lands that he now possessed.

Overgrazing by sheep resulted in environmental degradation by causing a reduction in the height, spacing, and species diversity of native vegetation and the appearance of bare soil between plants. Over twenty to thirty years, animals in the numbers mentioned stripped all vegetation by browsing and grazing. Instead of normal regrowth occurring—live oak in open woodland—spiny and woody plants invaded the denuded soil. Then followed invasions of "secondary growth consisting primarily of armed species of plants: wild maguey (*lechuguilla:* Agave lechuguilla), yucca (*Palmas sylvestsres:* Yucca spp.), cacti (*tunal, nopal:* prickly pear cactus: Opuntia spp.), thorn bushes (*espinos:* possibly ocotillo: Fouqueria spp.), mesquite (*mesquites:* Prosopis spp.) and *cardones* (possibly the introduced thistle *Cynara cardunculus*)."[50]

As its name implies, mesquite-dominated dense scrub became the most noticeable type of vegetation in the Valle. Grazing pressures induced substantial sheet erosion and gullying in the hills and deposits of debris in the flatlands. Deprived of vegetation for water catchment and recharge, springs began drying up throughout the region. In the seventeenth century, the Valle del Mezquital came to resemble the badlands of the stereotypical Mexican landscape, with its bare gullies and mesquite scrub vegetation.[51]

SILVER AND THE CHICHIMECAS

Spanish settlement and commercial pastoralism marched steadily northward to extend the area under New Spain's control.[52] The colonial state subsidized and encouraged the founding of missions and presidios to open up the way north and to domesticate surviving Indians who could be used as a labor force. Feral horses and cattle in ever increasing numbers pushed ahead of the Spanish frontiersmen into the North American interior. Indian groups

49. Ibid., 83, table 4.4.
50. Ibid., 90.
51. Ibid., 98.
52. Wolfgang Trautman, "Geographical Aspects of Hispanic Colonization on the Northern Frontier of New Spain," *Erdkunde* 40, no. 4 (1986): 241–50.

captured and used wild horses in a rapid changeover from a pedestrian to a mounted society.

The central line of advance led northward into the Mesa del Norte, the great interior plateau bounded by the western and eastern Sierras Madre. Most of the Mesa del Norte was semiarid, falling below the five-hundred-millimeter isohyet. Prickly pear and woody deciduous shrubs merged into the Chihuahuan Desert, with its dominant creosote bush, lechuguilla agave, sotol, and mesquite vegetation. Cattle could browse on mesquite, which offers seed fat and protein-rich seed pods, but pastoralists and cattle avoided the arid interior of the desert. Instead, livestock raisers moved northward along the western edge of the plateau. The foothills of the Sierra Madre Occidental invited grazing along a corridor of higher grasslands with perennial streams and small springs. On the eastern edge of the plateau, hampered by the rain shadow of the Sierra Madre Oriental and lack of grassland, slow northward movement continued, with sheep as the favored animal.

In September 1546, when Captain Juan de Tolosa convinced Zacatecos Indians to lead him to the silver deposits that were to become the site for the mine in Zacatecas, the northern frontier suddenly took on new importance. Nueva Galicia, the northern province of the interior, became the scene of intense activity as entrepreneurs, miners, settlers, and muleteers, funded by investors, made their way to the new mine. The rush to the mine touched off violent resistance by bands of armed Indians in the opening phase of the Chichimeca War, a bloody frontier conflict lasting over fifty years.[53] Full pacification of the silver frontier did not occur until the turn of the seventeenth century. Spanish losses in this war "greatly exceeded, in property, as well as lives, . . . any previous Spanish-Indian conflict on the mainland of North America."[54]

Time after time, bands (cuadrillas) of armed Indians, usually numbering forty to fifty men, attacked wagon and pack trains moving north along the Camino Real to Zacatecas or to mines farther north. If not beaten off by armed guards, they killed or took prisoner the Spanish, mestizos, African slaves, and Indians attached to the train and looted the supplies. Other raiding bands attacked and burned isolated ranch houses and killed or captured their defenders.

The Indians rarely obtained and used firearms. Their most potent weapon was a wooden bow propelling slender obsidian-tipped arrows whose shafts readily pierced layered buckskin armor and all but the closest-woven Spanish mail. They fired their bows accurately and rapidly and then struck at close quarters with short spears and clubs. Even on foot, Chichimeca warriors were

53. Philip Wayne Powell, *Soldiers, Indians, and Silver: The Northward Advance of New Spain, 1550–1600* (Berkeley and Los Angeles: University of California Press, 1952), 10–15.
54. Ibid., 52.

a formidable match for mounted Spanish crossbowmen, lancers, and har-quebusiers, who were usually on the defensive. Losses to the raiders were steady and terrifying. During the first decade of the struggle, raiders had killed about two hundred Spanish frontiersmen and ten times that number of mestizos, Africans, and friendly Indians in their service.

The Spanish applied the derogatory term *Chichimeca* (singular, *Chichime-catl*) to the eight or nine separate Indian groups or nations who fought them. Each spoke, but did not write, a distinctive language. The northernmost and most aggressive of these nations included the Guachichiles of the east be-tween Saltillo and San Luis Potosí, and the Zacatecos, whose lands sur-rounded the new silver mines. To the south, warriors from the Pames, Otomis, Guamares, Tepehuanes, Tecuexes, and Cazcanes joined in this war of resistance.[55] All were hunter-gatherers organized into kinship groups, called *rancherías* by the Spanish.

Scattered across the harsh interior landscape of the northern interior, all these groups shared a common material culture. Under peaceful circum-stances, they grew maize and squash, but under the pressure of war de-pended far more on gathering wild plants. They consumed the fruit *(tuna)*, leaves, heart, and flowers of the cactus (eaten both raw and cooked); the mesquite plant, from which they ground a flour to bake a white bread in un-derground ovens; the fruit of the yucca palm; and juice of the agave as a sub-stitute for water. They fished and hunted birds, rabbits, deer, snakes, and rats. They eagerly killed and ate feral and domesticated Spanish cattle and horses.

As the Chichimecas learned to use stolen horses, they became more for-midable. A Spanish pioneer observed in 1585, "They are no longer content to attack the highways on foot, but they have taken to stealing horses and fast mares and learning to ride horseback, with the result that their warfare is very much more dangerous than formerly, because on horses, they make raids and flights with great speed."[56] The Chichimeca raids could not stop Spanish determination to mine silver, but they certainly made life in the northern mining settlements and *estancias* more precarious and costly and, on occasion, forced the evacuation of more isolated sites.[57]

As the conflict continued, the Indians developed better tactics and strat-egy, leadership, and confidence to the point that, by the 1570s, they readily attacked Spanish towns. Coordination between various groups grew more ef-fective. As their tactics evolved, they employed spies to inspect Spanish de-fenses, adopted the Spanish surprise attack at dawn, and routinely stole and

---

55. Ibid., 32–39. See also Charlotte M. Gradie, "Discovering the Chichimecas," *Americas* 51 (1994): 67–89.

56. Quoted in Powell, *Soldiers, Indians, and Silver,* 50.

57. Ibid., 74.

killed livestock in advance of an attack. Between raids, they retreated to remote bases at higher elevations. In the first twenty years of the war, the official Spanish military response was weak and usually ineffective, in part due to lack of funds. Occasionally, the authorities mounted well-equipped punitive expeditions that succeeded in capturing and brutally punishing hostile Indians. More often, local ranchers and miners provided their own defense.

The Chichimeca War was marked by little or no negotiation between the parties in its earliest stages and by the utmost hatred, ferocity, and cruelty displayed on both sides. The Indians brutally tortured, killed, or enslaved their captives; the Spaniards maimed, killed, or enslaved their captives. To the Spanish, the Indians were savages who were hostile to civilization and Christianity. Their nomadism, primitive technology, near nudity and body paint, reliance on hunting and gathering, bellicosity, and addiction to warfare all condemned them as primitives in the eyes of the Spanish. To the Indians, the Spanish were alien invaders who routinely tortured, abused, and ill-treated those Indians who submitted to them. The Chichimecas were especially hostile to Christianity and prone to desecrate churches and to steal church vessels and plates. They assumed, after bitter experience, that the Spanish lacked good faith in any negotiations or arrangements they made with Indians.[58]

How best to end the war set off an ongoing debate between the hard-line soldiers, ranchers, miners, and frontiersmen and the Church officials and members of the religious orders, who called for a more conciliatory, peaceful approach to dealing with the Indians. The latter especially protested the illegal practice of enslaving those Chichimeca captives who were not executed. Usually, the soldiers who captured men, women, and children received a share of their human booty. They were free to sell them to the highest bidder. Selling slaves at high prices—which reached one hundred gold pesos on the Mexico City slave market for a twenty-year-old Indian female captive—was the only means of profit for generally ill-paid soldiers on the frontier.

As the Chichimecas intensified their assaults in the 1570s, they met much more determined Spanish military action under Viceroy Don Martin Enriquez de Almanza. Enriquez put more funds, soldiers, and attention toward the war effort. He garrisoned a string of *presidios* along the Mexico City–Zacatecas road; put wagons into larger, escorted trains on a regular basis; helped fortify and garrison Spanish towns in the north; and commissioned some of the friendlier Indian captains to lead auxiliary troops. Even these measures did not suppress the Chichimecas. By this time, too many soldiers and others were actually profiting from the slave trade and the war itself.

58. Ibid., 53.

Greater security did encourage many ranchers to persevere and expand. Huge numbers of Mesa del Norte cattle provided essential meat, tallow, and hides for the mining centers. Ranchers also took up mule breeding in response to the need for surefooted draft animals for the transport network centered on the mines. The famed sixteenth-century rancher Francisco de Ibarra, whose lands lay between Zacatecas and Durango, reportedly owned 130,000 head of cattle in 1578 and yearly branded 42,000 calves. Small ranchers were those with fewer than 20,000 head.[59]

Finally, by 1585, a new viceroy, the Marques de Villamanrique, acting under direct royal command, devised a new strategy. In a conciliatory approach, one urged strongly by Church officials, Villamanrique began to negotiate peace treaties with the principal Chichimeca leaders. Spanish negotiators promised food, clothing, agricultural implements, and peaceful settlement with affiliation to religious orders. Simultaneously, the viceroy reduced the frontier soldiery and ended the Spanish campaigns that had become slave-raiding expeditions. Within five years, most of the leading Indian bands had submitted, and conditions became peaceful in the area between the two mountain ranges of the interior.[60] Another decade passed before more remote and intractable Indians living in the mountains finally agreed to end the Chichimeca War, by 1600.

The frontier could advance to the north without hindrance. The Indian groups moved from their lands and congregated into settlements, where they were assimilated. Those ranchers and settlers who had persisted claimed their reward.

THE FAR NORTH

Beyond Durango, ranchers moved their stock into the colder temperate zone with grama grass suitable for summer grazing and winter forage for cattle. As early as 1610, a party of settlers commanded by Juan de Onate brought herds of cattle, sheep, and goats across the Rio Grande to found Santa Fe in the highlands of northern New Mexico.[61] By the early 1700s, the entire Mesa del Norte was devoted to government-protected, labor-intensive mixed cattle, sheep, and goat pastoralism.

A second prong of the advance lay to the west and northwest: to the Pacific and onward to California. Today, this region comprises the Mexican states of Durango, Sinaloa, Sonora, southwestern Chihuahua, and Baja California and the United States regions of southern Arizona, New Mexico, and

59. Jordan, *North American Cattle-Ranching Frontiers,* 130.
60. Powell, *Soldiers, Indians, and Silver,* 181–94.
61. Jordan, *North American Cattle-Ranching Frontiers,* 146.

portions of Texas.[62] Between 1530 and 1565, seven Spanish explorers led expeditions *(entradas)* farther and farther north into the northwest and reported their findings in detail. These were Nuño Beltrán de Guzmán (1530–1531), who traveled among the Totorames and Tahues of Sinaloa; Diego de Guzmán (1533), who traveled among the Cahitas and Guasaves of northern Sinala and Sonora; Cabeza de Vaca (1535), who, with only three companions, trekked west from Florida to reach the Rio Grande and traveled through northern Chihuahua and southern New Mexico, the lands of the Jumanos, Opatas, and Pima Bajas; Fray Marcos de Niza (1539), a Franciscan friar who produced the first observations of the Pimo Altas in northwestern Sonora, southern Arizona, and Cibola (or Zuni); and the well-known expedition of Francesco Vasquez de Coronado (1540) through the Sonora Valley to Cibola. Some years later, Francisco de Ibarra (1563–1565), after prospecting for silver deposits north of Zacatecas, pressed on to a two-year expedition into the Sierra Madre among the Axacees, Tepehuanes, and Ximimes.[63]

Over varied itineraries and different topography and ecosystems, these first Europeans unanimously wrote about well-settled, productive lands in which the inhabitants made good use of various forms of irrigation to raise substantial surpluses. They encountered towns with several hundred structures and several thousand persons in residence. Drawing from these accounts and from archaeological evidence, recent estimates put the total population of the region at about 1 million persons in 1530.[64] The early explorers reported road and communication networks over which trade in pottery and other commodities flowed. They noted sophisticated political systems of considerable size and extent with elites demonstrably in charge. They found evidence of complex religious belief and worship systems attended by shamans or priests.

This testimony, however, conflicts with the writings of the Jesuits who began to organize missions throughout this region in the 1590s. The Jesuits found far fewer people, in scattered tiny settlements, abandoned buildings, and unused irrigation works. Daniel T. Reff estimates an overall population decline of 30 to 50 percent from the time of first contact. Some Indian ethnic groups suffered a depletion in their numbers as high as 90 percent.

Spanish expeditions immediately brought new diseases to the region. The first expedition of Guzmán in 1530 into the coastal province of Axtatlan (northern Nayarit and southern Sinaloa) touched off a pandemic that killed

---

62. Daniel T. Reff, *Disease, Depopulation, and Culture Change in Northwestern New Spain, 1518–1764* (Salt Lake City: University of Utah Press, 1991), 5, fig. 1. Data and arguments for the following section are drawn from this work.

63. Ibid., 18 and ff.

64. Denevan, *The Native Population of the Americas in 1492*, xxviii, table 1.

more than eight thousand of his troops and Indian allies and proceeded to devastate the Totorame peoples of the region. A combination of dysentery, typhoid, and possibly malaria produced intense fever, chills, bloody stools, and prostration among the sufferers. Heavy mortality from this onslaught was immediately followed by the measles pandemic of 1530–1534, which affected the Totorames, Ximimes, Axacees, and Tahues over a much wider area along the coast from Guadalajara to as far north as the Temazula River.[65] At least three subsequent pandemics with heavy mortality are recorded as having occurred prior to the arrival of the Jesuits.

After 1591, the gathering of Indians into missions, the opening of the northern silver mines, and the regularization of contact with the disease reservoirs of central Mexico had a fatal effect on the Indian population. During the first half of the seventeenth century, pandemics recurred a dozen times. The total Indian population of northwest Mexico fell to about 10 percent of what it had been in 1530.

Spanish settlement and ranching moved readily into the space left by Indian deaths. By 1530, Spanish ranchers found and used the only passable route through the barrier wall of the Sierra Madre Occidental. From Guadalajara in the Bajío, they led their herds through Tepic to Nayarit and the dry, tropical deciduous thorn forests of the lowlands and foothills along the coast. Spanish stock raisers discovered that they could burn this forest yearly and thereby encourage luxuriant vegetation for grazing.

Beyond the Rio Mayo, Indian populations still survived, although they remained subject to periodic pandemics. In the 1590s, Jesuit fathers founding missions displaced entrepreneurial secular ranchers to become the leading pastoralists along the Pacific Coast. Among the most important material benefits that the Jesuits offered their new converts were cattle and sheep raising. For populations weakened by recurring disease, European livestock afforded protein ready to hand, unlike game that had to be arduously pursued. The Jesuits distributed a weekly ration of beef to their followers at every mission station. Required fieldwork on communal mission lands also ensured that large surpluses of maize, wheat, beans, and cotton could be produced. Together with cultural demoralization, economic security attracted Indian converts to the Jesuits.[66]

In the 1620s, Jesuit brothers who had reached the Sonoran Desert turned inland to find river valleys with abundant grass in the lands of the Pima and Opata Indians. In the 1680s, Father Eusebio Francisco Kino placed his first mission colony on the upper San Miguel River among the Pima Indians in

65. For the area of the outbreaks, see Reff, *Disease, Depopulation, and Culture Change in Northwestern New Spain,* 105, fig. 9 and 110, fig. 10.

66. Ibid., 277–79.

northern Sonora. By his death in 1711, he had stocked nearly twenty missions and trained Pima vaqueros to work cattle in northern Sonora and southern Arizona.

In the 1690s, Jesuits ferried hundreds of cattle to Loreto in Baja California to begin a chain of small mission stations reaching up the enormous peninsula. Not until after the expulsion of the Jesuits in 1767, however, did Spanish colonists finally reach the extensive, fertile prairies of California proper. Beginning at San Diego, Franciscan brothers set up a chain of missions stretching northward to Sonoma. Cattle driven from Sonora and from Baja California were the progenitors of rapidly increasing herds. By 1800, twenty-one missions owned herds that totaled sixty-seven thousand cattle— three times the number of Indian converts.[67]

INTRODUCED LIVESTOCK AND THEIR ENVIRONMENTAL IMPACT

Invasion by new grazing and browsing animals, previously unknown, radically changed the human and natural landscape of colonial Mexico. Domesticated livestock of any kind had not existed. In the wild, there were deer and, in northern Mexico, bison, but beyond this there were no large ungulates. How do we assess and understand this massive human and environmental transformation?

How we perceive the colonial pastoral landscape in Mexico is as much a social, cultural, and aesthetic judgment as it is a biological assessment. The Spanish introduced a modified Mediterranean agropastoral economy to Mexico as they embraced what proved to be ideal conditions for livestock raising. Their choice, made with no reservations or debate, reflected the long-sustained rewards that the Mediterranean system had offered human society on the Iberian Peninsula. Scholarly views of colonial Spanish pastoralism, especially among anglophone scholars, have suffered from an inherited "old and deep-seated bias by North European scholars and travelers against Mediterranean pastoralism."[68] Since the eighteenth century, northern European visitors to the Mediterranean lands have reacted to what they perceived as an impoverished landscape, arid and treeless by comparison with their homelands. This bias extended to their view of the landscape of colonial Mexico and has continued to the present.

There is another powerful bias against grazing livestock found most noticeably among many of today's environmentalists. From this perspective, to replace Indians who practiced horticulture or mixed cultivation, hunting,

67. Jordan, *North American Cattle-Ranching Frontiers,* 162.

68. Butzer and Butzer, "Transfer of the Mediterranean Livestock Economy," 172. For a recent study that supports this argument, see A. T. Grove and Oliver Rackham, *The Nature of Mediterranean Europe: An Ecological History* (New Haven: Yale University Press, 2001).

and gathering on the lands of New Spain by domesticated and feral European livestock was both tragic and ecologically wrong. For others, perhaps equally concerned for environmental health, the landscape of livestock rearing has its ecological integrity and its own aesthetic appeal. Open rangeland has its own fierce defenders as a culturally and ecologically satisfying system. Livestock rearing is also, for better or worse, very much a part of the national cultural heritage of Mexico and the American Southwest.

Tracking an interpretive course through this difficult terrain is not easy. At one level, the movement of large grazing and browsing ungulates into a new habitat is a purely natural phenomenon that has occurred many times before without human intervention. According to Terry G. Jordan:

> Grasslands and herbivore animals evolved together, so that grazing is a natural ecological factor, and moderate grazing yields more grass than complete protection. The animals, by eating grass, stimulate herbage production, create contour trenches or slopes with their trails, fertilize with their manure and carcasses, disperse seeds, and prove beneficial in various other ways. After millennia of grazing under natural conditions, the dominant herbaceous growth remains palatable to grazing animals, suggesting a symbiotic relationship.[69]

Nevertheless, the onset of large hooved grazing and browsing animals invariably changes the invaded habitat.

Ungulates modify competition among plant species and, over time, change plant cover in grazed areas. The newcomers push back woodlands and scrub or woody vegetation and create mosaics of open spaces. As they graze and browse, they thin out underbrush within those formations of woodlands. They feed selectively among preferred grasses and other vegetation in the new environment. They can and do eat some species of plants to extinction—especially vulnerable are native perennial floral species that are replaced by annual grasses. Ungulates may feed selectively on the more aggressive plants and give other species an opportunity to survive. Alternatively, their grazing may permit the invasion of exotic species. Grazers and browsers avoid less palatable plants unless fodder is scarce. Plants with effective chemical defenses or spiny, thorny plants may increase in number and territory. High nutrient concentrations from deposits of dung and urine "provide conditions that favor aggressive, unattractive weedy species and destroy habitats of species sensitive to these influences."[70]

Other effects of grazing by heavy hooved animals include soil trampling and compaction. Compaction increases soil density and reduces pore space.

---

69. Jordan, *North American Cattle-Ranching Frontiers,* 10. Here, Jordan relies heavily on Lincoln Ellison, "Influence of Grazing on Plant Succession of Rangelands," *Botanical Review* 26 (1960): 1–78.

70. Avi Perevolotsky and No'am G. Seligman, "Role of Grazing in Mediterranean Rangeland Ecosystems," *Bioscience* 48, no. 12 (1998): 1013.

The rate of water infiltration is reduced and that of surface runoff increased. Recharge of springs and underground water may be reduced. Soil compaction may also encourage sheet erosion and gullying.

Wild ungulates, over time, reduce net primary production and total biomass in the new region. It is generally assumed that grazing reduces species diversity, but that is not at all a settled question. Some ecologists have recently argued that the reverse is true. In their view, ungulates create patches and mosaics in the landscape that encourage biodiversity by comparison with wooded areas.[71] The evolved grazed habitat has its own ecological integrity and stability.[72]

Domesticated ungulates, managed in herds for profit by commercial pastoralists, are not permitted to work out a purely ecological relationship to their new habitats. Despite the continuing existence of herds of feral cattle, pigs, and horses, most of the new livestock in Mexico were managed by ranchers who were attuned to market signals. Like ranchers everywhere they tried to control the fertility, health, and productivity of their herds. They sharply restricted the numbers of males in favor of females in their herds. They killed off predators. They found and improved sources for water and salt. When they sold animals for meat, they deprived the habitat of fertilization by their carcasses.[73] Although prohibited from doing so by Spanish authorities, most ranchers burnt their ranges in the dry season to favor grass regrowth over woody brush.[74] Their most effective management tool, of course, was to control herd size by varying the number of animals per unit of land (the stocking ratio).[75]

Much of the debate over the environmental consequences of Spanish livestock centers on the question of stocking rates and grazing pressure on existing vegetation. Did the Spanish colonial ranchers maintain their herds

71. Ibid., 1111. According to Perevolotsky and Seligman, "Total protection [of grasslands from grazing] on the other hand, leads to stagnation of growth and more or less complete dominance of a few species. Species diversity decreases and productivity drops sharply." See also J. Looman, "Grassland as Natural or Semi-Natural Vegetation," in *Geobotany*, edited by W. Holzner, M. J. A. Werger, and Isao Ikushima (The Hague: Kluwer, 1983), 5:177.

72. Perevolotsky and Seligman, "Role of Grazing in Mediterranean Rangeland Ecosystems." The authors state, "It should be realized, however, that grazing does not exercise an exclusively destructive influence upon the grazed vegetation. It can work positively in a number of ways, provided the grazing pressure is kept to a limit." See also S. J. McNaughton, "Grazing as an Optimization Process: Grass-Ungulate Relationships in the Serengeti," *American Naturalist* 113 (1979).

73. Jordan, *North American Cattle-Ranching Frontiers*, 10.

74. Butzer and Butzer, "Transfer of the Mediterranean Livestock Economy to New Spain," 180.

75. D. H. White, "Stocking Rate," in *Managed Grasslands*, edited by R. W. Snaydon (Amsterdam: Elsevier, 1987), 227.

at stocking ratios far heavier than the habitat would allow? Elinor Melville is one of the strongest critics of Spanish colonial ranching. She argues that sudden, massive growth of livestock numbers, a "plague of sheep," caused irreversible damage to vegetation, soils, and water resources in Mexico. She relies on a model of "ungulate irruption" to support her analysis:

1. rapid, nearly geometric early fecundity of introduced ungulates
2. overshoot as the herds begin to outstrip their food supply
3. crash and herd die-off as high grazing pressure destroys forage
4. recovery as the surviving animals are sufficiently reduced in number to survive on pasture subject to less grazing pressure[76]

From this boom-and-bust pattern of colonial ranching—seemingly unmanaged—came the environmental degradation she describes (see above).

Other scholars argue differently. Using the same types of documentary sources, Karl and Elizabeth Butzer did not find significant environmental degradation in the Bajío. The Butzers conclude that, after fifty years of colonial ranching, "the impact of Spanish land use [in the Bajío], particularly of grazing, is not clearly apparent as of about 1590, either in the vegetation or in the hydrological cycle."[77] They based their conclusions on descriptions of vegetation found in Spanish land grants and on palynological (pollen grain) evidence from the region. Pollen cores suggest substantial Indian landscape disturbance preceding the conquest. The Spanish could graze large herds of sheep and cattle in the Bajío (800,000 cattle and 1 million sheep) because they resorted to long-distance transhumance and thereby lessened grazing pressure on the land.[78]

Work by Andrew Sluyter on the coastal plain and its piedmont at Veracruz, the original hearth for cattle ranching in New Spain, tends to support the Butzer argument. Sluyter finds that, at least for "semiferal criollo cattle" in this region, Spanish ranchers maintained high livestock densities right through to the nineteenth century by means of annual transhumance.[79] Sluyter concludes, "The Veracruz lowlands clearly did not undergo the sequence of environmental degradation predicted by the ungulate irruptions model. Lowland livestock increased exponentially during the sixteenth century, but they did not overshoot the range carrying capacity, did not devastate the environment, and did not suffer a population crash. Instead, the

76. Melville, *A Plague of Sheep*, 47–55.

77. Butzer and Butzer, "The Sixteenth-Century Environment of the Central Mexican Bajío," 120.

78. Ibid. These early land grants describe the same biotic zonation found today in the Bajío.

79. Sluyter, "From Archive to Map to Pastoral Landscape."

high densities of the sixteenth century persisted into the nineteenth."[80] In this region, because of the management strategies employed by colonial ranchers, high stocking ratios did not necessarily lead to overgrazing.

Whether the irruption pattern occurred across Mexico is uncertain. There is no doubt that herds grew exponentially from tiny numbers of imported livestock. Whether or not overshoot and excessive grazing pressure followed may be region-specific. First-generation ranchers in each region, unfamiliar with the new habitat, seemingly lost control of herd size when livestock proved to be so prolific. As time passed, pioneer ranchers steadily gained experience and information about forage and the life cycle of their herds to become more effective managers. In this sense, they undoubtedly had an interest in limiting damage to their forage base.

After a hundred years, the overall livestock numbers in New Spain do not appear as excessive or as alarming as those reported for the sixteenth century. The aggregate estimates supplied by the Butzers for the period 1620 to 1650 suggest an overall intensity that is less than commonly supposed. Throughout New Spain, 6 to 8 million sheep grazed on 50,000 square kilometers. These figures imply that between 120 and 160 sheep grazed per square kilometer, or 1.2 to 1.6 head per hectare. This is a low figure. In her estimates of stocking densities for sheep, Melville developed a scale of intensity in which she designated the level 0 to 130 sheep per square kilometer as the very lowest grazing rate. The next level, still classified as low, is 131 to 260 animals per square kilometer. These levels proceed upward to peak at 521–650, described as "very high," and culminate in the "saturated" category at 681 to 785 sheep grazing per square kilometer.[81]

Cattle and horses numbering between 1.5 and 2 million grazed on 75,000 square kilometers. These figures imply stocking densities of 20 to 27 animals per square kilometer, or .20 to .27 per hectare for the colony. Even under the most unfavorable conditions in Mexico in the dry north beyond the 500 millimeter isohyet, cattle ranchers in the Mesa del Norte grazed 17 cattle per

80. Ibid., 521.

81. Melville, A Plague of Sheep, 80. The highest point in the scale reflected the highest calculated rate of sheep grazing in the Valle del Mezquital for the sixteenth century. Melville divided this by six to fix points on a descending graduated scale. Sluyter calculates the stocking rate for sheep for Veracruz in 1619 at 260 head per square kilometer (2.6 per hectare) on the area specified in *estancias:* 230,000 head on 89,240 hectares. Cattle densities would have been 29 per square kilometer (.29 per hectare) on the area granted (585,000 head on 204,399 hectares). If, however, transhumance practices meant that the entire region of 525,000 hectares was available for grazing, the stocking ratios are close to the Butzers' estimates for all of New Spain. Under this scenario, if total lands were divided by the ratio of sheep to cattle grants, the following would apply: there would have been 140 sheep per square kilometer (1.4 per hectare) on 159,553 hectares and 16 per square kilometer (.16 per hectare) on 365,477 hectares. Sluyter, "From Archive to Map to Pastoral Landscape," 514.

square kilometer in the sixteenth century.[82] Light aggregate stocking densities for New Spain as a whole are consistent with widespread seasonal transhumance between summer and winter pastures practiced by ranchers. Episodes of intense overgrazing and browsing due to excessive stocking certainly occurred, but they were temporary and not systemic.

At the close of the first century of colonial rule, it is unlikely that Spanish commercial pastoralism had caused long-term devastating soil denudation and erosion across Mexico or "severe and long-term decline of primary and secondary production and degradation of the habitat."[83] Documentary studies comparing the earliest Spanish landscape observations with today's vegetation formations, limnological studies comparing pre- and postconquest sediments on lake bottoms, pollen studies looking for postconquest "weed explosion and arboreal decline," or alluvial geological studies tracking extreme flooding events in the pre- and postconquest periods do not show that Spanish land use was environmentally damaging.[84] If anything, the physical evidence suggests that Indian intensive agriculture caused greater ecological disturbance than the colonial pastoral economy. During the remaining two centuries of Spanish rule, pastoralism appears to have been sustainable at reduced postconquest colonial population levels. It was only toward the end of the eighteenth century that signs of ecological distress appeared.[85] (See below.)

We may also pose a counterfactual question: What would the landscape of New Spain have looked like after 1519 if the Spanish had not developed a widespread ranching industry? What if the Spanish had simply confined their livestock needs to horses and mules and not promoted cattle and sheep raising? What if they had actively killed off feral cattle and kept them from spreading? Under this scenario, the tracts formerly cultivated by Indians, measuring in excess of two hundred thousand square kilometers, would have been allowed to regrow vegetation virtually without human interference. Without grazing, browsing, and fire, there may have been an explosive growth of brushy, woody vegetation across the face of Mexico.[86] Net primary

82. Jordan, *North American Cattle-Ranching Frontiers,* 129. The figure is for Chihuahua: "After the initial years of grass 'harvesting,' 6 hectares (15 acres) of pasture would be required to support a single head of cattle."

83. Perevolotsky and Seligman, "Role of Grazing in Mediterranean Rangeland Ecosystems," 1009.

84. Butzer and Butzer, "Transfer of the Mediterranean Livestock Economy to New Spain," 177–81.

85. Ibid.

86. M. J. A. Werger, "Tropical Grasslands, Savannas, Woodlands: Natural and Manmade," in *Man's Impact on Vegetation,* edited by W. Holzner, M. J. A. Werger, and Isao Ikushima, vol. 5 of *Geobotany* (The Hague: Kluwer, 1983); Looman, "Grassland as Natural or Semi-Natural Vegetation," 5:119–20.

production certainly would have increased and soil erosion would have diminished. Some plant and animal species would have flourished; some would have declined. Perhaps there would have been a net gain in biodiversity, perhaps not. Seasonal fires, fed by massive fuel from oily brush, would have periodically burst across the landscape. Such a landscape might well have been less appealing and useful to the human inhabitants of colonial Spain, as they struggled to cross its thicketed expanses, than the pastoral landscape that did emerge.

SILVER MINING AND MERCURY POLLUTION

Industrial pollution in New Spain was also important. The scale, territorial extent, and intensity of colonial Spanish silver mining left an indelible mark on the Mexican environment. Over three centuries of uninterrupted colonial Spanish operation, silver mining altered soil, water, plants, animals, and birds. The human population of the mining centers found their lives shaped by the resources demanded by the mines and by rampant industrial pollution, primarily from mercury wastes. As yet, the true environmental costs of silver have not been fully explored or acknowledged by scholars.

The leading miners and metalworkers in preconquest Mexico were the Tarascans of west central Mexico (roughly the present-day state of Michoacan) who dug and processed copper and silver and washed gold from placers.[87] Alerted by the indigenous industry, the Spanish traversed the countryside outside Mexico City in an incessant attempt to find silver deposits and gold placers. This restless prospecting paid off. In the 1530s, Spanish prospectors discovered the deposits of silver close to Mexico City; in 1543, the mines at Guadalajara; and by 1546, the great northern strikes at Zacatecas and its vicinity.[88] Immediately, mining towns sprang up, often located in the most desolate of regions. Silver veins tended to be at higher altitudes; gold was mined from alluvial deposits near the coast. Almost all silver mines in New Spain were above two thousand meters. Avid prospecting continued for three centuries. Fourteen mining centers opened in the sixteenth century, with strikes at 143 separate working mines. Between 1600 and 1800, four new mining centers and an additional 310 operating mines opened.[89]

This was a sizeable industrial sector. Although not a state-owned enter-

87. West, "Early Silver Mining in New Spain."

88. Peter J. Bakewell, "Mining in Colonial Spanish America," in *The Cambridge History of Latin America,* edited by Leslie Bethell (Cambridge: Cambridge University Press, 1984), 2:108.

89. Alvaro Sanchez Crispin, "The Territorial Organization of Metallic Mining in New Spain," in *In Quest of Mineral Wealth: Aboriginal and Colonial Mining and Metallurgy in Spanish America,* vol. 33 of *Geoscience and Man,* edited by Alan K. Craig and Robert Cooper West (Baton Rouge: Geoscience Publications, Department of Geography and Anthropology, Louisiana State University, 1994), 163.

prise, it was heavily controlled and encouraged by the Crown. The Spanish king levied a 10 percent tax on metal production and an assay charge. The state controlled the supply and price of mercury, the critical reagent for refining silver, and could supply or withhold draft labor. The state also established forts and patrolled the main routes against hostile Indian attack.

Colonial mining demanded large amounts of labor and capital. Owners and managers were Spanish; some mestizos, but not many, did physical labor. An official report of 1597 counted 9,143 miners working in the mines of New Spain. Over two-thirds (6,261) were professional Indian miners and refiners who were paid wages; less than one-fifth (1,169) were drafted laborers; and the remainder (1,263) were black slaves.[90] Capital came from the mercantile community in each mining town, which gave credit on supplies and bought and shipped refined silver to the dozen or so silver merchants who lived in Mexico and who had the funds to buy large quantities of the output of the mines and carry it to the mints.

Colonial miners first exploited an open pit and then followed promising veins of ore that twisted deeper into the earth. Only slowly did they invest in digging adits (gradually sloping tunnels) to the lowest galleries in their mines. Silver production relied on pick- and bar-wielding skilled laborers to extract silver-bearing ore from narrow veins. Ore concentrate, broken out manually in chunks at the mine face, was brought to the surface on human backs for processing in a refinery attached to the mine. Most operating mines had at least one refinery attached and sometimes more.

For some ores with high lead content, smelting by means of blast furnaces was profitable and sometimes used. Most mine operators treated ore by the "cold" mercury amalgamation process, rather than by "hot" smelting. Known as the "patio" process, mercury amalgamation was by far the most efficient method to recover silver from relatively low-grade ores. When particles of silver in the ore came in contact with mercury, they dissolved in the mercury and formed an alloy called amalgam. Costs could be met if the miners recovered only one and half ounces of refined silver per one hundred kilograms of ore concentrate.

Each mine had a refinery that employed water- or animal-driven stamping mills. Each mill lifted shoes weighing up to 68 kilograms to crush the concentrate on stone platforms to sandlike consistency. Refinery laborers heaped the milled ore in piles of one to two metric tons on a patio, or capacious, stone-paved, flat surface. They added water to the ore to produce a thick slime. They then mixed into the heaped milled ore three reagents: common salt at 1 to 1.5 kilograms per one hundred kilograms of ore; roasted copper pyrites at 3.5 to 5.5 kilograms per pile; and mercury squeezed through the mesh of a cloth bag at 4.5 to 5.5 kilograms for each pile. La-

90. Bakewell, "Mining in Colonial Spanish America," 127.

borers spread out the mix to form a thin layer on the stones. For a period of six weeks to as long as three months, workers or sometimes mules periodically walked barelegged through the muddy mix to agitate it. After the technical supervisor judged fusion of the silver and mercury to be complete, laborers washed the mix with water in vats equipped with paddles. Under agitation, the heavier amalgam of mercury and silver settled and the lighter waste floated off. Refinery workers then heated batches of amalgam under a metal or clay hood. The mercury vaporized to leave pure refined silver behind. Much of the vaporized mercury could be recovered from the cooled hoods; but a greater amount dispersed into the air.

Every year, each mine consumed energy and resources drawn from the immediate vicinity of the mine, from the surrounding region, from all of Mexico, and even from Spain. Detailed information on the operation of the mines at Zacatecas, one of the earliest and richest mining centers in Mexico, illustrates the reach of mining operations. Located on the high central plateau 560 kilometers northwest of Mexico City, at twenty-four hundred meters elevation, Zacatecas was strung out along a stream in a narrow valley between two hills. In the early 1600s, the center's population consisted of fifteen hundred Spanish and three thousand Indians, blacks, and mestizos.[91] Almost all food and supplies had to be carried to Zacatecas, since land in the immediate vicinity of the mines was too dry and infertile to support cultivation.

Zacatecas, like other mining centers, stimulated the growth of colonial agriculture and pastoralism. As Peter J. Bakewell puts it, "The prosperity of wide agricultural areas of northern New Spain depended to a large extent on the mineral output and prosperity of Zacatecas and its district." Wheat and maize grown on the high plateau could be obtained from lands irrigated by year-round streams in a number of fertile, humid, low-lying river canyons not too distant from Zacatecas. Meat came from sheep and cattle herds consuming the rough pasture of the plateau in a widening radius outside Zacatecas. Hides for leather and tallow were essential supplies for the mines. Wine came from the vineyards of Parras just to the north. Vegetables and fruit were grown in bottomlands in valleys surrounding the city.[92]

Supplying Zacatecas rapidly depleted these sources. Additional food and materials had to be imported from more distant regions. Carters rolled their wagons and muleteers led their mule trains over what became the Camino Real, a permanent wagon road leading to central Mexico. Cartloads of wheat from the Bajío, two hundred kilometers to the southeast, arrived regularly at Zacatecas, and coined silver accompanied the empty carts on the return journey. In 1654, for example, municipal records show that the Bajío sent 4,000 *cargas* (7,499 hectoliters) of wheat to Zacatecas and received sixty thousand

91. Bakewell, *Silver Mining and Society in Colonial Mexico*, 268.
92. Ibid., 80.

silver pesos in payment.[93] Other, less essential foods traveled the Camino Real. Carters brought *muscavado* sugar two hundred kilometers from Jacona in Michoacan, as well as salt fish caught in Lake Chapala. Fish and shrimp arrived from Chiametla on the Pacific Coast.

Fortuitously, the patio process sharply reduced consumption of fuelwood at the mines. Refiners bought and used charcoal to heat the amalgam and for occasional smelting, but local supplies of mesquite (*Prosopis* spp.) and Holm oak (*Quercus ilex*) seemed adequate. At least miners did not complain of shortages of timber at Zacatecas. Nevertheless, cumulative demand, without any attempt at restorative forestry, did deplete forest cover in an ever widening circle at Zacatecas and each mining center.

The mines consumed raw materials. Salt, or rather a mixture of salt and earth, used in the amalgamation process came from two salt pans ninety kilometers east of Zacatecas. Magistral, a mixture of iron and copper pyrites, used as a reagent in amalgamation, came from ores dug in local mines around Zacatecas.[94] Mercury, however, was another matter, since there were only a few working mines in colonial Mexico and their production fell far short.

The principal source of mercury for the mines in Mexico was Almaden, the great mercury mine in southern Spain; in the eighteenth century, Idrija in Slovenia in the Hapsburg domains served as another, less significant source.[95] Every year, the galleon fleet brought hundreds of wooden casks holding two to three triple-wrapped leather sacks, each containing five hundred kilograms of mercury. From Veracruz, the mercury casks were transported by wagon or mule train to Mexico City, and from the capital they were sent to individual mining centers as determined by treasury officials.

Perhaps the most important environmental consequence of mining was mercury pollution. It is likely that mercury pollution from the silver mines of Mexico and Peru constituted the single largest source of industrial pollution in the entire early modern world. In the 258 years between 1558 and 1816, mercury imports into colonial Mexico, almost entirely from Spain's Almadén mine, totaled 64,470 metric tons. In the latter sixteenth century and the seventeenth century, imports averaged 121 metric tons per year (totaling 17,129). During the eighteenth century and the early years of the nineteenth, the annual average mercury imports rose nearly fourfold, to 401 tons

93. Ibid., 58–80.

94. Ibid., 146–48.

95. Silver mines in Peru, especially Potosí, obtained part of their requirements for mercury from the Huancavelia mercury mine. Total production between 1571 and 1812 has been estimated at 1.1 million quintals (approximately 61,625 metric tons). Richard L. Garner, "Long-Term Silver Mining Trends in Spanish America: A Comparative Analysis of Peru and Mexico," *American Historical Review* 93, no. 4 (1988): 243. Huancavelia mercury did not move north to Mexico.

per year (totaling 47,341).[96] Moreover, during the nineteenth century, mercury imports continued to rise as silver output from the Mexican mines soared.

Each of Mexico's 453 silver mines, stretching from Chihuahua in the north to Tegucigalpa in the extreme south, was a source for long-term, cumulative deposition of mercury into the environment. Although recycling of mercury occurred, ultimately all the mercury imported into Mexico dissipated. Miners assumed that 1 to 1.5 kilograms of mercury would be lost for each 1 kilogram of silver produced. Some losses were due to spillage in transit; some to mercury residue in the wastewater. Other losses resulted from binding of mercury in insoluble compounds to sulfide, chloride, or other salts in the ore. Some, perhaps most, of the losses occurred in vaporization of mercury. Whatever the specific path, all imported mercury moved into air, water, or soil sinks.

Obviously, the consequences for human health were great. Men working in the refinery were at great risk of chronic and perhaps even acute mercury poisoning. Those laborers who stirred the milled ore and its infusion of mercury on the patio undoubtedly absorbed mercury through their skin (especially into cuts and lesions), breathed mercury-laden vapors, and ingested mercury-infused dust on their hands when they ate. Any workers in the refinery would have similar absorption of mercury over time.[97] All miners and all who lived in the mining center were also at risk.

Today the effects of chronic inorganic or organic mercury exposure are well known: "Symptoms may include a metallic taste and excessive production of saliva; inflammation of the membranes of the mouth; loosening of the teeth; the formation of a blue line on the gums; pain, numbness and tremor in the extremities; loss of weight and appetite; and mental and personal changes marked by depression and a tendency to withdraw."[98] Acute mercury poisoning is marked by lung damage, nausea, vomiting, diarrhea, heightened blood pressure and heart rate, skin rashes, and even death from respiratory failure.[99]

96. This total was supplied by John J. TePaske in a personal communication. For the years 1564–1700, TePaske derives his figures from Bakewell, *Silver Mining and Society in Colonial Mexico.* Average exports of mercury are calculated from quinquennial figures for New Spain on p. 254, table 10a. Only 936 metric tons of mercury came from Peru and 3,479 metric tons from Idrija in present-day Yugoslavia—all in the eighteenth century. Almadén in Spain shipped by far the largest amount to Mexico in the colonial period.

97. Mark R. Malecki, "Regulating Mercury in Miners' Eating Areas," *Public Health Reports* 113, no. 2 (1998): 179–82.

98. "Mercury Poisoning," Encyclopædia Britannica Online. See also "Mercury Fact Sheet," U.S. Agency for Toxic Substances and Disease Registry.

99. A 1996 clinical study of those suffering from "elemental mercury intoxication" revealed "significant depression of performance [and] intellectual functioning[;] impairments of attention, non-verbal short-term memory and visual judgements of angles and directions[;] psy-

There is no question that day after day, year after year, at each mining center, waste mercury moved into the air, the water, and the soil.[100] Food and water consumed by humans, animals, and birds was contaminated.[101] Plants growing in the region absorbed inorganic mercury. Bacteria in water and soil combined mercury with carbon to form organic or methylmercury that could rise through the food chain. Local market demand encouraged production of food crops and garden crops in the vicinity of the mines. Fish in the freshwater streams of the mining regions absorbed mercury.

This was unremitting deposition, since the mines rarely, if ever, shut down, but operated year after year without pause. Although occupational illness of the largely Indian miners of New Spain does not seem to have been noticed by observers at the time, it is hard to conceive how successive generations of miners and their families could have avoided the harmful effects of mercury exposure. Recent studies of mercury-afflicted peoples today in the gold-mining regions of the Brazilian Amazon and of Inuit groups in the Canadian Arctic have documented declines in the health and well-being of these communities.[102]

An as-yet-unanswered question is the extent to which mercury from the mines found its way through the freshwater drainage system to the lowland

---

chomotor retardation and personality changes including depression, anxiety, desire to be alone, lack of interest and sensitivity to physical problems." M. S. Hua, C. C. Huang, and Y. J. Yang, "Chronic Elemental Mercury Intoxication: Neuropsychological Follow-up Case Study," *Brain Injury* 10, no. 5 (1996).

100. Jerome O. Nriagu, "Mercury Pollution from the Past Mining of Gold and Silver in the Americas," *Science of the Total Environment* 149 (1994).

101. For methylmercury concentrations and devastating symptoms in birds, see N. Fimreite, "Accumulation and Effects of Mercury on Birds," in *The Biogeochemistry of Mercury in the Environment,* edited by Jerome O. Nriagu (Amsterdam: Elsevier and North-Holland Biomedical Press, 1979). Tissue samples taken from deer feeding in the area around the Idrija mercury mine in Slovenia during the early 1990s revealed that total mercury content was one hundred times higher than the content detected in control animals. A. Ganamus, M. Horvat, and P. Stegnar, "The Mercury Content among Deer and of Browsed Foliage as a Means of Ascertaining Environmental Pollution of the Mining Regions of Idrija—a Case Study from Slovenia," *Zeitschrift fuer Jagdwissenschaft* 41, no. 3 (1995). Humans on-site suffered similar exposure during the five hundred years of the mine's operation before it closed in 1995. Despite attempts to reduce risk by limiting work hours and controlling waste, miners at the Idrija mine in Slovenia in the early 1960s who were identified as having mercury poisoning numbered between 10 and 14 percent of all workers employed at the mine. A. Kobal and T. Dizdarevic, "The Health Safety Programme for Workers Exposed to Elemental Mercury at the Mercury Mine in Idrija," *Water, Air, and Soil Pollution* 97 (1997): 192.

102. Margaret A. Wheatley, "Social and Cultural Impacts of Mercury Pollution on Aboriginal Peoples in Canada," *Water, Air, and Soil Pollution* 97 (1997); Philippe Grandjean et al., "Methylmercury Neurotoxicity in Amazonian Children Downstream from Gold Mining," *Environmental Health Perspectives* 107 (1999); M. Roulet et al., "Effects of Recent Human Colonization on the Presence of Mercury in Amazonian Ecosystems," *Water, Air, and Soil Pollution* 112 (1999).

areas of Mexico.[103] It is likely that dissolved and perhaps even particulate mercury from the mines reached the river deltas and bays of both the Atlantic and Pacific Coasts. What is certain, however, is that the atmosphere picked up and carried gaseous and particulate mercury throughout Mexico and into worldwide atmospheric wind patterns.[104] A recent estimate is that about 60 percent of the mercury used in the patio process dissipated into the atmosphere at the time of amalgamation. Between 1568 and 1816, the annual average flux for Mexico would have been 150 metric tons of mercury per year, for a total release of 38,882 tons.[105]

ECOLOGICAL AND ECONOMIC CRISIS

Between the early sixteenth and early nineteenth centuries, from conquest to independence, the livestock and mining sectors were two principal drivers of the colonial economy of Mexico. Both industries had profound effects on the landscape, ecology, and human society of Mexico. For three centuries, the economy of colonial Mexico supported a steadily growing population and generated a surplus of production shipped to other colonial markets in North America and to Spain. Both industries were closely tied to the emerging world economy. Mexican silver helped fuel the economic development and political centralization of the early modern world. For nearly three centuries, Spanish exploitation of Mexican resources was apparently sustainable. Obviously, silver was a nonrenewable resource and once gone, was gone. However, the land continued to support several million livestock each year and to produce food grains and other products to feed and clothe a

103. P. Benes and B. Havlik, "Speciation of Mercury in Natural Waters," in *The Biogeochemistry of Mercury in the Environment,* edited by Jerome O. Nriagu (Amsterdam: Elsevier and North-Holland Biomedical Press, 1979).

104. Evidence from core samples bored in a Spanish ombotrophic peat bog covering a four-thousand-year period is suggestive. Atmospheric mercury traveled six hundred kilometers from the Almadén mine to the bog. Depositions of mercury found in the core samples mirror the working of the Almadén mine. A. Martinez-Cortizas et al., "Mercury in a Spanish Peat Bog: Archive of Climate Change and Atmospheric Metal Deposition," *Science* 284, no. 5416 (1999).

105. Nriagu, "Mercury Pollution from the Past Mining of Gold and Silver in the Americas," 179. Nriagu calculates that the total colonial Spanish American flux between 1580 and 1820 would have averaged 316 metric tons per year, for a total of 75,840 metric tons of mercury for the 240 years. Currently, annual worldwide mercury emissions from human activities total between 2,000 and 3,400 metric tons. John Douglas, "Mercury and the Global Environment," *EPRI Journal* 19, no. 3 (1994): 16. For fluxes, budgets, and schematic diagrams of the mercury biogeochemical cycle, see Anders W. Andren, "The Global Cycle of Mercury," in *The Biogeochemistry of Mercury in the Environment,* edited by Jerome O. Nriagu (Amsterdam: Elsevier and North-Holland Biomedical Press, 1979).

steadily growing population risen fourfold, from 1.5 million in the mid-1600s to 6 million by 1800.[106]

By the mid- to late 1700s, signs of ecological distress and economic strain appeared. Part of this distress appears to have resulted from a significant shift in long-term climate patterns. Both documentary and proxy evidence from the Basin of Mexico suggest that the Aztec period (1345–1521) and the early years of the Spanish conquest through 1590 were relatively wet. There were few drought years, and in some years rainfall was copious to the point of causing high lake levels and even flooding in central Mexico.[107] By the end of the sixteenth century, however, the climate of central Mexico was progressively drier. Given the tight linkage between annual summer precipitation and agriculture throughout Mexico, this was a serious disability. In contrast to the moister conditions earlier, Mexican climate in the seventeenth through the nineteenth centuries was "characterized by prolonged drought interspersed by brief wetter episodes."[108]

The colonial drying trend culminated in a series of devastating drought years during the late 1700s and early 1800s. The weather diary of Don Felipe de Zuniga y Otiveras records increasing dryness in the critical months of May and June, when rain was needed for the newly planted maize crops. The years 1775, 1776, 1777, 1778, 1779, and 1780 "were too dry for maize producers in the valley of Mexico."[109] A respite over the next three years, in 1781–1784, ended in 1785 with a nine-month drought and autumn frosts. Catastrophic crop failures brought on the famine of 1785–1786, the "Year of Great Hunger."[110] Drought conditions continued over the next decades. Late spring droughts in 1791, 1793, and 1797 caused harvest failures and in-

106. Nicholas Sanchez-Albornoz, "The Population of Colonial Spanish America," in *The Cambridge History of Latin America*, edited by Leslie Bethell (Cambridge: Cambridge University Press, 1984), 2:34; Richard L. Garner and Spiro E. Stefanou, *Economic Growth and Change in Bourbon Mexico* (Gainesville: University Press of Florida, 1993), 15–17.

107. Georgina H. Endfield and Sarah L. O'Hara, "Conflicts over Water in 'The Little Drought Age' in Central Mexico," *Environment and History* 3 (1997): 257; Sarah L. O'Hara and Sarah E. Metcalfe, "Reconstructing the Climate of Mexico from Historical Records," *The Holocene* 5, no. 4 (1995): 489.

108. O'Hara and Metcalfe, "Reconstructing the Climate of Mexico from Historical Records," 489.

109. Arij Ouweneel, *Shadows over Anáhuac: An Ecological Interpretation of Crisis and Development in Central Mexico, 1730–1800*, 1st ed. (Albuquerque: University of New Mexico Press, 1996), 83. See also C. Gibson, *The Aztecs under Spanish Rule*, appendix 5: "1785. Rainy season delayed; drought in May; almost all maize destroyed by severe frost August 27; shortages began in September; sharp increase in price in last months of the year" (45).

110. Endfield and O'Hara, "Conflicts over Water in 'The Little Drought Age' in Central Mexico," 261; Susan L. Swan, "Mexico in the Little Ice Age," *Journal of Interdisciplinary History* 11 (1981): 638.

creased mortality.[111] The extreme droughts after 1785–1786 took place in a four-year sequence between 1808 and 1811, when crop failures brought famine conditions at the onset of the revolution.

By the late colonial period, Mexicans were pressing the limits of the land as signs of environmental degradation accompanied drought. For example, in the Michoacan region of western Mexico, in the Bajío region of central Mexico, and elsewhere, data from sediment cores and archives reveal increased soil erosion and degradation of vegetation. Fuelwood supplies became harder to obtain because of progressive deforestation. Flooding grew more violent. Long-term pressure from Spanish colonial plow agriculture, livestock grazing, and urban energy demands seems to have had a cumulative effect on the land.[112]

Rising human numbers in late colonial Mexico stimulated intensified land use as settlement and cultivation expanded into previously marginal and less fertile lands. Hacienda owners invested in improving land by clearing and irrigating formerly grazed tracts to add fields for plow cultivation of wheat.[113] Whether this tendency brought an overall reduction in livestock raising during the eighteenth century is not clear, in the absence of systematic research on this point. Ranchers may have kept their herd sizes constant and either raised their stocking ratios or pushed cattle and sheep into previously unused lands. Either alternative would have contributed to possible land degradation.

Prices in the land market moved upward at about 1 percent per year (a seventy-year doubling) throughout the century, with generally greater increases for nonirrigated, less desirable land. As demand for land grew, legal and extralegal conflicts over land, at times violent, flared up more conspicuously in the eighteenth century than ever before. Many of these struggles grew out of attempts by Indian communities to resist land purchases and usurpation by owners of large haciendas. Often they involved Indian attempts to recover communal lands lost in earlier periods to Spanish colonialists.[114]

Food security in New Spain became precarious by the end of the eighteenth century as Mexican estate owners, tenant farmers, and Indian communities struggled to grow more food. Building stocks of food grains to meet the shock of drought years became difficult. Yields of the basic crops probably did not increase. There is no evidence that estate owners experimented

111. Ouweneel, *Shadows over Anáhuac*, 91.

112. Georgina H. Endfield and Sarah L. O'Hara, "Degradation, Drought, and Dissent: An Environmental History of Colonial Michoacan, West Central Mexico," *Annals of the Association of American Geographers* 89 (1999); Butzer and Butzer, "Transfer of the Mediterranean Livestock Economy to New Spain," 178–79.

113. Garner, "Long-Term Silver Mining Trends in Spanish America," 68.

114. Endfield and O'Hara, "Degradation, Drought, and Dissent."

with, adopted, or even discussed new techniques to improve yields. Whether smallholders, especially Indian farmers, worked harder in a form of involution to produce more is an unanswered question. The only noticeable response was to press cultivation into marginal lands.[115]

Maize was not only the preferred staple food for Indians and a minority of Spanish, mestizos, and blacks but also the basic feed grain for livestock. Over the century, maize production rates probably grew at a rate equivalent to the rise in population (.8 to 1.2 percent per year), from 175,000 to 265,000 metric tons annually. There is some evidence that, by the end of the century, the supply of maize had become inelastic as prices rose at three times the level of the increase in supply.[116] Maize farming tended to be "relegated to marginal lands cultivated by poor tenants [where] production failed to keep pace with population growth."[117]

Late colonial Mexico, like a number of other early modern societies, had begun to press hard against its land and natural resources. Rising scarcities of food, fuel, water, and fertile land were symptoms of a serious ecological crisis.

CONCLUSION

The Spanish conquest and occupation of Mexico set in motion a pioneer expansion characteristic of other early modern settlement frontiers. From their initial bases centered on the coast at Veracruz and the valley of Mexico City, Spanish explorers, soldiers, priests and friars, miners, ranchers, and traders steadily enlarged the area of Spanish settlement. Spanish frontiersmen built roads, colonial towns, presidios or forts, mission stations, and mining stations as they settled new lands. When less-tractable Indians resisted, the colonial state supplied limited, but continuing, military and diplomatic support for its frontiersmen.

Colonial Mexico diverged somewhat from the model of intensifying land use that distinguished most settlement frontiers. Where Spanish settlers occupied lands formerly occupied and cultivated by Indian populations, land use became less, rather than more, intensive. The stream of migrants arriving in Mexico from Spain or from the Caribbean islands was not sufficient to replace the massive numbers of Indians who died from epidemic disease—even over the course of three centuries.

Silver profits drove frontier expansion in colonial Mexico. Often, exploratory parties ranging beyond the frontier line made silver strikes and es-

115. Garner and Stefanou, *Economic Growth and Change in Bourbon Mexico*, 67.
116. Ibid., 41.
117. Ibid., 46. Garner is quoting John Tutino from his case study of Silao parish in the upper Bajío.

tablished mining centers well beyond existing Spanish colonial settlement and control. Profits to be made by the state and by individuals drew Spanish and Indian settlers as well as African slaves to the new mines. The need to protect these remote centers from Indian attack, to provision and supply them, and to bring out the refined metal meant that settlement followed the roads leading to the mines.

Mining for silver drove the colonial economy and put in motion trade and production aimed at supporting the highest possible output of each mine. The mines had both direct and diffused impacts on the natural environment—especially from vast amounts of mercury used in the refining process and diffused into soils, water, and air.

Commercial pastoralism—ranching—was the other stimulus to frontier expansion. Ranchers were among the most avid of pioneer settlers in New Spain. Arriving with a long-standing bias toward and understanding of livestock raising, and avid desire for meat, hides, and wool, the Spanish bred enormous herds in just a few years. Dispersal of multitudes of cattle, sheep, horses, mules, burros, and goats across the landscape and their continued grazing and browsing altered the vegetation and, to some extent, the soil cover of much of Mexico. In some regions, overstocking clearly put unsustainable pressures on the land—pressures leading to environmental degradation within a relatively short time span. For most of Mexico, however, a new agropastoral economy proved to be sustainable and resilient until signs of an ecological crisis developed in the last decades of colonial rule.

The insertion of Eurasian livestock into habitats and lands where such animals had been absent since prehistory was one of the most important imprints made by Spanish rule on the environment of Mexico—second only to the inadvertent destruction of most of the Indian populations by disease, which in turn permitted free use of abandoned lands for grazing.

Chapter 11

Sugar and Cattle
in Portuguese Brazil

Beginning in the early sixteenth century, the Portuguese monarchy organized and encouraged colonial settlement on the Atlantic Coast of Brazil. For European settlement to succeed, the land had to be emptied. Its existing inhabitants, the Brazilian Indians, were either assimilated, put to work as dependents or slaves, driven from their lands, or killed. As in other New World populations, high death rates from introduced diseases greatly aided the Portuguese in this great colonial project. Most of the known Indian groups died out completely from disease, enslavement, and war. Groups that did survive suffered enormous losses. Ruthless colonial wars aimed at removing and exterminating Indians who showed any sign of organized resistance continued well into the nineteenth century.[1]

This was an audacious enterprise for a nation with a total home population of 1.5 million persons in the mid-1500s already stretched thin by ambitious colonial expansion in Asia and Africa. The total land area in Brazil open to exploration and settlement after conquest was 8.5 million square kilometers—ninety-six times the size of Portugal (eighty-five thousand square kilometers). Needless to say, the Portuguese did not succeed in settling or colonizing more than a portion of this vast area—even over three centuries. At independence, in 1826, Brazil's colonial population—3.6 million Europeans and black Africans and eight hundred thousand still-unassimilated Indians—averaged only one-half person per square kilometer. It was simply impossible for the small colonial population to exploit fully the abundant natural resources of Brazil's vast territories, much less to clear, settle, and plow

1. B. J. Barickman, " 'Tame Indians,' 'Wild Heathens,' and Settlers in Southern Bahia in the Late Eighteenth and Early Nineteenth Centuries," *Americas* 51 (1995). See also J. Hemming, *Amazon Frontier: The Defeat of the Brazilian Indians* (Cambridge: Harvard University Press, 1987).

forests and savannas. By far the most extensive changes in Brazil's lands have occurred in the nineteenth and twentieth centuries.

The first Portuguese mariners who landed on the eastern shore of Brazil in 1500 found themselves on the edge of a massive subtropical and tropical forest covering about a million square kilometers. In 1500, the Brazilian Atlantic forest stretched along the eastern coast from eight degrees south to twenty-eight degrees south latitude, and extended inland in a band one hundred kilometers wide at its northern tip, gradually increasing to five hundred kilometers in the south. Today, that entire forest has been reduced to bits and remnants of the original formation.[2] Running the length of the forest, just a few kilometers inland, rises a near continuous headwall, or palisade, several hundred to as many as a thousand meters high. Behind this, other hill chains lie parallel to the coast. Moisture-laden eastern trade winds from the warm equatorial Atlantic blow steadily much of the year against this escarpment and bring consistently heavy rainfall.

Moving directly west and inland from the shoreline, the early Portuguese first encountered mangrove formations followed by stands of great broadleaf evergreens as much as forty meters tall with trunks twelve meters in circumference. This was true canopied and layered tropical forest with epiphytes and lianas, which extended up the face of the palisade wall. On the palisade heights, there grew a less imposing cloud forest of differing species. Beyond the heights, in montane valleys, the Portuguese found once again broadleaf evergreens merging with broadleaf deciduous formations. On the western edge of the Atlantic forest, they reached the semiarid thornbrush scrubland and grasslands of the *sertão*, or outback. To the south in the subtropical highlands, where frosts began, were stands of *Araucaria angustifolia*, the hardy conifer that invades grasslands—probably a precursor to the broadleaf evergreens.

When the Portuguese arrived, the Atlantic forest, far from uninhabited and pristine, was already under systematic human assault. The bellicose, confident Tupis consisted of several distinct tribes of coastal Indians speaking a shared language.[3] About one thousand years before, the Tupis had migrated from the interior to the coast and driven out earlier inhabitants of the Atlantic forest. Although they seem to have been expanding in numbers throughout the ensuing centuries, the Tupis had not reached any sort of re-

2. Warren Dean, *With Broadax and Firebrand: The Destruction of the Brazilian Atlantic Forest* (Berkeley and Los Angeles: University of California Press, 1995).
3. J. Hemming, *Red Gold: The Conquest of the Brazilian Indians*, rev. ed. (London: Papermac, 1995), 54.

source crisis. In 1500, there were about 1 million Brazilian Indians living along the coast in the three thousand kilometers from Natal in Rio Grande do Norte in the north to São Vincente and São Paulo in the south.[4] Overall density probably did not exceed three to four persons per square kilometer.

All European observers agree that the Tupis were extraordinarily muscular, energetic, and healthy people whose varied diet was obviously adequate to their needs. Neither in their religious observances nor in their everyday practices was there evidence of any attention to conservation. By and large, the Tupis had a buoyant view of the unlimited resources available to them and did not concern themselves overmuch with the future.[5]

The coastal Indians of Brazil were shifting cultivators of manioc, beans, peanuts, tobacco, and some maize, who had substantially altered composition of the forest. The Tupis planted burnt-over forest plots for two to three seasons before abandoning the plot to fallow for perhaps twenty to forty years and moving to a new burnt patch. Tupi males were avid hunters. Armed with bows and arrows and lethal war clubs, they hunted and consumed all the larger animals of the forest—jaguars, deer, turtles, crocodiles, tapir, agoutis, sloths, armadillos, and monkeys. Both men and women trapped and gathered dozens of species of fish and shellfish in the estuaries and along the beaches. The Tupis also smoked meat, dried fish, and roasted manioc meal; they kept these supplies in large caches.

The communal wooden longhouses of Tupi villages contained on average six hundred persons living in an enclosed stockaded site measuring from five hundred to as much as a thousand meters across. They favored estuarine sites with easy access to the resources of sea and shore as well as forest. From details embedded in sixteenth-century chronicles, Warren Dean estimates that each village controlled a hinterland of about seventy square kilometers, or an average of about nine persons per square kilometer. Between villages were uninhabited buffer zones that reduced the overall density. Postulating .2 hectares of forest cleared per person per year, the entire village hinterland would have been cut and burnt in just over a half century. But it is likely the Tupis returned more frequently to regrown areas that were easier to clear and less dangerous to burn. Archaeological and other evidence suggests that

4. Ibid., 486–501, appendix. Hemming has done a region-by-region and group-by-group estimate of the 1500 population. His total for all Brazilian Indians was 2,432,000 persons. The stretch of coast mentioned includes the territories actually occupied by Portuguese settlements before 1600. See his map 1, on p. xviii. The regions of sixteenth-century encounter include São Paulo State, 146,000 Indians; Southern Mato Grosso, 118,000; Guanabara, Rio de Janeiro, 97,000; Espírito Santo, Ilhéus, 160,000; Minas Gerais, 91,000; Bahía 149,000; São Francisco Valley, 100,000; and Northeast Coast, 208,000, for a total of 969,000. Simply assuming a region of contact 100 kilometers deep for a region of 300,000 square kilometers puts the density at 3.2 persons per square kilometer.

5. Dean, *With Broadax and Firebrand*, 36.

the Tupis moved their village sites relatively frequently, such as when, among other reasons, they were defeated in their constant internecine warfare, the village wooden longhouses went up in flames, or hostile factions emerged within the village.[6]

Early modern Europeans were fascinated and repelled by the seeming innocence of the Tupis. Much to their discomfort, both Tupi men and women were unabashedly naked. They did paint their bodies with decorative black and red dyes, and wore brilliantly colored feather headdresses and decorations, but they needed no more covering than that in the warm climate of coastal Brazil. To the consternation of early modern Europeans, Tupis of both sexes bathed daily, and frequently several times a day. According to Jean de Léry, a French Huguenot pastor who came to Brazil as part of the first Protestant mission to the Indians, "Whenever they come upon springs and clear rivers, crouching on the edge or else getting in, they throw water on their heads with both hands, and wash themselves and plunge in with their whole bodies like ducks—on some days more than a dozen times."[7]

In contrast to peaceable Indian groups like the Tainos of the Caribbean, the Tupis were impressively devoted to war. Energetic, brutal, stylized warfare was the primary preoccupation of Tupi society. As the sixteenth-century historian Pero de Magalhães Gandavo comments, the Tupi "are well set up, lusty and of good stature; a very brave people who esteem death lightly, daring in war and very little prudence. They are very ungrateful, inhuman and cruel, inclined to fight and extremely vindictive."[8] This was warfare carried out for vengeance and honor, not for territorial conquest, as Tupi groups eagerly fought among themselves or launched raids against neighboring peoples. A Tupi war party readily traveled several hundred kilometers overland through the forest on foot, or in forty- to fifty-man war canoes along the rivers, to raid the settlements of their foes.

Lacking metals, Tupi warriors wielded heavy sword-clubs of hardened wood with keenly sharpened edges, which measured one and a half to two meters long, and bucklers of thick, dried tapir leather. Their most formidable weapon was the longbow. Tupi men were superb archers capable of accurate rapid fire with long, straight bamboo or reed arrows. Occasional, deadly pitched battles occurred between the opposing Indian parties, in which several thousand combatants engaged in desperate hand-to-hand combat. Only after sanguinary losses on both sides could one army prevail and either drive off or capture the defeated survivors.

To the Europeans, the most horrific aspect of Tupi culture was its ferocity

---

6. Ibid., 30–33.

7. Jean de Léry, *History of a Voyage to the Land of Brazil, Otherwise Called America* (Berkeley and Los Angeles: University of California Press, 1990), 66.

8. Pero de Magalhães Gandavo, *The Histories of Brazil* (Boston: Milford House, 1972), 85.

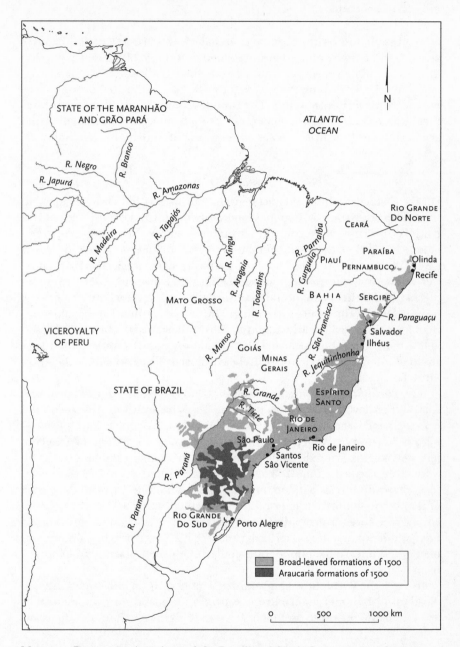

Map 11.1 Portuguese America and the Brazilian Atlantic forest, 1750. Adapted
from A. J. R. Russell-Wood, *A World on the Move: The Portuguese in Africa, Asia, and
America, 1415–1808* (New York: St. Martin's Press, 1993), p. 142, and Warren Dean,
With Broadax and Firebrand: The Destruction of the Brazilian Atlantic Forest (Berkeley
and Los Angeles: University of California Press, 1995), map 1, p. 3.

as expressed most vividly in ritual cannibalism. The Tupis kept war captives alive for some time before they were killed by a single blow from a war club in a great public ceremony. Immediately their bodies were dismembered and roasted over fires on the *boucan*, or grill. All present ate portions of the enemy with great enthusiasm. The proudest boast of the Tupi warrior was that he had eaten the kinsmen of those whom he fought. Dozens of firsthand accounts record the grisly details of the eating of humans by the Tupis.[9]

BRAZILWOOD

For the first half century, contact between Europeans and Tupis occurred in the context of trade, not conquest and settlement. Unlike the Tainos of Hispaniola, the Tupis wore colorful bird plumes and polished stones of green jadeite but had no gold ornaments and seemed to have no access to gold or silver. Without the prize of precious metals to drive them, the Portuguese were slow to create permanent settlements and, instead, created trading posts visited by fleets financed by consortia of Lisbon merchants.[10] Both the terrain and the Tupis were forbidding. The densely settled Tupis could more than hold their own in early violent clashes even against the firearms, horses, and armor of the Europeans. The fact that encounters were limited constrained infection. Pandemics with heavy mortality did not attack the Tupis until the 1550s.

The Portuguese obtained valuable brazilwood, exotic jaguar skins, parrots, and enslaved war captives from the Tupis in return for much-coveted iron tools and weapons. Portuguese and French ships came to barter for supplies of brazilwood, which grew in abundance in the north in an area centered on Recife, around Rio de Janeiro, and in southern Bahia. The brazilwood tree was a legume *(Caesalpinia echinata)* that grew successfully in second-growth forests both on the coast and inland. The Tupis used the core of the tree to color their cotton fibers. When cut open and exposed to the air, the tree core turns rapidly from golden color to a bright orange-red and then, when put in water, to reddish violet.[11] This New World brazilwood supplemented uncertain supplies of a similar tree called brazilwood exported from Asia.

In 1502, the Portuguese king awarded a monopoly on brazilwood to a syndicate of Lisbon merchants. Rising European demand for dyes for textiles and inks made the trade profitable at a rate of eighty to a hundred thousand

9. De Léry devotes an entire chapter to this subject (*History of a Voyage to the Land of Brazil, Otherwise Called America*, 122–33).

10. Harold B. Johnson, "The Portuguese Settlement of Brazil, 1500–1800," in *The Cambridge History of Latin America*, edited by Leslie Bethell (Cambridge: Cambridge University Press, 1984), 1:255–56.

11. Dean, *With Broadax and Firebrand*, 45.

pounds sterling per year. The French also used brazilwood in making cabinets and fine furniture. Ignoring the royal Portuguese monopoly, interloping French traders sailed for the coast of Brazil and traded for brazilwood. The brazilwood traders also profited by the sale of Indian slaves, primarily war captives bought and saved from barbecuing by the Tupis, and colorful and exotic parrots, parakeets, and other fauna, as well as thousands of jaguar skins.

Portuguese and French factors bartered laborsaving steel knives and axes, iron fishhooks, and other artifacts with the Tupis for supplies of brazilwood. Tupis found and cut brazilwood trees with their new axes, stripped the bark and cortex, cut them into shorter sections weighing twenty to thirty kilograms, and hand carried them to the traders at their landing sites. Dean estimates that brazilwood shipped over the sixteenth century averaged 8,000 metric tons per year.[12] This figure implies that several thousand Tupis labored to supply the equivalent of 320,000 twenty-five-kilogram sections. Over the century, nearly 2 million brazilwood trees were felled. At four trees per hectare, and with each measuring fifty centimeters in diameter, this would have affected some six thousand square kilometers of forest.

Although the Tupis were more than willing to cut and haul brazilwood in return for trade goods valuable to them, they were intrigued and surprised by the covetousness of the Europeans. De Léry observed, "Our Tupinamba are astonished to see the French and others from distant countries go to so much trouble to get their *araboutan* or brazilwood." After a lengthy exchange, a Tupi elder commented astringently:

> "Truly," said my elder (who as you will judge was no dullard), "I see now that you Mairs (that is[,] Frenchmen) are great fools; must you labor so hard to cross the sea, on which (as you told us) you endured so many hardships, just to amass riches for your children or those who will survive you? Will not the earth that nourishes you suffice to nourish them? We have kinsmen and children, whom, as you see, we love and cherish; but because we are certain that after our death the earth which has nourished us will nourish them, we rest easy and do not trouble ourselves further about it."[13]

This comment echoed many similar opinions expressed by inhabitants of the New World as they tried to comprehend the avarice of these strangers and the social logic that lay behind it. Even as the Tupis struggled with these notions, they were being caught up in the entangling appeal of early modern markets. Undoubtedly, they better understood the obsessions of the Euro-

12. Ibid., 46; José Jobson de Andrade Arruda, "Colonies as Mercantile Investments: The Luso-Brazilian Empire, 1500–1809," in *The Political Economy of Merchant Empires,* edited by James D. Tracy (Cambridge: Cambridge University Press, 1991), 373.

13. De Léry, *History of a Voyage to the Land of Brazil, Otherwise Called America,* 100–101.

peans from their own experiences of accumulation. In the end, however, this knowledge did not save them from the brutalities of Portuguese settlement.

SETTLEMENT AND POPULATION

In 1530, the king of Portugal sent a five-ship fleet under Martim Afonso de Sousa carrying four hundred settlers, seeds, domestic animals, and plants to coastal Brazil. The Crown's decision to settle Brazil was in large part due to the intensifying French legal challenge to the papal grant of sole access to Brazil and the aggressive French pursuit of brazilwood.[14] After two years spent cruising along the coast, attacking French brazilwood traders, trading with the Indians, and searching for reports of precious metals, de Sousa decided to place the first colony in the far south at São Vicente, near the modern port of Santos and in a settlement inland near São Paulo.

King João III (r. 1521–1557), to encourage colonization, divided the four thousand kilometers of coastline into fourteen "captaincies" whose reach extended inland to the papal boundary. Each grantee was given hereditary rights over his vast lands. He could reserve up to sixty-five kilometers of coast for himself as a private estate, make grants of lands to others, found towns, and administer civil and criminal justice. All products could be freely exported, save for brazilwood and a few spices. The grantee could enslave and work any number of Indians in Brazil or on his ships but could export only twenty-four per year to Portugal.[15]

One difficulty lay in finding colonists from among a Portuguese home population that numbered no more than 1.5 million in the 1530s. Only *degredados*—convicted criminals or political exiles—were easily obtained. As a result, the first settlers were relatively few. In the 1540s, before the arrival of a royal governor, Indian attacks wiped out two initial settlements at Bahia and São Tome and severely curtailed growth in the others. Although the Tupis were at a disadvantage against Portuguese harquebuses and cannons, they could and did overwhelm the colonists' defenses by sheer numbers and aggressive attacks. The Tupis had been more than willing to cut brazilwood to trade, but as soon as the settlers began to enslave Indians to work on their newly planted holdings, hostilities broke out.

Private proprietary settlement proved to be a temporary expedient as the royally appointed captains faltered in the face of determined Indian resistance. Within twenty years, the Portuguese king sent a royal governor to take charge of the colony. In 1549, Tome de Sousa arrived with a cadre of officials in a large fleet organized and paid for by the king. The viceroy's fleet carried a complete biological and cultural package. The passengers totaled nearly

14. Johnson, "The Portuguese Settlement of Brazil," 1:260.
15. Hemming, *Red Gold*, 36; Johnson, "The Portuguese Settlement of Brazil," 1:260.

1,000 Portuguese settlers, including 400 exiled convicts and political prisoners, 300 soldiers and officials, 200 free colonists, and 6 Jesuits. The cargo also included cattle and other domesticated animals and birds from the Atlantic islands, as well as seeds and cuttings for European grains, fruits, and vegetables. Although not listed on the manifests, quantities of pathogens sufficient to cause the subsequent epidemics of the 1550s also rode with their hosts across the Atlantic.

The third royal governor, Mem de Sa, an experienced soldier, shifted from a defensive to an offensive posture against the Indians. He led a series of devastating campaigns against the Tupi-speaking Indian groups that controlled the Atlantic Coast from Recife to Ilhéus. De Sa announced that peaceful Indians who accepted Christianity under the newly arrived Jesuit auspices would be free and could not be enslaved. Others, however, would either be extirpated or enslaved. In one punitive raid, de Sa led a party of Portuguese and friendly Indians against the Tupinikins, who had rebelled against the colonists at Ilhéus on the southern coast. In de Sa's own words:

> I went with the few people who followed me, and on the very night I entered Ilheus I went on foot to attack an *aldeia* that was seven leagues from the town. It was on a small hill all surrounded by water from flooding, which we crossed with much difficulty. Before morning, at two o'clock, I attacked the village and destroyed it and killed all who tried to resist. On the return I came burning and destroying all the villages that lay behind. The heathen assembled and were following me all along the beach. I made some ambushes against them in which I surrounded them, and they were forced to plunge swimming into the sea off the open coast. I ordered other Indians and chosen men to follow them for almost two leagues. They fought there in such a way that no Tupinikin remained alive. And they brought them all on to land and placed them along the beach in order, and their bodies occupied almost one league [four miles].[16]

By the end of this sortie, de Sa had destroyed over three hundred villages, and the surviving Tupinikins had either fled inland or agreed to settle in mission villages run by the Jesuits.

These first battles were a portent of the next three centuries. As the Portuguese pushed inland, they faced violent resistance from hostile Indians long accustomed to warfare, who had to be subdued and either enslaved or driven to flight. In the end, it was not firearms per se that prevailed but grim, unrelenting, aggressive campaigns that included elements of surprise, night attacks, and terror in one blood-drenched encounter after another. Having discovered that the palm-thatched buildings of the Indians burnt readily, the Portuguese systematically torched any village they occupied or passed. The Portuguese recruited and employed Indian allies to devastating effect and in-

16. Hemming, *Red Gold*, 88.

cited internecine warfare between politically fragmented Indian groups. This genocidal warfare resulted in the nearly complete extinction of many ethnic groups.[17] All this was accomplished with relatively few Portuguese troops acting with characteristic daring and brutality.

As in other encounters elsewhere in the New World, newly introduced Eurasian diseases aided the Portuguese. Tupi military victories against the early Portuguese settlers occurred partly because the coastal Indians avoided mass infection by Old World pathogens for a surprisingly long time. Only in the 1550s did the normally remarkably healthy and vigorous Tupis begin to succumb to hemorrhagic dysentery together with influenza, followed in short order by plague (which had struck Portugal in 1561), smallpox, and measles.[18] A virulent smallpox epidemic from 1562 to 1565 swept through the entire coastal region and reached into the interior. Disease mortality combined with the losses from Portuguese military victories caused the Indian population to drop precipitously. From a 1500 population calculated to be 2.4 million, the post-1570 total, according to one estimate, dropped to only one-third that number, or about eight hundred thousand.[19]

Ironically, throughout the greater part of the Atlantic forest, Portuguese colonization actually created a respite from human use. The productive landscape of Tupi agriculture present in 1500 had been largely abandoned a century later. No longer curtailed by Indian fires and axes, forest growth returned.[20] The original inhabitants, the Tupi speakers, had disappeared and the new European and African settlers formed only a tiny population. The Indian population had been virtually cleared out within a radius of three hundred kilometers from each coastal town. Constant Portuguese slave raiding, warfare, and disease depleted the population of the interior. Surviving Indians who fled into the interior gave up horticulture and relied primarily on hunting and gathering in order to remain mobile.

By the 1580s, the colonists had implanted an archipelago of port towns and settlements sufficient to support the Portuguese claim for Brazil. Portuguese Brazil boasted of 60,000 persons, of whom 30,000 were European migrants.[21] By far, the greater number of colonists was to be found in Pernambuco, with its 12,000 settlers, and Bahia, also with 12,000 settlers. As attacks or disease emptied Tupi lands, free Portuguese settlers moved in to take possession. To obtain legal title, squatters had to show that they occupied

17. Maria Luiza Marcilio, "The Population of Colonial Brazil," in *The Cambridge History of Latin America*, edited by Leslie Bethell (Cambridge: Cambridge University Press, 1984), 2:40.
18. Hemming, *Red Gold*, 139–45.
19. Marcilio, *The Population of Colonial Brazil*, 2:41.
20. Dean, *With Broadax and Firebrand*, 62–64.
21. Johnson, "The Portuguese Settlement of Brazil," 1:279, table 1. Johnson shows a total of 29,400 Portuguese settlers distributed among eight captaincies for 1585.

and were working the land. Royal grantees, their governors, and even municipal councils gave out land grants—as large as a square league, or 4,356 hectares—to those settlers who promised to increase production on the land.[22]

Portuguese migrants and imported African slaves continued a modest but steady influx into the colony throughout the seventeenth century. By the end of the century, the total colonial population of Brazil was about 300,000 persons, of whom 100,000 were white European settlers and about 150,000 were black African slaves.[23] Assimilated Indians constituted the remainder. In 1700, that colonial society occupied a settlement area of about sixty-five thousand square kilometers (6.5 percent of the Atlantic forest area). Within this ecological footprint, the settlers had made considerable changes in the forest habitat.[24]

Discovery of gold in 1695 touched off a wave of migration into Brazil. During the course of the eighteenth century, 400,000 persons ignored royal restrictions and migrated to Brazil—far more than had ever done so before.[25] Most of these migrants found their way to the mining regions in the south. The import of black slaves rose just as steeply. From an estimated half million blacks imported into Brazil during the 1600s, the cumulative total nearly quadrupled, to 1.8 million captives arriving during the 1700s.[26]

After three centuries of Portuguese colonization and settlement, the human population in Brazil had nearly doubled—in contrast to the demographic profile of postconquest Mexico and the Caribbean. The European and African migration replaced and eventually exceeded the number of Indians who died. In 1500, just prior to European contact, there were an estimated 2.4 million Indians living in the region that would become Portuguese Brazil.[27] By 1819, just before Brazil formally became an independent nation, the colony's population totaled 4.4 million: 2.5 million free white, mulatto, black, and Indian subjects; 1.1 million black slaves; and approximately 800,000 unassimilated Indians living in Amazonas and Para.[28]

---

22. Between 1624 and 1654, the Dutch West Indies Company forcibly occupied Recife and the northern captaincies of Brazil. Their rule was effectively neutralized by the revolt of Portuguese sugar planters and other colonists in the mid-1640s. While in control, the Dutch continued the production and export of sugar. Their presence did not change the long-term trends of Portuguese rule and is not treated directly in this chapter. See C. R. Boxer, *The Dutch in Brazil, 1624–1654* (Oxford: Clarendon Press, 1957).

23. Marcilio, *The Population of Colonial Brazil*, 2:47, 54.

24. Dean, *With Broadax and Firebrand*, 90.

25. Marcilio, *The Population of Colonial Brazil*, 2:47–48.

26. Ibid., 52–54.

27. Hemming, *Red Gold*, 492.

28. Marcilio, *The Population of Colonial Brazil*, 2:63, table 5.

SUGAR

Although brazilwood and timber were still exported, the primary economic base and link with Lisbon was sugar. The goal of all colonists with sufficient capital was to plant sugar and export it. Pernambuco and Bahia, the leading sugar centers, had favorable climates, rich black and dark red soils, cheap labor from Indian slaves, and low-cost maritime transport, as well as the support of the Portuguese Crown.[29] Rainfall of between one thousand and two thousand millimeters was steady all along the coast. The introduced Creole variety of sugarcane was free of many of the diseases and parasites common in Madeira and the Canaries.

By the 1580s, 115 to 120 sugar mills (engenhos) processed six thousand metric tons of sugar a year to be shipped to Portugal. Brazil quickly outstripped Madeira, the Canaries, and the Antilles, becoming the foremost producer and exporter of cane sugar in the world.[30] Sugar was extraordinarily profitable. By one calculation, every variety of sugar sent from Brazil to Lisbon in the late sixteenth century increased in value 2.5 to 4 times. That is, the merchant who purchased one cruzado worth of sugar at the Brazilian port obtained 2.5 to 4 cruzados at the wholesale price at Lisbon. By 1600, Brazil's exports of sugar were valued at a cost price of 2.16 million pounds sterling equivalent (out of 2.4 million pounds sterling for all exports combined).[31]

Portuguese sugar plantation owners were not nobles but rather commoners who seized on sugar as a means of upward mobility and prosperity. Many succeeded in getting rich, but the Crown did not grant hereditary noble titles to even the most successful of the planters. Planters lived in their great houses on their estates, although proximity to the nearest port settlement enabled them to move back and forth readily enough from the estate to the town. Portuguese sugar planters were scarcely overworked, but they were required to pay close attention to a complex agricultural and industrial enterprise, which had considerable capital tied up in it. Mill machinery, cauldrons, oxen, oxcarts, tools and implements, buildings, and the labor force constituted a large investment.

Brazilian planters discovered early on the importance of scale. The sizeable capital tied up in sugar meant that the best profits came from extensive cane fields and continually busy sugar mills. Plantations were large, a square

29. Stuart B. Schwartz, "Colonial Brazil, c. 1580–c. 1750: Plantations and Peripheries," in *The Cambridge History of Latin America*, edited by Leslie Bethell (Cambridge: Cambridge University Press, 1984), 2:424. Johnson shows 120 *engenhos* located in eight captaincies along the coast. Of these, over half, 66, were in Olinda and Igaracu in Pernambuco and 36 were in Salvador and Vila Velha in Bahia ("The Portuguese Settlement of Brazil," 1:279, table 1).

30. Ibid. See also Stuart B. Schwartz, *Sugar Plantations in the Formation of Brazilian Society: Bahia, 1550–1835* (Cambridge: Cambridge University Press, 1985).

31. De Andrade Arruda, "Colonies as Mercantile Investments," 378.

league or more, and originated in land grants. Cane and food cropping occupied only a portion of these vast estates; the remaining land was given over to forest and rough grazing. Beneath the grand mill-owners was a second group of Portuguese or Brazilian-born white cane-tenants who worked part of the plantation lands on sharecropping or rent contracts. Other small growers held title to their cane fields and contracted for milling with the plantation owner. Each plantation paid wages to a cadre of fifteen or twenty overseers, sugar masters, blacksmiths, carpenters, and other technicians who tended to be free Portuguese or mestizos.

Cane growing in Brazil was a year-round, labor-intensive process with little downtime. Sugarcane matured in fifteen to eighteen months after first planting, but regrew within nine months for another harvest. After several harvests, the juice yield dropped to the point that the cane had to be replanted with fresh cuttings. In Bahia, for example, gangs of slave laborers dug trenches and planted new cuttings in July and August and followed this by a second planting in February and March each year. Each new crop of cane had to be weeded at least three times. Each mill owner tried to schedule his new plantings and those of his cane growers so that fields could be continuously cut over a period of as long as ten months each year. From late July to early May, only repairs, shortages of firewood, holy days, and poor weather interrupted cutting and provided relief to the workforce and animals.[32] When the cane was ripe, slaves cut it with sickles, tied the stalks in bundles, and placed them on oxcarts or boats for transport to the mill. Cane had to be crushed within twenty-four hours or the juice began to ferment.

The crushing mills were driven by either waterwheels or oxen. In the early 1600s, Brazilians adopted an advanced design for their mills with three vertical, metal-covered rollers driven by cogs from a single large drive wheel. The three-roller device was cheaper and squeezed more juice from the cane than the edge-wheel, single millstone system used previously. Sugar mills operated eighteen hours a day, with only six hours for cleaning and repairs. Workers sent the cane through the rollers and ran the sugarcane juice by means of a wooden pipe or channel to a large metal cauldron in the boiling house.

In a lurid scene often likened by observers to the fires of hell, the sugar master supervised the boiling and refining of sugar in the boiling house. In the early 1600s, instead of using a single vat, Brazilian planters adopted a new technique in which they ladled the juice from one to another in a sequence of progressively smaller copper cauldrons with progressively hotter fires. The sugar master and his workers brought the raw juice to near boiling in the largest cauldron so that impurities could be skimmed off. In the next cauldron, they heated the juice again and added either lime or wood ash to help

32. Schwartz, "Colonial Brazil, c. 1580–c. 1750," 2:432–36.

clarification. At the third smaller cauldron they again heated and strained the liquid sugar. They moved the batch through more intensely heated smaller kettles in which the liquid was cooked until it reached a syrupy consistency. Finally, at the last stage, the sugar master declared the batch ready for cooling and molding. This new technique smoothed and speeded the industrial processing of sugar. Sugar boiling in this fashion remained virtually unchanged in Brazil and other New World sugar regions for the next three centuries.

After the syrup cooled, workers poured it into large cone-shaped or bell-shaped pottery molds set by the hundreds on racks with the flared end upward, which were kept in another building, the purging house. The liquid in the pots hardened for about two weeks before workers opened a plugged hole in the bottom of the pot and bored a hole through the sugar. They packed the open face of sugar at the flared end with white clay dampened with water. The water percolated slowly through the pot and carried off any remaining impurities and molasses. After as many as six percolations over a four- to six-week period, sugarhouse workers upended the pot and dropped the now-crystallized loaf of sugar on a board. They separated the white-clayed sugar of the face of the loaf from the golden brown *muscavado* in the middle and the dark-colored sugar at the bottom of the inverted pot. Workers broke up the sugar and packed it in paper-lined wooden crates for shipping; filled crates weighed about 290 kilograms each.

The by-products from claying sugar were another source of profit for the planter. Accumulated wastewater when solidified could be reboiled to produce a poor grade of sugar or, more commonly, simply could be consumed as molasses. In a separate industrial process, planters could distill the molasses to make rum. As a taste for rum developed in Brazil and in Europe, sales and exports increased.

Sugar growing demanded a large, hard-disciplined, and cheap labor force. Each plantation and sugar mill needed on average one hundred field hands, and the largest had work for two hundred slaves. Tenant growers worked a handful to as many as forty slaves, depending on the size of their fields. Free Portuguese and mestizo settlers were unwilling to do fieldwork themselves. They could be hired in supervisory and in technical positions, but not as field hands. Planters turned to the Indian population for the thousands of laborers they needed.

Generally unimpressed by money wages, Tupi men would not willingly labor on sugarcane estates. No amount of metal tools or other goods could entice them to do the tedious field labor of cultivating sugar. Agriculture was for women, and they were warriors and hunters. Early Portuguese settlers at first paid ransoms for the lives of Tupi war captives in order to use them as domestic and field slaves. This practice soon degenerated into inciting Indian tribes to attack others in order to obtain captives for the Portuguese. Finally, the colonists simply engaged in continuous slave raiding among the neighboring Indian groups.

Despite explicit legal opinions that Indians could be enslaved only when captured in a "just" war approved by church and Crown, sugar's appetite for labor led to interpretations that allowed slave raiding at will. Adult Indians were also permitted to sell themselves into slavery. By the 1580s, slaving expeditions into the interior of Bahia brought back two thousand to three thousand captives each year in order to sustain a workforce of some forty thousand Indian slaves in that region alone.[33] Indiscriminate slave raiding exacerbated tensions between the coastal Indians and the Portuguese colonists.

In one armed clash and campaign after another, the colonists steadily wore down Indian resistance. For example, the Portuguese warred with the Potigar tribe for control of the Paraíba River in the area to the north and west of Pernambuco. Between 1574 and 1599, the Potigars supported by the French traders valiantly struggled against Portuguese attacks. After the signing of a peace treaty in 1599, the Portuguese then employed the Potigars as allies in campaigns against the Aimores, another defiant group.[34] Faced with death or enslavement, some remnant groups retreated into the forest, only to be harassed by slavers raiding deeper into the interior. Some groups attempted alliances with the colonists and assisted them in their wars with the French and with hostile Indian groups, only to confront later assaults and betrayals by the Portuguese. Others sought refuge with the Jesuits, who constituted the only organized opposition to wholesale Indian enslavement in Brazil. Moving into mission settlements carried a high price in terms of conversion to Christianity and pressure to give up many of the most prominent features of their culture. Mission Indians were safer, but not entirely secure, from seizure by slavers.

By the 1550s, disease mortality sharply reduced the numbers of Indian slaves and the pool of those who could be recruited. Those Indians confined and concentrated by the Portuguese either as slaves on plantations (40,000 in Bahia alone) or as converts in mission villages organized by the Jesuits were quickly infected. In 1552, at Bahia where the Jesuits had established missions and made converts, bloody dysentery with flulike symptoms killed many Tupis. Two years later, 8,000 Tupis died at Rio de Janeiro from the same affliction. In 1562, bubonic plague killed large numbers of the 40,000 enslaved Indians working for the planters in Bahia.[35] These pandemics were accompanied by starvation, as the surviving Indians failed to plant manioc. Shortly thereafter, in the 1580s and later, smallpox struck repeatedly at Indians in the mission settlements.

33. Hemming, *Red Gold*, 152.
34. Ibid., 161–73.
35. Ibid., 139–46.

Imported African slaves offered an alternative labor supply for sugar growers. Indian slaves were less productive, weaker, and more likely to die from overwork than black slaves. In the seventeenth century, male black Africans could produce enough sugar to earn their replacement cost in thirteen to sixteen months. Imports between 1570 and 1630 averaged 4,000 primarily adult, male African slaves per year. Mortality due to overwork, disease, and abuse, though lower than that experienced by the Indians, remained high, and natural increase was very low. In the late sixteenth century, the total black population in the colony was no more than 15,000. Imports rose to 7,000 to 8,000 per year in the next half century, and by 1650, the black population had reached 150,000. Most black slaves worked as field hands; some who had artisanal skills fared better, and others, mostly mulattos, were domestic servants and, if female, concubines.[36]

Throughout the seventeenth century, the Portuguese sugar colonies dominated the world market. Brazilian sugar exports far outstripped those from Hispaniola, the Canaries, and other sugar-producing regions. In 1650, Brazilian exports rose to 28,500 metric tons and, in 1670, to 27,200 tons.[37] Output dropped off in the 1680s and, thereafter, hovered around 20,000 tons per year until the mid-1700s. It was only in the 1680s that northern European sugar planters in the Caribbean began to surpass Brazilian output. In 1700, British, French, and Dutch colonies processed and shipped approximately 34,000 metric tons of sugar to home markets in Europe.[38]

Sugar growing, with its cane fields, provision gardens, and woodlots, created the same landscape found in the Antilles. In Brazil, however, more land was readily available than on the Caribbean islands. Profitable sugar production relied on unrestrained exploitation of the Atlantic forests. The popular belief was that cane could flourish only on forest soils, and forests must be felled to grow sugar. Sugarcane cuttings planted by hoe in burnt-over forest fields produced consistently high yields without any need for expensive fertilizer or irrigation. When sugar yields started to decline after fifteen to twenty years, planters abandoned those cane fields and carved out new ones from burnt and cleared forestlands. Ample forest reserves supplied fuelwood for the boilers of the sugar mills.

Warren Dean calculates that, by 1700, Brazilian sugarcane fields occupied only about 120 square kilometers of land in an average harvest year, but that,

36. Schwartz, "Colonial Brazil, c. 1580–c. 1750," 2:436–42.
37. See J. H. Galloway, *The Sugar Cane Industry: An Historical Geography from Its Origins to 1914* (Cambridge: Cambridge University Press, 1989), 51, fig. 4.2.
38. In 1700, Barbados, Nevis, Antigua, Montserrat, and Jamaica shipped 24,521 metric tons to home markets, while French planters at Martinique, Guadeloupe, and Saint Christophe (half of Saint Kitts) probably added another 5,000–6,000 tons. The Dutch added 4,090 tons, sent from Suriname. Figures from Noël Deerr, *The History of Sugar* (London: Chapman and Hall, 1949), 1:193–243.

over the previous 150 years, as planters had opened new fields and abandoned old ones, they had stripped 1,000 square kilometers of primary forest for sugar.[39] Local forest degradation around the sugar centers expanded as the industry continued its operations year after year. Fuelwood required for crystallizing the cane juice would have consumed timber from another 1,200 square kilometers of secondary growth and mangrove formations and prevented forest regrowth in the vicinity of sugar production areas.[40]

During the eighteenth century, sugar production declined for a time and then recovered by the end of the century to around twenty thousand metric tons per year. Presumably another 2,400 square kilometers of primary or secondary forest fell to sugar over the century. After independence in the 1820s, planters added new cane fields in response to the abrupt end of sugar production in San Domingue (present-day Haiti). Exports from Brazil went soaring to 99,000 metric tons in 1823.[41] That expansive surge in production would have demanded more than 5,000 square kilometers in cane fields and additional cutting for firewood. Total clearing between 1700 and 1850 would have been 7,400 square kilometers.

TOBACCO

After sugar, tobacco, which was grown primarily in Bahia, had long been the most important cash crop of colonial Brazil. The hinterland of the port of Cachoira at the mouth of the Paraguaçu River was the leading center; smaller zones existed in the coastal plain of the Bay of All Saints and a few other places in Bahia and Pernambuco. Coastal Brazil's sandy, clay soils and hot, humid climate were ideal for growing the tropical variety of tobacco *(Nicotiana tabacum)*.[42] Tobacco growing did not compete with sugar for land or resources but offered an opportunity for men of modest circumstances to make a comfortable living on much smaller holdings. Tobacco planters bought and used slaves and cattle but needed far fewer of them. There was little overlap between sugar and tobacco planters.

Tobacco demanded intensive garden-style cultivation. The planting season began in February, when planters pastured cattle in their tobacco fields

39. Dean, *With Broadax and Firebrand*, 80. Dean's calculations assumed end-of-the-century production of 19,000 metric tons of sugar. At an average 3 percent extractive rate of juice from cane, this would require 633,333 tons of cane produced at 50 tons per hectare for 12,666 hectares, or 126 square kilometers.

40. Ibid., 80.

41. Deerr, *The History of Sugar*, 1:112.

42. In the temperate zone in North America, the native tobacco plant was *Nicotiana rustica*, a smaller and hardier plant with a less flavorful character. Linda Wimmer, "African Producers, European Merchants, Indigenous Consumers: Brazilian Tobacco in the Canadian Fur Trade, 1550–1821" (Ph.D. diss., University of Minnesota, 1996), 205.

to obtain liberal applications of manure—a critical input. In May, after the rainy season had begun, they plowed and tilled the fields and planted tobacco seeds saved from the previous year in planting beds. Three to four weeks later, laborers transplanted the seedlings to the fields. The growing plants required constant weeding and hand removal of a wide variety of insect pests. Workers periodically removed lateral shoots in order to discourage flowering. When the plants reached the desired size, they were topped or capped. Harvesting occurred in September, when workers broke the leaves off the plant by hand and left them in the field overnight to dry. Then they hung up the leaves by their stems in bunches in the curing shed. A second and sometimes a third harvest of less desirable leaves followed.

After hanging and drying the bundles of leaves in the curing shed, workers gradually twisted them into long ropes measuring seven to eight centimeters in diameter that were again hung up to dry. As the ropes dried, a juice or extract dripped from them. Workers gathered this rendered juice and mixed it with additives like molasses, aniseed, basil, and lard. They brushed this sticky liquid, called *mel*, or honey, over the hanging ropes as they dried. This gave the tobacco a rich, distinctive flavor and aroma and helped preserve the dried leaves. After drying and coating each rope, workers wound it tightly around a wooden stick or dowel three-quarters of a meter in length to the required thickness and weight. They wrapped three of these rolls together in a package in palm leaves tied with cords of vine. Then the planter encased the package in hides and branded it with the grower's mark, quality—first, second, or third—and place of origin. This was the "roll" of Brazilian tobacco; it weighed approximately 116 kilograms if it was to be shipped to Europe or North America and 43.5 kilograms if bound for Africa.[43]

Tobacco's environmental imprint was negligible. The tobacco crop in the early 1700s occupied less than 1,000 hectares of land—only a fraction of the 12,000 hectares devoted to sugar fields. In 1800, Bahia's nearly six thousand metric tons of tobacco exports could have been grown on 1,236 hectares.[44]

43. André João Antonil and Afonso de E. Taunay, *Cultura e opulencia do Brazil por suas drogas e minas, com um estudo bio-bibliográfico* (São Paulo: Companhia melhoramentos de São Paulo, 1923), 325, n. 10.

44. The area required to produce 3,263 metric tons of tobacco for export (27,750 rolls) in the early 1700s was probably no more than 685 hectares at a yield of 4.76 tons per hectare. This is based on Andreoni's (Antonil's) figure of 27,500 rolls of tobacco in an average year exported from Bahia and Pernambuco in the early 1700s. The average yield is calculated from data given in Catherine Lugar's table (omitting the figure for less than one acre). Lugar used Andreoni's description and assumed that tobacco plants were set at intervals of 43 to 56 centimeters and rows were about 114 centimeters apart. Lugar, "The Portuguese Tobacco Trade and Tobacco Growers of Bahia in the Late Colonial Period," in *Essays Concerning the Socioeconomic History of Brazil and Portuguese India*, edited by Dauril Alden and Warren Dean (Gainesville: University Presses of Florida, 1977), 34, table 1. Average yield per plant was 368 grams after processing. In

By contrast with sugar, tobacco consumed far less land, human and animal energy, and fuel, but it was an essential Portuguese trade commodity with large returns. Brazilian tobacco, considered the best in the world, played an important role in the Atlantic economy as a means of payment for slaves on the African coast and for furs in French North America.[45] Better quality Brazilian tobacco found a ready market in Lisbon for domestic consumption and for reexport to the rest of Europe.

CATTLE

Sugar and the other export crops depended on plentiful supplies of oxen, horses, and mules for use as draft animals. Portuguese settlers introduced European domestic animals to Brazil, just as the Spanish had done earlier in Mexico and the Caribbean. Unlike the Spanish experience, however, the Portuguese found that European ungulates did not flourish in the wild in Brazil. If, as seems likely, cattle, horses, sheep, goats, and pigs were landed and released by transient European ships, they did not survive. Later experience suggests that the Tupis killed these animals before they could propagate. European livestock diffused across the landscape as domesticated, not feral, animals that were bred and controlled by Portuguese ranchers. Although cattle were subsidiary to sugar in economic terms, the impact of cattle raising on the habitat of Brazil was wider than that of sugarcane and other crops. Throughout the colonial period, far more land felt the hooves and teeth of cattle than the hoes of slave laborers.

The first cattle known to have come to Brazil landed with the first settlers of the Martim de Sousa fleet in 1530–1531.[46] The cattle, loaded in Madeira, were probably standard Andalusian longhorn cattle bred for use as draft animals and for beef rather than milk production. Cattle remained scarce until the first royal viceroy, Tome de Sousa, made landfall at the Bay of All Saints and established his capital at Salvador. The new herd of cattle, small enough to be managed by a single herdsman, soon recovered from the voyage on the luxuriant grasses of the crescent-shaped coastal plain *(reconcavo)* surrounding the bay. Within a few years, the governor had given out land grants—three-square-league *sesmarias*—consisting of all available land within the *reconcavo*. These *sesmarias* became the earliest ranches in Brazil. Sugar planters obtained the grants and rapidly bred large herds of cattle and horses. Not long afterward, a second cattle-raising center formed to the north when sugar planters at Olinda and Recife in Pernambuco began raising cattle.

1800, Bahia exported 5,885 metric tons of tobacco. At 4.76 tons per hectare, this works out to 1,236 hectares required for export production.

45. Ibid.

46. Rollie E. Poppino, "Cattle Industry in Colonial Brazil," *Mid-America* 31 (1949): 219.

Also among the earliest successful cattle ranchers were the Jesuits, whose order had been given royal grants for lands in the vicinity of the capital to support their to-be-established schools and colleges. In 1552, the royal governor gave Father Manuel da Nobrega, the head of the Jesuits, twelve heifers. Additional pious donations of livestock came from the royal governor and wealthier colonists. Within a few years, each Jesuit school and mission village had its herd of livestock. The Jesuit herds were among the most prolific of the colony. Seeking additional pasture, the Jesuits and their Indian converts began to push their herds beyond the immediate coastal plain into the interior.

As sugar planters gained confidence, it became clear to them that land in the immediate hinterland of these settlements was too valuable to be used for grazing when sugarcane paid so well. Cattle raising became a specialty differentiated from sugar planting. Would-be ranchers could easily obtain land grants (sesmarias) from the colonial state that would permit them to occupy new lands north of Salvador and south of Recife. Further expansion into new grazing lands, however, required seizing and holding land against Indian resistance. Expansion along the cattle frontier was a protracted process marked by "exploration, extermination of the Indians, large land grants, and the establishment of cattle ranches."[47]

Enslaving Indians in the interior prepared the way for cattle ranchers. From the mid–sixteenth century on, organized slave raiders, known as *bandeirantes*, pushed aggressively into the interior in a search for Indian settlements. Virtually every year, companies of *bandeirantes* gathered supplies and weapons and mobilized Indian allies and slaves as porters, fighters, and guides to assist them in traversing the trails and rivers of the *sertão* (outback). Trekking under the most arduous conditions, the *bandeirantes* covered hundreds of kilometers in search of their prey. If fortunate, they surprised Indian villages and seized numerous captives with little or no resistance. Placing them in manacles and chains, the raiders forced their hapless captives to march back to São Paulo or other coastal cities to be sold as slaves. If unfortunate, the *bandeirantes* met determined and effective Indian fighters who had learned of their passage and who, on occasion, defeated and killed the slavers. On the whole, however, the slavers prevailed. Deaths from the violence of the raids, massacres, and forced marches, as well as from contact with diseases carried by the *bandeirantes*, were a leading contributor to the decline in Indian numbers in the interior.

The small southern town of São Paulo—its inhabitants numbering no more than two thousand persons in 1600—was the organizing center for the *bandeirantes*. At their location thirty miles over steep, forbidding trails from the port of Santos, the "Paulistas," as the people of São Paulo were called, found the soil too poor and roads too difficult to grow sugar with expensive

47. Schwartz, "Colonial Brazil, c. 1580–c. 1750," 2:460.

African slaves. Instead, they turned to harvesting Indians as slaves. By 1585, the settlers of São Paulo had enslaved and killed off the Indians in the immediate vicinity of the town. In that year, the town council authorized a raid into the interior against the Guarani-speaking Indians known as the Carijos. Spanish Jesuits moving east from the interior were simultaneously converting and settling the Carijos in mission settlements in Spanish territory. The town council bluntly asserted the need for slaves:

> This land is in great danger of being depopulated because its inhabitants do not have [Indian] slaves as they used to, by whom they have always been served. This is the result of many illnesses . . . from which over 2000 head of slaves have died in this captaincy in the past six years. This land used to be ennobled by these slaves, and its settlers supported themselves honourably with them and made large incomes.[48]

During the 1580s and 1590s, São Paulo captains led several extended expeditions against the Carijos. Jeronimo Leitao spent six years moving slowly up the Tieté River attacking and destroying Carijo villages along its banks. The Spanish Jesuits claimed that he and his *bandeirantes* devastated three hundred villages and killed or enslaved thirty thousand of their inhabitants.[49]

From this sanguinary beginning, the *bandeirantes* pushed deeply and steadily into the interior in their search for Indians to capture and sell. Repeated forays and raids gave the Paulistas unexcelled knowledge of the terrain, topography, and routes of the mountainous regions of the south. Indian losses to the *bandeirantes* sharply reduced the hazards and costs for pioneer cattle ranchers.

Armed, mounted cowboys, or *vaqueiros,* were the shock troops of the colonial advance. They defended their herds from raiding Indians or bandit groups and, when necessary, could be mobilized to serve as militiamen in wars with the Indians. The *vaqueiros* tended to be free, mixed-race white-Indians *(caboclos)* or black slaves who were given considerable freedom and responsibility to care for their herds. After they obtained land grants, the ranchers pushed forward into new grazing lands by setting up a line of small corrals with huts for their cowboys. One or two *vaqueiros* guarded a small contingent of ten cows and a bull for each pioneer corral to serve as the basis for breeding a larger herd. This system worked well against isolated raids, but not against serious Indian resistance. When that occurred, the colonial state and the landowners together had to send in military force to push back the Indians.[50]

---

48. Hemming, *Red Gold,* 245, 591, quoting a passage in the municipal records of the São Paulo council.

49. Hemming, *Red Gold,* 245.

50. Poppino, "Cattle Industry in Colonial Brazil," 225.

When the ranchers moving north from Bahia reached the banks of the Rio Real in Sergipe, the Indians of that region attacked, drove them back, and stopped further occupation of the coast for twenty years. Finally, in the 1590s, with the aid of government-sponsored assaults, the ranchers moved their herds into Sergipe and to the banks of the São Francisco River.[51] There, they met fellow colonists who had driven their cattle south from Pernambuco. With the coast secured, colonial ranchers began to push their herds up the courses of the Jiguirica, Paraguaçu, Jacuipe, and other rivers debouching on the coast, ranging as far north as the Paraíba.

Most desirable, however, was the three-hundred-kilometer lower valley of the São Francisco, which stretched as far as the great barrier of the Paulo Affonso Falls. Cattle thrived in the well-watered lower valley. In contrast to that found in the progressively drier middle and upper segments of the river, rainfall here varied between one thousand and two thousand millimeters per year. The grasses and tropical, semideciduous forest formations of the river's wide floodplain offered abundant grazing. Every year in November, after the onset of the rains in the upper reaches of the river in Minas Gerais, the São Francisco's volume rose; it remained high until March. High waters flooded the lower valley floor to a width of as much as twenty-five kilometers and covered the valley bottom with a rich, fine, black silt. During the subsequent dry season, numerous salt beds formed on the valley floor and provided salt licks for cattle. Since the Crown enforced a monopoly and exacted high prices on salt made on the coast, this was especially fortuitous as far as the ranchers were concerned.

With its proximity to the largest sugar-producing regions, and its ample grazing lands, the lower São Francisco River valley soon became the leading livestock region in colonial Brazil. By 1640, there were over two thousand corrals recorded for this area. As the lower São Francisco and the most desirable lower valleys of the other rivers filled with cattle, cattle ranchers began to head upriver and to encounter a new, drier habitat. When they moved beyond the Paulo Affonso Falls on the São Francisco, and past similar climatic bounds on other rivers, rainfall decreased to five hundred millimeters or below, and there was six months of drought each year. The pioneers found stunted, thorny scrub forest (known as *caatinga*). They discovered that if they burnt the *caatinga*, patches of nutritious grasslands replaced it and could supplement browsing in the thorny brush. It was the Paulistas who first explored the upper sections of the São Francisco River and who began raising cattle in this region.

After the mid-1600s, cattle ranchers moved their rapidly growing herds into the backlands, or *sertão*. The Indians of the *sertão* looked on grazing cattle as large, slow-moving game to be killed with little effort and eaten. The

51. Schwartz, "Colonial Brazil, c. 1580–c. 1750," 2:460.

ranchers viewed the backlands Indians as dangerous predators of their cattle and pursued them as vermin. When the ranchers met serious opposition from the Indians, they called in help from the colonial authorities on the coast. The latter turned to the notorious *bandeirantes* of São Paulo, the Paulistas, who had for several generations raided Indian villages in the interior for slaves. Shiploads of these ruthless Indian fighters sailed from São Paulo to Bahia to mount punitive expeditions against the Indians in the backlands during the late seventeenth century. The Indians fought hard but eventually were either killed, enslaved, or driven from potential cattle areas.[52] In some instances, the Jesuits, who remained enthusiastic livestock raisers, were able to head off attacks on groups of Indians who had converted to Christianity and settled in new mission stations. Each of the new missions in the interior maintained large herds of cattle.

With the Indians gone, the ranchers were free to move. Adapting to the sparse vegetation, the ranchers dispersed their cattle over vast areas while exercising tight control over riverbanks and water holes. They obtained land grants over enormous tracts of land—far larger than the legally stipulated three square leagues of the *sesmarias*. The proprietors of small ranches, or *curraes*, with one corral and living quarters, grazed herds of 200 to 1,000 cattle. Larger ranches, or *fazendas*, with multiple corrals, maintained herds of 1,000 to 3,000 cattle. The largest were larger than entire provinces in Portugal.

The career of Domingo Afonso (known simply as "Sertao"), a celebrated slave raider and Indian fighter along the São Francisco, illustrates the perils and possible rewards of the cattle frontier. Afonso was one of the first Portuguese to cross the São Francisco River and settle in the rolling hills of interior Piauí, between the Parnaíba and Gurguéia Rivers, in the 1680s and 1690s. Afonso and his partner, Colonel Francisco Dias d'Avila, along with their families and retainers, drove away most of the Indian tribes in the land between the two rivers. As a historian contemporary to the time wrote, "He [Afonso] entered those lands previously not penetrated by Portuguese and inhabited only by wild heathen, with whom he had many battles, emerging from one dangerously wounded but from all of them victorious, killing many heathen and making the rest retreat to the interior of the *sertão*."[53] At his death in 1711, Afonso bequeathed to the Jesuits 30 cattle ranches in Piauí that stocked 30,000 cattle and 1,500 horses on 1.2 million hectares.[54]

Miguel de Carvalho, a lay priest who traversed the settled region of Piauí

---

52. J. Hemming, "Indians and the Frontier in Colonial Brazil," in *The Cambridge History of Latin America*, edited by Leslie Bethell (Cambridge: Cambridge University Press, 1984), 2:519.

53. Hemming, *Red Gold*, 353–54; the quote is on 615, taken from Sebatiao da Rocha Pitta, *Historia da America Portugueza, desde o anno de 1500 do seu descobrimento ate o de 1724* (Lisbon, 1730), bk. 6, p. 385.

54. Schwartz, "Colonial Brazil, c. 1580–c. 1750," 2:460.

for four years in the 1690s, compiled a detailed census and description of the region as part of a March 1697 report to the bishop of Pernambuco. As yet there was no settled town, but the ranchers had just built a small adobe church at a central point to serve the region. Between them, Afonso and d'Avila owned or claimed to own all the land in Piauí. They rented most of it to individual ranchers at 10 milreis per year. There were 129 ranches in total, with 441 men working them. The ranches were scattered, with two to three leagues distance between them. Few ranchers had more than 2–3 black stockmen to help them, and many had only one. *Vaqueiros* could set up on their own if they chose. If they quit a ranch, they had to leave behind the same number of cattle they had taken responsibility for, but they could claim one-fourth of any surplus cattle bred during their tenure. Ranchers and *vaqueiros* alike lived on meat, milk, and honey: According to de Carvalho, "They usually roast the meat, as they have no cooking pots. They drink water from wells and lakes, always turbid, and impregnated with nitrate. The climate is very stormy and rather unhealthy, so that these wretched men live dressed in hides and look like Tapuyas [non-Tupi Indians]."[55]

As de Carvalho's report implies, this was extensive pastoralism on widely scattered ranches. A very few *vaqueiros*, who lived and camped among their herds, sufficed to care for the cattle of the interior. Throughout the year, the *sertão* cattle that grazed and browsed on unfenced ranges were kept from straying by their herders. The *vaqueiros* rounded up and corralled their herds in the spring of each year, after calving. They treated illnesses and wounds, cared for the young calves, branded the yearlings, and castrated young males. They killed ill or decrepit animals, consumed or sun dried the meat, and dried the hides for use. Leather served for clothing, boxes, containers, saddles, and rope. At roundup, the owners sorted the animals for retention or sale. The ranchers organized herds and put sale animals on the trail to markets in the coastal cities or to the gold mines. Well-marked cattle trails ran along each of the twenty or so river valleys bisecting the grazing lands.

The cattle produced in the *sertão* were of vital economic importance to the colony. Writing in the early 1700s, Jean Antonio Andreoni stated, "According to the information that I have obtained from several persons who have traveled through the *sertão*," there were five hundred *curraes*, or ranches, in interior Bahia and more than eight hundred in Pernambuco, with a total of about 1.3 million cattle, or an average of a thousand head per ranch.[56] According to Andreoni, a constant stream of cattle poured into the coastal

---

55. C. R. Boxer, *The Golden Age of Brazil: Growing Pains of a Colonial Society, 1695–1750* (New York: St. Martin's Press, 1995), 235; Hemming, *Red Gold*, 352, 614.

56. Antonil and Taunay, *Cultura e opulencia do Brazil por suas drogas e minas*, 467–79. (Andreoni wrote under the pseudonym André João Antonil.) Andreoni did not say that he was using an average figure, but his number for ranches in Bahia and Pernambuco, although appearing separately from his totals (479), suggest that this was the case.

cities: "The cattle trains that normally come to Bahia consist of 100, 160, 200 or 300 head of cattle. Some of these arrive almost every week at Capoame, a place eight leagues distant from the city where there is pasture and where the merchants buy them. At some times of year there are weeks when cattle trains arrive every day."[57]

Some of these cattle, purchased by planters, went immediately to work as draft animals for sugar, tobacco, and cotton growers. Continuing expansion of the cattle frontier sent a plentiful supply of oxen to the planters. In the 1690s, the price of a team of oxen was half what it had been in the 1590s.[58] The majority were slaughtered and their meat sold fresh; some were destined for sun and salt drying, their tallow and their hides sold. Tanneries in the port cities produced leather from raw hides to meet domestic demands for this ubiquitous product. Sun-dried hides *(meyo de sola)*, however, were a major export product from Brazil to tanneries in Portugal and elsewhere in Europe. Andreoni put the number ordinarily shipped each year at 110,000 hides, with a value representing 5.4 percent of the colony's total exports.[59]

GOLD AND DIAMONDS

During the first two centuries of colonial settlement, the Portuguese in Brazil, in contrast to the Spaniards in Mexico, continually searched for, but did not find, viable sources of gold or silver. Among the most assiduous prospectors were *bandeirantes,* who invariably carried gold pans and mining tools on their Indian slaving raids. Finally, however, in 1695, news came to the governor of Rio de Janeiro concerning major gold strikes at Rio das Velhas, deep in the interior of southern Brazil.[60] Over the next half century, numerous other strikes occurred across a broad area in Minas Gerais, Mato Grosso, Goiás, and several districts in interior Bahia.

There were no easy routes to the mines. The distances, extending to thousands of kilometers, were enormous. The longest, and most accessible route for cattle and horses, began with the lower São Francisco River, in Bahia at

57. Hemming, *Red Gold,* 353; English translation of Antonil and Taunay, *Cultura e opulencia do Brazil por suas drogas e minas,* 483.

58. Schwartz, "Colonial Brazil, c. 1580–c. 1750," 2:462.

59. Antonil and Taunay, *Cultura e opulencia do Brazil por suas drogas e minas,* 488–89. Andreoni's tabulated total for the combined value of the annual exports of sugar, tobacco, gold, hides, and brazilwood amounts to 3,743,992,800 reis (the standard money of account for the period). Hides sold for 201,800,000 reis. An additional number of hides used to enclose the 27,500 rolls of tobacco shipped from Bahia each year, and which were valued at 1,300 reis for each roll, also went to the tanners in Europe. This added at a minimum 37,750,000 reis to the contribution of tobacco to total exports and pushed the percentage to 6.4 percent (328–29).

60. A. J. R. Russell-Wood, *A World on the Move: The Portuguese in Africa, Asia, and America, 1415–1808* (New York: St. Martin's Press, 1993), 547.

Salvador. At the great falls, the gold seekers shifted to an overland track that led several hundred kilometers along the São Francisco to the Rio das Velhas. The latter culminated in the gold-mining region of Mato Grosso. Other, shorter, more direct trails from São Paulo were accessible only by foot: travelers had to climb steep hills, traverse dense forest, and cross fast-moving rivers. Hostile Indians, wild animals, poisonous snakes, and harmful flora exacted a steady toll on all who tried to reach the mines.

Few were discouraged by distance or hardship. Thousands of hopeful prospectors suffered along the arduous track into the hilly mountain regions. The population of the mining districts grew rapidly. By the 1720s, the mining districts contained half the colonial population of Brazil. The fascination with gold attracted a sharp increase in migration from Portugal. A majority of the new settlers, however, had no choice in the matter. Typically for colonial Brazil, the free white minority and a few mulatto miners relied on numerous black male slaves to do the heavy work. For example, there were thirty thousand black slaves working the mines in Minas Gerais by 1720.[61] As many as sixty thousand black slaves labored in the gold and diamond mines prior to independence.[62] As the mines produced gold, successful prospectors could afford to pay the high cost of transporting black slaves from the coast.

Most Brazilian gold was placer gold—flakes and grains found in the sand and gravel of riverbeds and banks. Prospectors panned for gold by oscillating a metal pan filled with river sand and water. Higher density gold particles sank; lighter sand particles washed over the sides of the shallow pan. In more elaborate operations, workers, usually black slaves, dug up riverbeds and placed the gravel in a series of sluice boxes that sifted out progressively smaller particles of gold. At a final trough, workers panned the residue. Sometimes miners used hydraulic pressure to move sand and gravel from the riverbanks into sluice boxes. Sometimes they dammed up the river and diverted its waters to get better access to the gold-bearing sands. In some areas, lode or vein mining involved following gold-bearing seams into hillsides or down into the earth.

The economic benefits to the colony were enormous. Gold and the thought of striking it rich touched off a massive migration from Portugal to Brazil in the eighteenth century. In the mining districts, returns from gold encouraged the growth of a diversified economy able to produce shelter and food and to meet other needs of the district's inhabitants. Successful miners made fortunes; successful traders, artisans, farmers, and ranchers grew prosperous by meeting the needs of the mining towns. A majority of miners prob-

61. Ibid., 570.
62. Marcilio, *The Population of Colonial Brazil*, 2:53.

ably died in poverty and obscurity. Those who best kept their fortunes combined mining with farming, ranching, and mercantile activity.

The feverish search for gold resulted in a totally unexpected discovery. In 1729, miners panning for gold on the upper reaches of the river Jequitinhonha in Minas Gerais found white crystalline stones settling among the gold flakes and dust remaining in their basins and sluices. These proved to be diamonds. Their quality matched those mined in Mughal India, which at the time was the only source of diamonds for the world market. The town of Truijico rapidly became a bustling center for diamond mining. By 1723, King João V (1706–1750) had issued regulations that defined the boundaries of a special diamond district in Minas Gerais and appointed two of his most trusted civilian officials, both Crown lawyers, to rule the new district.

As soon as shipments of Brazilian diamonds reached Lisbon in the early 1730s, the world diamond price plummeted, along with the prospect of enormous revenues to the Crown. In response, King João V banned all mining for diamonds and sent troops to arrest and expel anyone found working the riverbeds in the district. Finally, in 1740, when diamond prices had sufficiently recovered, the Portuguese rulers issued the first of a series of four-year monopoly contracts to two private entrepreneurs that permitted them to restore diamond mining on a limited scale. On payment of an annual fee per head, they could employ six hundred slaves in the mines confined to the river Jequitinhonha and its vicinity.[63] All other miners and prospectors were forbidden access to the district in an edict enforced by troops of dragoons stationed there. In 1771, the marquis de Pombal abolished the private contracts and put the diamond mines under direct royal control, with officials in charge of all operations. This system, with its greatly enhanced returns to the royal treasury, remained intact until Brazilian independence in 1821.

The techniques of diamond mining were nearly identical to those employed in gold placer mining described above. Diamonds were found, in fact, only where gold occurred. The principal difference lay in control over the mine workers, who, if not closely watched, would conceal the stones they found, smuggle them out, and sell them on the illegal contraband market. To prevent this, one white or free mulatto stood over eight crouching black slaves as they picked through the sluiced gravel for stones and gold. Although rewarded for any large stones found, the slaves could do much better by smuggling, but the penalties imposed were severe.

When found, rough stones went immediately into the royal intendant's safe. Each year, the intendant sent the stones under armed guard to Rio de Janeiro. There, official diamond shipments were placed on naval vessels assigned to guard the Rio-to-Lisbon fleet on its annual Atlantic crossing. On

63. Boxer, *The Golden Age of Brazil*, 211–12.

arrival in Lisbon, royal officials appropriated the largest and choicest stones to sell or place in the Crown treasury. The contractors were permitted to sell the remainder in lots carefully regulated so as to keep the price up.

After 1771, all stones were property of the treasury, and royal officials assumed control of the sales. Leading mercantile firms from Amsterdam and London were the buyers. At these centers, expert craftsmen cut and polished the stones, which were traded throughout the world. Between 1740 and 1821, those diamonds officially recorded and legally traded amounted to 3.1 million carats.[64] Another unknown, but certainly large, mass of diamonds traveled to Europe through clandestine channels.

Gold and diamond mining carved a distinctive landscape from the Atlantic forest. Observers wrote of denuded hillsides, in mature mining areas, disfigured by giant gullies, of silted streambeds and "pockmarked moors." Hardest hit were the wet-seeking (hygrophilic) tree, brush, and plant species found among the streams that were mined. Replacement vegetation consisted of sparse weed and brush cover. Digging and washing for gold and diamonds overturned and destroyed an estimated four thousand square kilometers of forest in the mining regions.[65]

Surrounding the core mining region lay a wider area of new settlement that grew to an estimated ninety-five square kilometers by 1800. In the early phase of the gold rush, ranchers in the São Francisco River valley drove herds over long distances to satisfy the miners' insatiable appetite for beef. Later, pioneering ranchers discovered areas with grass and water favorable for livestock in two areas closer to the mines. Cattle raising flourished in the grasslands west of São Paulo leading to the Gurupuava Plains and those to the northeast between the Sierra Mantiquerra and the Sierra do Mar.[66]

Extended supply lines to the coast resulted in high prices and periodic shortages and scarcity at the mines. Supply breakdowns encouraged many immigrants to the region to take up cultivation of maize and manioc to sell

64. Ibid., 220, 225. During the contract period between 1740 and 1771, legal shipments of Brazilian rough diamonds recorded in Lisbon amounted to 1.7 million carats (approximately 34.2 kilograms) and drew a sale price of 15.5 million milreis. Under direct royal control, total shipments slowed somewhat but reached 1.4 million carats (27.8 kilograms) by 1821.

65. Dean, *With Broadax and Firebrand*, 97–98. According to Dean, "The area devastated by gold and diamond mining may be roughly estimated. Modern surveys of the region suggest that the Mineiros [miners] obtained perhaps a gram of gold from a cubic meter of gold-bearing material and overburden and this layer averaged 50 centimeters deep. Thus the total volume of gold obtained during the eighteenth century would have overturned 4,000 square kilometers of the Atlantic Forest region. This suggests the destruction of about 20 percent of the gold-bearing arc extending for 450 kilometers between Diamantina and Lavras, in a band that varied in width but averaged about 30 kilometers from the ridgeline eastward and about 15 kilometers westward."

66. Ibid., 93, map 4; and 111.

as cash crops at the mines. Mestizo settlers, known by townspeople as *caboclos*, dispersed into the hinterlands around the mines. They were free to occupy, clear, and burn tracts of the regrown Atlantic forest in a return to the shifting cultivation of the Brazilian Indians.[67] The miners also required meat, timber, charcoal, fuelwood, medicinal plants, and many other commodities that could be extracted from the forest. The *caboclos* developed a distinctive backlands culture that drew unemployed townspeople, vagrants, failed miners, escaped slaves, and fleeing criminals, among others, to a life free from the harsh constraints of the towns. African slaves who had escaped the mines formed distinct communities of their own called *quilombos*.

The *caboclos* practiced aggressive, mobile, slash-and-burn cultivation that ate into the regrown forest. They shifted into newly burnt and cleared fields at two- to three-year intervals. In so doing, they could evade the demands of the state for taxes and conscription for their sons. They could take advantage of the nutrients in the ashes and obtain maximum soil fertility. Many of these forest pioneers simply abandoned any thought of cultivation for the market and lapsed into cultivation purely for subsistence—especially those who had little reason or desire to have close contact with towns and legal authorities.

But there was another, sound ecological reason for taking up new fields so frequently. Brazilian leaf-cutter ants moved into cultivated fields within two to three seasons. In a few years, ant mounds five to eight meters across and one-half meter high could occupy an eighth or more of a farmer's field. The ants consumed fungal masses that they cultivated in massive underground burrows. The fungus had to be fed fresh leaves, which were brought in by worker ants. Planted maize and manioc were the preferred targets. The ants could devastate an entire field of manioc in one or two nights. There were no known methods of eradicating the ants. The farmer's best response was to move.[68]

Brazilian gold and, to a lesser extent, diamonds certainly benefited the colony, the home Portuguese economy, and the Portuguese empire. Gold enabled Brazilian mints to issue coins that served as the basis for a new monetary economy. Gold exports increased the purchasing power of the colony with respect to Portugal and Europe. Many Portuguese subjects profited greatly from participating in the legal and contraband trade in gold and diamonds.[69] However, the transfer of 400,000 migrants to Brazil—amounting to one-fifth of the 2 million population of 1700—even though a benefit for Brazil, was probably a loss for the tiny metropolitan country. Most of the gold extracted in Brazil moved directly across the Atlantic as either legal or con-

67. Ibid., 98–101.
68. Ibid., 109–11.
69. De Andrade Arruda, "Colonies as Mercantile Investments," 385–95.

traband shipments. Despite continued leakage due to smuggling, the Portuguese Crown obtained lucrative new revenues from Brazil by imposing a tax of one-fifth on all gold and diamonds mined. The diamond tax at first was levied on a portion, and later on all, of the diamonds.

TRIBUTE TO THE OLD WORLD

The material advantages that Portugal and western Europe gained from Portugal's Brazilian colony are readily apparent. The economic return to the metropolitan state and its people—what might fairly be called tribute—far offset outlays made for colonial administration and supplies.[70] In effect, colonization added Brazil's enormous lands and natural resources directly to Portugal's national territory. Brazil's exports paid the cost of buying and importing slave workers from Africa. Brazil thereby obtained the human labor it needed for export production and resource extraction without straining the small Portuguese home population.

The flow of material and money across the Atlantic increased steadily until the final years of the colony. The sheer quantity of goods transported annually to Lisbon from Brazil is impressive. For example, the fleet of 1749, although lacking a convoy from Bahia, consisted of 70 ships: 20 merchant vessels and 2 warships sailing from Rio de Janeiro, 39 merchant vessels and 1 warship from Pernambuco, and 5 merchant vessels and 3 warships from Maranhão in the far north. The fleet carried 10 metric tons of sugar, 698 tons of cacao, nearly two hundred thousand hides, 542 tons of brazilwood, several thousand assorted timbers, planks, and boards, and other minor goods. Since for some unexplained reason there was no Bahia fleet that year, tobacco is not listed on the manifests. Most valuable was the gold and diamonds. The ships carried gold valued at 14.8 million gold cruzados, divided into 11 million minted coins (cruzados) and 6.2 metric tons of gold dust and bars. Private individuals owned 85 percent of the gold; the Crown, the remainder. There were 76,414 carats of diamonds belonging to the diamond contractors.[71]

Sugar, tobacco, cacao, cattle hides and leather, and timber were the mainstays of Brazilian exports. Between 1560 and 1821, Brazilian planters shipped at a minimum 4 million, and more likely 5 million, metric tons of

70. Ibid.; James Lang, *Portuguese Brazil: The King's Plantation* (New York: Academic Press, 1979).

71. Boxer, *The Golden Age of Brazil*, 351–53. Calculated from the lists Boxer provides. Conversions used to calculate metric weights include the Portuguese dram at 3.59 grams, sugar chests at 40 *arrobas*, 14.5 kilograms per *arroba*, the quintal at 58.75 kilograms, and sections of brazilwood at 25 kilograms. See Lang, *Portuguese Brazil*, 139, for a different presentation of the totals.

sugar to Lisbon.[72] Only a portion of that annual import stayed in Lisbon; traders from Amsterdam reexported the bulk of this to feed that city's refineries. During the first half of the eighteenth century, between 1,400 and 3,000 metric tons of the highest quality Bahian tobacco reached the Lisbon market.[73] Much of this tobacco moved directly to Amsterdam, the greatest single tobacco market in Europe. Another large shipment of tobacco went to Angola to pay for imports of slaves to Brazil.

During the eighteenth century, gold and diamonds outstripped all the older exports in value. Brazil emerged as the leading gold producer in the entire early modern world. Brazil's mines extracted an average 9.7 metric tons of fine gold per year. Officially recorded gold mined between gold's discovery in 1695 and Brazil's independence reached a total of 967.4 tons.[74] Miners and traders concealed a large additional amount of gold that remained untaxed. As yet, no one has devised a reliable way to estimate the quantities of smuggled gold.[75] Brazilian production far outstripped the total of 590 metric tons of fine gold extracted throughout the Spanish colonies—in the Caribbean, Mexico, and South America—between 1500 and 1800. Production remained at high levels until a downturn after 1800. The diamond mines produced somewhere between 3 and 5 million carats of diamonds in the late colonial period. Brazil became a direct challenger to the monopoly long held by Indian production. The Portuguese Crown took most of the profits from diamonds. Thanks to these Brazilian mining revenues, King João V was widely reputed to be the richest king in Europe. Most of this imported gold moved directly into European trade and payment channels to offset Portugal's trade deficits. Brazilian gold added liquidity to the maturing and monetizing world economy of the eighteenth century.

72. As yet, no complete year-by-year tabulation of Brazilian sugar production or exports seems to have been completed. Deerr gives annual figures for 15 selected years between 1560 and 1820 (*The History of Sugar*, 112). The annual average for those years is 22,128 metric tons. For 261 years, that average yields a total of 5.8 million tons—probably too high. Dropping the high production figure for 1820, when output soared to 75,000 tons, the average for 14 years falls to 18,352, for a total of 4.8 million tons.

73. Extrapolated from Schwartz, "Colonial Brazil, c. 1580–c. 1750," 2:459, fig. 2. Direct shipments to Portugal for that period fluctuated between one hundred thousand and two hundred thousand *arrobas*, at 14.5 kilograms per unit.

74. John TePaske, personal communication. For the period 1695–1700, the total production was 4.3 metric tons of fine gold. Harry Cross puts the minimum production of gold for Brazil at 10.9 tons per year in the period 1712 to 1755. Harry Cross, "South American Bullion Production and Export 1550–1750," in *Precious Metals in the Later Medieval and Early Modern Worlds*, edited by John F. Richards (Durham, N.C.: Carolina Academic Press, 1983), 417, table 8. The figures given by Russell-Wood are much lower than these (*A World on the Move*, 594, table 1).

75. Warren Dean suggests that an amount equal to that officially recorded was smuggled out: that is, another thousand tons. *With Broadax and Firebrand*, 91.

THE ENVIRONMENTAL IMPACT

What ecological impact did the Portuguese have on Brazil? Were there dramatic changes to the landscape and habitats of Indian Brazil as it existed in 1500? Certainly, as in other parts of the New World, the Portuguese transported a package of biological invaders. As discussed earlier, they brought with them a lethal array of pathogens and their hosts that irreversibly changed the disease patterns of Brazil. They introduced numerous Eurasian and African cultivars similar to those the Spaniards brought to the Caribbean. They inserted new domesticated animals that changed the landscape of Brazil. These introductions did not stop, but continued throughout the colonial period. For example, malaria and yellow fever from Africa made its way into the Atlantic forest of Brazil by the 1700s. In short, the Portuguese swept Brazil into the Columbian exchange of the early modern world.[76]

Beyond the effect of these introductions, the Portuguese irrevocably changed the 1-million-square-kilometer Atlantic forest that stretched along the eastern coast from Recife to Porto Alegre. To the Portuguese, this great forest, with its dense canopy and immense trees in hundreds of strange shapes and hues, was awe inspiring. The forest symbolized the great potential wealth of Brazil. It was a resource that could never be exhausted. Simultaneously, the forest was a menacing presence that stood in the way of comfortable, safe human settlement. These emotions combined to encourage unrestrained clearing and exploitation and to dispel any notion of conservation or limits.

At first, the Portuguese contributed unwittingly to forest regrowth. As their violence and imported diseases killed off the Brazilian Indians, human activity in the forest declined accordingly. Continuing Indian genocide steadily reduced hunting, gathering, and burning. Trees, plants, animals, and birds formerly consumed by the Indians recovered to form a new, more luxuriant ecosystem.

Within the settled zone, however, colonization had the reverse effect. Migrants from Europe and their slaves from Africa assaulted the Atlantic forest far more intensively than had the Indians. The ecological footprint created by settlement continued to expand in size throughout the three centuries of the colonial period. By 1821, the settled area probably amounted to 200,000 square kilometers, or one-fifth of the total 1 million square kilometers covered by the Atlantic forest.

This does not mean that the Portuguese cleared the entire area of settlement and converted forest completely to cultivated lands and sites for human habitation. For example, in the sugar-growing regions, the actual land devoted to sugarcane in any single year was only about 120 square kilome-

---

76. Russell-Wood, *A World on the Move*, 158–63.

ters. Surrounding the fields was a halo of abandoned cane fields where forest regrowth had begun, which constituted an area ten times greater. Warren Dean posits that, in the southeast, mining, farming, and cattle raising might have occupied a deforested area 30,000 square kilometers by the end of the eighteenth century.[77] But this accounts for only a portion of the total settlement area where second-growth forest was present. When planters abandoned cane fields or when *caboclos* left three-year fields for new burntover plots, secondary growth emerged. By the end of the colonial period, most of the land within this larger footprint still retained some form of wooded cover, but it was depleted in varying degrees by human action.

It was the cumulative effect of transient land use that was important. In an ever increasing arc, Portuguese settlers and their dependents whittled away at the forest. Planters and *caboclos* alike routinely abandoned fields to occupy newly cut and burnt tracts. They made no effort to conserve soil fertility or to invest in the land, since new, more fertile forest tracts were readily at hand. The result was an uninhibited attack on the forest that appeared wasteful to many observers at the time.

The colonists made other demands on the flora and fauna of the forest. Backwoodsmen of all sorts, ranging from Indians to *bandeirantes* to *caboclos,* hunted and sold the skins and furs of jaguars, deer, otters, agoutis, snakes, alligators, and tapir. They killed forest birds for colorful plumes. These same groups gathered resins, waxes, glues, and other materials from the forest. By the end of the colonial period, backwoodsmen annually had gathered and sold 4 metric tons of ipecac—whose rhizome is an emetic—from the forests of Minas Gerais after those around Rio de Janeiro had been stripped of the plant.[78] Hunting and gathering for both the colonial and world market depleted those species targeted, and touched off a chain of complex changes in linked ecosystems in and beyond the area of settlement.

Colonists continually depleted the forest by their lavish use of firewood. I have already referred to the fuel needs of sugar planters, who, unlike their Caribbean counterparts, never resorted to burning cane stalks as fuel. The entire colonial culture relied on cheap and abundant wood supplies. Town dwellers, who kept domestic and commercial fires going around the clock, relied on a wholesale market fed daily by carts loaded with firewood and charcoal. *Caboclos* forest pioneers kept kitchen fires lit around the clock. They burnt great stores of fuelwood to dry manioc (to evaporate the poison), to process bacon and hams, and to make soap. Backlands farmers consumed at least a ton of firewood per person per year.[79]

The settlers drew on the forest's seemingly inexhaustible source of wood

77. Dean, *With Broadax and Firebrand,* 115.
78. Ibid., 130.
79. Ibid., 195.

for building houses and furniture, boats, rafts, canoes, fence posts, tool handles, yokes, and all sorts of containers. Each year, sugar planters assembled
thousands of wooden sugar chests from planks cut from a softwood species,
the *jequitiba*. Each of the giant chests, measuring 1.75 meters by .65 meters,
contained .15 cubic meters of wood.[80] When the chests had been unloaded
and disassembled in Lisbon, the boards constituted a useful wood product
supplied to Portugal from its colony. Timber from the forest also supported
a colonial shipbuilding industry of modest size that supplied vessels for a
coastal trade between Brazilian ports and for the annual transatlantic fleet.

Strangely, however, despite the vast stands and the wondrous size and remarkable qualities of dozens of Brazilian tree species, the Portuguese failed
to build an export timber industry. Although the annual fleets regularly carried choice timbers for the royal shipyards and an assortment of cut lumber,
the overall quantities were modest. Throughout the colonial period, Portugal continued to obtain the bulk of its imported timber from the Baltic lands
and North America. In the early nineteenth century, Brazilian timber accounted for less than 10 percent of the kingdom's total annual wood imports.[81]

Several reasons help explain this notable failure. There were technical difficulties in finding the most appropriate techniques for cutting, processing,
and using the extraordinarily heavy, dense woods of Brazil. There were thousands of new and different species totally unfamiliar to Europeans. But the
primary reason lay in official policies that killed the industry. From 1652 onward, the Portuguese Crown imposed a harshly restrictive monopoly over the
choicest timber trees found on private lands anywhere in the colony. A visitor stated the problem:

> The country produces an inexhaustible supply of the finest timber, suitable for
> all purposes of civil and naval architecture; but the cutting and disposing of it
> is a monopoly of the Crown. The first object of every man, who obtains a grant
> of woodland, is to destroy the best trees as fast as he can; because he is not only
> forbidden to send them to market, but may have additional mortification of
> being obliged to entertain the King's surveyor, whenever he thinks fit to pay
> him a visit, with a numerous retinue, for the purpose of felling the timber,
> which he as owner of the estate has not the power to prevent.[82]

Instead of processing the best timber trees and putting them to use, landowners simply cremated them when they cleared land, rather than reveal their
presence to the royal authorities.

Beyond the bounds of the rain forest, on the drier plateaus, in the river val-

---

80. Shawn William Miller, "Brazil's Colonial Timber: Conservation, Monopoly, and the Accumulation of Colonial Wealth, 1652–1822" (Ph.D. diss., Columbia University, 1997), 74.
81. Ibid., 111, table 4. The average is based on annual imports between 1796 and 1819.
82. Ibid., quoting John Barrow, who spent considerable time in Rio de Janeiro in 1792.

leys, and on the mountains of the *sertão*, the Portuguese profoundly changed the Brazilian ecosystem simply by introducing domesticated livestock. Throughout the colonial period, ranchers, responding to market forces, built up their herds of cattle, horses, and mules to number in the millions. They pressed against the ecological margin by dispersing their herds in ever thinner densities into drier and less favorable habitats. Year after year, livestock grazed indigenous grasses and browsed shrubs and bushes. Year after year, they trampled and compacted the soils and deposited nutrients from their manure. Seeking to restore nutrients and fertility to the grasslands, the ranchers burnt the grazing lands every year—something that the Indians apparently did not do. It is difficult to determine whether the annual firing or the accepted level of cattle-stocking densities at this early period caused degradation of the soil and vegetation. What is certain, however, is that the introduction of great numbers of ungulates into lands where they had not been present before caused a cascading set of ecological changes across a wide swath of interior Brazil.

CONCLUSION

With unremitting effort and considerable luck, the Portuguese rulers added the fertile lands and natural resources of the Brazilian coast and much of the interior to those of their tiny homeland. The abundant products of Brazil moved across the Atlantic every year in the Brazil fleet to enrich both king and subjects at home. The colonists opened a moving frontier of pioneer settlement, which continued to expand during the nationalist period. They planted, grew, and exported sugar and tobacco as leading suppliers of those commodities in the early modern centuries. They imported Africans to work as slaves. They developed an enormous livestock-raising industry. In addition, they discovered gold and diamonds in mines rich enough to make Brazil the leading supplier of these commodities in the eighteenth century.

Like settlement in other regions of the New World, the Portuguese settlement in Brazil set in motion an array of environmental changes. Some of these changes resulted from the biological invaders carried by each migrant and each ship that made the Atlantic passage. Others resulted from land use and resource extraction practices by the early modern Portuguese that were more intensive than those of the Brazilian Indians. In areas of relatively high population concentration, such as the sugar regions of Bahia and Pernambuco, and later the mining regions of Minas Gerais, the colonists dramatically altered the land and its ecosystems before 1800. Less obvious but continuing cumulative effects from colonial hunting, gathering, timber cutting, and above all, livestock raising decisively altered the flora and fauna of the settlement region and beyond.

Chapter 12

Landscapes of Sugar in the Antilles

Sugar drove the repeopling of the New World tropics, whose previous inhabitants had succumbed to new disease. Sugar was the main driving force for frontier expansion and intensifying land use in the humid tropics of the New World. Imports of cane sugar, grown in the tropical regions of the Western Hemisphere, became one of the leading economic inducements to European settlement and exploitation of the New World territories. During the early modern centuries, profits from sugar shaped and stimulated the Atlantic trading system. Cane sugar's access to buoyant home and colonial markets depended in part on reliable maritime freight transport. Between 1500 and 1800, steady gains in efficiency, safety, and cost of transatlantic shipping encouraged New World commodity production for Europe.

Sugar imposed its own configuration on frontiers of settlement. Directly and indirectly, sugar attracted European settlers to the Caribbean and Brazil's Atlantic Coast—but they remained a minority in relation to the people who really did the work of land clearing and planting. Sugar's labor needs were the engine that brought the largest numbers of migrants to the region—the African slaves purchased and transported to the new plantations.

By the late sixteenth century, black slaves transported from West Africa replaced dwindling numbers of Indian slaves in the sugar regions. Blacks were available in large numbers at low prices, as a result of the sophisticated slave-trading routes between Africa and the New World. The full-blown Atlantic plantation system suffered from a demographic imbalance. The slave labor force did not replace itself. Planters did not find it economic to encourage slave reproduction in the plantations.[1] Instead, vigorous slave markets and

1. Philip D. Curtin, *The Rise and Fall of the Plantation Complex: Essays in Atlantic History* (Cambridge: Cambridge University Press, 1998), 11.

trading ensured that new bodies were always available to replace losses. The plantation's harsh discipline and confinement of slaves, firmly backed by the colonial government, ensured reliability. Northern European states, financiers, and entrepreneurial planters combined cheap slave labor from Africa with the favorable climate and natural resources of the tropical West Indies to produce massive amounts of sugar.[2]

The emerging plantation system created a distinctive sugar landscape marked by intensifying land use. The highly intensive monocrop growing of sugarcane put a great strain on soil fertility. Sugar processing consumed immense quantities of fuelwood and it depleted estate lands commonly set aside for forest and woodland. Even the best-informed planters found it difficult to maintain productivity on their plantations. Plantation agriculture magnified human impact on the land. Sugar growing encouraged further frontier expansion in the form of other cash crops—cotton, tobacco, pimento, cacao, ginger—often cultivated in somewhat smaller estates. (Ironically, escaped slaves from the plantation system merged with remnant Indian groups who had settled remote and inaccessible mountain or swamp refuge areas ahead of the settlement frontier.)

The export sugar plantation sector had a symbiotic relationship with commercial pastoralism. Although sheep did not flourish in these moist, humid regions, cattle and horses did. Ranching was the default form of land use in the Caribbean and northeastern Brazil in regions yet to be cleared for sugar and in areas where markets or state policy had caused recession and land abandonment. With their need for draft animals, plantations were a reliable market for cattle, horses, and mules. Despite temporary retreats or pauses, century after century the area cleared for plantations expanded steadily at the expense of grazing ranges for livestock.

With the necessary land, capital, labor, technical skills, and machinery, and with accessible markets, even absentee owners could make enormous profits—and, on occasion, suffer heavy losses. Planters had to raise large sums of capital to pay for clearing land, planting crops, putting up buildings, buying the requisite tools and implements, and funding operations until harvests could be obtained each year. They had to recruit and pay managers and overseers skilled in both cultivation of the crop and in after-harvest processing. They had to have credit sufficient to ship their product and wait months for its sale each year. For most planters, financing remained a tricky problem, subject as they were to the vagaries of price for their product each year.

2. Robin Blackburn stresses the "conjunction of slavery, colonialism, and maritime power [that] permitted the more advanced European states to skew the world market to their own advantage." *The Making of New World Slavery: From the Baroque to the Modern, 1492–1800* (London: Verso, 1997), 6. Blackburn's discussion of the sugar colonies focuses on issues of slavery rather than on those of natural resources and the environment dealt with in this chapter.

From its inception, New World sugar growing was an industrial, monocrop mode of production. Europeans grew sugar for export on heavily capitalized, large estates or plantations in tropical and subtropical latitudes. That they relied on forced labor on plantations was largely an accident of the social forces driving European conquest and colonialism in these regions, not the technical demands of raising and processing sugarcane. Sugar reasonably could have been produced in large quantities for export by European settlers cultivating smallholdings and cooperating in the operation of sugar mills. Instead, opportunities to amass relatively large estates and access to cheap supplies of forced labor from Africa encouraged the rise of plantations. Nothing in the cultivation or processing of sugarcane prevented smallholding, free cultivators from successfully growing sugar, as had long been the practice in India and China.[3]

Distant authorities and, increasingly, absentee owners exercised political and economic control over New World sugar production. Plantation owners depended heavily on land grants and other subsidies from the state. Generally, plantations emerged in new lands opened up for exploitation by conquest and domination. Cheap, fertile land was available in areas thinly occupied by marginal peoples, such as shifting cultivators, or in areas where the indigenous populace had died off or been driven out. European colonial rulers distributed large tracts of land bearing private property rights to individual owners, syndicates, and joint-stock companies. Where the state could not directly manage production on the land, it turned to large landowners to generate colonial revenues. Under new European property rights, land markets quickly emerged that permitted consolidation of landholdings behind the sugar frontier.

During the seventeenth century, Europe embraced three new, exotic stimulants: tea from China, coffee from Mocha, and cocoa from the New World. Each could be brewed and consumed as a nonalcoholic beverage. But tea, coffee, and cocoa were all bitter and devoid of caloric energy if taken alone, as they were in their original homes. When heated and combined with sugar and milk or cream, these caffeinated drinks delighted European taste. When consumers added sugar, a calorie-rich, intensely sweet substance, and milk or cream, containing fat and protein, all three beverages became sources of important nutrients and stimulants in the early modern European diet. As new tropical colonies shipped more cocoa and coffee, and as more tea arrived from China, consumer prices declined to the point that, by the eighteenth century, even ordinary people could afford these hot drinks on a regular basis. The novel mood-altering tropical products encouraged a new public culture of sociability in coffee and teahouses. Unlike consumers of

3. See, for example, Sucheta Mazumdar, *Sugar and Society in China: Peasants, Technology, and the World Market* (Cambridge: Harvard University Asia Center, 1998).

wine or beer, the coffee, tea, and cocoa drinkers could conduct business with heightened intellectual powers and energy.[4]

Simultaneously, sugar became more readily available and cheaper. In England—the most avid market for tropical sugar in Europe—the price of each variety of sugar declined by half during the seventeenth century and by another third in the period 1700 to 1750. Per capita consumption of cane sugar reached 1.8 kilograms annually in the late 1600s. During the 1700s, per capita annual consumption rose to 11 kilograms by the end of the century. By that date, sugar had truly become a grocery item of mass consumption bought on a regular basis by people of varied income levels.[5]

Land clearing and planting for sugar expanded steadily between the late fifteenth and early nineteenth centuries. The sugar frontier strode steadily from the tiny islands of the Lesser Antilles to the largest of the Greater Antilles and onto the South American mainland by the end of the early modern period. Responding to the world market, sugar planters cleared and cultivated lands previously considered marginal on each island or in each new region. Beyond the sugar plantations extended an arc of land occupied by small estate cash-crop producers, cattle ranchers, and subsistence smallholders drawn from the free or fugitive (maroon) black and mulatto communities. The tropical forests and woodlands of the Caribbean and northeastern Brazil fell to satisfy a growing, Europe-centered craving for sugar.

THE LESSER ANTILLES: BARBADOS

Throughout the 1500s, Spain claimed royal ownership and governance of the entire West Indies island chain but did little to consolidate its rule. The Spanish Crown could not mobilize the funds, manpower, or ships to defend its Caribbean possessions. The islands of the Spanish West Indies were isolated from the main shipping routes between Spain, Mexico, and Peru and attracted few settlers. Large portions of the Greater Antilles and nearly all of the Lesser Antilles had lost their Taino or Carib inhabitants and were populated only by feral cattle, pigs, and horses. Still-defiant Carib and mixed black-Carib populations remained on the smaller Leeward and Windward Islands to the east: Tobago, Saint Vincent, Grenada, and Dominica.

The northern Europeans—British, French, and Dutch—who were poised to move aggressively into the Spanish New World domain, did not have sufficient force at their disposal to dispossess the Spanish. Instead, both British and French regimes confined themselves to encouraging privateers to send

---

4. The most powerful statement of this connection is in Sidney Wilfred Mintz, *Sweetness and Power: The Place of Sugar in Modern History* (New York: Viking, 1985).

5. Carole Shammas, *The Pre-industrial Consumer in England and America* (Oxford: Clarendon Press; New York: Oxford University Press, 1990), 77–86.

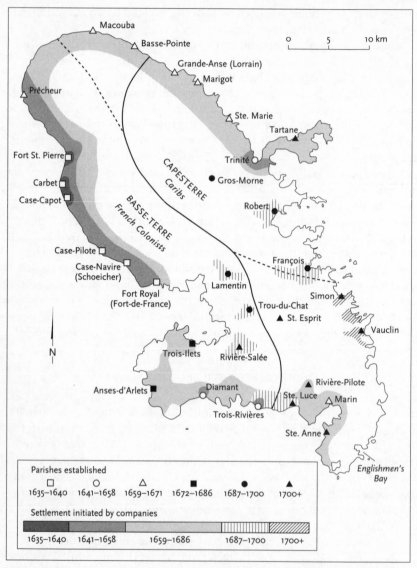

Macouba

Basse-Pointe

Grande-Anse (Lorrain)

Marigot

Prêcheur

Ste. Marie

Tartane

Fort St. Pierre

Trinité

Carbet

Gros-Morne

Case-Capot

CAPESTERRE
Caribs

Robert

BASSE-TERRE
French Colonists

Case-Pilote

François

Case-Navire
(Schoeicher)

Lamentin

Simon

Fort Royal
(Fort-de-France)

Trou-du-Chat

St. Esprit

Vauclin

N

Trois-Ilets

Rivière-Salée

Anses-d'Arlets

Diamant

Rivière-Pilote

Ste. Luce

Marin

Trois-Rivières

Ste. Anne

*Englishmen's
Bay*

0   5   10 km

Parishes established

☐   ○   △   ■   ●   ▲
1635–1640 1641–1658 1659–1671 1672–1686 1687–1700 1700+

Settlement initiated by companies

1635–1640 1641–1658 1659–1686 1687–1700 1700+

Map 12.1 Progress of settlement in Martinique in the seventeenth and
eighteenth centuries. Adapted from Clarissa Kimber, *Martinique Revisited: The
Changing Plant Geographies of a West Indian Island* (College Station: Texas A & M
University, 1988), map 19, p. 114.

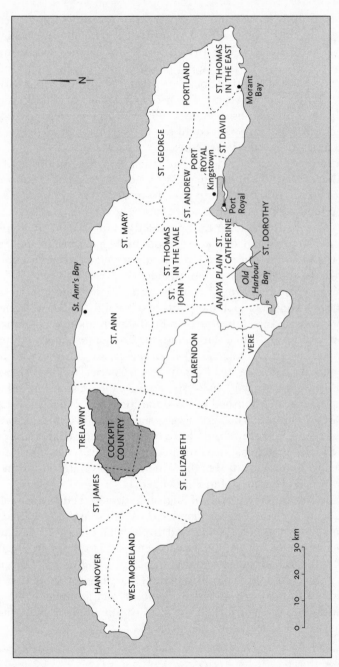

Map 12.2 Jamaica in the eighteenth century. Adapted from David Watts, *The West Indies: Patterns of Development, Culture, and Environmental Change since 1492* (Cambridge: Cambridge University Press, 1987), fig. 7.3, p. 295.

raiding fleets from Plymouth and Dieppe against Spanish shipping, especially the treasure ships of the annual Spanish fleet returning to Seville. In
1596, however, a tripartite French, British, and Dutch alliance, acting under
the terms of the Treaty of The Hague, did attempt to break Spanish sea
power and succeeded in severing Spain's maritime communications with its
New World colonies for two years.[6] The prolonged truce negotiations that
ensued reaffirmed Spanish trade monopolies with its colonies but also established the principle that Spain could not prevent trade or settlement in
unoccupied territories in the West Indies.

By the early 1600s, ample evidence had reached northern Europe of the
potential value of New World products. The ready sale and eager consumption of the first crop of tobacco sent back from Virginia stimulated the interest of merchant-adventurers in Britain, France, and Holland. They seized
on the idea of privately financing European settlers who would create plantations in order to grow and ship exotic crops in demand in Europe. Such
plantations would fare best if placed in sparsely populated or even unoccupied areas like the smaller West Indian islands.

In 1624, two separate groups of colonists, one English and one French,
landed on the tiny 269-square-kilometer island of Saint Kitts. Two well-known
London merchants financed the fourteen Englishmen under the command
of Thomas Warner. After initial settlement, the London backers obtained a
lease for 10,000 acres (4,047 hectares) from the earl of Carlisle, who held
Saint Kitts and Barbados by royal grant from Charles I. The thirty-five
French, commanded by Urbain de Roissy, a naval captain, were backed by a
state trading company established by Cardinal Richelieu. Long known as a
retreat for pirates, Saint Kitts had good water supply, good volcanic soils, and
productive salt pans. A few hundred Caribs resided on the island but offered
no resistance to the intruders. Both European parties divided up the island's
territory (the British took control of the Wingfield River water supply in the
center) and agreed to a joint defense if needed.[7]

Three years later, in 1627, a party of English settlers backed by the wealthy
London merchant William Courteen landed on nearby Barbados, which had
long been abandoned. Barbados was a relatively small island of 440 square
kilometers (compared to 76,484 square kilometers for Hispaniola). The new
settlers built a fort called Jamestown and began planting crops. The same
year, another party of English colonists, under Henry Hawley, landed on the
windward side of Barbados, founded Bridgetown, and immediately began
quarreling with their compatriots on the leeward side of the island. Within

6. David Watts, *The West Indies: Patterns of Development, Culture, and Environmental Change since
1492* (Cambridge: Cambridge University Press, 1987), 131.

7. Ibid., 142–43.

a few years, other English migrants settled on Nevis, Antigua, and Montserrat and began raising tobacco. Violent Carib resistance frustrated English efforts to colonize Barbuda and Saint Lucia.

The first settlers on Saint Kitts and Barbados survived by gathering fruits, hunting feral hogs to extinction, and adopting basic West Indian cassava and sweet potato horticulture. Caribs on Saint Kitts taught the settlers the rudiments; the English on Barbados imported a few Tainos from the South American mainland as their tutors. The settlers began the laborious process of clearing forest and scrub for their *conuco* plots and for growing tobacco. The latter was an ideal cash crop. It was a native West Indian plant that matured within a year and did not require plow cultivation; it could be grown readily by a single planter with one or two laborers. Processing consisted mainly of drying and twisting the tobacco into ropes without the use of expensive tools or machinery. Tobacco's primary drawback was its tendency to exhaust the soil. Entrepreneurial planters also turned to growing the cotton native to the Caribbean and the northern coast of South America. There was heavy English demand for cleaned and ginned cotton if the techniques could be mastered.

Saint Kitts and Barbados settlers were so successful in planting and shipping cash crops that, by 1642, about ten thousand migrants lived on Saint Kitts and forty thousand on Barbados.[8] Elite English and French settlers were able to purchase a four-hectare land grant outright from their respective land companies. Under the terms of their grant, they were obliged to bring along one indentured servant for each four-hectare tract they owned or leased. The impoverished majority, primarily young males, migrated under a form of indenture in which they contracted with a landowner or lessor to work for three to as many as five years. At the end of that period, the indentured worker would be freed and would be entitled to a four-hectare land grant himself. The flow of ships reaching Barbados and Saint Kitts also brought cattle, primarily for draft purposes, horses, sheep, and pigs.

Within four decades, between 1640 and 1680, Barbados planters shifted to sugar production. High prices and limited supply of crystalline sugar in Europe encouraged planters on Barbados to experiment with sugar. As early as 1665, sugar production on Barbados's newly cleared fields reached a five-year annual average of 9,525 metric tons. High sugar prices in those years, never to be equaled, gave Barbados planters a windfall profit. Barbados remained the leading sugar producer in the West Indies until about 1700, when sugar from other islands surpassed its total. Despite a perceptible decline from the highs of the previous century, between 1700 and 1779 the annual

8. Ibid., 173, table 4.4.

production averaged 7,543 metric tons of cane sugar from the same limited set of plantation cane fields.[9]

Barbados became a model for efficient growing and processing of sugar in the West Indies. After they obtained the requisite technical knowledge, plantation owners on Barbados first stripped the island's vegetation and turned it into a vast sugarcane field. Thereafter, every year, they imported technical and managerial staff, new and replacement field-workers, draft cattle and horses, food and provisions (from New England and Europe), fuel for boiling sugar, all manner of consumer items from furniture and dishes to clothing and books, and even feed for livestock. Adroitly coordinating these inputs, Barbados planters put in place a "simplified, totally exploitative, and potentially unstable agricultural system."[10] The planters proved willing to adapt new technical innovations to compensate for pressure on the island's resources.

Sugar enabled Barbados to support an extremely dense and crowded population. The detailed census of 1680–1684 counted a total population of 81,704 persons on Barbados, or a density of 186 persons per square kilometer—a density that did not decrease for the next century or more.[11] Barbados became an offshore platform, an industrial site that decade after decade exported crystalline cane sugar efficiently and profitably to Amsterdam for the growing consumer markets of Europe and North America.

In the early 1640s, James Drax, a successful Barbados planter, obtained the plans for a Brazilian three-roller sugar mill and a set of copper cauldrons from Pernambuco and began growing cane sugar. In 1645, when the Portuguese regained control of coastal Brazil from the Dutch, they expelled a group of Sephardic Jews skilled in sugar refining, who then migrated to Barbados. Under the impetus of this technological transfer, the larger planters on Barbados were all growing sugarcane by midcentury. Barbados sugar planters quickly realized that they needed economy of scale. Since Barbados had limited land, one obvious solution was to buy up the properties of the smaller tobacco and cotton growers. Consolidation of holdings proceeded very quickly as planters put together estates of fifty to more than two hundred hectares. Land prices soared on the island as wealthy Cavalier and Roundhead officers who had survived the English Civil War migrated to Barbados.

Would-be sugar planters had another option. They could buy land grants to blocks of forested, unoccupied land in the interior of the island and clear these holdings for cane. In the 1640s, most Barbados estates were located on the coast. Within a decade, the entire island was divided into demarcated es-

9. Production data from ibid., 284–87, tables 7.1 and 7.2.
10. Watts, *The West Indies*, 219.
11. Ibid., 311, table 7.5.

tates. Employing all possible sources of labor, including swelling numbers of black African slaves, planters first logged out timber and dyewood trees such as the lignum vitae *(Guaiacum officinale)*, then felled usable but less valuable timber trees, and finally clear-cut and burnt the remaining vegetation. With immense effort, they pulled and burnt stumps to prepare the land for cane. The increasing demand for fuel for sugar-boiling operations also put pressure on the island's forests.

Of necessity, however, planters could not devote all their lands to sugarcane fields, nor could they afford to clear all tree cover. Instead, they had to reserve a considerable portion of their estates for pastures and woodlots. For example, in 1647, planter William Hilliard put 93 hectares, or 46 percent, of his total 202.3-hectare plantation into cash crops: sugarcane fields, 80.9 hectares (40 percent); tobacco, 8.1 hectares (4 percent); ginger, 2 hectares (1 percent); and cotton, 2 hectares (1 percent). Hilliard set aside 28.3 hectares (14 percent) for "general provision" gardens, in which he grew potatoes, plantains, cassavas, bonavist peas, and other garden crops. His pastures covered 32.4 hectares (16 percent), and woodlands covered 48.6 hectares (24.3 percent).[12]

In two short decades, by the mid-1660s, sugar planters cleared much of the island's tree cover and left only their woodlots standing. They stripped away the ecologically intricate, stable tropical seasonal and rain forest of Barbados. Only the most inaccessible patches of hill forest on steep slopes remained. Even the woodlots came under pressure by the end of this period. A 1667 report summed up the situation: "At the Barbados[,] all the trees are destroyed, so that wanting wood to boyle their sugar, they are forc'd to send for coales from England."[13] Two tree species became extinct, one an endemic palmetto and the other the mastick *(Mastichodendron sloaneanum)*, a prized timber tree.

Where previously numerous land birds had lived in the forest canopy, all disappeared. Land birds remain scarce on Barbados today. All the larger mammals, including the monkey native to Barbados, suffered the fate of the forest. In the aftermath of forest clearing, alien heliophytic shrubs and grasses extended their range. Two introduced ornamentals, the flowering Barbados Pride *(Caesalpinia pulcherrima)* from the Cape Verde islands and the tamarind *(Tamarindus indica)*, escaped to a wild state. Along the coast, the introduced coconut tree *(Cocos nucifera)* spread rapidly to become a highly regarded food-producing plant.

Deforestation on Barbados caused the expected local environmental effects. Evapotranspiration intensified and the island's climate became hotter

12. Ibid., 194.
13. Quoted in ibid., 186.

and drier. Removal of the forest cover "gave rise to a severe diminution of the island's total nutrient reserve."[14] The bulk of magnesium, calcium, phosphorus, and other nutrients resided in the vegetation itself in a tropical ecosystem like Barbados. When the island forests were cleared and burnt, nutrient-rich ashes were added to the topsoil only temporarily as leaching rates intensified. Stripped of the forest canopy, Barbados soils were open to weathering impact from raindrops, compaction, and increased runoff in the rainy season. These processes, when added to the cumulative demands of sugarcane itself, noticeably began to affect soil fertility. Early clogging of the Bridgetown harbor revealed heavy soil erosion as well.

When supplies of firewood were depleted on Barbados and then on adjoining islands, the planters turned to a new expedient. They began to use bagasse, or cane trash, the fibrous cane stalks left by the crushing mill. The residue from the mill was stacked up to dry before being used in the furnaces of the sugarhouse. Planters began using only one fire in the sugarhouse—located under the smallest kettle, where the greatest heat was required—and then transferring the heat by means of a long, covered flue to the rest of the kettles. This innovation, which came to be called the "Jamaican train," increased efficiency and saved on fuel.

Clearing, planting, and harvesting the expanding cane fields depended on a continuing flow of humans to Barbados. Conventional wisdom among planters held that they required five field hands per hectare of cane cultivated. Voluntary indentures continued but did not meet the demand. Aware of the economic potential of Barbados sugar, successive British rulers in the 1640s and 1650s sent involuntary migrants to work in the cane fields. During and after the English Civil War (1642–1649), thousands of war prisoners were transported to and indentured in Barbados. After 1649, Cromwell's wars in Ireland and Scotland produced some twelve thousand prisoners to be auctioned to Barbados agents, who made a tidy profit reselling them to sugar planters. The planters' average initial cost of twelve pounds per prisoner was readily regained during the years of indenture.

Much of the heavy work of clearing forest and planting cane fell to these British migrants. Brutality, overwork, and scanty rations caused high death rates during service. One indentured servant, who came to Barbados in a draft of thirteen hundred in 1652, wrote that he alone of that group survived indenture. Even planters did not expect to live more than twenty years after arrival. Among other causes of premature death were the occasional epidemics, such as one in 1647–1649 thought to be the plague.[15] Together with

14. Ibid., 221.
15. Ibid., 200, 214–15.

food shortages that caused near-starvation, deaths among whites in this episode were judged to have numbered six thousand to ten thousand.

By the 1660s, the flow of indentured servants from England, whether voluntary or involuntary, diminished. No longer could freed indentured servants look to receive land grants from the colony. Peace ended the prisoner supply. By this time, freed indentured servants and small estate owners who had sold their properties were encouraged to migrate to Jamaica and other islands in the West Indies or to the North American colonies. The planters were more than willing to reduce a sickly, potentially troublesome white population in favor of healthier black Africans who were slaves for life.[16]

Early on, the Barbados planters had looked to black African slaves to fill out their workforce. The Dutch traders offered reliable supplies at good prices until the Navigation Act of 1660 put a monopoly in the hands of the new Company of Royal Adventurers Trading to Africa, under Charles II. Male adult slaves in the 1640s cost twenty-five pounds, or double the price of indentured servants. In later years, the price of a black slave dropped to thirteen or fourteen pounds, or about that of an indentured servant. Slave food and clothing were usually cheaper, especially since Africans would willingly raise some of their food in small plots assigned them. As the slave trade offered abundant supplies of black slaves at a descending price, African slaves replaced indentured Europeans as workers on the Barbados plantations.

A slave count done in the early 1660s put the total population at 32,644 (10,236 men, 17,121 women, and 5,287 children). Twenty years later, the carefully done census of 1684 recorded the total black slave population at 62,136 persons and white colonists at 19,508, for a ratio of just over 3 black people to 1 white person on the island.[17] In the 1700s, as more intensive labor was required to keep up a modicum of soil fertility, the ratio stabilized at 4 blacks to 1 white. By 1773, there were 18,532 whites, 534 freedmen (a new category), and 68,548 slaves on Barbados—a population only slightly enlarged from that of a century before.

Obsessed with costs, the planters began to reduce slave rations and increase the workload for field hands. Barbados planters preferred to borrow money and buy new male slaves rather than encourage slave births and viable families as a means of maintaining their workforces. Heavy mortality among slaves and low reproduction rates meant that the influx of slaves had to con-

16. Philip R. Coelho and Robert A. McGuire argue that Old World diseases introduced into Barbados and the Caribbean in the mid–seventeenth century—yellow fever, hookworm, malaria, and others—afflicted Europeans at a devastating rate. But Africans were far more resistant to these diseases and their resistance to disease enhanced their economic value as slaves. "African and European Bound Labor in the British New World: The Biological Consequences of Economic Choices," *Journal of Economic History* 57 (1997): 92–98.

17. Watts, *The West Indies*, 218, 311, table 7.5.

tinue nearly every year to maintain the island workforce. During the twenty-five years between 1651 and 1675, slave ships landed an average of 1,920 Africans on Barbados each year; a hundred years later, between 1751 and 1775, the annual average was 3,372. Overall, for the entire 125-year period, 339,900 captive African slaves ended their lives on Barbados.[18]

Sugar production on Barbados depended on a wide assortment of other imports. Ships from England and from the North American colonies regularly carried hundreds of replacement draft cattle and horses for the island. Apart from disease, cattle and horses were especially prone to die from overwork as they turned the booms on the three-roller crushing mills. Some relief from the heavy expense of importing draft animals could be found in the use of windmills. Deforestation meant that nearly every spot on the island was subject to intensified trade winds. Barbados sugar planters imported parts and designs and erected windmills to power sugar mills. Occasionally, even the trade winds failed and completely reliable power could be obtained only with adequate numbers of healthy horses and oxen. Barbados imported pine and oak boards, shingles, bricks, and other building materials from the North American colonies. All tools, implements, nails, and other necessary hardware were imported from England.

The North American colonies sent regular shipments of food to Barbados: hundreds of barrels of wheat flour, maize, and rice; barrels of lard, butter, and cheese; bushels of beans, peas, and onions; and barrels of beef and pork and even dried and salt cod, pickled alewives, and other fish. Some provisions continued to arrive from England, but prices were better and transport easier from the mainland colonies. These processed foods were supplemented by shipments of live pigs, sheep, and poultry.[19] The shipments provided a critical nutritional supplement to the diets of planters and slaves alike. Without this regular provisioning, Barbados could not have supported its crowded population or have grown sugar for export.

How did the Barbados planters produce every year thousands of tons of crystalline sugar and additional tonnages of rum and molasses? Barbados was a limited resource base. Virtually all usable tracts of land in Barbados's 440 square kilometers were employed as cane fields, slave food plots, pasture, or space for human settlement. One answer lies in active, innovative land management. When yields and profits declined, the planters acted.

18. Ibid., 364, table 8.6; 366.

19. Richard Pares, *Yankees and Creoles: The Trade between North America and the West Indies before the American Revolution* (Cambridge: Harvard University Press, 1956), 25–26. Pares reports the 1771 quantities for major exports to the West Indies from the two leading ports in that item. For example, New London and New Haven together shipped 2,829 cattle and 4,467 horses in 1771 to the Caribbean. Dried fish from Salem, Marblehead, and Boston together totaled 145,381 quintals shipped in the same year.

By 1685, yields in many Barbados estates had been reduced by half. Recognizing that cane required longer to mature in tired soils, the planters on Barbados extended the time from planting to harvest from fifteen to eighteen months. Planters began to abandon the practice of ratooning (obtaining several yields from the same planting of cane). Yields became so low that it was more profitable to replant every year. Better to use additional slave labor than to accept meager yields from regrowth.

Simultaneously, the planters turned to animal manuring. So intense was the demand for dung that some smaller estate holders turned to enclosing their cattle, horses, sheep, and pigs. They collected the dung, mixed it with maize stalks, cane trash, grasses, and other green manures and sold it by the wicker basket to the sugar planters.[20] Dung had to be hand carried and spread on the cane fields and, therefore, required additional field labor on each sugar plantation. By 1720, however, many planters took to generating dung on their own land, since prices for manure had risen so high. Attention to manuring cane lands was necessary to restore soil fertility.

Soil erosion was also a severe problem, especially with the practice of straight-line trenching to plant cane cuttings. This technique ignored contours and thereby provided chutes for water and soil to wash downslope. To combat this problem, planters had their slaves build retaining walls and haul back soil at the foot of slopes "in carts, or upon negros' heads; our negros work at it like ants and bees."[21] By the early 1700s, the planters had also begun to use a different planting system. Cane-hole planting required marking off a field in squares 1.5 meters to a side. Within each square, field hands scraped square depressions .6 to 1 meter along each side at a depth of 12 to 15 centimeters. When cane was planted in each depression or hole, there existed a two-dimensional system of ridges to contain soil loss.[22]

Shrewd land management could only go so far. In the end, Barbados could continue to grow cane so intensively only because of the continuing inflow of people, animals, provisions, and materials. Energy and nutrients flowed in from outside the island's ecosystem. Neither human workers nor animals were replaced by natural reproduction on the island, and new migrants were constantly needed. Both people and animals converted imported provisions into energy and waste products. The latter restored nutrients to the soil. The decomposing bodies of humans and livestock added their nutrients to the soil of Barbados. Barbados became and remained a factory island, an assembly point for the manufacture of sugar.

From Barbados, British colonists cleared land and planted sugar in other

20. Watts, *The West Indies,* 223.
21. Quoted in ibid., 397.
22. Watts, *The West Indies,* 410.

islands of the Lesser Antilles. Colonists on the tiny British-held Leeward Islands—Nevis (130 square kilometers), Antigua (280 square kilometers), Anguilla (88 square kilometers), Barbuda (161 square kilometers), and Montserrat (84 square kilometers)—first had to overcome serious Carib resistance, which began to subside only in the 1670s. By that time, colonists could import slaves and clear forests in order to grow sugar commercially. For example, Christopher Codrington, a Barbados planter who began to grow sugar on Antigua in 1674, provided the Barbados template for other colonists on the island to follow. By the 1680s, sugar exports from the Leeward Islands averaged 3,300 metric tons per year; by 1700–1704, the average annual yield had doubled to 6,858 tons, coming close to the average figure for Barbados.[23]

Antigua, one of the most successful of these small island colonies, had a population of about ten thousand colonists and black slaves in 1700. Well over half the island was under intensive cultivation—mostly in sugar. The processes of land clearing, timbering, burning, plowing, planting, and livestock foraging were well on the way to destroying the original vegetation. Alien plant and animal imports followed the pattern described for Barbados.[24]

Later, the British acquired other islands in the Lesser Antilles. The Treaty of Paris in 1763, signed at the end of the Seven Years' War, gave England sovereignty over Saint Vincent, Dominica, Grenada, and Tobago (the Ceded Islands), formerly held by France. The West Indies sugar lobby in London pressed to have these islands immediately opened up for development by making cheap land available. English settlers from Barbados and other intensively cultivated islands moved quickly to these new sugar frontiers. Within ten years, nearly 110,000 hectares of land on the four islands had been sold to colonists.[25] By the early 1770s, average annual production for the new lands was 12,972 metric tons per year. Some of the lands already under cultivation in Grenada had been multicropped for indigo, coffee, cotton, cocoa, and food growing. These were immediately brought under the single-minded, Barbados-style sugar monoculture.

The intensive Barbados model heavily influenced sugar production elsewhere in the Caribbean. Barbados was first; Barbados was profitable; and Barbados had found a reliable labor force. On one West Indies island after another, English, French, and later, Spanish planters deforested the land and planted cane in a sequence of sugar frontiers.

23. Ibid., 285, table 7.1.

24. David R. Harris, *Plants, Animals, and Man in the Outer Leeward Islands, West Indies: An Ecological Study of Antigua, Barbuda, and Anguilla* (Berkeley and Los Angeles: University of California Press, 1965), 99–101.

25. Watts, *The West Indies*, 294–95.

MARTINIQUE

The French were slow to move to the Barbados model of sugar monoculture in their West Indian possessions. For many decades, production and export of sugar lagged behind that of the British islands. French sugar planters were hampered by tight state control and by badly conceived monopolies imposed on the slave trade and export trade in sugar. French official policy prohibited trade with the English North American colonies, and trade with Quebec was unpromising. Seventeenth-century French Canada was underpopulated and underdeveloped. The French sugar colonies relied more than the British on provisions and materials sent from the metropolis, since they could not import cheap provisions from British North America; of necessity, they were more self-sufficient in growing food.

Colbert and, following him, other French metropolitan authorities encouraged a pattern of diverse cash and subsistence crops less precariously dependent on the vagaries of the European market. They favored a pattern of smaller estates owned and managed by resident French settlers. Large sugar estates, with their heavy reliance on slave labor, reduced the numbers of French colonists who could support themselves in the new colonies. Having fewer French colonists in residence left the islands vulnerable to slave revolts and to British attacks. French settlers who arrived in the West Indies were far more willing than their English counterparts to grow indigo, cocoa, cotton, coffee, and food crops as well as sugar. Not until later in the eighteenth century did they move gradually toward a tightly focused sugar economy.

In 1639, a new French governor on Saint Kitts claimed Martinique, Marie Galante, La Désirade, Les Saintes, Dominica, and Grenada as French possessions. None, save Martinique, attracted French settlers. Small Carib groups occupied these islands until the 1700s. Seventeenth-century French agricultural colonization centered on the largest islands of the Lesser Antilles, Martinique and Guadeloupe.[26]

26. French sugar planters expanded into Martinique's twin island, Guadeloupe, in a near identical trajectory that generated similar environmental outcomes. Slightly larger than Martinique at 1,706 square kilometers, Guadeloupe, with its limestone and volcanic soils, high rainfall, and lush vegetation, offered rich prospects for French colonization. Guadeloupe's two sections give it a butterfly shape: two great wings linked by a narrow body. A massive mountain chain crowned by Soufrière, an active volcanic peak 1,467 meters in height, dominates Basse-Terre, the larger region. The smaller region, Grande Terre, has level and low-lying terrain. French settlers landed first on Basse-Terre and occupied its coastal plains in the seventeenth century. A five-year war with the Caribs eventually resulted in Carib retreat to the island of Dominica. Settlement on Grande Terre did not really advance until the eighteenth-century sugar enterprise took off.

In 1671, the date of an official census, Guadeloupe's population numbered 7,351 persons: 3,023 French or other European settlers, 4,267 blacks (3,190 slaves), and 61 Caribs. Lucien-René Abénon, *La Guadeloupe de 1671 à 1759: Étude politique, économique et sociale* (Paris: L'Har-

Martinique, 1,090 square kilometers in area, is a high island dominated by two volcano massifs in the interior. Much of the terrain is hilly with steep gradients; the island is traversed by short rivers leading to the sea and has few plains areas.[27] The climate, in common with that of Barbados and the other Lesser Antilles, is humid tropical with variable rainfall, from one thousand to two thousand millimeters per year carried by the trade winds.

When the initial French pioneers arrived, Martinique's natural, spontaneous vegetation was still rich, complex, and diverse. The animal and bird life was similar to that of other West Indies islands. Forests comprised 79 percent of the total vegetation cover. There were three distinct formations: the highest montane forest probably covered 3,000 hectares (5 percent); evergreen rain forests in the upland interior, about 25,000 hectares (22 percent); and the seasonal forests, about 55,000 hectares (52 percent). The montane forests occupied sites above nine hundred meters, and their species composition reflected the cooler temperatures, greater moisture, and higher wind speeds of these elevations. The largest trees in the double canopy were *Tomavita plumieri,* which grew to be twenty meters in height.[28]

Evergreen rain forests growing at three hundred to one thousand meters elevation consisted of three dozen or more tree species. At the highest level of the three-story canopy were massive trees thirty-five to forty meters in height. The largest included the chestnuts *(châtaigniers),* such as *Sloanea massoni,* and other large-bole trees, such as *Dacryodes excelsa* and *Talauma dodecapatela,* with boles up to three meters in circumference.[29] Rope lianas and epiphytes abounded at all levels.

Seasonal forests generally occupied drier and warmer habitats under five hundred meters elevation and had somewhat less standing biomass than the rain forests. The total number of tree species fell off to about twenty. The tallest trees in the double layers of these forests grew to thirty meters height. Enough deciduous species interspersed with evergreens to vary leaf abun-

---

mattan, 1987), 31, 111–22. Cultivation was still limited. The majority of the colonists grew mixed crops of tobacco, ginger, indigo, and provision crops *(vivres)* on their small estates. Other, larger planters had begun to specialize in sugarcane (140). Just as on Martinique, over the next few decades Guadeloupe shifted to a plantation economy. By 1730, the island's population had climbed by a multiplier of five, to 35,168 (7,633 white colonists, 26,301 African slaves, and 1,234 free mulattos) (190–202). There were 252 sugar works on the island, which produced 6,320 metric tons of sugar in 1730 (ibid.).

27. C. T. Kimber, *Martinique Revisited: The Changing Plant Geographies of a West Indian Island* (College Station: Texas A & M University, 1988), 13–18. For a detailed systematic description of Martinique's environment on the arrival of the French settlers, see Jacques Petitjean Roget, *La société d'habitation à la Martinique: Un demi siècle de formation, 1635–1685* (Lille: Atelier Reproduction des thèses Université de Lille III, distributed by H. Champion, 1980), 207–309.

28. Kimber, *Martinique Revisited,* 50, fig. 5.

29. Ibid., 47, fig. 4.

dance noticeably by the seasons. Lianas and epiphytes were fewer and thorny plants more abundant. (The French colonists referred to all these forests as one type, i.e., *les grands bois* or *les bois de haute futaie*.)

On the western and southern coastal plains and piedmont could be found large areas of dry woodlands in areas subject to severe annual drought and hot wind. The half dozen or more smaller tree species—some deciduous and some evergreen—grew in an uneven, interrupted canopy layer that rose to 15 meters at most. Such trees as red birch *(Bursera simaruba)* and *Caeseria decandra* later proved useful for both fuel and timber for the colonists.[30]

The remaining vegetation consisted of evergreen swamp woodlands along the rivers or on the coasts and covered perhaps four thousand hectares. Mangrove swamps with *Rhizophora mangle* were prominent. There were also bushlands, or woody shrub communities, less than four meters in height in comparatively small areas, and a distinctive dense thicket, or littoral hedge, at the margin of the sea.

Carib Indians migrated to Martinique from the South American mainland in the prehistoric period. When they did so, they brought with them a number of mainland cultivars, including their staples of manioc and sweet potato. In the late fifteenth century, about eight thousand or so Carib Indians probably lived on Martinique. They were hunter-gatherers organized into "local, self-sufficient, extended matriarchal families" who inhabited shared homesteads of thirty to one hundred people.[31] The Caribs, like the Tainos of Hispaniola, grew manioc and sweet potatoes in *conucos* cleared every year by burning. Probably more than two-thirds of Martinique's land area—the coastal areas and the lower slopes of the mountains—was affected by Carib burning and shifting cultivation. The Martinique Caribs obtained much of their diet from the sea by hunting sea turtles and conches and by fishing from their seagoing dugout canoes. The Caribs were generally far more warlike and aggressive than the Tainos and engaged in long-distance raiding of other islands.

From Hispaniola, the Spanish claimed possession of Martinique and the rest of the Lesser Antilles. Imported diseases and Spanish slave raiding reduced the Carib population of Martinique to about half its original size, or about four thousand persons, as early as the mid–sixteenth century. The Caribs offered determined violent resistance to Spanish raids. They tolerated, however, a limited, transient European presence on the island. Privateers and buccaneers landed periodically for fuel, food, and refuge and established small-scale settlements on the coasts. These visitors introduced pigs that ran wild on the island in considerable numbers. Pig rooting undoubtedly modified ground vegetation across the island. Other early introductions included the banana, plantain, sugarcane, and coconut—all adopted by the Caribs. European sojourners planted plots of tobacco and indigo. By the mid-1500s, the greatest single environmental change stemmed from land abandonment as the numbers of Caribs declined. It is likely that these areas, formerly under *conuco* cultivation, reverted to "well-developed forests and woodlands" by the early 1600s.[32]

In 1635, a newly formed French private company chartered by the king, the Compagnie des Isles de l'Amérique, first settled Martinique with overflow settlers from Saint Christophe, the original French colony on Saint Kitts. Syndicates of private merchants took up portions of land granted the company by the Crown and agreed to pay rent in tobacco or cotton. Settling in person, these new proprietors landed first at Saint Pierre, on the northwest coast, and then began to disperse along the western coastline. By 1640, there were a thousand French settlers on Martinique. The company ceded each colonist on arrival a plot of land varying from a few to as many as twenty-six hectares. The land was free of charge, but the gift obligated the holder to cultivate a substantial portion of it within three years.[33] The colonists immediately began clearing land for settlement and cultivation.[34]

After initial resistance failed to drive off the settlers, the Martinique Caribs retreated east to the interior. For three decades, a longitudinal line agreed on by a formal treaty divided the island between Basse-Terre, the western side of French activity and Capesterre, the eastern half left to the Caribs.[35] As more colonists arrived, however, the demand for coastal lands intensified and relations with the Caribs worsened. Between 1658 and 1660, the settlers attacked and drove the Caribs from the fertile northeastern coastal regions of Capesterre. Those few remaining Caribs living on the northeastern coast fled to the nearby island of Dominica. This removal opened up the east coast for pioneer settlement.

Within fifty years, the total population had grown to 15,600 persons. In 1685, 6,200 French colonists, largely from northwestern France, owned 9,400 African slaves. By that date, only a handful of Caribs remained on Martinique's south coast. Most settlers were smallholder, owner-cultivators living on their holdings, who employed one or two indentured French laborers or black slaves to grow tobacco, ginger, cotton, annatto, and *Cassia fistula* as cash crops, along with provision gardens and grains. The indentured laborers were committed to three years of service, after which they could obtain a plot of land on their own. Settlers also maintained significant numbers of

32. Ibid., 109.
33. For a detailed description of the first five years of settlement, 1635–1640, see Petitjean Roget, *La société d'habitation à la Martinique*, 513–700.
34. Ibid., 560–65.
35. Kimber, *Martinique Revisited*, 115.

livestock in a mixed farming system brought from home. As Africans became available at a thriving slave market at Saint Pierre, colonists replaced their indentured servants with purchased slaves.

A ship carrying Dutch Jews that had been expelled from Pernambuco on the Brazilian coast by the Portuguese arrived in 1654, bringing technical knowledge of sugar planting and processing. Favorable prices for sugar and declining prices for tobacco encouraged sugar planting on Martinique. The sugar sector directly competed for land with the smallholders' mixed-farming sector.

A land market emerged in 1644 as colonists began to sell land. However, to restrain speculation, the Martinique Council ruled in 1665 that any ceded lands not in cultivation within six months of taking possession would be confiscated. The state tried to limit the market in other ways. In 1670, the council reserved as state property an eighty-meter strip of land (the Cinquante Pas de Roi) running inland from the high-tide mark all along the coast of the island.[36] This belt of land guaranteed access to the sea and a free route for travel and communication along the coast between settlements. Artisans and traders were granted small parcels of land in this strip.

Once under way, land clearing progressed without faltering. According to an official survey *(terrier)* done in 1671, the company had ceded to settlers 23,770 hectares, or 21.8 percent of the 109,000 hectares of land on the island. Ceded lands lay in an arc around the northwest to the northeast coasts and along the southern coast. The colonists had at that point cleared almost half, or 10,000 hectares (9.2 percent), for cultivation.[37] Of the total cleared area, sugarcane occupied 2,447 hectares, tobacco 1,019 hectares, cleared pasture or savanna 2,406 hectares, and provision gardens 3,192 hectares. The remainder was urban settlement (1,675 hectares) and uncleared woods *(bois)* covering 11,885 hectares.

The first half century of French settlement, land clearing, and European-style farming had a pronounced impact on Martinique's environment. In this early period, the colonists employed classic slash-and-burn techniques to bring land under cultivation. They attacked the dry woodlands and seasonal forests of the coasts and lower hills but made little impact on the rain forests of the high interior. The heaviest concentration of cleared land was in and around Saint Pierre on the northwest coast, where colonists cultivated 80 to 90 percent of the ceded land.[38]

By opening previously closed canopy vegetation, the pioneers created niches for the expansion of heliophytic and xerophytic scrub woodland in

36. Ibid., 117.
37. Ibid., 128, table 19.
38. Ibid., 120, map 20.

the seasonal forest areas. The type of clearing and fallowing employed also encouraged expansion of savannas at the expense of dry woodland. Woody, shrubby plants like the beach mahot *(Hibiscus tiliaceus)* and several other mahots moved aggressively into fields abandoned by the settlers.[39]

In a familiar sequence, the colonists introduced an array of new cultivars and animals to Martinique. These included the cash crops already mentioned and various European and African fruits and vegetables. To the herds of feral pigs, the settlers added other ungulates. By 1684, their herds included 5,483 cattle, 1,180 horses, 111 mules, and 2,166 sheep and goats.[40] The savannas existing at the time were too small to afford adequate grazing for these animals. Instead, the settlers turned toward unfenced forest and woodland grazing.

In addition to grazing and browsing, woodcutting by the colonists put heavy pressure on the island's woodlands. Charcoal was the preferred domestic and iron-working fuel. Charcoal burners targeted the dense hardwoods *(Simaruba amara* and *Bucida buceras)* of the dry woodlands, which burned slowly and evenly. Making charcoal for cooking alone probably consumed seven hundred to eight hundred metric tons of wood per year.[41] Woodcutters cut into coastal and riverine mangrove formations to obtain the wood of the red mangrove *(Rhizophora mangle)* for charcoal burning and for the tanning agent in its bark used in preparing hides for leather. As the number of sugarcane estates and mills grew, woodcutting to feed the furnaces under the sugar vats kept pace. Hardest hit were the dry and seasonal woodlands adjacent to the sugar fields.

Timber demands for house construction and for boat and shipbuilding were substantial. From the seasonal forests growing along the riverbanks, builders cut hardwood species such as *bois olive (Geoffroea inermis), gommier rouge (Bursera simaruba)*, and *bois agouti (Vitex divaricata)*. The latter was especially rot resistant and used often for ships. For barrel staves, tool handles, and similar purposes, the colonists favored *genipa (Genipa americana)* for its "fine-grained, easily worked wood." During the earliest years, suitable hardwoods were readily accessible; in later years, timber cutters moved increasingly higher, toward fringes of the highland forests of the interior. Hardwood rain forest species used for construction included *bois pistolet (Guarera ramiflora)*, abundant from 400 to 900 meters in elevation; *bois du bouis (Chrysophyllum argenteum)*, which grew 8 to 12 meters tall at 200

39. Ibid., 123.
40. Ibid., 125.
41. According to Kimber's calculation, 4 pounds of wood is required to make 1 pound of charcoal, and 1 pound would cook a meal for four persons. Using this formula, she arrives at 2.5 English tons of wood used per day and 812 tons per year for a population of 16,500 (123). The same ratio using .5 kilograms per day of charcoal for four persons works out to 712 metric tons per year for the 1685 population of 15,600.

to 700 meters in elevation; *acomas (Homalium racemosum)* found at 200 to 400 meters in elevation; *rois bandar (Richeria grandis);* and several others.[42]

Several resin-impregnated trees that resisted insect and water penetration were especially durable. These species also tended to have colorful, dense woods that contained dyeing principals. The most sought after of these trees was lignum vitae, known as gaiac and used for carving pulleys for ship's rigging, machinery cogs, and girders. Most of the lignum vitae harvested traveled to France as one of Martinique's early exports. The Loire ports received thirty-five thousand metric tons of the wood in 1672 and twenty-five thousand the next year. However, as harvesting continued, the tree became scarce and exports peaked at that level and dropped off thereafter. By the mid-1700s, gaiac remained on official price lists, but shipments had nearly ended.[43]

Martinique's brilliantly colored hardwoods that could be used for inlay work attracted European cabinet and furniture makers. A number of joiners set up shop on the island and built distinctive furniture. Traders regularly shipped to France considerable quantities of these much-sought-after hardwoods. The three most popular species in this early period were *Tabebuia pallida*, with its pink or gray semihard wood; *Coccoloba diversifolia*, a reddish wood; and *Rochefortia cuneata*, with its blue-green hue. The last had become rare by the turn of the eighteenth century. By that point, however, local cabinetmakers and wood merchants had identified and were cutting more than thirty species of trees with colored wood attractive to the trade.[44]

As soon as they landed, the Martinique colonists began exploiting the rich hunting and fishing resources of the island. Within a short time, the settlers exhausted the protein resources of the island that had sustained the Caribs for generations and had to rely on domesticated animals for meat. The colonists and their slaves hunted the largest indigenous land fauna—the iguanas *(Iguana delicatissima)*, agoutis *(Dasyprocta antillensis)*, opossums *(Didelphis marsupialis insularis)*, and rice rats *(Megalomys desmarestii)*—to scarcity and virtual extinction in the first two decades. They killed large numbers of any edible birds and parrots they discovered. Along the coast, the colonists enthusiastically killed and ate marine turtles: green sea turtles *(Chelonia mydas)*, hawksbills *(Eretmochelys imbricata)*, and loggerheads *(Caretta caretta)*, among others. They hunted manatees *(Trichechus manatus)* to virtual extinction. They gathered conchs, crayfish, and oysters so avidly that these resources could not reproduce. Localized fishing of sixteen fish species continued but with diminishing returns.[45]

42. Ibid., 122, 123.

43. Ibid., 189. Kimber in a private communication reports that in 1992 there were only two known specimens of lignum vitae on the island.

44. Ibid., 122. See the list in Kimber, *Martinique Revisited*, 184–86, table 21.

45. Ibid., 24. The role of the green sea turtle in the food budgets of the European-dominated early modern Caribbean population has not been fully recognized. Exports of live

By the end of the first century of colonial settlement on Martinique, in the 1730s, land use on the island had radically changed. Sugar planting replaced smallholders' diversified mixed farming. The state had ceded all land in the plains and piedmont regions of Martinique. In these settled regions, small and midsize landholders struggled to survive as the markets for tobacco and their other cash crops fell off. Many were forced to move their households and slaves to other islands or to the Carolinas, where cheap, easily workable, fertile land was still available. Only sugar planters could put together the wherewithal to expand. They steadily enlarged their lands by buying up nearby smaller holdings in a continuing process of consolidation. In contrast to the 5- to 40-hectare holdings of the earlier period, sugar plantations averaged 170 hectares, and a few were over 1,000 hectares.

In the conventional West Indies pattern, Martinique planters reserved land for a grinding mill, a boiling house, and the habitations of owner, managers, and slaves, aside from the sugarcane fields and fallows, grazing lands, slave provision lands, and woodlands. The topography of Martinique and the elongated shape of its original landholdings dictated that plantation lands contain lands at different elevations. At each level, there were differing soil, sun, and wind exposures and microclimates. The configuration of sugarcane fields varied accordingly. Planters assigned the roughest and steepest lands, often crossed by steep ravines, or *mornes,* to slaves for growing manioc or plantain in provision gardens or kept these lands as woodlots.

By 1731, the number of sugar plantations had risen to 431. Fields planted in sugarcane totaled 15,450 hectares (14 percent of the island's total area), a sixfold increase since 1671.[46] Martinique's sugar production was 14,450 metric tons, three times the output of Barbados and equal to that of Jamaica in the same year.[47] Sugar output peaked in 1753 at 20,390 metric tons and then declined in the 1760s, fluctuating between 8,000 and 12,000 tons annually for the remainder of the eighteenth century. The introduction of a new, more productive variety of sugarcane from the Pacific helped restore output to the 20,000-ton mark in the 1820s, where it remained.

Sugar's labor needs paid for the import of African slaves, whose numbers rose fourfold in fifty years (from 9,400 in 1685 to 40,000 in 1736) and doubled again in the next fifty years to 80,000 in 1783. Apart from labor on the plantation cash crops, the slaves put their own impress on the land. By terms of the *code noir,* planters had to provide each of these slaves with specified

---

turtles to Europe for consumption were also large. See James Jerome Parsons, *The Green Turtle and Man* (Gainesville: University of Florida Press, 1962).

46. Noël Deerr, *The History of Sugar* (London: Chapman and Hall, 1949), 1:233. Deerr uses the term *sugar works.* I assume that each plantation had such a mill and boiling house, and I use *plantation* as a synonym.

47. Ibid. The production figure is for 1732. Deerr lists 14,450 English tons for production.

numbers of plantain and manioc plants that could be grown for their own use. Consolidated areas, known as provision gardens, occupied more than 5,000 hectares in the 1780s. But many slaves also grew these plants, as well as sweet potatoes and yams, along roadsides and in isolated patches in the ravines of the plantation uplands. Various surveys estimated the numbers of manioc hills at 22 million in the 1730s and 38 million in the 1780s.[48] This style of food cultivation marks an intriguing reversion to the *conuco* cultivation of the long-departed Caribs.

Blessed with more land than their counterparts in Barbados, the Martinique planters were more profligate and less inclined to invest in careful conservation of resources. Rather than fertilize sugarcane fields, they adopted a system of extended fallowing that permitted reversion of exhausted fields to scrub and brush cover. This system of heavy use followed by abandonment without fertilization "led to substantial soil erosion and soil exhaustion."[49] Reduced output of sugar in the latter part of the eighteenth century in large measure reflects lowered yields on Martinique by comparison with other islands.

Most plantations relied heavily on the island's nineteen thousand cattle and horses (the population in 1783), whose primary task was to drive the sugar-grinding mills. (Before the nineteenth century, no sugar planters adopted the plow; instead, growers relied on slaves laboring with hoes to plant cane.) These large ungulates, plus another eleven thousand to twelve thousand sheep and goats, stressed the vegetation of the island. Although feral livestock roaming the interior had virtually disappeared, the island's livestock grazed and browsed in wooded areas when the limited savannas and unimproved pastures failed to satisfy them. Martinique's pastures were "uncultivated spontaneous, herbaceous vegetation on inaccessible or rough land rather than true planted grassland pasture."[50]

A few planters tried to improve animal feeds by importing new legumes and grasses. They experimented with the European lucerne *(Medicago sativa)*, yellow sweet clover, or melilot *(Melilotus officinalis)*, and the West Indies plant *Desmodium latifolium*, naturalized in the botanical garden at Saint Pierre. Guinea grass *(Panicum maximum)* and para grass *(Bracheria purpurascens)*, West African imports that arrived in the mid-1700s, had great potential for eight to ten cuttings of hay each year if planted annually. However, the majority of planters seem not to have systematically followed through on the potential of these nutritious imports.

Martinique planters did invest substantially in water control. If at all possible, they irrigated their cane fields. They built dams on upper ravines to

48. Kimber, *Martinique Revisited*, 199–200.
49. Ibid., 205.
50. Ibid., 189.

trap rainy-season stream flows and mounded earth to create small tanks or ponds (often used to water livestock as well). They also adopted alternatives to animal traction whenever feasible. Windmills located on the windward coast remained fewer than twenty but still saved their owners heavy expenditure. Water mills proliferated. By 1769, there were 116 water-driven grinding mills in operation. In the northern part of the island, many streams were perennial and could supply waterwheels directly. To tap seasonal water flow was a different matter. Planters built dams and reservoirs, which could be drawn on nearly year-round, and canals, aqueducts, and flumes to move water to the grinding mills.

The canals were sizeable. On the Carbet-to-Saint Pierre, leeward side of the island, three canals moved water from the Carbet River to large sugar plantations. The Delajus Canal, for example, brought water 1.6 kilometers along the contour lines of the slope, and then went underground beneath Charlotte Ravine to empty into a plantation reservoir near Lajus Ravine. Building the canal, tunnel, and flume required three years of slave labor.[51]

Rapid growth in the sugar sector up to the 1730s extended the settlement frontier on Martinique. By and large, however, sugar plantations did not extend far into the higher interior. Less fertile, marginal lands on the higher slopes were available for pioneering. In these areas, a secondary form of export planting on smaller estates spread. Start-up costs for clearing and pioneering were high, but colonists discovered that tree and bush crops could flourish in the hills. Cacao proved to be profitable, and plantings grew rapidly after 1700. Cacao berries could be transported at a reasonable cost by pack animals and wagons even from remote highland estates. Upland planters used sheltering trees from the original forest vegetation to provide shade for cacao seedlings in forest clearings. During the six years necessary for cacao trees to bear fruit, slaves interplanted them with manioc, plantain, and vegetables. By 1727, 14 million cacao trees occupied 9,477 hectares of land; in that year, however, a violent hurricane and earthquake destroyed 6 million trees. An unidentified root fungus immediately killed off most of the surviving cacao trees. Exports fell by 95 percent. It was not until a South American variety of cacao was reintroduced that cacao made a partial comeback.[52]

The cumulative impact of single-minded cash cropping on Martinique's environment was dramatic. By the first half of the nineteenth century, up to three-quarters of "the island plant cover had been cleared, burned, or otherwise destroyed beyond recognition." The 1783 survey revealed that 24.1 percent of the island's lands were cropped every year (see table 12.1). The nearly 58,000 hectares, or 53 percent of the island, classified as *plaine* (sugar

---

51. Ibid., 178.
52. Ibid., 201–3.

TABLE 12.1 Profile of Martinique, 1783

Land Use	Number of Hectares	Percentage of Island Area
Croplands		
Sugarcane	14,555	13.3
Coffee	4,505	4.1
Cacao	1,107	1.0
Cotton	873	0.8
Provisions	5,426	5.0
TOTAL AREA IN CROPS	26,466	24.1
Fallow and Disturbed Lands		
Plaines (sugar fallow lands)	10,733	9.9
Savannas and pastures	13,588	12.4
Mornes (ravines)	33,652	30.7
TOTAL FALLOW AND UNDISTURBED	57,973	53.0
Natural Vegetation		
Forests	14,698	13.4
TOTAL LAND USE	99,137	90.5
Unsurveyed Residual	10,463	9.5
TOTAL ISLAND AREA	109,600	100.0

SOURCE: Data derived from Kimber, *Martinique Revisited*, 196, table 92.

fallows), savanna, pasture, and *morne* (ravines) no longer bore any semblance of the island's precolonial plant cover. Instead, a mix of pioneer bushy shrubs and weedy tree products of arrested and early succession stages flourished. Many of these were unpalatable to livestock. In the drier zones on the leeward side of the island, dry brushlands and mixed cactus scrub dominated. Numerous invading wild plant species thrived in the disturbed ecosystems found on Martinique. Some, like bamboo *(Bambusa vulgaris)*, were, from the colonist's perspective, welcome and useful; many were not.[53] Only the forest area (13.4 percent) retained much of its original vegetation, and that was heavily disturbed.

Those planters who survived financially replaced cacao with Arabian coffee seedlings. Within ten years, 10 million coffee bushes had been planted on sixty-five hundred hectares. The coffee sector hovered around this level for the rest of the century, with a peak in the 1770s and a low point in the 1780s. The 1783 survey counted 498 coffee estates, with an average nine

53. Ibid., 209. See p. 192 for the introduction of bamboo.

hectares planted in coffee bushes, and 101 cacao estates, with an average of eleven hectares in cacao trees.

SAINT DOMINGUE

At the turn of the eighteenth century, French sugar planters acquired abundant new lands to clear and plant. Saint Domingue (present-day Haiti), a new French colony, comprised the western third of Hispaniola. Sparsely populated, at 27,750 square kilometers it was ten times the size of Martinique and Guadeloupe combined. The French, having informally settled along the western coast of Hispaniola without protest by Spanish authorities, secured legitimate royal title by the terms of the Peace of Ryswick in 1697. General European peace after the Treaty of Utrecht in 1713 encouraged additional French migrants to settle in Saint Domingue.

New lands on Saint Domingue held obvious attractions, and land clearing proceeded rapidly. By 1739, there were over 350 large sugar estates in the colony, and most of the well-watered, well-drained land had been taken up. Sugar was not the only crop grown; estates growing indigo and coffee were also numerous and profitable. The remaining available land lay within the rain shadow of the island's mountain range. For the next two decades, the French state invested more than 6 million livres in a large irrigation project. Irrigation engineers sent out from France planned and carried out the digging of irrigation canals on the Artobonite Plain, the Cul de Sac Plain and the Plain of Les Cayes. By 1760, 40,000 irrigated hectares had been planted with cane. In 1775, there were 648 plantations with an average of 120 to 160 hectares in operation on Saint Domingue. Another round of expansion occurred in the 1780s, when planters ventured into the difficult terrain of the northern coast, where rainfall was plentiful, and claimed new lands to plant cane.

By midcentury the plantations of Saint Domingue produced more sugar than those of Jamaica or any of the other English Antilles colonies. Sugar shipped from Saint Domingue to France went from an annual average of 5,012 metric tons in 1710–1714 to 42,400 tons in 1742 and to 68,407 tons in 1785–1789.[54] In part, yields from newly opened cane fields tended to be higher than those from islands where no new lands were left. In part, French investment surged because of a considerable price advantage. Lower French tariffs on imported sugar meant that unrefined sugars, both *muscavado* and white-clayed sugar, could be sold throughout Europe at prices 30 to 50 percent lower than those from English colonies.[55] France used less sugar domestically and, for much of the century, exported far more than did En-

54. Watts, *The West Indies*, 287, table 7.5.
55. Ibid., 272.

gland. French traders were permitted after 1727 to sell their sugar direct to other European markets without reexporting through French ports.

Slaves poured into Saint Domingue to support the expansion of sugar. By 1767, after construction of the irrigation projects, 264,471 slaves, mostly engaged in sugar cultivation, labored in the colony. In that year, there were only 20,378 European settlers and 5,897 black freedmen. By 1791, there were approximately 480,000 slaves, 28,000 freedmen, and only 32,650 colonists— a white-to-black ratio of 1 to 15.6. The extreme imbalance of this ratio, more pronounced than for any other sugar colony in the eighteenth century, made possible a mass slave revolt in the context of the French Revolution, the collapse of French rule on Saint Domingue, and the precipitous decline of sugar exports from Hispaniola.[56]

JAMAICA

Far greater scope for sugar cultivation lay in the larger islands of the Greater Antilles. Jamaica's 11,424 square kilometers—much of it cultivable plain— was over ten times the area of Martinique. Aggressive warfare by the mid-sixteenth-century English state, deeply embroiled in a long, bitter ideological struggle with Spain, opened the sugar frontier on Jamaica. Thereafter, state funding, encouragement, and protection nurtured Jamaican settlement. During the 1700s, Jamaica became a leading Caribbean sugar producer and one of the richest colonies in the British empire. Nonetheless, even by 1800, with so much more land available, Jamaica's sugar plantations occupied but a fraction of the island's potentially fertile lands. On Jamaica, sugar and cattle formed a symbiotic connection in a frontier society. Much of the island remained in forests and pastures suitable for cattle raising. Ranching continued to be the second most important sector of the island's economy and an equally important form of land use.

In 1654, the English Protector Oliver Cromwell set in motion his "Western Design"—a surprise assault on the Spanish colonies in the West Indies. Cromwell appointed William Penn as admiral and Robert Venables as general of the expedition. Their orders were to sail across the Atlantic and attack and seize one or more of the Spanish island or mainland colonies in the Caribbean as circumstances dictated.[57] Carrying five understrength regiments, the English fleet arrived at Barbados at the end of January 1655. There, Penn and Venables enlisted additional recruits among settlers on Bar-

56. See ratio calculations in ibid., 308–25.

57. S. A. G. Taylor, *The Western Design: An Account of Cromwell's Expedition to the Caribbean,* 2d ed. (London: Solstice Productions, 1969), 3–7; Richard S. Dunn and the Institute of Early American History and Culture, *Sugar and Slaves: The Rise of the Planter Class in the English West Indies, 1624–1713* (Chapel Hill: University of North Carolina Press, for the Institute of Early American History and Culture, Williamsburg, Va., 1972), 151–52.

bados, Nevis, Saint Kitts, and Montserrat who hoped to gain new lands and prosperity in the about-to-be conquered Spanish lands. In April 1655, the English attempted a landing and assault on San Domingo, capital of Spanish Hispaniola, which ended in disaster and the loss of over a thousand men.

The disheartened commanders did not try again but sailed for Jamaica to attack what appeared to be a much easier target. Jamaica was a backward and nearly forgotten piece of the Spanish colonies in the New World. After the Spanish conquest, the Taino population, perhaps sixty thousand persons, died of disease or were captured by slave raiders. Few colonists came to replace them. By the end of the Spanish period, Jamaica's total population did not exceed twenty-five hundred persons—half of them white and half of them black African slaves. Although the Spanish elite owned vast estates in theory, these estates were little cultivated or developed.[58] The Spanish settlements clung to the plains of the south coast, while the north coast was nearly deserted. The leading Spanish prelate in Jamaica reported in 1611:

> The whole of the rest of the island which is about 50 leagues long and little more than 15 wide is uncultivated and uninhabited, though there are many hunting grounds of horned stock in which the colonists have their shares in proportion to the ranches they formerly had stocked with tame cattle[,] from which have sprung those that are now wild in these grounds. Nearly the whole year is taken up in killing cows and bulls only to get the hides and fat, leaving the meat wasted. There are also large herds of swine raised in the mountains, which are common to all who may wish to hunt them as is ordinarily done, obtaining therefrom a great quantity of lard and jerked pork.[59]

Spanish Jamaica's main exports were cattle hides and hog lard obtained by hunting feral animals. Jamaica, despite one and a half centuries of Spanish settlement, was less a garden than a huge trackless wilderness. Whatever impact the Tainos had had on the island's flora and fauna had long since been erased. Natural vegetation and animal life was luxuriant and abundant. Some new plants and animals had invaded the island. The most noticeable ecological change occurred with the introduction and proliferation of free-ranging European horses, cattle, and pigs that survived admirably in the wild.

Jamaica extends 231 kilometers in length from east to west and 48–64 kilometers north to south. There are three distinct natural divisions of the island: the dry coastal zone, the central montane region, and the wet northern coast.[60] Along the southern coast, most of the rain falls in two bursts, in the months of May and October, for an average of under 750 millimeters per year. Inland from the beach was a dry scrub woodland "made up of hard-

---

58. Dunn and the Institute of Early American History and Culture, *Sugar and Slaves*, 151.

59. Quoted in Michael Craton and James Walvin, *A Jamaican Plantation: The History of Worthy Park, 1670–1970* (Toronto: University of Toronto Press, 1970), 13.

60. Asprey and Robbins, "The Vegetation of Jamaica," 370.

leaved, dry limestone shrubs with cacti, halophytes and salt-resistant trees not encountered inland."[61] Along the shoreline in the bays and inlets were frequent mangrove groupings with red, white, and black mangroves similar to those found throughout the West Indies.

Some tracts in the five largest southern coastal plains (Clarendon, Anaya, Saint Catherine, Liguanea, and Ayala) were cultivated, but the far greater portion was sparse woodland, virtually a savanna. The tree cover included the smallish lignum vitae, the gru gru palm *(Acrocomia aculeata)*, and larger trees such as the yokewood *(Catalpa longissima)*, measuring up to 28 meters high, and even the deciduous cotton tree *(Ceiba pentandra)*, rising to 40 meters.[62]

Those intrepid mid-seventeenth-century Spanish settlers—or the English who followed them—who decided to traverse the island from the southern to the northern coast probably would have taken the only well-defined route across the interior plateau. An eighty-kilometer packhorse trail began at the edge of the Anaya Plain (fronting on Old Harbour Bay) directly north along the valley of the Rio Minho and climbed to Los Vermejales, a fertile, well-watered savanna at a height of 900 meters, before beginning the long descent to the northern coast at Saint Ann's Bay.[63] Apart from a few isolated settlements, the track lay in uninhabited country. Travelers on this route first encountered a dry, largely evergreen limestone forest growing on a series of rocky limestone hills and ranges. On the lower reaches nearer the coast, the dominant trees, up to 14 meters tall, were the red birch, found in similar woodlands on Martinique, and the tall cotton tree. As travelers pushed higher to a level where rainfall increased, the forest became more abundant, with a continuous 14- to 20-meter canopy and a substory standing 7 to 10 meters tall. They saw scattered individual trees, such as *Chlorophora tinctoria*, reaching as high as 28 meters.

Climbing to 350 meters elevation brought the travelers into the dramatic landforms of the "Cockpit Country," where the terrain was covered with large bowl-shaped circular depressions, or *dolinas,* 170 meters deep. The bottoms of these *dolinas* were filled with bauxite soils and suffused with subterranean streams and caves. The submontane forest cover, benefiting from rainfall of up to 1,900 millimeters, was moist evergreen forest with a 20-meter canopy. This higher forest was "far more mesophytic and luxuriant than the dry type, having more forest trees, epiphytes and lianes, aroids, bromeliads and orchids."[64]

61. Ibid., 383.
62. Ibid., 389.
63. S. A. G. Taylor, *The Western Design,* 40 and frontispiece map, where the trail is clearly marked.
64. G. F. Asprey and R. G. Robbins, "The Vegetation of Jamaica," *Ecological Monographs* 23, no. 4 (1953): 385. Above nine hundred meters elevation, the lower montane moist forest declined into an upper montane drier regime of much smaller trees and shrubs. Above fifteen

At Los Vermejales, the track climbed upward into true montane forest on the 600- to 900-meter central upland plateau of Jamaica. Annual rainfall sharply increased to 2,500 millimeters or more. In the lower montane rain forest, the settlers marched under a 28-meter main canopy and a secondary 15- to 17-meter canopy. They passed giant trees such as the *Psidium montanum,* soaring to 41 meters in height with a great trunk that measured as much as 4 meters in circumference. During the last quarter of the trail, as the pioneers descended steadily toward the northern coast, they moved through a continuing tropical rain forest, but one with higher canopies and even greater proliferation of lianas and epiphytes. This heavy lowland tropical forest persisted until within a few kilometers of the coastline.[65]

The tiny Spanish settlement offered no effective resistance when the British fleet arrived. Within a week, on May 11, 1655, Cromwell's troops entered Villa de la Vega, the Spanish capital, abandoned by its defenders. On the 17th, the Spanish governor, Don Juan Ramirez, signed the "capitulations" that set out the terms for the Spanish surrender and the English assumption of control over Jamaica.[66] Venables and a few of his men returned to England within a few months, but the remainder of the army settled along Jamaica's south coast; their main base was located near Villa de la Vega.

Most Spaniards left Jamaica for Cuba as refugees. A few stayed and, rejecting the terms of the capitulation, fought a five-year guerilla war of raids and ambushes against the English. The Spanish commander Christobal de Arnaldo Ysassi, appointed governor of Jamaica by the Spanish ruler, skillfully mobilized hundreds of newly released black slaves by recognizing their own leaders as commanders. Especially lethal to the English troops were those slaves who had served the Spanish under relatively favorable circumstances as mounted hunters of feral cattle and hogs.

Casualties from guerilla raids continued, but deaths from disease were far greater. Dysentery and malaria struck hard. By January 1656, of the 7,000 men who had landed in May the previous year and the subsequent 800 reinforcements, only 2,600 remained—over 5,000 had died.[67] Cromwell, determined to hold on to his new colony, sent a new commander with 1,200 vet-

---

hundred meters, in the eastern Blue Mountains, where the upper ridges are enveloped in clouds for at least six hours per day, was evergreen mountain mist forest, which still exists today. Widely spaced trees formed an uneven, open upper canopy at thirteen to fifteen meters and a subcanopy at ten meters, with scattered shrubs and a "close and often luxuriant cover of herbs, ferns and bryophytes."

65. The hypothetical reconstruction breaks down at this point. Asprey and Robbins had no relic stands of true lowland tropical moist forest on Jamaica to draw inferences from, since all had been long since destroyed. They infer that the northern lowland forest cover was a more abundant extension of the montane forest. Ibid., 395.

66. S. A. G. Taylor, *The Western Design,* 16–17.

67. Ibid., 91–92.

eran soldiers to Jamaica in a convoy that arrived in December 1656. Also in that year, with official encouragement, some 1,400 planters, their families, and servants, sailed from overcrowded Nevis for Jamaica. The newcomers settled at uninhabited Morant Bay on the eastern tip of the island.

Despite their depleted numbers, in 1657 and 1658 the English defeated and drove off two successive Spanish counterattacks from nearby Cuba. These were the battles that decided the war, although Spanish and black guerilla raids continued until the Spanish commander finally gave up the struggle and left for Cuba in 1650.

The new Restoration government had no dispute with Cromwell's goals in the Caribbean. Charles II put in place liberal policies intended to encourage land settlement, clearing, and cultivation in Jamaica. In August 1662, Lord Windsor, the newly appointed royal governor who had been sent to establish a civil administration, reached Jamaica accompanied by a large body of new migrants. Windsor disbanded the Cromwellian army and retained only a small garrison force. Few English soldiers of the 9,000 who had landed left Jamaica. Those who survived battle and disease formed the core of a new settler colony. About 3,000 additional settlers had come from Nevis and England.

A census taken in October 1662, just after Windsor's arrival, listed a settler population of 4,721 (including 645 women and 408 children) and 552 black slaves. These figures imply that a total of at least 7,000 migrants had perished from disease or war in the course of just seven years. Thus far, the remaining settlers had planted only 1,179 hectares of land.[68] The tiny population clustered along the southeastern coast in each of the well-defined coastal savannas stretching from the Clarendon Plain in the west to Morant Bay at the eastern tip of the island. The approximately 1,000 pioneer settlers in Guanaboa Vale, the upland valley just north of the Anaya Plain, marked the extent of settler penetration into the interior.

In 1664, a new royal governor, Thomas Modyford, formerly a Barbados planter, opened Jamaica up for settlement. Arriving with him were more than a thousand mostly poor settlers from Barbados. Modyford brought royal orders to open to prospective planters some 400,000 acres (161,868 hectares) of land earlier reserved as Crown lands. During his seven-year tenure, Modyford issued eighteen hundred land patents, totaling 120,000 hectares.[69] A settler arriving on Jamaica could immediately claim 12 hectares for himself, plus 12 hectares for his wife, each of his children, each indentured servant, and each slave. Settlers were required only to cultivate the land and to pay a quit rent of one penny per acre every year—but only on im-

68. Ibid., 205–6.

69. Dunn and the Institute of Early American History and Culture, *Sugar and Slaves*, 154; Craton and Walvin, *A Jamaican Plantation*, 18–23.

proved or "manured" land. These incentives attracted more settlers. bringing the population in 1672 to 7,768 whites and 9,504 black slaves.

Modyford also was involved intimately with the English buccaneers who had made Port Royal in Jamaica their headquarters after the conquest. By the mid-1660s, 1,500 buccaneers had sailed from Port Royal to raid and plunder Spanish shipping and settlements around the Caribbean. Modyford, unable to dislodge the buccaneers forcibly, allied with them. He commissioned Henry Morgan to lead a series of flamboyant raids in which his men sacked Spanish ports in Nicaragua, Cuba, Panama, and Venezuela. The governor profited from a share in these raids. Charles II favored the buccaneers even to the extent of knighting Henry Morgan. In 1675, when Morgan returned to Jamaica, the king also named him second in command to the royal governor, Lord Vaughn.[70] In addition, a series of short-term governors appointed by the Stuarts tried to stifle any aspect of self-governance by the planters of Jamaica in their legislative assembly.

The strength and visibility of Henry Morgan and the buccaneers on Jamaica, with their well-deserved image of lawlessness and cruelty, did a good deal to discourage prospective settlers. The more sober planter elite of Jamaica struggled to evict them from Port Royal and to restore the island's reputation as well as its liberties. Only after the Glorious Revolution of 1688–1689 did the planters prevail and evict the buccaneers. A powerful lobby of England-returned Jamaica planters persuaded the new regime to repudiate Stuart support for the buccaneers and to concede local governance to the Jamaican Assembly. The buccaneers moved to Saint Domingue, the French colony on Hispaniola.

Now, however, war depressed colonization on Jamaica. For a quarter of a century, from 1689 to 1713, the Caribbean was an active theater of war between the English and the French. To human we may add natural disasters: the massive earthquake of 1692 that destroyed Port Royal, and a malaria epidemic in the 1690s that killed many colonists. The settler population of Jamaica, over ten thousand in 1689, dropped to less than seven thousand until the end of the war.[71]

Steadily and surely, sugar triumphed on Jamaica during these difficult decades. The structural transformation of the Jamaican economy was virtually complete by the end of the war. In the thirteen years between 1671 and 1684, the number of sugar plantations rose from 57 to 286, and sugar output increased tenfold, from 1,000 hogsheads (470 metric tons) to 10,000 hogsheads (4,699 metric tons).[72] Increases in sugar demanded increases in

70. Dunn and the Institute of Early American History and Culture, *Sugar and Slaves*, 157.
71. Ibid., 165.
72. Ibid., 169, table 17.

labor. Since European indentured servants were no longer available, planters imported black African slaves at an ever increasing rate. In 1689, there were about thirty thousand slaves on the islands; in 1713, about fifty-five thousand, with no increase in whites.

Sugar planters were by far the wealthiest of any Jamaican landholders, holding estates worth 5.2 times the late-seventeenth-century average value.[73] Disease and debt forced smaller landowners—many of whom, lacking the capital for sugar, had grown foodstuffs, cotton, and cacao—to sell their holdings to the wealthier sugar planters. The purchasers added new lands to their already large estates but often simply held their purchases on speculation without cultivating them. The only smaller landowners who survived were those who had taken up cattle ranching, with its symbiotic relationship to sugar. Ranchers could count on a steady market for their cattle from sugar planters who needed draft cattle to haul carts laden with sugar at every stage, and who wore out cattle driving the presses for the sugar mills. Ranchers could also rely on a steady export market for hides.

After 1713, the indices of economic growth—accumulated wealth, shipping, number of white settlers, number of black slaves, head of livestock, lands under patent and cultivation, and tonnage and value of sugar and other exports—all moved steadily, if not rapidly, upward. Plantation profits on Jamaica, lower than those of the earlier-settled islands of the Lesser Antilles before 1739, grew to equal them in the mid–eighteenth century, when they averaged 13 to 14 percent annually. Between 1749 and 1834, through war and peace, profits on a sample of Jamaican plantations averaged 9.4 percent per year, almost exactly the average of the British West Indian islands.[74] By the third quarter of the eighteenth century, Jamaica had become the leading sugar producer and the wealthiest colony in the British empire.

Jamaica's profits were enhanced by its self-sufficiency. In contrast to the earlier sugar colonies of the lesser Antilles, throughout the eighteenth century Jamaica met most of its energy, livestock, and food needs domestically, not from imports. For fuel and energy, Jamaican planters relied on their woodlots and occasionally on burning bagasse, but there is no indication of wood shortages. Planters imported minimal amounts of livestock and instead depended on local livestock ranchers for their needs (see below).

While it is true that imported foods were significant and generally regarded as essential by white Jamaicans, by far the greatest part of the slave diet came from their own efforts on their provision grounds and from the products of hunting and fishing. A 1995 study shows that, throughout the eigh-

73. Ibid., 171, table 18.
74. J. R. Ward, "The Profitability of Sugar Planting in the British West Indies, 1650–1834," *Economic History Review* 31, no. 2 (1978): 85, table 6; and 87, table 9.

teenth century, on average only 16 percent of the per capita daily diet could have come from foodstuffs imported to Jamaica. Although whites relied on imported foodstuffs for 73 percent of their daily intake, the far greater slave population obtained only 10.4 percent of their foods from imports.[75]

However, without the resources of the sea, it is doubtful that the growing colony on Jamaica could have flourished as it did. The most productive fishery was that of sea turtles harvested annually. Colonists ate all four varieties but favored the green sea turtle. These massive herbivores migrated annually from the Honduras and Nicaraguan coasts between May and September to their breeding grounds on the Cayman Islands and the Isle of Pines. Between May and September every year, the females crawled up on the sandy beaches and laid their eggs in holes they covered with sand. After hatching, females and hatchlings withdrew to the shores of Cuba, where they could find adequate plant food—absent in the Caymans—on which to graze. Those adults who had migrated from the Central American coast apparently returned to their original feeding grounds for the winter season.[76]

In 1655, Admiral Penn, British commander of newly seized Jamaica, sent an expedition to the Cayman Islands rookeries to bring back turtle meat and eggs to supply his followers. By 1688, a total of forty sloops and 120 to 150 men hunted turtles year-round to supply Jamaica's markets. During the nesting season, they could easily fill a single vessel with thirty to fifty hatching females and their eggs in a single night. During the remainder of the year, they had to follow the turtle herds to their feeding grounds off the coast of Cuba, where it might take six weeks to fill a ship. Permanent settlers on the Cayman Islands also made their living by turtling.[77]

Each year, the Jamaican fleet returned with thirteen thousand or more green sea turtles to be sold at Port Royal. Their catch was one of the most important sources of meat for the island's population. William Dampier, seafarer, buccaneer, and naturalist, who visited the island for varying periods in the 1670s and 1680s, commented:

---

75. Yu Wu, "Jamaican Trade, 1688–1769: A Quantitative Study" (Ph.D. diss., Johns Hopkins University, Ann Arbor: University Microfilms, 1995), 547, table 10.36; 548, table 10.37; and 548, table 10.38. Wu's import figures derive from the detailed annual Naval Office Shipping Lists compiled by the admiralty in Kingston every year. He has sampled eleven years in full. My figures are based on averaging the calories imported for each of the eleven years and deriving a percentage of twenty-five hundred calories per day, Wu's minimum baseline for men, women, and children. If the total were raised higher for daily consumption to account for higher manual labor—up to three thousand, for example—the percentages would be even lower.

76. See articles in Karen A. Bjorndal, *Biology and Conservation of Sea Turtles*, rev. ed. (Washington: Smithsonian Institution Press, 1995).

77. E. Wayne King, "Historical Review of the Decline of the Green Turtle and the Hawksbill," in *Biology and Conservation of Sea Turtles*, edited by Karen A. Bjorndal (Washington: Smithsonian Institution Press, 1995). Lewis quotes many of the existing sources, including Hans Sloane, William Long, and others.

The Green Turtle are so called, because their shell is greener than any other. . . . These Turtles are generally larger than the Hawks-Bill; one will weight *[sic]* 2 or 3 hundred pound. . . . Green Turtle are the sweetest of all kinds; But there are degrees of them, both in respect to their flesh and their bigness. . . . The Turtle that live among the Keys, or small islands on the South Side of Cuba, are a mix'd sort, some bigger, some less; and so their flesh is of a mix't *[sic]* colour, some green, some dark, some yellowish. With these Port Royal in Jamaica is constantly supplied, by Sloops that come hither with nets to take them. They carry them alive to Jamaica, where the Turtles have wires made with Stakes in the Sea, to preserve them alive; and the Market is every day plentifully stored with Turtle, it being the common food there, chiefly for the ordinary sort of people.[78]

Heavy market hunting depleted the herds and reduced the importance of turtle in the Jamaican diet—but only after a century or more of cheap meat and eggs. By the late eighteenth century, the fishery had dropped to eight or nine boats that hunted green sea turtles on the Cuban shore. Early in the nineteenth century, Jamaican turtlers resorted to sailing to the Moskito Cays off Nicaragua to find the turtles. By 1900, the Cayman Islands nesting population was extinct. Of the estimated 6.5 million green sea turtles of the mid-seventeenth-century breeding herd in the Cayman Islands, only a remnant survived.[79]

In the early 1770s, Edward Long, owner of Lucky Valley Estate, one of Jamaica's largest sugar plantations, and heir to one of the leading planting families, wrote the *History of Jamaica*, a three-volume history and gazetteer published in London in 1774.[80] In his stocktaking of the past century of English settlement, Long praised the beauties of Jamaica's cultivated landscapes and natural vistas, defended plantation slavery against its abolitionist critics, protested the ill effects of absentee ownership, and lauded the economic benefits Jamaica brought to the British home economy. In this much-cited and -quoted work, Long of-

---

78. William Dampier and John Masefield, *Dampier's voyages; consisting of a New voyage round the world, a Supplement to the Voyage round the world, Two voyages to Campeachy, a Discourse of winds, a Voyage to New Holland, and a Vindication, in answer to the Chimerical relation of William Funnell* (London: E. Grant Richards, 1906), 131–32. Dampier described each of the four species of sea turtles and their habits in considerable detail. He carefully noted the grazing habits of the green sea turtle: "Green Turtle live on Grass, which grows in the Sea, in 3, 4, 5, or 6 fathom water, at most of the places mentioned. This Grass is different from Manatee-grass for that is a small blade; but this is a quarter of an inch broad and six inches long" (132).

79. J. B. C. Jackson, "Reefs since Columbus," *Coral Reefs* 16, supplement (1997): S26.

80. Edward Long, *The history of Jamaica, or, General survey of the antient [sic] and modern state of that island with reflections on its situation, settlements, inhabitants, climate, products, commerce, laws, and government: in three volumes, illustrated with copper plates* (London: Printed for T. Lowndes, 1774). For detailed maps and discussion of the 1,486-acre Lucky Valley Estate in upland Clarendon, see B. W. Higman, *Jamaica Surveyed: Plantation Maps and Plans of the Eighteenth and Nineteenth Centuries* (Jamaica: Institute of Jamaica Publications, 1988), 84–89.

fered an assessment of the colony's economy, politics, and society at the time that he wrote and a set of proposals for future growth. To the gratitude of future historians, he included statistical information taken from contemporary records and checked against his own observations.

Long saw Jamaica as an unfinished project. By his count, Jamaica's 1768 population stood at 189,063 persons, including 17,949 resident whites, 4,200 free blacks and mulattos, and 166,914 slaves.[81] In his view, "Jamaica is in want of people; the kingdom would be considerably benefited by encouraging the population of it; and therefore ought to promote it by every favourable and prudent measure."[82]

After more than a hundred years of English settlement and land clearing, much of Jamaica was still an undeveloped frontier. Based on a recently published map, Long assumed the total land area of Jamaica to be 3.5 million acres (1.4 million hectares), "or near four times as much land as all the other British sugar islands put together." Long judged that about one-quarter of the island was in productive use, with "land opened, cleared of its wood, and applied either to pasturage or cultivation of some sort[;] the whole may be rated at six hundred thousand acres" (243,000 hectares, or 17.1 percent). Another 125,000 acres (101,000 hectares, or 7.1 percent) consisted of natural savannas used for grazing. Of the remainder, about 300,000 acres consisted of "rocky, unplantable parts, roads, river-courses, and gullies" that would remain unproductive. This left over two-thirds the island—2.35 million acres (951,000 hectares)—available for clearing, settlement, and cultivation. He concluded, "If this computation is near the truth, there is room sufficient in it [Jamaica] for more than double the settlements it now contains."[83] And Long left no doubt that he considered such expansion to be a good and necessary task that should be encouraged by any means possible.

81. Long, *The History of Jamaica*, 1:377–78. It is not certain whether Long included the 500 "Maroon Negroes in the free towns" and the 3,700 "Free blacks and mulattoes" under the total of 166,914 for "Negroes, servants" on p. 377. He states that he included the 1,700 "Mulattoe slaves" in the 166,914 figure, but not the other two categories. If he did so, the total population should be lowered to 184,863. Long also counts 500 "transients or unsettled whites" and 3,000 "Soldiers and seamen resident, at an average about" in his enumeration. Part of Long's concern, which he had in common with other Jamaican planters, was the white-black ratio. Recent slave insurrections added force to these fears. Long, however, calculated the number of able-bodied men capable of military service, or "fencibles," in the white population at 12,000 and those in the black population at 55,000, a ratio of one to five. In his view, "the essential difference between a small body of men, disciplined and armed, and a much larger body kept in subjection and unarmed, seems greatly to overpoise the natural superiority of the latter" (378). His aim to increase white migration was more concerned with land clearance and exports than with security.

82. Ibid., 1:513. Although Long did not make the calculation, a population density of just under seventeen persons per square kilometer implies that he was right.

83. Ibid., 1:350. This figure is a one-fifth overestimate, since the measured total today is only 1,124,000 hectares, or 2,777,365 acres.

Part of the problem was sugar. Sugar's dominance discouraged migration of ordinary English settlers who could not hope to raise the funds sufficient to grow the crop. Sugar planters "swallowed up by degrees all the little settlements around; which, from their contiguity, and being ready cleared for canes or pasturage, the lordly planter has found convenient to be purchased, and added to his territory." In 1773, Jamaica's 680 sugar plantations occupied 300,000 acres (121,408 hectares) of land "exclusive of waste wood-land" presumably included as part of the estate. Of this total, only 20 to 23 percent of the plantation-owned land was actually in cane fields.[84] The sugar estates consumed the labor of 105,000 black slaves, 40,000 "Road and Mill Cattle," and 25,000 horses and mules.

On average, between 1768 and 1771, these plantations produced 75,000 hogsheads (55,071 metric tons) of sugar, 30,000 puncheons (3 million gallons or 11.4 million liters) of rum, and 300,000 gallons (1.1 million liters) of molasses.[85] Each year's output of sugar, rum, and molasses sold for 1.4 million pounds sterling.[86] Sugar planting unquestionably generated the bulk of Jamaica's wealth, but Long was concerned by the 2,000 "Annuitants and proprietors non-resident," who no longer had a direct personal involvement in either the running of their estates or the governance of the colony.[87]

However, the colony was still more diversified than might appear. There were nearly 1,500 other landowning planters on the island. Of these, 110 primarily raised cotton, 30 grew ginger, 8 grew indigo, and in a recent development, 150 grew coffee. Taken together, these minor cash crops sold for only seventy-five thousand pounds sterling on the export market.[88] About 600

84. Long further comments, "It is evident that this extrusion of poorer settlers from their small possessions of thirty to one hundred acres has operated like the demolition of many small farms in Britain, to build up one capital farm, and may justly be considered as another cause of depopulating this island." Ibid., 1:386, 494. The plantation-owned land in cane fields amounted to between 60,000 acres (24,281 hectares) and 70,000 acres (28,329 hectares).

85. Ibid., 1:229. Long lists 13,200 puncheons of rum (84 gallons), which converts to 7.75 pounds per gallon or 295.3 kilograms per puncheon by weight. See also Wu, "Jamaican Trade," 613–17. For 1769, the adjusted weight for a hogshead of sugar is 1,618.8 pounds (614).

86. Long, *The History of Jamaica*, 1:496. This amounts to 1,875,000 pounds Jamaican. The conversion was 1.4 pounds Jamaican to 1 pound sterling. Long put the price of a hogshead of sugar at 20 pounds Jamaican currency or 14.3 pound sterling, and the price of a puncheon of rum at 12.5 pounds Jamaican (2s.6d Jamaican per gallon).

87. Ibid., 1:378. For Long's lengthy list of problems with absentee owners, see 1:386–91. See also Richard B. Sheridan, *Sugar and Slavery: An Economic History of the British West Indies, 1623–1775* (Baltimore: Johns Hopkins University Press, 1974). For 1775, Sheridan finds that 30.1 percent of the total 775 sugar plantations that had been recorded in the Jamaica Assembly report "Account Produce" were owned by absentees and minors.

88. Long, *The History of Jamaica*, 1:496–97. Production included 800 casks of coffee weighing 300 pounds each, 1,000 bags of cotton weighing 180 pounds each, and 500 bags of ginger weighing 500 pounds each. Pimento, much of it grown on cattle pens, totaled 3,085,000 pounds (1,399 metric tons).

planters produced provisions or foodstuffs for the domestic market and 500 raised cattle in "breeding penns." Together, these various planters owned another 300,000 acres (121,408 hectares) of land on which they employed 40,000 black slaves. The cattle keepers owned sixty-seven thousand head of livestock, the other planters only four thousand.

It was this sector of Jamaica's economy that Long hoped would attract new settlers:

> If poor and industrious persons were sufficiently encouraged to settle in the interior parts of it [Jamaica], necessity would oblige them to go upon the cultivation of cacao, ginger, aloes, coffee, pimento, and other articles, which require no great labour, are not burthensome in the carriage, and which have all a sufficient demand at home, to recompense those who do not look for vast and sudden fortunes. By degrees, and with good management, they would improve in the culture of many of those articles, in which we are at present rather defective; the careful would grow tolerably rich and considerable works of many valuable commodities, as cacao, cochineal, and indigo[,] might be attempted with small capitals. So that, whilst the great stocks, and lands most convenient to navigation, are employed in sugars, the small capitals, and more inland parts, might be dedicated to the humbler, though not less useful, commodities.[89]

In short, Long foresaw these new pioneers moving briskly inland to clear land and develop the resources of the island's interior. Unlike the sugar planters, too many of whom were absentee owners living in Britain, the new settlers would live on their holdings and become active land managers and members of colonial society.

In Long's Jamaica, the five hundred or so cattle pens, with herds numbering sixty-seven thousand head, constituted an important pastoral segment of the island's economy. Well before the end of the seventeenth century, the great herds of wild cattle disappeared, although much-depleted numbers of wild pigs continued to roam in the unsettled tracts of the interior during the eighteenth century.[90] Many of the early English settlers used profits from hunting the free-roaming cattle and pigs to finance their planting costs. Others rounded up feral cattle to stock their new ranching operations. As sugar and other plantations expanded into the most fertile lands in the river deltas and basins and the more humid valleys of the south, "ranching spread into the hills and mountains of the interior, including rough karstic areas, former refuges of the dwindling feral herds."[91] Livestock ranch-

89. Ibid., 513.

90. Ibid., 1:384. Long comments on the problem of dealing with "young Creole lads," who, "for want of other employment," became "hog-hunters and idle vagabonds."

91. Terry G. Jordan, *North American Cattle-Ranching Frontiers: Origins, Diffusion, and Differentiation* (Albuquerque: University of New Mexico Press, 1993), 81.

ers were second only to sugar planters in capital and profits, and it was much easier for men with limited capital to become pen keepers.

The cattle pens had their own distinctive form of land use. In contrast to the ranchers who developed the extensive cattle ranges of New Spain, Jamaican ranchers operated modestly sized livestock farms. The term *pen* replaced the Spanish *hato* or *estancia* to mean the facilities and land of a livestock ranch, with its owner's dwelling and outbuildings, provision garden, slave quarters, central corrals, and stock pens located in the pastures. Jamaican law demanded one white livestock herder for each hundred head of cattle. Under the influence of its British livestock men, the Jamaican system evolved into a more intensive practice of confining cattle nightly in the palisaded enclosures located in each pasture. Pen keepers regularly moved the pens in order to plant provision gardens on the heavily manured sites. British insistence on castration of calves made it easier to control the animals. Because annual roundups for branding and culling were unnecessary, herders operated on foot rather than on horseback in the Spanish American tradition.[92]

Jamaican pastoralists fattened cattle for the island's beef consumers (either settled or transient whites, not slaves) and raised cattle, horses, and mules to meet the needs of planters for motive power.[93] In the 1770s, 680 sugar plantations averaged ninety-six head of livestock, by Long's figures. As the animals wore out, their continuing replacement at eighteen pounds Jamaican per unit was a considerable expense.[94] Most planters found it easier to rent or buy livestock from pen keepers than to raise their own—although a number of pens were actually owned by larger sugar planters.

The average cattle pen on Jamaica in the late eighteenth century and the nineteenth century had 281 hectares of land. Pastures were 54 percent of the total, divided about equally between ordinary pasture grass and seeded African guinea grass. Pen keepers left on average 30 percent of the total in woodland and *ruinate* (a Jamaican term meaning regrown secondary scrubland). Plantain and other food crops took up only 6 percent of the total. The remainder went primarily to pimento, with trees distributed among the pastures that formed a cash staple for pens.[95] Pen keepers also planted logwood to serve as fences and boundaries and sold it to the dyewood market. "Penguin fences," a hedge formed of the prickly *Bromelia pinguin*, were a common alternative. If the pen had woodlands with high-value timber trees, especially

92. Ibid., 80.

93. B. W. Higman, "The Internal Economy of Jamaican Pens, 1760–1890," *Social and Economic Studies* 38 (1989).

94. Verene A. Shepherd, "Livestock and Sugar: Aspects of Jamaica's Agricultural Development from the Late Seventeenth to the Early Nineteenth Century," *The Historical Journal* 34, no. 3 (1991): 238.

95. Higman, "Internal Economy of Jamaican Pens," 73.

mahogany, pen keepers employed their slaves as timber cutters and sawyers to ship planks.

One of the largest cattle pens was Goshen, with 1,586 hectares, located at the foot of the Don Figueroa Mountains in Saint Elizabeth Parish on the western side of Jamaica. When Francis George Smyth purchased Goshen in 1780, the pen sustained a large herd of about 1,500 livestock.[96] In 1781, Smyth sold 209 livestock—130 cattle and some calves, 51 horses, and 28 mules. That year, the total plantation income was 4,212 pounds Jamaican (around 19 to 20 pounds per head).[97] In 1783, Smyth added a lucrative sideline by selling timber and other woodland products: 3,782 feet of mahogany plank, 600 feet of boards, and 39 metric tons of fustic, a yellow dyewood.[98] The total area designated as pastures was surprisingly small. Pastures, divided into twenty-four named and bounded fields, covered only 38 percent of the total area: 188 hectares planted to guinea grass and 406 hectares left in common pasture grass. Apart from small areas given over to the plantation buildings, slave quarters, and a few hectares in cotton, the remainder of the pen was undeveloped woodland or possibly *ruinate*.[99]

At the other extreme was the tiny 65-hectare Breadnut Island Pen on the coast in Westmoreland Parish on the far west end of Jamaica. Thomas Thistlewood, a cattle keeper who had arrived from England in 1750, had scraped together enough funds to purchase the holding in 1765 for 275 pounds.[100] Thistlewood moved to his new property in 1767 to live there and

96. Higman, *Jamaica Surveyed*, 201. In this volume, Higman supplies survey maps and data about several other cattle pens.

97. Possibly pounds sterling instead, since this is not specified by Higman, but more likely Jamaican currency.

98. This is dyer's mulberry, a large, tropical American tree (*Chlorophora tinctoria* or *Morus tinctoria*) of the mulberry family, Moraceae. The dye produces yellow in wool fixed with chromium salts.

99. For a description of the midsize, 474-hectare Vineyard Pen in Westmoreland Parish, see Philip D. Morgan, "Slaves and Livestock in Eighteenth-Century Jamaica: Vineyard Pen, 1750–1751," *William and Mary Quarterly*, 3d ser., 52 (1995). Thomas Thistlewood was the pen manager for one year. During his tenure, the pen had 251 cattle and 16 horses, as well as sheep, goats, and pigs. There were forty-two slaves at the pen.

100. Douglas Hall and Thomas Thistlewood, *In Miserable Slavery: Thomas Thistlewood in Jamaica, 1750–86* (Basingstoke: Macmillan, 1989), xvi. The property was actually half of the pen attached to Paradise sugar plantation. Thistlewood and a partner contributed half the 550-pound purchase price and shared the land equally. Another sale and repurchase by the original owners to save the cost of an official survey occurred in 1567 (149). During his adult life, Thistlewood kept a detailed daily diary that contains ten thousand closely packed pages. This is the documentary basis for Hall's book. In its laconic style, the Thistlewood diary has much valuable information about land use and land management at the time, as well as about the lives of slaves and other topics not covered in detail in this present study. The slaves on the pen were supposedly in better circumstances than those laboring in the sugar fields. Nevertheless, Thistlewood's continued mention of whippings, brandings, and sexual assaults on his female slaves simply confirm the degradation and pain of slavery.

actively manage the pen, which he did for nearly twenty years, until his death in 1786. On the 28 hectares of solid land on Breadnut Island Pen, Thistlewood kept a small herd of livestock for sale. In January 1777, his inventory listed 3 horses, 28 cattle, 45 sheep, and 2 hogs, as well as various geese, turkeys, and other poultry.[101] However, he made as much or more of his income from other activities. In his provision gardens, he and his slaves raised vegetables and flowers for sale and for consumption on the pen. He frequently hired out his thirty or so slaves for day labor to neighboring plantations and pens or for such projects as road building. He also lived off the land by such devices as employing one of his slaves as a full-time fisherman sent out every day in a dugout canoe to cast lines and set fish traps. Thistlewood and his slaves hunted and ate waterfowl from the swamp. He was an enthusiastic gardener and importer of new varieties of fruits, vegetables, and flowers. In June 1775, he listed 300 varieties of plants then growing in his gardens and provision grounds.[102] His reputation as a first-rate gardener seems to have given him much higher social status with wealthier planters and pen owners than one might expect.

Edward Long devoted a lengthy chapter in his *History* to a discussion of Jamaica's external trade and its importance for the British empire. He listed the quantities and values of the goods exported and imported each year in the early 1770s to various ports in Great Britain, North America, the Spanish colonies, and Europe. He calculated a small positive merchandise trade balance for Jamaica (46,628 pounds sterling). From these and other data, Long then worked out Jamaica's annual economic benefit to Great Britain. Taking into account profits made by Britons in the slave trade to and from Jamaica, in carrying freight to and from the island, in marine insurance and brokerage, in absentee ownership of plantations, in interest on loans, in sale of British goods to Jamaica, and in the share of profits made by Ireland and North America in the Jamaica trade, Long put the "annual profits which the nation may be supposed to gain by her commerce with this island" at 1.25 million pounds sterling.[103]

Long went on to mention less easily measured returns. For example, Britain consumed nearly all the sugar exported from the British West Indies:

What immense sums have been saved to the nation by our entering so largely into the cultivation of the sugar cane! Before our West Indies islands were set-

101. Ibid., 249.
102. Ibid., 238.
103. Long, *The History of Jamaica,* 1:508. While certainly not a definitive computation of the annual economic returns to Great Britain, Long's economic reasoning seems to have been remarkably sophisticated. Richard Sheridan, an economic historian specializing in British West Indian colonial history, redid Long's numbers with slightly different categories to arrive at a figure of 1.55 million pounds sterling each year. Sheridan, *Sugar and Slavery,* 383, table 16.1.

tled, we paid to the Portuguese from 4l. to 5l. per hundred weight for muscavado sugars, no better in quality than what are now sold for 30s. to 35s.; and if
we but consider the difference in the value of money now, and at the period I
allude to, the great saving to this kingdom will appear in a very striking
light.[104]

Moreover, Long argued that the Jamaican profits could and should increase:
"If we should carry our ideas still further, and imagine double the acres to be
occupied in the island and equally cultivated, it would then yield a profit of
full two millions and a half yearly to our mother country; a grand prospect
this of future maturity."[105] Long draws a direct correlation between continuing frontier expansion and intensified land use on Jamaica and imperial
profits.

BENEFITS TO WESTERN EUROPE

Sugar flowed to Europe in ever widening streams. For the five years between
1770 and 1774, sugar exports from the plantations of the West Indies islands
and mainland Caribbean plantation colonies averaged 186,000 metric tons
each year (see table 12.2). If we add 20,000 tons from Brazil, the New World
total reached 206,000 tons each year.[106] However, production steadily increased after that. In most established sugar colonies, slaves cleared and
planted new lands to increase sugarcane production. Even the destruction
of sugar plantations in Saint Domingue during the French Revolution did
not stop the advance of sugar but stimulated production elsewhere.

In the five-year period (1815–1819) after the end of the Napoleonic Wars,
the West Indies and other Caribbean sugar colonies combined shipped an average of 271,000 metric tons of sugar to Europe's markets each year.[107] The
collapse of exports from Saint Domingue was partly compensated by heavy
shipments from Spanish Cuba. French planters fleeing revolution on Saint
Domingue bought new lands in Cuba and began anew. By 1815, Cuban output averaged 41,000 metric tons per year. Brazilian output soared from
nearly 29,000 metric tons in 1808 to 75,000 tons in 1820. Total New World

104. Long, *The History of Jamaica*, 1:515.

105. Ibid.

106. For 1776, Deerr finds 20,400 metric tons (*The History of Sugar*, 112). Stuart B. Schwartz
lists 1.4 million *arrobas* shipped at 16.4 kilograms per *arroba* for 1676, or 20,580 tons. *Sugar Plantations in the Formation of Brazilian Society: Bahia, 1550–1835* (Cambridge: Cambridge University
Press, 1985).

107. Table derived from Watts, *The West Indies*, 286–87, tables 7.2 and 7.3, with interpolated
data from Deerr, *The History of Sugar*, various tables. Deerr and Watts use long tons at 2,240
pounds for data from the British colonies and metric tons for the remainder.

TABLE 12.2 Sugar Exports from the West Indies

	1770–1774 Average (in Metric Tons)	1815–1819 Average (in Metric Tons)
British colonies		
Antigua	7,794	9,558
Barbados	6,766	12,376
British Guiana	2,592	20,406
Dominica	1,902	2,222
Grenada	9,407	11,383
Jamaica	42,311	81,034
Montserrat	2,404	1,613
Nevis	2,836	3,233
Saint Kitts	9,580	6,947
Saint Lucia	0	3,252
Saint Vincent	2,619	12,741
Tobago	1,403	5,251
Trinidad	0	6,934
BRITISH TOTAL	89,614	176,950
French colonies		
Guadeloupe	7,898[a]	16,033
Martinique	11,344	17,362
Saint Domingue	61,247	0
FRENCH TOTAL	80,489	33,395
Spanish colony		
Cuba	1,250	41,271
SPANISH TOTAL	1,250	41,271
Dutch colony		
Suriname	6,658	7,820
DUTCH TOTAL	6,658	7,820
Danish colony		
Saint Croix	8,230[b]	11,666[c]
DANISH TOTAL	8,230	11,666
TOTAL SUGAR EXPORTS	186,241	271,102

[a] 1767 only.
[b] 1779 only.
[c] 1820 only.

exports to Europe in the immediate post-Napoleonic years were about 330,000 tons per year.[108]

Sugar imports on this scale added significant caloric energy to the European diet at a critical time. At the end of the eighteenth century, Europe was approaching a food crisis.[109] Even in good times, the average calorie intake was barely adequate, but by the end of the eighteenth century, Europeans were subsisting on a diet that provided 2,700 kilocalories per day for an adult male. People ate less of the more nutritious foods, and meat and dairy products were seldom seen on the plates of the lower classes. Given the harsh disease environment, the heavy workloads, and the fact that even simple day-to-day activities required the expenditure of many times the calories required today, this level of consumption did not provide adequate quantities of energy, protein, and nutrients for a secure biological standard of living.

Sugar, along with rum, wheat, rice, codfish, and a variety of minor imports, directly supplemented the European food budget. The population of the British Isles was the greatest consumer of sugar. Of the 330,000 metric tons of New World sugar carried to Europe in 1816, the British market bought 28.5 percent (94,000 metric tons). In the 1790s, the annual per capita consumption in England and Wales added the equivalent of 140 kilocalories to the average diet.[110]

Conventional summing of private or social income derived from the sugar colonies ignores the food issue. Debates as to whether the rate of return on investment was higher or lower than funds put to work in Europe, or whether the opportunity cost of investing in the Caribbean was properly considered, miss the point. Political control over the Caribbean colonies offered Europe access to new, unique human and natural resources that were otherwise inaccessible.

The planters, and ultimately European society, obtained enormous benefits from the strange conjuncture of slave labor and bounteous natural resources in the sugar colonies. Planters' ready access to imported black African slaves at relatively cheap prices drove out European laborers. On the sugar frontier, millions of black slaves burnt and cleared new lands. Black

108. Schwartz, *Sugar Plantations in the Formation of Brazilian Society*, 428. According to Schwartz, "In 1808, Bahia exported 20,000 crates, Pernambuco 14,000, Rio de Janeiro 9,000 and Sao Paulo only 1,000." Each crate contained forty *arrobas* at 16.4 kilograms per *arroba* for a total of 28,846 tons. Generally Schwartz's numbers are not systematic and are sometimes hard to interpret. Deerr shows 20,400 tons for 1806, and then only 9,000 for 1809, 6,200 for 1812, and suddenly 75,000 for 1820 (*The History of Sugar*, 112).

109. John Komlos, "The New World's Contribution to Food Consumption during the Industrial Revolution," *Journal of European Economic History* 27 (1998): 68.

110. Carole Shammas, *The Pre-industrial Consumer in England and America* (Oxford: Clarendon Press; New York: Oxford University Press, 1990), 82–83, table 4.3.

slaves hoed the ground to prepare it for planting, and planted, weeded, cut, hauled, and ground sugarcane. Slaves grew much of their own food in provision gardens and hunted and fished for food for themselves and their masters. Slaves cut and shaped timber for use and for export. Slaves built the buildings, dug the ditches and canals for irrigation, and herded the livestock bred on these islands. Left virtually uninhabited by the Spanish, each of the sugar islands in the Antilles served as a sharply bounded empty container in which vast numbers of slaves could be confined and made to labor till death. It was the human energy of Africa that shaped the landscapes of sugar.

The sugar colonies added millions of hectares of land to Europe's land area. The British, French, Dutch, Danish, and Spanish colonists and their compatriots at home obtained a windfall effect as they consumed the abundant natural resources of the Antilles and the Guianas. Underestimated and certainly unmeasured is the extent to which the natural flora and fauna of the region contributed to the nutrition of white and black residents in these colonies throughout this period. The Caribbean's tropical climate, rainfall, winds, soils, ground- and surface water, forests, grasslands, and fauna directly augmented the temperate-zone natural resources of western Europe.

Some exports to Europe extracted natural resources such as timber and dyewoods in which the pattern was one of depletion and movement to new sources. The highest value exports were tropical crops that could not be grown in Europe, such as cacao and pimento. Coffee was rapidly developing as a major export crop in the late eighteenth century in Suriname and Jamaica. But it was sugar that created and sustained this system of intensive plantation agriculture. Sugarcane flourished in the climate and soils of the Caribbean and could not be grown in northern Europe. And sugar was the ultimate reward for European predation.

CONCLUSION

The landscape of sugar became the dominant landscape in and around the Caribbean in the early modern period. From its earliest manifestation on Barbados, the West Indies sugar frontier steadily extended its bounds during the seventeenth and eighteenth centuries and into the nineteenth century. Northern European pioneer settlers seized, occupied, cleared, and planted sugarcane on island after island, from the tiniest in the Lesser Antilles to Jamaica and Saint Domingue. In favorable conditions on the South American mainland, such as in Suriname and British Guiana, other colonists moved inland from the coast to plant sugar along major river valleys.[111] By the late

111. The discussion in this chapter has not touched on the mainland sugar colonies, British Guiana, Dutch Suriname, and French Guiana, which can be considered part of the Caribbean

eighteenth century, the sugar frontier had reached even Spanish Cuba, the largest of the Antilles, as French refugees from slave insurrections settled on that island.

The sugar settlement frontier had its own peculiarities. The smallholding pioneer settlers originally present in each colony—and in some cases officially encouraged, as occurred on the French islands—did not survive long. Instead, freewheeling land markets combined with the profits to be made in sugar—as well as the steep initial investment necessary—encouraged consolidation into large estates or plantations. Small cadres of elite planters gained a grip on the land and on power and profits that they never relinquished.

The question of human-induced environmental change is another matter. What were the environmental costs of this highly successful, if brutal and socially repugnant, effort to grow sugar in the Caribbean? To a certain extent, the answer is clear: creating the landscape of sugar involved drastic alteration of land and habitat. The Antilles, relatively isolated islands in the premodern world, even if inhabited by humans, sheltered unique ecosystems with many species endemic to them. The suddenly intensified human landings, settlement, and maritime traffic put these island ecosystems under enormous pressure. Alien species carried by humans took up residence and often pushed aside or even killed off endemic island flora and fauna. Human predation and resource extraction further exacerbated these effects. Finite island boundaries reduced possibilities for survival in refuge areas. In short, the Antilles were vulnerable to massive environmental disruption by European intruders.

The process began under the Spanish, as described in the previous chapter. Rapid Indian die-offs on each island and subsequent diffusion of European livestock and other alien plants and animals created a new tropical environment. Since the Spanish settlers remained scattered and relatively few in number, they placed little pressure on these altered ecosystems. It is likely that flora and fauna, allowed to recover by the collapse of Taino and Carib land use, were more rather than less abundant during the sixteenth century than in the pre-Columbian epoch.

It was only after northern European conquest and settlement in the mid–seventeenth century that sugar planting drastically altered the Caribbean habitat and landscape. David Watts summarizes these effects as follows:

system even though, strictly speaking, they faced on the Atlantic. For an extensive and detailed study of Dutch Suriname, see Cornelis Ch. Goslinga, *The Dutch in the Caribbean and on the Wild Coast, 1580–1680* (Gainesville: University of Florida Press, 1971); Cornelis Ch. Goslinga and Maria van J. L. Yperen, *The Dutch in the Caribbean and in the Guianas, 1680–1791* (Assen, Netherlands: Van Gorcum, 1985).

The introduction of commercial estates into most [West Indian] territories also has instigated several additional trends of environmental decline. The immense, and customarily fast and complete[,] removal of much of the region's natural lowland forest through felling and burning to make way for these, in itself brought about a massive nutrient loss, and this then was reemphasized and reaccentuated by successive crop harvest. Most of the chosen commercial cultigens were high in nutrient demand, and they were raised year after year with very little being put back into the soil in return. After a short time, yields began to fall, in association with the decline in soil quality; and then, as soil structure failed, a more general pattern of soil loss was initiated. This form of agriculture was essentially unbalanced[;]. . . with a few notable exceptions, it came to be purely extractive and exploitative of the available natural resources.[112]

As Watts asserts, sugar cultivation was inherently exploitative and rapacious in its consumption of soil fertility as well as energy from woodlots, animals, and people. Forest clearing followed by the planting of sugarcane and other cash crops shaped a new West Indian habitat that only faintly resembled that of either the pre-Columbian landscapes or the Spanish colonial ecosystems of the sixteenth century. Without a doubt, this was an impoverished landscape by comparison with the abundant natural vegetation and animal life found by the Spanish.

From another perspective, however, the issue is more complex. If we look carefully at sugar landscapes and ecosystems at any point in the latter part of the eighteenth century, we do not find vistas of vast, unrelieved fields of sugarcane similar to the expanses of wheat or maize fields in the United States Midwest. Virtually every sugar estate devoted only a portion of its lands, often as little as one-third, to cane fields. The remainder consisted of pastures or savanna, woodlots, and rough ground dedicated to slave manioc and plantain provision gardens that did not exhaust the soil as did sugarcane. Moreover, save on the tiniest islands, topography dictated that some wooded reserves remained beyond the reach of aspiring sugar planters. Sugar did far better on lower, more level lands. In short, the eighteenth-century plantations were not as monochromatic or as ecologically sterile as has been suggested.

Nearly all then-contemporary European observers, whether planters or others, commented on the aesthetic appeal and diversity of these sugar landscapes, with their varied plant communities and abundant vegetation. To these observers, sugar landscapes revealed highly productive land to be viewed in the same light as the rich cultivated fields of the French or British countryside. In fact, it was not unusual for British estate owners at home to be absentee owners of West Indian plantations as well. They applied the same

112. Watts, *The West Indies*, 536.

principles of careful estate management to each of their holdings.[113] To present-day observers looking back, the taint of plantation slavery distorts our reaction to the sugar landscape. It is unlikely that sugar produced by independent European smallholders would have created a landscape any more diverse or productive—although socially such a landscape would have been much more appealing to our own sensibility.

On the smallest islands of the Lesser Antilles, the settlement frontier had long since closed. On Antigua or Nevis or Barbados, sugarcane fields took up a far greater percentage of the island's area than on Jamaica or even Martinique. Problems of soil exhaustion and soil erosion began early and were more severe on Barbados than on Jamaica. Jamaican planters could leave exhausted sugarcane fields fallow and shift their production to new fields— Barbados planters could not. Sheet or gully soil erosion does not seem to have been a serious problem in Jamaica during the 1700s. Barbados, unlike Jamaica, could not produce sufficient food for its slave population, livestock for motive power, or wood for its sugar boilers but instead relied on steady imports. Jamaica, however, did generate the bulk of its food supplies, energy, and livestock from the island's resources. Woodlots were still not so depleted in the larger islands that planters had to pay serious attention to coppicing, replanting, or other silvicultural practices. As land clearance for sugar planting continued, and as pressures for greater production on each estate accelerated, the sugar frontier closed and signs of serious ecological stress came. Even on islands as large as Jamaica, sugar planting in the Antilles was not sustainable unless planters and the colonial state adopted effective land management and conservation strategies. That radical change had not yet begun to occur by the early decades of the nineteenth century.

113. Susanne Seymour, Stephen Daniels, and Charles Watkins, "Estate and Empire: Sir George Cornewall's Management of Moccas, Herefordshire, and La Taste, Grenada, 1771–1819," *Journal of Historical Geography* 24 (1998). I thank Professor Kimber for this reference.

PART IV

The World Hunt

Chapter 13

Furs and Deerskins
in Eastern North America

European maritime contact with the New World thrust commercialized human predation across the North Atlantic Ocean. Commercial hunting proved to be the most lucrative way to exploit the northernmost regions of the Americas. Much of the early impetus for maritime travel to North America came from the profits to be made from hunting, killing, processing, and shipping animal skins back to Europe. Europeans found several prey species—beavers, foxes, marten, and other furbearers, and deer—that yielded high-value commodities for the home market with its pent-up demand for fur. Windfall exploitation of abundant New World fur-bearing animals raised the European standard of living.

By the early sixteenth century, supplies of furs were dwindling across Europe and prices had risen sharply. The European beaver, for example, was nearly extinct in southern Europe and fast disappearing elsewhere. Even rabbit skins were hard to get and were expensive.[1] Sable and marten, the costliest furs, were prohibitive in price for all save the very few. In England, fashionable taste was shifting away from fur-lined gowns toward "fabrics of an almost unbelievable richness."[2] Nevertheless, cloth did not provide the warmth of fur in the increasingly cold winters. In 1604, a Venetian living in London commented, "The weather is bitterly cold and everyone is in furs although we are almost in July."[3]

Unlike sugar and tobacco, producing furs required no heavy investment in land conversion and cultivation. Peltries demanded only a modest invest-

---

1. Elspeth M. Veale, *The English Fur Trade in the Later Middle Ages* (Oxford: Clarendon Press, 1966), 172–76.
2. Ibid., 143.
3. Ibid., 141.

ment in relation to their potential return. The indigenous peoples of North America supplied the human energy and skill needed for the hunt and its aftermath. Successive Indian groups were a cheap, readily available labor force that engaged in ever more arduous labor in return for inexpensive trade goods. If necessary, Indian groups bartered for beaver and other furs from more remote Indians with access to better hunting grounds. European colonists, even fur traders, did very little actual hunting and trapping themselves. Traders, farmers, and artisans saw little appeal in the rigors of the hunt. Somewhat later, by the late seventeenth century and through the eighteenth century, the warmer southern region of North America developed a new export product. Overshadowed by the far better known trade in beaver, fox, and other furs, deerskins became a staple product of the American Southeast. Market demand by the early modern European leather industry soared as domestic supplies of deerskin dwindled. European traders turned to North America, where the most plentiful deer by that time were those in the southern colonies. The indigenous peoples in the American Southeast responded to new market stimuli and became primary producers of semiprocessed deer hides in ever increasing numbers.

The territorial reach of the fur trade far exceeded the extent of European settlement and direct contact. Long before any direct trade with Europeans occurred, Indian groups in the interior traded furs for goods brought by Indian middlemen. Some Indian groups became middlemen who acquired fur for trade goods from interior Indian hunters and exchanged them for more trade goods, especially European weaponry, with Europeans. Conflicts over middleman status could and did lead to war and the expulsion of the losers from their territories. In this "protohistoric era" of indirect trade, Indians moved perceptibly toward commercial hunting.[4] Archaeological data confirm that even the Indians of the Canadian subarctic were acquiring and using European trade goods by the end of the seventeenth century. During the "historic era," that followed, European fur traders traveled to Indian settlements and began direct trading relations. As contact intensified, the arrival of other, competing European fur traders generated new pressures to kill and overkill more animals.

THE SIXTEENTH-CENTURY FUR TRADE

Early-sixteenth-century voyages to engage in North Atlantic cod fishing and whaling put European seamen in frequent contact with Indians along the northern coastline of North America. French, Basque, and Portuguese sailors exchanged gifts with the Micmacs of the Maritime Provinces and the

4. J. C. Yerbury, *The Subarctic Indians and the Fur Trade, 1680–1860* (Vancouver: University of British Columbia Press, 1986), 10–13.

Montagnais groups of southern Labrador.[5] Gift exchanges soon evolved into a trading pattern. The Indians wore and used furs and pelts that had substantial value in European eyes. Beaver, bear, lynx, fox, otter, marten, badger, muskrat, and mink pelts could be conditioned then cut and pieced together to make warm and decorative fur garments. The skins of shorthaired seals, moose, elks, and deer, if properly treated, made exceptionally strong and supple leather garments. The coastal Indians were willing to exchange furs for European manufactured goods.

In these early encounters, the most desirable objects offered to the Indians were iron knives, hatchets, and kettles; wool blankets and other European textiles; and glass beads for decoration. Marten skins, rare and expensive in Europe, were plentiful in New England and could be obtained very cheaply in exchange for axes, knives, and other trade goods.[6]

In the latter part of the century, profits from the casual trade encouraged merchant-adventurers to invest in fur trading rather than fishing or voyages to the New World. In 1583, French merchants in La Rochelle, Saint Malo, and Rouen financed five fur-trading voyages to North America. Two years later, ten ships made the crossing. One Stephen Bellinger, a trader from Rouen, "brought home . . . divers beastes skynnes as beavers, otters, martense, lucernes, seals, buff, dere, skynnes. All drest and paynted on the innter side with divers excellent colors."[7]

The eastern Algonkian Indians—Micmacs and Montagnais among others—living along the Gulf of Saint Lawrence and in Nova Scotia were involved in low-intensity fur trading throughout most of the sixteenth century.[8] These Algonkian-speaking hunters had recently driven the horticultural Iroquois out of the Saint Lawrence River valley in a conflict over control of the growing fur trade. The Montagnais became the dominant middlemen, or trading specialists, who extracted furs from hunters in the interior in the Saguenay River drainage system in exchange for trade goods. The Montagnais in turn supplied those Spanish, Basque, Dutch, and French trading vessels that sailed up the Gulf of Saint Lawrence as far as Tadoussac, an Indian trading center located where the Saguenay River enters the Saint Lawrence.

In the last half of the sixteenth century, a new, intense European demand for beaver pelts stimulated fur trading in the New World. Molded and shaped hats made of felt from the inner fur of the beaver became popular for higher-status men in the late 1500s in western Europe and remained in

5. Laurier Turgeon, "French Fishers, Fur Traders, and Amerindians during the Sixteenth Century: History and Archaeology," *William and Mary Quarterly*, 3d ser., 55, no. 4 (1998).

6. Paul C. Phillips, *The Fur Trade*, 1st ed. (Norman: University of Oklahoma Press, 1961), 1:16–17.

7. Ibid., 1:21. Quote is from Richard Hakluyt's *Discourse Concerning Western Planting*.

8. Kenneth M. Morrison, *The Embattled Northeast: The Elusive Ideal of Alliance in Abenaki-Euramerican Relations* (Berkeley and Los Angeles: University of California Press, 1984), 12–19.

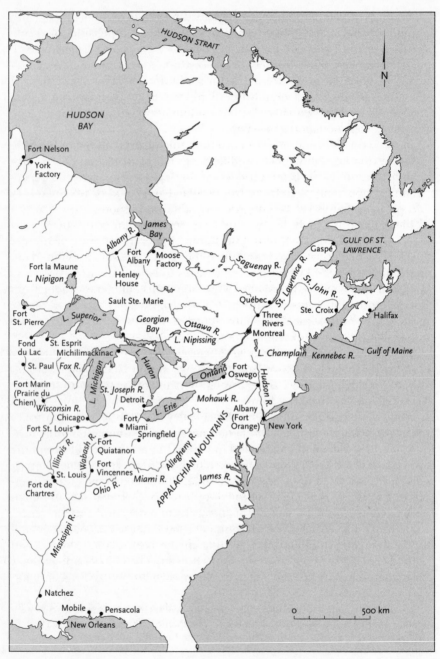

Map 13.1 North American fur trade routes. Adapted from W. T. Easterbrook and Hugh G. J. Aitken, *Canadian Economic History* (Toronto: Macmillan Co. of Canada, 1967), pp. 164–65.

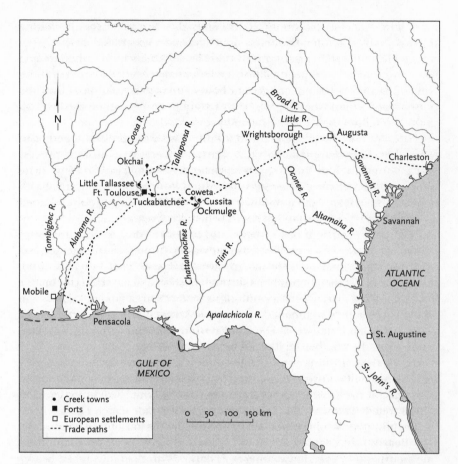

Map 13.2 Creek country and contiguous European settlements, 1772. Adapted
from Kathryn E. Holland Braund, *Deerskins and Duffels: The Creek Indian Trade with
Anglo-America, 1685–1815* (Lincoln: University of Nebraska Press, 1993), map 2,
p. 91.

fashion throughout the early modern period. The North American beaver
became the most valuable furbearer of the New World and prey to one of the
longest sustained hunts for a single species in world history. Demand for
beaver hats continued undiminished for three hundred years, until manu-
facturers perfected the cheaper and glossier silk hat in the 1840s. Thereafter,
prices for high-quality beaver pelts declined steadily in the face of technological innovation in hat making.

Beaver pelts consist of coarse, two-inch-long outer, or guard, hairs that
cover the inner, extremely fine down of the coat. The one-inch-long inner

hairs have microscopic hooks at the ends that are ideal for the felting process. Skilled master hatters bought cleaned and graded beaver wool sheared from the skin. Journeymen boiled lesser quality wool with water and urine to enhance its felting qualities; the best quality needed no preparation. Next, the workers passed a large taut bow, similar to a violin bow, over the pile of wool. When vibrated, the bow's magnetic force aligned the hairs all in the same direction. Using heat and pressure, the hatter shaped the wool into batts of felt. Two large and two joining batts were pressed together to form a hat. After shaping or blocking, the hat underwent a finishing process that involved dyeing, stiffening, waterproofing, reblocking, ironing, trimming, and final shaping. The result was a durable, waterproof, warm hat with no discernible seams and a smooth nap that could be shaped and reshaped according to fashion, a hat that could be worn for years on end.[9]

Prices and profits on beaver pelts rose together. Most sought-after were beaver robes consisting of five to as many as eight pelts sewn together and worn for some time by their Indian owners. These "coat," or *castor gras,* beaver robes lost their guard hairs through friction and left the inner beaver wool pliant and workable as a result of its wearer's sweat and oils. Less valuable was the stiff "parchment," or *castor sec,* scraped skin that carried both guard hairs and inner wool. The latter required careful combing and separation from the skin before it could be used in felting.

During the sixteenth century, Dutch traders shipped the best-quality parchment skins via fifteen- to twenty-vessel fleets that left Amsterdam in the spring each year for the Russian port of Archangel on the White Sea; from there the skins traveled to Moscow. Furriers in Moscow held a trade secret. They combed out the inner wool from beaver skins while leaving the long guard hairs on the skin. Beaver pelts combed in this way fetched a higher price for use in trimming garments or even for wearing as a "natural" fur than uncombed beaver skins from North America. After the furs had been processed, the Dutch traders shipped two profitable goods with the return voyage each year.[10] Both combed beaver pelts and separated, high-quality beaver wool returned a profit despite the costs of shipping to Archangel and back. Paris, with its high concentration of skilled hatters, remained the primary market for processed beaver fur—at least until the flight of the Huguenots to London in 1685.

BEAVER AND OTHER FURBEARERS

The beaver is one of those wild animals whose singular appearance and work habits have become firmly engrained in United States and Canadian popu-

9. The manufacturing process is described by Hugh Grant, "Revenge of the Paris Hat: The European Craze for Wearing Headgear Had a Profound Effect on Canadian History," *The Beaver* 37 (1989).

10. E. Rich, "Russia and the Colonial Fur Trade," *Economic History Review,* 2d ser., 7 (1955).

lar culture (and indeed, world culture)—so much so that historians of the
fur trade rarely think it necessary to describe its physical characteristics, life
cycle, habitat, or industrious work ethic. This omission tends to minimize the
extraordinary importance of the beaver in the shaping of the North American landscape and to elide the ecological significance of its market-driven
near-extinction.

The densely furred, reddish brown to black North American beaver (*Castor canadensis*) is one of the largest rodents in the world. Adult beavers of both
sexes are about the same size: from 600 to 800 millimeters in body length and
twelve to twenty-five kilograms in weight. They have broad, flat, naked tails
(100–130 millimeters wide) that add another 250–400 millimeters in length.
They have unwebbed front feet with strong digging claws and webbed hind
feet for swimming. Their strongly developed front teeth never stop growing
but are worn down by incessant chewing and gnawing. Beavers are herbivores that feed on the cambium, bark, leaves, twigs, and roots of deciduous
softwood trees—willow, aspen, poplar, birch, and alder—as well as on roots
of aquatic plants such as water lilies. They are semiaquatic animals who prefer to live in burrows or lodges beside or in streams and small lakes near an
abundant growth of their favored tree species. Strong swimmers, they reach
a speed of six to seven kilometers per hour and routinely remain underwater for five minutes or more.

Beavers are social animals that live in family groups of four to as many as
eight animals. Each group centers on a monogamous, mated breeding pair
of adults who take care of young that are less than two years of age. Mating
takes place once a year, about January or February, followed by a gestation
period of 100 to 110 days. The litters, born April to June, usually number two
to four kits that nurse for three months. Kits live with their parents until they
reach sexual maturity, at which time their parents expel them from the
colony to establish their own households nearby. Beavers in captivity can survive from thirty-five to fifty years, but the life span in the wild is probably
shorter.[11] In short, beavers are both prolific and long-lived and have few dangerous predators.

These animals are energetic hydrologic engineers who work continuously
to shape their home environment. Ponds afford them security and food storage for winter. They cut trees and bushes by gnawing and drag or float logs
and poles for use in construction. Using earth, mud, stones, brush, and
poles, beavers build dams to create or augment ponds and lakes, build submerged lodges on islands in the ponds or on the banks of rivers, and even
dig waterways (beaver canals) that permit them to float logs readily from a

---

11. Ronald M. Nowak and Ernest P. Walker, *Walker's Mammals of the World*, 5th ed. (Baltimore: Johns Hopkins University Press, 1991), s.v. "Beaver."

distant source. Over years and decades, undisturbed beaver colonies continually augment and extend these works to an impressive scale.

In favorable habitats like northern hardwood forests, beavers can reach prodigious numbers. Reasonably credible estimates suggest that *Castor canadensis* numbered between 60 to 100 million animals before European settlement in North America. Some inkling of the cumulative impact of dense beaver populations on the North American landscape can be inferred from a mid-nineteenth-century study of an area where beavers were under minimal pressure from trappers.

Lewis Morgan, later to become prominent as an early ethnologist and anthropologist, began studying beavers in the mid-1850s. Morgan was involved in the construction of a railroad built to reach iron deposits in an uninhabited area in northern Michigan on the south shore of Lake Superior. The railroad cut through a "beaver district"; as a result of the railroad "opening this wilderness in advance of all settlement, the beavers were surprised, so to speak, in the midst of their works, which, at the same time, were rendered accessible for minute and deliberate investigation."[12] Morgan chose as his study area a mixed deciduous and coniferous rectangular tract measuring 9.6 by 12.9 kilometers. Within this 124-square-kilometer region traversed by two small rivers, the Carp and the Ely, Morgan found "sixty-three beaver dams, without reckoning the smallest, from those which are fifty feet [15 meters] in length, and forming ponds covering a quarter of an acre of land, to those which are three hundred and five hundred feet [91 to 150 meters] in length, with ponds covering from twenty to sixty acres [8.1 to 24.3 hectares] of land."[13] In this small region, beavers also built lodges on the banks of natural ponds and lakes. They constructed dozens of canals that enabled them to move timber and brush readily by water to their lodges. One of the longest canals, 153 meters in length, was designed to supply beaver burrows along its route and a lodge at the entrance to a natural pond.

Morgan also commented on the ubiquitous "beaver meadows" shown on the map of the study tract. These were low-lying areas adjacent to beaver ponds, where, in the wet seasons, standing water had killed off the tree growth and permitted a "rank, luxuriant grass" to flourish. The beaver meadows were "a series of hummocks formed of earth and a mass of coarse roots of grass rising about a foot high, while around each of them is a narrow strip of bare and sunken ground."[14] However, as Morgan was careful to emphasize, all these works required constant maintenance and repair by the at-

---

12. Lewis Henry Morgan, *The American Beaver: A Classic of Natural History and Ecology* (New York: Dover Publications, 1986), 8.

13. Ibid., 80.

14. Ibid., 203–4.

tentive beaver colonies that benefited from them. When hunting killed off beaver colonies in a region, the dams and canals deteriorated and rapidly altered those ecosystems associated with the beaver.

In addition to beaver pelts, European merchants encouraged Indian hunters to supply them with pelts from other furbearers. All were carnivores with smaller populations than those of the beaver and were more difficult to hunt. Their furs were not used for making hats but for garments or linings that offered warmth, comfort, and display in the traditional fashion. Second only to the beaver in annual numbers harvested was the raccoon *(Procyon lotor)*, whose fur was warm but considered less fashionable and valuable. Also targeted were highly valued pelts from the marten *(Martes americana)* and the fisher *(Martes pennanti)*, both close relatives of the Siberian sable. Along stream and riverbanks were found the mink *(Mustela vison)*, the river otter *(Lutra canadensis)*, and the less valuable muskrat *(Ondata zibethicus)*.

Furs from several species of fox found a market: red fox *(Vulpes vulpes)*, kit fox *(Vulpes macrotis)*, swift fox *(Vulpes velox)*, gray fox *(Urocyon cinereoargenteus)*, and in the far north, arctic fox *(Alopex lagopus)*. Pelts from two large cats, the lynx *(Felis lynx)* and the smaller and ubiquitous bobcat *(Felis rufus)*, sold readily in Europe. Killing the gray wolf *(Canis lupus)* and especially the rare wolverine *(Gulo gulo)* required both skill and perseverance on the part of the hunter. Long before contact with Europeans, Indian hunters pursued the black bear *(Ursus americanus)*, the largest, most dangerous, and most respected of their prey animals. Every year, several thousand black bear furs, along with those of a few brown bears *(Ursus arctos)* and even polar bears *(Ursus maritimus)*, reached Europe.

THE SEVENTEENTH-CENTURY SAINT LAWRENCE FUR TRADE

Pursuit of the beaver can best be described in terms of the river systems Europeans used to penetrate the interior. In the north, Indians employed light birch-bark canoes to transport packs of heavy furs along subsidiary streams to converge on a main river route that would take them to a European trading center. Use of the canoe permitted portaging around rapids and falls. To the north, the French followed the Saint Lawrence, Saguenay, and Ottawa River systems inland; further south, the Dutch relied on the Hudson River and its tributaries to gain access to Indian hunters and to transport their furs. The English moved up the Connecticut and Delaware Rivers to trade for furs. Toward the end of the century, the English, organized under a royal charter into a new company, sailed north into Hudson Bay and established trading posts in its vicinity.

The first organized French fur-trading expeditions in the early 1600s encountered eastern Algonkian Montagnais who offered them furs in return for trade goods. After Samuel de Champlain sailed up the Saint Lawrence River and founded Quebec in the narrows of the great river, the French could actively trade for furs with the Montagnais from a permanent base.

The intensified French trading presence in the seventeenth century had a perceptible impact on the eastern Algonkians and their habitat. Prior to contact with the French, they had hunted beaver for meat and for furs to wear as warm clothing, but apparently not with the intensity they displayed after exposure to market incentives. For the Algonkians—as for nearly all North American Indians—to hunt moose, bears, beavers, and other prey was a spiritual quest, a "holy occupation," during which "animals, in the Indian cosmology, consciously surrendered themselves to the needy hunter."[15] They did so, however, only if the hunter consulted his own "soul-spirit" for guidance in a dream before the hunt. If the dream were properly divined, the hunter's soul spirit, who had been in contact with the wildlife spirits, would lead the hunter to the game that had agreed to be slain.[16] Generally, the hunter felt a strong sense of kinship and even friendship with his game animals. He observed elaborate taboos and rules for deferential treatment of the slain animal's carcass. If he were careless in these observances, or if he killed too many animals, bad luck would follow. The animal spirits, angered and hostile, would punish the greedy or unobservant hunter by denying him willing prey.[17]

These cultural inhibitions that imposed dignity and restraint on Algonkian hunters faltered when juxtaposed with the seductive appeal exerted by commodities of the fur trade. Algonkian material culture became dependent on French trade goods. Iron tools and kettles replaced those of stone, wood, bark, and bone. Harquebuses and pistols replaced bows and arrows in hunting and warfare. European blankets, shirts, stockings, and other

15. Calvin Martin, *Keepers of the Game: Indian-Animal Relationships and the Fur Trade* (Berkeley and Los Angeles: University of California Press, 1978), 115. An intriguing theory, first advanced by Martin in the mid-1970s, is that this spiritual universe shattered in the sixteenth century. In advance of full-blown participation in the fur trade, the Algonkians went through a profound spiritual crisis. Confronted with catastrophic diseases brought by the Europeans, which their shamans or healers could not cure, they blamed the wildlife spirits for their affliction. This occurred partly, as Martin argues, because wild animals themselves were probably carriers of some of these diseases. Restraints based on mutual respect and deference dissolved. The Algonkians went to war with their animal tormentors. At this juncture, the fur traders offered material incentives and a rationale for the further killing and punishing of treacherous wildlife. With the rationale for their spiritual world ripped apart, the ideological assault mounted by Christian missionaries contributed further to the demoralization of the Algonkians. Since Martin published *Keepers of the Game*, other anthropologists have decisively rejected its validity and usefulness. See the rebuttal articles assembled in Shepard Krech III, *The Ecological Indian: Myth and History* (New York: W. W. Norton and Company, 1999).

16. C. Martin, *Keepers of the Game*, 123–25.

17. Ibid., 128–29.

items of clothing partially replaced beaver robes and deerskins. Flint and steel replaced the wooden drill for making fire. The practice of burying weapons and other possessions with dead warriors was a continuing drain on these goods.[18]

To obtain trade goods, the Algonkians traded beaver but also moose, lynx, otter, marten, badger, and muskrat hides. Avid consumers, the Indians hunted harder and killed more of these animals than they ever had before. In 1634, a French Jesuit, Father Paul Le Jeune, spent the winter with a band of Montagnais who were actively hunting beavers for the trade. Le Jeune observed that when the Montagnais found a beaver lodge, they "kill all, great and small, male and female." Le Jeune opined that they "will finally exterminate the species in this Region, as has happened among the Hurons, who have not a single Beaver."[19] Le Jeune further suggested that the Indians set up family-managed hunting territories for sustainable management, and that they restrict their kill to males of an appropriate size.[20]

The older practice of coalescing into groups of families for the winter and summer hunting seasons changed. Formerly, the head of the hunting bands had allotted territories each season to individual hunters. Instead, under the constraints of commercial hunting, individual families began to select sites for camping and to mark out their hunting territories. They asserted property rights in this territory by marking blazes on trees. Ownership of family territories was inherited by patrilineal descent. Growing scarcity of game encouraged this type of dispersal; so also did the French preference for dealing with individual hunters rather than groups.[21]

By mid–seventeenth century, beaver and other furbearers were severely depleted in the eastern Algonkian lands. Overhunting had serious consequences for the Algonkian food supply as moose, bears, beavers, and other larger fauna were killed off. Game birds such as geese and partridges came under heavy assault, especially from the growing use of guns for hunting. According to Nicolas Denys, Victor Hugo Paltsits, and William Francis Ganong:

> The musket is used by them more than all other weapons, in their hunting in spring, summer and autumn, both for animals and birds. With an arrow they killed only one Wild Goose; but with the shot of a gun they kill five or six of

18. Alfred Goldsworthy Bailey, *The Conflict of European and Eastern Algonkian Cultures, 1504–1700: A Study in Canadian Civilization*, 2d ed. (Toronto: University of Toronto Press, 1976).

19. Quoted in Krech, *The Ecological Indian*, 181.

20. Ibid., 182.

21. Bailey, *The Conflict of European and Eastern Algonkian Cultures*, 84–88; Janet E. Chute, "Frank G. Speck's Contributions to the Understanding of Mi'kmaq Land Use, Leadership, and Land Management," *Ethnohistory* 45, no. 3 (1999).

them. With the arrow it was necessary to approach the animal closely; with the gun they kill the animal from a distance with a bullet or two.[22]

The spiritual and material world of the Algonkian Indians offered impressive coherence, meaning, and well-being for its inhabitants. The fur trade, perhaps the single most important conduit for contact with the technically superior Europeans, devastated that world. Adaptation to demands of the market was simply one aspect of a larger cultural challenge.

Two common narcotics—one old and one new—stimulated Algonkian consumer demand and pushed them to hunt more voraciously. Smoking tobacco (*Nicotiana rustica*, the only crop grown by Algonkian men) was in active use and was traded widely before the French arrived. Having become acquainted with Brazilian tobacco on the Brazilian Atlantic Coast during the early sixteenth century apparently led to the French including it as part of the bundle of trade goods on offer to the Algonkians in New France. Tobacco from Brazil was made from the tropical tobacco plant *Nicotiana tabacum*. This was a larger tropical variety that dried to a more flavorful product than the indigenous variety. A large part of the Brazilian product's appeal lay in its additives: Portuguese growers added molasses and spices in a mix that sweetened and imparted a distinctive flavor to their product.

All Algonkian groups preferred Brazilian tobacco imported by the French to the native-grown and traded variety. Brazilian trade tobacco supplanted the indigenous product in leisure and recreational smoking, in use as a work drug to combat fatigue and hunger, and as a ceremonial drug in male councils. The indigenous variety retained its place in religious ceremonies. So pronounced had Algonkian taste become in this regard that the Hudson's Bay Company was forced to obtain Brazilian tobacco for its own fur purchases and to abandon attempts to introduce Chesapeake tobacco from the English colonies.[23]

Alcohol was far more damaging and costly. Very early on, the coastal Indians became addicted to wine and brandy offered by the French. Although frequently protested by the French missionaries and often banned, brandy remained a staple trade good offered for furs. Heavy alcohol consumption resulted in deeply felt depression and malaise in the Indian populations. Drunkenness prevailed during annual trading sessions. Many Algonkians died from alcohol poisoning or the effects of alcohol-induced diseases. Males killed each other in drunken quarrels and assaulted their parents and

22. Bailey, *The Conflict of European and Eastern Algonkian Cultures*, 52, citing Nicolas Denys, Victor Hugo Paltsits, and William Francis Ganong, *The Description and Natural History of the Coasts of North America (Acadia)* (Toronto: Champlain Society, 1908), 443.

23. Linda Wimmer, "African Producers, European Merchants, Indigenous Consumers: Brazilian Tobacco in the Canadian Fur Trade, 1550–1821" (Ph.D. diss., University of Minnesota, 1996), 202–14.

wives. Drunken women and men engaged in promiscuous and often public sex. After addicts sold all their furs for brandy, they and their families starved through the winters.[24]

Alcoholism and malnutrition reduced Algonkian resistance to infectious diseases. A major smallpox epidemic in 1639–1640 killed off thousands of Indians. A French Jesuit observer at Tadoussac in 1646 reported, "There were reckoned, formerly on the shores of this port, three hundred warriors or effective hunters, who made with their families about twelve or fifteen hundred souls[,] . . . humbled by diseases which have almost entire[ly] exterminated [them]. . . . Jesus Christ . . . seems to wish to repeople this tribe with a goodly number of Savages who land there from various places."[25] When beset by disease, the Indians often migrated to seek help from the French and further exposed themselves to infection.

Commodification in a new market setting was important, but it alone would not have wreaked such havoc. Disease, alcoholism, and war enveloped the fur trade in a miasmic cloak that corroded all aspects of Algonkian society and culture. The end result was a dependency that grew more pervasive and demeaning over time. By the latter 1600s, the eastern Algonkians were trading furs for biscuits, bread, peas, and prunes.[26] They had become dependent on European foodstuffs to make it through the long, boreal winter without starvation.

HURONS AND MOHAWKS

Important though the Montagnais and other eastern Algonkian Indians were for the French fur trade, the numbers of furs traded by them dwindled, and they soon were outstripped by the Hurons, the northernmost of the Iroquoian-speaking peoples, who established an alliance with the French in 1611. The Hurons, numbering about eighteen thousand persons in as many as twenty-five villages, the largest of them fortified, had concentrated their settlements at the southeastern corner of Georgian Bay of Lake Huron.[27] From this strategic site, located at the northern extremity of maize-growing climatic limits, the Hurons were well placed to control the major water routes that provided easy access to the hunting tribes of the north.

During the sixteenth century, the Hurons were a horticultural people who employed shifting cultivation to produce surpluses of maize every year. They enjoyed a higher standard of living than Indian groups to the north and

24. Bailey, *The Conflict of European and Eastern Algonkian Cultures,* 66–74.
25. Quoted in ibid., 83.
26. Ibid., 55–57.
27. Bruce G. Trigger, *The Children of Aataentsic I: A History of the Huron People to 1660* (Montreal: McGill-Queen's University Press, 1976).

west, who lived purely by hunting. They were skillful and assiduous traders and negotiators who bartered their maize surplus for furs and other luxury goods and who acted as middlemen for the trade between north and south. The Huron language had become a widely understood trading language employed in and around the Great Lakes region.

After Champlain established a French settlement at Quebec in 1608, he acted decisively to fend off an Iroquois threat to seize control of the fur trade of the Saint Lawrence River valley. Responding to overtures from the Hurons, Champlain led an allied Huron, Algonkian, and French force south along the Richelieu River to the southern end of Lake Champlain. There, in July 1609, his firearms were decisive in the Battle of Lake Champlain against a Mohawk war party. Next year, Champlain, at the head of another allied force, used his firepower to win a bloody battle with the Mohawks on the Richelieu River. After an intricate series of negotiations stretching over five years, in 1616 Champlain and the Hurons agreed on an alliance in the fur trade and united in opposition to the Iroquois. This alliance, which endured until the destruction of the Hurons at midcentury, permitted peaceful use of the Saint Lawrence River and made possible an annual fur-bartering expedition from Huronia to Quebec.

In the spring of each year, 200 to 250 Huron men loaded their furs on about sixty large canoes. The flotilla spent six weeks making its way down the Ottawa River to the Saint Lawrence to Quebec for an annual exchange of furs for goods with the French. Relationships between the Hurons and the French resembled more traditional exchange patterns between the Hurons and other Indian groups. There was no competition from other European fur traders. Before actually trading, both sides devoted several days to feasts, speeches, and the exchange of costly presents. The rituals reaffirmed the treaty of friendship between the Hurons and the French.

Each year, the Hurons sold twelve thousand to fifteen thousand beaver pelts, along with high-quality lynx, marten, otter, fox, and other furs. Lacking price information, they accepted the price for furs set by the French. If they perceived that the trade goods offered were too little, they phrased their request for more in terms of "an appeal for further proof of friendship" instead of haggling over individual furs. The French eagerly sought beaver since the price for a good quality beaver pelt in France rose from 2.5 livres in 1558 to 8.5 livres in 1611 and to 10 livres in 1618, where it remained for most of the century.[28] The Hurons were most anxious to obtain metalware—iron knives, axes, and awls—and glass beads. During this early period, the French refused to offer firearms. The Hurons did not demand or consume much alcohol.

28. Ibid., 1:364, 356.

When the exchanges were complete, the Hurons paddled back along the Saint Lawrence to the Ottawa River and home. A handful of French traders accompanied the Hurons on their return journey to spend the winter in one of their settlements and to help in defense against the Mohawks.

In the early years, the Hurons brought furs of beavers they had killed themselves, as well as those they had acquired by trading with other Indian groups. However, by 1630, they had hunted out the beaver on their own hunting grounds.[29] The Huron trading network extended as far north as James Bay, as far west as Lake Michigan, and to the southeast as far as Lake Erie and the territory of the Susquehannock Indians. Each year, several hundred Hurons traveled by canoe for weeks at a time to barter maize and trade goods with the Nipissings, Ottawas, Ojibwas, and neutral Indian groups in both the Lake Huron area and the Ottawa River valley. The finest pelts came from the Canadian Shield to the north. Algonkian-speaking hunting groups from the north spent the winter on Huron lands in order to have access to more reliable food supplies and a market for their furs.

By the 1620s, cargoes sent from New France to the metropolis exceeded twenty thousand pelts per year and reached a high point at thirty thousand beaver pelts in 1627.[30] Two-thirds of the French fur supply came from the Hurons; the French obtained the other one-third from the Montagnais and other coastal Algonkian speakers. The latter included the Abenakis of northern Maine.

The Hurons, unlike the Montagnais, Micmacs, and other Algonkian-speakers on the coast, seemingly retained their social organization and culture without overt damage. Their system of matrilocal residence apparently remained intact. With their new iron tools, they cleared more of the forest and produced more, rather than less, maize for themselves and for trade. Craft expression flourished in traditional pottery and tobacco-pipe making but also in a new form of ornamental metalworking.

The Hurons drank a little alcohol in the course of the welcoming ceremonies at Quebec but did not bring supplies back with them, nor did they suffer from alcoholism. The leading scholar of the Hurons comments:

> The Huron's lack of interest in alcohol correlates with their unbroken self-esteem. In their relations with the French, the Huron were still their own masters. Their role in the fur trade was built on earlier trade relations and the cultural fluorescence that this trade made possible was a realization of tendencies that had been inherent in their traditional culture, rather than a disruptive or degrading process. All of these developments contributed to a sense of achievement and well being. The Huron had no reason to resent the French or to feel

29. Ibid., 1:350.
30. Ibid., 1:356.

inferior to them. On the contrary, they seem to have felt more justified than ever in regarding other peoples as being inferior to themselves.[31]

The Hurons were also assisted in their rejection of alcohol by the Jesuits, who, before 1649, did as much as they could to prevent the French from offering brandy as a trade good.

Unfortunately for the Hurons, this happy condition did not last. Before 1634, the Hurons seem not to have been afflicted with European diseases, nor were they prone to infectious disease. However, between 1634 and 1640, they were assaulted by several severe epidemics. Prolonged encounters with influenza and other unknown diseases killed some Hurons and weakened many more in the years 1634 to 1637. The greatest blow came from smallpox—carried by a group of Saint Lawrence Indians who had visited the New England Abenakis—which hit the Hurons in 1639. Before the disease waned, approximately half the population, or nine thousand Hurons, had died. Despite these tragic losses, those Hurons who survived traded vigorously to keep up the level of their annual fur deliveries to the French. The average number of furs shipped from New France rose perceptibly in the 1640s to thirty thousand or more pelts each year.[32]

In the end, conflict over the fur trade destroyed and dispersed the Hurons. By the first decade of the seventeenth century, the Mohawks and the other Iroquois nations, traditional enemies of the Hurons, had developed an "economic lifeline" to the Dutch in the Hudson River valley.[33] Control over access to Albany ensured that nearly all pelts traded with the Dutch— whether hunted by the Mohawks themselves or pillaged from others— brought cloth, guns, wampum (shell beads strung by New England Indians), and metalware to the Mohawk consumer. As these goods replaced traditional handicrafts, the Iroquois became dependent on these imports.

Most damaging was the Iroquois demand for brandy. Unlike the Hurons, Mohawk men drank enthusiastically to excess, with devastating results. To some extent, drinking replaced long-practiced vision quests and trancelike states as a means to spiritual fulfillment. However, both group "brandy feasts" and individual drinking released pent-up aggressions in a context that excused drink-inspired violent behavior.[34]

31. Ibid., 1:433.

32. Ibid., 2:589–99, 603.

33. Daniel K. Richter and the Institute of Early American History and Culture, *The Ordeal of the Longhouse: The Peoples of the Iroquois League in the Era of European Colonization* (Chapel Hill: University of North Carolina Press, for the Institute of Early American History and Culture, Williamsburg, Va., 1992), 75.

34. Ibid., 86; Maia Conrad, "Disorderly Drinking," *American Indian Quarterly* 23 (summer 1999): 1–11.

The more aggressive Mohawks resorted to warfare to supplement their own hunting. They met their growing desire for European trade goods by raiding both the Huron and the Algonkian Indians to the north. In this new style of raiding, they seized furs and trade goods, as well as captives who could be assimilated into their own society as slaves or dependents. The latter device helped to remedy their own losses from smallpox, which were similar in magnitude to those of the Hurons.[35] As a result of Dutch firearm sales, the Mohawks were better armed than the Hurons.

For most of each year in the 1640s, the Mohawks kept as many as ten raiding parties active along the Saint Lawrence. A peace negotiated by the French with the Mohawks in 1645 soon broke down. Between 1646 and 1650, the Mohawks (joined by the Senecas) attacked and destroyed Huron settlements with the aim of destroying the confederacy. By 1649, the terror-stricken Hurons, weakened by their inability to grow food because of raids, burnt their own villages and dispersed as refugees either to Quebec or west to Lake Superior and Lake Michigan.

NEW ENGLAND AND NEW YORK IN THE SEVENTEENTH CENTURY

Along the New England coast, the early English colonists, like the French, seized upon furs as a cash crop to pay off their investors. The Pilgrim community at Plymouth made substantial profits from furs traded locally and by means of trading missions sent to barter with the Abenakis on the Kennebec River in Maine. The discovery that they could barter wampum—beaded in belts worn by high-status Indian sachems and other leaders—and trade the wampum for furs enhanced their profits. In 1632, they shipped 3,361 pounds of beaver pelts (equal to 2,305 prime beaver pelts) to England for sale.[36] As early as 1627, the first English colonists, funded by Bristol merchants, had peopled a fishing settlement at the mouth of the Pemaquid River and were trading for furs with the Abenakis.[37]

The Connecticut River proved to be the most durable and profitable area for the English fur trade. Between the spring of 1633 and the spring of 1634, a massive smallpox epidemic killed thousands of Indians between Maine and southern Connecticut. Of an estimated twelve thousand Indians then living in the Connecticut River valley, as many as three-quarters may have died. The survivors were disorganized and unlikely to offer any serious resistance

35. Trigger, *The Children of Aataentsic I*, 2:627.
36. For an overview of Indian-European interaction, see Neal Salisbury, *Manitou and Providence: Indians, Europeans, and the Making of New England, 1500–1643* (New York: Oxford University Press, 1982).
37. Neill De Paoli, "Beaver, Blankets, Liquor, and Politics: Pemaquid's Fur Trade, 1614–1760," *Maine Historical Society Quarterly* 33, nos. 3–4 (1993–1994): 172.

to settlers from the Massachusetts Bay Colony.[38] In the wake of these losses, the fur trade virtually halted.

In 1635, William Pynchon, given a license by the Massachusetts Bay Colony, moved into this vacuum and established a fur-trading post upriver, beyond the fall, or tidal, line adjacent to Agawam, a settlement inhabited by Indians of that name. At Agawam, renamed Springfield, Pynchon and his son extracted furs from upland western and northern New England and sent them on to European markets.

For four decades, William Pynchon was the most visible and successful fur trader in New England. The Pynchons themselves, or their approved English subtraders, offered wampum and trade goods to local Indian hunters—Agawams, Woronocos, Norwottucks, and Pocumtucks—and to those who became middlemen for more distant producers. Pynchon, by offering higher prices, also enticed Mohican Iroquois to bring their furs to Springfield, in preference to the Dutch post at Albany. At this early phase of the English colonist–Indian encounter, Pynchon and the inhabitants of Springfield seem to have negotiated with each other fairly and in a general spirit of goodwill and respect. Pynchon, whose linguistic and diplomatic abilities figure prominently, did not assume that "God's Grace and the King's charter" automatically gave the Puritans "full and final legal authority over the heathen Indians."[39] The Indians made good use of English trade goods; and the Puritans sold their furs to London. Both sides needed what the other offered and both sides benefited from the exchange.[40]

Springfield's role as a fur entrepôt was brief, lasting less than thirty years, and its total contribution not all that impressive by comparison with that of Quebec. Shipments in the 1630s and 1640s may have been higher, but the annual average for the decade 1651 to 1661 was 1,625 pounds, or 1,114 beaver pelts. In the 1660s, beaver supplies dropped substantially to an average of 487 pounds, or only 334 pelts, per year.[41] By the 1680s, the Connecticut River valley fur trade had dwindled into insignificance largely because of reduced beaver populations in the New England hunting grounds.

The most prolific and durable route to furs lay below New England, in the Hudson River valley. After the results of the 1609 voyage of Henry Hudson became known, Dutch merchants from Amsterdam fitted out two ships, under Hendrick Christiansen and Adrian Block, respectively, and sent them on repeated voyages to trade for furs and to explore the Hudson River and the

38. Peter A. Thomas, *In the Maelstrom of Change: The Indian Trade and Cultural Process in the Middle Connecticut River Valley, 1635–1665* (New York: Garland, 1990), 54–55.

39. Marty O'Shea, "Springfield's Puritans and Indians," *Historical Journal of Massachusetts 26*, no. 1 (1998): 46–47.

40. Ibid.

41. P. A. Thomas, "In the Maelstrom of Change," 287, fig. 7. Detailed account books for the years before 1651 have not survived.

coastline of Connecticut and New York. In 1614, the merchants organized themselves as the Company of New Netherland, with exclusive trading rights granted by the States General. The trading company built two trading posts: one on Manhattan Island and the other upriver on the Hudson, called Fort Orange, near the future site of Albany.[42] Access to supplies of wampum, made from the periwinkle shells found by the Montauks on Long Island, proved to be a trading asset for the Dutch. These early ventures were promising enough for the Dutch West India Company, chartered in 1621, to win approval from the States General to take over the Hudson River fur trade and trading posts as a small part of wide mandate for trade.

During their first year of operation, in 1624, Dutch West India Company traders shipped 7,246 beaver skins, 850 otter skins, and other miscellaneous furs from Manhattan Island to Amsterdam. For the next forty years, the Dutch sustained a profitable trade in beaver and other furs. They drew from a wide catchment area that extended to the Delaware River valley to the south, and into the Iroquois country of what is now interior New York State, and beyond. The Dutch managed to trade successfully with both the Mohawks and their avowed enemies, the Mohicans, throughout this period. Until the destruction of the Hurons, Dutch output was only a fraction of the French trade, amounting to several thousand beaver pelts a year, but considerably greater than that of the English. With the Mohawks as trading partners, the Dutch boosted their trade to a peak of 46,000 furs in 1657.[43] This was the highest shipment before the English conquest and annexation of New Netherland in 1664.

After the conquest of New York removed the Netherlands as a colonial contender, the English developed a vigorous fur-trading system competitive with that of the French. Colonial merchants continued to buy, bundle, and ship beaver and other furs from ports in New England and the Atlantic Coast states. In spite of continuing observations about depleted animal populations, Indians found sufficient furbearers to support an ongoing export fur industry in these regions.

With the Dutch removed from the scene, the British controlled Albany, the leading fur entrepôt for New York and New England, and its outlet to the sea, Manhattan, at the mouth of the Hudson River. Surviving Dutch fur merchants and new English traders located at Albany relied on the Mohawk Indians to deliver large numbers of beaver and other furs to them every year. James, duke of York, who held the patent for the newly conquered colony from Charles II on annual payment of forty beaver skins, permitted direct shipment of furs to Holland, where prices were generally better than in En-

42. Phillips, *The Fur Trade*, 1:149.
43. Allen W. Trelease, *Indian Affairs in Colonial New York: The Seventeenth Century* (Ithaca, N.Y.: Cornell University Press, 1960), 131.

gland. Albany merchants actually held formal rights to a monopoly of the fur trade confirmed by a charter granted by the governor of New York in 1686—a charter that was frequently evaded but which symbolized the predominance of Albany during the seventeenth century.[44]

The Mohawks and other Iroquois remained the dominant trading partners of the Albany merchants. The Iroquois domain in the seventeenth century stretched from the Mohawk River valley to the Buffalo area. To extend their hunting territories, the Mohawks attacked the Indians of southern Ontario and those to the south of Lake Erie. They also moved south into the valley of the Delaware River, attacked Indian groups living there, and took beaver pelts as tribute to trade at Albany.

The Iroquois, as did most other Indians, preferred English trade goods to those of the French. English strouds, or woolen blankets, were not only cheaper, but also warmer and more serviceable than those made by the French. English rum was cheaper and stronger than French brandy. These preferences strengthened the Five Nations in their hostility to the French and their military challenge to the French role in the northern fur trade (see below).

FRENCH AND OTTAWAS IN THE GREAT LAKES REGION

Flowing from Lake Ontario, the Saint Lawrence River offered a direct water route to the interconnected waterways of the Great Lakes and the Mississippi River valley. From the 1650s through the 1680s, several French explorers ventured deep into the interior as far west as Lake Superior and the valley of the Mississippi. Some of these men traveled without official authorization; most went with the encouragement of the French colonial authorities. Among those reporting and publicizing their discoveries were Jesuit missionaries who, by the 1640s, had reached the strategic juncture of Lake Huron and Lake Superior at Sault Sainte Marie and, by the 1670s, had mapped all the Great Lakes.[45]

To gain uninterrupted access to furs produced by the Great Lakes Indians, the French first had to develop an alliance with the Ottawas, whom Champlain initially had encountered in 1615. At their villages on the shores and islands of Lake Huron, the Ottawas were gatekeepers of interlake canoe transport and central actors in the wider Indian system of waterborne trade and diplomacy. The Ottawas held their strategic positions partly by their much-respected military prowess and belligerence but primarily because of their mastery of deepwater canoeing and navigation on the Great Lakes.

44. Phillips, *The Fur Trade*, 1:250.
45. Ibid., 1:220–21.

During the early seventeenth century, the approximately five thousand Ottawas divided into four named totemic groups.[46] To the east, fifteen hundred Kiskakons, descended from the black bear, spent the warmer southern months at the mouth of Nattawaga River on the southern shore of Georgian Bay. The Kiskakons were closely tied to and allied with the Iroquoian Tionnontates, or Petuns, whose villages lay to the south in the interior. The most ardent warriors of the Ottawas, the Kiskakons watched and defended the overland trails by which raiding parties from the Ottawas' inveterate enemies, the Five Nations Iroquois, would approach the lake.[47] On the southwestern coast of Lake Huron on the shores of Thunder Bay, seven hundred Nassaukuetons, descendants of Michachou, the great hare, scanned the water approaches from Lake Erie in the south. In the north, nearly two thousand Kamigas, descendants of the white sucker fish, from their villages at Michilimackinac on the coasts and islands of the Straits of Mackinac, controlled the route between Lake Michigan and Lake Huron. Finally, one thousand Sinagos, claiming descent from the gray squirrel, lived in summer fishing villages on the eastern end of Manitoulin, the immense island in northern Lake Huron. The Sinagos kept watch over the river routes flowing from Lake Nipissing into Lake Huron. They were also the guardians of the spiritual center of Ottawa culture and society on Manitoulin.[48] Manitoulin Island was the site for annual Ottawa councils that drew together the entire Ottawa nation.

Part of the Ottawa homeland lay in the boreal forest zone, with its truncated frost-free season, and part in the southern broadleaf forest zone that permitted reliable agriculture. The Ottawas followed a seasonal cycle of migration between summer settlements—used for fishing, trade, meetings, and ceremonies—and dispersed, small winter camps for hunting and trapping. In the summer, the Ottawas grew limited crops of beans and hardy "flint corn" but did not rely on these crops for the bulk of their food. They gathered berries and fruits and tapped maple trees for sap to make sugar.

Fishing supplied the most reliable portion of the Ottawa diet. Fishing in Lake Huron's rough waters was dangerous work that demanded great skill, courage, and canoes designed and built for open waters. The Ottawas cast

46. William James Newbigging, "The History of the French-Ottawa Alliance, 1613–1763" (Ph.D. diss., University of Toronto, 1995), 49. Newbigging gives the population estimates from Reuben Gold Thwaites, ed., *The Jesuit Relations and Allied Documents: Travels and Explorations of the Jesuit Missionaries in New France, 1610–1791* (Cleveland: Burrows Brothers, 1896–1901).

47. Ibid., 44. The Ottawas formed one branch of the Anishinabeg peoples, Central Algonkian speakers, who carried out this migration. The closely related Ojibwas occupied the Canadian forest north of Lakes Huron and Superior, and the Potawatomis went west to the broad-leaved Carolinian forest of southern Lake Michigan.

48. Ibid., 90–94.

and recovered gill nets weighted with sinkers and marked by floating buoys. They also used dip nets where fish came close to the surface.[49] When spring and fall spawning seasons brought masses of large lake fish into shallow waters, the Ottawas gathered a bountiful harvest. During the two-month spring spawning season, they caught lake sturgeons *(Acipenser fulvescens)*, channel catfish *(Ictalurus punctatus)*, white suckers *(Castotomus commersoni)*, and walleyes *(Stizostedion vitreum)*. In the shorter, two-week fall spawning season, they took lake trout *(Salvelinus namaycush)*, the smaller cisco or lake herrings *(Coregonus artedii)*, and above all, whitefish *(Coregonus clupeaformis)*. Women cleaned and smoked most of the catches for later consumption.

More than any other Great Lakes Indian nation, the Ottawas were superb long-distance paddlers and canoe handlers. Their experience fishing prepared them for traversing open waters across Huron and the other lakes with a boldness, speed, and endurance that few Indians could match. Building new lake canoes each year was one of the most important symbolic and economic acts of Ottawa society. In late winter, work parties of Ottawa women carefully cut and rolled wide sections of bark from white birches. From black spruce trees, they stripped thin, flexible roots for lashing and gum for sealing the canoes. Men found white cedar windfalls to split into narrow segments used for the canoe ribs, gunwales, and sheathing. Working together, both men and women constructed new canoes with high sterns and bows designed to survive open lake waters. When complete and watertight, the women applied dyes and designs to the canoes that denoted the four clan totems, as well as designs denoting either the sun or the spirit of water, called Michipichy.[50]

Ottawa males were determined hunters. During the long winter season, Ottawa hunters traveled hundreds of miles on foot and in their canoes up rivers in search of game. After extended fasting and dreaming ceremonies, they set off in the autumn on the dangerous task of hunting black bears, which, if successful, resulted in a great community feast and celebration. More prosaically, they stalked deer, moose, caribou, and elks for meat and for their hides, which they used for clothing. They shot ducks, cranes, geese, passenger pigeons, and other fowl with bows. They netted turtles and hunted wild turkeys for meat. They hunted wolves, mink, otters, marten, and muskrats for flesh and fur. In particular, Ottawa hunters devoted much time and energy to hunting beavers for meat and fur. During the winter months, after they had experienced favorable dream portents, groups of Ottawa hunters set out to find beaver ponds and inhabited lodges. They smashed holes in the dams to drain off the pond water under the ice, then broke into the lodges and netted and killed fleeing beavers. The Ottawas, in other

49. Ibid., 76.
50. Ibid., 64–70.

words, avidly hunted beaver and other furbearers long before the Europeans demanded beaver pelts.

The Ottawas were dominant figures in an intricate trading network that tied together Indians throughout the Great Lakes region. Various products circulated in what seems to have been largely an exchange of presents of accepted traditional value rather than a price-setting market. Much of the actual exchange of goods seems to have occurred in the presence of, and with the encouragement of, the Ottawas. They also seem to have carried exchange goods to the extremities of the system.

The more numerous Ojibwas, allied to the Ottawas by language and descent, fished and hunted along rivers to the north but were not cultivators. Instead, they and other northern Indians obtained maize, corn, beans, squash, and tobacco raised by Indians under more favorable climatic conditions to the south. The Ojibwas sent their furs and skins to those Indian groups to the south who were less devoted and energetic hunters. There were also specialized products. Ottawa women wove durable, colorful, and well-designed reed mats that were much in demand throughout the region.[51]

From their first acceptance of an iron-bladed ax from Champlain in 1615, the Ottawas entered willingly into a mutually advantageous trading relationship and a solidifying political and military alliance with the French. In return for furs, the French offered valuable iron implements and tools, blankets, and other trade goods, but above all else, muskets. The Ottawas were willing to trade their own furs and those obtained in their trade network for French goods. There is considerable evidence that, throughout this period, the Ottawas prevented the Ojibwas and other tribes from attempting to travel themselves to the French posts on the Saint Lawrence and, instead, acted as middlemen and exchanged trade goods with them.

For several decades, the Ottawas, along with Tionnontate Indians, sent joint flotillas of canoes laden with furs on the long, endurance-testing water route from Manitoulin Island to the French River, then inland to Lake Nipissing and, via portage, to the Matawwa River and then to the Ottawa River, where they traded their furs for trade goods via Huron intermediaries.[52] Trading in this fashion brought highly valued goods and, in this early stage, left Ottawa society and culture intact and vital.

However, in the aftermath of the midcentury destruction of the Iroquois and the Hurons, the Ottawas made direct contact with the French. The Ottawa-French relationship moved quickly toward a full-blown alliance. Removal of the Huron buffer brought new Iroquois attacks from the east that drove the Kiskakon Ottawas from Nottawasaga Bay, along with may of their

51. Ibid., 79.
52. There is no direct evidence that the Ottawa actually entered the Saint Lawrence or traded directly with the French before 1649. Personal communication from Bruce Trigger.

Tionnontate allies, to take refuge with the Sinago Ottawas on Manitoulin Island. Despite this reverse, the Ottawas vigorously defended their remaining territory against repeated Iroquois attacks throughout the 1650s and resumed their fur-trading journeys to Montreal.

In 1654, Ottawas and Tionnontates who came to Montreal with furs agreed to take back with them two young venturesome French traders, Médard Chouart des Groseilliers and Pierre-Esprit Radisson. Two years later, Groseilliers and Radisson returned to Montreal with sixty canoes full of prime furs worth a hundred thousand livres. In 1665, Nicholas Perrot made his headquarters at Sault Sainte Marie and began buying furs from the Great Lakes Indians. In 1670, Perrot returned to Montreal accompanied by nine hundred Ottawas in canoes loaded with furs. During the 1660s, several Jesuit missionaries accompanied the Ottawa fur flotillas back to Lake Huron and established Saint Ignace, a permanent mission station at Michilimackinac.[53]

THE IMPERIAL CONFLICT

Two British interventions in the latter half of the seventeenth century—the creation of direct sea links between Hudson Bay and England and the conquest of the Dutch Hudson River territory—neatly encircled the French fur-trading system of the Saint Lawrence River valley. From 1664 to 1763, the British and French struggled for imperial dominance in North America. This conflict found its most direct expression in ferocious competition for the fur trade. The great prize was access to the Indians and the still-plentiful furbearers of the Great Lakes and upper Mississippi territories. This greater European imperial struggle swept all northeastern Indian groups into its sphere. Every Indian group in the region was forced to align itself with one or the other colonial regime and, periodically, to die in its wars.

Between 1689 and 1763, Britain and France fought each other in four separate European wars that spilled over into North America: the War of the League of Augsburg (King William's War), 1689–1697; the War of Spanish Succession, 1702–1713; the War of Austrian Succession, 1739–1748; and the Seven Years' War, 1754–1763. Between 1689 and 1763, these European conflicts thrust North American colonists and Indians alike into hostilities for one year in every two. At the end of the War of Spanish Succession, the Treaty of Utrecht removed France from Newfoundland, Acadia, and the subarctic territories of northern Canada. The Treaty of Louisburg in 1763 marked the final defeat of the French and left most of North America, save for Louisiana, to British colonial rule. The Indians mobilized by each side did much of the fighting and suffered most of the losses in these conflicts.

In addition to these larger wars, Indians engaged in internecine warfare

53. Newbigging, "The History of the French-Ottawa Alliance," 159–65.

at a frequency and intensity seemingly beyond what they had known prior to the French intervention. Seeking security in a time when little was to be had, defeated Indian groups engaged in kaleidoscopic relocations and removals in reaction to adversity and threatened extinction. Rather than offer greater opportunities for advantage and maneuver, the two European contenders for territory and trade, in the end, diverted Indian energies into diplomacy and war. This, in turn, reduced whatever economic benefits they had previously enjoyed by supplying furs for the European market.

The French responded to British encirclement by linear extension of the Saint Lawrence system deep into the interior of North America.[54] Men like Jean Talon, intendant general of New France for eight years under Colbert, and his successor, Louis de Baude, comte de Frontenac (governor from 1672 to 1682 and 1689 to 1698), saw the potential richness of the fur territories to the west and acted vigorously to encourage and promote the expansion of French trade. Talon argued, rightly, that the western lakes and rivers afforded water routes that permitted easy access to and control of these new fur territories.[55]

The French imperial vision coincided with the interests of the Ottawas in the Great Lakes region. During the 1670s, the Ottawas pressed the French to establish a trading settlement at Michilimackinac. If the French would do so, the Ottawas could obtain guns and other trade goods without making the exhausting trip to Montreal every summer, and they could control the distribution of guns among the Great Lakes Indians. Finally, in 1683, shaking free of Colbert's restraints, Frontenac, the governor of New France, sent Daniel Grasolon Duluth with fifteen French-manned canoes to set up a trading post on the Straits of Mackinac. This action cemented the Ottawa-French alliance that survived intact until 1763.

From this base, the French sent more fur traders and began to build a network of trading posts throughout the Great Lakes region. Nicholas Perrot and Louis Jolliet founded a trading post at present-day Green Bay to trade on the Wisconsin River. In the 1680s, Duluth journeyed to the headwaters of the Mississippi and thereafter established successful fur-trading posts on Lake Superior, near the mouth of the Kaministiguia River, on Lake Nipigon, and on the Albany River.

French discovery of the Mississippi set the outer bounds of the western fur trade. In 1673, Louis Jolliet and Father Marquette portaged between the Fox and Wisconsin Rivers and followed the Wisconsin to the upper Mississippi River. Jolliet and Marquette traveled down the Mississippi, past its confluence with the Missouri and the Ohio, to the vicinity of the Arkansas River intersection before returning. In the 1680s, Robert Cavalier de La Salle, an active

54. Phillips, *The Fur Trade*, 1:220.
55. Ibid., 1:222.

fur trader and confidant of Frontenac, devised a grand scheme to reach the mouth of the Mississippi and to claim the Mississippi River valley for a French empire in the west. La Salle and his companion Henri de Tonty canoed down the Illinois River to its junction with the Mississippi and continued downstream to finally reach the Gulf of Mexico. On April 9, 1682, La Salle formally claimed the entire Mississippi Basin for the king of France.

THE FRENCH-IROQUOIS WARS

During the late seventeenth century, however, the Iroquois, not the British, were the major enemy of New France. It was the Iroquois Confederacy that directly and aggressively threatened the growing network of French settlements and New France's Indian allies. The French and Iroquois, each aiming to dominate the lands and peoples of the Great Lakes interior, clashed in raids and counterraids that rose in intensity and scale to reach the level of all-out war.[56] The French fought to control the western fur trade. The Iroquois, encouraged, supported, and supplied by the British at Albany, fought to prevent French intrusion into hunting lands they considered their own and to keep the French from arming and dominating non-Iroquois that the Iroquois had marked for future conquest and assimilation as war captives. They also fought to have access to the fur trade of the interior and the flow of trade goods imported to pay for those furs—especially guns, which were increasingly important for Iroquois military operations. Obtaining control over the fur trade was part of a complicated mixture of motives that shaped Iroquois diplomacy and war, but it was not their only goal.[57]

During the 1670s and 1680s, the Five Nations Iroquois became progressively more upset by French incursions into lands located around Lake Ontario and Lake Erie that the Iroquois used as their primary hunting grounds. They feared that French forts built in this region would encourage their Indian allies—enemies to the Iroquois—to freely hunt in these tracts and deplete their food and fur resources.[58] Simultaneously, they suffered dismaying population losses in at least five major epidemics. To recover these losses, they would have to follow their usual practice of going to war and taking captives who could be assimilated into their society.[59]

56. W. J. Eccles, "The Fur Trade and Eighteenth-Century Imperialism," *William and Mary Quarterly*, 3d ser., 40 (1983): 342–44.

57. José António Brandão, *Your Fyre Shall Burn No More: Iroquois Policy towards New France and Its Native Allies to 1701* (Lincoln: University of Nebraska Press, 1997); Francis Jennings, *The Ambiguous Iroquois Empire: The Covenant Chain Confederation of Indian Tribes with English Colonies, from Its Beginnings to the Lancaster Treaty of 1744*, 1st ed. (New York: W. W. Norton, 1984).

58. Brandão, *Your Fyre Shall Burn No More*, 117–22.

59. Ibid., 115, table B1.

In the 1680s, the French became increasingly perturbed over attempts by English and Dutch traders accompanied by Iroquois to open direct access to the western fur trade.[60] Governor Denonville, acting under direct orders from Louis XIV to bring the Iroquois under French royal authority, attacked the Senecas in the summer of 1687. The Iroquois responded with an attack on Niagara and a massacre at La Chine, a French settlement near Montreal. This war soon merged into the War of the League of Augsburg, which broke out in 1689.

Between 1687 and 1697, "the Iroquois launched thirty-three raids against the French alone, sent armies of a thousand men or more against the colony three times, and captured or killed close to six hundred people."[61] They mounted an additional sixteen assaults against the Indian allies of the French. This was an enormous effort for a force of slightly over 2,000 Iroquois warriors.[62] The French settlers, aided by 1,500 regular troops sent from France, mounted thirty-three raids of their own with the assistance of their Indian allies. The Iroquois suffered greater losses—between 2,158 and 2,351 persons killed, captured, or lost, most of them male warriors. The Iroquois followed their customary practice of assimilating some Indian, but generally not French, captives into their society and reemployed them as warriors. Despite this, the number of Iroquois warriors probably fell by half during the decade.[63]

When, in 1697, the war ended in Europe, the Iroquois, deprived of further English support, reluctantly entered into peace negotiations with the French that were to last four years. Finally, in August 1701, Louis-Hector de Callières, governor-general of New France, convened a grand assembly of 1,300 Indians at Montreal to confirm a comprehensive treaty. In addition to the representatives of the Five Nations Iroquois, those of twenty-eight Indian tribes allied with the French were also present.

The French recognized that the Iroquois could be a useful buffer between themselves and the British colonies if neutralized. The Iroquois, exhausted by the war, no longer hoped to drive out the French and had discovered that the British were unreliable in their support. The Iroquois negotiators recognized that they would be able to play the French off against the British in the future. Therefore, the Iroquois willingly agreed to a clause in the peace treaty by which they declared that, in any future war between the French and the British, they, the Iroquois, would remain neutral. At one stroke, the greatest single threat to French western expansion and the fur trade vanished.[64]

60. Phillips, *The Fur Trade*, 1:260–61.
61. Brandão, *Your Fyre Shall Burn No More*, 125.
62. Ibid., 157.
63. Ibid., 126.
64. Eccles, "The Fur Trade and Eighteenth-Century Imperialism," 344.

THE FRENCH WESTERN FUR TRADE

Each imperial contender adopted a distinctive approach to extending its share of the fur trade. The French colonial state actively organized a state monopoly system that sent individual traders in canoes out to a system of trading posts for direct purchases of furs from their Indian producers. The British regime left its traders free to organize a purchasing system that relied heavily on Indian hunters and middlemen. Wide-ranging Iroquois warriors acquired furs by direct hunting, trade, and frequently, plunder, and brought the proceeds directly to Albany to exchange for trading goods. The French approach encouraged continuing westward exploration and territorial claims in new fur-producing regions. The British approach conserved energy for settlement and development of territories already held.

By the late seventeenth century, French interests dictated a vigorous westward expansion of the fur trade. Montreal, rather than Quebec, became the dominant trading center. The movement west of surviving Hurons and other defeated enemies of the Mohawks extended the reach of the fur trade. Merchants in New France sent skilled woodsmen, the French, and mixed French-Indian *coureurs de bois* to trade with these new sources of furs. The *coureurs de bois* canoed long distances up the river system to trade directly with the Ottawas and other new middlemen around the Great Lakes.[65]

French monopoly control provided stable capitalization, trade goods, quality control, and the processing and shipping services necessary to send furs to metropolitan markets. The actual collection of furs from the Indians was the task of licensed individual fur traders, who were given a high degree of freedom to barter and trade where it was most profitable.

As they fought the Iroquois, the French tightened their grip on the Great Lakes fur trade by a long drawn-out process of trial and error. They planted dozens of colonial settlements throughout the region. Invariably the sites were at strategic locations along water transport routes. Some French settlements were solely mission stations, some were fur-trading posts; many combined both functions. French forts and garrisons protected the largest trading settlements.

Acting from long experience, French fur traders established intimate, generally amicable, and profitable relationships with one Indian group after another. As Perrot did with the Ottawas, the French traders lived with and adopted the dress, food, and habits of their hosts and often took Indian wives. They learned to speak their hosts' language acceptably. These intimate ties certainly facilitated the exchange of furs for trade goods and benefited both parties. French fur traders pressed eagerly westward to the Great Lakes,

65. Phillips, *The Fur Trade*, 1:203.

south to the Mississippi River valley, and finally north to the Hudson Bay drainage system.

For the six decades remaining to French imperial rule in North America, the *coureurs de bois* enlisted Indian hunters and traders; exchanged guns, woolens, alcohol, tools, implements, and other trade goods for furs and skins; and packed and carried their stocks back to Montreal. The eighteenth-century western French fur trade settled into a pattern that relied on nineteen major fur-trading entrepôts in the Great Lakes region and four in Louisiana territory. Together these twenty-three posts sent an annual flow of furs east. These were carried by canoe to Montreal to be bulked and shipped across the Atlantic to La Rochelle in France.

Operating under strict official regulation, traders at these posts could purchase 5,685 100-pound packs of furs each year (568,500 pounds).[66] Detroit was the largest supplier of furs, sending a total of 900 packs (15.8 percent) of all allocations. Next was Michilimackinac, the famed fur-trading center that mediated traffic between Lake Huron and Lake Michigan, which sent 650 packs (11.4 percent). Then followed Baie des Puants (Green Bay), located on the Fox River where it runs into an arm of Lake Michigan, which sent 550 packs (9.7 percent) of the annual allocation.

Fur traders from Montreal formed into small companies, often in partnership with post commanders, and purchased either monopoly leases (farms) for these posts or licenses to import a fixed amount of trade goods to the post. The Crown reserved trading at six of the easternmost posts—La Belle Rivière, Niagara, Frontenac, Rouille, La Présentation, and Domaine du Roi—for salaried royal agents. Altogether, the royal monopoly purchased 845 packs of furs, or 14.9 percent of the annual total.

Judging by output, French westward expansion was a success. The intake of beaver furs rose decisively from the modest 15,000 to 20,000 pelts of the annual shipments in the first half of the seventeenth century. During the 1680s, fur traders delivered an average of 73,000 beaver furs (weighing 100,850 livres) each year at Montreal's official warehouses.[67] In the 1690s, beaver fur deliveries spiraled upward to the point of glut during the Iroquois-French wars. For the entire seventeenth century, data for eighteen selected years put the annual average intake of beaver furs at 75,000 pelts (104,173 livres). Although subject to considerable fluctuations, totals continued to rise in the eighteenth century. Between 1700 and the final French defeat in

66. Richard C. Harris and Geoffrey J. Matthews, *Historical Atlas of Canada* (Toronto: University of Toronto Press, 1987), vol. 1, pl. 40.

67. Calculated from Harold Adams Innis, *Fur Trade in Canada: An Introduction to Canadian Economic History* (Toronto: University of Toronto Press, 1956), 149–52, appendix A. Each beaver fur weighed on average 680 grams. Beaver furs were recorded by weight, so the number of furs is an approximate number.

1763, traders sent, on average, 122,000 beaver furs (weighing 169,381 livres) each year to Montreal.[68]

Although beaver was the fur most in demand in European markets, furs and skins from other animals actually made up the greater part of exports sent from New France. Between 1728 and 1755, the value of fur shipments sent to La Rochelle from Quebec averaged 875,000 or so livres tournois per year. Beaver furs contributed 43 percent to this total, other furs 41 percent, and deer and elk skins and hides 17 percent.[69] Relative proportions are similar when calculating the numbers of animals slaughtered. Over the same period, in a single year, hunters killed on average around 286,000 animals to meet this annual export demand. Beaver populations clearly bore the greatest hunting pressure: the 114,000 beaver skins exported represented 38.8 percent of the total kill. Hunters pursued other furbearers with far less intensity. Only raccoons, at 25.6 percent, approached the beaver total, followed by marten at 11.1 percent, bears at 4.4 percent, river otters at 2.6 percent, and four types of foxes at 1.7 percent. Deer represented just under 7 percent, with an average of around 20,000 skins taken per year.[70]

THE EXPANDING ENGLISH FUR TRADE IN THE EIGHTEENTH CENTURY

Toward the end of the seventeenth century, both British and French fur traders were looking to the prolific fur-bearing animals of the far north, the Canadian subarctic. The colder regions of the subarctic—the boreal forest and tundra wetlands—produced the thickest and most valuable beaver pelts and other furs.

In the 1660s, two French fur traders had ventured north of Lake Superior overland to Hudson Bay. Pierre Radisson and Jean-Baptiste de Groseilliers tried to interest French merchants and officials in establishing a maritime route to Hudson Bay. Rebuffed by the French, they eventually were patronized by King Charles I of England. An exploratory voyage in 1668 was the stimulus for the founding of the Hudson's Bay Company in 1670. Chartered by the king, the joint-stock company received sole right to trade in Hudson Bay and its hinterland. The first Hudson's Bay Company expedition sailed in

68. Ibid. Based on data for twenty-nine of the sixty-three years in question.

69. Thomas Wien, "Castor, peaux, et pelleteries dans le commerce canadien des fourrures, 1720–1790," in *"Le Castor Fait Tout": Selected Papers of the Fifth North American Fur Trade Conference, 1985,* edited by Bruce G. Trigger, Toby Morantz, and Louise Dechene (Montreal: Lake St. Louis Historical Society, 1987). Average value and percentages calculated from data on p. 92, table 4. Data for ten years only. The numbers are certainly not reliable to the last pelt or hide but are probably reasonably close to the actual count. A ±10 percent margin of error seems a reasonable assumption. Numbers given in the text are rounded.

70. Ibid., 89, appendix A, table 2.

1671, found three sites for future trading posts on rivers flowing into the bay, and returned with three thousand pounds of beaver skins.[71]

The English had opened up a new, direct maritime route into Hudson Bay that, by making expensive canoe travel by European traders unnecessary, reduced costs substantially. The French responded by forming a rival trading company for Hudson Bay and sending ships to trade. Over the next decades, varying levels of threat and force marked the conflict over control of trade and the region. Control of the posts commanding the major rivers entering into the bay changed hands on numerous occasions. Not until the Treaty of Utrecht in 1713 expelled the French from Hudson Bay did the British gain clear and unchallenged supremacy over the northern water route. Despite the difficulties of French competition, the Hudson's Bay Company had been generally successful in sending back cargoes of furs and was extremely profitable.

After Utrecht, the Hudson's Bay Company traders operated from four posts surrounding James Bay—Forts Richmond, Eastmain, Moose, and Albany—and three posts on the southwestern shore of Hudson Bay: Forts Severn, York, and Churchill. From the posts, they developed durable trading partnerships with the Algonkian-speaking Crees and Siouan-speaking Assiniboines of the boreal forest regions, who served as middlemen for more distant tribes. From its earliest years of operation, York Factory attracted furs from Plains Indians like the Mandans, Bloods, Blackfoot, and Sioux, some of whom made a thousand-mile round-trip to the factory. By 1720, when the Plains Indians were adapting to horses, they were less inclined to make the difficult canoe trip to Hudson Bay, and the Crees and Assiniboines dominated the trade. Newly established in 1717, Fort Churchill became the westernmost Hudson Bay trading establishment. Here, despite stiff Cree resistance, English traders slowly built up direct trade with the Chipewyans and other Athabascan-speaking subarctic Indians.[72]

The seven trading posts bordering the James and Hudson Bays were located in low-lying boreal forest, muskeg, or tundra, which had little in the way of game or furbearers. Only great flights of geese twice a year, partridges, and rabbits could be looked to for a food supply. The Cree Indians visited the area yearly for goose hunting but did not live there. Productive agriculture posed real difficulties that far north. To provision the posts, the Hudson's Bay Company hired bands of Cree Indians to hunt year-round. What came to be called "Home Guard Cree," as distinct from the middleman

71. Phillips, *The Fur Trade*, 1:270.

72. Arthur J. Ray and Donald B. Freeman, *"Give Us Good Measure": An Economic Analysis of Relations between the Indians and the Hudson's Bay Company before 1763* (Toronto: University of Toronto Press, 1978), 45–51; Yerbury, *The Subarctic Indians and the Fur Trade*, 16–50.

fur-trading groups, settled down near the posts. They were paid with trade goods, including arms and munitions, and guaranteed food security in wintertime. These contract hunters ranged widely to obtain moose, caribou, deer, and geese to supply the posts. This put increased hunting pressure on these animals throughout radial hinterlands of extraordinary area.

Hudson's Bay Company traders regularly collected and shipped large numbers of beaver pelts and other furs from this new resource. In addition to beaver, Indians traded marten, wolverine, wolf, red fox, bear, wildcat, and muskrat pelts—all luxuriant, cold-weather furs fetching good prices. Marten, for which the company paid a price that was kept at one-third the price of prime beaver furs, were taken in numbers that at times approached those of beavers. Albany Fort, for example, averaged 6,600 marten and 10,500 beaver pelts per year between 1750 and 1763.[73] Beaver retained its value, however, and between 1700 and 1763 the fort shipped nearly a million beaver pelts, an average of over 15,000 per year.

By midcentury, the beaver catch had begun to drop as beaver populations were hunted out. Albany Fort averaged 19,000 beaver pelts a year in the first two decades of the century, which dropped to an average of 15,600 pelts annually between 1720 and 1749, followed by declining average annual yields of 10,700 for the period 1750 to 1763.[74] Simulations of prices and the annual Fort Albany yield and dynamics of the beaver population in the fort's hinterland corroborate the notion of depletion.[75]

Nevertheless, in spite of these trends, the Hudson's Bay Company traders bought, baled, and shipped sufficient numbers of high-quality northern furs to average 8,205 pounds sterling each year in customs valuations in London. Subarctic furs accounted for just under one-third (32.7 percent) of all North American colonial fur imports into England in the period 1700 to 1775.[76]

To the south of the French corridor, the English fur trade flourished in the six decades before the French defeat in 1763. From Charleston to Boston, ports along the Atlantic seaboard served as entrepôts for the fur trade. Even the Carolinas and Virginia sent a few thousand beaver furs each year to London (see below). Philadelphia drew furs from hunters in the Delaware River valley and in Pennsylvania. Boston was a catchment for furs taken by the Abenakis and other Indians to the Northeast. The leading fur

73. Calculated from Ann M. Carlos and Frank D. Lewis, "Indians, the Beaver, and the Bay: The Economics of Depletion in the Lands of the Hudson's Bay Company, 1700–1763," *Journal of Economic History* 53 (1993): 477, table 2.

74. Ibid., 474–75, table 1. York Fort, the highest-yielding post, had its best returns during 1720 to 1740, with an annual average of 33,616 pelts. For the period 1750 to 1763, this average slipped to just under 18,000 pelts per year.

75. Ibid., 480, fig. 3.

76. Data from John Lawson, *A New Voyage to Carolina* (Chapel Hill: University of North Carolina Press, 1967), 108–9, appendix E.

exporter in the British colonies, however, was Manhattan, the officially designated entrepôt for furs collected at the head of the Hudson River in Albany and Schenectady. From 1700 to 1775, New York's production was double that of New England, its nearest competitor. New York averaged 4,156 pounds sterling in furs sent each year to Britain, 16.6 percent of the annual average sent by the colonies for the period.[77]

As before, the Mohawks and other Iroquois were the primary trading partners for the English and Dutch traders of the interior. Some, but probably not a majority, of the furs collected in New York were the product of direct hunting by Iroquois warriors. A considerable portion of the furs bought by upstate traders was actually contraband smuggled by Christian Iroquois settled in New France near Montreal.[78] These Indians traded for western Indian furs before they reached Montreal and brought them down Lake Champlain to get better prices and better quality English trade goods at Schenectady and Albany. The French authorities turned a blind eye to this illegal commerce because, by this means, French fur traders obtained English strouds, kettles, firearms, and other goods to be sent west for exchange with Indian suppliers there.

Another growing portion of furs came from western Indians who traveled to Lake Ontario to exchange their furs directly with English traders. In 1724, New York's Governor Burnet built a fort at Oswego where the Oswego River (then the Onondaga River) empties into Lake Ontario. From Oswego, a water route led to Schenectady, interrupted only by a 4.8-kilometer portage between the Mohawk River and Wood Creek. Large numbers of Albany traders began journeying every year to buy furs from the Ottawas, Miami, Ojibwas, and other Great Lakes Indians who had been dissuaded by the lengthier journey to the Hudson River.[79]

CREEK DEER HUNTERS

The warmer southern regions of North America did not produce furbearers with coats as lustrous, thick, and longhaired as those in the colder north. Early British settlers found beaver dams throughout Virginia and the Carolinas. During the seventeenth and eighteenth centuries, coastal Atlantic Indian tribes such as the Tuscaroras and Westos hunted beavers and supplied pelts for export. Generally, however, the numbers were small and the pelts less valuable. Virginia, for example, sent only two thousand beaver pelts each

---

77. Calculated from Carlos and Lewis, "Indians, the Beaver, and the Bay," 477, table 2.

78. Jean Lunn, "The Illegal Fur Trade Out of New France, 1713–1760," *Canadian Historical Association Report of the Annual Meeting* (1939).

79. Richter and the Institute of Early American History and Culture, *The Ordeal of the Longhouse*, 248–52.

year to London between 1699 and 1714, and Charleston exported only about six hundred pelts per year.[80] Instead, colonists discovered that the immense herds of white-tailed deer in the south could be made profitable.[81]

In Virginia, the Carolinas, Georgia, and Florida, the deer population was enormous during the seventeenth century. All observers contemporary to the time commented on the extraordinary abundance of deer, elks, and even wild bison that slowly had returned to the Southeast. Such was the abundance and ease of the New World that deer could be freely taken by anyone without punishment or permission. Deer taken from the interior and at higher elevations were larger, fatter, and more desirable than those found in the heat of the coastal plain.[82] Postcontact Indian depopulation permitted deer and other wildlife numbers to escalate. For two centuries, successive waves of disease thinned the numbers of the indigenous horticulturists and hunters of the North American Southeast.[83] Few natural predators, apart from wolves and panthers, threatened the deer herds in a landscape seemingly made for browsing creatures.

The contrast with the Old World deer population is striking. American deerskins began arriving in England just as domestic herds of deer declined. Those deer herds that remained in England were semidomesticated. They survived only because an aristocratic hunting culture stringently enforced game laws and set aside land for protected deer parks and forest reserves. Even with these protections, widespread poaching and illegal sale of deer meat and deer hides continued to deplete the deer population. However, these were capricious and covert sources for the leather industry. Over time, deer parks and reserved forests gave way to the needs of the rural iron industry and agricultural expansion.[84]

The British leather industry turned to New World deerskins to manufacture durable, popular men's leather breeches, gloves, bookbindings, and other applications that demanded strong, supple, lightweight leather. Supplies of cattle hides from Europe were also constricted by an epidemic disease wasting cattle herds between 1710 and 1714 and recurring thereafter.

80. Timothy Silver, *A New Face on the Countryside: Indians, Colonists, and Slaves in South Atlantic Forests, 1500–1800* (Cambridge: Cambridge University Press, 1990), 98.

81. For an overview of the deerskin hunt, see Krech, *The Ecological Indian*, 151–71.

82. Lawson, *A New Voyage to Carolina*, 126–27.

83. For lists of episodes of epidemic and pandemic disease among the American Indians, see Henry F. Dobyns, William R. Swagerty, and the Newberry Library Center for the History of the American Indian, *Their Number Become Thinned: Native American Population Dynamics in Eastern North America* (Knoxville: University of Tennessee Press, 1983), 7–32. The first major pandemic of smallpox in 1520–1524 caused the greatest loss of life and disruption of Indian societies across the New World.

84. Roger B. Manning, *Hunters and Poachers: A Social and Cultural History of Unlawful Hunting in England, 1485–1640* (Oxford: Clarendon Press; New York: Oxford University Press, 1993).

Spared this disease, England banned import of hides and cattle from Europe. American deerskins increasingly made up shortages in raw materials for the domestic English industry.[85]

As was the case earlier with northern furbearers, Indians offered a cheap, easily mobilized source of labor to hunt and process deerskins. In the colonial South, Indians, who had long depended on deer for much of their meat and clothing requirements, began to kill and process deerskins for export. Almost all Indians in this region became producers for the deerskin market. Market demand originating in Charleston and other coastal port cities rapidly diffused throughout an extensive region and among many different groups of Indians. Along the coast, the Saponi peoples in the Roanoke River area of Virginia and the diverse Catawba groups in the Carolina Piedmont soon became active hunters.[86] By the turn of the century, Choctaws from the lower Mississippi region were in direct contact with English and French traders.

Production of hides for the deerskin trade depended on a relatively small population of Indian hunters and processors spread over a vast area stretching from the Atlantic Coast inland for a thousand miles to the lower Mississippi River valley. By 1700, the remnants of many groups of Indian tribes had coalesced into various "nations," or groups defined by shared kinship, cultural, linguistic, and political ties. The fast-declining Indian population of the southeastern United States—living in the area between Virginia and Florida, and between the Atlantic Coast and eastern Texas—is estimated to have numbered 130,600 at the turn of the century.[87]

The Creeks, who ranged widely over the best hunting grounds in the Southeast and who generally were conceded to be the finest hunters, numbered approximately 4,000 warriors among a total population of 14,000 to 20,000 in the 1770s.[88] Although the Creeks adapted quickly and successfully to the new incentives of the deerskin trade, they, like other Indian hunters in the Southeast, faced a basic contradiction.[89] Economic and political forces made it imperative that they deliver a maximal number of deerskins every

---

85. Kathryn E. Holland Braund, *Deerskins and Duffels: The Creek Indian Trade with Anglo-America, 1685–1815* (Lincoln: University of Nebraska Press, 1993), 42.

86. James Hart Merrell and Institute of Early American History and Culture, *The Indians' New World: Catawbas and Their Neighbors from European Contact through the Era of Removal* (Chapel Hill: University of North Carolina Press, for the Institute of Early American History and Culture, Williamsburg, Va., 1989).

87. Peter H. Wood, "The Changing Population of the Colonial South: An Overview by Race and Region, 1685–1790," in *Powhatan's Mantle: Indians in the Colonial Southeast,* edited by Gregory A. Waselkov, M. Thomas Hatley, and Peter H. Wood (Lincoln: University of Nebraska Press, 1989), 38–39, table 1.

88. Braund, *Deerskins and Duffels,* 9.

89. Hudson, "Why the Southeastern Indians Slaughtered Deer," 157–76. The Choctaw followed a path similar to that of the Creeks. See Richard White, *The Roots of Dependency: Subsistence,*

year. They became market hunters linked into the world market who used muskets to avidly pursue as many deer (and bear) as possible during their annual fall and winter season. Guns could be obtained only by offering deerskins to French, English, or Spanish traders. For the Creeks and other Indian groups who survived, muskets were essential for self-defense against Indians employed by the English as slavers in earlier years and in intra-Indian warfare throughout the eighteenth century.

Simultaneously, Creeks and other Indians believed that they existed in a special relationship to the deer, bears, and other animals they pursued. These animals had to be treated with respect or the consequences would be severe. Many taboos and rules regulated Creek behavior toward game animals, both before they were taken and after death. If hunters killed deer carelessly or disrespectfully, serious harm, including withdrawal of the herds and the onset of disease for humans, might be the result. Therefore, Creek hunters employed ancient ceremonies for purification by sweating and steaming and by singing, dancing, and dreaming as preparation for the hunt. Various potions were ingested; others were rubbed on the skin. The hunters carried charms like the physic-nut in buckskin pouches to aid their efforts. To the best of their ability, the hunters tried to treat their prey with respect and honor. They obeyed taboos against taking the skins of sick or dying deer.

Mutual respect also implied some restraint—that the hunters would kill deer sufficient for their needs, but no more. The imperatives of production for a world market made restraint difficult. Conforming to these pressures, each Creek warrior hunted with great ferocity and determination until his domestic needs and his market role were fulfilled.

Each hunter and his wife and children in a nuclear family formed a production unit. In October, the hunters and their families traveled on horseback to dispersed hunting camps and remained there until the end of February each year. The Creek warriors hunted with muskets, on foot in groups of men from the same clan. They depended on their knowledge of deer habits and habitats to stalk their prey day after day in a familiar hunting range. As one English observer commented, "Their manner of rambling through the woods to kill deer, is a very laborious exercise, as they frequently walk twenty-five to thirty miles through rough and smooth grounds, and fasting, before they return to camp loaded."[90] This sustained effort resulted in fifty to as many as seventy-five deer slain each season by each hunter.

In a good year, Creek hunters might harvest two hundred thousand to three hundred thousand deerskins, of which perhaps half were sold to

Environment, and Social Change among the Choctaws, Pawnees, and Navajos (Lincoln: University of Nebraska Press, 1983), 1–146.

90. Braund, *Deerskins and Duffels*, 67, quoting James Adair, *Adair's History of the American Indians* (Johnson City: Watauga Press, 1930; reprint, New York: Argonaut Press, 1966), 432.

traders. Damaged hides and home consumption of deerskin dictated that perhaps half of the skins taken were not traded but consumed at home.[91] Dried and smoked deer meat was the main source of year-round protein for the Creeks and their families.

Creek women, who formed the other side of the production unit, processed the skins for sale and for domestic use. Semiprocessed skins for the trade were cleaned of flesh and fur, stretched, sun dried, and smoked in an abbreviated treatment. Each finished export hide weighed between one and two pounds. Skins for domestic use went through additional steps such as soaking in a solution of water and deer brains, pounding, stretching, drying, smoking, and dyeing to become a soft, pliable, lightweight leather. Traditional female skills in leather working necessarily survived the transition to commercial production. So also did traditional skills in subsistence agriculture and pottery making.

The Creeks became enthusiastic consumers of the trade goods offered in payment for deerskins by English and French traders. William Bartram commented, "[They] wage eternal war against deer and bear, to procure food and cloathing [sic], and other necessaries and conveniences; which is indeed carried to an unreasonable and perhaps criminal excess, since the white people have dazzled their senses with foreign superfluities."[92] As did other Indians in the Southeast, the Creeks obtained smoothbore muskets (Birmingham muskets), powder, and shot; metal tools such as axes, knives, hatchets, needles, scissors, and especially iron kettles; red, blue, white, or striped heavy woolen blankets (duffles); lighter weight strouds, which were cheaper woolen cloths in scarlet or blue used for men's leggings and breechcloths and women's skirts; decorative glass beads and face paint; and finally, rum. The Creeks negotiated price lists for all these items with the British and French colonies that remained relatively stable throughout the century. Muskets, at six deerskins per gun, and duffel blankets, at four to six deerskins each, were the most expensive items.[93]

The new consumerism meant that most native manufactures fell away and the society depended on imported goods. Creek hunters lost older bow- and arrow-making skills and did not learn the technology of fabricating muskets—although they could make repairs. Traders extended credit to Creek hunters in the form of trade goods in the spring of each year. Debts were to be paid a year hence, when hides were brought back to the village. Trade goods were expensive by any measure, and debts mounted as the season's catch often failed to pay off previous credit extended by the trader. To maintain their standard of living, the Creeks continually warred against the

91. Braund, *Deerskins and Duffels,* 71.
92. Quoted in ibid., 121.
93. Ibid., 121–38.

Choctaws, the Florida tribes, and the Cherokees. Creek leaders engaged in ongoing negotiations with the English and French governments and with traders to improve the terms of trade.

Creek society adapted willingly and easily to the new economic regime. The Creeks maintained their social cohesion and sense of identity and acted decisively to control their destiny in the eighteenth century. For much of the century, deerskin production, however arduous, was seen as beneficial to the Creek. The relatively unchanged nature of women's roles played a critical part in Creek stability. Greater inequities in personal property were noticeable, but communal property in land persisted. The matrilineal kin system maintained its strength. Younger men, emboldened by rum, defied their elders and engaged in horse thievery or clashed with both white and red neighbors.

Still, chiefs and elder males maintained their effective influence and power. Even frequent bouts of drunkenness by groups of men and women, with their consequent loss of social constraints, did not rip apart the society—dismaying as these often violent displays were to outsiders. Creek society, with its air of hospitality, generosity, and corporate responsibility for each individual, retained much that European observers found appealing.

EIGHTEENTH-CENTURY DEERSKIN TRADE TRAJECTORY

New World deerskin production began to be substantial by 1700. Charleston, South Carolina, first settled under royal charter in 1670, took an early lead in this trade. By 1700, Charleston's five thousand inhabitants were well acquainted with the interior and its Indian residents. The colonists had settled on deerskins as the only commercially viable staples that could be exported (apart from Indian slaves). Between 1699 and 1704, Charleston shipped an annual average of 49,000 heavy deer pelts to London. By the late 1750s, Charleston's exports of pelts had more than doubled, to over 137,000 hides exported each year.[94] The founding of Augusta in 1735, and the subsequent organization of well-capitalized trading companies operating in Creek, Chickasaw, and Choctaw territory, stimulated Indian production. In the 1750s, Savannah shipped 100,000 or more hides per year.[95] The French entrepôts at Mobile and New Orleans sent an average of 50,000 pelts per year to the port of La Rochelle between 1720 and 1780.[96] In 1764, John Stuart, the

94. Converse D. Clowse, *Measuring Charleston's Overseas Commerce, 1717–1767: Statistics from the Port's Naval Lists* (Washington, D.C.: University Press of America, 1981), 54–55, table B-11.
95. Braund, *Deerskins and Duffels*, 98, n. 89.
96. Daniel H. Usner and Institute of Early American History and Culture, *Indians, Settlers, and Slaves in a Frontier Exchange Economy: The Lower Mississippi Valley before 1783* (Chapel Hill: University of North Carolina Press, for the Institute of Early American History and Culture, Williamsburg, Va., 1992), 246.

British colonial officer charged with administering the newly defined South-eastern Indian territories controlled by the British, estimated that the nearly fourteen thousand Indian adult male hunters ("guns") under his control could produce up to 800,000 pounds of deerskins per year. This figure converts to 457,000 hides per year at an average weight of 1.75 pounds per dressed pelt.[97]

From these and other figures, we can suggest that the eighteenth-century export of deerskins from Virginia, the Carolinas, Georgia, Florida, and Louisiana conformed to the classic pattern of market-driven raw materials exploitation. At a conservative estimate, pelts shipped by British, French, and Spanish traders each year rose from 50,000 at the turn of the century, to 150,000 in the 1730s, to peak at 250,000 to 300,000 per year in the 1760s and early 1770s. In the 1780s, after the American Revolution, production dwindled to 175,000 with the depletion of deer herds and the expansion of colonial settlement and agriculture. By the turn of the century, the deerskin trade had begun to collapse entirely.[98]

British customs records for imported hides and skins from the Americas have a similar trajectory. The three-year average for 1699–1701 for skins and hides was 23,000 pounds sterling; for 1722–1724, 34,000 pounds sterling; for 1752–1754, 46,000 pounds sterling; and for 1772–1775, 111,000 pounds sterling.[99]

For Indian market hunters, the American Revolution of 1776–1783 was a turning point that dissolved the prewar institutions of the deerskin trade. The British market for skins, which had provided credit and trade goods, disappeared. War left the Creeks and other Indian hunters short of guns, ammunition, and clothing. The Creek leader Alexander McGillivray devised new trade ties and a new trade path to exiled loyalist merchants in Spanish-held Florida. Panton, Leslie, and Company shipped about 125,000 skins per year from Pensacola to Britain in the 1780s and 1790s. In 1783 and 1790, the new American regime negotiated treaties that confirmed Creek hunting rights in return for their conceding large hunting grounds for settlement. Slowly, however, the trade began to reopen, with a few American traders operating from Augusta. In 1796, the United States government set up official deerskin trading posts along the Creek border and offered an alternative outlet for Creek deerskins in return for the usual trade goods.

Well before the century's end, the hunting economy of the Creeks, as well

97. Braund, *Deerskins and Duffels*, 70.
98. Ibid., 72.
99. Ralph Davis, "English Foreign Trade, 1700–1774," in *The Growth of English Overseas Trade in the Seventeenth and Eighteenth Centuries*, edited by Walter E. Minchinton (London: Methuen, 1969). These figures were for all of British North America, Spanish America, the West Indies, and West Africa. The bulk of the imports represented in these figures consisted of American deerskins. Imports from the Americas far exceeded those from any other world region.

as that of the Choctaws and Chicksaws in the lower Mississippi, had begun to collapse, and Indian hunters faced a "severe socioeconomic crisis."[100] The catch declined as deer were either hunted out or pushed out by the livestock of encroaching settlers. Deer were localized in their habitats and did not readily move to new locations when their existing ranges were threatened. The Creek nation began building up substantial debt as the payment for skins never fully repaid the advances they received for trade goods. At the same time, the prices of trade goods rose and the value of deerskins dropped nearly 50 percent.

By this time, the American government was convinced that the day of the Indian commercial hunter had ended. The Creeks, Choctaws, Cherokees, and other Indians in the Southeast would have to accept civilization and become agriculturists like the white settlers. In 1805, the Creeks ceded 2 million acres of land and permitted construction of a federal road on their lands in return for a yearly annuity to be paid the chiefs.

Gradually, a split in the Creek nation developed between the traditionalists and those warriors, often mixed blood, who opted for livestock and settled agriculture. A visit by the charismatic Shawnee warrior Tecumseh in 1811 led to the Creek civil war of 1813–1814, American intervention, and a final massacre and defeat at Tohopeka. With the subsequent treaty, the United States seized 30 million acres of Creek lands for settlement and reduced the remaining Creeks to being American dependents. Creeks still hunted deer for a limited market, but both the deer and the commercial hunt essentially were finished.[101]

IMPACT OF THE FUR TRADE ON INDIANS

Easily one of the most complicated and unresolved historiographical issues in North American history concerns the effects of the fur trade on those Indian groups caught up in it.[102] Every year, Europeans enlisted tens of thousands of Indians to serve as hunters, processors, carriers, and traders of huge numbers of furs and skins for export from North America. Three intertwined questions lie at the heart of the matter: First, did involvement in the fur trade lead invariably to Indian weakness, dependence, and varying de-

100. Usner and Institute of Early American History and Culture, *Indians, Settlers, and Slaves in a Frontier Exchange Economy*, 285.

101. Braund, *Deerskins and Duffels*, 164–88.

102. For a discussion of the broader interpretation of Indian responses to European intervention in their world, see Trigger, "Early Native North American Responses to European Contact: Romantic versus Rationalistic Interpretations," *Journal of American History* 77, no. 4 (1991): 1195–1215. Trigger assesses the claims of cultural relativists versus rationalists in this article. He argues that a "cognitive reorganization" accompanied greater familiarity with Europeans and their ways that resulted in a rationalizing behavior on the part of Indians.

grees of cultural disintegration and despair? Second, did Indians change their cultural beliefs, institutions, and behavior in dramatic ways in response to the stimuli of price-driven markets and the availability of new, industrially produced commodities? And third, as a corollary to the second question, did the stimuli and pressures of the fur trade cause Indians to abandon ecologically sound hunting practices and beliefs in an indiscriminate slaughter of newly valuable prey animals? All these issues resonate directly with our most sensitive ideological and moral concerns in the twenty-first century. All scholars and writers on the history of the fur trade offer more-or-less explicit answers to these questions.

One general point seems indisputable. By the early nineteenth century, after more than two centuries of fur trading, all Indian groups in the eastern half of North America were enmeshed to varying degrees in a dependent relationship with European regimes and settler societies. All had suffered population declines, severe cultural shocks, and loss of previously vital institutions and skills. For example, even formerly powerful and impressive groups such as the Five Nations Iroquois had fallen into political and material dependency as early as the 1730s.[103] The Iroquois no longer negotiated with European authorities and traders from a position of relative strength and equality but from one of inferiority and weakness. They needed the cloth, guns, implements, alcohol, and tobacco purveyed by fur traders far more than the European society at large needed their furs. The Iroquois had lost the skills to make the craft objects that had previously sustained them.

Much of this decline can be traced to the onslaught of disease among unprotected populations. Certainly, hammer blows from introduced European diseases buffeted the Iroquois, as they did every Indian society in North America. Whether epidemics preceded direct contact is open to argument, but there is no question as to the numerous deaths and cultural and social disruption caused by new diseases in the seventeenth and eighteenth centuries. For example, the first smallpox epidemic, in 1616, sharply reduced populations of Indians along the northeast Atlantic Coast.[104] Only the fact that Indian groups were widely dispersed and thinly settled throughout the landscape and had limited contacts with Europeans saved them from greater suffering and losses. However, confident societies and cultures can and do shake off disease and, even after suffering heavy mortality, recover their numbers and reassert their identity.

European colonization of North America subjected the Indians to a new relationship with alien invaders who became increasingly more powerful

103. Richter and the Institute of Early American History and Culture, *The Ordeal of the Longhouse*, 268.

104. Dean R. Snow and Kim M. Lanphear, "European Contact and Indian Depopulation in the Northeast: The Timing of the First Epidemics," *Ethnohistory* 35, no. 1 (1988).

and uncompromising and more brutal in their demands. The fur trade was only one, albeit an extremely important, aspect of this unequal relationship. Indians' involvement as economic actors in the fur market was probably not a sufficient cause of Indian decline and dependence. No reasonable scholars deny the intrinsic appeal of metal blades and tools as replacements for those of stone, or woolen cloth as a replacement for or, more often, supplement to deerskin and fur clothing and blankets. In its initial phases, the exchange of furs for trade goods was not inequitable. When Indians swapped furs stripped and processed from animals that they had killed in the hunt for metal tools, cloth, guns, powder, and shot, the transaction enabled them to dispose of surplus goods in exchange for the means to live better and more comfortably.[105]

For two centuries, Indians were conservative consumers who restrained their wants in both variety and quantity. Trade goods focused on a very narrow basket of commodities that Indians emphatically told traders they wanted: muskets, balls, powder, brass kettles, knives, hatchets, needles, scissors, flints, woolen cloth and linen shirts for women and men, vermilion and verdigris for body painting, glass beads, mirrors, burning glasses for starting fires, steel and brass wire, glass bottles, clay pipes, tobacco, and rum or brandy. No item was acceptable that did not conform to a nicely calibrated consumer preference expressed by the Indians for specific decoration, material, and quality.

Eventually each of these items either wore out or was used up and had to be replaced by entering the market again. Archaeological evidence suggests that Indians consumed considerable amounts of trade goods as burial items placed with the deceased. But there is little evidence that any group amassed large quantities of trade goods as household possessions. Nor were Indians especially price sensitive. Numerous anecdotes record Indian hunters responding to higher fur prices by simply bringing in fewer furs to trade rather than acquiring more trade goods. If Indians were cautious consumers, slow to find new wants and desires, then it is difficult to see how commodification alone could have destroyed Indian cultures and institutions or have sent them into a frenzy of market-driven slaughter of game animals.

Only alcohol, among the standard trade goods, caused some Indians to consume to excess. Although old to Eurasia, fermenting and distilling alcohol was a new, complex technology for North American Indians. Alcohol's addictive and consciousness-transforming qualities, with its tendency to encourage violence, hit Indian societies with explosive force. Unlike Eurasian societies, Indians had no time to evolve those social rituals and cultural attitudes that erected defenses against the worst aspects of the drug before they had access to it in quantity. Alcohol consumption rent the stability and har-

105. Trigger, "Early Native North American Responses to European Contact," 1207.

mony of Indian communities.[106] Alcohol use was clearly destructive and probably acted as a depressant on people who already had much to be depressed about.

There is some evidence that European brandy and rum occupied a larger share in the trade goods offered to Indians as they became accustomed to it. For example, eau-de-vie and wine represented only 4 to 5 percent of the trade goods offered by French traders from Montreal during the seventeenth century. Much of this was consumed in the ceremonials of trade meetings and sociability rather than carried back to home villages for consumption. In general, the French, inhibited by Jesuit intervention, were less prone to offer alcohol than were the English or Dutch. The eighteenth century, however, saw rapid growth in Indian consumption of alcohol in exchange for furs.[107]

When they obtained rum or brandy from traders or, more frequently, as gifts on ceremonial occasions, younger male Indians tended toward immediate binge drinking that ended badly, in assaults and homicides.[108] Often, Indian hunters traded quantities of their season's furs for large amounts of rum, brandy, or whiskey at the expense of badly needed trade goods. Considerable anecdotal evidence suggests that on occasion Indian alcohol purchases so reduced the quantities of other trade goods obtained that hardship and suffering resulted in the following season. As mentioned above, some groups, like the Hurons, managed to contain and neutralize alcohol and minimize its abusive effects.

Since Indians never learned to ferment or distill their own alcohol, their desire for rum or brandy stimulated additional hunting for furs beyond that needed to acquire other trade goods. However, that desire had practical limits imposed by seasonal migrations. Indians did not store and transport bulky and heavy jugs of rum or brandy for regular consumption. Instead, they drank publicly, in groups, shortly after obtaining the intoxicant. This practice limited their consumption to the more spectacular forms of alcohol use reported by European observers.

Alexander Henry, a British fur trader, canoed west beyond Lake Superior to the Lake of the Woods in 1775. He reported an encounter with a band of Ojibwa Indians who had offered him and his men a warm welcome:

> From this village we received ceremonious presents. The mode with the Indians is, first, to collect all the provisions they can spare, and place them in a heap; after which they send for the trader, and address him in a formal speech.

106. For a systematic discussion of this issue, see Peter Mancall, *Deadly Medicine: Indians and Alcohol in Early America* (Ithaca, N.Y.: Cornell University Press, 1995).

107. Louise Dechêne, *Habitants et marchands de Montréal au XVIIe siècle: Essai* (Montréal: Boréal, 1988), 158.

108. Conrad, "Disorderly Drinking," 2.

They tell him, that the Indians are happy in seeing him return into their country; that they have been long in expectation of his arrival; that their wives have deprived themselves of their provisions, in order to afford him a supply; that they are in great want, being destitute of every thing, and particularly of ammunition and clothing; and what they long for, is a taste of his rum, which they uniformly denominate milk.

The present in return consisted in one keg of gunpowder of sixty pounds weight; a bag of shot, and another of powder, of eighty pounds each; a few smaller articles, and a keg of rum. The last appeared to be the chief treasure, though on the former depended the greater part of their winter's subsistence. In a short time, the men began to drink, while the women brought me a further and very valuable present, of twenty bags of rice. This I returned with goods and rum, and at the same time offered more, for an additional quantity of rice. A trade was opened, the women bartering rice, while the men were drinking. Before morning, I had purchased a hundred bags, of nearly a bushel measurement each. Without a large quantity of rice, the voyage could not have been prosecuted to its completion. The canoes, as I have already observed are not large enough to carry provisions. . . .

When morning arrived, all the village was inebriated; and the danger of misunderstanding was increased by the facility with which the women abandoned themselves to my Canadians. In consequence, I lost no time in leaving the place.[109]

Henry's description of this encounter clearly delineates the intensity of Indian desire for rum and its importance in the ceremonial exchanges of the fur trade. The passage suggests, however, that the Ojibwas contained alcohol use within certain manageable bounds for the time that the entire village, male and female, required to consume the keg of brandy. Sexual license occurred, but Henry does not mention any violence.

In the end, however, no matter how resolutely Indians regulated their consumer behavior, when they became commercial hunters they entered an inherently unstable and unsustainable realm. One after another, Indian ethnic groups drawn into trading furs for goods suffered the fate of all human groups who gain a livelihood by extraction of natural resources for the world economy. In responding to market signals, the Indians necessarily changed their patterns of hunting in order to obtain the specialized products most in demand. When European traders asked for beaver, marten, otter, and other luxuriant furs, Indian hunters pursued those furbearers longer and harder than they had before. When traders sought deerskins, Indians hunted deer. Each hunting group altered the diversity and resilience of its seasonal round of hunting, fishing, gathering, and horticulture in order to put more effort into hunting preferred species. Invariably, market demands translated into

109. Bruce M. White, "The Woman Who Married a Beaver: Trade Patterns and Gender Roles in the Ojibwa Fur Trade," *Ethnohistory* 46, no. 1 (1999): 114.

heavier hunting of preferred prey species that caused slow or fast depletion of their numbers.

It is likely that the Hurons, Iroquois, and other groups that depended more on horticulture had less to risk if they systematically depleted their own hunting grounds. This would be true also of former hunters who had settled down to become mission Indians. Hunting-and-gathering Indians, like the Crees and Montagnais, were less apt to hunt their prey into extinction. For example, the Montagnais in the eighteenth century protested that Hurons and Abenakis associated with French merchants from Quebec or Trois-Rivières were killing off their game.[110] The protests imply that the Montagnais, even had they tried to apply restraint themselves, could not have saved their hunting grounds and prey from market forces imposed by other Indian hunters.

Kinship and gender relations shifted in important ways. Men spent more time away, hunting nearly year-round. Pressures on women for speeded-up production of furs and skins grew. The group also made a new effort each season to carry these goods to traders—whether Indian or European—who could offer trade goods. Under some circumstances, Indians could also obtain trade goods by supplying provisions to itinerant European traders or to fur-trading posts. When the food they supplied involved the products of horticulture or gathering, women played a key role in the trade, as in the example of Ojibwa women trading wild rice for powder, shot, and rum given above.

Whether Indians before European contact were "conservationists" who killed only what they could use, or if in fact they frequently killed a greater number of prey animals than they actually consumed, is a thorny question. Indian attitudes and practices varied among ethnic groups and within each group according to the prey animal sought and to the circumstance. There is a recurring pattern, however, of a steadfast belief in the abundance of nature and its capacity to regenerate what they had consumed, whether wasteful or not. Some evidence exists from the postcontact period that, when Indians hunted animals with no market value, such as caribou, they routinely killed more animals than they really needed and consumed only the choicest parts of the carcasses.[111] To categorize the precontact Indian as a noble "ecologist and conservationist" reflects more on our contemporary fears and concerns for environmental issues than anything else.

The cumulative record of the fur trades in North America is clear and unambiguous. Once Indians were touched by the stimulus of market demand, any restraints they had previously maintained eroded rapidly. Pursuit of the

110. Personal communication from Denys Delâge.

111. Krech, *The Ecological Indian*, 186. See also Jeanne Kay, "Wisconsin Indian Hunting Patterns, 1634–1836," *Annals of the Association of American Geographers* 69, no. 3 (1979).

material rewards offered by the fur traders forced Indians to hunt preferred species steadily, despite declining numbers. As animals thinned out, the hunters pushed themselves to the limits of their skill and energy to sustain their yields. Whether or not the Indians had entered the market relationship as sensitive conservationists is irrelevant. What they became were commercial hunters caught up in the all-consuming market.

Could Indians have simply reduced their commercial hunting as furbearer populations declined? Could they have returned, with somewhat better metal tools and implements, to older forms of production and consumption? Why did so many Indian groups like the Five Nations and the Ottawas seek new hunting grounds or try to obtain furs by trade or coercion from more remote Indian groups when their own hunting lands were depleted? Raising these questions overlooks the critical role played by another complex technology introduced by the Europeans—that of firearms. In contrast to historians of New Zealand and Africa who assign central importance to the adoption of firearms, North American historians have tended to minimize their impact. Contrary to often-expressed opinion, matchlock and, later, flintlock muskets were superior tools for hunting and war that Indians enthusiastically adopted and used. With all their admitted deficiencies, even the earliest harquebuses were potent tools that offered accuracy and killing power beyond that of bows and arrows. No better testimonial to this is the speed with which Indian hunters abandoned their bows in favor of muskets for the hunt and for war. By mid– to late seventeenth century, wide adoption of the flint-striking mechanism and weight reduction put an even more imposing weapon into the hands of the Indian hunter and warrior.[112]

In diplomatic negotiations and in trade, the Indians always looked to obtain muskets, powder, and shot—as did the Ojibwas in the example given above. Unfortunately, Indians did not seek out and develop iron-working and toolmaking skills that would have permitted them to repair or even make their own firearms. They remained dependent on the exchange of furs for guns and on European blacksmiths and gunsmiths for repairs.

Muskets made war more deadly in the seventeenth and eighteenth centuries in North America. Without musket, powder, and ball, Indian warriors were defenseless. They could not give up their guns and survive. Therefore, they had to hunt, trade, or plunder furs to obtain guns and munitions. Inter-Indian relationships became more brittle and dangerous in this period than they had been before contact. The fur trade, more than any other European enterprise, thrust Indians into new, unstable, and insecure relationships be-

112. For development of the arguments expressed here, see Carl Parcher Russell, *Guns on the Early Frontiers: A History of Firearms from Colonial Times through the Years of the Western Fur Trade* (Berkeley and Los Angeles: University of California Press, 1957), 10–16 and generally.

tween themselves and Europeans and with other Indian groups. Dozens of Indian groups suffered catastrophic defeats, massacres, and dispersal as pitiable refugees at the hands of Indian and, especially, European enemies. Ultimately, if we are to look for the root causes of Indian debility and dependence, they are to be found in the continuing, ruthless exercise of European military power followed by the advancing settler frontier—not the fur trade.[113]

ENVIRONMENTAL CHANGES

In the usual pattern of commercial hunters, Indians hit the most promising and closest hunting grounds first, killed off all save the most hidden or remote animals, and then moved outward to find new hunting areas. As group after group responded to market signals in the form of trade goods and trading opportunities, the pattern of intensive, devastating hunting recurred. Some furbearer species were more numerous and resilient and recovered their numbers; others, less resilient, became extinct.

Hardest hit was the beaver. Writing at midcentury, in September 1749, the Swedish naturalist Peter Kalm offered this assessment:

> Beavers are abundant all over North America and they are one of the chief articles of trade in Canada. . . . It is certain that these animals multiply very fast; but it is also true that vast numbers of them are annually killed and that the Indians are obliged to undertake distant journeys in order to catch or shoot them. Their decreasing in numbers is very easily accounted for, because the Indians, before the arrival of the Europeans, only caught as many as they found necessary to clothe themselves with, there then being no trade with the skins. At present a number of ships go annually to Europe, laden chiefly with beaver's skins; the English and French endeavor to outdo each other by paying the Indians well for them, and this encourages the latter to extirpate these animals. All the people in Canada told me that when they were young all the rivers in the neighborhood of Montreal, the St. Lawrence river not excepted, were full of beavers and their dams; but at present they are so far destroyed that one is obliged to go several miles up the country before one can meet one.[114]

Pursuit and the near extinction of the beaver in North America followed an east-to-west trajectory: in the 1660s, few beavers were to be found in coastal New England and along the lower Saint Lawrence River. As table 13.1 shows, the number of beaver pelts exported rose steeply throughout the

113. For a full development of this theme, see Ian Kenneth Steele, *Warpaths: Invasions of North America* (New York: Oxford University Press, 1994).

114. Pehr Kalm and Adolph B. Benson, *Peter Kalm's Travels in North America: The English Version of 1770* (New York: Dover, 1987), 534. The newly formed Swedish Academy of Sciences sent Kalm on a botanizing mission to North America at the suggestion of Carl von Linné (Linnaeus).

eighteenth century, peaking at an annual yield of 264,000 furs in the final two decades. Nineteenth-century harvests fluctuated below that level until beaver populations crashed in the 1890s.[115] The number of beavers killed to meet domestic needs of the Indians themselves and for the colonial market probably added another 50 percent to the total. Beaver harvests continued at or above this level. By 1825, beavers were extinct in southern Wisconsin, although "moderate numbers of beaver continued to be trapped in northern Wisconsin and Michigan's Upper Peninsula in the 1820's and 1930's."[116] By the 1840s, beaver populations were under pressure from Indian hunters in the Far West in Oregon and in the Canadian subarctic in the Mackenzie River drainage area. Beaver and other furbearer populations certainly plummeted as the fur frontier advanced westward.

Attached to their immediate waterways and lodges, beavers were a sedentary animal that could not readily migrate away from danger. When hunters wiped out beaver colonies, abandoned dams crumbled and created hollows of fertile soil that benefited incoming pioneer farmers. The "beaver meadow complex," formed by the temporary succession of sedges (*Carex* spp.) and bluejoint grass (*Calamagrostis canadensis*) in abandoned beaver ponds was especially important as a source of ready hay for pioneer livestock. These beaver meadows yielded up to four metric tons of hay per acre in the early period before settlers cleared land to sow English hay.[117]

The environmental effects of beaver extinction were considerable. Beavers were a keystone species whose actions determined the configuration of the entire ecosystem. They were "ecological engineers," whose tireless work created ponds that "acted as settling basins and were an important factor in the aggradation of small stream valleys."[118] The ponds retained large amounts of organic matter and eventually, by a process similar to eutrophication, became wetlands or bogs. Beaver ponds also created patches or small landscape units with distinctive vegetation (which Morgan labeled beaver meadows).[119] Beavers affected the biogeochemical cycles of temperate forest

---

115. Milan Novak et al., *Furbearer Harvests in North America, 1600–1984* (Ontario: Ministry of Natural Resources, 1987), 37–41. By 1898, the annual total had plunged to thirty-five hundred.

116. Jeanne Kay, "Native Americans in the Fur Trade and Wildlife Depletion," *Environmental Review* 9, no. 2 (1985): 119.

117. Gordon Graham Whitney, *From Coastal Wilderness to Fruited Plain: A History of Environmental Change in Temperate North America, 1500 to the Present* (Cambridge: Cambridge University Press, 1994), 304.

118. Ibid; C. G. Jones, J. H. Lawton, and M. Shachak, "Organisms as Ecosystems Engineers," *Oikos* 69, no. 3 (1994).

119. C. A. Johnstone and R. J. Naiman, "Boundary Dynamics at the Aquatic-Terrestrial Interface: The Influence of Beaver and Geomorphology," *Landscape Ecology* 1, no. 1 (1987).

TABLE 13.1 Furs Harvested in North America (Annual Averages)

	1700–1763	1780–1799	Percentage Change	1830–1849	Percentage Change
Beaver	179,268	263,976	47.3	77,654	-70.6
Raccoon	91,637	225,115	145.7	322,759	43.4
Marten	51,315	88,856	73.2	130,283	46.6
Fox	18,411	20,360	10.6	79,056	288.3
Bear	16,033	26,833	67.4	13,229	-50.7
Mink	15,730	20,680	31.5	144,719	599.8
Otter	11,525	36,326	215.2	20,169	-44.5
Muskrat	10,432	177,736	1,603.8	849,865	378.2
Lynx/bobcat	10,179	17,277	69.7	35,443	105.1
Fisher	3,373	8,480	151.4	10,412	22.8
Wolf	1,830	16,461	799.5	8,899	-45.9
Wolverine	608	1,430	135.2	1,318	-7.8
TOTAL	410,341	903,530	120.2	1,693,806	87.5

SOURCES: Data for 1700–1763 come from table 13.2, this volume. Twenty-year averages for 1780–1799 and 1830–1849 are calculated from Novak et al., *Furbearer Harvests in North America, 1600–1984.*

regimes by shifting storage of chemical elements from surrounding forest vegetation to pond sediments.[120]

A sampling of recent research suggests other possible consequences of the beaver's disappearance: Species diversity in plants, animals, and birds fostered by beaver ponds probably declined with their drying up.[121] Ducks and other waterfowl lost attractive habitat when beaver ponds drained, and they probably lost numbers as well.[122] Osprey *(Pandion haliaetus),* who built large nests in dead tops of trees and snags near beaver ponds, lost these niches.

120. R. J. Naiman et al., "Beaver Influences on the Long-Term Biogeochemical Characteristics of Boreal Forest Drainage," *Ecology* 75, no. 4 (1994).

121. J. W. Snodgrass, "Temporal and Spatial Dynamics of Beaver-Created Patches as Influenced by Management Practices in a South-Eastern North America Landscape," *Journal of Applied Ecology* 34, no. 4 (1997); R. L. France, "The Importance of Beaver Lodges in Structuring Littoral Communities in Boreal Headwater Lakes," *Canadian Journal of Zoology* 75, no. 7 (1997); A. M. Grover and G. A. Baldassarre, "Bird Species Richness within Beaver Ponds in South-Central New York," *Wetlands* 15, no. 2 (1995).

122. D. J. Brown, W. A. Hubert, and S. H. Anderson, "Beaver Ponds Create Wetland Habitat for Birds in Mountains of Southeast Wyoming," *Wetlands* 16, no. 2 (1996); D. R. Diefenbach and R. B. Owen Jr., "A Model of Habitat Use by Breeding American Black Ducks," *Journal of Wildlife Management* 53, no. 2 (1989); P. Nummi, "The Importance of Beaver Ponds to Waterfowl Broods: An Experiment and Natural Tests," *Annales Zoologgici Fennici* 29, no. 1 (1992).

River otters probably diminished in numbers as beaver ponds drained.[123] Freshwater fish declined in abundance and variety.[124]

However, reports of extinctions were exaggerated. Beavers did not disappear. In some out-of-the-way tracts, such as that discovered by Lewis Morgan in the mid-1850s, beavers flourished in great numbers (see above). Beavers were sufficiently numerous to permit continuous trapping by white settlers and substantial harvesting of beaver pelts throughout the nineteenth and on into the twentieth century. In fact, the total beaver harvest was probably as high or higher after 1800 as before. Even along the Atlantic Coast, where beavers supposedly had long been hunted out, Indian and white hunters and trappers continued to bring in beaver pelts, as well as those of other furbearers. For example, in 1763, in Newfoundland, English trappers sold about 5,700 furs, of which about 2,500 were beaver.[125]

Raccoons were even more resilient than beavers. (See table 13.2.) Although raccoon kills rose to astronomical levels by mid–nineteenth century—up to 323,000 animals per year—the species did not become extinct in its original territories. Harvests at this level certainly had a severe local impact on raccoon populations. However, the ability of raccoons to adapt to human settlement permitted the species to survive its slaughter for furs. Raccoon populations today reach densities as high as twenty animals per square kilometer.[126] Partly protected by their aquatic habitats, river otters, mink, and muskrats suffered heavy losses but survived.

Other less social and numerous furbearers were more vulnerable to sustained human predation. The original marten population, found in the colder regions of eastern North America, was probably between 2.4 and 4.7 million.[127] If this estimate is at all close to the actual total, fur trade harvests should have been sustainable. By the late eighteenth century, fur-trade hunters averaged only 89,000 marten, each year—3.7 percent of the lower bound of the estimate. By mid–nineteenth century, as white settlers began

123. D. G. Newman and C. R. Griffin, "Wetland Use by River Otters in Massachusetts," *Journal of Wildlife Management* 58, no. 1 (1994); A. P. Dyck and R. A. MacArthur, "Spacing, Movements, and Habitat Selection of the River Otter in Boreal Alberta," *Canadian Journal of Zoology* 72, no. 7 (1994).

124. I. J. Schlosser, "Dispersal, Boundary Processes, and Trophic-Level Interactions in Streams Adjacent to Beaver Ponds," *Ecology* 76, no. 3 (1995).

125. Ingeborg Marshall, *A History and Ethnography of the Beothuk* (Montreal: McGill-Queen's University Press, 1996), 75.

126. Nowak and Walker, *Walker's Mammals of the World*, 5th ed., s.v. "Raccoons."

127. My estimate is based on a total area of approximately 4.7 million square kilometers with a presumed density of .5 to 1 adult marten per square kilometer. The area includes all of Canada from the Maritimes to and including Manitoba, and all U.S. states from the East Coast as far west as and including Minnesota, Iowa, and Missouri, with the latter, Kentucky, and Virginia marking the southern boundary.

TABLE 13.2 Eighteenth-Century Fur Exports by Species,
1700–1763 (Annual Averages)

	English Fur Exports	French Fur Exports	Total English and French Fur Exports	Percentages
Beaver	65,427	113,841	179,268	43.8
Raccoon	18,339	73,298	91,637	22.4
Marten	19,641	31,674	51,315	12.5
Fox	13,566	4,845	18,411	4.5
Bear	3,616	12,417	16,033	3.9
Mink	7,840	7,890	15,730	3.8
Otter	4,231	7,294	11,525	2.8
Muskrat	9,783	649	10,432	2.5
Lynx/bobcat	3,872	6,307	10,179	2.5
Fisher	1,235	2,138	3,373	0.8
Wolf	1,002	828	1,830	0.4
Wolverine	470	138	608	0.1
TOTAL	149,022	261,319	410,341	100.2

SOURCES: Murray G. Lawson, *Fur, a Study in English Mercantilism, 1700–1775* (Toronto: University of Toronto Press, 1943); Innis, *The Fur Trade in Canada;* Wien, "Castor, peaux, et pelleteries dans le commerce canadien des fourrures, 1720–1790"; Phillips, *The Fur Trade.*

trapping to supplement their incomes, the annual average harvest rose to 130,000 animals—still only 5.4 percent of the total population. Nevertheless, by the end of the nineteenth century, the population crashed and marten became extinct throughout the eastern regions where they had formerly flourished.[128]

The localized intensity of commercial hunting devastated marten populations. Marten today have maximum densities of between .5 and 1.7 adult animals per square kilometer of optimal habitat. They are among the most "habitat specialized mammals in North America" and require cold-climate landscape mosaics of old-growth conifer forests to flourish.[129] The size of their home ranges and their solitary nature imply that recolonizing an area with a few survivors would have been difficult, if not impossible.

Hunting for the fur trade pushed several other species toward extinction by the early nineteenth century. Despite seemingly low annual harvests, wolves and wolverines were hit hard. The total pre-fur-trade popula-

128. Marjorie A. Strickland, "Harvest Management of Fishers and American Martens," in *Martens, Sables, and Fishers: Biology and Conservation,* edited by Steven Buskirk (Ithaca, N.Y.: Cornell University Press, 1994), 150, fig. 9.1.

129. Steven Buskirk and Roger A. Powell, "Habitat Ecology of Fishers and American Martens," in *Martens, Sables, and Fishers: Biology and Conservation,* edited by Steven Buskirk (Ithaca, N.Y.: Cornell University Press, 1994), 296.

tion of wolves was unlikely to have reached 100,000 animals in eastern North America and was probably much less.[130] Annual harvests of 16,500 wolf pelts per year in the late eighteenth century seem to have drastically depleted the population. In addition to the fur hunting by Indians, white settlers' pursuit of wolves as vermin would have pressed the animals to rapid extinction in a westward moving pattern. The wolverine suffered a similar fate. With population densities of around 1 adult animal to 200 square kilometers, losing even a few thousand animals each year was sufficient to wipe out a small original population with little or no chance of self-regeneration.

In short, the demands of the fur trade depleted beaver numbers to near extinction in much of eastern North America by the first decades of the nineteenth century and had profound consequences for the North American landscape. Fur trade hunting drastically cut the numbers of a dozen or more carnivorous furbearers. Some species recovered from remnant populations; some did not and remain extinct in much of eastern North America today. We can only speculate as to the intricate and widely diffused ecological effects caused by killing off such an array of carnivores.

The final phase of wildlife extinctions accompanied the advance of the pioneer settlement frontier. Once established, white settlers began to supplement their income by systematically trapping and hunting furbearers. To this, we may add the settlers' indiscriminate killing, often for bounty, of wolves, bears, and other large animals perceived to be a threat to livestock and humans.[131]

As with the beaver in the north, so went deer in the south. Indian commercial hunting steadily depleted the deer herds of the American Southeast.[132] If we assume that the number of deer killed each year was twice the number of exported deerskins, the scale of Indian commercial hunting becomes clearer. In the 1760s and early 1770s, Indian hunters in the Southeast probably harvested more than half a million animals per year. From its earliest years, this hunting pressure revealed itself in the contraction of deer ranges. The easily obtained coastal herds declined rapidly, followed by those of the piedmont. The Virginia and North Carolina colonial legislatures tried to formalize Indian practice by establishing open and closed seasons on deer

130. Nowak and Walker, *Walker's Mammals of the World*, 5th ed., s.v. "Dogs, Wolves, Coyotes and Jackals." Wolf population densities from contemporary studies vary from 1 per 520 square kilometers in some parts of Canada, to 1 per 73 square kilometers to 1 to 273 square kilometers in Alberta. In the Great Lakes region, researchers found stable maximum densities of 1 per 26 square kilometers. If we simply assume 1 per 100 square kilometers, the total for the cold eastern region of North America, as defined earlier, would have been 47,000.

131. Whitney, *From Coastal Wilderness to Fruited Plain*, 301–6.

132. Silver, *A New Face on the Countryside*, 96–97.

hunting east of the mountains.[133] Indian hunters were forced to range more widely each decade to pay off their accounts with the traders. Indian prosperity and well-being moved in the same secular trend over the century as that of the deer herds of the Southeast.

CONCLUSION

The rhythms of the fur trade powerfully redefined human relationships with wildlife, the forest, and the natural world in eastern North America. The interlinked ecological effects of specialized commercial hunting were most obvious in terms of the disappearance of beaver as a keystone species and deer as a highly visible ungulate and the main prey of many carnivores. Removal of the larger carnivores had an important, albeit less visible, effect as well.

The impact on human society was profound. Profits from the fur trade financed European colonization and settlement in North America. The fur trade undercut Indian resistance to European land clearing and pioneer settlement. As their entanglement in the fur trade grew, Indians became more directly dependent on Europeans and less able to resist encroachments on their lands. Disease spread by traders reduced their numbers. In effect, the fur trade emptied the landscape of humans and larger fauna in advance of the settler frontier.

As furbearers declined, so did the Indians who hunted them. Supplying furs in exchange for commodities in the marketplace, however, was not, by itself, necessarily fatal to Indian hunters, who generally displayed high levels of sophistication in this new form of exchange. Some Indian groups, such as the Hurons, flourished within the market. There is every evidence that Indians could have sustained their way of life with only modest adjustments necessary as they hunted for the world market.

In large measure, it was noneconomic forces that destroyed the Indians, not commodity production and exchange relationships. The epidemics of European-induced disease that killed many and weakened the survivors pushed Indians toward dependency. Alcohol, the European-introduced intoxicant, and the technology required to produce it also weakened and demoralized Indian societies.

It might be that producing for the fur trade made it possible for the Indians to strengthen and sustain a way of life that they otherwise would have lost much earlier and under more brutal circumstances. Unlike the Russian practice in Siberia, the North American fur and skin trade was not directly coercive. The tsars extracted furs as annual tribute from the indigenous peoples of Siberia. In contrast, the British, French, and Dutch colonial regimes

133. Ibid., 94–95.

traded goods with real value for furs and skins in a voluntary exchange with North American Indians. As workers in a global industry, laboring for low wages, North American Indians occupied a useful and profitable niche. Had they not been armed and encouraged to hunt for the fur trade, they might have suffered the fate of the Indians of Portuguese Brazil, who were either destroyed in genocidal wars or captured and impressed into servitude by the colonists and settlers of that region.

In the end, it was not participation in the fur trade that destroyed the Indians, but the European drive for colonial domination. Both British and French colonial regimes put heavy diplomatic and military pressure on successive Indian groups as they sought to create and retain allies in their struggle for territory and power. European interventions destabilized inter-Indian relations, intensified fears and insecurities, and touched off an unprecedented level of warfare in North America. The availability of ever more lethal and effective muskets from fur traders forced every Indian group to trade furs for weapons. Dissemination of muskets brought a new intensity and deadliness to Indian warfare. The final blow to most Indian groups was the advancing European settlement frontier.

During the early modern centuries, the European stocks of wild animals were much depleted in the face of expanding settlement, industrial development, and above all, agriculture. From the beginning of the sixteenth century until the end of the nineteenth, millions of lustrous beaver and other furs from North America flowed to the workshops of European furriers and hatmakers. For four centuries, Europeans protected themselves from the cold with the warmest materials available in the premodern era—and, in the case of processed beaver fur, one of the most durable. During the late seventeenth century and through the eighteenth, North American deerskins supplied lightweight, comfortable, and durable leather for trousers, gloves, and other clothing. In exchange, European traders shipped what had become cheap and abundant cloth, firearms, alcohol, and other trade goods to purchase these fabrics. The consumers and societies of western Europe were the ultimate beneficiaries of this system.[134] The forested lands of eastern North America became, in effect, a European forest preserve from which vast numbers of wildlife could be extracted and consumed.

134. For other broad comparative views, see Denys Delâge, *Bitter Feast: Amerindians and Europeans in the American Northeast, 1600–64* (Vancouver: UBC Press, 1993); and Eric R. Wolf, *Europe and the People without History* (Berkeley and Los Angeles: University of California Press, 1982).

Chapter 14

The Hunt for Furs in Siberia

By the late 1500s, after Russia's conquest of the khanate of Sibir, Siberia's vast lands lay open to exploration, conquest, and exploitation. Most of Siberia's soils, vegetation, and climate did not hold out great appeal to the Russian peasant cultivator. Instead, Siberia offered the products of the hunt to Russian frontiersmen. Russians had long hunted or purchased from indigenous hunter societies the furs of the north. Furs were one of the most valued consumption items in Russia and one of its most profitable exports.

For centuries, the temperate-zone Christian, Islamic, and Confucian worlds have demanded high-quality furs. In these colder climates, furs were valued for their luxuriously warm comfort, their visual and tactile appeal, and their scarcity and high cost. Fur wearing permitted the wearer to display high social status, power, and wealth. The primary medieval sources of supply for the finest furs were the coldest and most remote lands in northeastern Europe and northwestern Siberia. According to Janet Martin, "It was here that fur-bearing animals grew the thickest, softest pelts in the purest winter hues."[1]

Killing furbearers—as well as processing, assembling, and grading their pelts and transporting them to distant markets—was a long-standing staple of the Russian economy and a principal source of income for the nascent Russian state. In the mid–fourteenth century, the princes of Moscow, taking advantage of the weakening hold of the Mongol Golden Horde, established control over their own fur supply network. Moscow's rulers extended their military domination over the tribal peoples of Perm and Pechora to the northeast, who were required to pay tribute in fine furs. The Moscow state

---

1. Janet Martin, *Treasure of the Land of Darkness: The Fur Trade and Its Significance for Medieval Russia* (Cambridge: Cambridge University Press, 1986), 1.

negotiated arrangements with the Tatars of Kazan to permit passage of their furs through the Crimea to the Black Sea colonies of Italian merchants. Other furs found their way through Lithuania to the Hanse towns on the Baltic. Moscow became the leading fur supplier to the Ottoman realm and western Europe, as luxury furs like ermine, marten, and sable rose in popularity. Both European and Russian traders busied themselves in this vast traffic, bringing silver and gold as payment for furs.

By the beginning of the sixteenth century, despite fluctuations in routes and changing fashions in furs, the basic structural features of the northern fur trade were firmly fixed. Buoyant and growing demand by consumers fed the entire enterprise. For the consuming societies, furs continued to be a comfortable means by which to meet that most compelling human need: the visible display of high status and power combined with the appeal of warmth and comfort. Groups of foreign traders journeyed to Russian entrepôts equipped with silver and technical knowledge of northern furs. The furs were graded by species and quality by a customary schema. Russian and Tatar princes and merchants acted as middlemen in the trade. They obtained furs as tribute or in payment for iron goods, salt, or other trade goods from the indigenous peoples of the northern woods or, increasingly, Russian fur trappers. Russian traders and royal agents assembled, stored, and graded the pelts at entrepôts, which were also sites of growing state power.

Shortly after Ivan's annexation of Kazan, Russia established for the first time a direct maritime trade link with western Europe. In 1554, an English trading ship in search of an Arctic route to China landed by accident at Archangel, the White Sea port. The English captain and chief merchant, Richard Chancellor, who was brought to Moscow, opened what proved to be a successful set of negotiations with Ivan IV. The tsar gave the English traders a charter guaranteeing them free trade in his domains. The resulting Muscovy Company, a joint-stock trading company with an official monopoly on the Russian trade, established trading missions in Moscow and at Kholmogory, just south of Archangel on the Dvina River. The company sent ships each year on direct voyages between London and Archangel.

Despite a short sailing season limited by Arctic ice, Archangel proved to be an important outlet for Russian furs that generated greater profits for the Russian state monopoly. English traders also bought naval stores such as tar, timber, and hemp rope, as well as wax and hides, in return for English cloth and other goods. There remained a favorable Russian balance in the exchange that forced the English to pay the remainder with silver and gold—largely from the New World discoveries.[2]

2. Artur Attman, *The Russian and Polish Markets in International Trade, 1500–1650* (Göteborg: Institute of Economic History of Gothenburg University, 1973), 176–88.

WESTERN SIBERIA

Demand increased, but annual yields of fur in the lands around the White Sea were not keeping pace. Siberia offered the prospect of new, abundant sources of the best quality furs for both consumption and export.[3] The Russian occupation of Kazan opened up new opportunities for movement into Siberia. Driven by the prospect of fur profits, Russian frontiersmen followed the river systems north and east across the vast tracts of Siberia above the fifty-fifth parallel. Russian parties of explorers and traders trekked by boat along the rivers and by horseback, foot, and sledge on portage from one river to another. At strategic junctures, the Muscovite state, following closely after the frontiersmen, established fortified towns and administrative centers (ostrogs), to which it appointed military governors (voevody).

The first task was to annex the Tatar khanate of Sibir, already a tributary to the Russian tsar. In 1582, under the aggressive leadership of the Stroganov family, Russian forces crossed the Urals to attack Sibir, the capital, located on the Ob River. Eight hundred cossack mercenaries led by Yermak Timofeyevich defeated Kuchum, the Tatar khan, drove him into exile, and occupied Sibir. Despite continuing and bitter Tatar resistance that resulted in the death of Yermak and much of his force, the Russians persevered. In 1584, Tsar Fydor, Ivan's son and successor, sent military governors and official forces to consolidate Russian control over the Sibir khanate and its people.[4]

Moscow moved quickly to seize control of western Siberia, the lands drained by the Ob River. Private groups of Russian fur trappers and traders had already ventured along the rivers of this vast region and begun both hunting and trading for furs. With the defeat of the Tatars, Russian official and irregular expeditionary forces established fortified posts at Tobolsk in 1587, Surgut and Tara in 1594, and Obordosk the next year. Mangazeya on the Taz River, established in 1601, and Tomsk, established in 1604, became staging points for the move eastward toward the Yenisey-Tunguska River basin. Directives and funds from Moscow organized and legitimated mixed official and trader attempts to explore the Yenisey River. The tsar ordered the founding of Turkhansk at the confluence of the Yenisey and the Lower Tunguska River in 1607 and the founding of Yeniseysk to the south, just north of the confluence of the Upper Tunguska and Yenisey, in 1619.

By 1620, Russians were the dominant power in western Siberia—an area

3. Robert O. Crummey, *The Formation of Muscovy, 1304–1613* (London: Longman, 1987), 21; Henry R. Huttenbach, "Muscovy's Penetration of Siberia: The Colonization Process 1555–1689," in *Russian Colonial Expansion to 1917*, edited by Michael Rywkin (London: Mansell, 1988), 76.

4. James Forsyth, *A History of the Peoples of Siberia: Russia's North Asian Colony, 1581–1990* (Cambridge: Cambridge University Press, 1992), 32–33.

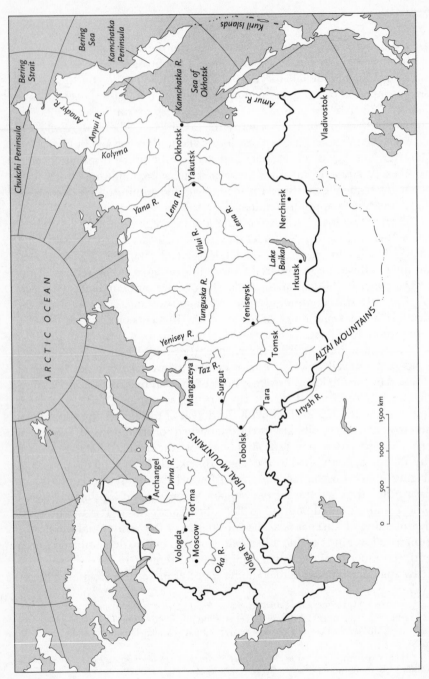

Map 14.1 Expansion and settlement of tsarist Russia

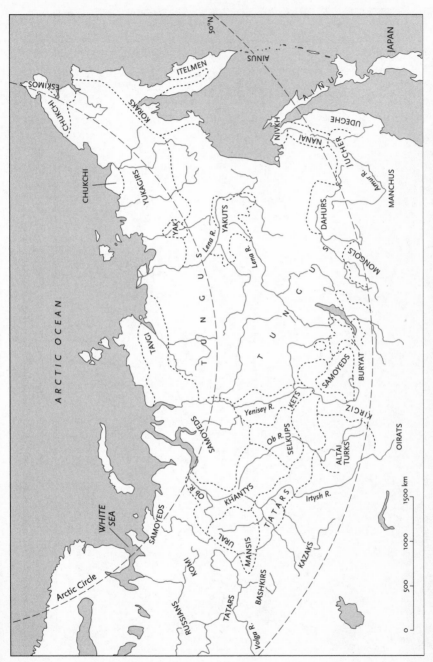

Map 14.2 Peoples of northern Asia, c. 1600. Adapted from James Forsyth, *A History of the Peoples of Siberia: Russia's North Asian Colony, 1581–1990* (Cambridge: Cambridge University Press, 1992), map 2, p. 17.

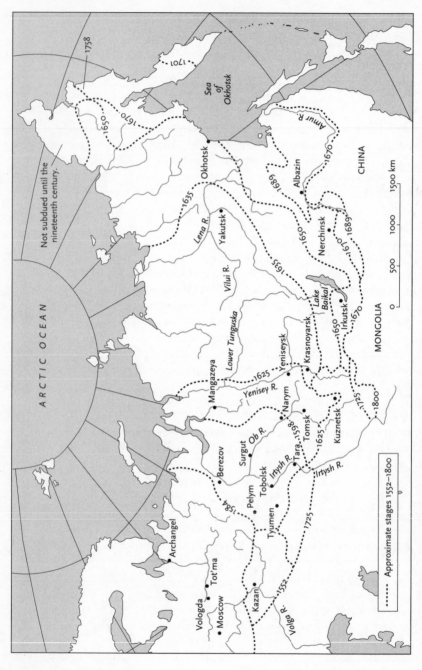

Map 14.3 Russian conquest of Siberia. Adapted from James Forsyth, *A History of the Peoples of Siberia: Russia's North Asian Colony, 1581–1990* (Cambridge: Cambridge University Press, 1992), map 6, p. 103.

of 2 million square kilometers. The tsar's writ ran from the Arctic Ocean to the Altai Mountains in the south and from the Urals to the valley of the Yenisey in the east. Conquest had more than doubled the territorial extent of the tsardom of Moscow.

Western Siberia's lands divided into two distinct natural regions: the frozen tundra to the north and the taiga, or marshy wet coniferous forest, below. These were Arctic and sub-Arctic lands, not all that promising for sedentary cultivation or Russian settlement. The tundra stretches forty-five hundred kilometers from one end of Siberia to the other. Above the permafrost line, the tundra lands are frozen all year round. Low temperatures and limited sunshine permit only lichens, mosses, small woody shrubs, and small herbaceous plants to grow. Having 240 days of snow each year limits animal life as well. Polar bears, foxes, rodents, owls, reindeer, and aquatic birds share space with seals and walruses on land.

South of the tundra, the western plain of Siberia is primarily taiga, a sparse forest of fir, spruce, and cedar growing over peat bogs of moss and lichen. The taiga, generally wet terrain with many lakes, streams, and marshes, is inundated in the spring by pack-ice blockages at the mouth of the Ob and other rivers. Wildlife, common to all of Siberia, includes larger mammals such as the brown bear, wolf, elk, reindeer, and lynx. The smaller furbearers—the sable, marten, beaver, ermine, and squirrel—also can be found. To the south, in the vicinity of Tomsk, the terrain dries out and aspen and birch replace conifers. These thin out into woodland-steppe formations and eventually to steppe grassland.

The small bands of Russian invaders threaded their way along western Siberia's rivers, founded fortified posts, and tried to impose new, one-sided relationships on the peoples they encountered. At first, the Siberians reacted violently to Russian demands and attacked the invaders, only to suffer bloody casualties and ignominious defeat. The killing power of Russian muskets and cannon was far superior to any weapons the Siberian natives employed. In sharp contrast to the Tatars, who terrorized and enslaved Russian settlers west of the Urals, the Siberian peoples were few, vulnerable, and divided.[5] After they submitted, the Russians forced or enticed the tsar's new subjects to help them with further expansion by serving as interpreters, guides, boatmen, and porters. Many were willing to serve as armed allies or auxiliaries and attack those neighbors with whom they had long-standing grievances.

After the Russians had demonstrated their military strength, their terms were simple. Each of the newly subdued Siberians had to offer ritual submission by means of a sworn oath to the tsar's authority. And, to confirm this, each adult male had to deliver a specified number of furs and pelts in

5. Yuri Slezkine, *Arctic Mirrors: Russia and the Small Peoples of the North* (Ithaca, N.Y.: Cornell University Press, 1994).

payment of the *iasak,* an annual tax. These were the essentials, but soldiers and colonists often forced the tsar's new subjects to help build forts, housing, and boats, to contribute other labor, or to supply foodstuffs. Russians seized and enslaved women to provide sex and domestic services for the male invaders. Although the Russians did offer gifts—metal utensils, knives, blankets, flour, tea, and especially alcohol—in return for furs, the exchange was certainly inequitable.

The total population of western Siberia in the last half of the sixteenth century probably did not exceed a hundred thousand persons, who were organized into small groups of preliterate hunter-gatherers. About half the population consisted of an estimated sixteen thousand Finno-Ugrian speakers thinly distributed across much of the western Siberian taiga. The Khantys and the Mansis—two distinct, but very similar, groups speaking mutually intelligible forms of the same language—divided the marshy spruce forestlands between the Ob and the Urals. They were organized into separate lineages, or clans, headed by a hereditary chief. Clan heads occupied forts protected by earth ramparts and stockades and amassed wealth in terms of silver objects and furs.[6] They had access to some iron and steel objects through trade. Their weapons included longbows and arrows, spears, and, for protection, mailed coats and helmets.

Ordinary Khantys and Mansis lived in log huts in the wintertime and moved to temporary hunting quarters for the summer hunting season. They used dugout or bark canoes for transport in the summer and skis for the six months or more of snow-covered winter. They hunted, but did not domesticate, reindeer for their meat and hides. They hunted and trapped sables, marten, ermines, and foxes and wore and traded their furs. Fresh, dried, and smoked fish taken from the rivers and streams supplied a considerable portion of their diet. The Khantys and Mansis, like nearly all the indigenous peoples across Siberia, apparently did not make or consume alcohol in any form.

In their spiritual beliefs, the Khantys and Mansis worshipped a Nature god, Num Torem, as well as spirits that lived in all natural phenomena. Religious rites conducted by shamans in sacred clearings involved sacrifice of reindeer and other animals. Each person had his or her own totem animal represented by designs tattooed on the person. The Khantys and Mansis were split into exogamous moieties defined by clan totems. Hunters were supposed to refrain from killing their particular totem animal. Like virtually all Siberian natives, they venerated the brown bear, who was known as the "master of the forest" and only occasionally killed and eaten. When this occurred, special rituals designed to propitiate the bear's spirit were performed before and during the village feast.

6. Forsyth, *A History of the Peoples of Siberia,* 10.

Also in western Siberia were the Samoyeds, Uralic language speakers whose numbers were similar to those of the Khantys and Mansis.[7] The Samoyeds' habitat extended across both tundra and taiga. In the extreme northern tundra, their culture was one shared by virtually all the indigenous peoples who lived in the harsh climate and terrain of northern Siberia. The Samoyeds fished and hunted seals and walruses in the long fjords of the Ob, Yenisey, and other rivers flowing into the Arctic Ocean.[8] They kept herds of domesticated reindeer to pull light wooden sledges and for clothing, meat, and milk. Their white, bushy-coated Samoyed dogs assisted in herding the reindeer. They hunted wild reindeer for meat and hides. They lived in hide-covered conical pole tents up to nine meters in diameter. These were portable and frequently were moved as groups engaged in seasonal migrations.

To the south, other groups of Samoyeds lived in the swampy taiga forests as far as the middle Ob River. In this habitat, the Samoyed lifestyle and material culture were closer to those of the Khantys and Mansi peoples. Each branch of the Samoyeds was loosely organized into confederations of lineages or clans. The latter controlled marriage patterns; access to hunting, fishing, and grazing grounds; dispute settlement, and if necessary, organization for war. For the latter purpose, temporary chiefs were accepted.

The annual flow of furs from western Siberia grew steadily and soon added substantial amounts to the tsar's revenues and generated considerable wealth for private Russian hunters and trappers. Pushed by depleted stocks of sable in western Russia, and encouraged by rising demand from Moscow, unofficial hunters and trappers, the *promyshlenniks,* and their hired armed guards moved restlessly eastward along the rivers. With extraordinary speed, the fur hunters dashed across Siberia in just a few short decades.[9]

CENTRAL AND EASTERN SIBERIA

Russian expeditions plunged eastward into the vastness of central Siberia along the three great tributaries of the Yenisey: the Lower, Central, and Upper Tunguska Rivers. In the 1620s, a band of cossacks followed the Lower Tunguska 2,400 kilometers to its source. There they found themselves on the bank of the upper Lena River. From its source near the western shore of Lake Baikal, the Lena River flows 4,400 kilometers northeastward to its great

7. Other, much smaller groups were the Selkups, who spoke a Samoyedic language and lived in the southeastern part of western Siberia along the tributaries of the Ob River, and the Kets, found in the Yenisey River valley.

8. Ibid., 16–17.

9. Huttenbach, "Muscovy's Penetration of Siberia."

delta on the shore of the Arctic Sea. The cossacks did not hesitate but sailed downstream (north) to explore the Lena. In 1632, they founded Yakutsk in the middle reaches of the Lena, and 720 kilometers further north on the lower Lena they built the fort of Zhigansk. The next year, the Russians reached the Lena Delta and the open sea. By the end of the decade, the cossacks had explored and built several forts on the Vilui River, the Lena tributary that flows eastward across central Siberia from its source near the Lower Tunguska. As soon as the Russians were established on the Lena, they made their by now customary demands on the indigenous peoples for ritual submission and payment of *iasak* in furs.

Midway between the Yenisey and the Lena Rivers, the sparse fir, spruce, and cedar forests of the western Siberian taiga ended. Spruce, for example, is unable to survive temperatures below minus thirty-eight degrees centigrade. From that point eastward, larger, denser forests composed of larch and pine species covered central and eastern Siberia as far as the Pacific Coast. The European larch *(Larix decidua* or *Larix europaea)* at maturity stands twenty-four to forty-two meters tall. The larch is a conifer, has reddish gray bark, and sheds its short, needlelike leaves in the fall as deciduous species do. The Scots pine *(Pinus sylvestris)* attains a height of twenty to forty meters, has a straight trunk as much as a meter in diameter, red-brown bark, and blue-green foliage at the extremities.

Two distinct peoples—the Tungus, or Evens, and the Yakuts—inhabited the 5 million square kilometers of larch and pine taiga lands comprising central Siberia. The territory and population of the Altaic-speaking Tungus, of whom there were an estimated thirty-six thousand, were by far the largest. The Tungus were originally forest dwellers in the central Siberian larch forests; they had dispersed far from their presumed homeland near Lake Baikal. They were highly mobile hunters and herders of domesticated reindeer. They used bows and arrows, protective metal armor and helmets, and iron knives and swords. They were organized into twenty or more named tribes, or clusters of clans, without hereditary chiefs.[10]

The Yakuts were a Turkic people who spoke a unitary language and are thought to have migrated from the open steppe to their compact territory in the lowlands on the upper Lena River where it intersects with the Aldan River. Here, larch forests were interspersed with meadowlands. The Yakuts, who maintained large herds of horses and cattle, practiced short-distance seasonal transhumance by moving with their animals to summer grazing lands. They were organized into a single grouping of independent clans. Each clan had a hereditary chief and shared in a common language for all Yakuts. Each clan had control over communal grazing lands and hunting and fishing grounds. At contact with the Russians, the well-organized Yakuts

10. Forsyth, *A History of the Peoples of Siberia,* 48–55.

seem to have been in the process of expanding by colonizing new lands and assimilating Tungus and other splinter ethnic groups into their domain.[11]

The fort and town of Yakutsk, built in the Yakut homeland on the Lena River, quickly became the leading Russian administrative and trade center for central Siberia. In just over a decade, by 1650, the town and its hinterland had two thousand Russians in residence. Confiscations of Yakut horses and cattle provided both mobility and meat to the colonists. Prosperous fur traders trekked to Yakutsk from European Russia to obtain the abundant furs of the region directly at the source. The traders tended to employ private Russian trappers rather than attempt to buy furs from the Yakuts or Tungus, who were overly burdened with *iasak* demands. The stream of furs sent on the yearlong river journey to Moscow increased steadily in volume.[12]

A lengthy report dated September 6, 1633, by Petr Beketov, commander of a hundred-man company *(sotnik)*, to Tsar Mikhail Federovich describes the founding of Yakutsk. The report nicely illustrates the mode and scale of Siberian conquest. According to Beketov's narration, the military governor of Yeniseysk sent him with a company of musketeers and hunter-traders *(promyshlenniks)* on "distant service" to the Lena River with supplies for one year.

The expedition actually took two and a half years, during which Beketov and his followers "suffered every deprivation," but "brought under your Sovereign Tsarist mighty hand on the Lena River many diverse Tungus and Iakut lands."[13] From their inhabitants, Beketov succeeded in collecting *iasak*, or tribute in furs, including "61 forties and 31 sables [2,471 pelts], 25 Iakut sable *shubas* [coats], 10 sable *plastinas* [pelts sewn together,] 2 beavers, 7 red fox, and one red fox pup."[14] The remainder of the report details battles with Yakut chiefs, their ultimate submission to him, the tribute exacted, and the hostages taken, as well as forts constructed and manned. At no time does Beketov appear to have had more than one hundred men under his command, and he frequently mentions sorties with far fewer participants.

In September 1633, Beketov built a fortification *(ostrog)* at Yakutsk on the Lena River "in the heart of the whole Iakut territory."[15] From here, he sent out parties to demand submission by the various Yakut princes:

11. Ibid., 55–57.

12. Ibid., 61.

13. Petr Beketov, "September 6, 1633, Report to Tsar Mikhail Fedorovich from the Steltsy Sotnik [Musketeer Commander] Petr Beketov Concerning His Expedition on the Lena River," in *Russia's Conquest of Siberia, 1558–1700: A Documentary Record,* edited by Basil Dmytryshyn, E. A. P. Crownhart-Vaughan, and Thomas Vaughan, vol. 1 of *To Siberia and Russian America* (Portland, Ore.: Western Imprints, the Press of the Oregon Historical Society, 1985), 136.

14. Ibid., 1:137. Sable and other furs were generally counted and packed in stacks of forty compressed between two boards. Forty to fifty sable pelts were required for a coat.

15. Ibid., 1:144.

On November 8 [1633], in accordance with the Sovereign's ukas, I, Petr[,] sent servitors on the Sovereign's service from the new ostrozhek on the Lena River to the Iakut prince Ineno-Oiun to collect iasak for the sovereign. The servitors traveled four days to reach Ineno-Oiun[,] and when they returned they reported [that] . . . this Iakut prince did not want to come under the Sovereign's mighty hand nor go to the ostrozhek, and he and his people began to attack the servitors. The servitors invoked God's mercy and fought them, and with the luck of the Sovereign they killed many Iakuts in that foray and shed their blood for the Sovereign Tsar and Grand Prince Mikhail Fedorovich *[sic]* of all Russia.

In the struggle they captured Prince Ineno-Oiun himself, and other . . . [missing]. In this battle the servitor Prokopii Vasilev was wounded by an arrow in his leg. They brought Prince Ineno-Oiun to the ostrozhek, and I, Petr, took him into the office and asked him why he had opposed the Sovereign Majesty. . . . The Iakut princeling said they had shot arrows at the servitors out of ignorance, that the Sovereign's men had never come to them before and that they had never even heard about the Sovereign Majesty. He said he hoped the Sovereign would have mercy now and forgive them for their transgressions. . . . I brought Prince Ineno-Oiun to take the oath, and he swore that he and all his people would serve loyally under the Sovereign's mighty hand for all time, and that they would pay iasak.[16]

The encounter closed when the Yakut prince handed over twenty sable pelts as his first payment of tribute to the tsar.

The lure of more furs sent Russian frontiersmen pressing on to the east with scarcely a pause. As the nineteenth-century tsarist historian Slotsov puts it, "The Iakutsk authorities, drawn to yasak *[iasak]* as surely as a magnet to the pole, went on sending out their scouts to track down any human retreat which had not yet been subjected to yasak."[17] Yakutsk, two-thirds of the way from the Urals across Siberia, became the jumping-off point for further Russian exploration and conquest. From Yakutsk, there were two onward routes. The first marched southeast 720 kilometers through mountainous country inhabited by Tungus peoples to the Pacific Ocean. In 1648, Russian contingents founded two coastal settlements, Okhotsk and Tauisk, on the shores of the Sea of Okhotsk.

The second, far more arduous, route to the northeast extended 2,400 kilometers across forest, tundra, and mountains as far as the Chukchi Peninsula thrusting out into the Bering Strait. The route followed an intricate pattern that made optimal use of the great rivers of the northeast. From Yakutsk, the Russians trekked overland to the source of the Yama River, took boats north along the Yama as it flowed to the Arctic, left the middle Yama for an over-

16. Ibid., 1:145.
17. Quoted in Forsyth, *A History of the Peoples of Siberia*, 75.

land trek to the source of the Aiazeya River, built boats and moved with the current as it flowed eastward, left the Aiazeya at its northward bend, trekked to the lower Kolmya River, floated with the northerly current of the Kolmya to its intersection with the Anyui, pushed against the current upriver eastward to the Anyui's source, and then trekked overland to float along the upper Anadyr River as it flowed eastward to the Bering Sea. As early as 1649, a Russian expedition traversed this route and founded the town of Anadyrsk on the upper Anadyr River, 300 kilometers from the coast.[18] By the mid-1600s only the Chukotsk and Kamchatka Peninsulas were left undisturbed.

Along this northeastern route, the Russians encountered a new set of indigenous peoples, whose population probably did not exceed forty thousand persons. First, they discovered a neolithic people they called collectively Yukagirs. From west to east, these were the Khoromos, Yandins, Uyandins, Shormobas, Omoks, Lawrens, Chuwans, and Anauls, who all spoke the same language, one unrelated to any other known human language. Each named group consisted of clans or patrilineages named after a single male founder. Under the guidance of a powerful shaman, the Yukagirs worshipped the clan ancestor.

These groups divided into the "reindeer Yukagirs" and the "settled Yukagirs." The reindeer Yukagirs, who had no domesticated reindeer, moved with the wild reindeer herds of the region from the taiga forests in May as they grazed the tundra vegetation, and they followed the herds back toward the forests in August each year. When the herds congregated for mating in the fall, the Yukagirs organized killing drives and slaughtered great numbers for meat and hides. The "settled Yukagirs" lived in log cabins or lodges along the rivers and subsisted by fishing and hunting elk. The Yukagirs, like nearly all peoples in Siberia at the time, believed strongly in the notion of spirit guardians or "master" spirits of natural phenomena. The spirit guardians of the reindeer and the elk in particular had to be propitiated by various rites and rituals.

Further to the northeast, where the Russians reached the mouth of the Kolmya River, they first encountered settlements of Asiatic Eskimos along the frozen shore. The Siberian Eskimos, like their counterparts across the Bering Strait, were a coastal, winter people whose life was consumed with hunting seals, walruses, and whales. Interspersed among the Eskimos were the Chukchi and Korak peoples. Some had adopted a life of sea hunting virtually identical to that of the Eskimos and lived in permanent coastal settlements. Others, who herded reindeer, spent the year in a transhumance pattern similar to that of the Yukagirs. The Chukchi and Korak peoples were the dominant inhabitants of the eponymous Chukchi Peninsula, the easternmost extremity of Siberia, which thrust into the Bering Strait.

18. See ibid., 134, map 7.

FURS, TRIBUTE, AND THE RUSSIAN STATE

Moscow's modest investment in ongoing Siberian conquest was more than amply repaid. The quantity of sable and other furs that flowed to Moscow from the new lands became one of the most valuable liquid assets of a cash-starved state. Devoid of domestic gold- or silver-producing mines, and lacking in much exportable agricultural and industrial production, the early modern Russian monarchy relied on the sale of furs to obtain coined and uncoined precious metals for its treasury. The tsar also used furs from his stores to reward exceptional service by his officials, nobles, and clergy; to make diplomatic gifts; and to make special purchases abroad of strategic or luxury goods.[19] Furs were not used to pay salaries or for other ordinary disbursements within Russia, because the tsar wanted to realize profits from the export price in Moscow.

Some thirty elite merchants in Moscow, appointed by the tsar, purchased furs, usually of the best quality, from royal stores and were permitted to export these furs to foreign markets. Foreign merchants arriving in Moscow had to give first refusal to the tsar's agents for their goods. Any purchases made from their stocks were paid in furs.

Moscow set up a network of customs posts at the border of Siberia, in every *ostrog*, and at portage points and other strategic locations along the main Siberian river routes.[20] The regime recruited heads of customs posts from older Russian fur-trading towns west of the Urals, such as Ustuig, Vologda, Sviazhsk, Tot'ma, Sol Vyehgodsk, and Moscow itself. These were "sworn men," or responsible notables with fur-trading experience, elected by the assemblies of these towns and sent for one- to two-year terms to Siberia. They were independent of the military governors. They were responsible for appropriating the best one of every ten pelts carried by traders or hunters, for storing these furs, and for shipping them to Moscow along with the tribute furs demanded from Siberian native hunters. Traders entering Siberia with goods for sale were charged a similar 10 percent tax, paid either in money or in kind.

Total yearly state revenue from Siberian furs grew steadily, from twelve thousand rubles in 1589 to a plateau of one hundred thousand rubles per year or more for the middle decades of the century, 1640 to 1680; the figure declined to an average annual return of seventy-eight thousand rubles in the 1690s.[21] These very large sums, calculated on the original Siberian price of

19. Raymond Henry Fisher, *The Russian Fur Trade, 1550–1700* (Berkeley and Los Angeles: University of California Press, 1943), 130.

20. George Vjatcheslau Lantzeff, *Siberia in the Seventeenth Century: A Study of the Colonial Administration* (Berkeley and Los Angeles: University of California Press, 1943), 135.

21. R. H. Fisher, *The Russian Fur Trade,* 114.

furs, not the export price, constituted between 7 and 10 percent of the state's rising income until the 1680s, when fur revenues began to drop off.[22] Fur revenues defrayed total state expenditures in Siberia, with a comfortable margin to spare.[23] By far, the greater portion of pelts taken by native hunters was appropriated by the tsarist state—not purchased by private traders.

The primary duty of Siberian military governors was to collect the *iasak,* levied in furs on every fit native Siberian adult male between eighteen and fifty years of age. Russian settlers were exempt from this tax, derived from an older Tatar practice that connoted subordination and defeat. Each group of Siberian natives that had submitted to the tsar was forced every year to pay the stipulated number of good-quality unfinished furs, preferably sable, which was the standard. In theory at least, each *iasak* payer should have hunted and trapped the furs himself. If sable pelts could not be obtained, the state would accept marten, beaver, otter, fox, ermine, lynx, wolf, or even squirrel at fixed ratios to sable.

The number of sables to be paid varied by district and over time. Originally set high, at ten to twelve sables per man per year, by the early 1600s the average was closer to five pelts. By midcentury the rate had dropped to three pelts per man in western Siberia. The state pragmatically adjusted its demand to the realities of declining sable populations.

Tsarist officials identified and fixed the territory occupied by each distinct ethnic and linguistic group as a tax district, or *volost.* Contiguous *volosts* were grouped into larger units with a Russian *ostrog* at the center that served as seat for the military governor. At the time of initial submission, as illustrated in the Beketov document quoted above, the Russians took two measures to ensure payment of the *iasak:* first, they exacted a solemn oath of allegiance to the tsar that included a commitment to pay the *iasak;* and second, they took one or two of the leading men from each *volost* hostage and kept them captive at the *ostrog.* Periodically the Russians exchanged their hostages for new ones. The Russians provided food for hostages, who were confined, often chained, and guarded to prevent escape or rescue. Nonpayment of the *iasak* by their group meant indefinite captivity or abuse and even death.

After the hunting season, by late fall and early winter, delegations of Siberians came from nearby *volosts* to the *ostrog* with the required number of furs to pay the *iasak.* They also presented additional furs to the military governor and his staff as a gift *(pominki)* in honor of the tsar. *Pominki* payments seem to have been retained as a personal perquisite by the *voevody* and his

22. Ibid., 120.

23. Ibid. For 1699, fur receipts in Siberia were 74,982 rubles against total expenditures of 54,086 rubles. The state collected an additional 56,538 rubles in money, so that the Siberian surplus that year was actually 77,434 rubles. Therefore, the fur revenues were almost entirely profit to the state.

staff. Before the natives handed over their *iasak* furs, the military governor was obliged to display the hostages from that *volost* as evidence of their good health and condition. Finally, the Russians feasted the natives with food and strong alcoholic drinks and gave them gifts. The latter consisted of beads, grain, iron knives and axes, and cloth—but not guns, ammunition, or alcohol. These gifts, although much anticipated by the *iasak* payers, were scarcely equivalent to what the Russians would have had to pay in barter if the Siberians were free to trade rather than forced to pay a tax. If any furs remained after the official payments, the governor or his staff usually offered to buy the surplus either for the treasury or for their private accounts.

To make collections from remote *volosts* or from some of the more mobile nomadic groups, especially in eastern Siberia, the Russians resorted to erecting networks of small blockhouses *(zimov'e)* in regions distant from the primary towns. Official parties traveled to collect the *iasak* at these points.[24] Around 1629, for instance, the *iasak* collectors sent to certain nomadic tribes from Mangazeya (on the Taz River) would enter a *zimov'e* (usually a simple cabin with a stove adapted for wintering) and there await the natives with the furs. The natives, two or three at a time, would approach the place and throw the furs through the window. On their side of the window, the *iasak* collectors would show the hostages, whom they had brought along for this purpose from the *ostrog*, and throw back some beads, tin, and bread. Both sides regarded each other with extreme suspicion, because, as is stated in one of the *voevody*'s reports, "the natives are afraid of being seized as hostages, while the serving men are afraid of being murdered." As this description suggests, *iasak* collection by tsarist officers was an adversarial, often brutal, expropriation of the products of the hunt from the weak indigenous peoples of Siberia. They hunted sable and other furbearers to avoid punishment, not for the incentives of trade goods and profit.

Submission to the Russians immediately forced Siberian natives into a new mode of hunting, carried out under duress, with a new set of priorities that designated sable as the most desirable prey animal. The *iasak* could be paid most efficiently by trapping or killing sable, followed by other furbearers according to the decreasing value assigned by the Russians. The *iasak* distorted the long-standing hunting patterns and the prey selections of the Siberians. The Khantys, Mansis, Samoyeds, Yakuts, Tungus, and Yukagirs had previously taken furbearers and either used or traded their furs, but not with the same desperate intensity. The energy they had expended in killing animals for meat was diverted to killing furbearers—especially sables.

The Siberian sable *(Martes zibellina)* shares many characteristics with the European pine marten *(Martes martes)* and the American marten *(Martes*

24. Lantzeff, *Siberia in the Seventeenth Century,* 128–29.

americana).[25] Sables occur across 7 million square kilometers of Siberia's cold taiga forests, from the Dvina River eastward to the Pacific Coast.[26] Sables are superbly equipped to withstand cold temperatures, with adaptations such as furred feet and use of protected microhabitats. However, they cannot thrive in areas with high summer temperatures or in broadleaf forests. It is likely that their range increased somewhat to the south with the fall in temperature during the early modern centuries.[27]

These animals are small, forest-dwelling carnivores; males weigh between .8 and 1.8 kilograms and females reach .7 to 1.5 kilograms. They have slender, long, supple bodies and elongated tails. Their winter fur consists of long, silky, lustrous guard hair with dense underfur. Their coat colors vary from light brown to dark brown. Their most important prey are voles *(Clethrionomys rutilis* or *Clethrionomys gapperi),* but they routinely kill and eat weasels *(Mustela sibirica* and *Mustela nivalis);* mice (Arvicolidae); pikas; small, tailless hares (*Ochotona* spp.); chipmunks *(Eutamias sibericus);* squirrels; the Siberian jay and other birds; and spawning salmon.[28] In winter, sables will even kill and eat grouse (Tetraonidae) sheltering in snow holes and, in deep snow, musk deer *(Moschus moschiferus)* ten times their weight. They also gather and consume pine nuts from the Siberian pine species *(Pinus siberica* and *Pinus pumila),* honey, and many types of bush berries and fruits. Adult sables are energetic hunters and foragers who cover long distances as they hunt by day and night.

Sables are solitary nesting and burrowing animals. Females select brood or maternal nests to occupy through much of the spring and into the summer. Both adult males and females in the summer and autumn move around to a number of nests and resting sites. Both sexes occupy permanent nests from December to April. These consist of sometimes lengthy burrows through the snow leading to round chambers usually placed under the trunk or roots of a tree.

The animals have few natural predators and may live up to fifteen years. Reproduction is on an annual cycle. Mating takes place from June to August, and birth of one to five kits per litter occurs in April or May. The total gestation period is actually 250 to 300 days because of delayed implantation; the actual development of the embryo requires only twenty-five to forty days.

25. Steven Buskirk, ed., *Martens, Sables, and Fishers: Biology and Conservation* (Ithaca, N.Y.: Cornell University Press, 1994), 2.

26. Nikolai N. Bakeyev and Andrei N. Sinitysn, "Sables in the Commonwealth of Independent States," in *Martens, Sables, and Fishers: Biology and Conservation,* edited by Steven Buskirk (Ithaca, N.Y.: Cornell University Press, 1994), 246.

27. Ibid., 248.

28. Steven Buskirk, "Diets of, and Prey Selection by, Sables *(Martes zibellina)* in Northern China," *Journal of Mammalogy* 77 (1996).

The young kits wean at seven weeks and attain adult body weight by five months.

Sables are fiercely territorial and sedentary animals. Barring fires or other disasters, they spend their entire lives in a well-defined range, within which they annually vary their nests and hunting territories. As the Russian biologists Solokov and Belousev comment, "The area inhabited by an individual sable is relatively small, 2–3 intermingled wood mounts, the heads of 2–3 neighboring rivulets, often a mountain taiga stream whose inflows drain an area of about 22–28 square versts [23.5 to 29.9 square kilometers]—this is the area where it [the sable] is born, lives and dies."[29] This may be an extreme statement of the sable's range, since other reports suggest that density may be as high as 1.5 sables per square kilometer in some pine forests and reduced to 1 animal per 25 square kilometers in larch forests.[30]

Sables were especially vulnerable to human predation during the winter when their burrows and nests were visible and their inhabitants could be readily caught and killed. However, collecting enough pelts to meet the *iasak* quota meant that Siberian hunters had to trek long intervals between one sable home range and another. Filling the annual quota for a single hunter killed off the sable population in areas measuring tens to hundreds of square kilometers. Because sables were solitary, territorial, sedentary, and slow-reproducing animals, once gone they were unlikely to be replaced by others. Each year, meeting the *iasak* required travel over wider tracts of territory with steadily growing stress and greater certainty that the quotas could not be met.

RUSSIAN HUNTERS AND TRADERS

Important as the state's tax demand on the native Siberian hunters was, however, Moscow's collection of sable and other furs did not come close to the furs taken by private traders who employed Russian trappers in Siberia. For example, in 1631 the tsar's fur treasury sent out furs worth 42,000 rubles: 18,000 rubles from tolls and 24,000 from the *iasak* on Siberian natives.[31] These data suggest that, in that year, the private Russian traders and hunters produced furs worth 180,000 rubles, or seven and a half times the value of the 24,000 rubles' worth of furs paid in *iasak* by Siberian native hunters. Of the total 204,000 rubles' worth of furs exported from Siberia in that year,

29. Quoted in S. U. Stroganov, *Carnivorous Mammals of Siberia* (Jerusalem: Israel Program for Scientific Translations, 1969, available from the U.S. Department of Commerce Clearinghouse for Federal Scientific and Technical Information, Springfield, Va.), 221.

30. Ronald M. Nowak and Ernest P. Walker, *Walker's Mammals of the World*, 5th ed. (Baltimore: Johns Hopkins University Press, 1991), s.v. *Martes zibellina*.

31. Paul Bushkovitch, *The Merchants of Moscow, 1580–1650* (Cambridge: Cambridge University Press, 1980), 117.

state-owned furs were valued at 42,000 rubles (20.6 percent) and private traders' furs totaled 162,000 rubles (79.4 percent).

Native hunters faced direct competition from the Russian trappers who poured into Siberia. Russian merchants traveled themselves or sent their agents to Siberia to engage in a brisk private trade, but the indigenous peoples seem to have had little part in it. Many private Russian hunter-traders (*promyshlenniks*), whose hunting grounds had been depleted, crossed the Urals to take furs from the rich Siberian hunting grounds. Some came as members of expeditions financed and organized by traders; some came in self-financed groups of hunters. Most were experienced hunters whose families and villages had long been involved in commercial hunting in the Russian north. Areas such as Pomorye, the region surrounding the White Sea, prospered from profits made by its hunters in Siberia. Customs records suggest that 2,000 or more Russian hunters moved into Siberia each season. Large numbers moved beyond the Lena River into eastern Siberia. For example, in 1642, 839 Russian hunters heading east passed through Yakutsk.[32]

In Siberia, fur hunting and trapping took place in winter, when pelts were generally in their best condition. Young sables born in March and April each year had grown sufficient hair on their coats by the following winter to be worth taking. Hunting parties traveled in boats on the rivers to the hunting grounds before the winter freeze. In contrast to most Siberian natives, who hunted furbearers with bow and arrow, the Russians adopted trapping methods on a large scale.

At the onset of winter, Russian hunting bands divided into two- or three-man teams with agreed-on territories. They built numerous trap pits that consisted of deep holes dug in the ground surrounded by a palisade of six-foot stakes. At a single narrow entrance, they suspended a board baited with fish or meat. As soon as the animal alighted on the entrance board, the board turned and threw the animal into the pit. Each group made dozens of traps that they checked regularly. The hunters bludgeoned any animals found, reset the traps, skinned their prey, and smoked the pelts. An alternative method involved nets and dogs. The hunter tracked individual sables in the snow to their nest in the ground or in a tree, put a net around the site, and waited—sometimes for a full day—for the sable to emerge and become entangled in the net. Then the dog would kill the trapped animal. At times, when confronted with groups of sable holes, hunters used smoke to drive the sables into the open.[33]

Such methods as these produced massive harvests when applied by large numbers of Russian hunters. In newly opened tracts, such as the Lena River area in the 1640s, each man in a hunting party might take as many as 120

32. R. H. Fisher, *The Russian Fur Trade*, 94.
33. Ibid., 156–57, supplies a description of methods from the early 1700s.

sables in a season.[34] Before the town burnt in 1643, Mangazeya on the Taz River was the dominant internal fur market for Siberia. In 1641, those private Russian traders returning to European Russia passed through customs at Mangazeya with 62,882 sable furs. Returns for the same year from Yeniseysk, to the south, amounted to 36,030 sable pelts carried by traders or hunters.[35] In 1702, the tsarist regime did a financial survey that produced total figures for pelts exported from Siberia at the end of the century. According to this record, in 1698 the total number of pelts sent to European Russian towns was 256,837, and for 1699 the number was 489,900.[36] Throughout the seventeenth century, a plausible Siberian harvest—including *iasak* and private hunting—would have ranged between 200,000 and 300,000 sable pelts every year.

Slaughtering fur-bearing animals in such numbers assuredly depleted animal populations. Since market demand and prices for Siberian furs increased steadily throughout the seventeenth century, it was cost-effective for many Russian hunters to search out hunting grounds bypassed in the initial rush eastward.[37] They were able to obtain profitable harvests in areas on the tributaries of the great rivers that still had sizeable animal populations. It was this steady process of hunting out all available areas behind the moving frontier that bolstered the total annual catch and helped exhaust the fur-bearing stocks in Siberia.

State pressure on indigenous hunters did not relent in spite of protests and declining *iasak* returns. Between the 1620s and 1690s, *iasak* collections from western Siberia declined by about 45 percent.[38] In 1638, Tsar Mikhail Federovich noted, "The voevodas [military governors] write to the Sovereign from Siberian towns that they cannot obtain any more furs. They report that these Siberian towns and *ostrogs* are experiencing a depletion of sables and other furbearing animals because the *iasak*-paying forest dwelling natives have trapped all the available animals."[39] The tsar's solution for that problem was to send his officers eastward to the Lena River area. By the 1690s, sables had vanished as far east as the vicinity of Yakutsk on the Lena River.[40]

During the 1690s, the Chinese market for furs, with its nearly insatiable

34. Ibid., 98.

35. Bushkovitch, *The Merchants of Moscow*, 121–22.

36. R. H. Fisher, *The Russian Fur Trade*, 180. In 1698, the tithe equaled 16,800 and the *iasak* 105,837; in 1699, the tithe was 42,200 and the *iasak* was 109,900.

37. Richard Hellie, "Furs in Seventeenth-Century Muscovy," *Russian History* 16 (1989). See p. 187, fig. 12, for the north and fig. 13 for Siberia. Prices at Moscow rose slowly but steadily throughout the century. See p. 186, fig. 11.

38. R. H. Fisher, *The Russian Fur Trade*, 102.

39. Basil Dmytryshyn, E. A. P. Crownhart-Vaughan, and Thomas Vaughan, *Russia's Conquest of Siberia, 1558–1700: A Documentary Record*, vol. 1 of *To Siberia and Russian America* (Portland, Ore.: Western Imprints, the Press of the Oregon Historical Society, 1985), 171.

40. R. H. Fisher, *The Russian Fur Trade*, 107.

demand, opened to Russian fur traders. The territorial interests of tsarist Russia and Qing China collided in the Amur River valley. China prevailed and forced Russia out of the Amur Valley in a dispute settled by the Treaty of Nerchinsk in 1689. One article of the treaty provided that private traders from each country could trade in each other's territory. The Chinese market paid high prices for all varieties of Siberian furs. Ermine and wolverine commanded better prices than sable or fox—although the latter sold well. In return, traders could bring back porcelain, silk, gold, silver, tea, precious and semiprecious stones, and ivory.[41] Given the distances involved, Siberian furs were the only commodity available to Russia to exchange for these highly prized goods.

In the late 1690s, Peter the Great, anxious to engross the potential profits of the China fur trade and concerned by the state's inability to obtain the finest-quality sables as the supply decreased, imposed a state monopoly on all export sales of furs from Russia and on all sable and fox furs in the domestic market. This new arrangement simply shifted the source of pressure and did not inhibit private Russians from hunting for furs. The new monopoly ended only in 1762, by which time dwindling harvests had reduced the monopoly's importance for state revenues.

Overall, Russian and foreign demand for sable drove Siberian expansion. Of the furs, sable was most heavily valued and traded. Over a 125-year period for which information survives, sable accounted for just under 95 percent of the total monies paid for furs in sales at Moscow.[42] The Moscow price of sable pelts, that benchmark of the Russian fur trade, rose steadily at a rate of 1.68 percent per year between 1600 and 1719. As Richard Hellie comments, "Certainly, this constant rise in the price of sable reflects relentless, ruthless trapping, without the slightest notion of conservation, of the Russians' most valuable fur crop."[43]

CONQUEST AND SETTLEMENT

Why did the Russians prevail so quickly and easily over such a vast territory? First, and perhaps most important, the indigenous peoples were few and poorly organized. A generally accepted official Russian count for tribute purposes puts the indigenous population of all Siberia at only 227,000 in the

41. Ibid., 225.

42. Hellie, "Furs in Seventeenth-Century Muscovy," 69–70, and table 4.8. All sable transactions totaled 2,469 (58.9 percent), from 4,191 total fur transactions. Total monies paid for sable in those transactions amounted to 1,631,047 rubles (94.7 percent) of a total expenditure of 1,723,205 rubles for furs.

43. Richard Hellie, The Economy and Material Culture of Russia, 1600–1725 (Chicago: University of Chicago Press, 1999), 62, fig. 4.4.

1600s.[44] Even allowing for substantial underestimation by the widely scattered Russian officials, it is doubtful that the total early modern Siberian population exceeded 300,000 persons.

For the Siberians, who were organized into hundreds of discrete groups that lacked centralizing state structures, unified, large-scale effective resistance to the Russians was impossible. With technological capacities that at best encompassed some use of iron and steel, their weaponry could not match Russian firearms. To varying degrees, each group fought. Some groups fought desperately and some occasionally won victories, but overall they could not defeat the Russians. Both resistance and flight remained futile.

New diseases also weakened and demoralized the indigenous peoples of Siberia. The worst of these was smallpox "because of its swift spread, the high death rates, and the permanent disfigurement of survivors."[45] Smallpox first reached western Siberia in 1630. In the 1650s, it moved east of the Yenisey, where it carried away up to 80 percent of the Tungus and Yakut populations.[46] In the 1690s, smallpox epidemics reduced Yukagir numbers by an estimated 44 percent. The disease moved rapidly from group to group across Siberia. Death rates in epidemics reached 50 percent of the population. The scourge returned at twenty- to thirty-year intervals, with dreadful results among the young. Venereal disease, called "the Russian disease" by the natives, spread widely as Russian intruders engaged in sexual relationships with native women. Venereal disease sharply reduced fertility and sent indigenous populations into decline. Other, airborne infections such as measles hit hard at the Siberians. Finally, alcoholism seems to have taken hold in populations that had not previously known its use, and it contributed to an increasing cultural and social malaise.[47]

Because the indigenous populations were so weak, the manpower required to defeat them was relatively low. Russian exploration and conquest was the work of small parties of audacious private trappers and state servicemen. Groups of only 20, 30, or 50 tsarist musketeers or cossacks routinely defeated larger forces of Siberians. Moscow sent relatively few men to Siberia. When, in 1636, the tsar was strapped for manpower by the race into central Siberia, he doubled the Siberian cadre of troops and officials, and the total number rose to a paltry 5,004 men (from 2,735 serving a decade earlier).[48]

44. Forsyth, *A History of the Peoples of Siberia*, 71, table 5.1.

45. Alfred W. Crosby, *Ecological Imperialism: The Biological Expansion of Europe, 900–1900* (Cambridge: Cambridge University Press, 1986).

46. James Forsyth, "The Siberian Native Peoples before and after the Russian Conquest," in *The History of Siberia: From Russian Conquest to Revolution*, edited by Alan Wood (London: Routledge, 1991), 82–83.

47. Ibid., 82.

48. Lantzeff, *Siberia in the Seventeenth Century*, 67.

After the initial phase of conquest and fur trading, Russian settlers did find their way to even the most distant and remote parts of Siberia. Apart from state officials and soldiers, hunters, and trappers, Siberia began to draw peasant migrants. Parts of the southern taiga forest in western Siberia lent themselves to sedentary plow cultivation. These attracted Russian pioneer settlers, who clustered near the Ural Mountains in Tobolsk district. By 1670, there were 7,586 peasant farmsteads with some 34,000 settlers occupying land after cutting and burning the taiga forest in that region.[49] Another area of peasant settlement and grain cultivation was located on the upper Ob River around Tobolsk.

In central and eastern Siberia beyond the Yenisey River, large areas under permafrost discouraged widespread Russian peasant migration. Some agricultural settlement occurred around Yeniseysk in the 1620s, in areas of black earth around Krasnoyarsk in the 1630s, and in pockets of good soil along the Angara and Ilim Rivers in the 1650s.[50] Officials imported many of these peasants to grow grains to feed their settlements. Native Siberians' resentment over peasants grabbing and clearing their hunting grounds found expression in numerous complaints and even violent incidents.

The Russian population of Siberia grew steadily. The number of male peasants rose from 49,000 in 1678, to 173,912 in 1719, to 365,050 in 1762, and to 600,368 in 1811.[51] From these data, we can do a crude estimate of the growth of total agricultural area in Siberia. If each peasant pioneer occupied 20 hectares with his household area, arable land, hayfields, and woodlots (somewhat more than the 10–17-hectare average claimed by peasants in the Russian heartland), the totals for those years are as follows: 9,800 square kilometers in 1678, 34,782 square kilometers in 1719, 73,010 square kilometers in 1762, and 120,074 square kilometers in 1811. Although even the 1811 total is less than 1 percent of the total land area of Siberia (which covered 13.5 million square kilometers), in absolute terms the area of agricultural settlement was significant. Especially in western Siberia, Russian pioneers burnt and cleared forests, plowed for grain cultivation, and grazed their livestock—and thereby altered the existing habitat.

IMPACTS ON INDIGENOUS PEOPLES

As animal populations dropped in eastern Siberia, the living standards of the Tungus, Yakuts, and other eastern groups also worsened. Disease, the tsar's continuing demand for *iasak* payment in sable furs, and Russian brutality and

---

49. Forsyth, *A History of the Peoples of Siberia,* 45; David Moon, "Peasant Migration and the Settlement of Russia's Frontiers, 1550–1897," *The Historical Journal* 40, no. 4 (1997): 877.
50. Ibid., 64.
51. Moon, "Peasant Migration and the Settlement of Russia's Frontiers," 863, table 1.

corruption all exacted a heavy toll on native populations across Siberia. A 1744 memorial written by Heinrich von Fuch, a political exile with extended experience among the Yakut and Tungus peoples of northeastern Siberia, eloquently protested their hardships suffered as furs became harder to harvest. When von Fuch departed Siberia, he "promised the Iakuts and Tungus, who had petitioned me, that I would report these conditions to Imperial authorities."[52] He points out, "At first there were plenty of furbearing animals there, but now there are no sables and not many foxes in those Iakut lands, from the shores of the [Arctic] ocean all the way south to the great Lena River."[53]

Moreover, contagious disease had devastated the Siberians—"when they are stricken with smallpox they die like flies." Even more devastating was the inflexibility of Russian officials who forced survivors to pay the *iasak* owed by their dead relatives. According to von Fuch:

> I personally knew several wealthy Iakuts who had to pay for four or five of their dead relatives. They were so impoverished that before I left they had to forfeit all their livestock and horses, and sometimes pawn their wives and children [to Russian officials]. Some of them hang or drown themselves. This is a natural consequence because a local native works very hard in the forest all winter and suffers hunger and cold until he traps enough to pay his iasak and make gift[s of furs] to the iasak collector and his assistants. If in addition to this he is forced to pay the iasak for those who have died or who have run off, first he loses all his livestock, then his wives and children. He cannot hunt without horses, so he commits suicide or runs off. Then the collectors find his relatives and force them to pay. The collectors take everything until the natives are destitute.[54]

Von Fuch recommended that the *iasak* payers be permitted to submit fixed numbers of squirrel and wolverine pelts instead of the diminished sable and fox.

Greedy Russian officials exacted large illegal bribes and gifts from the natives that were often equal to the amount of the *iasak* paid. If officials were not paid what they demanded, they "then take the native's wives and grown children to work for them. They also take the nets, axes, tools, boats, bows and arrows. Sometimes they take the clothes right off the backs of the natives, and beat and torture them secretly in their iurts [encampments]."[55] Perhaps most deplorably, according to von Fuch, the native peoples had no recourse, no representation, no means by which their ill treatment could be protested

52. Ibid., 187.
53. Dmytryshyn, Crownhart-Vaughan, and Vaughan, *Russia's Conquest of Siberia*, 1:170.
54. Ibid.
55. Ibid., 1:173.

effectively. The military governors were invariably influenced by their local native interpreters, who benefited from the existing corrupt system.

The native Siberian population did not disappear, in spite of Russian brutality and the ravages of smallpox and other diseases. For western and eastern Siberia combined, the total native population recorded in 1790 was 303,395 persons.[56] The 1790 total is slightly more than the estimated preconquest population of 227,000. Part of the increase may be accounted for by the inclusion of a growing number of mixed-race, Russian-indigenous persons counted as Siberians by officials.

KAMCHATKA AND THE PACIFIC

The search for new sources of fur led the Russians to further eastward advances in the first half of the eighteenth century. In 1696, a cossack commander, Vladimir Atlasov, led an overland expedition out of Anadyrsk fort on the Anadyr River in northeast Siberia on an eighteen-hundred-kilometer trek south into the Kamchatka Peninsula. Two years later, Atlasov returned with 3,640 sable pelts taken as *iasak* from the Itelmen—the natives of Kamchatka—or trapped by members of the expedition. The numerous Kamchatka sables were larger than ordinary Siberian varieties, and their furs brought higher prices at market. The Russians soon returned to obtain more furs. Over the next quarter century, a steady stream of Russian cossacks followed the long, arduous route to Kamchatka, forced the Itelmen to submit to the tsar in time-honored fashion, and exacted *iasak.*

The Kamchatka Peninsula is one of the most unstable regions on earth, with its twelve active volcanoes and the earthquakes and tidal waves associated with frequent volcanic eruptions. In the 1690s, the birch and larch forests of the Kamchatka River plain supported a sizeable human population, perhaps thirteen thousand Itelmen people (called Kamchadals by the Russians). These Paleo-Siberian language speakers used bone and stone implements, hunted reindeer, fished salmon, hunted seals, and carried out modest horticulture. The Itelmen were a warrior people accustomed to tough internecine warfare among themselves, who lived in villages fortified by palisades to protect themselves against interlineage raiding.[57]

The lengthy circuitous land route to Kamchatka was made hazardous by attacks from the northern Korak peoples, who had obtained firearms by this time. Lack of a defined sea route impeded exploitation of the peninsula's resources. Finally, in 1716–1717, after several failed attempts, the cossack Kozma Sokolov successfully navigated from Okhotsk to the peninsula, and

---

56. Forsyth, *A History of the Peoples of Siberia,* 115, n. 14.
57. Ibid., 132–33.

the land route was virtually abandoned. Okhotsk became Russia's chief Pacific port until the mid–nineteenth century.[58]

Apparently unchecked by the imperial authorities, the cossacks treated the Itelmen with contempt and cruelty that went well beyond the usual Russian practice in Siberia. They extorted furs far in excess of the numbers specified for payment of the *iasak* and brutally punished those Itelmen who did not meet their demands. If the Itelmen could not hand over the demanded furs, the cossacks seized and enslaved Itelmen women and children. In 1724, the Russians at the Upper Kamchatka and Big River forts possessed among them 209 Itelmen slaves.[59] The cossacks also forced Itelmen to use their sled dogs and canoes to transport seaborne supplies to Russian forts.

Itelmen resentment against cossack brutality caused numerous small-scale violent attacks that the cossacks punished ferociously. This ongoing hostility triggered three large-scale rebellions, in the periods 1706 to 1713, 1731 to 1732, and 1741 to 1742. Even though the Itelmen acquired firearms and developed effective war chiefs, they did not prevail. Punitive campaigns and massacres of the Itelmen followed each of these uprisings. Despite the unrest, the flow of sable furs from Kamchatka continued and the sable population declined steadily. Itelmen numbers dropped too: from 13,000 when the Russians arrived in the 1690s to about 6,000 by 1767. The smallpox epidemic of 1768–1769 reduced that number to about 3,000 at its end. Many of the Itelmen were in fact of mixed Russian-Itelmen descent by that time.[60]

SEA OTTERS IN THE PACIFIC

Russian interest in the Pacific Coast intensified when Peter the Great sent Captain Vitus Bering on the first Kamchatka exploration in 1725, just before the tsar's death. Bering sailed along the Kamchatka coast as far north as what came to be called the Bering Strait, before turning back.[61] The second Kamchatka expedition (1733–1734), led by Bering and A. I. Chirikov, brought a wave of new settlers to Okhotsk and the Pacific Coast. In 1738, Bering sent ships from Okhotsk to Kamchatka and then to the Kuril Islands. In 1739, a second expedition to the south reached Hokkaido in Japan. On June 4, 1741, Bering sailed from Kamchatka for America across the Bering Sea. He commanded one twenty-four-meter sailing vessel built in Okhotsk, the *Svyatoy Petr,* and Chirikov commanded its sister ship, the *Svyatoy Pavel.* Although the

58. James R. Gibson, *Feeding the Russian Fur Trade: Provisionment of the Okhotsk Seaboard and the Kamchatka Peninsula, 1639–1856* (Madison: University of Wisconsin Press, 1969), 9–11.

59. Forsyth, *A History of the Peoples of Siberia,* 135.

60. Ibid., 140–43.

61. T. Armstrong, "Bering's Expeditions," in *Studies in Russian Historical Geography,* edited by James H. Bater and R. A. French (London: Academic Press, 1983), 175–95.

ships became separated, each commander landed on North American soil safely by mid-July—Bering in the Gulf of Alaska and Chirikov near Prince of Wales Island. Chirikov returned safely to Kamchatka by mid-October. Bering landed erroneously on an uninhabited island (Bering Island) two hundred kilometers east of Kamchatka. After his ship wrecked offshore, Bering died from an illness, and the crew spent nearly a year there until they built a new vessel and sailed home. The rebuilt ship sailed to Kamchatka in August 1742, wintered over, and finally arrived in Okhotsk in June 1743.

The reconstructed *Svyatoy Petr* returned with several hundred sea otter pelts taken on Bering Island during the crew's long sojourn. They reported that great numbers of sea otters were to be found along the coasts of the islands in the Bering Sea. So luxurious were these furs that they brought the astounding price of eighty to one hundred rubles each when sold in Siberia. The best sea otter pelts were nearly 2 meters long and .7 meters in width when stretched before drying. Their fur was rich jet black and glossy, with a slight intermixture of white hairs that conveyed a muted silver color in the background. The normal price steadied at about double that of sable pelts, or four rubles per skin. So much in demand were sea otter furs in China that formerly land-bound Siberian traders and hunters took to the sea in pursuit of the sea otter.

The sea otter *(Enhydra lutris)* lives in shallow waters with kelp and shellfish beds along the coasts of the northern Pacific from Hokkaido in northern Japan to southern California. Grouped in schools of seventy-five to a hundred, sea otters eat crabs and fish in summer and sea urchins and mollusks in winter. They are slow to reproduce, since females bear only one pup each year. Although mammals, they spend most of their lives in the water and come ashore to rest primarily at night and in times of hard winds and foul weather. During fair weather they go far to sea and sleep afloat. Generally, they were best hunted at sea during the fair weather season of the North Pacific, from May to June of each year. So soundly did they sleep that they could be approached within very close range by experienced hunters.

Russian entrepreneurs paid to have sailboats hastily built and designed at Okhotsk and other ports. Each boat carried forty to seventy crew members operating on shares. A single trip lasted two years or more because the hunters spent the winter on the Commander Islands. Here, they hunted sea cows for meat and sea lions and fur seals for their hides. The following summer, the boats sailed to the Aleutians, where they operated from one of the small beaches. They forced the Aleuts to join the hunting parties formed by the Russians and to net or harpoon sea otters. The crews put to sea in the Aleut *baidaras* or umiaks, which were made from the hides of sea cows and held six to eight men. In the course of a summer, they could take 100 or more pelts per crew member for the return to Okhotsk. A full load of furs returned ten thousand to thirty thousand rubles, or twice the cost of outfitting an expedition.[62]

Between 1743 and 1800, Russian hunters made 101 officially counted voyages to the Aleutian Islands, the Commander Islands, and Alaska. The half-century harvest (1743–1798), from which tsarist officials took their 10 percent tax, amounted to 186,754 pelts. As early as 1750, sea otters had disappeared from the coast of the Kamchatka Peninsula; by 1780, they had disappeared from the Kuril Islands; and by the 1790s, their numbers on the Aleutians had perceptibly dropped. The North Pacific shores of Alaska marked the terminus for the Siberian hunt for furs.

ENVIRONMENTAL EFFECT OF THE RUSSIAN CONQUEST

The Russian advance into Siberia noticeably changed the faunal composition of the entire region from the Ob River to the Kamchatka Peninsula. With every passing decade, Russian and native hunters further depleted the sable population all the way across Siberia. Was this a significant loss that caused major changes in Siberian ecosystems? Probably not. The sable was not a keystone species equivalent to the American beaver or even a dominant carnivore in Siberia.[63] That role can be assigned to larger animals such as the bear or wolf. The sable's disappearance might have reduced pressure on its many prey species. However, so many species prey on smaller rodents that the effect would be virtually impossible to measure. The Siberian weasel may have increased its numbers and pines might have had better seed distribution when sables stopped eating, and thereby killing, pine nuts.[64] The ecological consequences of the sable's departure were diffuse and hard to detect in the historical record.

Perhaps more significant is the fact that, with the Russian advance into Siberia, other furbearers, especially carnivores, came under new hunting pressures. Over twenty species of furbearers were sold, many for substantial prices, on the Moscow market.[65] Moscow transactions data, however, understate the intensity with which Russian and native hunters pursued bears, wolves, wolverines, foxes, bobcats, cats, otters, minks, ermines, and weasels. Some furs, like ermine, were preferred and were sold to the Chinese market. Most of the remainder were immediately fabricated into clothing or sold on

62. J. R. Gibson, *Feeding the Russian Fur Trade*, 24–33.

63. For a discussion of keystone species, see M. E. Power et al., "Challenges in the Quest for Keystones," *BioScience* 46 (1996).

64. I am grateful to Steven Buskirk for making these points in a personal communication.

65. Hellie, *The Economy and Material Culture of Russia*, 53–54. Foxes, at 11.2 percent of recorded transactions, and marten (5.8 percent) were prominent in sales at Moscow. Noncarnivores included beavers, at 5.6 percent of the total transactions, and squirrels, at 7.7 percent. Transactions involving other animals combined were no more than 2 to 3 percent, if that.

local and regional markets for domestic consumption. As sable catches declined, it is likely that Russian and native Siberian hunters put more effort into taking these other species. Human predation can easily have a deleterious effect on relatively small populations of carnivores, whose average population densities are only 3 percent of those of their prey.[66] The end result of this stepped-up effort would have been the depletion of the wolf, usually considered a keystone carnivore because of its size and effect on herbivores, and similar reductions in virtually all smaller carnivores. Whether surges in herbivore prey populations occurred in early modern Siberia as a result— and if so, to what extent—is an unanswered question.

Finally, as the hunt thrust out into the Pacific Ocean, the war on the sea otters had a significant ecological effect on the coastal fauna around its rim. The sea otter is a "conspicuous predator in nearshore communities of the northeastern Pacific Ocean" and can be considered a keystone species for those communities.[67] When sea otters were plentiful, they preyed heavily on the invertebrate herbivore the sea urchin *(Strongylocentrotus polyacanthus)*, whose populations live in shallow waters. When sea otters reduced sea urchin populations, these herbivores no longer heavily grazed kelp or macroalgae *(Alaria fistulosa, Laminaria* spp., and *Agarum* spp.), and kelp forests grew luxuriantly. The kelp canopy in turn provided important food and cover for a wide range of fish and other species. Intensified human hunting in the Aleutians reversed this sequence. Sea urchin populations shot up and grazed kelp and other macroalgae to a remnant layer and reduced fish and other coastal marine populations.[68]

CONCLUSION

A century and a half after the 1552 conquest of Kazan, the Russian tsar ruled over all Siberia. The early modern Russian state rarely wavered in its expansionist resolve as, decade after decade, Moscow mobilized resources and deployed military force in service of expansion into Siberia. Russian frontiersmen, some of them directly employed by the state and some of them private

---

66. Steven Buskirk and Gilbert Proulx, "Furbearers, Trapping, and Biodiversity" (manuscript, 2000).

67. James A. Estes, Norman S. Smith, and John F. Palmisano, "Sea Otter Predation and Community Organization in the Western Aleutian Islands, Alaska," *Ecology* 59 (1978): 822. This is the classic statement of the sea-otter-as-keystone-species argument.

68. James A. Estes and David O. Duggins. "Sea Otters and Kelp Forests in Alaska: Generality and Variation in a Community Ecological Paradigm," *Ecological Monographs* 65, no. 1 (1995). Despite criticisms, the theory remains robust and its applications have been extended beyond the original rocky shore habitats investigated by Estes. R. G. Kvitek et al., "Changes in Alaskan Soft-Bottom Prey Communities along a Gradient in Sea Otter Predation," *Ecology* 73 (1992).

entrepreneurs, carried out an audacious feat of exploration and ruthless conquest.

The tsars, heads of a centralizing and aggrandizing regime, maintained continuity of purpose from reign to reign. In large measure, Moscow's determination can be explained by the fact that the world fur market continued to send out strong demand signals. The regime reaped high returns from the furs demanded of Siberian natives as a tax. A large, perhaps even dominant, share of fur profits went to the private sector. Violent, hardy, private fur trappers and traders had much to gain by pushing deeper and deeper into Siberia to gain access to untapped stocks of sables and other furbearers. The profits obtained in the form of furs amply repaid the costs of this great national venture.

Whatever their numbers, the indigenous peoples of Siberia did not flourish or prosper under early modern Russian rule. The pressures they endured and the cultural and social devastation that ensued was nearly identical to those faced by the Indians of North America, described in the previous chapter. Aside from the strains they suffered in paying the *iasak,* the natives of Siberia became increasingly dependent on Russian-produced and -traded consumer goods. They developed a taste for and need for bread, became addicted to alcohol and tobacco, and relied on firearms and purchased ammunition. They lost possession of their choicest hunting grounds and fishing rights after taking fraudulent loans from settlers. They found the settlers competing with them in gathering such edible forest produce as the nuts from the cones of Siberian pine as well as honey from wild bees. Many natives were reduced to dependency and beggary on the outskirts of Russian settlements.[69] Others retreated to more distant, less productive areas, in the hope that they could avoid these pressures.

Active, commercial hunting by both Russian settlers and indigenous peoples stripped the larger carnivores from the Siberian landscape. What for Russians began in the sixteenth century as commercialized hunting of sables in western Siberia had, by the late eighteenth century, intersected with the world hunt for sea mammals in the northern oceans.

69. Forsyth, *A History of the Peoples of Siberia,* 157–58.

Chapter 15

Cod and the New World Fisheries

From the Baltic to the Barents Sea, the fishing grounds of the northeastern Atlantic and Arctic had long produced valuable catches of cod for European markets. Fishermen had identified and were exploiting each of the major populations of cod in the northwestern Atlantic. Since the thirteenth century, there had been a long-distance trade in stockfish—dried and salted cod—dominated by merchants of the Hanseatic League. From Icelandic waters, European fishermen pushed onward to discover gratifyingly copious stocks of cod, a familiar resource, off Labrador and Newfoundland.

In the 1490s, Basque fishermen apparently sailed regularly across the icy waters of the North Atlantic to take codfish from coastal waters ("the banks") of Newfoundland, Nova Scotia, and southern Labrador. Between 1497 and 1502, the exploratory voyages of the English John Cabot and Portuguese Gaspar Corte-Real made visible, and excited interest in, the transatlantic route to the northeast coast of North America.[1] Greater numbers of fishing vessels from a greater number of European ports sailed each year to the fishing grounds off Newfoundland. The New World fishery became a new industry that consumed considerable European capital and entrepreneurial energy. The fisheries tapped into a vast natural resource virtually unused by the sparse Indian and Eskimo populations of the region.

Cod, with its rich protein, was one of the great prizes of the New World. The New World fisheries were a self-renewing resource of the greatest abundance.[2] Every year over the next half millennium, the fishing fleets of the

1. Felipe Fernández-Armesto, K. N. Chaudhuri, and Times Books, *The Times Atlas of World Exploration: Three Thousand Years of Exploring, Explorers, and Mapmaking* (New York: Harper-Collins, 1991), 74–75.
2. A recent book on the cod fisheries is Mark Kurlansky, *Cod: A Biography of the Fish That*

Old World caught coldwater New World codfish, preserved them, and carried them home to put cheap, nutritious protein on the food markets of western Europe. Cod became a staple food for African slaves laboring in the sugar fields of the West Indies. Cod enriched the diet of the colonial settlers of New York, New England, and Canada. Even after three centuries of intense fishing, the great stocks of codfish seemed inexhaustible to the humans who preyed on them.

THE PREY

The adult Atlantic codfish *(Gadus morhua)* is a species of coldwater fish belonging to the order Gadiformes, akin to haddock, pollock, hake, and whiting. The adult fish has a heavy body and large head, blunt snout, and a distinctive barbel under the lower jaw tip. It has a square tail with three dorsal and two distinct anal fins. Colors vary from grayish to reddish tones speckled with small, round, indistinctly edged spots. A distinctive, pale lateral line runs down the body. Atlantic cod studied today mature sexually at a median age of 1.7 to 2.3 years and have body lengths measuring 32 to 41 centimeters. They may live twenty or more years and attain lengths up to 1.3 meters and bodyweights as high as 25 to 35 kilograms. The largest recorded codfish caught in modern times was taken in 1895 and weighed 95.9 kilograms.[3]

The cod is an ideal fish for human consumption. Its flesh is white, firm, and gelatinous without being fatty, and the relatively few bones are easily removed. Raw cod flesh is 17.8 percent protein. Most important, codfish can be preserved almost indefinitely by sun drying and salting. When the water is removed, the salted, dried cod is 62.8 percent protein.[4] Cod can also be preserved wet for a limited period after being caught, by heavy salting (pickling) of the eviscerated, headless carcass. Cod eggs, or roe, are nutritious and palatable either fresh or smoked. Cod livers produce an edible oil rich in vitamins.

Cod follow annual migration patterns tied to the reproductive cycle and seasonal temperature changes in the water. Mature and juvenile cod spend

Changed the World (New York: Walker and Company, 1997); A. R. Michell puts New World fishing in the general context of the early modern European fisheries of Western Europe. "The European Fisheries in Early Modern History," in *The Economic Organization of Early Modern Europe*, edited by E. E. Rich and Charles Wilson (Cambridge: Cambridge University Press, 1977).

3. Michael P. Fahay and Northeast Fisheries Science Center, *Essential Fish Habitat Source Document* (Woods Hole, Mass.: U.S. Department of Commerce National Oceanic and Atmospheric Administration, National Marine Fisheries Service, Northeast Region, Northeast Fisheries Science Center, 1999), 2.

4. Agricultural Research Service, U.S. Department of Agriculture, Nutrient Data Laboratory Home Page, USDA Nutrient Database for Standard Reference (Release 13), 1999. In 100 grams of salted, dried Atlantic cod, there are 62.82 grams of protein.

their winters offshore along the submerged continental shelf clustered on rough-textured banks or shallow grounds with water 40 to 130 meters in depth (rarely, as deep as 200 meters) and at temperatures usually between −1.5° and 10° C. The blood plasma of cod freezes at −0.7°C; however, the juvenile and adult fish produce antifreeze proteins that permit survival in waters nearly down to the freezing point of seawater (1.8°C).

In late winter or early spring, cod follow one of a number of distinct migration routes separated by deepwater trenches. Upon arrival inshore, the cod stocks concentrate in dense numbers along the coast in predictable locations, or grounds, of fifty meters depth or less. Currently off Newfoundland, huge, dense schools of cod leave the deeper wintering areas in early spring "and follow tongues of deep, relatively warm, oceanic waters ('highways') across the shelf to summer feeding areas inshore."[5]

In early June to July, depending on location, the codfish temporarily abandon their zooplankton diet when they make contact with massive schools of capelin *(Mallotus villosus)*, small, silvery, smeltlike fish heading toward the shore to spawn. Voracious after their own spawning, codfish pursue the capelin inshore, where they are vulnerable to the hand lines and jiggers of inshore fishermen. The inshore season lasts from one hundred days in southern waters to less than sixty days off Labrador. Concentrations of cod move inshore along the coast during the summer and return to deeper, offshore waters along the banks in the winter. Some larger cod prefer colder and deeper water and return to the offshore banks by early autumn to spend the winter.

The peak spawning season occurs as migration begins, but spawning may take place anytime between November and July. Fertilized females release several million eggs in water temperatures between 5° and 7°C. The buoyant pelagic eggs drift on the water surface for an average of two to three weeks before hatching larvae. Optimal temperatures for incubation are between 2° and 8.5°C; the upper bound is 12°C. The emergent larvae, 3.3 to 5.7 millimeters in length, also pelagic, drift from a near-surface depth to depths of 75 meters. The larvae feed on zooplankton until they reach 20 millimeters in length and their fin rays are formed. Optimal temperatures range from 4° to 12°C. The larvae are vulnerable to a wide range of predators, including spiny dogfish, sea raven, hake, halibut, flounder, and adult cod.

As they age, larvae move deeper, until they reach the ocean bottoms as first-year juvenile codfish. Juveniles, especially in the first and second years, cluster in areas of spawning activity at depths of 25–75 meters. Often, they cluster to try to avoid cannibalism by adult cod. Larger juveniles overwinter on the banks with adult cod. Both juveniles and adults consume a varied diet, including zooplankton, especially copepods, as well as shrimp, crabs, and

5. Fahay and Northeast Fisheries Science Center, *Essential Fish Habitat Source Document*, 1.

small fish such as capelin, herring, and juvenile redfish. Cod predators, apart from humans, primarily are large sharks.

Self-sustainable stocks of *Gadus morhua* are found across the North Atlantic and Arctic Oceans. In the northeast, there are six distinct cod habitats: At the northern limits of its range, between 80° and 62° north latitude, the northeast Arctic cod stock inhabits the Barents Sea as far north as Svalbard and migrates south to spawn along the west coast of Norway.[6] The western Greenland stock extends south from Disko Bay (69° north) to the tip of Greenland (60° north) at Cape Farewell.[7] The Icelandic–eastern Greenland stock centered on 65° north latitude has spawning grounds located between Iceland's west coast and Greenland.[8] Two self-sustainable Faroe Island stocks have been identified along the 62° parallel.[9] The North Sea stock stretches between the 61° and the 51° parallels.[10] Just to the east, two distinct bodies of cod live in the Baltic Sea.[11] All these stocks had long been known and exploited by European fishermen before the opening of the New World cod fisheries in the late 1400s.

6. Odd Nakken, "Causes of Trends and Fluctuations in the Arcto-Norwegian Cod Stock," in *Cod and Climate Change: Proceedings of a Symposium Held in Reykjavík, 23–27 August 1993*, edited by Jakob Jakobsson and the International Council for the Exploration of the Sea, ICES Marine Science Symposia, v. 198 (Copenhagen: International Council for the Exploration of the Sea, 1994), 213, fig. 1.

7. Erik Buch, Svend Aage Horsted, and Holger Hovgard, "Fluctuations in the Occurrence of Cod in Greenland Waters and Their Possible Causes," in *Cod and Climate Change: Proceedings of a Symposium Held in Reykjavík, 23–27 August, 1993*, edited by Jakob Jakobsson and International Council for the Exploration of the Sea, ICES Marine Science Symposia, v. 198 (Copenhagen: Denmark International Council for the Exploration of the Sea, 1994).

8. Sigfus A. Schopka, "Fluctuations in the Cod Stock off Iceland during the Twentieth Century in Relation to Changes in the Fisheries and Environment," in *Cod and Climate Change: Proceedings of a Symposium Held in Reykjavík, 23–27 August 1993*, edited by Jakob Jakobsson and the International Council for the Exploration of the Sea, ICES Marine Science Symposia, v. 198 (Copenhagen: International Council for the Exploration of the Sea, 1994).

9. S. H. I. Jakupsstovu and Jakup Reinert, "Fluctuations in the Faroe Plateau Cod Stock," in *Cod and Climate Change: Proceedings of a Symposium Held in Reykjavík, 23–27 August 1993*, edited by Jakob Jakobsson and the International Council for the Exploration of the Sea, ICES Marine Science Symposia, v. 198 (Copenhagen: International Council for the Exploration of the Sea, 1994).

10. Henk Heesen and Niels Daan, "Cod Distribution and Temperature in the North Sea," in *Cod and Climate Change: Proceedings of a Symposium Held in Reykjavík, 23–27 August 1993*, edited by Jakob Jakobsson and the International Council for the Exploration of the Sea, ICES Marine Science Symposia, v. 198 (Copenhagen: International Council for the Exploration of the Sea, 1994).

11. Ole Bagge and Fritz Thurow, "The Baltic Cod Stock: Fluctuation and Possible Causes," in *Cod and Climate Change: Proceedings of a Symposium Held in Reykjavík, 23–27 August 1993*, edited by Jakob Jakobsson and the International Council for the Exploration of the Sea, ICES Marine Science Symposia, v. 198 (Copenhagen: International Council for the Exploration of the Sea, 1994).

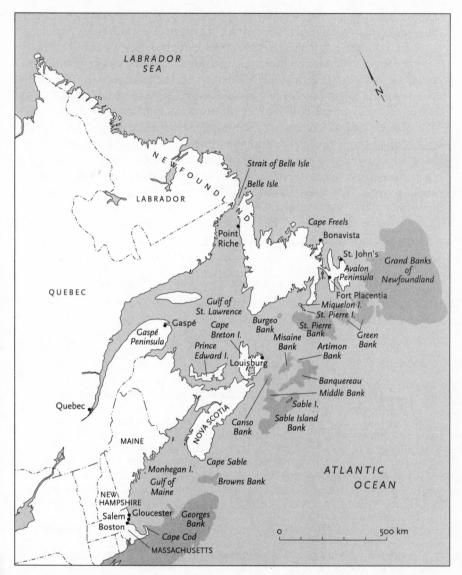

Map 15.1 North Atlantic and New England fishing grounds. Adapted from W. T. East-erbrook and Hugh G. J. Aitken, *Canadian Economic History* (Toronto: Macmillan Co. of Canada, 1967), p. 28.

In the northwest, the New World cod habitats do not extend as far north into the Arctic Ocean as do those in the northeast. New World cod habitats, however, are found much further to the south. Self-sustaining cod stocks are found in several areas. The Labrador and Newfoundland stocks inhabit the area from 61° to 43° north along the east coast of Labrador to the banks off the east and southern coasts of Newfoundland.[12] Between 52° and 45°, the Gulf of Saint Lawrence shelters two cod stocks, a northern and a southern, each of which spends the spring and summer months in the gulf for spawning but migrates to areas just outside it for the winter.[13] An eastern and a western stock inhabit offshore waters along the Scotian shelf, off the southeastern coast of Nova Scotia between 46° and 42° latitude.[14] The Gulf of Maine stock (44° to 42°) is found in the offshore waters marked by Cape Sable (in Nova Scotia) to the north and Cape Cod to the south.[15] The Georges Bank stock (42° to 40°) is linked to the southern New England–mid-Atlantic stocks that terminate at 35°, at Cape Hatteras.

THE EARLY NEW WORLD COD FISHERY

Breton, Norman, and Spanish and French Basque fishermen dominated New World cod fisheries throughout the sixteenth century. A smaller number of Portuguese and English vessels crossed the North Atlantic each season.[16] The fishery divided into two approaches: the offshore, or banks, fish-

12. C. T. Taggert et al., "Overview of Cod Stocks, Biology, and Environment in the Northwest Atlantic Region of Newfoundland, with Emphasis on Northern Cod," in *Cod and Climate Change: Proceedings of a Symposium Held in Reykjavík, 23–27 August 1993*, edited by Jakob Jakobsson and the International Council for the Exploration of the Sea, ICES Marine Science Symposia, v. 198 (Copenhagen: International Council for the Exploration of the Sea, 1994).

13. Ghislain A. Chouinard and Alain Frechet, "Fluctuations in the Cod Stocks of the Gulf of St. Lawrence," in *Cod and Climate Change: Proceedings of a Symposium Held in Reykjavík, 23–27 August, 1993*, edited by Jakob Jakobsson and International Council for the Exploration of the Sea, ICES Marine Science Symposia, v. 198 (Copenhagen, Denmark International Council for the Exploration of the Sea, 1994).

14. Kenneth T. Frank, Kenneth F. Drinkwater, and Fredrick H. Page, "Possible Causes of Recent Trends and Fluctuations in Scotian Shelf/Gulf of Maine Cod Stocks," in *Cod and Climate Change: Proceedings of a Symposium Held in Reykjavík, 23–27 August 1993*, edited by Jakob Jakobsson and the International Council for the Exploration of the Sea, ICES Marine Science Symposia, v. 198 (Copenhagen: International Council for the Exploration of the Sea, 1994).

15. Fredric M. Serchuk et al., "Fishery and Environmental Factors Affecting Trends and Fluctuations in the Georges Bank and Gulf of Main Atlantic Cod Stocks: An Overview," in *Cod and Climate Change: Proceedings of a Symposium Held in Reykjavík, 23–27 August 1993*, edited by Jakob Jakobsson and the International Council for the Exploration of the Sea, ICES Marine Science Symposia, v. 198 (Copenhagen: International Council for the Exploration of the Sea, 1994).

16. Portuguese participation in the early New World cod fisheries seems to have been limited. Darlene Abreu-Ferreira, "Terra Nova through the Iberian Looking Glass: The Portuguese-

ery and the inshore, or sedentary, fishery. The first produced wet, salted, actually pickled fish; and the second, sun-dried, salted fish.

As its name implies, the offshore fishery exploited the banks located well offshore from Labrador, Newfoundland, Nova Scotia, and New England.[17] European fishermen preyed on stocks of fish found lying near the ocean bottom in a dozen or more shallow offshore banks. Well-provisioned ships loaded with salt set off from Atlantic ports as early as January each year. Consumers in France, Italy, Spain, and Portugal had long been accustomed to, and enjoyed, pickled fish. In addition, sea salt could be had cheaply in the Bay of Biscay and along the coasts.

Ships and crews were not large for the period. Ships known as bankers ranged from forty to one hundred tons capacity and carried fifteen to twenty men, who were both seamen and fishermen. Captains steered by latitude, guided by readily available charts. They identified the banks by soundings as well as by sightings of seabirds hovering over concentrations of fish.

During the voyage, the crew erected an outboard staging along one side of the ship. When they reached the banks, the leather-apron-clad crew members, each sheltered by an upright half-hogshead stood on the outboard staging to fish. Each man cast two lines simultaneously to within a few feet of the bottom. Baiting his hooks with cod entrails or pieces of herring, each might take twenty-five to as many as four hundred codfish a day. Most of the cod caught in the sixteenth and seventeenth centuries probably ranged between four and fifteen kilograms—substantially larger than those taken today. The very largest specimens were close to two meters in length and more than a hundred kilograms in weight.

When caught, the fish were dressed, thrown in a salting tub for several days, and then packed in the hold between layers of salt.[18] As soon as the boat was full, carrying from twenty thousand to twenty-five thousand heavily salted "wet," or "green," codfish, the captain returned to his home port to sell them. If he arrived in time for the Lenten season in France and the Mediterranean countries, his profits soared. Banker vessels could make two or even three trips to the offshore fishery before the season closed.

Sun drying and lightly salting offered an alternative means of preserving the catch. By the 1540s, the sedentary, or inshore, fisheries had begun on the eastern coast of Newfoundland. Sun-dried cod kept better and found an excellent market in the Mediterranean countries. The inshore fishers timed

Newfoundland Cod Fishery in the Sixteenth Century," *Canadian Historical Review* 79, no. 1 (1998).

17. Charles de La Morandière, *Histoire de la pêche française de la morue dans l'Amérique septentrionale (des origines à 1789)* (Paris: Maisonneuve et Larose, 1962), 1:27–32.

18. Harold Adams Innis, *The Cod Fisheries: The History of an International Economy*, rev. ed. (Toronto: University of Toronto Press, 1954), 47–48.

their spring departure from European Atlantic ports to precede the massing of capelin and cod inshore in early summer. Inshore vessels were large, up to 250 or even 300 tons capacity, and had crews of up to 150 men. At the end of a five- to six-week, two-thousand-mile voyage, the fishing vessels pushed through offshore ice to land in one of dozens of sheltering harbors and coves on Newfoundland or along the mainland.

After securely mooring their ship, the crew built a covered timber wharf with tables for cleaning fish, huts for the crew, and several chest-high, thirty-meter or more, open wooden drying racks along the shore. As soon as the shore facilities were complete, the crew unloaded fifteen or more open fishing boats, ten to twelve meters in length, equipped with sails and oars. They dug mussels from the beach for bait, then caught herring and, when they arrived, spawning capelin.

Early every morning, each small boat, crewed by three to four men, set out to fish the shallows just off the coast. They used hand lines up to sixty meters in length, to which were attached weights and baited hooks. The cod were readily hooked; they were hauled into the boat and the lines recast. When the crew had a full boatload, they returned to the fishing wharf. On the wharf, a "header" dexterously gutted and decapitated each fish and carefully saved the liver for its oil in a separate container. Next, a "splitter" cut the fish lengthwise and removed the backbone. Young helpers stacked and brushed the fish sections with salt on a wooden board. After salting, the stacked fish were taken to the drying table and exposed to the sun.

As the season progressed, freight vessels turned up in each harbor to buy dried fish and carry them back to European markets. By September, this annual cycle was largely complete as each fishing vessel packed up the last of its catch in its own hold and sailed for home.

By the late 1500s, New World cod fishing had become an important industry for early modern Europe. Basque maritime entrepreneurs flourished in the fisheries. For example, Adam de Chibau, a prominent French Basque merchant, mobilized funds from a consortia of fellow merchants to send eight fishing vessels on repeated voyages to Newfoundland between 1601 and 1611. These were evidently profitable. De Chibau maintained a high and influential position as a burgess in local society and left an estate worth 30,000 ducats when he died.[19]

Interest in the industry's potential ran high in official and mercantile circles, and reports about the cod fishery proliferated. For example, in 1578, the English traveler Anthony Parckhurst described in a letter to M. Richard Hakluyt "the sundry navies that come to Newfoundland or Terra nova [sic],

19. Michael M. Barkham, "French Basque 'NewFound Land' Entrepreneurs and the Import of Codfish and Whale Oil to Northern Spain, c. 1580 to c. 1620: The Case of Adam de Chibau, Burgess of Saint-Jean-de-Luz and 'Sieur de St. Julien,' " *Newfoundland Studies* 10, no. 1 (1994).

for fish."[20] Parckhurst lists, in what was probably an underestimate, 150 French and Breton vessels totaling 7,000 tons capacity, 50 Portuguese vessels at 3,000 tons, more than 100 Spanish vessels at 5,000 to 6,000 tons, and 50 English vessels with unspecified tonnage, for a total of 350 or more boats with 17,000 or more tons capacity fishing for cod in that year. Research published in 1997 suggests that the totals were probably much larger. In 1580, an English intelligence operative estimated in a report that 500 French vessels engaged in the New World fisheries.[21]

After 1580, when the Danish monarch imposed hefty license fees on boats in Icelandic waters, numerous English West Country fishermen shifted from Icelandic to North American waters. During this period, however, Spanish and Portuguese New World fishing for cod dwindled to insignificance. To some extent, this decline was due to the wars between Spain and England. In the last two decades of the sixteenth century, English raiders and pirates harassed and captured Spanish and Portuguese fishing vessels off Newfoundland.[22] When the war ended in 1604, the Anglo-Spanish treaty of that year granted English traders permission to bring New World codfish into Iberian markets.[23] Thereafter, Spanish fishermen could not compete successfully with the French and English.

The annual flow of wet and dry codfish was a welcome addition to the European diet. Vigorous distribution networks and far-flung markets for New World cod quickly emerged. For example, Bordeaux, along with Rouen and La Rochelle, was a major center for outfitting and supplying New World fishing vessels (largely Basque) and a leading entrepôt for returning ships laden with cod. By midcentury, Bordeaux traders were buying tons of cod and shipping it along the rivers of Aquitaine to Cahors, and to Toulouse and Mont-de-Marsan. By then, cod had "become the market leader among commercially-available salt fish in the country around Bordeaux, overtaking sardines, herring and salmon, not to mention its medieval competitor, hake from Brittany."[24]

Cod's appeal lay partly in its palatability. Consumers preferred it to the other salt fish. Partly it was price. Cod, for example, sold for less than half the price of hake in this period. River toll records and notarial sales contracts for salt fish show that cod had become a consumer staple by the end of the century.[25]

20. Innis, *The Cod Fisheries*, 9–10.
21. Laurier Turgeon, "Bordeaux and the Newfoundland Trade during the Sixteenth Century," *International Journal of Maritime History* 9, no. 2 (1997): 8.
22. Ralph Greenlee Lounsbury and the Kingsley Trust Association, *The British Fishery at Newfoundland, 1634–1763* (New Haven: Yale University Press, 1934), 28–31.
23. Innis, *The Cod Fisheries*, 92.
24. Turgeon, "Bordeaux and the Newfoundland Trade during the Sixteenth Century," 21.
25. Ibid., 22; 28, table 4.

SEVENTEENTH CENTURY

During the seventeenth century, English fishing fleets, directly supported by the English state and mercantile communities, moved aggressively to gain a foothold in the inshore dried fish industry in the southeastern corner of Newfoundland. The English fleet challenged the French industry in size and scale. Dried cod from Newfoundland became the basis of a three-cornered trade between Newfoundland, Spain, and England. In Harold Innis's trenchant comment, "Cod from Newfoundland was the lever by which [England] wrested her share of the riches of the New World from Spain."[26]

Slowly, small populations of more or less permanent inhabitants grew up around the fishing harbors in Newfoundland and Nova Scotia. These "winterers" stayed behind when the fishing boats left and lived off the land. The French established colonies with small contingents of troops in Nova Scotia and on the Avalon Peninsula at Fort Placentia in Newfoundland. The British set up a colony at Saint John's. However, settlement was not critical to the annual operation of the inshore fisheries. Year after year, the fleets came, caught and processed their catches, and departed.

Exploitation of the New World fisheries grew substantially when English and French mariners discovered the prolific fishing grounds of New England. During the sixteenth century, European fishermen had hardly touched the New England stocks. It was only after a series of exploratory voyages made by English and French mariners that the value of this resource became better known. The first English expedition, that of Bartholomew Gosnold in 1602, arrived in Maine waters and sailed south along the coast until it reached the great peninsula of present-day Massachusetts. As a member of the party commented, "Neere this Cape we came to anchor in fifteene fadome, where wee tooke great store of Cod-fish, for which we altered the name, and called it Cape Cod."[27] Gosnold returned with high praise for the richness of the New England coastal waters, which he deemed superior to those of Newfoundland.[28] Stimulated by these reports, merchant syndicates and individual entrepreneurs organized several more English voyages and attempts to found colonies of settlement. In the same years, Virginian colonists from Jamestown sent fishing expeditions north to the New England banks to obtain badly needed food for their settlement.

The French, too, were actively involved in reconnaissance. From New

26. Innis, *The Cod Fisheries*, 52.

27. Faith Harrington, " 'Wee Tooke Great Store of Cod-Fish': Fishing Ships and First Settlements on the Coast of New England, 1600–1630," in *American Beginnings: Exploration, Culture, and Cartography in the Land of Norumbega*, edited by Emerson W. Baker (Lincoln: University of Nebraska Press, 1994), 194.

28. Raymond McFarland, *A History of the New England Fisheries, with Maps* (Philadelphia: University of Pennsylvania; New York: D. Appleton and Company, 1911), 31–32.

France, Samuel de Champlain commanded a carefully planned and executed exploration of the New England coast in 1605. Champlain's surveys resulted in the publication of accurate maps of the New England coast that included descriptions of harbors, water depths, and location of fishing banks.
All these accounts praised the virtues of New England. The southern fisheries
boasted relatively shallow fishing grounds close to shore, numerous large
codfish for the taking, and good shore sites for drying and processing.

In the 1620s, cod fishing off New England's shores—although it engaged
only a fraction of the number of boats that sailed for Newfoundland—had
become an alternative destination for West Country English fishermen. By
the end of the decade, there were at least ten seasonal fishing stations in use
from Maine's Monhegan Island in the north as far south as Cape Ann off
Massachusetts. Each year between January and March, forty to fifty fishing
vessels left Plymouth, Falmouth, or other English West Country ports for the
New England banks; they returned by September fully laden with codfish.

In the 1640s, partly as a result of the English Civil War, colonists who had
begun to settle coastal villages started a commercial fishery that soon supplanted that of the English fishermen.[29] Operating in smaller boats,
seventeenth-century colonial cod fishers tapped the mid-Atlantic and Gulf of
Maine cod stocks. They set up shore stations to produce dried cod from inshore fisheries. By 1675, there were reportedly 440 boats and one thousand
colonial fishermen operating in the New England inshore fishery.[30] This
fleet was producing some 60,000 quintals (6,250 metric tons) of dried fish
per year.

Enterprising New England traders profited by sending their own vessels
bearing dried fish, timber, and other commodities directly to Mediterranean
Europe and the West Indies. In the latter part of the century, New England
merchants also carried flour, meat, and other provisions, as well as West Indies sugar and rum, north to Newfoundland settlements.

The New World cod fisheries grew in size, capital investment, and production in the seventeenth century. In 1677, for example, 109 English vessels sailed to Newfoundland for the inshore fishery. When they arrived, they
deployed 892 four-man boats. Settlers wintering on Newfoundland put another 337 fishing boats in the water. The total number of cod landed by English fishermen in that year produced 238,000 quintals (12,138 metric tons)
of dried codfish for British or wider European markets. The average return

29. Douglas R. McManis, *Colonial New England: A Historical Geography* (New York: Oxford
University Press, 1975), 102–7; Daniel Vickers and the Institute of Early American History and
Culture, *Farmers and Fishermen: Two Centuries of Work in Essex County, Massachusetts, 1630–1850*
(Chapel Hill: University of North Carolina Press, for the Institute of Early American History and
Culture, Williamsburg, Va., 1994), 98–99.

30. Vickers and the Institute of Early American History and Culture, *Farmers and Fishermen*,
100.

load per vessel was 2,183 quintals (111.4 metric tons) of dried fish, and the average production per five-man rowed fishing boat was 194 quintals that year.[31] In general, each five-man boat (three in the boat and two ashore) employed in the British inshore dry cod fishery was expected to produce about 200 quintals (10.2 metric tons) of dried fish each season.[32]

Newfoundland settlers ("planters") put one-third (340) of the boats in the water, and seasonal vessels from England represented two-thirds (708), for an average of 1,048 each season—a presumed workforce of 5,240 fishermen. The average catch was 214 quintals (10.9 metric tons) per boat, or 11,232 tons in a good year. These averages disguise considerable fluctuation between good seasons and poor seasons. Annual catches sank as low as 125,000 quintals (6,375 metric tons) in 1684 and went as high as 347,000 quintals (17,697 metric tons) in the bumper year of 1692.[33] Since the numbers of boats were relatively constant, these variations probably reflect natural fluctuations in cod numbers rather than the intensity of the fishing effort—at least in this period.

French production and capacity was similar to that of the English. In 1664, an official inventory prepared for Colbert listed seventeen ports that had sent 352 fishing vessels to the New World. Of these vessels, the report specifically identified 120 as bankers (pêche errante), which had brought back wet, salted fish from the offshore fishery, and 232 as pêche sédentaire of the inshore fishery, which had caught and processed dried fish.[34] If we presume a per-vessel average return of 2,000 quintals of either dried or wet fish carried back to France, then in a good year, a fleet of that size should have produced 264,000 quintals (13,464 metric tons) of heavily salted wet cod and 464,000 quintals (23,673 metric tons) of dried codfish. The total combined would have been 37,137 tons of cod in a good year.

In 1704, the fishing convoy returning from inshore fishing at the French settlement of Plaisance consisted of 43 vessels of 5,741 metric tons crewed

31. C. Grant Head, Eighteenth Century Newfoundland: A Geographer's Perspective (Toronto: McClelland and Stewart, 1976), 63. Head writes, "In 1677, the total cod landings in English Newfoundland produced more than 220,000 quintals of dried fish, and this was probably typical of that decade." The number of vessels and boats comes from table 3 in D. H. Cushing, The Provident Sea (Cambridge: Cambridge University Press, 1988), 70. I have used Pope's adjusted figures for the 1677 catch (see below).

32. Peter Pope, "Early Estimates: Assessment of Catches in the Newfoundland Cod Fishery, 1660–1690," in Papers Presented at the Conference Entitled "Marine Resources and Human Societies in the North Atlantic since 1500," October 20–22, 1995 (St. John's, Newfoundland: The Institute of Social and Economic Research, Memorial University of Newfoundland, 1997), 11.

33. Ibid., 30, table 2. I have recalculated Pope's figures using the total catch figures he provides to arrive at a nine-year average. For 1682, I used 203,500 quintals, splitting the difference between his higher and lower estimates for that year.

34. De la Morandière, Histoire de la pêche française de la morue dans l'Amérique septentrionale, 1:315. The figure for inshore vessels is 132, which I take to be an error for 232.

by 1,508 men. This fleet brought 123,000 quintals (6,273 metric tons) of dried fish to French ports. This works out to 2,860 quintals (146 metric tons) per vessel, or 81.6 quintals (4.2 metric tons) per man fishing, considered to be "fort abondante."[35]

These data suggest that in the seventeenth century the English and French fishing fleets carried an average of 35,000 metric tons of dried cod-fish and 12,000 tons of wet codfish for sale to European consumers each year. A smaller quantity of less desirable codfish was beginning to be taken up by Barbados and other West Indies sugar islands to feed a growing slave population. The Canary and Madeira Islands also imported fish, as well as other commodities, from New England. In addition, a growing settler population along the North American coast, over 100,000 persons by 1700, certainly consumed a share of the catch.[36]

THE EIGHTEENTH CENTURY

French and British exploitation of the New World cod fisheries intensified in the eighteenth century. The flow of fish to Europe and the Caribbean quadrupled. The French New World fisheries continued despite two significant imperial defeats inflicted by the British in 1713 and 1763. Although the terms of the 1713 Treaty of Utrecht forced the French out of Newfoundland and Nova Scotia, they retained Cape Breton Island and the right to catch and dry fish along the western shore of Newfoundland. That the French negotiated tenaciously for New World fishing rights as part of the postwar settlement attests to the economic value of the cod fishery.

After 1713, the French consolidated their maritime holdings by establishing the city of Louisburg on Cape Breton Island as a headquarters for the inshore fishery, and by occupying Ile Saint Jean (Prince Edward Island) and the Gaspé Peninsula.[37] French fishing vessels also traveled north to Labrador. In 1719, five hundred fishing vessels sailed from a dozen French ports for the North American cod fishery. Approximately half engaged in inshore fishing for cod to dry and half in offshore banks fishing for wet cod.[38] A few additional vessels sailed out from Quebec. For a half century, the French cod

---

35. Ibid., 1:498.

36. The population of New England was about 93,000 in 1700. McManis, *Colonial New England*, 68–69, table 1. For English Newfoundland, there was a total of 3,450 permanent inhabitants in 1715; see Head, *Eighteenth Century Newfoundland*, 256. Total population in New France in 1700 was less than 6,000 persons. Quebec, by far the largest town, had only 2,000 settlers in 1700. Raymond Douville and Jacques Donat Casanova, *Daily Life in Early Canada*, 1st Amer. ed. (New York: Macmillan, 1968), 82.

37. De la Morandière, *Histoire de la pêche française de la morue dans l'Amérique septentrionale*, 2:643–82.

38. Innis, *The Cod Fisheries*, 169.

fishery flourished as a vigorous competitor to the English fishery. In 1745, clearly a good year, the French fishery produced 1.1 million quintals (56,100 metric tons) of dried fish for sale in Mediterranean markets, 15,600 tons of wet cod (3.9 million fish weighing 4 kilograms each, counted individually for the Parisian market), and 689,400 gallons of cod liver oil.[39]

The Treaty of Paris in 1763 forced the French to give up their colonial settlements on the mainland as well as Cape Breton and Prince Edward Islands. The French did retain possession of the two small islands of Saint Pierre and Miquelon, just south of Newfoundland, as a fishing base.[40] The British permitted French fishing vessels seasonal landing privileges along the shore of Newfoundland between Point Riche in the west to Bonavista in the north. Despite these setbacks, by the 1770s the French fleet had nearly returned to its former numbers and productivity. French inshore fishermen marketed an average of 361,258 quintals (18,425 metric tons) of dried salt cod per year and the banks fishermen brought back another 100,000 to 130,000 quintals (5,100 to 6,630 metric tons) of wet fish for the Parisian market.[41]

After 1713, the English fishery grew rapidly. Newfoundland remained a busy island fishing platform off the coast of North America that produced an ever increasing tonnage of fish for Europe and the West Indies. The diplomatic accord turned over the inshore fishery on Newfoundland's southern coast, previously worked by the French, to English fishermen. Political stability encouraged English expansion into previously untapped inshore fisheries along the inland coast from Cape Freels to Cape Saint John. The number of three-man fishing boats put in the water each season rose to around twenty-two hundred by the early 1770s. The annual catch from the enlarged inshore cod fishery of Newfoundland produced double the seventeenth-century levels, or 500,000 quintals (25,500 metric tons) of sun-dried fish, in the 1740s. Thereafter, average production rose only slightly, to 550,000 quintals (28,050 metric tons) in the 1770s.[42]

English fishermen and their backers, stimulated by rising market demand, sent vessels for the first time to the offshore banks to fish directly from shipboard. Unlike the French, they had no home market for heavily salted wet cod and required dried fish for the southern European market. The English bankers necessarily had to salt their catch heavily at sea to keep it from spoiling in the weeks required to fill their holds. But in a new departure, the bankers then pulled in to Newfoundland beaches, washed off their fish and

39. Ibid., 168.

40. Ibid., 183–85; de la Morandière, *Histoire de la pêche française de la morue dans l'Amérique septentrionale*, 2:731.

41. Innis, *The Cod Fisheries*, 182.

42. Head, *Eighteenth Century Newfoundland*, 65, 70, 140.

had them sun-dried before export. An official report of 1726 describes the process:

> The Country Ships that come here to fish upon the Banks, generally leave England [in February] & are in the some time [sic] in March, the first thing they doe is Land their Stores, & make choice of a Stage & flakes belonging to it, what they call a Ships Room. . . .
> Their first trip to the Bankes [sic] is generally the beste, the coldness of the Season allowing them to stay the longer out: as they catch the fish they Split them & Salt 'em then lay 'em down in the Ships hold, where they lay till they goe into the Harbour, they [sic] they take them out & Spread them upon the Fleakes, where they lay for a day or two if the Weather will allow. . . . Some time after this they lay them together in small heaps about a dozen or 14 of them . . . & Spread them again in the mornings; after that they put them up into larger heaps, what they call piles, & from thence leave them as they require & the Weather will allow, until they are fit to goe aboard ship.[43]

By the early 1770s, the English offshore fishery deployed 150 to 200 bankers, which together generated around 100,000 quintals (5,100 metric tons) of dried fish each year.

SETTLEMENT ON NEWFOUNDLAND

Newfoundland moved slowly toward a colony of settlement. Had fishing not been available to settlers, the island's harsh climate and skimpy soil would have discouraged European settlement. Cod fishing provided an adequate living—especially for migrants from Ireland, who became a substantial portion of the settled population. The island's summer fishing-season population jumped from six thousand persons in the early eighteenth century to twenty-five thousand by the 1740s and remained at that level for the remainder of the century.[44] Gradually the proportion of wintering to migratory summer residents grew to half in the 1770s. Women and children constituted only one-fourth of the resident population—single male laborers continued to dominate through the century.

After 1713, other resources were exploited commercially for the first time. Settlers constructed weirs and used seines to catch Atlantic salmon when they came up streams to spawn in July. They strung large nets along the coastal headlands in December, waited for shoals of seals to approach, and then pulled up the nets at the right moment. Seal oil, like cod oil, was very much in demand. Both salmon fishing and sealing provided substantial additional

43. Ibid., 73–74.
44. Head, *Eighteenth Century Newfoundland*, 56, 232.

income, especially in the northern areas of the island. Relatively small numbers of furs also augmented Newfoundlanders' income.[45]

Settlers were slow to move inland from the coast, even though colonists were given clear title to lands they occupied and cultivated. Clause VII of the Parliamentary Act to Encourage the Trade to Newfoundland in 1699 provided permanent title for lands used by settlers and offered protected seasonal use of beach sites to migratory fishermen. Total cultivated land on the island was just over a thousand hectares in the early 1770s. Given low yields and poor soil, the cultivated area did not produce enough food for the year-round inhabitants, let alone the summer migratory influx. Massive amounts of food imports were essential. Bread, biscuits, flour, pork, beef, peas, butter, molasses, and rum were the staples.[46] In 1763, American traders and shippers sent to Newfoundland ports over 1 million pounds of breadstuffs, 653 barrels of pork, 19,580 gallons of molasses, and 57,420 gallons of rum—the latter from the West Indies. English West Country merchants shipped breadstuffs, peas, sugar, beer, cider, and cheese. Irish traders sent hundreds of barrels of butter, pork, and beef. Just how dependent Newfoundland was on imports became apparent when American imports ceased and English shipping dwindled during the American Revolutionary years.

The slow pace of settlement and cultivation, however, did not prevent steady, cumulative deforestation. In 1500, the forests, while not all that impressive in size, did cover most of the island's land surface. In the coastal areas frequented by fishermen, mature conifers, eighty to one hundred years old, reached twenty to thirty feet high and had diameters measuring four to five inches at breast height. Trees in the interior forests were considerably larger. By the 1770s, the coastal forests had been stripped away for fuel and building needs and the interior forests were under active assault.[47]

THE NEW ENGLAND FISHERY

Like that of Newfoundland, the colonial New England cod fishery burgeoned during the 1700s. Unlike in Newfoundland, however, the fisheries were not the only, or even the principal, form of commercial production. Under the stimulus of continued immigration—which caused New England's population to rise from 93,000 persons in 1700 to 539,000 in 1770—land clearing on the settler frontier proceeded at an impressive pace during the century.[48] Domestic and foreign demand for fish and timber, two of the region's principal exports, continued to run high.

45. Ibid., 74–76.
46. Ibid., 130, 146.
47. Ibid., 45–46.
48. McManis, *Colonial New England*, 68–69.

Between 1675 and 1725, the New England fishery transformed itself from a purely regional inshore fishery into a much larger long-distance maritime industry. New England retained its local fisheries but also sent large deep-water fleets to compete with British and French fishing vessels in the waters of first Nova Scotia and then Newfoundland and Labrador. New England shipowners and entrepreneurs invested in more expensive, larger ketches and schooners. They adopted the fast, seaworthy, fore-and-aft-rigged, two-masted, 20- to 100-ton fishing schooner developed on the New England coast.[49] Depending on the season and the captain's strategy, vessels might sail to the Newfoundland offshore grounds or they might work Georges Bank off Cape Cod or any of the other smaller grounds off the New England coast.[50] Another several hundred boats were engaged in the mackerel and herring fisheries.

Boston and Salem, whose merchants financed the trade and owned many vessels, exported the bulk of dried codfish. Marblehead and Gloucester emerged as the busiest of the twenty or so fishing towns along the coast in Massachusetts, New Hampshire, and Maine. During the pre–Revolutionary War years, the New England cod fisheries employed nearly five thousand men in more than 665 vessels.[51] The average annual catch from 1768 to 1772 grew to more than 300,000 quintals (15,300 metric tons) of dried cod per year.[52] In the early 1770s, New England ships sent an average of 123,308 quintals (6,289 metric tons) of dried salt cod per year to southern European markets.[53] Together, southern European and West Indies markets paid an annual average of 152,155 pounds sterling for New England fish in the period 1768–1772.[54]

During the American Revolution, pressure on the fishing grounds eased as seafaring energies were diverted to war, and the total catch fell off con-

49. Vickers and the Institute of Early American History and Culture, *Farmers and Fishermen*, 143–52.

50. Robert Greenhalgh Albion, William A. Baker, and Benjamin Woods Labaree, *New England and the Sea* (Middletown: Wesleyan University Press, for the Marine Historical Association Mystic Seaport, 1972), 28–29.

51. McFarland, *A History of the New England Fisheries*, 112.

52. Laurier Turgeon, "Fluctuations in Cod and Whale Stocks in the North Atlantic during the Eighteenth Century," in *Papers Presented at the Conference Entitled "Marine Resources and Human Societies in the North Atlantic since 1500," October 20–22, 1995* (St. John's, Newfoundland: Institute of Social and Economic Research, Memorial University of Newfoundland, 1997), 90.

53. James G. Lydon, "Fish for Gold: The Massachusetts Fish Trade with Iberia, 1700–1773," *New England Quarterly* 54 (1981): 544–45, table 2. The figure is based on compilation of customs figures from New England and Newfoundland.

54. John J. McCusker, Russell R. Menard, and the Institute of Early American History and Culture, *The Economy of British America, 1607–1789, with Supplementary Bibliography* (Chapel Hill: University of North Carolina Press, for the Institute of Early American History and Culture, Williamsburg, Va., 1991), 108.

siderably. After 1783, French, British, and American fishing fleets returned in their former numbers.

THE MARKET FOR CODFISH

Europeans came to rely on cheap, ample supplies of North American dried and salted fish as a staple of their diet in the early modern centuries. This was especially timely, since, throughout Europe after 1500, meat consumption declined dramatically from its late medieval levels.[55] During the sixteenth century and most of the seventeenth, the price of codfish in North American and European markets moved upward. Daniel Vickers has constructed a combined index for codfish prices in North America and Spain for the period 1505–1892. The base period is 1784–1800 = 100. The index is worked out in prices converted to silver equivalents. From a low of 19 in 1505, the cod price index climbed to 72 in 1598. The index spiked at 101 in 1629. For the next forty years, until 1669, it remained at a plateau, with an annual average of 85.[56] After 1670, the cod price index began a slow decline, until prices reached a mid-eighteenth-century trough in the 40 to 60 index range. Presumably, this decline resulted from greatly increased output from the fisheries. Interruptions in fishing caused by the American and French Revolutions and the Napoleonic Wars forced cod prices to over 100 during the period 1790 to 1815.

Contemporaries fully recognized the importance of cod. In a report to the English Admiralty published in 1615, Richard Whitburne writes:

> And . . . I should here set downe a valuation of that fish (cod) which the French, Biscaines, and Portugals fetch yeerely from this coast of Newfoundland and the Banke . . . usually making two voyages every yeere thither . . . (to which places and to the coast of Canady [Canada] which lieth neere unto it and yeerely sent from those countries more than 400 saile of ships).
>
> It would seeme incredible, yea some men are of opinion, that the people of France, Spain, Portugall and Italy could not so well live if the benefit of the fishing upon that coast and your Majesties other dominions were taken from them.[57]

New World dried and salt cod became an important element in what is today recognized as the healthful Mediterranean diet.

In an average year during the seventeenth century, 47,000 metric tons of

55. Massimo Livi Bacci, *Population and Nutrition: An Essay on European Demographic History* (Cambridge: Cambridge University Press, 1990), 93–95.

56. Daniel Vickers, "The Price of Fish: A Price Index for Cod, 1505–1892," *Acadiensis* 25, no. 2 (1996): 101. I have calculated the average index for 1629–1669 from appendix 1.

57. Harold Adams Innis, *Select Documents in Canadian Economic History* (Toronto: University of Toronto Press, 1929), 16. Whitburne was present in Newfoundland in 1615.

codfish arrived in European markets. When sold, the codfish could, in theory, have supplied 136.3 billion kilocalories per year, or 373.4 million kilocalories per day, to European consumers.[58] Most of the loads went to France, Spain, and Italy, which together had a combined population of approximately 40 million persons in 1650. If we assume that 80 percent went to markets in these three countries, the equivalent of 376 million 100-gram portions would have been sold. This works out to 9.4 portions consumed per person per year, each with an energy value of 290 calories and 62 grams of protein for dried cod, or 18 grams of protein for wet cod.

In theory, then, codfish should have been readily available and affordable for ordinary consumers. This does seem to have been the situation. Data compiled in the 1930s by Earl Hamilton on commodity prices and wages for the early modern period confirm this. For example, for the period 1601 to 1650 in Andalusia in Spain, calculations made from Hamilton's annual data show that the average price of dried codfish was 4 *maravedi* (a Spanish copper coin) per 100 grams, tuna fish was 4.5 *maravedi,* and mutton was 5.7 *maravedi.*[59] That is, of the most common types of meat and fish, codfish was the cheapest. It was routinely sold in Andalusian markets in this period.

Even an ordinary urban laborer could afford it. Over the fifty-year period, a day laborer in Andalusia averaged 150.2 *maravedi* wages per day. A 100-gram portion of dried codfish would have consumed only 2.7 percent of his day's wages; a 250-gram portion, only 6.7 percent. Codfish prices in other regions in Spain were similar to those in Andalusia. Rising imports of codfish and declining prices during the eighteenth century imply that codfish retained its role as a cheap and accessible food for most Europeans.

New World cod imports rose steadily in the course of the eighteenth century. The combined average annual French and English output of dried codfish for the period 1701 to 1789 was 41,354 metric tons.[60] To this we may add

58. John Komlos, "The New World's Contribution to Food Consumption during the Industrial Revolution," *Journal of European Economic History* 27 (1998). According to table 3 on p. 74, the Newfoundland fishery sent 40 percent of its total exports, or 21,228 metric tons of fish, to England every year, and these fish contributed 50 million kilocalories per day to the British diet. This works out to 859,713.6 kilocalories per year per metric ton, or only 859.7 kilocalories per kilogram. This seems low, since USDA Nutrition Laboratory figures given earlier show 290 kilocalories per 100 gram portion of dried salt codfish. I have used the figure 2,900 kilocalories per kilograms, or 2.9 million kilocalories per ton.

59. Earl J. Hamilton, *American Treasure and the Price Revolution in Spain, 1501–1650* (Cambridge: Harvard University Press, 1934). Average prices for dried codfish are calculated from annual data in appendix 5, table A. According to the customary measurement (Libra carnicera) of codfish, 32 ounces = 920.32 grams, or 28.76 grams per ounce (177). Wages are calculated from appendix 7, table C. Coins are *maravedis* of pure copper, issued from 1603 through 1650.

60. Turgeon, "Fluctuations in Cod and Whale Stocks in the North Atlantic during the Eighteenth Century," 166, table 1. Turgeon found combined data for English and French catches for a total of thirty-one years between 1677 and 1789.

an average 9,072 metric tons for the New England fishery. The dried fish total, 50,246 tons, was 143 percent higher than the 35,000-metric-ton average
for the seventeenth century.[61] If we assume that wet fish shipments continued at one-third the volume of dried fish shipments, this would have added
13,800 tons, for a combined total of 55,000 tons (rounded). Using the calculation applied earlier for the seventeenth century, for a population grown
to 49 million, this would have made available 11.2 100-gram portions of
dried codfish per capita per year—a distinct increase from 9.4, the
seventeenth-century figure.

The catches were moving upward. Between 1785 and 1790, combined English and French fleets shipped 54,437 metric tons per year and New England
vessels carried 20,027 tons, for a total of 74,464 tons.[62] If we assume that wet
fish shipments continued to average about one-third the volume of dry fish
shipments, this puts the combined dry and wet fish total in the latter half of
the century at about 100,000 metric tons per year—roughly double that of
the seventeenth century. With 80 percent, or 80,000 tons, delivered in these
countries, the number of portions rose to 16.3 per capita in the 1780s. As
codfish deliveries increased, prices dropped, to the benefit of the consumer.

IMPACT OF THE COD FISHERY

Was the early modern catch sufficiently large to have an impact on cod stocks
and the maritime ecosystem? Most historians and biologists have assumed
that catch levels prior to twentieth-century industrial fishing were well within
a sustainable yield for the entire stock of codfish in the waters off the North
American coast. Only after five centuries, when the annual catch quadrupled
to over 800,000 metric tons during the 1960s, did the population crash due
to overfishing.[63]

Early modern cod landings were well below the late-twentieth-century figure. D. H. Cushing, basing his calculation on intermittent data on numbers
of fishing vessels, concludes that, each year, "up to 250,000 tonnes of fish
fresh from the sea were taken from about 1580 to 1750."[64] Peter Pope, who

61. Vickers and the Institute of Early American History and Culture, *Farmers and Fishermen*,
154, table 4.

62. The highest combined English and French totals occurred in the five years between
1785 and 1789, when the annual live catch averaged 245,502 metric tons live weight for these
two fleets alone (Turgeon, "Fluctuations in Cod and Whale Stocks in the North Atlantic during
the Eighteenth Century," 106).

63. Pope, "Early Estimates," 26.

64. Cushing, *The Provident Sea*, 74–75. Cushing assumed that each quintal equaled 112.2
pounds. However, a quintal of dried fish "from the sea (after heading, splitting and drying)"
equaled 227 kilograms (500 pounds) of fresh fish (ix). Under this formula, divide the number
of quintals of dried fish by .224, or multiply by 4.46, to arrive at the live catch weight. To convert live catch weight into dried fish output, multiply by .224. De la Morandière, however, as-

used both catch and total fleet tonnage data, concludes that "the total live catch at Newfoundland in this period appears to have been in the order of 200,000 metric tonnes."[65] This figure is four times the 50,000 metric tons adopted by biologists who had earlier reconstructed historical trends for cod catches.

Pope suggests that fishing at the 200,000-metric-ton level had been going on since the last half of the sixteenth century. He states that human predation at this scale probably did not have much of an impact on total cod stocks in the region, but that "European fishers may have already been putting pressure on local stocks by 1600."[66] These pressures probably made cod scarce on Newfoundland's English shore, "and fishers made, on average, only about 60 percent of the catch per boat that they had come to expect."[67]

Landings did not remain at the 200,000-metric-ton level but continued to rise. By the late 1780s, European deliveries alone amounted to 75,000 metric tons of dried fish and another 25,000 tons of wet cod (see above). Additional landings fed domestic markets in Canada and the North American colonies. The European numbers alone imply a 180 percent increase, to a 360,000-ton live catch, and the total catch might well have doubled to 400,000 tons.[68]

At the same time, fishing pressure diffused over a wider area and bore upon new cod stocks. A new commercial fishery grew up in New England in the late 1600s that exploited previously ignored codfish stocks in the mid-Atlantic, Gulf of Maine, and Georges Bank regions. Doubling the catch probably did not double landings of the Newfoundland stock—although it is likely that landings from that stock had increased by the late eighteenth century.

More recently, however, scholars have "begun to challenge commonly held assumptions concerning the time frame over which Newfoundland cod have been overexploited."[69] It has long been observed that the overall size of codfish catches had begun to shrink by mid–eighteenth century.[70] Even

---

serts that dressing and drying would remove 80 percent of the water from each carcass. In his view, a 2-kilogram codfish after drying would weigh only 350 grams. According to his calculations, the ratio drops to .175 for conversion. De la Morandière, *Histoire de la pêche française de la morue dans l'Amérique septentrionale,* 1:183.

65. Pope, "Early Estimates," 24.

66. Ibid., 27.

67. Ibid.

68. Dried weight is multiplied by 4.46, and the weight of wet cod is unadjusted.

69. Jeffrey A. Hutchings, "The Nature of Cod *(Gadus morhua):* Perceptions of Stock Structure and Cod Behavior by Fishermen, 'Experts,' and Scientists from the Nineteenth Century to the Present," in *Papers Presented at the Conference Entitled "Marine Resources and Human Societies in the North Atlantic since 1500," October 20–22, 1995,* edited by Daniel Vickers (St. John's, Newfoundland: Institute of Social and Economic Research, Memorial University of Newfoundland, 1997), 170.

70. Cushing, *The Provident Sea,* 75.

in this early period, catches at inshore fisheries declined if fished too severely. Some of the Newfoundland bays seemed to have had limits to the sustainable local catch. According to C. Grant Head:

> [There is] a tendency for the total inshore catch to not exceed a certain maximum for any long period of years. Note especially the case of Trepassy and St. Mary's, where at cycles of ten to fifteen years catches rose above 18,000 quintals, but never remained above that magnitude for more than about five years. . . . In Placentia Bay, this magnitude can be placed at about 60,000 quintals, on the Southern Shore at about 80,000 quintals, at St. John's at about 50,000, in Bonavista Bay at 30,000 and in Fogo and Twillingate district at 25,000. It is here suggested that these figures represent a maximum sustainable yield of the inshore fishing resources of each area, using the traditional fishing technology.[71]

In response to local scarcities, cod fishers moved to new, unexploited coastal regions. In the mid– to late eighteenth century, they moved across the Strait of Belle Isle to the inshore waters of eastern Labrador. In the late eighteenth century, resident Newfoundlanders intensified fishing along the island's Petit Nord, or North Shore. Perhaps the most dramatic spatial expansion came with intensified, industrialized offshore fishing.

Fish biologists have articulated a more sophisticated understanding about codfish stocks and their population configurations and dynamics. They have been negotiating between two extreme views: One long-standing popular and scientific view holds that all codfish in the entire North Atlantic region belong to a single stock that, until very recently, was thought to be nearly inexhaustible. Since codfish are "cosmopolitan wandering vagrants" within this vast region, each codfish is interchangeable with another. Only the total number of fish taken by human predation matters. In the other view, long held by fishermen with a local ecological understanding honed over generations of close observation, cod are territorial animals "unwilling to wander and[,] when they do, instinctively driven to return to their place of birth to reproduce."[72] This model implies that there are discrete cod substocks, or breeding populations, identified with particular inshore spawning grounds and annual migration patterns that can be depleted by excessive fishing.

The emerging view is of a complex system in which there are self-sustaining stocks—Newfoundland, Gulf of Maine, Saint Lawrence, Georges Bank, mid-Atlantic—that constitute separate breeding populations (listed above). However, codfish within each stock are not an undifferentiated mass. The larger stocks contain breeding populations that must be managed as separate entities. The substocks exhibit complex migratory patterns in the course of each year. According to Jeffrey A. Hutchings, "Cod tend to differ

71. Head, *Eighteenth Century Newfoundland*, 66.
72. Hutchings, "The Nature of Cod," 172.

in the timing and nature of their spawning and feeding behaviour. They also tend to differ by age; some age groups engage in feeding migrations and return to spawning areas while others remain more stationary."[73] Younger cod are more likely to remain inshore while larger cod migrate to feed.

The timing, distance, and direction of migrations may be determined by the size, age structure, local food supplies, and competition for food by other species. If food supplies change, migrations may also change. Some individuals may move from one stock to another. Heavy fishing at particular spawning sites may well have sharply depleted specific substocks and even encouraged migration. As human fishing removed larger, more mature fish from each substock, the chances of abrupt swings in the reproductive rate increased. In short, even at the seemingly "moderate" levels of the 1600s and 1700s, fishing altered the age (and perhaps gender) structures, size, weight, and spawning and feeding habits, and the overall size of codfish stocks in the North Atlantic.

Apart from annual fishing, the codfish stocks were subject to other forces that helped determine their size, distribution, and rate of reproduction in the early modern period. It is possible that early modern whaling in this region had a positive effect on codfish numbers. Basque whalers largely fished out bowhead and right whales *(Balaena mysticetus)* and *(Balaena glacialis)* from the waters around Newfoundland and Labrador by the early 1600s.[74] Thereafter, northern French Basques continued the whale fishery in the area around the Gulf of Saint Lawrence, but at a much reduced catch level. Both whales and cod occupy a similar position on the trophic food web. They both feed heavily on crustacean zooplankton—primarily copepods, euphausiids, and mysids. Eliminating large herds of whales could well have freed zooplankton for cod consumption and fostered an increase in codfish stocks by the end of the sixteenth century.[75]

COLDER WATERS

A larger issue is that of climate change. What effect did Little Ice Age cooling have on the northern oceans generally and on the cod fisheries of the New World specifically? Evidence adduced by Hubert Lamb, and more recently by A. E. J. Ogilvie and J. Jonsson, from historical annals, cod fisheries catch data, and coastal sea ice accumulation around Iceland, Greenland, and the Faroe Islands strongly suggests that a substantial cooling of the north-

73. Ibid., 173.
74. See chapter 16.
75. John J. Burns et al., *The Bowhead Whale* (Lawrence, Kans.: Society for Marine Mammalogy, 1993), 229–32.

eastern Atlantic took place in the early modern centuries.[76] This change had a demonstrable, unfavorable effect on the Icelandic–eastern Greenland codfish stocks.

Generally speaking, even though cod is a boreal fish, warmer water temperatures (below an upper limit) favor higher rates of reproduction in codfish. Cod also will shift their grounds from colder, less favorable waters to warmer waters when necessary. It is likely that Icelandic cod populations were reduced from what they had been in the warmer medieval period. Codfish in the Icelandic stock seem to have responded unfavorably to colder water temperature in this period—probably because of the vulnerability of the cod eggs and larvae to colder conditions. Female cod spawn in temperatures from $5°$ to $7°C$. Larvae require temperatures above $5°C$ and do better at even higher temperatures. The larval food supply could have been hard hit as well. If normal Atlantic Ocean waters were invaded by extremely cold polar waters that transported and preserved ice, the primary production of phytoplankton would have been sharply reduced and zooplankton populations would have collapsed, as they did in the 1960s.[77]

For Iceland, Jonsson assembled smoothed annual trends in cod catches, estimated by a qualitative index derived from the Icelandic annals, and compared these with reconstructed ocean temperatures from monthly sea ice data. His data show distinct correlations between reduced fishing output and colder temperatures. For the post-1600 period, Icelandic cod catches are "in fairly good agreement with estimated temperature variations, showing long-term fluctuations of 50–60 years."[78] During the first half of the seventeenth century, water temperatures rose in some years to above $5°C$, and cod catches rose accordingly. In the second half of the century, temperatures plummeted to a low of $2.5°C$ in the mid-1690s, and catches fell in response.[79]

---

76. H. H. Lamb, "Climatic Variation and Changes in the Wind and Ocean Circulation: The Little Ice Age in the Northeast Atlantic," *Quaternary Research* 11 (1979): 12, fig. 9; A. E. J. Ogilvie, "Documentary Evidence for Changes in the Climate of Iceland, A.D. 1500 to 1800," in *Climate since A.D. 1500*, edited by Raymond S. Bradley and Philip D. Jones, rev. ed. (London: Routledge, 1995), 105, fig. 5.4. See also D'Arrigo and Jacoby, "Dendroclimatic Evidence from Northern North America," 302, fig. 15.4.

77. J. Jonsson, "Fisheries off Iceland, 1600–1900," in *Cod and Climate Change: Proceedings of a Symposium Held in Reykjavík, 23–27 August 1993*, edited by Jakob Jakobsson and the International Council for the Exploration of the Sea, ICES Marine Science Symposia, v. 198 (Copenhagen: International Council for the Exploration of the Sea, 1994), 14.

78. Ibid., 15.

79. Lamb, "Climatic Variation and Changes in the Wind and Ocean Circulation," 15. The coldest episode appears to have been "between 1675 and 1700[, when] the water temperatures prevailing about the Faroe Islands presumably were on overall average $4°$ to $5°C$ below the average of the last 100 years, an anomaly 4 or 5 times as great as that shown by the thermometer observations of the time in central England, where the coldest decade (1690s) averaged about $1.5°C$ below the warmest decades in the earlier part of this century."

Warmer temperatures in the first half of the eighteenth century improved catches—with the usual year-to-year fluctuations. Another period of severe cold in the 1750s reduced catches so much that many Icelanders died of hunger. Better conditions followed for the period 1766–1779, only to be succeeded by colder temperatures and reduced catches for the remainder of the century. During the first half of the nineteenth century, there was a "gradual, but irregular, increase in temperatures" that resulted in better catches.[80]

Presumably the same colder conditions and broad pattern of temperature fluctuations with southward movement of polar waters occurred in the northwestern Atlantic during the early modern centuries. However, Newfoundland, unlike Iceland, does not lie at the northern limits of the cod's range. The waters undoubtedly became colder, but their impact on cod eggs, larvae, and food supplies may not have been as pronounced. Maybe cod reproduction was affected and populations were reduced overall in New World stocks because of the colder climate after 1500—but it is simply not possible to demonstrate this.

To date, no long-term correlation between temperature and catches similar to that done for the Iceland fisheries has been constructed for Newfoundland or any of the New World fisheries. Before 1700, annual catch data are intermittent at best and vary from one national fishery to another. Short-term attempts to link catch data with temperature are suggestive but show anomalies. For example, Pope has calculated the catch rate per boat from both planters and seasonal fishermen at Newfoundland for the especially cold last quarter of the seventeenth century. He has catch and boat data for nine years between 1675 and 1698. Seven years show an average rate of 185 quintals (9.4 metric tons) dried fish produced per boat—well below the 200-quintal (10.2-ton) norm.

However, in 1692, English fishermen pulled in catches that averaged 350 quintals (17.8 metric tons) per boat, and in 1698 their catches averaged 285 quintals (14.5 metric tons).[81] The 1692 catch may be attributed to a warmer period for the spawning season after a cold December and January. But the winter of 1697–1698 "became famous for its severity," with its painfully low temperatures and twenty to thirty heavy snowfalls seen in New England. Massachusetts Bay froze from January to March. A half century later, Peter Kalm, the Swedish naturalist, found Americans agreeing that the winter of 1697–1698 "was the coldest and severest which they had ever felt."[82] Moreover, none of these correlations attempts to account for the possibility that

80. Jonsson, "Fisheries off Iceland," 8, fig. 2.
81. Pope, "Early Estimates," 30, table 2.
82. Karen Ordahl Kupperman, "Climate and Mastery of the Wilderness in Seventeenth-Century New England," in *Seventeenth-Century New England: A Conference*, edited by the Colonial Society of Massachusetts (Boston: The Society, distributed by the University Press of Virginia, 1984), 31–32.

fog, storms, and ice dangers could have reduced fishing activity and catches in an age of oar and sail.

Temperature changes certainly must have had an influence on the distribution and population dynamics of the cod stocks of the northwestern Atlantic. Tracking these changes, however, with incomplete information is another matter. Even today, using much more precise and full climate data, fish catch numbers, and a variety of fish-tracking data, it is difficult for biologists to identify short-term and long-term effects of temperature changes on cod populations. Niels Daan observes:

> We have to be aware that climate influences not just cod, but also all other species of the Subarctic ecosystem. Therefore any relation between climate and cod stocks will be mediated through a complex structure of abiotic and biotic processes operating in the ecosystem. As a consequence, we cannot expect simple mechanics; in fact, the effects of climate change are likely to be so complex and unpredictable that we cannot just accept without question any simple relationship which might appear to explain much of the variation observed in cod stocks.[83]

CONCLUSION

The New World fishing industry is an example of the steady evolution of human maritime capacity since the medieval centuries, and, more generally, of the growing capacity of early modern economic institutions and the ever greater reach of the world market. After 1500, several western European societies developed new large-scale, offshore, commercial fisheries for New World cod. Never before in human history had fishing fleets regularly, every year, made such voyages—traversing thousands of kilometers of open, dangerous water across the North Atlantic—to return with great loads of codfish. To operate at this distance demanded extraordinary entrepreneurial, organizational, seafaring, and shipbuilding skills. The industry's demand for capital was large; so also was its need for labor. The tonnage of North American cod taken, processed, and consumed in Europe and its colonies climbed steadily.

In the face of prolonged colder temperatures throughout the early modern centuries, overall codfish stocks, despite local scarcities, remained abundant and easily caught. Fishing intensity and total catches fluctuated, but the resource continued. Overall output moved steadily upward decade after

83. Niels Daan, "Trends in North Atlantic Cod Stocks: A Critical Summary," in *Cod and Climate Change: Proceedings of a Symposium Held in Reykjavík, 23–27 August 1993*, edited by Jakob Jakobsson and the International Council for the Exploration of the Sea, ICES Marine Science Symposia, v. 198 (Copenhagen: International Council for the Exploration of the Sea, 1994), 269.

decade. Every year thousands of tons of highly palatable, nutritious protein fed people of all classes in North America and Europe. The average sizes of codfish caught, however, did decline from century to century. Continued, steadily intensifying, and basically unregulated fishing changed the age composition, the average size, and probably the behavior of codfish in the various New World stocks. So numerous were codfish and so resilient, however, that it took five hundred years for human fishing to cause the stocks to crash—as they did in the 1980s.

Chapter 16

Whales and Walruses
in the Northern Oceans

Before 1500, favorably situated coastal communities around the world killed and consumed whales in a largely passive, opportunistic enterprise. Shore-based fishing communities in Arctic waters off the east and west coasts of North and South America, Siberia, South Africa, New Zealand, Japan, and northern Europe intercepted whales as they made their migratory rounds each year.[1] The whales taken were those vulnerable species that appeared regularly in coastal waters and were slow-moving enough to be taken by men in small boats wielding harpoons and lances or even nets. The greater part of the catch went for subsistence needs, although all whaling groups were engaged in limited trading and exchange networks. For these communities, whales were a substantial source of meat, as well as oil for illumination and heat and whalebone for artifacts. The total catch was relatively modest and does not seem to have posed a serious threat to whale stocks. If climatic changes or other developments changed the numbers or direction of whale migrations, these communities were forced to adapt. They did not really have the means to pursue whales throughout their migratory journeys.[2]

Commercialized early modern whale hunting was a departure. For the first time in human history, hunters actively pursued whales on the open sea in regions far distant from their homes. Each summer season, European and North American whalers made the dangerous voyage into western Arctic and

---

1. Richard Ellis, *Men and Whales,* 1st ed. (New York: Knopf, 1991).

2. For right whale hunting by Indians along the southeastern Atlantic coasts of North America, see Lewis H. Larson, *Aboriginal Subsistence Technology on the Southeastern Coastal Plain during the Late Prehistoric Period* (Gainesville: University of Florida Press, 1980), 145–62. I am indebted to my colleague Peter Wood for this reference. For Northwest Pacific coast whale hunting among the Tlingit-speaking peoples of North America, see Alvin M. Josephy, *America in 1492: The World of the Indian Peoples before the Arrival of Columbus* (New York: Knopf, 1992), 55–60.

sub-Arctic waters to the limits of pack ice in search of whales, walruses, and seals. Simultaneously, the intensified, systematic shore-based whaling along the eastern coast of North America, on both Japanese coasts, and along northern Europe added to the catch. Industrial whaling in the northern oceans heavily exploited a resource that, like the codfish, had been only lightly hunted by humans. Whales and, to a lesser extent, walruses and seals became new commodities in the early modern world economy. Europe, in particular, obtained access to abundant marine resources that were free for the taking. In its new form, whaling was a spectacular and profitable aspect of the world hunt—a market-driven enterprise. Demand for whale oil and whalebone was sufficient to send increasing numbers of men and ships into northern waters. By mid–eighteenth century, the hunt for whales enlarged to include new stocks of different species in the southern oceans.

THE PREY

The prey that first drew commercial European hunters into northern Arctic waters was the walrus *(Odobenus rosmarus)*, hunted for its extended ivory tusks, tough, thick hide, and copious fat. Immense numbers of walruses, a gregarious species, lived in the pack ice in herds of several thousand closely packed individuals. Walruses are large animals. Adult males reach 270 to 356 centimeters in length, 150 centimeters in height, and weigh between eight hundred and seventeen hundred kilograms; females are somewhat smaller. This species is generally cinnamon brown with coarse hair covering a tough, wrinkled skin that is about 2–4 centimeters thick over most of the body; beneath this lies a layer of blubber that on the chest measures about 10 centimeters thick. The walrus has a ponderous, rounded body with thick fore flippers and hind flippers, each having five digits. It has a rounded head with small eyes and a muzzle with a large, thick mustache. Both sexes have distinctive tusks, which reach 100 centimeters in length in males and 80 centimeters in females. Nearly the entire tusk is ivory (dentin), and a single tusk in an older male can weigh five kilograms or more.

Shallow waters across the Arctic Ocean and its adjoining seas constitute the usual habitat of the walrus. Walruses haul themselves out of the water to rest on the ice and, in summer, sometimes on beaches and rocky islets. The animals live in huge herds ordered by dominance hierarchies established by males. They migrate south as the pack ice expands in the winter and return north in the spring as the ice recedes. They feed by diving to depths of ten to fifty meters to forage on the ocean bottom for clams and mussels and a wide array of other invertebrates and, occasionally, take fish and seals. They mate in winter and have a total gestation period of fifteen to sixteen months. In early summer, from mid-April to mid-June, mothers give birth to a single calf. Lactation lasts up to two years, and extremely strong mother-calf bonds are maintained. Full maturity comes at 9–11 years for females and 15 years for males. Maximum longevity is about 40 years.[3]

Early modern whalers hunted two closely related species of large whales: the bowhead, or Greenland, whale *(Balaena mysticetus)* found in Arctic and sub-Arctic waters, and the right whale *(Balaena glacialis)*, distributed world-wide along the coasts of Europe, Asia, Africa, and the Americas. Occasionally, the gray whale *(Eschrichtius robustus)* was captured. Later, by mid–eighteenth century, American whalers pursued sperm whales *(Physeter macrocephalus)* worldwide in a new phase of the industry. However, bowhead and right whales, not distinguished as separate species until the 1860s, remained primary targets before 1800. Over several centuries, open-water whalers, sailing in previously uncharted northern seas, developed a narrowly focused understanding of the behavior and habitat of these animals.

Why were these two species of whales the primary quarry? First, they were immense creatures. Mature animals could reach eighty to one hundred metric tons in weight but were, for all their size, inoffensive and timid. Second, they were valuable. Each bowhead or right whale contained thick layers of blubber that could be converted to oil, and had hundreds of extended 3–5 meter baleen, or whalebone, plates of a tough, pliable, strong plasticlike material for industrial use. (European whalers reserved all possible space on their ships for blubber, oil, and whalebone. They consumed only a little of the meat, if any, and simply discarded the remainder.) A single carcass was a rich prize that could be had merely for the cost of hunting it down. Third, they were vulnerable. Both species were slow swimmers who followed regular migratory routes in pursuit of food in the summer and winter seasons. Often these routes brought them close to shore. Air breathers, they spent time on the surface, often sleeping, where they could be sighted and attacked. Fourth, they could be retrieved when killed. Most bowheads and right whales did not sink when they were killed, but stayed buoyant; their carcasses could be processed in the water or towed back to shore. Finally, they were abundant. Various reconstructions put the Arctic bowhead population prior to industrial whaling at approximately 50,000 to 60,000 and the right whale population at about 80,000 animals worldwide.[4] With these numbers, the bowhead whales formed the largest standing stock of biomass of any mam-

3. Ronald M. Nowak and Ernest P. Walker, *Walker's Mammals of the World*, 5th ed. (Baltimore: Johns Hopkins University Press, 1991), s.v. "walrus."

4. For bowhead whales, see Douglas A. Woodby and Daniel B. Botkin, "Stock Sizes Prior to Commercial Whaling," in *The Bowhead Whale*, edited by John J. Burns, J. Jerome Montague, Cleveland J. Cowles, and the Society for Marine Mammalogy (Lawrence, Kans.: Society for Marine Mammalogy, 1993), 387. For right whales, see Roger Payne, *Among Whales* (New York: Scribner, 1995), 269, citing M. Klinowska, "Dolphins, Porpoises, and Whales of the World," in *The IUCN Red Data Book* (Gland, Switzerland: IUCN, 1991). See also Kim E. W. Shelden and David J. Rugh, *The Bowhead Whale, Balaena mysticetus: Its Historic and Current Status* (Seattle: National

mal in the Arctic, estimated at 2 million metric tons—far more than that of the other two numerous mammals north of the fifty-seven-degree parallel: ringed seals and caribou.[5] Surprisingly, for such a large animal, bowheads, along with other baleen whales, are only at the third trophic level. On average, each bowhead whale consumes about a hundred metric tons of zooplankton each year. Bowhead whales engulf huge quantities of tiny crustaceans (copepods, euphausiids, and mysids) that in turn feed on phytoplankton, algae, and other primary biomass in the ocean.[6]

Bowhead populations are conventionally divided into five stocks, or distinct regions of commercial exploitation. (These may have been distinct breeding populations, but marine biologists are not certain on this point.)[7] From west to east, these are the Okhotsk Sea and Bering Sea stocks in the western Arctic and northern Pacific, and the Davis Strait, Spitsbergen, and Hudson Bay stocks in the eastern Arctic and northern Atlantic. Early modern European whalers first hunted the Spitsbergen and later the Davis Strait whales, but commercial hunting of the small Hudson Bay stock and the western Arctic bowheads did not begin until mid– to late nineteenth century. Two methods of extrapolation suggest a minimum size of 25,000 bowheads for the Spitsbergen population in the early sixteenth century, and 11,000 for the Davis Strait stock, for a total of 36,000 bowhead whales.[8] It is these relatively few animals and their descendants who became the quarry for a three-hundred-and-fifty-year hunt that ended in their extinction in eastern Arctic waters.

The bowhead derives its name from the bowlike shape of its enormous mouth that constitutes two-sevenths to one-third of its total body length. Lacking a dorsal fin, the bowhead has two short, broad flippers and extended tail flukes that average one-third of body length. The whale's paired blowholes are protected by a high crown that affords a defense against ice. The arch, or bow, of the mouth rises to accommodate the baleen plates used to trap zooplankton in the whale's mouth. These plates form in two rows, one on each side of the mouth. Each main plate, or lamina, has adjacent minor

Marine Mammal Laboratory, National Marine Fisheries Service, National Oceanic and Atmospheric Administration, 1997).

5. John J. Burns et al., *The Bowhead Whale* (Lawrence, Kans.: Society for Marine Mammalogy, 1993), 1. The editors calculate that sixty thousand bowhead whales, if similar to modern bowheads, would total 2,020,000 metric tons, and that the stock would have consumed 5,720,000 tons of planktonic food annually. This is a greater amount of food than required for an estimated 7 million seals, which would consume 560,000 metric tons, or required for 4.3 million caribou, which would consume 800,000 tons.

6. Lloyd F. Lowry, "Foods and Feeding Ecology," in *The Bowhead Whale*, edited by John J. Burns, J. Jerome Montague, Cleveland J. Cowles, and the Society for Marine Mammalogy (Lawrence, Kans.: Society for Marine Mammalogy, 1993), 229–30.

7. Woodby and Botkin, "Stock Sizes Prior to Commercial Whaling," 387.

8. Ibid., 401, table 10.4. The Hudson Bay stock is put at 575 animals.

plates and baleen hairs to aid in closure. The total number of plates in each animal may reach 330 or more on each side.

The bowhead is predominantly black in color with a consistent white chin patch and scattered, nonpigmented white streaks or mottling across its body. Beneath the epidermis and dermis lies a dense, thick layer (up to 28 centimeters) of adipose and fibrous tissue referred to as blubber. The innermost layer of the skin, or hypodermis, is a soft tissue that connects the skin with the muscles and other organs. (The hypodermis permits whalers to readily strip the layer of blubber intact from the carcass.) The eyes, covered with movable lids, are located low on either side of the head. The ear channels lie just below the eyes. This warm-blooded, air-breathing mammal has enormous lung capacity and the strength to sustain itself in extended dives as it searches for subsurface plankton clouds.[9]

Bowheads inhabit largely icy Arctic waters in the region of the Atlantic between 60 and 85 degrees north and in the Pacific between 50 to 75 degrees. They tend to live on the edge of the ice pack. They swim under the ice surface in leads of open water and are powerful enough to breach ice cover up to sixty centimeters thick in order to breathe. Each spring season, segregated by sex and age class, bowheads move in loosely assembled herds north to reach largely ice-free continental shelf waters; they retreat slowly southward in the autumn as the ice cover advances. Migration speeds are slow, with travel averaging four kilometers per hour.

Bowhead whales are gregarious animals who communicate among themselves with a remarkable repertoire of low-frequency calls and songs as well as by blows and slaps on the water.[10] These whales live long—forty years or even far more—and have few natural enemies. Only the fast-swimming killer whales (Orcinus orca) are known to attack bowheads. Ice entrapment is the other occasional threat to bowheads, who can reach a point where they simply cannot break thickened ice cover.[11] As befits their size, bowheads have a slow reproductive cycle and a low annual reproductive rate.[12] Females sexually mature late, when they are about fifteen years of age (and measure 12.5

9. Jerrold T. Haldiman and Raymond J. Tarpley, "Anatomy and Physiology," in *The Bowhead Whale*, edited by John J. Burns, J. Jerome Montague, Cleveland J. Cowles, and the Society for Marine Mammalogy (Lawrence, Kans.: Society for Marine Mammalogy, 1993).

10. Bernd Wursig and Christopher Clark, "Behavior," in *The Bowhead Whale*, edited by John J. Burns, J. Jerome Montague, Cleveland J. Cowles, and the Society for Marine Mammalogy (Lawrence, Kans.: Society for Marine Mammalogy, 1993).

11. L. Michael Philo, Emmett B. Shotts Jr., and John C. George, "Morbidity and Mortality," in *The Bowhead Whale*, edited by John J. Burns, J. Jerome Montague, Cleveland J. Cowles, and the Society for Marine Mammalogy (Lawrence, Kans.: Society for Marine Mammalogy, 1993).

12. William R. Koski et al., "Reproduction," in *The Bowhead Whale*, edited by John J. Burns, J. Jerome Montague, Cleveland J. Cowles, and the Society for Marine Mammalogy (Lawrence, Kans.: Society for Marine Mammalogy, 1993).

Map 16.1 Whaling areas of the Northern Hemisphere

to 14 meters in length). Adult females calve every three to four years. Mating and conception occur in late winter and early spring. Gestation, while not known with certainty, is estimated to last thirteen to fourteen months. The nursing calves, which are born in April and May, accompany their mothers during the spring migration to the summer feeding grounds. Weaning occurs by twelve months or so. Bowhead calves grow slowly by comparison with other whale species.

Right whales, slightly smaller, share many of the physical and behavioral characteristics of bowheads. This species' mouth is nearly as large, but not as arched, as that of the bowhead. Right whales have similar baleen plates, are black in color with an irregular white belly patch, and lack a dorsal fin. Most strikingly, they are born with callosities, or "keratinous lumps and bumps," distributed across the face and head.[13] Since these callosities do not change over time, they permit confident identification of individuals. Unlike bowheads, the right whale is widely dispersed. Right whales have been found

13. Richard Ellis, *Men and Whales*, 1st ed. (New York: Knopf, 1991), 7. This work has excellent illustrations of various types of whales.

in every ocean and along the coasts of every continent, including Antarctica. Today, they exist in remnant populations totaling no more than one or two thousand animals.[14]

INDIGENOUS ARCTIC WHALING

Between 1200 and 1600 C.E., throughout the circumpolar Arctic and sub-Arctic, the Inuit (Eskimo) peoples were the most skilled and aggressive hunters of whales and other marine mammals. In contrast to the reindeer-hunting peoples of northern Eurasia or the caribou-hunting Indians of North America, the Inuits relied on the sea as their main source of subsistence. Highly specialized Inuit technology and intimate knowledge of the harsh, ice-locked environment permitted them to survive and even to live in relative comfort—much to the amazement of those Europeans who first ventured into the northern oceans. The latter were intrigued by how the Eskimos used oil from marine mammals for heat and light, stayed warm and mobile in fur and skin clothing, and took shelter in rapidly constructed snow houses that provided warmth in a frozen environment. They admired the fast and buoyant sealskin kayaks propelled by double-bladed paddles and the speed and endurance of sled dogs that pulled enormous loads on efficient, runnered sledges with seeming ease. They were impressed by the Eskimos' navigational and hunting skills displayed in the trackless land of ice and snow as they pursued the walrus, seal, and polar bear.

The indomitable Eskimos, with their cheerful resilience and skill in coping with the Arctic's hazards, became a symbol of a relatively benign, admirable, savage state for the early modern world. As European explorers and whalers recorded more ethnographic detail about Eskimo life, Inuits became stock figures in an emerging taxonomy of savage peoples. The Eskimo hunter who braved the Arctic ice and ocean waters in search of marine mammals became a trope for a superb, but limited, form of human adaptation to the most severe environment in the world.

The fully developed Arctic medieval and early modern hunting culture that depended on marine mammals and engaged in intensive whaling is known by archaeologists as the Thule culture. First appearing in the northern Bering Strait region and the Chukchi Sea coast of Alaska about 900 C.E., the Thule supplanted the Punuk and the Birnirk cultures. Over the next few hundred years, it spread rapidly westward into Siberia, as well as eastward

---

14. Robert L. Brownell et al., *Right Whales: Past and Present Status: Proceedings of the Workshop on the Status of Right Whales, New England Aquarium, Boston, Massachusetts, 15–23 June 1983* (Cambridge, Eng.: International Whaling Commission, 1986).

across all of Arctic North America as far as Labrador and Greenland.[15] Evidence for a warming trend around 1000 to 1200 C.E. has led to speculation that reduced sea ice may have opened up summer routes for migratory whales all the way across from the Bering Sea to Greenland. The ensuing abundance of whales may have encouraged dispersal of Inuits and the Thule culture. Other archaeologists have posited population growth and internecine warfare as possible push factors.[16]

The Russian anthropologist I. I. Krupnik has suggested a cyclical series of adaptations to Arctic climatic change in which warming trends attracted whales and walruses into northern waters and thereby permitted Eskimos to hunt these large mammals. During cooling trends, the large mammals retreated to southward waters, and the importance of fishing and of hunting caribou, reindeer, and seals rose.[17] The Eskimos hunted and used all accessible Arctic land and sea animals, from birds and foxes to whales. The emphasis put on each species depended on both the relative effort needed under specific circumstances and the energy return expected. The latter phase of Thule culture, between 1400 to 1600 C.E., was a cooling period during which Arctic hunters found whales less abundant and adapted accordingly.[18]

Despite contraction of the whales' ranges, however, whaling retained its central significance for Thule-era peoples. Favorably situated coastal settlements continued to hunt whales and walruses until the seventeenth century. Simply put, the economic return for whale hunting was very large indeed. According to Krupnik:

> Eskimo subsistence, like most human economies, did not escape a general evolutionary tendency toward using ever more productive, stable, and at the same time, more labor-intensive, resources in the environment. Hunting the largest sea mammal[s] such as whales and walrus required more complex hunting technology and organization, but compared to other subsistence activities yield[ed] a maximum harvest in the shortest period of time. Yet, without sufficient labor resources to store large amounts of meat quickly, the hard-won

15. Sam W. Stoker and Igor I. Krupnik, "Subsistence Whaling," in *The Bowhead Whale,* edited by John J. Burns, J. Jerome Montague, Cleveland J. Cowles, and the Society for Marine Mammalogy (Lawrence, Kans.: Society for Marine Mammalogy, 1993), 584. Thule cultural dominance of the Arctic reached its height in the thirteenth through sixteenth centuries, known as the "Baleen Period" in American archaeology. See also Robert McGhee, "Thule Prehistory of Canada," in *Handbook of North American Indians,* edited by William C. Sturtevant (Washington: Smithsonian Institution, 1978).

16. Ibid.

17. I. I. Krupnik, *Arctic Adaptations: Native Whalers and Reindeer Herders of Northern Eurasia* (Hanover, N.H.: University Press of New England, for Dartmouth College, 1993), 189–90.

18. Ibid. Krupnik speaks of the "decline of aboriginal whaling, the resumption of sealing and caribou hunting, and the desertion of large coastal villages during this period throughout the entire Eskimo ecumene from Chukotka to Greenland" (188).

catch would rot. So, utilizing such "feast-or-famine" meat supplies also required considerable additional energy to create large food reserves.[19]

Only settled, relatively densely populated communities could mobilize the human energy to hunt whales successfully. Whaling was very much a community endeavor, with communal sharing of the proceeds among all its members. Successful whale-hunting communities probably obtained well over half their food and fuel requirements from butchered whales. Calculations made on faunal remains from two Somerset Island sites in the Canadian Arctic suggest that food from whales "equaled the food from all other animals combined."[20] Feeding sled dogs—each of whom, when working, required as much food as an adult human—was made considerably easier by success in the whaling season.

The huge size of the bowhead whale, the primary target for Arctic hunters, meant that success could be measured by annual kills of only a few animals for each community. Along the Chukchi Peninsula, for example, archaeologists working with identifiable remains at coastal settlements estimate the annual kill at about 10 to 15 bowheads per year before European contact. Along the Alaskan coast, the total may have reached 45 to 60 animals. In the eastern Canadian Arctic, the annual kill was about 25 to 30 whales per year. Along the Labrador coast, hunters took 4 to 5 animals per year. For the entire west coast of Greenland, indigenous hunters took perhaps 10 animals per year; no estimate has been made for the east coast. In short, the total estimate for Arctic hunters in the late Thule period is no more than 120 to 130 animals captured per year.[21] This includes both the Spitsbergen and Bering Sea stocks of bowhead whales.

Archaeological remains show that hunters deliberately pursued immature animals whose carcasses were more manageable when landed. Yearling bowhead whales—seven to ten meters in length and 5,000 to 13,000 kilograms in weight—were the preferred targets. One reason may well have been that, despite the admitted sophistication of Eskimo whaling technology, capturing fully adult bowheads stretched its limits. For bowheads, body weight did not increase in linear fashion as body length extended. A mature adult might gain another seven to ten meters in length, reaching a total of 17 meters, but gain proportionately far more weight, reaching 80,000 to 85,000 kilograms.[22] Contrary to popular belief, selection of immature animals was probably not as damaging to the whale herds as taking mature animals in

19. Ibid., 190.

20. Allen P. McCartney and James M. Sevelle, "Thule Eskimo Whaling in the Central Canadian Arctic," *Arctic Anthropology* 22 (1985): 42.

21. Stoker and Krupnik, "Subsistence Whaling," 591–97.

22. Allen P. McCartney, "Whale Size Selection by Precontact Hunters of the North American Western Arctic and Subarctic," in *Hunting the Largest Animals: Native Whaling in the Western*

their reproductive years—especially for large mammals with such slow rates of reproduction. Selective capture of yearlings was probably less disruptive than attacking the adult population.[23]

The total array of organizational skills and technical innovations that made whale hunting successful was impressive: Inuit whalers used *umiaks*, walrus- or sealskin-covered boats (with flotation devices under the seats) that carried six to eight paddlers, a steersman, and one or two harpooners in the bow. Several of these boats, working in unison, approached a sighted whale in silence in order to make the first harpoon strike at close range. The harpoon, attached to a thirty-meter seal-hide line, had a roughly two-meter wood or bone primary shaft with an attached short foreshaft of the same materials and a detachable swivel head of bone or ivory. Inserted in the head was a slate or iron blade. The harpoon head detached from the harpoon proper when it struck the whale and swiveled within the wound to hold firmly within the animal's flesh. The harpoon shaft floated free and was recovered later. The harpoon line was attached to two or three floats made of whole, inflated sealskins that created a drag equivalent of 90 to 135 kilograms. At the strike, the harpooner threw the floats and line overboard. These floats marked the whale's whereabouts when it dived and helped the whalers to anticipate its next surfacing, when it could be attacked again. Whalers also used more powerful sea anchors or chutes made out of whalebone or baleen to exhaust the whale and slow its escape. As often as necessary, the whalers put more harpoons into the whale as the pursuit continued.

At the kill, the whalers, who sometimes climbed on the beast's back, drove four-meter-long lances with sharpened stone heads into the brain, the heart, or the lungs of the animal. Lancers in faster and more maneuverable kayaks sometimes aided boat crews in the kill.[24] Once the whale had been killed, the whalers lashed its fins close to its body and towed it to the shore. If possible, they hauled the whale out of the water using dogs, men, and lines; if not, they butchered the carcass in shallow water using large flensing knives with blades of polished slate. Butchering and hauling the proceeds required the services of nearly the entire community for a day or more. The meat and *muktuk* (blubber with skin attached) was stored in pits dug in the permafrost.

In a good year, whaling produced surpluses that could be traded with other, nonwhaling Eskimo communities more reliant on caribou or reindeer. Whale oil provided badly needed fat for caribou hunters, whose diet consisted of lean meat most of the year, and helped to balance out years when caribou stocks fell or were nonexistent. Surplus caribou skins, with

Arctic and Subarctic, edited by Allen P. McCartney and the Canadian Circumpolar Institute (Alberta: Canadian Circumpolar Institute, University of Alberta, 1995), 99.

23. Krupnik, *Arctic Adaptations,* 238.

24. Ibid., 586–88.

their hollow hairs, offered whale hunters desirable fur and skins for high-insulating, cold-weather clothing. These were the principal items exchanged in vigorous trading networks across the Arctic.[25]

It is doubtful that human predation in the Thule period had more than a slight impact on the stocks of whales in the Arctic. Climatic change and food availability would have been the major determinants of the numbers of whales—not human hunting.[26] As stated earlier, the total catch by Arctic whalers was probably no more than a hundred or so animals per year. Limited catches partly reflected the limitations of the whaling technology employed and the modest numbers of people involved.

Existing archaeological remains do not support the notion that precontact Eskimo populations were much larger than those counted in the nineteenth and twentieth centuries. There is no evidence of large-scale mortality from new diseases of the sort seen in societies to the south and, therefore, no reason to suspect large precontact populations.[27] It is unlikely that more than a few thousand people across Arctic and sub-Arctic Eurasia were directly involved in whale hunting in any single year, and probably there were fewer. And, even with some offtake of whale oil by larger populations in a trading network, the overall human pressure on whale stocks was modest—a situation that would change rapidly in the next centuries.

THE BASQUES

The Basques, who inhabit the coastline of the Bay of Biscay, in a region bisected by the national boundary between France and Spain, have enthusiastically hunted whales since the early medieval centuries. Overall, forty-seven coastal villages and towns in French and Spanish Basque country relied on offshore whaling to supplement fishing until the supply of right whales ended in the early nineteenth century. Many towns have municipal seals and coats of arms that proclaim a proud history of whaling.[28]

The Basques hunted migrating right whales that came close to shore between October–November and February–March. (Basque whale hunting

25. Gene W. Sheehan, "Whaling Surplus, Trade, War, and the Integration of Prehistoric Northern and Northwestern Alaskan Economies, A.D. 1200–1826," in *Hunting the Largest Animals: Native Whaling in the Western Arctic and Subarctic,* edited by Allen P. McCartney and the Canadian Circumpolar Institute (Alberta: Canadian Circumpolar Institute University of Alberta, 1995).

26. Sue E. Moore and Randall R. Reeves, "Distribution and Movement," in *The Bowhead Whale,* edited by John J. Burns, J. Jerome Montague, Cleveland J. Cowles, and the Society for Marine Mammalogy (Lawrence, Kans.: Society for Marine Mammalogy, 1993), 313.

27. Krupnik, *Arctic Adaptations,* 221.

28. Ellis, *Men and Whales,* 47.

was virtually identical to that practiced by the Eskimos of the Arctic against bowhead whales, described above.) Fishing cooperatives erected lookout towers and placed full-time lookouts on duty throughout the season. When whales were sighted, the whalers launched small rowing boats in pursuit. If fortunate and skillful, they got close enough to harpoon and kill their prey and then towed the carcass back to shore. Harpooners aimed first at calves, which were easily hit, so that the mothers would come to their aid and then be taken. Each whale taken was a bonanza for a small village, since the whale-bone, oil, and meat were all valuable and could be either consumed or sold.[29] The catch taken by these methods was modest in number. A fishing village that took a whale each year would consider itself fortunate. Catch statistics from the village of Zauraz in the Spanish Basque country for the period 1500 to 1550 show a total of thirty-three whales for the fifty years. However, this rate was halved in the second half of the century.[30]

The high point of offshore Biscay whaling seems to have been the six-teenth century, which was followed by a gradual decline in the catch there-after. Offshore whaling certainly continued but became subordinate. Prob-ably around 1500, if not before, Basque whalers set out from the Bay of Biscay in larger ships searching for new whaling grounds in the North Sea as far as Iceland.[31] Confident of their hunting skills and well aware of possible prof-its to be made, the Basques were the first to begin industrial, early modern whaling. Local investors and financiers from as far away as Bordeaux and New Rochelle put up the funds necessary to build and outfit specially equipped whaling vessels and pay their crews for extended periods of time. In part, this initiative accompanied the pursuit of codfish into northern wa-ters by Basque and other fishermen as stocks declined in the Bay of Biscay. To some degree, lowered catches by offshore whaling methods also may have pushed the expansion.

Basque whalers did not stop at Iceland. By the early sixteenth century, they had begun sailing directly across the Atlantic to exploit new cod fishing and whaling grounds off Labrador and Newfoundland. The first recorded voyage made by northern French Basques to Terranova, or "New Land," was in 1517. By the 1530s, as many as twenty Basque vessels made the transat-

29. Alex Aguilar, "A Review of Old Basque Whaling and Its Effect on the Right Whales (*Eu-balaena glacialis*) of the North Atlantic," in *Right Whales: Past and Present Status: Proceedings of the Workshop on the Status of Right Whales, New England Aquarium, Boston, Massachusetts, 15–23 June 1983*, edited by Robert L. Brownell, P. B. Best, John H. Prescott, the New England Aquarium Corporation, and the International Whaling Commission (Cambridge, Eng.: International Whaling Commission, 1986).

30. Ibid., 194, table 3.

31. Jean Pierre Proulx and the Canadian Parks Service, *Basque Whaling in Labrador in the Six-teenth Century* (Ottawa: National Historic Sites Parks Service, 1993), 12.

lantic journey each year.[32] The primary whaling site was the narrow Strait of Belle Isle between the west coast of Newfoundland and the Labrador coast. Material remains from the first whaling station in North America at the present-day harbor of Red Bay on the Labrador coast confirm the presence of Basque whalers. On Saddle Island, located in the mouth of Red Bay, archaeologists discovered foundations from several blubber-rendering tryworks sites, a site where coopers built casks for whale oil, hundreds of pieces of red Spanish roofing tile, Spanish majolica ceramics, glassware, iron tools, and a cemetery holding remains of 140 whalers.[33]

The most remarkable finds, however, have been those of several Basque whaling ships and boats sunk in Red Bay Harbor. Firmly identified is the *San Juan,* a three-masted, ninety-foot galleon sunk while loading barrels of whale oil during a gale in 1565 and whose insurance policy is still extant in Spanish archives. Contemporary references permit identification of another seven ports along the same stretch of coast, for a total of eight Labrador whaling settlements occupied. After a two-month journey across the Atlantic, large whaling galleons arrived in June or July of each year at Belle Isle for the four- to five-month summer and autumn season. A typical Basque whaler of 250 tons capacity might have a crew of fifty or more sailors, craftsmen, and skilled harpooners and flensers. The galleons were not used to hunt whales, but were moored in the harbor to serve as living quarters and storehouses. The whalers built, or used already built, tiled roof tryworks on land, where copper cauldrons were positioned over great ovens. Each whaling captain sent out fully equipped whaleboats (called shallops) with six- or seven-man crews to patrol the straits in regular shifts.

When a whale was sighted, the boat crew tried to get between the whale and the open sea and to come upon the animals from behind. At a distance of seven to eight meters or even closer, if possible, the harpooner thrust the detachable harpoon head into the whale's body. When the wounded whale began to dive, the crew paid out a three-hundred-meter line of rope attached to the harpoon head. Usually the whale surfaced before the entire rope was used up, but wooden floats were attached to the end of this line so that the whale could be kept in sight if this did happen.[34] Sometimes boats with additional lines were able to add their length to the original line.

This began a bloody, prolonged embrace between whale and boat crew in which the final outcome was not at all certain. Many whales escaped. They

32. Ibid., 15–16. Notarial documents in Bayonne, Bordeaux, and La Rochelle confirm these voyages.

33. James A. Tuck and Robert Grenier, *Red Bay, Labrador: World Whaling Capital, A.D. 1550–1600* (St. John's, Newfoundland: Atlantic Archaeology, 1989).

34. Proulx and the Canadian Parks Service, *Basque Whaling in Labrador in the Sixteenth Century,* 53–57.

dove under the ice and loosened the harpoon in their frantic maneuvers. If the harpoon held during several dives and surfacings, the boat crew was able to get close enough to the tiring whale for the harpooner to thrust lances aiming for the animal's heart or lungs. When he succeeded, the whale thrashed in its death paroxysm—the most dangerous point for the hunters in their small boat—and, when dead, usually floated on the surface of the water.

The whalers then towed the carcass to the harbor, where they lashed it to the side of the whaling galleon. Flensers with huge knives cut the blubber off the whale in strips and carried it into shore to be heated in the cauldrons of the tryworks. The resulting oil, cooled, skimmed, and strained, was poured into newly built wooden barrels. The Spanish barrel in use had a capacity of around 180 to 200 liters of oil and a loaded weight of 250 kilograms. The whalers also removed the baleen plates and stored them carefully on board ship.

Analysis of hundreds of whale skeletal remains found on land and underwater at Red Bay suggest that the Basque whalers killed roughly equal numbers of bowheads and right whales, whose ranges overlapped in this region. During the summer, the whalers probably took right whales at the northern extent of their range; in the later autumn months, referred to as the "second season," they captured bowheads as they migrated into southern waters.[35] By far the greatest number of whales identified were fully mature adult whales, not calves.[36] Sources contemporary to the time state that each whale carcass yielded between 70 and 140 barrels of oil.

Toward the end of the season in November and December, most whaling captains had succeeded in filling their vessels with whale oil and were preparing to return to their home ports in the Bay of Biscay. Whaling galleons, between two hundred and seven hundred tons displacement, could carry 600 to 1,500 Spanish barrels of whale oil on the return voyage. Perhaps twenty to thirty whaling galleons made the Terranova journey each season.[37] At an average of 85 barrels of oil per whale and 1,000 barrels per vessel, the median catch could have been 12 whales per voyage. Commercially valuable baleen plates probably averaged three hundred or so per whale and could be

35. Stephen L. Cumbaa, "Archaeological Evidence of the Sixteenth Century Basque Right Whale Fishery in Labrador," in *Right Whales: Past and Present Status: Proceedings of the Workshop on the Status of Right Whales, New England Aquarium, Boston, Massachusetts, 15–23 June 1983,* edited by Robert L. Brownell, P. B. Best, John H. Prescott, the New England Aquarium Corporation, and the International Whaling Commission (Cambridge, Eng.: International Whaling Commission, 1986).

36. Ibid., 189.

37. Aguilar, "A Review of Old Basque Whaling and Its Effect on the Right Whales *(Eubalaena glacialis)* of the North Atlantic," 195.

stowed somewhat differently than barrels of oil. Whales taken per season would have totaled between 240 and 360 animals.[38] The Basques' Labrador whaling fishery seems to have sustained this level between 1530 and 1620. The estimated cumulative total catch would then have been 21,600 to 32,400 bowhead and right whales for that period.[39]

There is little doubt that New World whaling, which continued uninterrupted for such a long time, contributed substantial revenues to the economy of the Basque region. Even the humblest apprentices received 2 to 3 valuable barrels of whale oil—each worth twelve or more ducats in the late sixteenth century—when they returned from the year's expedition. Ratios varied according to individual agreements, but one common arrangement gave the whaling crew one-third of the proceeds from the oil; the owner of the ship, another third; and the outfitters who had financed and provided equipment and supplies, the final third. Moreover, the odds of whalers returning to their home port seem to have been no worse than for other mariners of the time. Casualties from the whale hunt were seemingly rare.

The outfitters or investors in each voyage retained profits from the whalebone brought back, which were not divided with the crew. A whaling galleon returning with whalebone and 1,000 barrels of oil in the late sixteenth century could realize six thousand to twelve thousand or more ducats depending on conditions that year. If we consider that the average amount of insurance taken out on each ship (limited to 90 percent of value) in that period was between two thousand and twenty-five hundred ducats, the potential for profit among all concerned was considerable.[40]

Demand for whale oil and whalebone remained high even as the price of a barrel of whale oil rose from six ducats in the 1560s to twelve to fifteen ducats in the 1590s.[41] Most captains sailed directly to their home ports and sold their cargoes immediately. For the northern, or French, Basque region, the primary oil markets were at Bayonne and Saint-Jean-de-Luz; for the southern or Spanish, they were San Sebastian and Bilbao. Foreign merchants kept agents permanently in residence in these towns.

After meeting local demand, buyers sold oil to wholesalers who dealt with retail apothecaries throughout France and Spain. Others sent whale oil to industrial centers such as the textile and soap factories of the Languedoc region. For example, in the winter of 1565–1566, two merchants, Geronimo de Salamanca Santa Cruz and Antonio de Salazar, shipped whale oil valued at

38. Aguilar suggests a figure of three hundred to five hundred whales taken per season.

39. Ibid., 196. Aguilar suggests that "an approximate cumulative catch for the period 1530 to 1610 would be between 25,00 to 40,000 whales." I have redone the calculation to extend the period to 1620 and have simply extended the barrels of oil per whale and per ship specified.

40. Proulx and the Canadian Parks Service, *Basque Whaling in Labrador in the Sixteenth Century*, 65–79.

41. Ibid., 78.

twenty-eight thousand ducats (thirty-five hundred barrels at a price of eight ducats per barrel) to northern Europe.[42]

After 1620, the numbers of Basque whaling ships coming to Terranova dropped to perhaps ten or twelve a year and the whaling grounds shifted westward to the Gulf of Saint Lawrence. It is very likely that whaling at this level of intensity had little impact on the numbers of either bowheads or right whales passing through the Strait of Belle Isle. After 1620, it was northern French Basques who remained active in the hunt and who benefited from the French colonial presence at Quebec. However, the Treaty of Utrecht in 1713 completely barred their entry to these waters and ended independent Basque whaling in Terranova.[43]

EXPLORATION IN NORTHERN WATERS

It was not until the early years of the seventeenth century that Europeans fully understood the potential richness of the bowhead whaling grounds to the north of Terranova, in the Arctic waters around Greenland. To hunt in these grounds, whalers first needed navigational and cartographic information about previously unexplored northern oceans. This knowledge was hard-won by decades of repeated voyages into ice-filled seas by a small group of determined mariners. Under varying forms of state and private commissions and financing, French, Dutch, English, and Danish ships probed the Arctic Ocean to find a direct northern sea route to China and Japan free of Spanish or Portuguese control.

One alternative, first proposed by Sebastian Cabot in 1548, was to seek a northeast passage to China by sailing north along North Cape of Norway into the White Sea, and then east into unknown northeast Arctic waters. Cabot's initial voyage, and several subsequent English voyages, reached the islands of Novaya Zemlya and Vaygach but could not penetrate the pack ice of the Kara Sea.

Dutch ventures were more fruitful. The Dutch led the way in exploring and charting Arctic waters.[44] Willem Barentsz and Jacob van Heemskerck, two extraordinarily gifted navigators and courageous leaders, conducted two Arctic voyages in search of the northeast passage in 1594 and 1596. These were sponsored and organized by private Dutch merchants, the Dutch States General, and the municipality of Amsterdam. The first expedition failed to get past Novaya Zemlya's west coast. In the second voyage, van Heemskerck

42. Ibid., 77.
43. Ibid.
44. Gunter Schilder, "Development and Achievements of Dutch Northern and Arctic Cartography in the Sixteenth and Seventeenth Centuries," *Arctic* 37, no. 4 (1984).

and Barentsz in one ship, and Jan Cornelisz Rijp as captain of the other, set a more northerly course than any before them.

On June 7, 1596, they first sighted Bear Island, located midway between Norway's North Cape and Spitsbergen (the Svalbard Archipelago) and then, proceeding north by northwest, reached the northwest tip of Spitsbergen (which they called the "sharp mountains"). The two ships parted in July. Rijp returned successfully from Spitsbergen. Barentsz set sail for the northern tip of Novaya Zemlya and reached it in late August, but was caught by ice and forced to go ashore with his crew for the winter of 1596–1597. Barentsz and van Heemskerck and their crew built two small, open boats. They set out in June 1597 on a fifteen-hundred-mile journey around the tip of Novaya Zemlya and down its west coast, and eventually reached the Kola Peninsula by the end of August. Barentsz and two other members of the fifteen-man crew died en route. Gerrit de Veer, a crew member, published his journal of the voyage in Dutch in 1598. Widely read, it was translated into French, German, Italian, and Latin by 1600 and English by 1609. Barentsz became a Dutch national hero in part because of the vividness and literary qualities of Veer's journal. Awareness of the Arctic burst upon European consciousness.[45]

Simultaneously, other mariners looked for a northwest passage to Cathay. English merchant speculators in London sent Martin Frobisher on three voyages north of Labrador into the Arctic in the 1570s. John Davis, who headed three expeditions in the 1580s, explored the eponymous Davis Strait off the west coast of Greenland as far as Upernavik.[46] Following on these voyages, a few British mariners sailed as far north as Bear Island and sighted numerous walrus herds. Other English ships sailing from Hull moved from their accustomed waters around Iceland to Greenland and began to hunt walruses for their ivory and oil. The Muscovy Company sent vessels in search of a northwest passage to China and Asia.

In 1604, Stephen Bennet, captain of the *Speed*, reached Bear Island, where he found a great walrus herd on the northeast shore of the island. According to his log:

> It seemed very strange to us to see such a multitude of monsters of the sea ley like hogges upon heapes: in the end we shot at them, not knowing whether they could runne swiftly or seize upon us or no. . . . Some, when they were wounded

45. Richard Vaughan, *The Arctic: A History* (Dover, N.H.: A. Sutton, 1994), 54–62. Also Felipe Fernández-Armesto, K. N. Chaudhuri, and Times Books, *The Times Atlas of World Exploration: Three Thousand Years of Exploring, Explorers, and Mapmaking* (New York: HarperCollins, 1991), 158–59; Gerrit de Veer, Charles T. Beke, and Laurens Reinhart Koolemans Beijnen, *The Three Voyages of William Barents to the Arctic Regions (1594, 1595, and 1596)* (New York: B. Franklin, 1964).

46. Vaughan, *The Arctic*, 64–74.

in the flesh, would but looke up and lye downe againe. Some were killed with the first shot; and some would goe into the sea with five or sixe shot; they are of such incredible strength. When all our shot and powder was spent, wee would . . . with our carpenter's axe cleave their heads. But for all we could doe, of above a thousand we killed but fifteene.[47]

On this voyage, Bennet and his crew only took the heads for tusks. On subsequent voyages in 1605 and 1606, they spent the summers killing walruses and boiling down their blubber for oil. They found that lances were more effective and cheaper than muskets in slaughtering large numbers of walruses. From the 1606 voyage, they returned with twenty-two metric tons of oil and three hogsheads of walrus tusks.[48]

In May 1607, the Muscovy Company sent the *Hopewell,* commanded by Henry Hudson, to make another attempt to find a northwest passage. On his 1607 voyage, Hudson, using Barentsz's charts, reached the Spitsbergen Archipelago. Hudson found the pack ice crowding much of Spitsbergen's coasts. Nevertheless, he reported that Kongsforden, a bay on the west coast of the archipelago, was teeming with bowhead whales. One bowhead even nudged his ship and made it list.[49] Another Muscovy Company voyage to Bear Island in 1608 resulted in the capture of a young walrus kept alive until the ship returned to London, "where the king and many honourable personages beheld it with admiration for the strangeness of the same, the like whereof had never before beene seene alive in England. Not long after[,] it fell sick and died. As the beast in shape is very strange, so is it of strange docilitie, and apt to be taught."[50]

In 1610, the Muscovy Company ordered Jonas Poole, commander of the *Amitie,* to make direct for Spitsbergen to hunt walruses. Poole found landing on the archipelago difficult, given the great amount of coastal ice and high winds, but when he did land, his crew reported the existence of unfrozen freshwater ponds. Poole and his crew were impressed by the abundance of animal life, including a "great store of whales" as well as polar bears, reindeer, walruses, and fowl. The *Amitie* returned with blubber, hides, and tusks from 120 walruses, hides and meat from 51 reindeer and 30 polar bears, and 3 bear cubs taken alive.[51]

---

47. William Martin Conway, *No Man's Land: A History of Spitsbergen from Its Discovery in 1596 to the Beginning of the Scientific Exploration of the Country* (Cambridge: Cambridge University Press, 1906), 21. Also William Martin Conway et al., *Early Dutch and English Voyages to Spitsbergen in the Seventeenth Century, Including Hessel Gerritsz. "Histoire du pays nommé Spitsberghe," 1613, Translated into English, for the First Time* (Nendeln, Liechtenstein: Kraus Reprint, 1967).
48. Conway, *No Man's Land,* 21.
49. Vaughan, *The Arctic,* 79; Conway, *No Man's Land,* 22–30.
50. Conway, *No Man's Land,* 30.
51. Ibid., 37.

EARLY COASTAL WHALING

Interest in possible profits to be made by Arctic whaling coalesced rapidly. Potential cargoes of oil from whaling promised to far outstrip the amount of oil gained from walruses. Colder climate conditions in the Arctic also seem to have favored Spitsbergen as a site for whaling. Winter pack ice solidified and extended farther southward than usual. Cooler summers meant that less drift ice was released in the grounds frequented by bowhead whales off the northeast coast of Greenland. Instead, the bowheads were forced toward the ice edge off Spitsbergen's bays and harbors. These conditions continued for the next several decades.[52]

In 1611, the entrepreneurs of the Muscovy Company sent two ships to Spitsbergen equipped to hunt whales; there were six Basque harpooners aboard. The expedition managed to kill one whale and five hundred walruses, and to render their fat into oil onshore, but both ships foundered. An English walrus-hunting ship out of Hull saved the crews and cargoes (for a fee). In 1612, spurred by shrinking numbers of whales off Labrador, a Basque whaling galleon from San Sebastian reached Spitsbergen and returned with a full cargo of whale oil.[53]

The next season, in 1613, strong market demand for oil sent at least twenty-six whaling ships to Spitsbergen's west coast. Most of the 1613 fleet were Basque whalers, including ten from San Sebastian and a giant 800-ton vessel from Saint-Jean-de-Luz captained by Miguel de Aristega. Two were Dutch whalers from Amsterdam and another two were Dutch vessels chartered by merchants from Dunkirk. Another seven were English: the Muscovy company commissioned seven English whalers with twenty-four Basque harpooners aboard. The 260-ton English flagship the *Tiger* was heavily armed, fitted with twenty-one cannons. When they arrived at Spitsbergen, the English ships sent out whaleboats to hunt whales in Forlandsundet Strait (between Prince Charles Island and the archipelago) and set up tryworks for the blubber on the shore.

The *Tiger* intercepted and boarded seventeen Basque, French, and Dutch whalers. The English admiral confiscated their catch and expelled the whalers from Spitsbergen waters. In several cases, such as that of Miguel de Aristega's great ship, the captain was permitted to stay and fish provided he hand over one-half the oil obtained.[54]

In January 1614, the Dutch whaling investors, stung by the English actions

52. Chr. Vibe, "Animals, Climate, Hunters, and Whalers," in *Proceedings of the International Symposium, Early European Exploitation of the Northern Atlantic, 800–1700,* edited by Rijksuniversiteit te Groningen, Noordelijk Centrum (Groningen, Netherlands: Arctic Centre, University of Groningen, 1981), 207.

53. Vaughan, *The Arctic,* 80–81.

54. Ibid., 81.

of the previous season, had organized themselves into a chartered trading company called the Noordsche Compagnie, with chambers formed in Amsterdam and the other leading towns in the Netherlands. Under a charter from the States General, they obtained a monopoly on whale hunting in Arctic waters off Greenland and Novaya Zemlya. The new Dutch company agreed on production quotas for whale oil, minimum prices, and maximum wages for seamen.[55] It also armed and equipped eleven ships for Spitsbergen and obtained an escort of three Dutch warships provided by the States General. At the whaling grounds, a standoff resulted: the Dutch whaled in the northwestern bays of the archipelago and maintained tryworks at Amsterdam Island, and the English remained in the bays of west Spitsbergen.

In the aftermath of these events, the territorial question of right of access to the whaling grounds came into sharp focus. Whose property rights were to prevail in the subsequent whaling seasons? Would the Muscovy Company dominate by force of arms? Would the Arctic waters fall under the control of one or more European states that claimed sovereignty? Would there be open access to this fishery, allowing participation by any whalers? In this dispute, the French and Spanish Basques obtained almost no early support from their respective rulers and were hampered by having less reliable and less copious investment capital. The principal claimants were the English, the Danes, and the Dutch. By the 1614 summer season, the Muscovy Company had obtained royal authority to annex Spitsbergen on behalf of King James I.

In the 1615 season, King Christian IV of Denmark and Norway sent a naval squadron to Spitsbergen that unsuccessfully tried to claim his old, established rights to Greenland and to rename Spitsbergen Christianbergen. The next year, Christian sent diplomatic representations to the courts of Europe to publicize his claim, but they failed to obtain support.

The Dutch view prevailed. Following their nation's general ideological position, the Dutch whalers articulated a doctrine of freedom of the seas (mare liberum) for the whale fishery and rejected the notion of a closed sea (mare clausum).[56] Stated firmly and backed by sufficient naval power, the Dutch view opened up the abundance of the Greenland fishery to any and all whalers. Rather than fight a costly war on the northern seas, the English and Danish kings acquiesced in the face of Dutch determination. There seemed to be enough whales for all.

The first shore-based phase of Arctic bowhead whaling established Dutch dominance over other European powers. The Dutch Noordsche Compagnie

55. C. De Jong, "The Hunt of the Greenland Whale: A Short History and Statistical Sources," in *Historical Whaling Records: Including the Proceedings of the International Workshop on Historical Whaling Records, Sharon, Massachusetts, September 12–16, 1977,* edited by Michael F. Tillman, Gregory P. Donovan, and the International Whaling Commission (Cambridge, Eng.: International Whaling Commission, 1983), 3:290.

56. Ibid., 3:2.

maintained its home monopoly until successful challenges from aspiring independent Dutch whalers and merchants led to its demise in 1642. From the very first, the whaling merchants in Amsterdam organized and financed a Europe-wide distribution network for whale oil and whalebone from that city. Although it never totally dominated the whale oil market, Amsterdam seems to have been the most efficient and reliable source for the oil throughout Europe. Dutch whalers, unlike their English counterparts, could count on ready sale of their product to a market far wider than that offered by the domestic market alone.

Every season, the Noordsche Compagnie sent between twenty and thirty whaling ships to the bays and fjords of Spitsbergen. Dutch whalers also hunted the well-stocked whaling grounds along the coasts of Jan Mayen Island to the south. Each whaling ship anchored in protected waters with ready access to the furnaces and cauldrons of the tryworks on shore. As the Basques had done before them in Labrador, the Dutch sent out boats—often commanded by Basque harpooners—in pursuit when bowheads entered the bays. The whalers harpooned and lanced the whales and towed their massive carcasses to shore. They tied them to the stern of the waiting whaling ship. Flensers pulled off long strips of blubber, cut them into pieces, and strung them on a line to be dragged ashore to the tryworks. Onshore, the blubber, minced into very small pieces, was boiled, strained, cooled, and poured into the wooden casks that would be loaded onto the whaling ship for the return voyage.

The principal Dutch shore station, called Smeerenberg (Blubbertown), located on the sandy beaches of the southeast corner of Amsterdam Island, was a scene of intense activity every summer season between 1619 and the 1660s. Each of the eight Dutch towns or chambers with a share in the Noordsche Compagnie had its own tryworks there and kept a shore crew of as many as forty men at work all season.[57] Smeerenberg probably processed 350 to 450 whales each year, and its competitors perhaps half that number.[58]

57. Louwrens Hacquebord, "The Rise and Fall of a Dutch Whaling-Settlement on the West Coast of Spitsbergen," in *Proceedings of the International Symposium, Early European Exploitation of the Northern Atlantic, 800–1700,* edited by Rijksuniversiteit te Groningen, Noordelijk Centrum (Groningen, Netherlands: Arctic Centre, University of Groningen, 1981); L. H. van Wijngaarden-Bakker and J. P. Pals, "Life and Work in Smeerenberg: The Bio-Archaeological Aspects," in *Proceedings of the International Symposium, Early European Exploitation of the Northern Atlantic, 800–1700,* edited by Rijksuniversiteit te Groningen, Noordelijk Centrum (Groningen, Netherlands: Arctic Centre, University of Groningen, 1981), 133–52; and G. J. R. Maat, "Human Remains at the Dutch Whaling Stations on Spitsbergen: A Physical Anthropological Study," in *Proceedings of the International Symposium, Early European Exploitation of the Northern Atlantic, 800–1700,* edited by Rijksuniversiteit te Groningen, Noordelijk Centrum (Groningen, Netherlands: Arctic Centre, University of Groningen, 1981), 153–202.

58. De Jong, "The Hunt of the Greenland Whale," 91. Occasionally, the total numbers of whales taken is listed with a fraction, e.g., 12 7/16. It is not entirely clear whether that fraction

The shore workers kept their ovens operating day and night. Each oven consisted of a brick ring, or fire screen, measuring 2.7 meters in diameter, surrounded by an insulating wall of stone with a sand layer in between them. A great copper kettle was set in the brick fire screen. The fire burnt in a funnel-shaped stoke hole located on one side of the brick fire screen, so that the heat circulated around the sides of the kettle. A chimney leading from the stoke hole discharged smoke. The heated whale oil drained in gutters to fill the barrels in which it was shipped.[59]

An archaeological expedition to Spitsbergen in 1980 from the University of Groningen found substantial numbers of artifacts from the settlement.[60] Dutch archaeologists have studied the material remains left at Smeerenberg and evidence of the layout of the original tent encampments and the later semipermanent wooden structures, as well as remnants of forges and tryworks. They have found dozens of clay pipes, stoneware objects, bottles, more than one hundred leather shoes, and over one thousand pieces of cloth. Excavating the cemetery revealed 185 bodies, many with still-intact woolen clothing. A high percentage of the bones analyzed bear evidence of scurvy.

Soil samples and pollen analysis show that the settlement and tryworks heavily polluted the soil and vegetation of the area around Smeerenberg.[61] The men trampled the soil and it became very muddy. They carried with them alien cereals and pollens that were deposited in the soil as well. Decaying whale flesh and oil nourished the growth of closed grass vegetation in place of the original open moss cover. Gradually, more than a century after abandonment, the grass cover gave way again to open moss formations.

Pollen and other evidence obtained from stratified samples found in a peat section in a bird cliff four kilometers east of Smeerenberg permit reconstruction of local climate trends during the seventeenth century. These data reveal that the climate was cooling in 1615 and remained cool during the first half of the settlement period. Around 1645, the climate warmed

---

denotes a scavenged carcass, a whale divided between two ships, or a portion given up to a privateer. I have simply omitted the fractions in my calculations.

59. H. J. Zantkil, "Reconstructie van de behuizing op Smeerenburg," in *Walvisvaart in de gouden eeuw: Opgravingen op Spitsbergen,* edited by Louwrens Hacquebord and Wim Vroom (Amsterdam: De Bataafsche Leeuw, 1988). The article includes a black-and-white reproduction of a 1634 painting by Abraham Speeck, *Deens landstation aan de Noordelijke Ijszee* (The Land Station of the Northern Ice Sea), which depicts a Dutch tryworks (68).

60. Hacquebord, "The Rise and Fall of a Dutch Whaling-Settlement on the West Coast of Spitsbergen"; and Louwrens Hacquebord and Wim Vroom, *Walvisvaart in de gouden eeuw: Opgravingen op Spitsbergen* (Amsterdam: De Bataafsche Leeuw, 1988).

61. W. O. Van der Knaap, "De invloed van de landstations op hun directe omgeving; klimaatsverandering in de zeventiende eeuw," in *Walvisvaart in de gouden eeuw: Opgravingen op Spitsbergen,* edited by Louwrens Hacquebord and Wim Vroom (Amsterdam: De Bataafsche Leeuw, 1988).

somewhat during the last half of the settlement period, until 1660. After 1660, the climate cooled considerably, reaching a low point in 1670.[62] Chr. Vibe has suggested that the disappearance of bowhead whales from Spitsbergen and the abandonment of Smeerenberg resulted from a warming trend that permitted the whales to return to their normal summer grounds off the northeast coast of Greenland.[63] Since the climate by 1670 had become colder once again, this seems unlikely. That the whales who survived avoided the waters infested with whalers near Smeerenberg is a more likely scenario.

OPEN SEA AND DRIFT ICE WHALING

Between 1640 and 1670, all whalers were steadily forced away from sheltered coastal whaling into open waters. Whalers could no longer simply anchor offshore and send out their whaleboats to kill bowheads. The number of whales entering the bays of Spitsbergen and Jan Mayen Island dropped steadily as bowheads avoided areas where their fellows had been slaughtered. Pelagic whaling invariably led the whalers into the areas of drift ice favored by the bowhead. Whalers followed the borders of the drift ice west from Spitsbergen toward eastern Greenland. Aggressive pursuit of bowheads drew the whalers into difficult and risky navigation between giant ice floes and pack ice.

Whaling ships became more specialized and costly. The danger of collision with hidden ice formations forced redesign. The first special-purpose, fortified whaling ship was built in Amsterdam in 1660.[64] The new, more expensive ships had doubled planking on the hulls below the waterline and reinforced knees and ribs to withstand blows and pressure from ice. Every year, a few ships caught in the drift ice could not be freed and were abandoned by their crews. Generally, crew members moved onto the ice and waited in relative safety for rescue by fellow whalers. An elaborate set of rules quickly emerged that set out terms for proper treatment of such refugees.

At first, the open-sea whalers flensed their carcasses at sea and carried the blubber to be boiled on Spitsbergen and Jan Mayen Island. This expedient proved unsatisfactory as distances to the shore stations increased. The Dutch whalers then resorted to packing cut blubber into barrels and bringing it back for processing in their home ports. Amsterdam became a major processing and distribution center for whale oil. The tryworks at home were in-

62. Ibid., 145.

63. Vibe, "Animals, Climate, Hunters, and Whalers," 207.

64. C. De Jong, *Geschiedenis van de oude Nederlandse walvisvaart* (Pretoria: De Jong, 1972), 3:297.

dependent enterprises working on commission that processed other kinds of oil in the off-season.

The scale of Dutch whaling rose rapidly after the demise of the Noordsche Compagnie in 1642. With free entry into the industry, the number of whaling ships outfitted in the Netherlands more than doubled, to 70 in 1654, and doubled again, to 148 in 1670. In 1684, the Dutch Arctic whaling fleet reached its highest point. That year, 246 Dutch whalers sailed for Spitsbergen and captured 1,185 whales.[65]

Second to the Dutch were the Germans, whose interests closely converged with those of Dutch investors. As the Noordsche Compagnie dissolved, German shipowners from Hamburg, Bremen, and Emden began to outfit Arctic whalers, sometimes chartered Dutch vessels, and sent them out in considerable numbers. Hamburg developed tryworks to process bowhead blubber and distribution networks complementary to those of Amsterdam. From the 1640s, German whalers sailed to the Arctic nearly every season until the Napoleonic Wars. In the 1669 season, 37 whaling ships left Hamburg for the waters off Spitsbergen and returned with blubber from 260 whales.[66] In the peak year of 1684, German whalers brought 57 ships to the north, which killed 227 whales.

The Dutch also tolerated Danish whalers and permitted them to have a shore station on Spitsbergen. Christian IV of Denmark and Norway failed to sustain his claim to sovereignty over Spitsbergen, but Danish interest in extending whaling from Norway's North Cape continued. Between 1619 and 1622, Christian IV, acting as royal entrepreneur, sent several ships each year to Spitsbergen accompanied by a Danish warship. Christian IV did not use Danish ships but employed chartered Dutch ships and Basque whalers, and the proceeds were sold in Amsterdam. Thereafter, the Danish king issued licenses to Johan and Goddart Braem, two brothers who were Hamburg merchants, for a Danish monopoly on North Cape and Spitsbergen whaling.

Stiff Dutch opposition to these arrangements sharply curtailed Danish activities for a decade or more. Only after 1634 did the Danish company reach an accommodation with the Dutch Noordsche Compagnie and rebuild its shore stations at a new location on Danes Island called Copenhagen Bay. The Dutch and the Danes collaborated in sending armed naval vessels to drive French whalers from Spitsbergen. Even after the end of the Dutch monopoly in 1642, Goddart Braem kept the royal charter and monopoly for Danish whaling, until his death in 1655. By 1660, Danish investors had lost

65. Ibid.; De Jong, "The Hunt of the Greenland Whale," 91, table 1.

66. Harald Voigt, *Die Nordfriesen auf den Hamburger Wal- und Robbenfängern, 1669–1839*, Studien zur Wirtschafts- und Sozialgeschichte Schleswig-Holsteins, Band 11 (Neumünster: K. Wachholtz, 1987), 25, 28.

enthusiasm, and dwindling profits brought closure to the Danish whaling effort. Throughout this period, Danish whaling voyages rarely exceeded five in a season and often numbered fewer than that.[67] The Dutch and Germans were far more successful than the English and the French. After suffering considerable financial losses, the English Arctic whaling business declined precipitously in the 1620s. The Muscovy Company seems to have spent far more effort in fighting legal challenges from interloping English whalers at home than in developing its fleet. These problems were compounded by lessened demand for whale oil by English soap makers in London, who preferred oilseeds for their manufactures. Although occasionally English investors gambled on a whaling voyage, for the next century or more the English were a negligible presence in the hunt for bowheads.[68]

The French, despite Dutch hostility, remained active in Arctic whaling. In 1629, Cardinal Richelieu obtained a royal charter for a French company headed by the Basque whaler Jean Vrolicq, who commanded whalers sailing from French ports. The Dutch did not permit the French to set up shore stations on Spitsbergen and forced them into open-water whaling very early. The French also resorted to hunting for right whales near Iceland and Norway's North Cape. Lack of shore stations forced them to devise methods for trying whale oil on board ship.[69] Although little has been published about the French chartered company, it seems likely that it never operated more than a few whalers each year. The company survived until 1665, when its monopoly was ended.[70]

Freedom to engage in the industry did not attract many French investors and entrepreneurs in spite of the pool of expertise offered by the Basque port towns. Most French whalers sailed from Le Havre and Honfleur, not the Basque ports, and these were relatively few. Between 1668 and 1689, fifty-seven whalers returned to Le Havre and thirty-two whalers to Honfleur, for an average of only 4.2 voyages per year for the two ports.[71] Together, Le

67. Sune Dalgård, *Dansk-norsk hvalfangst, 1615–1660: En studie over Danmark-Norges stilling I europaeisk merkantil expansion* (København: G. E. C. Gad, 1962). An English summary is appended on pp. 419–29.

68. G. Jackson, "The Rise and Fall of English Whaling in the Seventeenth Century," in *Proceedings of the International Symposium, Early European Exploitation of the Northern Atlantic, 800–1700,* edited by Rijksuniversiteit te Groningen, Noordelijk Centrum (Groningen, Netherlands: Arctic Centre, University of Groningen, 1981). See also a description of an unsuccessful English voyage in 1656 in J. C. Appleby, "A 'Voyage to Greenland for the Catching of Whales.' "

69. Thierry Vincent and Nicolas-Victor Fromentin, *Le "Groënlandais": Trois-mats baleinier des mers polaires: Journal de bord du Capitaine Fromentin* (Luneray: Editions Bertout, 1994), 36.

70. Ibid., 57–58.

71. J. Thierry Du Pasquier, "The Whalers of Honfleur in the Seventeenth Century," *Arctic* 37, no. 4 (1984): 535.

Havre and Honfleur offered a much better market and distribution system for whale oil than did the Basque ports to the north.

French whalers tended to take larger catches than the Dutch. In seventeen voyages for which catch data exist, the total kill was 226 bowheads and right whales, with an average of 13.3 per ship—a much higher figure than for Dutch or German ships.[72] These higher totals primarily resulted from the Basque practice of boiling the blubber and storing it in casks on board ship before returning to port. This practice meant that they had room to store more whales. The French also stopped off in Iceland and hunted right whales more consistently than did the Dutch. In common with other European whalers, the French suffered remarkably few human casualties. Logbook notations for thirty-two voyages from Honfleur record that, among about thirteen hundred crewmen, only one man had been killed by a whale, three men had drowned, one man had been killed in a collision, and two men had died of illness.[73]

Beginning in 1661 in the Netherlands and 1669 in Germany, private individuals compiled detailed annual whaling statistics for the Greenland fishery. Each season as the whalers returned to Amsterdam, Hamburg, and other whaling ports, merchants, investors, and other interested parties recorded the particulars for each: the name and size of the ship; its commander; number of whales caught; output of blubber, whale oil, and baleen; and current prices. So popular was the practice that local printers even made up booklets with lists and columns to be filled in.[74] Those records preserved in archives permit a detailed reconstruction of the industry.

Arctic whaling became firmly emplaced in the consciousness of citizens of the Dutch Republic during its golden age. As we have seen, whaling was an important industry. Many Dutchmen had a direct economic interest in the industry either as investors or workers. However, what caught the popular imagination was the exotic appeal of dangerous voyages to the ice-filled seas of the far north to pursue marine animals as large as bowhead whales. Depicting northern whaling became a minor genre for Dutch painters and engravers. Examples of some of these paintings include *The Whaler "Prince William" on the River Maas, near Rotterdam,* by Lieve [Pietersz.] Verschuier (1630–1686), showing a whaler's safe return from the northern ice seas.[75] *Whaling in a Northern Ice Sea,* by Abraham van Salm (1660–1720), portrays eleven ships of a whaling fleet operating in an ice-filled northern sea. His

72. Ibid., 537, table 3.

73. Ibid., 534, table 1.

74. De Jong, "The Hunt of the Greenland Whale," 83.

75. George S. Keyes, Minneapolis Institute of Arts, Toledo Museum of Art, and Los Angeles County Museum of Art, *Mirror of Empire: Dutch Marine Art of Seventeenth Century* (Minneapolis: Minneapolis Institute of Arts; Cambridge: Cambridge University Press, 1990), 182–84.

painting shows the tails of two sounding whales pursued by men in boats and a ship caught in the ice and in the process of being abandoned by its crew.[76]

Despite increased costs and greater risks, open-water whale hunting in the drift ice between Greenland and Spitsbergen was successful and profitable. Dutch and German investors built and sent a rising number of specially designed ships to the Arctic. Between 1661 and 1719, the peak period for drift ice whaling in this region, Dutch and German whalers made 10,610 trips to the Arctic, averaging 176 voyages per year. Over the same period, 548 ships (5.2 percent) were lost in the ice or to privateers. Whales killed totaled 49,973, or an average of 832 bowheads per year. Whale blubber totaled just over 2 million tuns at an average of 40.3 tuns (1,145.3 liters per tun) per whale. Whale oil produced for the six decades was 4.9 million quarters (kardels), or barrels, at 232.8 liters per unit.[77] The average yearly output was 82,822 quarters or 19.2 million liters of oil. To this figure, we must add a modest contribution from the French, essentially Basque, whalers and a few others. Cornelis De Jong's estimate that Dutch and German whalers caught 95 to 98 percent of the Greenland bowheads in this period is probably accurate.[78]

FREDERICK MARTENS

We possess a detailed firsthand account of a late-seventeenth-century Greenland whaling voyage, compiled and later published by Frederick Martens, a native of Hamburg. His text, although relatively brief, illustrates the matter-of-fact experience of European whalers engaged in what had become a routine extractive enterprise in the ice-filled northern oceans. In addition, Martens was an intellectual who participated in European scientific reporting about distant regions. Following his narrative of the voyage, Martens's account contains a lengthy set of responses to a list of questions about Spitsbergen's weather, land, flora, and fauna posed by Henry Oldenburg, secretary of the Royal Society in London.[79]

76. Ibid., 144–46.
77. Calculated by De Jong, "The Hunt of the Greenland Whale," 98, table 9, n. 2.
78. Ibid., 91.
79. Adam White et al., A Collection of Documents on Spitzbergen [sic] and Greenland (London: Hakluyt Society, 1855), iii–v. Another firsthand account is to be found in the memoirs of Johann Dietz, also a German and a surgeon and barber. In a Hamburg tavern in the late 1680s, three Dutch mariners recruited Dietz from his post as a surgeon-barber to serve as ship's surgeon for the Hoffnung, a whaler from Rotterdam, at a wage of twelve thalers per month and rations. The Hoffnung, a well-armed Dutch whaler with twenty-six guns, sailed for Spitsbergen with a forty-five man crew. The Hoffnung had good fortune and killed nine bowhead whales and one right whale (in Dutch, a Nordkaper) in a relatively short time. This catch "was a remarkable success. It meant also a great deal of money for the ship, for one fish may richly repay all the expenses and still leave something over." Johann Dietz, Bernard Miall, and Ernst Consentius, Master Jo-

During the whaling season of 1671, Martens sailed as a ship's surgeon on the *Jonas im Walfisch,* captained by Peter Peterson of Friesland. The ship left the Elbe River at noon on April 15, heading north by northeast. By April 27, the ship had reached pack ice at the seventy-first parallel, turned back, and arrived within ten miles of Jan Mayen Island. Over the next ten days, it traced the ice border heading for Spitsbergen. Martens notes that, two days out from the archipelago, "we saw daily many ships, sailing about the ice: I observed that as they passed by one another, they hailed one another, crying Holla and asked each other how many fish they had caught. . . . When they have their full fraight of whales, they put up their great flag as a sign thereof: then if any hath a message to be sent, he delivers it to them." They had arrived in a region where the frost was constant, despite the summer sun that did not set, and where "their teeth chatter in their heads commonly, and the appetite is greater than in any other countreys."[80]

The *Jonas im Walfisch* did not put in to land when it reached Spitsbergen on May 7, but joined other whalers at sea to hunt for bowhead. On May 14, in sunny, calm weather, states Martens, "we told twenty ships about us" at "seventy-five degrees and twenty-two minutes." That same day, they spotted a whale and sent four boats after the animal, but lost it when it dived. On May 21, the *Jonas* sailed into the ice along with another Hamburg ship, the *Lepeler,* where both whalers fixed their ice hooks to "a large ice-field" and joined another thirty whaling ships in a "harbour or haven" in the ice-pack. On May 30, the captain of the *Jonas* sent out his "great sloop" further into the ice, where the party heard a whale blow and succeeded in killing it—their first catch of the season. They brought the whale back to the ship, where it yielded seventy barrels of fat. That same night, another captain lost his ship when it was crushed between two sheets of ice.[81]

On June 4, they missed yet another whale that dove precipitously, for there were so many ships in the vicinity that "one hunted the whales to the other, so they were frighted and became very shy." By June 13, they were sailing "somewhat easterly towards Spitzbergen," when "that night we saw more than twenty whales, that run one after another towards the ice; out of them we got our second fish, which was a male one; and this fish, when they

hann Dietz, Surgeon in the Army of the Great Elector and Barber to the Royal Court: From the Old Manuscript in the Royal Library of Berlin (London: Allen and Unwin; New York: Dutton, 1923), 122. With this success, the captain and crew, including Dietz, were able to go ashore at Spitsbergen and indulge in such diversions as a reindeer hunt. This good fortune extended to the return voyage, when the *Hoffnung* narrowly escaped being seized by a French raider. On Dietz's second voyage with the *Hoffnung* the next season, the catch was only five whales due to a near disaster in the northern ice that forced an early return. Dietz's account, somewhat more entertaining, agrees with Martens in nearly every detail.

80. Ibid., 4, 38.
81. Ibid., 5–6.

wounded him with lances, bled very much, so that the sea was tinged by it where he swam."[82]

The *Jonas* reached Spitsbergen on June 14 and anchored in South Bay. Here, they flensed the whale taken the day before, which yielded sixty-five barrels of fat. That night they sent out three boats into the English bay where they harpooned and lanced a whale but lost it under the ice. They did come across "two great sea-horses" (walruses) asleep on a sheet of ice, which they lanced and killed. On June 22, still at Spitsbergen, the men of the *Jonas* killed their third whale from among six that were sighted: "This fish was killed by one man, who flung the harpoon into him; and killed him also, while the other boats were busy in pursuing or hunting another whale. This fish run [*sic*] to the ice, and before he died beat about with his tail; the ice settled about him, so that the other boats could not come to this boat to assist him, till the ice separated again that they might row, when they tied one boat to another, and so towed the whale to the great ship." The carcass gave up forty-five barrels of blubber.

On June 29, they scavenged "a great quantity of the fat of a whale, three vessels [boats] full" that had been left by a whaler caught in the ice. On July 1, a *Jonas* boat crew harpooned a female bowhead who was "beating about with her tail and fins, so that we durst not come near to lance her." The stricken whale struck one harpooner with her tail "over his back so vehemently, that he had much ado to recover his breath again." The whale overturned another boat that approached her, "so that, the harpoonier was forced to dive for it, and hide his head under the water; the rest did the same; they thought it very long before they came out, for it was cold, so that they came quaking to the ship again." This seems to have been the fourth whale taken.[83] The same day they just missed one whale and lost another to a Dutch whaler that succeeded in harpooning him first.

In rapid succession, they took, on July 2, the fifth, a male bowhead, and two days later the sixth, another male. The latter filled forty-five barrels. During these days, notes Martens, "we saw more whales than we did in all our voyage."[84] On July 5, they struck another whale, which broke the harpoon line against a rock and escaped, but then the same day they killed the seventh whale, a female that yielded forty-five barrels.

In a brief respite, the *Jonas* dropped anchor in a sheltered Spitsbergen bay to cut up and put in barrels large pieces of blubber from two whales that had simply been flung in the hold in the press of the hunt. Cruising again on July 9, they took their eighth bowhead and "filled with him fifty-four kardels of fat." On July 12, they killed three polar bears swimming in the water and then

82. Ibid., 7.
83. Ibid., 9.
84. Ibid., 10.

rowed up to a herd of walruses resting on the ice and killed ten of them, but not without protest. The remaining walruses "came all about our boat, and beat holes through the sides of the boat, so that we took in an abundance of water; were forced at length to row away. . . . They pursued us as long as we could see them, very furiously."[85]

The *Jonas* continued to sail up and down the Spitsbergen coast, among drifting ice, but bowheads were becoming scarce in these waters. On July 15 the *Jonas im Walfisch* entered South Harbor, where twenty-eight whalers—eight German and twenty Dutch—lay at anchor.

A week later, on July 22, the *Jonas im Walfisch* left South Harbor for the uneventful voyage home. On August 20, the ship took on a Hamburg municipal pilot near Heligoland, and on August 29, it anchored in the Elbe River after a four-and-a-half-month absence. The hold was filled with at least four hundred sixty-four-gallon barrels of fat from the eight bowhead whales killed. Another two bowheads had been hit and wounded by harpoons and lances but not taken. The fat was processed into whale oil at Hamburg for sale in European markets. The whalebone, carefully extracted from each carcass, "doth only belong to the owners of the ship and the others that run their hazard, whether they catch few or many whales. The rest [i.e., the officers and crew], which take their pay by the month, receive their money when they come home whether they have caught many or none, and the loss or gain falls upon the merchants."[86]

THE EXPANDED EIGHTEENTH-CENTURY HUNT

During the first half of the seventeenth century, the Noordsche Compagnie had sent several expeditions to the west of Greenland in a futile search for a northwest passage to Asia or, failing that, valuable minerals, whales, seals, or other opportunities. In tandem with these exploratory ventures, Dutch traders, mostly from the North Sea island of Terschelling, began a modest barter trade with the Inuits of Greenland's west coast. They organized and equipped smaller vessels of fifty to one hundred tons, assembled ten- to fifteen-man crews, and stocked European consumption goods and tools as trade goods. Departing early in February or March, they made the long voyage to Greenland's west coast, where the Inuits bartered whale and seal blubber, whalebone, walrus and narwhale tusks, and furs for European products. The trading vessels also carried two whaleboats and equipment to hunt whales if the opportunity arose. In 1720, a Terschelling Island captain, Lourens Feykes Haan, codified the accumulated knowledge of western

85. Ibid., 11.
86. Ibid., 129.

Greenland by publishing in Amsterdam a detailed description of the lands and people of the strait.[87]

By the 1720s, Dutch-Inuit trade was steadily declining as Denmark sent settlers and assumed formal colonial powers in Greenland. Official disapproval by Danish authorities increased risks and reduced returns to the Dutch traders. Danish authorities, who wanted to reserve trading profits for their own nationals, argued that the barter trade "was morally prejudicial to the Inuit."[88] Largely in response to this pressure, the Terschelling Island trading captains switched to open-water whaling in the Davis Strait. News of abundant stocks of bowheads in this region filtered out to other whaling captains and investors whose catches off eastern Greenland and Spitsbergen were in a temporary slump.

In 1719, unofficial whaling statistics began to record voyages and whales taken in the Davis Strait as a separate category. The western whaling grounds became an important addition to the Greenland fishery but never fully replaced or even equaled the eastern grounds. During the 1720s, Dutch whaling voyages to the Davis Strait averaged 148 per year, compared to 258 per year made to the eastern whaling grounds. In the 1730s, the numbers were nearly equal; and in the 1740s, the balance had shifted heavily again, with an average 246 voyages per year to the eastern whaling grounds and only 64 to the west.[89]

With the additional catch afforded by the Davis Strait whaling grounds, Dutch and German whalers brought back profitable cargoes of whale blubber to Amsterdam and Hamburg for the rest of the century. No technical or business innovations occurred; the whaling fleets followed long-standing routes and long-established procedures. Between 1720 and 1800, Dutch and German whalers averaged 169 voyages per year to both eastern and western Greenland, for a total of 13,501 trips. In an average year, they killed 498 whales, whose carcasses produced 24,819 barrels of oil. The aggregate catch was 39,833 bowhead and right whales, for a total of 2 million barrels of whale oil placed on European markets.

In the 1780s, both Dutch and German whaling went into rapid decline. By the 1790s, only one-fifth the previous number of Dutch whalers sailed to the Arctic and no German voyages are recorded. The total catch declined accordingly. By this time, new competition from British and Scandinavian whalers began to press hard against the Dutch. The British, Danish, and Swedish governments put up handsome subsidies to encourage their own whaling fleets, and they heavily taxed imports of foreign whale oil.

British blockades and seizures put an end to voyages during the

87. De Jong, *Geschiedenis van de oude Nederlandse walvisvaart*, 3:303.
88. Ibid.
89. De Jong, "The Hunt of the Greenland Whale," 92, table 2.

Napoleonic Wars as the Royal Navy blockaded the French-held Netherlands from 1795 to 1813. In 1798, when thirty-one Dutch whalers tried to sail under neutral flags, the British seized twenty-nine of the vessels. Neither Dutch nor German whaling recovered, even after the liberation of the Netherlands in 1814 and restoration of peace in Europe.

BRITISH WHALING AND THE FINAL DEMISE OF THE GREENLAND BOWHEAD

Between the mid–seventeenth and mid–eighteenth centuries, various attempts to organize British whaling companies and make them profitable ended in failure. Britain's poor showing in northern whaling became a matter of injured national pride. If the Dutch could succeed in this lucrative endeavor, why could not British mariners and investors? One of the most vocal proponents of restored Greenland whaling was Henry Elking, who published in 1722 his *A View of the Greenland Trade and Whale Fishery, with the National and Private Advantages Thereof*, in which he argued forcefully that the Dutch, Germans, French, and Spaniards "are made rich" from whaling.[90] Even if the domestic British market was presently well supplied with whale oil, "we know how many other parts of Europe want the train oil, and the soap boiled of the same," which could be efficiently and cheaply supplied by British enterprise.[91]

Finally, in 1724, Elking received approval for a Greenland venture. Armed with a massive amount of capital, Elking commissioned new ships, docks, and warehouses and hired whaling specialists. In the course of eight years and 172 whaling voyages, his whalers brought back only 160 whales—far from enough to pay start-up expenses. In 1731, Elking ended the experiment.

This failure convinced Parliament that greater encouragement from the state was needed. In 1733, Parliament offered an annual subsidy or bounty of twenty shillings per ton for each British whaler exceeding two hundred tons capacity equipped and sent to the Arctic. When this did not work, the official rate increased to thirty shillings per ton in 1740 and finally to forty shillings in 1749.[92] At that threshold, investors' risk was much reduced and a boom in Arctic whaling began. From an average of four British voyages to

90. Quoted in G. Jackson, *The British Whaling Trade* (Hamden, Conn.: Archon Books, 1978), 42. See Henry Elking, *A View of the Greenland Trade and Whale Fishery, with the National and Private Advantages Thereof*. In *A Select Collection of Scarce and Valuable Economical Tracts, from the Originals of Defoe, Elking, Franklin, Turgot, Anderson, Schomberg, Townsend, Burke, Bell, and Others; with a Preface, Notes, and Index*, edited by J. R. McCulloch (London: n.p., 1859); William Scoresby, *An Account of the Arctic Regions, with a History and Description of the Northern Whale-Fishery*, reprint of the 1st ed. (Newton Abbot: David and Charles, 1969), 2:98–109.

91. Jackson, *The British Whaling Trade*, 43.

92. Scoresby, *An Account of the Arctic Regions, with a History and Description of the Northern Whale-Fishery*, 2:109.

Greenland each year, for the next quarter century (1750–1776) the average jumped to 57 voyages per year and, despite a slow decrease in the rate of subsidy, voyages more than tripled, to an average of 171 by the early 1790s.[93]

British northern whaling was once again competitive with the Dutch and German industry. Although London continued to fit out the greater number of whalers, a number of new ports formed private whaling companies. Liverpool, Whitby, Hull, and other English northern ports had a decided advantage in terms of location. This was even truer of Aberdeen and other Scottish ports, from which the round-trip distance to Greenland waters was much shorter.[94]

Between 1733 and 1800, British whalers made 4,006 voyages to the ice fields, killed approximately twelve thousand whales, and produced 1.4 million hectoliters (608,447 quarters or 123,688 English tuns) of whale oil and 5,303 metric tons of whalebone.[95] By the end of the century, the British exchequer had paid 1.98 million pounds sterling in subsidies to whalers.

During the Napoleonic Wars, the bowhead whale gained a respite. Whaling ventures during the two decades between 1795 and 1815 were intermittent and much reduced. When peace returned, however, the avid hunt for whales resumed. British, rather than Dutch or German, whalers dominated the final phase of Arctic whaling. Within thirty years, by midcentury, British whalers had exterminated the last remaining bowhead whales—the Spitsbergen stocks—to be found in the Atlantic.[96]

As postwar whaling renewed, reduced numbers of increasingly wary whale stocks forced British whalers into new grounds. By 1817, they entered the

93. Jackson, *The British Whaling Trade*, 264, appendix 3.

94. W. R. H. Duncan, "Aberdeen and the Early Development of the Whaling Industry, 1750–1800," *Northern Scotland* 3 (1977–1978).

95. Jackson, *The British Whaling Trade*, 264, appendix 3. English tuns of whale oil have been converted to the older quarter, or barrel, at 4.92 to the tun. These are volume measures. (Based on De Jong, "The Hunt of the Greenland Whale," 98, n. 2, in which a quarter is equal to 232.8 liters and a tun to 1,145.3 liters.) Historians of British whaling have not compiled the actual number of whales killed in the eighteenth century, although those data are available in logbooks and other primary sources. The number for whales killed is calculated by a ratio of 10.2 English tuns of oil, or 50.2 barrels of oil, per whale taken from the aggregate Dutch and German figures above for the same period.

96. The western Arctic stocks of bowhead whales in the Bering, Chukchi, and Beaufort Seas were left relatively undisturbed until American whalers found their way into that region in the 1840s. The estimated population of twenty thousand to forty thousand bowheads declined steadily until the industry collapsed in the early twentieth century. John R. Bockstoce and Daniel B. Botkin, "The Historical Status and Reduction of the Western Arctic Bowhead Whale *(Balaena mysticetus)* Population by the Pelagic Whaling Industry, 1848–1914," in *Historical Whaling Records: Including the Proceedings of the International Workshop on Historical Whaling Records, Sharon, Massachusetts, September 12–16, 1977*, edited by Michael F. Tillman, Gregory P. Donovan, and the International Whaling Commission (Cambridge, Eng.: International Whaling Commission, 1983).

dangerous waters of Baffin Bay and pressed on to the Canadian archipelago. British whalers sailed earlier in the season to intercept the earliest bowhead migrants, largely the nursing and immature animals, before they reached the dense drift ice in the north. Between 1815 and 1842, British whalers made 2,634 voyages, during which they killed 21,548 bowhead whales. From this northern fishery (as distinguished from the pursuit of the sperm whale in southern oceans), their efforts generated 2.8 million hectoliters (1.2 million quarters or 238,460 tuns) of whale oil and 12,249 metric tons of whalebone.[97] The whale oil became especially useful as a cheap fuel to light municipal street lamps, which, for the first time, were being introduced in British and European cities.

THE ANCILLARY HUNT FOR WALRUSES

Throughout the whaling grounds around Spitsbergen and the Davis Strait, whalers continually encountered large assemblages of walruses. They treated them with caution because the animals, when affronted, attacked small boats, using their bulk and swimming speed of up to thirty-five kilometers per hour to great effect. However, Eskimo, and later European, hunters found that walruses which had hauled out of the water onto pack ice or beaches were vulnerable. Hunters could thrust sharp iron lances or whaling harpoons through the tough hides of the walruses into their chest cavities and kill them. If their lances were long enough—up to three meters—this could be done by surprise with little danger to the hunter.

During the walrus summer breeding season, which, after 1600, coincided with the summer whaling voyages, whalers who reached Spitsbergen and other islands nearby found large numbers of walruses hauled out of the water. The walruses favored sandy, flat bays in well-protected fjords that were easy to reach at flood tide.[98] Since each walrus carcass produced about two hundred kilograms of blubber that could be boiled down to about a standard barrel of oil and pass for whale oil, whalers had some incentive to kill walruses if easily done. This might be a matter of killing a few animals simply to round out a load of whale blubber. Alternatively, it might mean on occasion a wholesale slaughter to take on nearly a full cargo of walrus blubber instead of whales. Whalers also took walrus tusks and sold them when they returned home.

Early in the seventeenth century, English whalers drove the annual walrus breeding herds away from their usual sandy beaches on Bear Island. In July 1604, an English whaling ship that landed on Bear Island found over

97. Totals calculated from Jackson, *The British Whaling Trade*, 270, appendix 9.
98. Nils Stora, "Russian Walrus Hunting in Spitsbergen," *Études/Inuit/Studies* 11, no. 2 (1987): 117–38.

1,000 walruses pulled out on the beaches. They killed 100 of them. The next year, in July 1605, the same ship was back to kill between 700 to 800 walruses. Three years later, the same ship returned in summer 1608 to slaughter 900 animals in only seven hours. In the 1610 season, English whalers killed another 800 walruses. Thereafter, walruses did not return to Bear Island to breed for many years.[99] Despite this and other similar assaults, however, it was more cost-effective to kill whales than to pursue walruses for their blubber.

The most avid walrus hunters on Spitsbergen and the other islands of the Svalbard Archipelago were the Russians, who did not participate in commercial whaling. Since at least as early as the tenth century, hunters from the region of Pomor on the White Sea had killed walruses for the European market. They sold hides and tusks to Norsemen and other medieval European seafarers who found their way around the North Cape to buy ivory and tusks, probably at the mouth of the Dvina River.[100] Walrus ivory from northern Russia—with tusks that could reach half a meter in length and weigh five or more kilograms—was used for knife, sword, and dagger handles and other carved durable objects. Walrus hides, cut into strips, made extremely strong cart straps and durable harnesses and ships' rigging. By the early sixteenth century, English traders from the Muscovy Company were buying these products at Archangel on the Dvina River.

As late as the sixteenth century, walruses still could be obtained in and around the White Sea, especially at the mouth of the Pechora River and along Kostin Sound. However, Russian walrus hunters had begun to sail north to Spitsbergen to hunt the far more numerous walruses in the Svalbard Archipelago. By the seventeenth century, walruses were so depleted in the White Sea region that the entire Russian effort shifted north. Moscow's efforts to centralize all Siberian trade at the capital prevented hunting in Siberian waters. In 1620, the Russian tsar issued an edict that forbade inhabitants of the Dvina and Pechora River areas from sailing east to the Kara Sea and entering Siberia by that route.

Instead, throughout the period from about 1600 to as late as 1830, Russian hunters sailed every year to the Svalbard Archipelago. Some Russian hunters who stayed only during the summer season were financed by peasant villages. Those more expensive expeditions that wintered year-round required funds from traders. Several Old Believer orthodox monasteries, most notably the island monastery of Solovetsk, funded and organized regular hunting expeditions, manning them with monks and lay adherents.

The annual fleet was composed of 60- to 160-ton sailing and rowing vessels *(lodya)* capable of bringing back substantial loads. Each carried teams of fifteen to twenty-five hunters led by a master hunter. The ships set out on the

99. Ibid., 131.
100. Ibid., 120–21.

voyage to Spitsbergen in June or July, arriving up to fifty days later. Those who did not winter returned with their catch at the end of September. Those who stayed over returned in October of the following year, some fifteen months after their departure. During the summer, the hunters relied on finding walruses on the beaches, where they could kill great numbers of them while they were sleeping. Generally, Russian hunters only took the heads with the tusks and skins, which filled their small boats, and left the walrus blubber.

Those hunters who stayed over took shelter at about ten or so established main camps, using either prefabricated huts brought on the boats or occupying huts still standing. They used stone or brick stoves fed by driftwood. They actively hunted walruses in small boats, moving among the ice floes to find them where they had hauled out on the ice. The hunting teams also sought out and killed seals and beluga whales *(Delphinapterus leucas)* for oil and skins and eiders *(Somateria mollissima)* for down. All these activities began in February, when daylight returned, and continued until November and the onset of the polar night. By that time, the ice on the fjords, snow blizzards, and darkness made it impossible to hunt on the water. Instead, the Russians turned their attention to trapping and killing polar bears and arctic foxes for their fur.[101]

Around the end of the eighteenth century, observers counted about 270 ships with twenty-two hundred Russian hunters gathered during the summer season at Spitsbergen.[102] What their annual catch might have amounted to is impossible to estimate. We do have figures from one Russian hunting party that wintered on Spitsbergen in 1784–1785. When they returned, they had tusks and hides from 300 walruses as well as oil and skins from 230 seals, 150 polar bear skins, and 1,000 fox skins. They carried 300 kilograms of eiderdown. They also had killed 100 beluga whales and 1 larger whale, presumably a bowhead.[103] If this level of efficiency were typical, then it is surprising that walruses and other prey animals persisted in the Svalbard Archipelago as long as they did. It was not until about 1850 that walruses were extinct in these marine ecosystems.

ECONOMIC BENEFITS

Europe received large material benefits from its slaughter of the Greenland whale. The massive living biomass of the bowhead whale was a resource free for the taking. Whaling was an industry that extracted from the flesh of wild

101. Mark E. Jasinski, "Russian Hunters on Svalbard and the Polar Winter," *Arctic* 44, no. 2 (1991).
102. Stora, "Russian Walrus Hunting in Spitsbergen," 126.
103. Ibid., 119.

animals a needed industrial commodity. Whales provided an extraordinary energy link between the smallest phytoplankton swarms of the northern oceans and humans. The whaler's costs were those of the hunter, not those of the pastoralist. The demand for oil suitable for use in lamps, for soap making, for curing leather, and for lubrication of machinery grew steadily.

Arctic whaling displayed the characteristic pattern of commercially driven resource extraction. No allowance was made for any sort of conservation or sustainable use of these stocks. The Arctic bowhead herds became an open-access resource without any discernible management or restraint on the part of the users. From the early sixteenth century to the mid–nineteenth, as bowheads were killed off, the whalers shifted to more and more distant, difficult, and dangerous regions. To move from shore whaling off Labrador to drift ice hunting in Baffin Bay challenged the skill and daring of whalers, who routinely sailed where no one had ever sailed ships of that size before.

Over the entire period, and in each phase of the hunt, there was a slow reduction in productivity as the number and size of whales caught declined. For example, in the 1670s, each Dutch whaling ship took an average each year of 6.4 whales and brought home on average 279.5 metric tons of blubber. One hundred years later, in the 1770s, the annual average catch per ship was only 2.2 animals that yielded 100.7 tons of blubber.[104] Whaling became more costly and uncertain but remained profitable until the final years of each phase.

Despite productivity trends, supplies of whale oil proved to be reliably available and consistently price-competitive with vegetable and other sources for oils in the early modern market. From 1661 to 1800, Dutch and German whalers brought back to Europe blubber sufficient to produce 5 million barrels of whale oil (11.6 million hectoliters). Replacing the whale oil consumed in the European economy every year with vegetable oil would have placed heavy demands on agriculture. Thousands of hectares of land would have been devoted to growing rape and other oilseeds in addition to or at the expense of growing food grains or other edibles. The thousands of tons of whalebone that landed in European ports became a consumption material that had no real equal in flexibility, strength, and versatility until the arrival of plastics in the late nineteenth century.

By any of the standard economic measures, whaling was more than a niche or specialty enterprise. The industry made a substantial contribution to the economy of early modern Europe. Chartering, insuring, provisioning, and supplying equipment to the combined Dutch and German whaling fleets each year demanded a heavy investment. By one estimate contempo-

104. De Jong, "The Hunt of the Greenland Whale," 99, table 11B.

rary to the time, preparing the typical Dutch whaler of the early eighteenth century to make the voyage cost 12,500 guilders: 6,500 Dutch guilders for casks, provisions, whaleboats, and gear; 3,000 guilders for the hire of the ship and insurance; and 3,000 guilders for payment of the forty-two-man crew.[105] If in an average year 175 ships sailed to the Arctic from Dutch and German ports, the initial investment needed was about 2 million guilders. This was a considerable sum if we consider that total private capital in the Netherlands in 1650 is estimated at 500 to 550 million guilders.[106]

Employment generated by whaling remained consistently high. Direct employment of seamen averaged around eighty-five hundred men per whaling season for the combined Dutch and German fleets in the seventeenth and eighteenth centuries.[107] Indirect employment of coopers, smiths, warehousemen, blubber boilers, shipyard workers, ships' chandlers, traders, and others was probably equal to that figure. Demand for whale oil and whalebone rose steadily. The price of whale oil, amid fluctuations, doubled from 35 guilders per quarter in the 1660s to 62 in the 1770s; whalebone nearly tripled, from 48 to 120 guilders per hundredweight in the same period.[108] Dozens of whale oil refineries and soap factories grew up along the Zaan River opposite Amsterdam and in Rotterdam. France imported by far the greatest share of Dutch refined whale-oil exports.[109]

Was Arctic whaling profitable for the nation? Certainly, contemporaries and near-contemporaries thought so. Early modern European states repeatedly sent warships to escort their whaling vessels, waived customs duties on incoming whale blubber, offered royal monopolies to whaling entrepreneurs, organized state-run whaling companies, and even offered subsidies to

105. Scoresby, *An Account of the Arctic Regions, with a History and Description of the Northern Whale-Fishery*, 2:150. Scoresby, a British whaling captain himself, relied on the statistical work of the Dutch whaling historian Cornelis Zorgdrager, who published his results in the eighteenth century. Cornelis Gijsbertsz Zorgdrager and Georg Peter Monath, *Beschreibung des groenlaendischen Wallfischfangs und Fischerey, nebst einer gründlichen Nachricht von dem Bakkeljau- und Stockfischfang bey Terreneuf und einer kurzen Abhandlung von Groenland, Island, Spitzbergen, Nova Zembla, Jan Mayen Eiland, der Strasse Davids u. a.* (Nuernberg: G. P. Monath, 1750). In his own calculations, Scoresby used the lower figure of 10,000 guilders suggested by another eighteenth-century Dutch student of whaling.

106. Jan Luiten Van Zanden, "Economic Growth in the Golden Age: The Development of the Economy of Holland, 1500–1650," in *The Dutch Economy in the Golden Age*, edited by Karel Davids and L. Noordegraaf (Amsterdam: Nederlandsch Economisch-Historisch Archief, 1993), 23, table 10.

107. Calculated at an average of forty-two men per crew for recorded sailings in the period 1670–1770. See De Jong, "The Hunt of the Greenland Whale," 91, table 1.

108. Scoresby, *An Account of the Arctic Regions, with a History and Description of the Northern Whale-Fishery*, 2:156.

109. Jonathan I. Israel, *Dutch Primacy in World Trade, 1585–1740* (Oxford: Clarendon Press; New York: Oxford University Press, 1990), 115, 268, 285–86.

encourage the industry. The Dutch were much envied and admired for their skill and profits.

William Scoresby, using Dutch statistical data, calculated for the period 1669–1778 that Dutch whalers received 274.8 million guilders for whale oil and whalebone at prevailing prices. Their expenses—including allowance for lost ships—totaled 218.6 million guilders, leaving a gross profit of 56.2 million guilders. This works out to an average of 525,523 guilders average profit per year on expenditures of slightly over 2 million guilders, or 26.2 percent.[110] This figure is probably high, as Scoresby admits, because his figure of 10,000 guilders per ship for expenditures is on the low side. If he had allowed a higher figure for construction and ownership of the vessels, the profit margin "would have been reduced to near one-half" or 12 to 13 percent.[111]

Obviously, as later historians have commented, this kind of all-encompassing calculation disguises short-term fluctuations and losses. Nevertheless, year after year, European investors put large sums of capital into building or renting, fitting out, manning, and sailing whalers to the Arctic. At the end of the day, the biomass of the Arctic translated into energy and profits for Europeans.

CONCLUSION

What were the environmental effects of three centuries of mayhem inflicted by European hunters on the walrus and the Greenland bowhead whale? (See table 16.1.) Human predation killed off both species in that region. From an original herd size estimated at 25,000 animals, the Atlantic walrus disappeared completely from the marine ecosystem around Spitsbergen by 1870.[112] No estimate for average or annual kills is really possible, but descriptive evidence implies incessant hunting, especially by Russian hunters, as well as ongoing kills by whalers seeking to round out their cargoes of whale oil.

Removal of 36,000 bowhead and 25,000 walruses from the marine ecosys-

110. Scoresby, *An Account of the Arctic Regions, with a History and Description of the Northern Whale-Fishery*, 2:157. I have combined the totals for the Greenland and Davis Straits fisheries that Scoresby separated out.

111. Ibid.

112. Louwrens Hacquebord, "Three Centuries of Whaling and Walrus Hunting in Svalbard and Its Impact on the Arctic Ecosystem," *Environment and History* 7 (2001): 176–77. Hacquebord offers the larger figure of 46,000 as the preexploitation herd size for bowhead whales, but assumes a lower annual food consumption figure of 76 metric tons per animal to arrive at 3.5 million tons of zooplankton consumed yearly.

TABLE 16.1 Greenland Whales Killed, 1500–1800

	Dutch	Germans	English	French	Basques	Danes	Total
1530–1607	—	—	—	—	25,000	—	25,000
1607–1661	24,000	—	2,000	2,000	2,000	1,000	31,000
1661–1719	31,000	11,000	—	3,000	2,000	—	47,000
1719–1800	34,500	5,500	—	1,000	1,000	—	42,000
1800–1850	1,000	—	16,500	—	—	—	17,500
TOTAL	90,500	16,500	18,500	6,000	30,000	1,000	162,500

tem made some 4 million metric tons of additional food available each year for other organisms. Bowhead whales feeding on tiny crustaceans or zooplankton consume about one hundred metric tons per animal per year. The beneficiaries of the whales' disappearance were polar cod *(Boreogadus saida)* and capelin *(Mallotus villosus)* as well as planktonivorous seabirds like little auks *(Alle alle)*. When cod and capelin increased, the numbers of fish-eating seabirds such as Brunnich's guillemots *(Uria lomvia)* and common guillemots *(Cepphus grylle)* must have risen. The same is true of the cod-eating populations of Greenland seals *(Phoca groenlandica)* and minke whales *(Balaenoptera acutorostrata)*.[113] Walruses feed on bivalves and decapod crustaceans, annually consuming, on average, around 20 metric tons per year per animal.[114] Their disappearance freed up food for bearded seals *(Erignathus barbatus)* and diving ducks such as eiders.

From a herd in the eastern Arctic originally made up of about 36,000 large animals that live forty years or more, Europeans killed between 150,000 and 200,000 bowhead whales. Logbook data from whalers suggest that between 15 and 20 percent of the whales struck were lost.[115] Of these many, if not most, were presumed to have died of their wounds. Year after year, several hundred whales were slaughtered in a harrying that surely disrupted and reduced their slow reproductive cycles. (See table 16.2.)

For animals that had few natural predators and few mortal dangers to overcome in the course of their long lives, human predation must have been

113. Ibid., 178.
114. Hacquebord, "Three Centuries of Whaling and Walrus Hunting in Svalbard and Its Impact on the Arctic Ecosystem," 176.
115. Woodby and Botkin, "Stock Sizes Prior to Commercial Whaling," 393.

TABLE 16.2 Peak Dutch and German Whaling, 1661–1800 (by Dates Ships Sailed)

| | 1661–1719 | | | | | | | |
| | Dates Ships Sailed | | | | | | | |
	1661–1669	1670–1679	1680–1689	1690–1699	1700–1709	1710–1719	Totals	Annual Averages
Number of ships								
German	0	561	553	492	544	573	2,723	45
Dutch	970	985	1,922	944	1,631	1,435	7,887	131
TOTAL	970	1,546	2,475	1,436	2,175	2,008	10,610	177
Ships lost								
German	0	19	26	36	44	15	140	2
Dutch	19	80	114	79	61	55	408	7
TOTAL	19	99	140	115	105	70	548	9
Whales caught								
German	0	3,747	2,376	1,129	2,343	1,431	11,026	184
Dutch	4,815	6,325	9,529	5,474	7,982	4,822	38,947	649
TOTAL	4,815	10,072	11,905	6,603	10,325	6,253	49,973	833
Tuns of blubber								
German	0	186,084	101,295	48,569	81,164	54,175	471,287	7,855
Dutch	231,565	275,304	370,190	209,982	279,439	176,274	1,542,754	25,713
TOTAL	231,565	461,388	471,485	258,551	360,603	230,449	2,014,041	33,567
Tuns of blubber per whale	48	46	40	39	35	37	40	
Whale oil (in quarters)								
German	0	279,126	151,943	72,854	121,746	78,263	703,932	11,732
Dutch	347,348	412,956	555,285	314,973	419,159	264,411	2,314,132	38,569
TOTAL	347,348	692,082	707,228	387,827	540,905	342,674	3,018,064	50,301

1720–1800

				Dates Ships Sailed						
	1720–1729	1730–1739	1740–1749	1750–1759	1760–1769	1770–1779	1780–1789	1790–1799	Totals	Annual Averages
Number of ships										
German	427	401	222	215	273	302	376	0	2,216	28
Dutch	2,239	1,847	1,712	1,677	1,620	1,289	541	360	11,285	141
TOTAL	2,666	2,248	1,934	1,892	1,893	1,591	917	360	13,501	169
Ships lost										
German	17	10	3	9	3	10	6	0	58	1
Dutch	57	34	28	36	26	37	5	31	254	4
TOTAL	74	44	31	45	29	47	11	31	312	5
Whales caught										
German	1,077	544	563	503	589	889	1,306	0	5,471	91
Dutch	4,762	4,386	8,011	5,336	4,500	3,878	2,697	792	34,362	573
TOTAL	5,839	4,930	8,574	5,839	5,089	4,767	4,003	792	39,833	664
Tuns of blubber										
German	44,179	25,792	24,598	16,573	21,862	46,584	46,805	0	226,393	2,830
Dutch	207,427	216,834	256,851	160,909	144,501	129,776	63,779	22,489	1,202,566	15,032
TOTAL	251,606	242,626	281,449	177,482	166,363	176,360	110,584	22,489	1,428,959	17,862
Tuns of blubber per whale	43	49	33	30	33	37	28	28	36	
Whale oil (in quarters)										
German	67,079	38,688	36,897	24,860	32,793	65,376	70,208	0	335,901	4,199
Dutch	311,141	325,251	385,277	241,364	216,752	194,664	95,668	34,274	1,804,391	22,555
TOTAL	378,220	363,939	422,174	266,224	249,545	260,040	165,876	34,274	2,140,292	26,754

SOURCE: De Jong, *Geschiedenis van de oude Nederlandse walvisvaart.* Calculated from tables in vol. 3.

especially trauma inducing. The extent of collective and individual trauma inflicted by the whalers on the survivors—highly intelligent, highly sociable animals—can only be surmised. By mid–nineteenth century, of the once prolific herds of bowheads in Greenland waters, only a few animals remained.

Conclusion

The global scale and impact of human intervention in the natural environment during the early modern period were unprecedented in history. Accelerating productivity during this time rested firmly on access to unused, and often previously unknown, natural resources. These resources became accessible and valuable as a more efficient world economy linked resource extraction with core areas over longer distances. New technological inventions and innovations, especially in maritime transport and industrial production, raised economic output. Global communications and connections between human societies in distant world regions reached an unprecedented level of ease and intensity. Demands for natural resources, for cultivable land, and for control over the natural world at the global scale escalated.

The early modern near-doubling of human numbers generated new pressures on the natural world. Especially critical, however, was a pronounced rise in organizational capacity and efficiency. Increasingly capable states ordered and directed human efforts to mobilize natural resources. States and corporate organizations extended their reach beyond their homelands to distant regions where resources exhausted at home still could be found in abundance.

Early modern states in Eurasia and colonial states in the New World and Africa sought to maximize the productivity of the lands under their control. Without state protection and support, those groups and individuals who actually carried out the daily operations of changing the land or hunting for the market would have been far less productive and far less enterprising. Certainly, early modern states tried at times to restrain expansion so that they could control resource exploitation and its profits, and often they encountered difficulties in so doing. Admittedly, states were imperfect instruments whose policies were never executed entirely as planned. Nevertheless, as many of the foregoing case studies show, those who exploited new lands and resources depended on the protected space, the public order, that early modern states offered them. Without this support, the investment and capital for pioneers—and indeed the volunteers themselves—would not have materialized.

As the case studies detailed in each chapter reveal, shared long-term historical processes—settlement frontiers, biological invasions, and the world hunt—imposed shattering changes on regional ecosystems around the world. During the early modern period, there was an irresistible, and seemingly irreversible, trend toward more intensive human control and use of the land and the natural environment. As this occurred, those intricate local assemblages of vegetation and fauna that had long flourished with far less human intervention lost complexity, lost diversity, lost numerous species, and sometimes even were eradicated completely.

Simultaneously, hundreds of groups of indigenous peoples in all regions of the world experienced devastating losses. They suffered disease and high mortality, loss of land, loss of material well-being, and above all, loss of confidence and cultural certainty. Hunter-gatherers, shifting cultivators, and pastoral nomads fit awkwardly into the tightening strands of the early modern world.

Human intervention aimed at cultivation or other measures designed to increase economic productivity resulted in a loss of biomass and biodiversity for both animals and plants on land and in marine ecosystems. (The invasions of new, exotic species, with their lethal effects on indigenous species, appear to have led to a simplification of ecosystems, not the reverse.) These processes, once under way, have continued with little restraint or diversion in the nineteenth and twentieth centuries.

Another, less obvious but important theme is that of the continuing oscillation between abundance and scarcity of natural resources. Pioneers who moved to settlement frontiers confronted a perplexing and exhilarating abundance of vegetation, wildlife, freshwater, and fertile soils in sharp contrast to the resource scarcities they had left behind in their former homes. Around the world, pioneers found nearby expanses of woods and forests that offered wood for fuel and construction simply for the effort of cutting it. They found scarce minerals that could be readily mined with rudimentary tools. Above all, they found land that could be cleared, plowed, and planted, or that could be used for livestock grazing and browsing. Of course, much waste occurred when pioneers were unfamiliar with plants and animals and their economic potential.

Pioneer settlers encountered a profusion of wild animals, birds, and fish that could be readily slaughtered, eaten, or skinned for their hides and other useful materials. In early years, their numbers seemed inexhaustible. Edible wild animals ranging from sea turtles to waterfowl to deer and eland were a mainstay of settler diets. Without these initial caloric inputs, it is unlikely that human dispersal would have been as extensive or rapid. Unfortunately, thoughts of conservation or of restraint came, if at all, well after the virtual extirpation of the animals in question.

The numbers of wildlife were truly astonishing. We have generally lost from our collective memory any notion of the scale and size of wildlife populations before intensified human predation. Only now are ecologists rethinking their perceptions of normal sizes of wildlife populations by rediscovering both documentary and material evidence from the past. The authors of a recent interpretive article on coastal ecosystems comment:

> Few modern ecological studies take into account the former natural abundance of large marine vertebrates. There are dozens of places in the Caribbean named after large sea turtles whose adult populations now number in the tens of thousands rather than the tens of millions of a few centuries ago. Whales, manatees, dugongs, sea cows, monk seals, crocodiles, codfish, jewfish, swordfish, sharks and rays are other large marine vertebrates that are now functionally or entirely extinct in most coastal ecosystems. Place names for oysters, pearls and conches conjure up other ecological ghosts of marine invertebrates that were once so abundant as to pose hazards to navigation but are witnessed now only by massive garbage heaps of empty shells.[1]

The authors argue that severe exploitation in the past lies behind recent, mysterious collapses of coastal marine ecosystems. They also suggest that present-minded ecologists are too prone to accept the depleted populations of the past few decades as normal, instead of vestigial. Save in the most rigorously protected national nature reserves, today's world landscapes have lost the abundant variety of larger animals and birds that marked those same areas five hundred years before.

Abundance created a windfall mind-set in frontier societies. When food, energy, and materials sources were depleted, the frontier could simply move on to new, "untouched" resources available simply by appropriation. Many pioneer settlers made little effort to conserve resources or develop sophisticated ecological understanding of their new environments. In the early stages of frontier life, they wasted resources in ways that outside observers at the time deplored.

However, many other settlers who did not move on displayed a strong

---

1. See J. B. C. Jackson et al., "Historical Overfishing and the Recent Collapse of Coastal Ecosystems," *Science* 293, no. 5530 (July 27, 2001): 629.

sense of stewardship. Most came from regions where scarcity forced assiduous management of land and resources. They applied these standards as they learned the intricate details of microclimate, soil texture and fertility, vegetation cover, topography, and water cycles of their new homeland. Those pioneer settlers who stayed put tended to become reflective, serious land managers.

Following early modern frontier expansion, great expanses of the world's lands and resources were subject to new sets of rules governing human use. Slowly, but perceptibly, the early modern world began moving toward state-approved and -legitimated property rights regimes over land and resources. Although the new regimes differed widely in terminology and taxonomy, their overall effects were similar.[2]

Groups in areas of new settlement rapidly applied finely tuned property rights regimes over land and resources. Land, in particular, was divided, allocated, located, mapped, and occupied. Former frontier societies delineated discrete rights over land, wildlife, minerals, and freshwater. The loosely defined, highly particularized property rights regimes of indigenous peoples disappeared, to be replaced by property rights in land that were acceptable to states that claimed to control the territory involved. Fast-evolving property rights regulated which individuals and groups could benefit from occupancy, cultivation, timbering, or any of dozens of other conceivable economic processes that created value. As this occurred, these newly defined land rights acquired value that could be expressed in monetary terms and that could be bought, sold, rented, or mortgaged in ever expanding markets. However, to be effective, the new rights ultimately depended on recognition and affirmation by a legitimate state.

As the frontier receded, the real task was that of sustained resource management, of land management. How could new, productive landscapes be conceived, arduously improved, and painstakingly maintained for decades and for centuries? How could losses or desolation be repaired or restored? What were the shared aesthetic and cultural attitudes and practices that articulated best practices for land managers? How could these best be passed from one human generation to another? Could individual smallholding cultivators remain fiercely individualistic? Alternatively, should they come together in joint management of community resources in common property regimes while retaining individually owned and managed plots and homesteads? What were the solutions encouraged, permitted, or forbidden by the state? There were no optimal blueprints or answers for these questions.

2. John F. Richards, "Toward a Global System of Property Rights in Land," in *Land Property and the Environment,* edited by John F. Richards (Oakland, Calif.: Institute of Contemporary Studies Press, 2001).

Rather, settlers, learning by trial and error, devised more or less satisfactory patterns of land use that combined productivity with sustainable practices.

On the one hand, property rules provided security for land managers by giving them and their heirs some assurance of return on their labor and investment. On the other hand, property rules also generated ownership claims to land that, given a buoyant economy, could be salable at ever rising prices. Speculation and profit in rising land markets rarely lead to wise and sustainable long-term land use. State-backed property rights in land were a tool that could be used to protect community values and resist the land market or, alternatively, could be employed by individuals and groups to profit from market demand. Either option was possible.[3] Evolving land markets were, however, a characteristic of intensified land use in the early modern period.

Energy became a problem in the early modern period. Densely settled societies with dynamic economies began to encounter problems in finding fuel for domestic and industrial purposes. The universal fuel was biomass gathered from trees, bushes, and grasses, as well as straw and crop stubble, or, alternatively, animal dung. As the population, especially urban numbers, grew, the demands for fuel rose relentlessly. Nearly all forms of industrial production required heat—some, such as salt boiling or beer making, a great deal of heat. In colder climates, household fuel in the winter was a matter of life or death.

For most purposes, the best option was wood burnt either directly or converted to charcoal. The problem was simply that daily demands for fuel meant incessant wood cutting and gathering in an ever widening arc around each rural homestead and each village, town, and city. Cutting for fuel also coincided with clearing additional land for cultivation to grow food in areas near towns and cities.

Unless carefully protected and regulated, trees and bushes were not permitted to regrow naturally in the face of this intense demand. Forests protected by royal, ecclesiastical, or noble authority could be saved from depredation and could yield controlled amounts of fuel each year while preserving the woodland—but this was never a fully adequate solution to voracious energy appetites.

Invariably, prices of fuelwood spiraled upward, reflecting the effort required to fetch it at lengthening distances and the scarcity of the more desirable, hotter or better burning varieties. To some extent, higher prices attracted supplies for urban markets from more distant areas with still-thick tree cover. If water carriage by canal, river, or coastal shipping was possible, forests several hundred miles away could be exploited.

Ultimately, however, higher prices imposed rationing. Poorer consumers shifted to less efficient, less desirable forms of biomass fuel. Clever innovations in stoves that were adapted to these practices and that reduced fuel consumption helped, but they only slowed the trend. Conservation, minimal consumption, and eventually, population restraints became a necessity in societies across Eurasia in the eighteenth century.

One way out of the energy impasse could have been a radical restructuring of land use to provide for continually producing woodlots on a very large scale. However, despite the rise of silvicultural knowledge and practice, only Tokugawa Japan appears to have done this relatively successfully—but only with strict rationing and conservation measures. No other early modern society adopted or contemplated such a formidable reshaping of its landscape. To do so demanded a high degree of foresight on the part of the state, as well as vision and discipline in local communities.

The only other alternative was to move to another fuel source. During the seventeenth century, the Netherlands shifted to peat as its primary source of energy. As we have seen, the Dutch developed new methods for extracting, processing, carrying, and burning peat. Water transport on canals helped to keep prices down and availability high. Even with this expedient, however, the Dutch began to reach the limits of their domestic supply of peat by mid– to late eighteenth century.

Ultimately, coal burning proved to be the way out of the energy cul-de-sac. As the chapter on the British Isles describes, Britain was the first society in the world to substitute fossil fuel for biomass as its primary energy source. By 1800, coal was the leading domestic and industrial fuel in the British Isles. With coal as the new energy source, with steam power as a new prime mover, and with worked iron as a principal industrial material, all the components of the industrial revolution were in place.

What of the frontier, then: was it unending? In the early nineteenth century, yes. There were still ample lands yet to be settled in various parts of the world, from the American Midwest to interior Brazil to the Burma delta. Today, in the early twenty-first century, the frontier is no longer unending. From our perspective, the title of this volume is ironic. There are few, if any, possibilities for settlement frontiers around the globe today.

We have moved into a postfrontier phase in which resources are no longer abundant, but are limited and scarce. Humans are now the stewards and managers of the world's lands and ecosystems. Wise and responsible management from local scale to the global scale is the only possible strategy. The ultimate test of our emergent global society is how we shape the domesticated landscape that human action has created over the past half millennium.

Abénon, Lucien-René. *La Guadeloupe de 1671 à 1759: Étude politique, économique et sociale.* Paris: L'Harmattan, 1987.

Abreu-Ferreira, Darlene. "Terra Nova through the Iberian Looking Glass: The Portuguese-Newfoundland Cod Fishery in the Sixteenth Century." *Canadian Historical Review* 79, no. 1 (1998): 100–15.

Adshead, S. A. M. "An Energy Crisis in Early Modern China." *Late Imperial China* 3 (1974): 20–28.

———. *Material Culture in Europe and China, 1400–1800: The Rise of Consumerism.* New York: St. Martin's Press, 1997.

Aguilar, Alex. "A Review of Old Basque Whaling and Its Effect on the Right Whales (*Eubalaena glacialis*) of the North Atlantic." In *Right Whales: Past and Present Status: Proceedings of the Workshop on the Status of Right Whales, New England Aquarium, Boston, Massachusetts, 15–23 June 1983,* edited by Robert L. Brownell, P. B. Best, John H. Prescott, the New England Aquarium Corporation, and the International Whaling Commission, 191–99. Cambridge, Eng.: International Whaling Commission, 1986.

Albion, Robert G. *Forests and Sea Power: The Timber Problem of the Royal Navy, 1652–1862.* Cambridge: Harvard University Press, 1926.

Albion, Robert Greenhalgh, William A. Baker, and Benjamin Woods Labaree. *New England and the Sea.* Middletown: Wesleyan University Press, for the Marine Historical Association Mystic Seaport, 1972.

Allen, Robert C. *Enclosure and the Yeoman.* Oxford: Clarendon Press; New York: Oxford University Press, 1992.

———. "Tracking the Agricultural Revolution in England." *Economic History Review* 52, no. 2 (1999): 209–35.

Anderson, Roger Y. "Long-Term Changes in the Frequency of Occurrence of El Niño Events." In *Climate since A.D. 1500,* edited by Raymond S. Bradley and Philip D. Jones, 193–200. Rev. ed. London: Routledge, 1995.

Andrade, Antonio. "Political Spectacle and Colonial Rule: The *Landdag* on Dutch Taiwan, 1629–1648." *Itinerario* 21, no. 3 (1997): 57–93.

Andren, Anders W. "The Global Cycle of Mercury." In *The Biogeochemistry of Mercury in the Environment,* edited by Jerome O. Nriagu, 1–21. Amsterdam: Elsevier and North-Holland Biomedical Press, 1979.

Antonil, André João, and Afonso de E. Taunay. *Cultura e opulencia do Brazil por suas drogas e minas, com um estudo bio-bibliográfico.* São Paulo: Companhia do melhoramentos de São Paulo, 1923.

Appleby, Andrew B. *Famine in Tudor and Stuart England.* Stanford, Calif.: Stanford University Press, 1978.

Appleby, John C. "A 'Voyage to Greenland for the Catching of Whales': English Whaling Enterprise in the Seventeenth Century." *International Journal of Maritime History* 9, no. 2 (1997): 29–49.

Armstrong, James C., and Nigel A. Worden. "The Slaves, 1652–1834." In *The Shaping of South African Society, 1652–1840,* edited by Richard Elphick and Hermann Giliomee, 109–83. Middletown, Conn.: Wesleyan University Press, 1989.

Armstrong, T. "Bering's Expeditions." In *Studies in Russian Historical Geography,* edited by James H. Bater and R. A. French. London: Academic Press, 1983.

Asprey, G. F., and R. G. Robbins. "The Vegetation of Jamaica." *Ecological Monographs* 23, no. 4 (1953): 359–412.

Attman, Artur. *The Russian and Polish Markets in International Trade, 1500–1650.* Göteborg: Institute of Economic History of Gothenburg University, 1973.

Atwell, William. "The T'ai-ch'ang, T'ien-ch'i, and Ch'ung-chen Regimes." In *The Cambridge History of China,* edited by Denis Crispin Twitchett and John King Fairbank, vol. 7, pt. 1, pp. 585–640. Cambridge: Cambridge University Press, 1988.

———. "A Seventeenth-Century 'General Crisis' in East Asia?" *Modern Asian Studies* 24, no. 4 (1990): 661–82.

Averill, Stephen C. "The Shed People and the Opening of the Yangzi Highlands." *Modern China* 9 (1983): 84–126.

Bagge, Ole, and Fritz Thurow. "The Baltic Cod Stock: Fluctuation and Possible Causes." In *Cod and Climate Change: Proceedings of a Symposium Held in Reykjavík, 23–27 August 1993,* edited by Jakob Jakobsson and the International Council for the Exploration of the Sea, 254–68. ICES Marine Science Symposia, v. 198. Copenhagen: International Council for the Exploration of the Sea, 1994.

Bailey, Alfred Goldsworthy. *The Conflict of European and Eastern Algonkian Cultures, 1504–1700: A Study in Canadian Civilization.* 2d ed. Toronto: University of Toronto Press, 1976.

Bakewell, Peter J. *Silver Mining and Society in Colonial Mexico: Zacatecas, 1546–1700.* Cambridge: Cambridge University Press, 1971.

———. "Mining in Colonial Spanish America." In *The Cambridge History of Latin America,* vol. 2, edited by Leslie Bethell. Cambridge: Cambridge University Press, 1984.

Bakeyev, Nikolai N., and Andrei N. Sinitsyn. "Sables in the Commonwealth of Independent States." In *Martens, Sables, and Fishers: Biology and Conservation,* edited by Steven Buskirk, 246–54. Ithaca, N.Y.: Cornell University Press, 1994.

Barickman, B. J. " 'Tame Indians,' 'Wild Heathens,' and Settlers in Southern Bahia in the Late Eighteenth and Early Nineteenth Centuries." *Americas* 51 (1995): 325–69.

Barkham, Michael M. "French Basque 'NewFound Land' Entrepreneurs and the Import of Codfish and Whale Oil to Northern Spain, c. 1580 to c. 1620: The Case of Adam de Chibau, Burgess of Saint-Jean-de-Luz and 'Sieur de St. Julien.'" *Newfoundland Studies* 10, no. 1 (1994): 1–43.

Barraclough, Geoffrey, and Richard Overy, eds. *Hammond Atlas of World History.* 5th ed. Maplewood, N.J.: Hammond, 1999.

Bauerenfeind, Walter, and Ulrich Woitek. "The Influence of Climatic Change on Price Fluctuations in Germany during the Sixteenth Century Price Revolution." *Climatic Change* 43, no. 1 (1999): 303–21.

Beattie, Hilary J. *Land and Lineage in China: A Study of T'ung-ch'eng County, Anhwei, in the Ming and Ch'ing Dynasties.* Cambridge: Cambridge University Press, 1979.

Behringer, Wolfgang. "Climatic Change and Witch-Hunting: The Impact of the Little Ice Age on Mentalities." *Climatic Change* 43, no. 1 (1999): 335–51.

Beketov, Petr. "September 6, 1633, Report to Tsar Mikhail Fedorovich from the Steltsy Sotnik [Musketeer Commander] Petr Beketov Concerning His Expedition on the Lena River." In *Russia's Conquest of Siberia, 1558–1700: A Documentary Record,* edited by Basil Dmytryshyn, E. A. P. Crownhart-Vaughan, and Thomas Vaughan. Vol. 1 of *To Siberia and Russian America.* Portland, Ore.: Western Imprints, the Press of the Oregon Historical Society, 1985.

Benes, P., and B. Havlik. "Speciation of Mercury in Natural Waters." In *The Biogeochemistry of Mercury in the Environment,* edited by Jerome O. Nriagu, 175–202. Amsterdam: Elsevier and North-Holland Biomedical Press, 1979.

Berry, Mary Elizabeth. *Hideyoshi.* Cambridge: Harvard University Press, 1982.

Bethell, Leslie. *The Cambridge History of Latin America.* 11 vols. Cambridge: Cambridge University Press, 1984.

Bjorndal, Karen A. *Biology and Conservation of Sea Turtles.* Rev. ed. Washington: Smithsonian Institution Press, 1995.

Black, Jeremy. *A Military Revolution? Military Change and European Society, 1550–1800.* London: Macmillan, 1991.

Blackburn, Robin. *The Making of New World Slavery: From the Baroque to the Modern, 1492–1800.* London: Verso, 1997.

Blaikie, Piers M., and H. C. Brookfield. *Land Degradation and Society.* London: Methuen, 1987.

Blaut, James M. *The Colonizer's Model of the World: Geographical Diffusionism and Eurocentric History.* New York: Guilford Press, 1993.

Bockstoce, John R., and Daniel B. Botkin. "The Historical Status and Reduction of the Western Arctic Bowhead Whale *(Balaena mysticetus)* Population by the Pelagic Whaling Industry, 1848–1914." In *Historical Whaling Records: Including the Proceedings of the International Workshop on Historical Whaling Records, Sharon, Massachusetts, September 12–16, 1977,* edited by Michael F. Tillman, Gregory P. Donovan, and the International Whaling Commission, 83–106. Cambridge, Eng.: International Whaling Commission, 1983.

Bolitho, Harold. "The *Han.*" In *The Cambridge History of Japan,* vol. 4, edited by John Whitney Hall. Cambridge: Cambridge University Press, 1988.

Boomgaard, Peter. "The VOC Trade in Forest Products in the Seventeenth Century." In *Nature and the Orient: The Environmental History of South and Southeast Asia,* edited by Richard Grove, Vinita Damodaran, and Satpal Sangwan, 375–95. Delhi: Oxford University Press, 1998.

Borisenkov, Ye. P. "Documentary Evidence from the U.S.S.R." In *Climate since A.D. 1500,* edited by Raymond S. Bradley and Philip D. Jones, 171–83. Rev. ed. London: Routledge, 1995.

Boserup, Ester. *Population and Technological Change: A Study of Long-Term Trends.* Chicago: University of Chicago Press, 1981.

Boxer, C. R. *The Dutch in Brazil, 1624–1654.* Oxford: Clarendon Press, 1957.

———. *The Golden Age of Brazil: Growing Pains of a Colonial Society, 1695–1750.* New York: St. Martin's Press, 1995.

Braddick, Michael J. *State Formation in Early Modern England, c.1550–1700.* Cambridge: Cambridge University Press, 2000.

Brading, D. A. *Haciendas and Ranchos in the Mexican Bajio, Leon, 1700–1860.* Cambridge: Cambridge University Press, 1978.

Bradley, Raymond S., and Philip D. Jones. *Climate since A.D. 1500.* Rev. ed. London: Routledge, 1995.

———. " 'Little Ice Age' Summer Temperature Variations: Their Nature and Relevance to Recent Global Warming Trends." *Holocene* 3 (1993): 367–76.

Brandão, José António. *Your Fyre Shall Burn No More: Iroquois Policy towards New France and Its Native Allies to 1701.* Lincoln: University of Nebraska Press, 1997.

Braund, Kathryn E. Holland. *Deerskins and Duffels: The Creek Indian Trade with Anglo-America, 1685–1815.* Lincoln: University of Nebraska Press, 1993.

Bray, Francesca. "Agriculture." Pt. 2 of *Biology and Biological Technology,* edited by Francesca Bray. Vol. 6 of *Science and Civilisation in China,* edited by Joseph Needham. Cambridge: Cambridge University Press, 1984.

Brewer, John. *The Sinews of Power: War, Money, and the English State, 1688–1783.* 1st Amer. ed. New York: Knopf, 1989.

Briffa, K. R., P. D. Jones, F. H. Schweingruber, and T. J. Osborn. "Influence of Volcanic Eruptions on Northern Hemisphere Summer Temperature over the Past 600 Years." *Nature* 393 (1998).

Briffa, K. R., P. D. Jones, R. B. Vogel, F. H. Schweingruber, M. G. L. Baillie, and S. G. Shiyatov. "European Tree Rings and Climate in the Sixteenth Century." *Climatic Change* 43, no. 1 (1999): 151–68.

Brimblecombe, Peter. *The Big Smoke: A History of Air Pollution in London since Medieval Times.* London: Methuen, 1987.

Brockington, Lolita Gutiérrez. *The Leverage of Labor: Managing the Cortez Haciendas in Tehuantepec, 1588–1688.* Durham: Duke University Press, 1989.

Brooks, George E. *Landlords and Strangers: Ecology, Society, and Trade in Western Africa, 1000–1630.* Boulder: Westview Press, 1993.

Brotton, Jerry. *Trading Territories: Mapping the Early Modern World.* Ithaca, N.Y.: Cornell University Press, 1998.

Brown, D. J., W. A. Hubert, and S. H. Anderson. "Beaver Ponds Create Wetland Habitat for Birds in Mountains of Southeast Wyoming." *Wetlands* 16, no. 2 (1996): 127–33.

Brown, Philip C. *Central Authority and Local Autonomy in the Formation of Early Modern Japan: The Case of Kaga Domain.* Stanford, Calif.: Stanford University Press, 1993.

———. "State, Cultivator, Land: Determination of Land Tenures in Early Modern Japan Reconsidered." *Journal of Asian Studies* 56, no. 2 (1997): 421–44.

Brownell, Robert L., P. B. Best, John H. Prescott, the New England Aquarium Corporation, and the International Whaling Commission. *Right Whales: Past and Present Status: Proceedings of the Workshop on the Status of Right Whales, New England Aquarium, Boston, Massachusetts, 15–23 June 1983*. Cambridge, Eng.: International Whaling Commission, 1986.

Buch, Erik, Svend Aage Horsted, and Holger Hovgard. "Fluctuations in the Occurrence of Cod in Greenland Waters and Their Possible Causes." In *Cod and Climate Change: Proceedings of a Symposium Held in Reykjavík, 23–27 August, 1993*, edited by Jakob Jakobsson and International Council for the Exploration of the Sea, 158–74. ICES Marine Science Symposia, v. 198. Copenhagen: Denmark International Council for the Exploration of the Sea, 1994.

Burns, John J., J. Jerome Montague, Cleveland J. Cowles, and Society for Marine Mammalogy. *The Bowhead Whale*. Lawrence, Kans.: Society for Marine Mammalogy, 1993.

Bushkovitch, Paul. *The Merchants of Moscow, 1580–1650*. Cambridge: Cambridge University Press, 1980.

Buskirk, Steven. "Diets of, and Prey Selection by, Sables *(Martes zibellina)* in Northern China." *Journal of Mammalogy* 77 (1996): 725–30.

———, ed. *Martens, Sables, and Fishers: Biology and Conservation*. Ithaca, N.Y.: Cornell University Press, 1994.

Buskirk, Steven, and Roger A. Powell. "Habitat Ecology of Fishers and American Martens." In *Martens, Sables, and Fishers: Biology and Conservation*, edited by Steven Buskirk, 283–96. Ithaca, N.Y.: Cornell University Press, 1994.

Buskirk, Steven, and Gilbert Proulx. "Furbearers, Trapping, and Biodiversity." Manuscript, 2000.

Butzer, Karl W. "The Americas before and after 1492: An Introduction to Current Geographical Research." *Annals of the Association of American Geographers* 82 (1992).

———. "Biological Transfer, Agricultural Change, and Environmental Implications of 1492." In *International Germ Plasm Transfer: Past and Present*, edited by R. R. Duncan, 3–29. Madison, Wisc.: Crop Science Society of America, 1995.

Butzer, Karl W., and Elizabeth K. Butzer. "The Sixteenth-Century Environment of the Central Mexican Bajio: Archival Reconstruction from Colonial Land Grants and the Question of Spanish Ecological Impact." In *Culture, Form, and Place: Essays in Cultural and Historical Geography*, edited by Kent Mathewson, 89–124. Baton Rouge: Geoscience Publications, Department of Geography and Anthropology, Louisiana State University, 1993.

———. "Transfer of the Mediterranean Livestock Economy to New Spain: Adaptation and Ecological Consequences." In *Global Land Use Change: A Perspective from the Columbian Encounter*, edited by B. L. Turner, 151–75. Madrid: Consejo Superior de Investigaciones Científicas, 1995.

Campbell, B. M. S., and M. Overton. "A New Perspective on Medieval and Early Modern Agriculture: Six Centuries of Norfolk Farming, c. 1250–c. 1850." *Past and Present* 141 (1993): 38–105.

Camuffo, D., and S. Enzi. "Reconstructing the Climate of Northern Italy from

Archives Sources." In *Climate since A.D. 1500,* edited by Raymond S. Bradley and Philip D. Jones, 143–70. Rev. ed. London: Routledge, 1995.

Capp, B. S. *Cromwell's Navy: The Fleet and the English Revolution, 1648–1660.* Oxford: Clarendon Press; New York: Oxford University Press, 1989.

Carlos, Ann M., and Frank D. Lewis. "Indians, the Beaver, and the Bay: The Economics of Depletion in the Lands of the Hudson's Bay Company, 1700–1763." *Journal of Economic History* 53 (1993): 464–94.

Ceste, Anne Allice. "A Frontier Minority in the Chinese World: The Li People of Hainan Island from the Han through the High Qing." Ph.D. diss., State University of New York at Buffalo, 1995.

Chang, Chia-cheng. *The Reconstruction of Climate in China for Historical Times.* Beijing: Science Press, 1988.

Chaunu, Huguette, Pierre Chaunu, and Guy Arbellot. *Séville et l'Atlantique, 1504–1650.* Paris: A. Colin, 1955.

Chevalier, François. *Land and Society in Colonial Mexico: The Great Hacienda.* Berkeley and Los Angeles: University of California Press, 1963.

Chouinard, Ghislain A., and Alain Frechet. "Fluctuations in the Cod Stocks of the Gulf of St. Lawrence." In *Cod and Climate Change: Proceedings of a Symposium Held in Reykjavík, 23–27 August, 1993,* edited by Jakob Jakobsson and International Council for the Exploration of the Sea, 121–39. ICES Marine Science Symposia, v. 198. Copenhagen: Denmark International Council for the Exploration of the Sea, 1994.

Christopher, A. J. *Southern Africa.* Folkestone, Eng.: Dawson; Hamden, Conn.: Archon Books, 1976.

Chute, Janet E. "Frank G. Speck's Contributions to the Understanding of Mi'kmaq Land Use, Leadership, and Land Management." *Ethnohistory* 45, no. 3 (1999): 481–540.

Clowse, Converse D. *Measuring Charleston's Overseas Commerce, 1717–1767: Statistics from the Port's Naval Lists.* Washington, D.C.: University Press of America, 1981.

Coad, J. G., and Royal Commission on Historical Monuments (England). *The Royal Dockyards, 1690–1850: Architecture and Engineering Works of the Sailing Navy.* Aldershot, Eng.: Ashgate; Brookfield, Vt.: Scolar Press, 1989.

Coelho, Philip R., and Robert A. McGuire. "African and European Bound Labor in the British New World: The Biological Consequences of Economic Choices." *Journal of Economic History* 57 (1997): 83–117.

Coleman, D. C. *Myth, History, and the Industrial Revolution.* London: Hambledon Press, 1992.

Colley, Linda. *Britons: Forging the Nation, 1707–1837.* New Haven: Yale University Press, 1992.

Conrad, Maia. "Disorderly Drinking." *American Indian Quarterly* 23 (summer 1999): 1–11.

Conway, William Martin. *No Man's Land: A History of Spitsbergen from Its Discovery in 1596 to the Beginning of the Scientific Exploration of the Country.* Cambridge: Cambridge University Press, 1906.

Conway, William Martin, Jacob Segersz van der Brugge, Hessel Gerritsz, Basil Harrington Soulsby, and John Abraham Jacob De Villiers. *Early Dutch and English Voy-*

ages to Spitsbergen in the Seventeenth Century, Including Hessel Gerritsz. "Histoire du pays nommé Spitsberghe," 1613, Translated into English, for the First Time. Nendeln, Liechtenstein: Kraus Reprint, 1967.

Cook, Noble David. "Disease and the Depopulation of Hispaniola, 1492–1518." *Colonial Latin American Review* 2 (1993): 213–46.

———. *Born to Die: Disease and New World Conquest, 1492–1650.* Cambridge: Cambridge University Press, 1998.

Cornell, Laurel L. "Infanticide in Early Modern Japan? Demography, Culture, and Population Growth." *Journal of Asian Studies* 55 (1996): 22–41.

Cornell, Vincent J. "Socioeconomic Dimensions of Reconquista and Jihad in Morocco: Portuguese Dukkala and the Sa'id Sus, 1450–1557." *International Journal of Middle East Studies* 22 (1990): 379–418.

Craig, Alan K., and Robert Cooper West. *In Quest of Mineral Wealth: Aboriginal and Colonial Mining and Metallurgy in Spanish America.* Vol. 33 of *Geoscience and Man.* Baton Rouge: Geoscience Publications, Department of Geography and Anthropology, Louisiana State University, 1994.

Craton, Michael, and James Walvin. *A Jamaican Plantation: The History of Worthy Park, 1670–1970.* Toronto: University of Toronto Press, 1970.

Crispin, Alvaro Sanchez. "The Territorial Organization of Metallic Mining in New Spain." In *In Quest of Mineral Wealth: Aboriginal and Colonial Mining and Metallurgy in Spanish America.* Vol. 33 of *Geoscience and Man,* edited by Alan K. Craig and Robert Cooper West, 155–70. Baton Rouge: Geoscience Publications, Department of Geography and Anthropology, Louisiana State University, 1994.

Crosby, Alfred W. "Conquistador y Pestilencia: The First New World Pandemic and the Fall of the Great Indian Empires." *Hispanic American Historical Review* 47, no. 3 (1967): 321–37.

———. *Ecological Imperialism: The Biological Expansion of Europe, 900–1900.* Cambridge: Cambridge University Press, 1986.

Cross, Harry. "South American Bullion Production and Export 1550–1750." In *Precious Metals in the Later Medieval and Early Modern Worlds,* edited by John F. Richards, 397–423. Durham, N.C.: Carolina Academic Press, 1983.

Crummey, Robert O. *The Formation of Muscovy, 1304–1613.* London: Longman, 1987.

———. "Muscovy and the 'General Crisis of the Seventeenth Century.'" *Journal of Early Modern History* 2, no. 2 (1998): 156–80.

Cumbaa, Stephen L. "Archaeological Evidence of the Sixteenth Century Basque Right Whale Fishery in Labrador." In *Right Whales: Past and Present Status: Proceedings of the Workshop on the Status of Right Whales, New England Aquarium, Boston, Massachusetts, 15–23 June 1983,* edited by Robert L. Brownell, P. B. Best, John H. Prescott, the New England Aquarium Corporation, and the International Whaling Commission. Cambridge, Eng.: International Whaling Commission, 1986.

Cunningham, Richard L. "The Biological Impacts of 1492." In *The Indigenous People of the Caribbean,* edited by Samuel M. Wilson and the Virgin Islands Humanities Council, 29–35. Gainesville: University Press of Florida, 1997.

Curtin, Philip D. *The Rise and Fall of the Plantation Complex: Essays in Atlantic History.* Cambridge: Cambridge University Press, 1998.

Cushing, D. H. *The Provident Sea.* Cambridge: Cambridge University Press, 1988.

Daan, Niels. "Trends in North Atlantic Cod Stocks: A Critical Summary." In *Cod and Climate Change: Proceedings of a Symposium Held in Reykjavík, 23–27 August 1993,* edited by Jakob Jakobsson and the International Council for the Exploration of the Sea, 269–70. ICES Marine Science Symposia, v. 198. Copenhagen: International Council for the Exploration of the Sea, 1994.

Dalgård, Sune. *Dansk-norsk hvalfangst, 1615–1660: En studie over Danmark-Norges stilling I europaeisk merkantil expansion.* København: G. E. C. Gad, 1962.

Dampier, William, and John Masefield. *Dampier's voyages; consisting of a New voyage round the world, a Supplement to the Voyage round the world, Two voyages to Campeachy, a Discourse of winds, a Voyage to New Holland, and a Vindication, in answer to the Chimerical relation of William Funnell.* London: E. Grant Richards, 1906.

Darby, H. C. *Draining of the Fens.* Cambridge: Cambridge University Press, 1940.

———. *The Medieval Fenland.* Cambridge: Cambridge University Press, 1940.

D'Arrigo, R. D., and G. C. Jacoby Jr. "Dendroclimatic Evidence from Northern North America." In *Climate since A.D. 1500,* edited by Raymond S. Bradley and Philip D. Jones, 296–311. Rev. ed. London: Routledge, 1995.

———. "Tree Ring Width and Density Evidence of Climatic and Potential Forest Change in Alaska." *Global Biogeochemical Cycle* 9 (1995): 227–34.

Davies, Brian. "Village into Garrison: The Militarized Peasant Communities of Southern Muscovy." *Russian Review* 51 (October 1992): 481–501.

Davis, Ralph. "English Foreign Trade, 1700–1774." In *The Growth of English Overseas Trade in the Seventeenth and Eighteenth Centuries,* edited by Walter E. Minchinton. London: Methuen, 1969.

———. *The Rise of the English Shipping Industry in the Seventeenth and Eighteenth Centuries.* London: Macmillan; New York: St. Martin's Press, 1962.

Davis, Simon J. M., and John V. Beckett. "Animal Husbandry and Agricultural Improvement: The Archaeological Evidence from Animal Bones and Teeth." *Rural History* 10, no. 1 (1999): 1–17.

de Andrade Arruda, José Jobson. "Colonies as Mercantile Investments: The Luso-Brazilian Empire, 1500–1809." In *The Political Economy of Merchant Empires,* edited by James D. Tracy, 360–420. Cambridge: Cambridge University Press, 1991.

De Jong, C. *Geschiedenis van de oude Nederlandse walvisvaart.* Pretoria: De Jong, 1972.

———. "The Hunt of the Greenland Whale: A Short History and Statistical Sources." In *Historical Whaling Records: Including the Proceedings of the International Workshop on Historical Whaling Records, Sharon, Massachusetts, September 12–16, 1977,* edited by Michael F. Tillman, Gregory P. Donovan, and the International Whaling Commission, 83–106. Cambridge, Eng.: International Whaling Commission, 1983.

de la Morandière, Charles. *Histoire de la pêche française de la morue dans l'Amérique septentrionale (des origines à 1789).* Paris: Maisonneuve et Larose, 1962.

de Léry, Jean. *History of a Voyage to the Land of Brazil, Otherwise Called America.* Berkeley and Los Angeles: University of California Press, 1990.

De Paoli, Neill. "Beaver, Blankets, Liquor, and Politics: Pemaquid's Fur Trade, 1614–1760." *Maine Historical Society Quarterly* 33, nos. 3–4 (1993–1994): 166–201.

de Silva, Shanaka L., and Gregory A. Zielinski. "Global Influence of the A.D. 1600 Eruption of Huaynaputina, Peru." *Nature* 393 (June 4, 1998): 455–58.

de Vries, Jan. "Measuring the Impact of Climate on History: The Search for Appropriate Methodologies." In *Climate and History: Studies in Interdisciplinary History,* edited by Robert I. Rotberg and Theodore K. Rabb, 19–50. Princeton, N.J.: Princeton University Press, 1981.

de Vries, Jan, and A. M. van der Woude. *The First Modern Economy: Success, Failure, and Perseverance of the Dutch Economy, 1500–1815.* Cambridge: Cambridge University Press, 1997.

de Zeeuw, J. W. "Peat and the Dutch Golden Age: The Historical Meaning of Energy-Attainability." *AAG Bijdragen* 21 (1978): 3–31.

Dean, Warren. *With Broadax and Firebrand: The Destruction of the Brazilian Atlantic Forest.* Berkeley and Los Angeles: University of California Press, 1995.

Dechêne, Louise. *Habitants et marchands de Montréal au XVIIe siècle: Essai.* Montréal: Boréal, 1988.

Deerr, Noël. *The History of Sugar.* London: Chapman and Hall, 1949.

Defoe, Daniel, and G. D. H. Cole. *A Tour through the Whole Island of Great Britain.* London: Dent; New York: Dutton, 1962.

Delâge, Denys. *Bitter Feast: Amerindians and Europeans in the American Northeast, 1600–64.* Vancouver: UBC Press, 1993.

Denevan, William M. *The Native Population of the Americas in 1492.* 2d ed. Madison: University of Wisconsin Press, 1992.

Denys, Nicolas, Victor Hugo Paltsits, and William Francis Ganong. *The Description and Natural History of the Coasts of North America (Acadia).* Toronto: Champlain Society, 1908.

Diaz, Henry F., and George N. Kiladis. "Atmospheric Teleconnections Associated with the Extreme Phases of the Southern Oscillation." In *El Niño: Historical and Paleoclimatic Aspects of the Southern Oscillation,* edited by Henry F. Diaz and Vera Markgraf, 7–28. Cambridge: Cambridge University Press, 1992.

Diaz, Henry F., and Vera Markgraf. *El Niño: Historical and Paleoclimatic Aspects of the Southern Oscillation.* Cambridge: Cambridge University Press, 1992.

Diefenbach, D. R., and R. B. Owen Jr. "A Model of Habitat Use by Breeding American Black Ducks." *Journal of Wildlife Management* 53, no. 2 (1989): 383–89.

Dietz, Johann, Bernard Miall, and Ernst Consentius. *Master Johann Dietz, Surgeon in the Army of the Great Elector and Barber to the Royal Court: From the Old Manuscript in the Royal Library of Berlin.* London: Allen and Unwin; New York: Dutton, 1923.

Dmytryshyn, Basil, E. A. P. Crownhart-Vaughan, and Thomas Vaughan. *Russia's Conquest of Siberia, 1558–1700: A Documentary Record.* Vol. 1 of *To Siberia and Russian America.* Portland, Ore.: Western Imprints, the Press of the Oregon Historical Society, 1985.

Dobson, Mary J. *Contours of Death and Disease in Early Modern England.* Cambridge: Cambridge University Press, 1997.

Dobyns, Henry F., William R. Swagerty, and the Newberry Library Center for the History of the American Indian. *Their Number Become Thinned: Native American Population Dynamics in Eastern North America.* Knoxville: University of Tennessee Press, 1983.

Douglas, John. "Mercury and the Global Environment." *EPRI Journal* 19, no. 3 (1994): 14–22.

Douville, Raymond, and Jacques Donat Casanova. *Daily Life in Early Canada.* 1st Amer. ed. New York: Macmillan, 1968.

Dreser, Clara. "A Century of North Atlantic Data Indicates Interdecadal Change: Surface Temperature, Winds, and Ice in the North Atlantic." *Oceanus* 39 (1996): 11–14.

Du Pasquier, J. Thierry. "The Whalers of Honfleur in the Seventeenth Century." *Arctic* 37, no. 4 (1984): 533–38.

Duin, Pieter van, and Robert Ross. *The Economy of the Cape Colony in the Eighteenth Century.* Leiden: Centre for the History of European Expansion, 1987.

Duncan, W. R. H. "Aberdeen and the Early Development of the Whaling Industry, 1750–1800." *Northern Scotland* 3 (1977–1978): 47–59.

Dunn, Richard S., and the Institute of Early American History and Culture. *Sugar and Slaves: The Rise of the Planter Class in the English West Indies, 1624–1713.* Chapel Hill: University of North Carolina Press, for the Institute of Early American History and Culture, Williamsburg, Va., 1972.

Dusenberry, William Howard. *The Mexican Mesta: The Administration of Ranching in Colonial Mexico.* Urbana: University of Illinois Press, 1963.

Dyck, A. P., and R. A. MacArthur. "Spacing, Movements, and Habitat Selection of the River Otter in Boreal Alberta." *Canadian Journal of Zoology* 72, no. 7 (1994): 1314–1324.

Eaton, Richard. *The Rise of Islam and the Bengal Frontier, 1204–1760.* Berkeley and Los Angeles: University of California Press, 1993.

Eccles, W. J. "The Fur Trade and Eighteenth-Century Imperialism." *William and Mary Quarterly,* 3d ser., 40 (1983): 341–62.

Edmonds, Richard L. *Northern Frontiers of Qing China and Tokugawa Japan: A Comparative Study of Frontier Policy.* University of Chicago, Dept. of Geography, 1985.

Elisonas, Jurgis. "Christianity and the Daimyo." In *The Cambridge History of Japan,* vol. 4, edited by John Whitney Hall. Cambridge: Cambridge University Press, 1988.

Elking, Henry. *A View of the Greenland Trade and Whale Fishery, with the National and Private Advantages Thereof.* In *A Select Collection of Scarce and Valuable Economical Tracts, from the Originals of Defoe, Elking, Franklin, Turgot, Anderson, Schomberg, Townsend, Burke, Bell, and Others; with a Preface, Notes, and Index,* edited by J. R. McCulloch. London: n.p., 1859.

Ellis, Richard. *Men and Whales.* 1st ed. New York: Knopf, 1991.

Ellis, Stephen G. "Tudor State Formation and the Shaping of the British Isles." In *Conquest and Union: Fashioning a British State, 1485–1725,* edited by Stephen G. Ellis and Sarah Barber, 40–63. London: Longman, 1995.

Ellison, Lincoln. "Influence of Grazing on Plant Succession of Rangelands." *Botanical Review* 26 (1960): 1–78.

Elphick, Richard, and V. C. Malherbe. "The Khoisan to 1828." In *The Shaping of South African Society, 1652–1840,* edited by Richard Elphick and Hermann Giliomee. Middletown, Conn.: Wesleyan University Press, 1989.

Elvin, Mark. "The *Bell of Poesy:* Thoughts on Poems as Information in Late-Imperial Environmental History." In *Studi in onore di Lionello Lanciotti,* edited by S. M. Carletti, M. Sacchetti, and P. Santagelo. Napoli: Istituto universitario orientale, 1996.

————. "The Environmental Policy of Imperial China." *China Quarterly*, no. 156 (1998): 733 ff.

————. *The Pattern of the Chinese Past*. Stanford, Calif.: Stanford University Press, 1973.

Elvin, Mark, and Liu Tsui-jung, eds. *Sediments of Time: Environment and Society in Chinese History*. Cambridge: Cambridge University Press, 1998.

Endfield, Georgina H., and Sarah L. O'Hara. "Conflicts over Water in 'The Little Drought Age' in Central Mexico." *Environment and History* 3 (1997): 255–72.

————. "Degradation, Drought, and Dissent: An Environmental History of Colonial Michoacan, West Central Mexico." *Annals of the Association of American Geographers* 89 (1999): 402–22.

Estes, James A., and David O. Duggins. "Sea Otters and Kelp Forests in Alaska: Generality and Variation in a Community Ecological Paradigm." *Ecological Monographs* 65, no. 1 (1995): 75–101.

Estes, James A., Norman S. Smith, and John F. Palmisano. "Sea Otter Predation and Community Organization in the Western Aleutian Islands, Alaska." *Ecology* 59 (1978): 822–33.

Evelyn, John. *Fumifugium*. Exeter: The Rota, 1976.

Evelyn, John, and John Nisbet. *Sylva: A Discourse of Forest Trees and the Propagation of Timber in His Majesty's Dominions*. London: Doubleday and Company, 1908.

Fahay, Michael P., and Northeast Fisheries Science Center. *Essential Fish Habitat Source Document*. Woods Hole, Mass.: U.S. Department of Commerce National Oceanic and Atmospheric Administration, National Marine Fisheries Service, Northeast Region, Northeast Fisheries Science Center, 1999.

Fernández-Armesto, Felipe, K. N. Chaudhuri, and Times Books. *The Times Atlas of World Exploration: Three Thousand Years of Exploring, Explorers, and Mapmaking*. New York: HarperCollins, 1991.

Fimreite, N. "Accumulation and Effects of Mercury on Birds." In *The Biogeochemistry of Mercury in the Environment*, edited by Jerome O. Nriagu, 601–28. Amsterdam: Elsevier and North-Holland Biomedical Press, 1979.

Fischer, D. H. *The Great Wave: Price Revolutions and the Rhythm of History*. New York: Oxford University Press, 1996.

Fisher, Alan W. *The Crimean Tatars: Studies of Nationalities in the USSR*. Stanford, Calif.: Hoover Institution Press, 1978.

Fisher, Raymond Henry. *The Russian Fur Trade, 1550–1700*. Berkeley and Los Angeles: University of California Press, 1943.

Fletcher, Giles, and Albert J. Schmidt. *Of the Rus Commonwealth*. Ithaca, N.Y.: Cornell University Press, for the Folger Shakespeare Library, Washington, D.C., 1966.

Flinn, Michael W., with David Stoker. *1700–1830: The Industrial Revolution*. Vol. 2 of *The History of the British Coal Industry*. Oxford: Clarendon Press, 1984.

Forbes, Vernon S. *Pioneer Travellers of South Africa: A Geographical Commentary upon Routes, Records, Observations, and Opinions of Travellers at the Cape, 1750–1800*. Cape Town: A. A. Balkema, 1965.

Forsyth, James. *A History of the Peoples of Siberia: Russia's North Asian Colony, 1581–1990*. Cambridge: Cambridge University Press, 1992.

————. "The Siberian Native Peoples before and after the Russian Conquest." In *The*

History of Siberia: From Russian Conquest to Revolution, edited by Alan Wood, xiv, 192. London: Routledge, 1991.

France, R. L. "The Importance of Beaver Lodges in Structuring Littoral Communities in Boreal Headwater Lakes." *Canadian Journal of Zoology* 75, no. 7 (1997): 1009–13.

Frank, Kenneth T., Kenneth F. Drinkwater, and Fredrick H. Page. "Possible Causes of Recent Trends and Fluctuations in Scotian Shelf/Gulf of Maine Cod Stocks." In *Cod and Climate Change: Proceedings of a Symposium Held in Reykjavík, 23–27 August 1993,* edited by Jakob Jakobsson and the International Council for the Exploration of the Sea, 110–20. ICES Marine Science Symposia, v. 198. Copenhagen: International Council for the Exploration of the Sea, 1994.

French, R. A. "Russians and the Forest." In *Studies in Russian Historical Geography,* edited by James H. Bater and R. A. French. London: Academic Press, 1983.

Frenzel, Burkhard, Christian Pfister, Birgit Gläser, and European Science Foundation. *Climatic Trends and Anomalies in Europe, 1675–1715: High Resolution Spatio-Temporal Reconstructions from Direct Meteorological Observations and Proxy Data: Methods and Results.* Stuttgart: G. Fischer, 1994.

Furushima, Toshio. "The Village and Agriculture during the Edo Period." In *The Cambridge History of Japan,* vol. 4, edited by John Whitney Hall. Cambridge: Cambridge University Press, 1988.

Galloway, J. H. *The Sugar Cane Industry: An Historical Geography from Its Origins to 1914.* Cambridge: Cambridge University Press, 1989.

Galloway, Patrick R. "Secular Changes in the Short-Term Preventive, Positive, and Temperature Checks to Population Growth in Europe, 1460–1909." *Climatic Change* 26 (1994): 3–43.

Ganamus, A., M. Horvat, and P. Stegnar. "The Mercury Content among Deer and of Browsed Foliage as a Means of Ascertaining Environmental Pollution of the Mining Regions of Idrija—a Case Study from Slovenia." *Zeitschrift für Jagdwissenschaft* 41, no. 3 (1995): 198–208.

Gandavo, Pero de Magalhães. *The Histories of Brazil.* Boston: Milford House, 1972.

Garner, Richard L. "Long-Term Silver Mining Trends in Spanish America: A Comparative Analysis of Peru and Mexico." *American Historical Review* 93, no. 4 (1988): 898–935.

Garner, Richard L., and Spiro E. Stefanou. *Economic Growth and Change in Bourbon Mexico.* Gainesville: University Press of Florida, 1993.

Gibson, Charles. *The Aztecs under Spanish Rule: A History of the Indians of the Valley of Mexico, 1519–1810.* Stanford, Calif.: Stanford University Press, 1964.

Gibson, James R. *Feeding the Russian Fur Trade: Provisionment of the Okhotsk Seaboard and the Kamchatka Peninsula, 1639–1856.* Madison: University of Wisconsin Press, 1969.

Glaser, Rudiger, Rudolf Brázdil, Christian Pfister, Petr Dobrovolnp, Mariano Barriendos Vallve, Anita Bokwa, Dario Camuffo, Oldrich Kotyza, Danuta Limanowka, Lajos Racz, and Fernando S. Rodrigo. "Seasonal Temperature and Precipitation Fluctuations in Selected Parts of Europe during the Sixteenth Century." *Climatic Change* 43, no. 1 (1999): 169–200.

Goldstone, Jack A. *Revolution and Rebellion in the Early Modern World.* Berkeley and Los Angeles: University of California Press, 1991.

Gordon, David. "From Rituals of Rapture to Rituals of Dependence: The Political Economy of Khoikhoi Narcotic Consumption, c. 1487–1870." *South African Historical Journal* 35 (1996): 62–88.

Gordon, Robert Jacob, P. E. Raper, and M. Boucher. *Robert Jacob Gordon: Cape Travels, 1777 to 1786*. Houghton, South Africa: Brenthurst Press, 1988.

Gorski, Philip S. "The Protestant Ethic Revisited: Disciplinary Revolution and State Formation in Holland and Prussia." *American Journal of Sociology* 99, no. 2 (1993): 265–316.

Goslinga, Cornelis Ch. *The Dutch in the Caribbean and on the Wild Coast, 1580–1680*. Gainesville: University of Florida Press, 1971.

Goslinga, Cornelis Ch., and Maria van J. L. Yperen. *The Dutch in the Caribbean and in the Guianas, 1680–1791*. Anjerpublikaties 19. Assen, Netherlands: Van Gorcum, 1985.

Gradie, Charlotte M. "Discovering the Chichimecas." *Americas* 51 (1994): 67–89.

Grandjean, Philippe, Robert A. White, Anne Nielsen, and David Clung. "Methylmercury Neurotoxicity in Amazonian Children Downstream from Gold Mining." *Environmental Health Perspectives* 107 (1999).

Grant, Hugh. "Revenge of the Paris Hat: The European Craze for Wearing Headgear Had a Profound Effect on Canadian History." *The Beaver* 37 (1989): 37–44.

Grove, A. T., and Oliver Rackham. *The Nature of Mediterranean Europe: An Ecological History*. New Haven: Yale University Press, 2001.

Grove, Jean M. *The Little Ice Age*. London: Methuen, 1988.

Grove, Jean, and Annalisa Conterio. "The Climate of Crete in the Sixteenth and Seventeenth Centuries." *Climatic Change* 30 (1995): 223–47.

Grove, Richard. *Green Imperialism: Colonial Expansion, Tropical Island Edens, and the Origins of Environmentalism, 1600–1860*. Cambridge: Cambridge University Press, 1995.

Grove, Richard H. "Global Impact of the 1789–93 El Niño." *Nature* 393 (May 28, 1998): 318–20.

Grover, A. M., and G. A. Baldassarre. "Bird Species Richness within Beaver Ponds in South-Central New York." *Wetlands* 15, no. 2 (1995): 108–18.

Guelke, Leonard. "Freehold Farmers and Frontier Settlers, 1657–1780." In *The Shaping of South African Society, 1652–1840*, edited by Richard Elphick and Hermann Giliomee, 66–108. Middletown, Conn.: Wesleyan University Press, 1989.

———. "Ideology and Landscape of Settler Colonialism in Virginia and Dutch South Africa: A Comparative Analysis." In *Ideology and Landscape in Historical Perspective: Essays on the Meanings of Some Places in the Past*, edited by Alan R. H. Baker and Gideon Biger. Cambridge: Cambridge University Press, 1992.

Guelke, Leonard, and Robert Shell. "Landscape of Conquest: Frontier Water Alienation and Khoikhoi Strategies of Survival, 1652–1780." In *Agriculture, Resource Exploitation, and Environmental Change*, edited by Helen Wheatley. Aldershot, Eng.: Variorum, 1997.

Guerra, Francisco. "The Earliest American Epidemic: The Influenza of 1493." *Social Science History* 12, no. 3 (1988): 305–25.

———. "The European-American Exchange." *History and Philosophy of the Life Sciences* 15, no. 3 (1993): 313–27.

Habib, Irfan. *An Atlas of the Mughal Empire: Political and Economic Maps, with Detailed Notes, Bibliography, and Index.* Aligarh, Delhi: Centre of Advanced Study in History, Aligarh Muslim University; New York: Oxford University Press, 1982.

Hacquebord, Louwrens. "The Rise and Fall of a Dutch Whaling-Settlement on the West Coast of Spitsbergen." In *Proceedings of the International Symposium, Early European Exploitation of the Northern Atlantic, 800–1700,* edited by Rijksuniversiteit te Groningen, Noordelijk Centrum, 79–132. Groningen, Netherlands: Arctic Centre, University of Groningen, 1981.

———. "Three Centuries of Whaling and Walrus Hunting in Svalbard and Its Impact on the Arctic Ecosystem." *Environment and History* 7 (2001): 169–85.

Hacquebord, Louwrens, and Wim Vroom. *Walvisvaart in de gouden eeuw: Opgravingen op Spitsbergen.* Amsterdam: De Bataafsche Leeuw, 1988.

Haldiman, Jerrold T., and Raymond J. Tarpley. "Anatomy and Physiology." In *The Bowhead Whale,* edited by John J. Burns, J. Jerome Montague, Cleveland J. Cowles, and the Society for Marine Mammalogy, 71–156. Lawrence, Kans.: Society for Marine Mammalogy, 1993.

Hall, Douglas, and Thomas Thistlewood. *In Miserable Slavery: Thomas Thistlewood in Jamaica, 1750–86.* Basingstoke: Macmillan, 1989.

Hall, John Whitney, Keiji Nagahara, and Kozo Yamamura. *Japan before Tokugawa: Political Consolidation and Economic Growth, 1500–1650.* Princeton, N.J.: Princeton University Press, 1981.

Hamilton, Earl J. *American Treasure and the Price Revolution in Spain, 1501–1650.* Cambridge: Harvard University Press, 1934.

Hanley, Susan B. "Tokugawa Society: Material Culture, Standard of Living, and Life Styles." In *The Cambridge History of Japan,* vol. 4, edited by John Whitney Hall. Cambridge: Cambridge University Press, 1988.

Harrington, Faith. " 'Wee Tooke Great Store of Cod-Fish': Fishing Ships and First Settlements on the Coast of New England, 1600–1630." In *American Beginnings: Exploration, Culture, and Cartography in the Land of Norumbega,* edited by Emerson W. Baker. Lincoln: University of Nebraska Press, 1994.

Harris, David R. *Plants, Animals, and Man in the Outer Leeward Islands, West Indies: An Ecological Study of Antigua, Barbuda, and Anguilla.* Berkeley and Los Angeles: University of California Press, 1965.

Harris, Richard C., and Geoffrey J. Matthews. *Historical Atlas of Canada.* Toronto: University of Toronto Press, 1987.

Hart, Marjolein C. 't. *The Making of a Bourgeois State: War, Politics, and Finance during the Dutch Revolt.* Manchester, Eng.: Manchester University Press, 1993.

Hasan, S. Nurul. "Three Studies of Zamindari System." *Medieval India—a Miscellany* 1 (1969).

Hatcher, John. *Before 1700: Towards the Age of Coal.* Vol. 1 of *The History of the British Coal Industry.* Oxford: Clarendon Press, 1993.

Head, C. Grant. *Eighteenth Century Newfoundland: A Geographer's Perspective.* Toronto: McClelland and Stewart, 1976.

Heesen, Henk, and Niels Daan. "Cod Distribution and Temperature in the North Sea." In *Cod and Climate Change: Proceedings of a Symposium Held in Reykjavík, 23–27 August 1993,* edited by Jakob Jakobsson and the International Council for the Exploration of the Sea, 244–53. ICES Marine Science Symposia, v. 198. Copenhagen: International Council for the Exploration of the Sea, 1994.

Heidjra, Ben J., and Anton D. Lowenberg. "Towards a Theory of Colonial Growth: The Case of the Dutch in Southern Africa." *Journal of Interdisciplinary Economics* 1 (1987): 249–76.

Heidjra, Martin. "The Socio-Economic Development of Rural China during the Ming." In *The Cambridge History of China*, edited by John King Fairbank and Denis Crispin Twitchett, 417–574. Cambridge: Cambridge University Press, 1998.

Hellie, Richard. *The Economy and Material Culture of Russia, 1600–1725.* Chicago: University of Chicago Press, 1999.

———. "Furs in Seventeenth-Century Muscovy." *Russian History* 16 (1989): 171–96.

Hemming, J. *Amazon Frontier: The Defeat of the Brazilian Indians.* Cambridge: Harvard University Press, 1987.

———. "Indians and the Frontier in Colonial Brazil." In *The Cambridge History of Latin America*, vol. 2, edited by Leslie Bethell. Cambridge: Cambridge University Press, 1984.

———. *Red Gold: The Conquest of the Brazilian Indians.* Rev. ed. London: Papermac, 1995.

Henige, David. "On the Contact Population of Hispaniola: History as Higher Mathematics." *Hispanic American Historical Review* 58 (1978): 217–37, 709–12.

———. *Numbers from Nowhere: The American Indian Contact Population Debate.* Norman: University of Oklahoma Press, 1998.

Herman, John N. "Empire in the Southwest: Early Qing Reforms to the Native Chieftain System." *Journal of Asian Studies* 56, no. 1 (1997): 47–74.

Higman, B. W. "The Internal Economy of Jamaican Pens, 1760–1890." *Social and Economic Studies* 38 (1989): 61–86.

———. *Jamaica Surveyed: Plantation Maps and Plans of the Eighteenth and Nineteenth Centuries.* Jamaica: Institute of Jamaica Publications, 1988.

Hill, J. R., and Bryan Ranft. *The Oxford Illustrated History of the Royal Navy.* Oxford: Oxford University Press, 1995.

Ho, Ping-ti. *Studies on the Population of China, 1368–1953.* Cambridge: Harvard University Press, 1959.

Hoch, Steven L. *Serfdom and Social Control in Russia: Petrovskoe, a Village in Tambov.* Chicago: University of Chicago Press, 1986.

Hoekstra, Rik. *Two Worlds Merging: The Transformation of Society in the Valley of Puebla, 1570–1640.* Amsterdam: Cedla, 1993.

Hoffman, Richard C. "Economic Development and Aquatic Ecosystems in Medieval Europe." *American Historical Review* 101, no. 3 (1996): 630–70.

Hollman, Thomas O. "Formosa and the Trade in Venison and Deer Skins." In *Emporia, Commodities, and Entrepreneurs in Asian Maritime Trade, c. 1400–1750*, edited by Roderich Ptak, 263–90. Stuttgart: F. Steiner, 1991.

Holmes, Geoffrey S. *The Making of a Great Power: Late Stuart and Early Georgian Britain, 1660–1722.* London: Longman, 1993.

Holzhauser, H., and H. J. Zumbuhl. "Glacier Fluctuations in the Western Swiss and French Alps in the Sixteenth Century." *Climatic Change* 43, no. 1 (1999): 223–37.

Hosttetler, Laura. "Qing Connections to the Early Modern World: Ethnography and

Cartography in Eighteenth-Century China." *Modern Asian Studies* 34, no. 3 (2000): 623–62.

Howell, David L. "Ainu Ethnicity and the Boundaries of the Early Modern Japanese State." *Past and Present,* no. 142 (1994): 69–93.

———. *Capitalism from Within: Economy, Society, and the State in a Japanese Fishery.* Berkeley and Los Angeles: University of California Press, 1995.

Hua, M. S., C. C. Huang, and Y. J. Yang. "Chronic Elemental Mercury Intoxication: Neuropsychological Follow-up Case Study." *Brain Injury* 10, no. 5 (1996): 377–84.

Huang, Philip C. *The Peasant Economy and Social Change in North China.* Stanford, Calif.: Stanford University Press, 1985.

Huber, Johannes. "Chinese Settlers against the Dutch East India Company: The Rebellion Led by Kuo Huai-i on Taiwan in 1652." In *Development and Decline of Fukien Province in the Seventeenth and Eighteenth Centuries,* edited by E. B. Vermeer, 265–96. Leiden: Brill, 1990.

Hudson, Charles M., Jr. "Why the Southeastern Indians Slaughtered Deer." In *Indians, Animals, and the Fur Trade: A Critique of Keepers of the Game,* edited by Shepard Krech. Athens: University of Georgia Press, 1981.

Hutchings, Jeffrey A. "The Nature of Cod *(Gadus morhua):* Perceptions of Stock Structure and Cod Behavior by Fishermen, 'Experts,' and Scientists from the Nineteenth Century to the Present." In *Papers Presented at the Conference Entitled "Marine Resources and Human Societies in the North Atlantic since 1500,"* October 20–22, 1995, edited by Daniel Vickers, 125–85. St. John's, Newfoundland: Institute of Social and Economic Research, Memorial University of Newfoundland, 1997.

Huttenbach, Henry R. "Muscovy's Conquest of Muslim Kazan and Astrakhan, 1552–56: The Conquest of the Volga: Prelude to Empire." In *Russian Colonial Expansion to 1917,* edited by Michael Rywkin. London: Mansell, 1988.

———. "Muscovy's Penetration of Siberia: The Colonization Process 1555–1689." In *Russian Colonial Expansion to 1917,* edited by Michael Rywkin, 70–102. London: Mansell, 1988.

Innes, Robert L. "The Door Ajar: Japan's Foreign Trade in the Seventeenth Century." Ph.D. diss., University of Michigan, 1980.

Innis, Harold Adams. *The Cod Fisheries: The History of an International Economy.* Rev. ed. Toronto: University of Toronto Press, 1954.

———. *The Fur Trade in Canada: An Introduction to Canadian Economic History.* Toronto: University of Toronto Press, 1956.

———. *Select Documents in Canadian Economic History.* Toronto: University of Toronto Press, 1929.

Israel, Jonathan I. *Dutch Primacy in World Trade, 1585–1740.* Oxford: Clarendon Press; New York: Oxford University Press, 1990.

———. *The Dutch Republic: Its Rise, Greatness, and Fall, 1477–1806.* Oxford: Clarendon Press, 1995.

Jackson, G. *The British Whaling Trade.* Hamden, Conn.: Archon Books, 1978.

———. "The Rise and Fall of English Whaling in the Seventeenth Century." In *Proceedings of the International Symposium, Early European Exploitation of the Northern Atlantic, 800–1700,* edited by Rijksuniversiteit te Groningen, Noordelijk Centrum, 55–68. Groningen, Netherlands: Arctic Centre, University of Groningen, 1981.

Jackson, J. B. C. "Reefs since Columbus." *Coral Reefs* 16, supplement (1997): S23–S32.

Jackson, J. B. C., Michael X. Kirby, Wolfgang H. Berger, Karen A. Bjorndal, Louis W. Botsford, Bruce J. Bourque, Roger H. Bradbury, Richard Cooke, Jon Erlandson, James A. Estes, Terence P. Hughes, Susan Kidwell, Carina B. Lange, Hunter S. Lenihan, John M. Pandolfi, Charles H. Peterson, Robert S. Steneck, Mia J. Tegner, and Robert R. Warner. "Historical Overfishing and the Recent Collapse of Coastal Ecosystems." *Science* 293, no. 5530 (July 27, 2001): 629–37.

Jacoby, G. C., Jr., and R. D. D'Arrigo. "Reconstructed Northern Hemisphere Annual Temperature since 1671 Based on High-Latitude Tree-Ring Data from North America." *Climatic Change* 14 (1989): 39–59.

Jakupsstovu, S. H. I., and Jakup Reinert. "Fluctuations in the Faroe Plateau Cod Stock." In *Cod and Climate Change: Proceedings of a Symposium Held in Reykjavík, 23–27 August 1993*, edited by Jakob Jakobsson and the International Council for the Exploration of the Sea, 194–211. ICES Marine Science Symposia, v. 198. Copenhagen: International Council for the Exploration of the Sea, 1994.

Jannetta, Ann Bowman. *Epidemics and Mortality in Early Modern Japan*. Princeton, N.J.: Princeton University Press, 1987.

Jasinski, Mark E. "Russian Hunters on Svalbard and the Polar Winter." *Arctic* 44, no. 2 (1991): 156–62.

Jennings, Francis. *The Ambiguous Iroquois Empire: The Covenant Chain Confederation of Indian Tribes with English Colonies, from Its Beginnings to the Lancaster Treaty of 1744*. 1st ed. New York: W. W. Norton, 1984.

Johnson, Harold B. "The Portuguese Settlement of Brazil, 1500–1800." In *The Cambridge History of Latin America*, vol. 1, edited by Leslie Bethell. Cambridge: Cambridge University Press, 1984.

Johnstone, C. A., and R. J. Naiman. "Boundary Dynamics at the Aquatic-Terrestrial Interface: The Influence of Beaver and Geomorphology." *Landscape Ecology* 1, no. 1 (1987): 47–58.

Jones, C. G., J. H. Lawton, and M. Shachak. "Organisms as Ecosystems Engineers." *Oikos* 69, no. 3 (1994): 373–86.

Jonsson, J. "Fisheries off Iceland, 1600–1900." In *Cod and Climate Change: Proceedings of a Symposium Held in Reykjavík, 23–27 August 1993*, edited by Jakob Jakobsson and the International Council for the Exploration of the Sea, 3–16. ICES Marine Science Symposia, v. 198. Copenhagen: International Council for the Exploration of the Sea, 1994.

Jordan, Terry G. *North American Cattle-Ranching Frontiers: Origins, Diffusion, and Differentiation*. Albuquerque: University of New Mexico Press, 1993.

Josephy, Alvin M. *America in 1492: The World of the Indian Peoples before the Arrival of Columbus*. New York: Knopf, 1992.

Kaempfer, Engelbert, and Beatrice M. Bodart-Bailey. *Kaempfer's Japan: Tokugawa Culture Observed*. Honolulu: University of Hawaii Press, 1999.

Kalland, Arne. *Fishing Villages in Tokugawa Japan*. Honolulu: University of Hawaii Press, 1995.

Kalland, Arne, and Brian Moeran. *Japanese Whaling: End of an Era?* London: Curzon Press, 1992.

Kalm, Pehr, and Adolph B. Benson. *Peter Kalm's Travels in North America: The English Version of 1770.* New York: Dover, 1987.

Kang, Etsuko Hae-jin. *Diplomacy and Ideology in Japanese-Korean Relations: From the Fifteenth to the Eighteenth Century.* Houndmills, Eng.: Macmillan; New York: St. Martin's Press, 1997.

Kay, Jeanne. "Native Americans in the Fur Trade and Wildlife Depletion." *Environmental Review* 9, no. 2 (1985): 118–30.

———. "Wisconsin Indian Hunting Patterns, 1634–1836." *Annals of the Association of American Geographers* 69, no. 3 (1979): 402–18.

Keith, Robert G., and J. H. Parry. *New Iberian World: A Documentary History of the Discovery and Settlement of Latin America to the Early Seventeenth Century.* 1st ed. New York: Times Books, Hector and Rose, 1984.

Kelly, William W., and Cornell University, China-Japan Program. *Water Control in Tokugawa Japan: Irrigation Organization in a Japanese River Basin, 1600–1870.* Ithaca, N.Y.: China-Japan Program, Cornell University, 1982.

Keyes, George S., Minneapolis Institute of Arts, Toledo Museum of Art, and Los Angeles County Museum of Art. *Mirror of Empire: Dutch Marine Art of Seventeenth Century.* Minneapolis: Minneapolis Institute of Arts; Cambridge: Cambridge University Press, 1990.

Kimber, C. T. *Martinique Revisited: The Changing Plant Geographies of a West Indian Island.* College Station: Texas A & M University, 1988.

King, E. Wayne. "Historical Review of the Decline of the Green Turtle and the Hawksbill." In *Biology and Conservation of Sea Turtles,* edited by Karen A. Bjorndal, 183–88. Washington: Smithsonian Institution Press, 1995.

Kivelson, Valerie. "Merciful Father, Impersonal State: Russian Autocracy in Comparative Perspective." *Modern Asian Studies* 31 (1997).

Knight, R. J. B. "New England Forests and British Seapower: Albion Revisited." *American Neptune* 46, no. 4 (1986): 221–29.

Kobal, A., and T. Dizdarevic. "The Health Safety Programme for Workers Exposed to Elemental Mercury at the Mercury Mine in Idrija." *Water, Air, and Soil Pollution* 97 (1997): 169–84.

Kolb, Peter. *The Present State of the Cape of Good Hope.* New York: Johnson Reprint Corporation, 1968.

Komlos, John. "The New World's Contribution to Food Consumption during the Industrial Revolution." *Journal of European Economic History* 27 (1998): 67–82.

Koski, William R., Ralph A. Davis, Gary W. Miller, and David E. Withrow. "Reproduction." In *The Bowhead Whale,* edited by John J. Burns, J. Jerome Montague, Cleveland J. Cowles, and the Society for Marine Mammalogy, 239–74. Lawrence, Kans.: Society for Marine Mammalogy, 1993.

Krech, Shepard III. *The Ecological Indian: Myth and History.* New York: W. W. Norton and Company, 1999.

———. *Indians, Animals, and the Fur Trade: A Critique of "Keepers of the Game."* Athens: University of Georgia Press, 1981.

Kruger, Daniel P. "Pastoral Strategies and Settlement Systems in Colonial South Africa." *Historical Geography* 24 (1995): 57–70.

Krupnik, I. I. *Arctic Adaptations: Native Whalers and Reindeer Herders of Northern Eurasia.* Hanover, N.H.: University Press of New England, for Dartmouth College, 1993.

Kupperman, Karen Ordahl. "Climate and Mastery of the Wilderness in Seventeenth-Century New England." In *Seventeenth-Century New England: A Conference,* edited by the Colonial Society of Massachusetts, 3–37. Boston: The Society, distributed by the University Press of Virginia, 1984.

Kurlansky, Mark. *Cod: A Biography of the Fish That Changed the World.* New York: Walker and Company, 1997.

Kvitek, R. G., J. S. Oliver, A. R. DeGange, and B. S. Anderson. "Changes in Alaskan Soft-Bottom Prey Communities along a Gradient in Sea Otter Predation." *Ecology* 73 (1992): 413–28.

Lamb, H. H. *Climate: Present, Past, and Future.* London: Methuen, 1972.

———. "Climatic Variation and Changes in the Wind and Ocean Circulation: The Little Ice Age in the Northeast Atlantic." *Quaternary Research* 11 (1979): 1–20.

Lambert, Audrey M. *The Making of the Dutch Landscape: An Historical Geography of the Netherlands.* London: Seminar Press, 1971.

Landsteiner, Erich. "The Crisis of Wine Production in Late Sixteenth-Century Central Europe: Climatic Causes and Economic Consequences." *Climatic Change* 43, no. 1 (1999): 323–34.

Lang, James. *Portuguese Brazil: The King's Plantation.* New York: Academic Press, 1979.

Lantzeff, George Vjatcheslau. *Siberia in the Seventeenth Century: A Study of the Colonial Administration.* Berkeley and Los Angeles: University of California Press, 1943.

Large, P. "Rural Society and Agricultural Change: Ombersley 1580–1700." In *English Rural Society, 1500–1800: Essays in Honor of Joan Thirsk,* edited by J. Thirsk, J. Chartres, and D. Hey, 105–137. Cambridge: Cambridge University Press, 1990.

Larson, Lewis H. *Aboriginal Subsistence Technology on the Southeastern Coastal Plain during the Late Prehistoric Period.* Gainesville: University of Florida Press, 1980.

Lavely, William, and R. Bin Wong. "Revising the Malthusian Narrative: The Comparative Study of Population Dynamics in Late Imperial China." *Journal of Asian Studies* 57, no. 3 (1998): 714–48.

Lawson, John. *A New Voyage to Carolina.* Chapel Hill: University of North Carolina Press, 1967.

Le Roy Ladurie, Emmanuel. *Histoire du climat depuis l'an mil.* Paris: Flammarion, 1967.

———. *Times of Feast, Times of Famine: A History of Climate since the Year 1000.* Garden City, N.Y.: Doubleday, 1971.

Lee, Robert H. G. *The Manchurian Frontier in Ch'ing History.* Cambridge: Harvard University Press, 1970.

Lennon, Colm. *Sixteenth-Century Ireland: The Incomplete Conquest.* New York: St. Martin's Press, 1995.

Levack, Brian P. *The Formation of the British State: England, Scotland, and the Union, 1603–1707.* Oxford: Clarendon Press; New York: Oxford University Press, 1987.

Levine, David, and Keith Wrightson. *The Making of an Industrial Society: Whickham, 1560–1765.* Oxford: Clarendon Press; New York: Oxford University Press, 1991.

Lewis, C. Bernard. "The Cayman Islands and Marine Turtle." *Bulletin of the Institute of Jamaica Science* 2 (1940): 56–65.

Lieberman, Victor. "Transcending East-West Dichotomies: State and Culture Formation in Six Ostensibly Separate Areas." *Modern Asian Studies* 31 (1997): 463–546.

Lindley, Keith. *Fenland Riots and the English Revolution*. London: Heinemann Educational Books, 1982.

Livi Bacci, Massimo. *Population and Nutrition: An Essay on European Demographic History*. Cambridge: Cambridge University Press, 1990.

Loades, D. M. *Tudor Government: Structures of Authority in the Sixteenth Century*. Oxford:
Blackwell, 1997.

———. *The Tudor Navy: An Administrative, Political, and Military History*. Aldershot,
Eng.: Ashgate; Brookfield, Vt.: Scolar Press, 1992.

Lombard-Salmon, Claudine. *Un exemple d'acculturation chinoise: La province du Gui
Zhou au XVIIIe siècle*. Paris: École française d'Extrême-Orient, 1972.

Long, Edward. *The history of Jamaica, or, General survey of the antient [sic] and modern state
of that island with reflections on its situation, settlements, inhabitants, climate, products,
commerce, laws, and government: in three volumes, illustrated with copper plates*. London:
Printed for T. Lowndes, 1774.

Looman, J. "Grassland as Natural or Semi-Natural Vegetation." In *Geobotany*, edited
by W. Holzner, M. J. A. Werger, and Isao Ikushima, 5:173–84. The Hague: Kluwer,
1983.

López de Gómara, Francisco, and Lesley Byrd Simpson. *Cortés: The Life of the Conqueror,
by His Secretary*. Berkeley and Los Angeles: University of California Press, 1964.

Lough, J. M., D. J. Barnes, and R. B. Taylor. "The Potential of Massive Corals for the
Study of High-Resolution Climate Variation in the Past Millennium." In *Climatic
Variations and Forcing Mechanisms of the Last 2000 Years*, edited by Philip D. Jones,
Raymond S. Bradley, Jean Jouzel, and the North Atlantic Treaty Organization, Sci-
entific Affairs Division, 355–71. Berlin: Springer, 1996.

Lounsbury, Ralph Greenlee, and the Kingsley Trust Association. *The British Fishery at
Newfoundland, 1634–1763*. New Haven: Yale University Press, 1934.

Lovell, W. George. " 'Heavy Shadows and Dark Night': Disease and Depopulation in
Colonial Spanish America." *Annals of the Association of American Geographers* 82
(1992): 426–43.

Lowry, Lloyd F. "Foods and Feeding Ecology." In *The Bowhead Whale*, edited by John
J. Burns, J. Jerome Montague, Cleveland J. Cowles, and the Society for Marine
Mammalogy, 229–30. Lawrence, Kans.: Society for Marine Mammalogy, 1993.

Lugar, Catherine. "The Portuguese Tobacco Trade and Tobacco Growers of Bahia in
the Late Colonial Period." In *Essays Concerning the Socioeconomic History of Brazil and
Portuguese India*, edited by Dauril Alden and Warren Dean, 26–70. Gainesville:
University Presses of Florida, 1977.

Lunn, Jean. "The Illegal Fur Trade Out of New France, 1713–1760." *Canadian Historical Association Report of the Annual Meeting* (1939): 61–76.

Luterbacher, J., R. Rickli, C. Tinguely, E. Xoplaki, E. Shüpbach, D. Dietrich, J.
Hüsler, M. Ambühl, C. Pfister, P. Beeli, U. Dietrich, A. Dannecker, T. D. Davies,
P. D. Jones, V. Slonosky, A. E. J. Ogilvie, P. Maheras, F. Kolyva-Machera, J. Martin-
Vide, M. Barriendos, M. J. Alcoforado, M. F. Nunes, T. Jánsson, R. Glaser, J. Ja-
cobeit, C. Beck, A. Philipp, U. Beyer, E. Kass, T. Schmith, L. Bärring, P. Jönsson,
L. Rácz, H. Wanner. "Monthly Mean Pressure Reconstruction for the Late Maun-

der Minimum Period (A.D. 1675–1715)." *International Journal of Climatology* 20, no. 10 (2000): 1049–1066.

Luterbacher, J., R. Rickli, E. Xoplaki, C. Tinguely, C. Beck, C. Pfister, and H. Wanner. "The Late Maunder Minimum (1675–1715): A Key Period for Studying Decadal Scale Climatic Change in Europe." *Climatic Change* (June 2001).

Lydon, James G. "Fish for Gold: The Massachusetts Fish Trade with Iberia, 1700–1773." *New England Quarterly* 54 (1981): 539–82.

Maat, G. J. R. "Human Remains at the Dutch Whaling Stations on Spitsbergen: A Physical Anthropological Study." In *Proceedings of the International Symposium, Early European Exploitation of the Northern Atlantic, 800–1700,* edited by Rijksuniversiteit te Groningen, Noordelijk Centrum, 153–202. Groningen, Netherlands: Arctic Centre, University of Groningen, 1981.

Macartney, George Macartney, and J. L. Cramer-Byng. *An Embassy to China: Being the Journal Kept by Lord Macartney during His Embassy to the Emperor Chien-lung, 1793–1794.* Hamden, Conn.: Archon Books, 1963.

MacDougall, Philip. *Royal Dockyards.* Newton Abbot: David and Charles, 1982.

MacFarlane, Alan. *The Savage Wars of Peace: England, Japan, and the Malthusian Trap.* Oxford: Blackwell, 1997.

Macleod, Murdo J. "Spain and America: The Atlantic Trade, 1492–1720." In *The Cambridge History of Latin America,* vol. 4, edited by Leslie Bethell. Cambridge: Cambridge University Press, 1984.

Maejima, I., and Y. Tagima. "Climate of Little Ice Age in Japan." *Geographical Reports of Tokyo Metropolitan University* 18 (1983): 91–111.

Malecki, Mark R. "Regulating Mercury in Miners' Eating Areas." *Public Health Reports* 113, no. 2 (1998): 179–82.

Mancall, Peter. *Deadly Medicine: Indians and Alcohol in Early America.* Ithaca, N.Y.: Cornell University Press, 1995.

Manley, G. "Central England Temperatures: Monthly Means, 1659 to 1973." *Quarterly Journal of the Royal Meteorological Society* 100 (1974): 389–405.

Mann, Michael E., Raymond S. Bradley, and Malcolm K. Hughes. "Global-Scale Temperature Patterns and Climate Forcing over the Past Six Centuries." *Nature,* no. 392 (1998): 779–87.

Manning, Roger B. *Hunters and Poachers: A Social and Cultural History of Unlawful Hunting in England, 1485–1640.* Oxford: Clarendon Press; New York: Oxford University Press, 1993.

Marcilio, Maria Luiza. "The Population of Colonial Brazil." In *The Cambridge History of Latin America,* vol. 2, edited by Leslie Bethell. Cambridge: Cambridge University Press, 1984.

Marks, Robert B. " 'It Never Used to Snow': Climatic Variability and Harvest Yields in Late-Imperial South China, 1650–1850." In *Sediments of Time: Environment and Society in Chinese History,* edited by Mark Elvin and Liu Ts'ui-jung, 411–46. Cambridge: Cambridge University Press, 1998.

———. *Tigers, Rice, Silk, and Silt: Environment and Economy in Late Imperial South China.* Cambridge: Cambridge University Press, 1997.

Marshall, Ingeborg. *A History and Ethnography of the Beothuk.* Montreal: McGill-Queen's University Press, 1996.

Martin, Calvin. *Keepers of the Game: Indian-Animal Relationships and the Fur Trade.* Berkeley and Los Angeles: University of California Press, 1978.

Martin, Janet. *Medieval Russia, 980–1584.* Cambridge: Cambridge University Press, 1995.

———. *Treasure of the Land of Darkness: The Fur Trade and Its Significance for Medieval Russia.* Cambridge: Cambridge University Press, 1986.

Martinez-Cortizas, A., X. Pontevedra-Pombal, E. Garcia-Rodeja, J. C. Novoa-Munoz, and W. Shotyk. "Mercury in a Spanish Peat Bog: Archive of Climate Change and Atmospheric Metal Deposition." *Science* 284, no. 5416 (1999): 639.

Mathes, W. Michael. "A Quarter Century of Trans-Pacific Diplomacy: New Spain and Japan, 1592–1617." *Journal of Asian History* 24 (1990): 1–29.

Mazumdar, Sucheta. *Sugar and Society in China: Peasants, Technology, and the World Market.* Cambridge: Harvard University Asia Center, 1998.

McCann, James C. "Climate and Causation in African History." *International Journal of African Historical Studies* 32, nos. 2–3 (1999): 261–79.

McCartney, Allen P. "Whale Size Selection by Precontact Hunters of the North American Western Arctic and Subarctic." In *Hunting the Largest Animals: Native Whaling in the Western Arctic and Subarctic,* edited by Allen P. McCartney and the Canadian Circumpolar Institute, 83–108. Alberta: Canadian Circumpolar Institute, University of Alberta, 1995.

McCartney, Allen P., and James M. Sevelle. "Thule Eskimo Whaling in the Central Canadian Arctic." *Arctic Anthropology* 22 (1985): 37–58.

McClain, James L. "Space, Power, Wealth, and Status in Seventeenth-Century Osaka." In *Osaka: The Merchants' Capital of Early Modern Japan,* edited by James L. McClain and Osamu Wakita, 44–79. Ithaca, N.Y.: Cornell University Press, 1999.

McCracken, Eileen, and Queen's University of Belfast, Institute of Irish Studies. *The Irish Woods since Tudor Times: Distribution and Exploitation.* Newton Abbot: David and Charles, 1971.

McCusker, John J., Russell R. Menard, and the Institute of Early American History and Culture. *The Economy of British America, 1607–1789, with Supplementary Bibliography.* Chapel Hill: University of North Carolina Press, for the Institute of Early American History and Culture, Williamsburg, Va., 1991.

McEvedy, Colin, and Richard Jones. *Atlas of World Population History.* London: A. Lane, 1978.

McFarland, Raymond. *A History of the New England Fisheries, with Maps.* Philadelphia: University of Pennsylvania; New York: D. Appleton and Company, 1911.

McGhee, Robert. "Thule Prehistory of Canada." In *Handbook of North American Indians,* edited by William C. Sturtevant, 369–76. Washington: Smithsonian Institution, 1978.

McGurk, John. *The Elizabethan Conquest of Ireland: The 1590s Crisis.* Manchester: Manchester University Press, 1997.

McManis, Douglas R. *Colonial New England: A Historical Geography.* New York: Oxford University Press, 1975.

McNaughton, S. J. "Grazing as an Optimization Process: Grass-Ungulate Relationships in the Serengeti." *American Naturalist* 113 (1979): 691–703.

McNaughton, S. J., and F. F. Banyikwa. "Plant Communities and Herbivory." In

Serengeti II: Dynamics, Management, and Conservation of an Ecosystem, edited by A. R. E. Sinclair and Peter Arcese, xii, 665. Chicago: University of Chicago Press, 1995.

Melville, Elinor G. K. *A Plague of Sheep: Environmental Consequences of the Conquest of Mexico.* Cambridge: Cambridge University Press, 1994.

Menzies, Nicholas K. *Forest and Land Management in Imperial China.* New York: St. Martin's Press, 1994.

———. "Forestry." In *Science and Civilisation in China,* vol. 6, pt. 3, sec. 42b, edited by Joseph Needham, 540–689. Cambridge: University Press, 1996.

Merrell, James Hart, and Institute of Early American History and Culture. *The Indians' New World: Catawbas and Their Neighbors from European Contact through the Era of Removal.* Chapel Hill: University of North Carolina Press, for the Institute of Early American History and Culture, Williamsburg, Va., 1989.

Michell, A. R. "The European Fisheries in Early Modern History." In *The Economic Organization of Early Modern Europe,* edited by E. E. Rich and Charles Wilson, 134–84. Cambridge: Cambridge University Press, 1977.

Michie, R. L. "North-East Scotland and the Northern Whale Fishing, 1752–1893." *Northern Scotland* 3, no. 1 (1977–1978): 61–85.

Miller, Shawn William. "Brazil's Colonial Timber: Conservation, Monopoly, and the Accumulation of Colonial Wealth, 1652–1822." Ph.D. diss., Columbia University, 1997.

Mintz, Sidney Wilfred. *Sweetness and Power: The Place of Sugar in Modern History.* New York: Viking, 1985.

Mitchison, Rosalind. *Lordship to Patronage: Scotland, 1603–1745.* Edinburgh: Edinburgh University Press, 1990.

Moody, T. W., F. X. Martin, and F. J. Byrne. *A New History of Ireland.* Oxford: Clarendon Press, 1976.

Moon, David. "Peasant Migration and the Settlement of Russia's Frontiers, 1550–1897." *The Historical Journal* 40, no. 4 (1997): 859–93.

———. *The Russian Peasantry, 1600–1930: The World the Peasants Made.* London: Longman, 1999.

Moore, Sue E., and Randall R. Reeves. "Distribution and Movement." In *The Bowhead Whale,* edited by John J. Burns, J. Jerome Montague, Cleveland J. Cowles, and the Society for Marine Mammalogy, 313–86. Lawrence, Kans.: Society for Marine Mammalogy, 1993.

Morgan, Lewis Henry. *The American Beaver: A Classic of Natural History and Ecology.* New York: Dover Publications, 1986.

Morgan, Philip D. "Slaves and Livestock in Eighteenth-Century Jamaica: Vineyard Pen, 1750–1751." *William and Mary Quarterly,* 3d ser., 52 (1995): 47–76.

Morrison, Kenneth M. *The Embattled Northeast: The Elusive Ideal of Alliance in Abenaki-Euramerican Relations.* Berkeley and Los Angeles: University of California Press, 1984.

Mostert, Noël. *Frontiers: The Epic of South Africa's Creation and the Tragedy of the Xhosa People.* 1st Amer. ed. New York: Knopf, distributed by Random House, 1992.

Moya Pons, Frank. *Después de Colón: Trabajo, sociedad y política en la economía del oro.* Madrid: Alianza, 1987.

Murphey, Rhoads. "Deforestation in Modern China." In *Global Deforestation and the Nineteenth-Century World Economy,* edited by Richard P. Tucker and John F. Richards, 111–28. Durham, N.C.: Duke University Press, 1983.

Nagahara, Keiji, and Kozo Yamamura. "Shaping the Process of Unification: Technological Progress in Sixteenth- and Seventeenth-Century Japan." *Journal of Japanese Studies* 14 (1988): 77–109.

Naiman, R. J., G. Pinay, C. A. Johnstone, and J. Pastor. "Beaver Influences on the Long-Term Biogeochemical Characteristics of Boreal Forest Drainage." *Ecology* 75, no. 4 (1994): 905–21.

Nakken, Odd. "Causes of Trends and Fluctuations in the Arcto-Norwegian Cod Stock." In *Cod and Climate Change: Proceedings of a Symposium Held in Reykjavík, 23–27 August 1993,* edited by Jakob Jakobsson and the International Council for the Exploration of the Sea, 212–28. ICES Marine Science Symposia, v. 198. Copenhagen: International Council for the Exploration of the Sea, 1994.

Naohiro, Asaho. "The Sixteenth Century Unification." In *The Cambridge History of Japan,* vol. 4, edited by John Whitney Hall. Cambridge: Cambridge University Press, 1988.

Neeson, Eoin. *A History of Irish Forestry.* Dublin: Lilliput Press, 1991.

Nef, John Ulric. *The Rise of the British Coal Industry.* London: G. Routledge, 1932.

Neumark, S. D. *Economic Influences on the South African Frontier, 1652–1836.* Stanford, Calif.: Stanford University Press, 1957.

Newbigging, William James. "The History of the French-Ottawa Alliance, 1613–1763." Ph.D. diss., University of Toronto, 1995.

Newman, D. G., and C. R. Griffin. "Wetland Use by River Otters in Massachusetts." *Journal of Wildlife Management* 58, no. 1 (1994): 18–23.

Newton-King, Susan. *Masters and Servants on the Cape Eastern Frontier, 1760–1803.* African Studies Series, no 97. Cambridge: Cambridge University Press, 1999.

Nicholson, Sharon E. "Climatic Variations in the Sahel and Other African Regions during the Past Five Centuries." *Journal of Arid Environments* 1 (1978): 3–24.

———. "The Methodology of Historical Climate Reconstruction and Its Application to Africa." *Journal of African History* 20 (1979): 31–49.

Nobuhiko, Nakai. "Commercial Change and Urban Growth in Early Modern Japan." In *The Cambridge History of Japan,* vol. 4, edited by John Whitney Hall. Cambridge: Cambridge University Press, 1988.

Novak, Milan, Martyn E. Obbard, James G. Jones, Robert Newman, Annie Booth, Andrew J. Satterthwaite, and Greg Linscombe. *Furbearer Harvests in North America, 1600–1984.* Ontario: Ministry of Natural Resources, 1987.

Nowak, Ronald M., and Ernest P. Walker. *Walker's Mammals of the World.* 5th ed. Baltimore: Johns Hopkins University Press, 1991.

Nriagu, Jerome O. "Mercury Pollution from the Past Mining of Gold and Silver in the Americas." *Science of the Total Environment* 149 (1994): 167–81.

Nummi, P. "The Importance of Beaver Ponds to Waterfowl Broods: An Experiment and Natural Tests." *Annales Zoologgici Fennici* 29, no. 1 (1992): 47–55.

O'Brien, Patrick. "Did Europe's Mercantilist Empires Pay?" *History Today* 46 (1996): 32–41.

———. "European Economic Development: The Contribution of the Periphery." *Economic History Review*, 2d ser., 35 (1982).

———. "The Foundations of European Industrialization: From the Perspective of the World." In *Economic Effects of the European Expansion, 1492–1824*, edited by José Casas Pardo, 463–502. Stuttgart: In Kommission bei F. Steiner, 1992.

Ogilvie, A. E. J. "Documentary Evidence for Changes in the Climate of Iceland, A.D. 1500 to 1800." In *Climate since A.D. 1500*, edited by Raymond S. Bradley and Philip D. Jones, 92–117. Rev. ed. London: Routledge, 1995.

O'Hara, Sarah L., and Sarah E. Metcalfe. "Reconstructing the Climate of Mexico from Historical Records." *The Holocene* 5, no. 4 (1995): 485–90.

Osborne, Anne. "Barren Mountains, Raging Rivers: The Ecological and Social Effects of Changing Landuse on the Lower Yangzi Periphery in Late Imperial China." Ph.D. diss., Columbia University, 1989.

———. "Highlands and Lowlands: Economic and Ecological Interactions in the Lower Yangzi Region under the Qing." In *Sediments of Time: Environment and Society in Chinese History*, edited by Mark Elvin and Liu Ts'ui-jung, 203–34. Cambridge: Cambridge University Press, 1998.

———. "The Local Politics of Land Reclamation in the Lower Yangzi Highlands." *Late Imperial China* 15 (1994): 1–46.

O'Shea, Marty. "Springfield's Puritans and Indians." *Historical Journal of Massachusetts* 26, no. 1 (1998): 46–72.

Ouweneel, Arij. *Shadows over Anáhuac: An Ecological Interpretation of Crisis and Development in Central Mexico, 1730–1800*. 1st ed. Albuquerque: University of New Mexico Press, 1996.

Overpeck, J., K. Hughen, D. Hardy, R. Bradley, R. Case, M. Douglas, B. Finney, K. Gajewski, G. Jacoby, A. Jennings, S. Lamoureux, A. Lasca, G. MacDonald, J. Moore, M. Retelle, S. Smith, A. Wolfe, and G. Zielinski. "Arctic Environment Change of the Last Four Centuries." *Science* 278, no. 5341 (1997): 1251–57.

Overpeck, Jonathan T. "Varved Sediment Records of Recent Seasonal to Millennial-Scale Environmental Variability." In *Climatic Variations and Forcing Mechanisms of the Last 2000 Years*, edited by Philip D. Jones, Raymond S. Bradley, Jean Jouzel, and the North Atlantic Treaty Organization, Scientific Affairs Division, 479–98. Berlin: Springer, 1996.

Overton, Mark. *Agricultural Revolution in England: The Transformation of the Agrarian Economy, 1500–1850*. Cambridge: Cambridge University Press, 1996.

———. "Re-establishing the English Agricultural Revolution." *Agricultural History Review* 44 (1996): 1–20.

Pallot, Judith, and Denis J. B. Shaw. *Landscape and Settlement in Romanov Russia, 1613–1917*. Oxford: Clarendon Press; New York: Oxford University Press, 1990.

Pané, Ramón, and José Juan Arrom. *An Account of the Antiquities of the Indians: Chronicles of the New World Encounter*. Durham: Duke University Press, 1999.

Pares, Richard. *Yankees and Creoles: The Trade between North America and the West Indies before the American Revolution*. Cambridge: Harvard University Press, 1956.

Parker, Geoffrey. *The Military Revolution: Military Innovation and the Rise of the West, 1500–1800*. 2d ed. Cambridge: Cambridge University Press, 1996.

Parsons, James Jerome. *The Green Turtle and Man.* Gainesville: University of Florida Press, 1962.

Payne, Roger. *Among Whales.* New York: Scribner, 1995.

Perdue, Peter C. *Exhausting the Earth: State and Peasant in Hunan, 1500–1850.* Harvard East Asian Monographs, no. 130. Cambridge: Council on East Asian Studies, Harvard University, distributed by Harvard University Press, 1987.

Perevolotsky, Avi, and No'am G. Seligman. "Role of Grazing in Mediterranean Rangeland Ecosystems." *Bioscience* 48, no. 12 (1998): 1007–24.

Perkins, Dwight Heald. *Agricultural Development in China, 1368–1968.* 1st ed. Chicago: Aldine, 1969.

Petitjean Roget, Jacques. *La société d'habitation à la Martinique: Un demi siècle de formation, 1635–1685.* Lille: Atelier Reproduction des thèses Université de Lille III, distributed by H. Champion, 1980.

Pfister, Christian. *Agrakonjunktur und Witterungsverlauf im westlichen Schweizer Mittelland, 1755–1797.* Liebefeld: Lang Druck, 1975.

———. *Das Klima der Schweiz von 1525–1860 und seine Bedeutung in der Geschichte von Bevölkerung und Landwirtschaft.* Bern: P. Haupt, 1984.

———. "Fluctuations climatiques et prix céréaliers en Europe du XVIᵉ au XXᵉ siècle." *Annales ESC,* no. 1 (January–February 1988): 25–53.

———. "Monthly Temperature and Precipitation in Central Europe, 1525–1979: Quantifying Documentary Evidence on Weather and Its Effects." In *Climate since A.D. 1500,* edited by Raymond S. Bradley and Philip D. Jones, 118–42. Rev. ed. London: Routledge, 1995.

Pfister, Christian, and Walter Bareiss. "The Climate in Paris between 1675 and 1715 according to the Meteorological Journal of Louis Morin." In *Climatic Trends and Anomalies in Europe, 1675–1715: High Resolution Spatio-Temporal Reconstructions from Direct Meteorological Observations and Proxy Data: Methods and Results,* edited by Burkhard Frenzel, Christian Pfister, Birgit Gläser, and the European Science Foundation, 151–71. Stuttgart: G. Fischer, 1994.

Pfister, Christian, and Rudolf Brázdil. "Climatic Variability in Sixteenth-Century Europe and Its Social Dimension: A Synthesis." *Climatic Change* 43, no. 1 (1999): 5–53.

Pfister, Christian, Rudolf Brázdil, Rudiger Glaser, Mariano Barriendos, Dario Camuffo, Mathias Deutsch, Petr Dobrovolnp, Silvia Enzi, Emanuela Guidoboni, Oldrich Kotyza, Stefan Militzer, Lajos Rácz, and Fernando S. Rodrigo. "Documentary Evidence on Climate in Sixteenth-Century Europe." *Climatic Change* 43, no. 1 (1999): 55–110.

Pfister, Christian, Rudolf Bràzdil, Rudiger Glaser, Anita Bokwa, Franz Holawe, Danuta Limanowka, Oldrich Kotyza, Jan Munzar, Laios Racz, Elisabeth Strommer, and Gabriela Schwarz-Zanetti. "Daily Weather Observations in Sixteenth-Century Europe." *Climatic Change* 43, no. 1 (1999): 111–50.

Phillips, Paul C. *The Fur Trade.* 1st ed. Norman: University of Oklahoma Press, 1961.

Philo, L. Michael, Emmett B. Shotts Jr., and John C. George. "Morbidity and Mortality." In *The Bowhead Whale,* edited by John J. Burns, J. Jerome Montague, Cleveland J. Cowles, and the Society for Marine Mammalogy, 275–312. Lawrence, Kans.: Society for Marine Mammalogy, 1993.

Pomeranz, Kenneth. *The Great Divergence: Europe, China, and the Making of the Modern World Economy.* Princeton, N.J.: Princeton University Press, 2000.

Pope, Peter. "Early Estimates: Assessment of Catches in the Newfoundland Cod Fishery, 1660–1690." In *Papers Presented at the Conference Entitled "Marine Resources and Human Societies in the North Atlantic since 1500," October 20–22, 1995.* St. John's, Newfoundland: The Institute of Social and Economic Research, Memorial University of Newfoundland, 1997.

Poppino, Rollie E. "Cattle Industry in Colonial Brazil." *Mid-America* 31 (1949): 219–47.

Porter, John. "A Forest in Transition: Bowland, 1500–1650." *Transactions of the Historic Society of Lancashire and Cheshire for the Year 1974* 125 (1975): 40–60.

———. "Waste Land Reclamation in the Sixteenth and Seventeenth Centuries: The Case of South-Eastern Bowland, 1550–1630." *Transactions of the Historic Society of Lancashire and Cheshire for the Year 1977* 127 (1978): 1–24.

Portilla, Miguel León, and Lysander Kemp. *The Broken Spears: The Aztec Account of the Conquest of Mexico.* Boston: Beacon Press, 1962.

Post, John D. *Food Shortage, Climatic Variability, and Epidemic Disease in Preindustrial Europe: The Mortality Peak in the Early 1740s.* Ithaca, N.Y.: Cornell University Press, 1985.

Powell, Philip Wayne. *Soldiers, Indians, and Silver: The Northward Advance of New Spain, 1550–1600.* Berkeley and Los Angeles: University of California Press, 1952.

Power, M. E., D. Tilman, J. Estes, B. A. Menge, W. J. Bond, L. S. Mills, G. Daily, J. C. Castilla, J. Lubchenco, and R. T. Paine. "Challenges in the Quest for Keystones." *BioScience* 46 (1996): 609–20.

Prem, Hans J. "Disease Outbreaks in Central Mexico during the Sixteenth Century." In *Secret Judgments of God: Old World Disease in Colonial Spanish America,* edited by Noble David Cook and W. George Lovell, 20–48. Norman: University of Oklahoma Press, 1991.

———. "Spanish Colonization and Indian Property in Central Mexico, 1521–1620." *Annals of the Association of American Geographers* 82 (1992): 444–59.

Proulx, Jean Pierre, and the Canadian Parks Service. *Basque Whaling in Labrador in the Sixteenth Century.* Ottawa: National Historic Sites Parks Service, 1993.

Quinn, W. H., and V. T. Neal. "The Historical Record of El Niño Events." In *Climate since A.D. 1500,* edited by Raymond S. Bradley and Philip D. Jones, 623–48. Rev. ed. London: Routledge, 1995.

Ratekin, Mervyn. "The Early Sugar Industry in Espanola." *Hispanic American Historical Review* 34 (1954): 1–19.

Ravina, Mark. "State-Building and Political Economy in Early-Modern Japan." *Journal of Asian Studies* 54 (1995).

Ray, Arthur J., and Donald B. Freeman. *"Give Us Good Measure": An Economic Analysis of Relations between the Indians and the Hudson's Bay Company before 1763.* Toronto: University of Toronto Press, 1978.

Reardon-Anderson, James. "Land Use and Society in Manchuria and Inner Mongolia during the Qing Dynasty." *Environmental History* 5, no. 4 (2000): 503–30.

Reff, Daniel T. *Disease, Depopulation, and Culture Change in Northwestern New Spain, 1518–1764.* Salt Lake City: University of Utah Press, 1991.

Reid, George C. "Solar Forcing of Global Climate Change since the Mid–Seventeenth Century." *Climatic Change* 37 (1997): 391–405.

Rich, E. "Russia and the Colonial Fur Trade." *Economic History Review*, 2d ser., 7 (1955): 307–28.

Richards, John F. "Early Modern India and World History." *Journal of World History* 8 (1997): 197–209.

———. Introduction to *Land Property and the Environment*, edited by John F. Richards. Oakland, Calif.: Institute of Contemporary Studies Press, 2001.

———. *The Mughal Empire*. Vol. 1 of *The New Cambridge History of India*. Cambridge: Cambridge University Press, 1993.

———. "Mughal State Finance and the Premodern World Economy." *Comparative Studies in Society and History* (1981): 285–308.

———. "Only a World Perspective Is Significant: Settlement Frontiers and Property Rights in Early Modern World History." In *The Humanities and the Environment*, edited by Jill Conway, Kenneth Keniston, and Leo Marx. Cambridge: MIT Press, 1998.

———. "Toward a Global System of Property Rights in Land." In *Land Property and the Environment*, edited by John F. Richards. Oakland, Calif.: Institute of Contemporary Studies Press, 2001.

Richter, Daniel K., and the Institute of Early American History and Culture. *The Ordeal of the Longhouse: The Peoples of the Iroquois League in the Era of European Colonization*. Chapel Hill: University of North Carolina Press, for the Institute of Early American History and Culture, Williamsburg, Va., 1992.

Roberts, Luke Shepherd. *Mercantilism in a Japanese Domain: The Merchant Origins of Economic Nationalism in Eighteenth-Century Tosa*. Cambridge: Cambridge University Press, 1998.

Rodrigo, F. S., M. J. Esteban-Parra, and Y. Castro-Diez. "On the Use of the Jesuit Private Correspondence Records in Climate Reconstructions: A Case Study from Castile (Spain) for 1634–1648." *Climatic Change* 40 (1998): 625–45.

Rogers, Graham. "Custom and Common Right: Waste Land Enclosure and Social Change in West Lancashire." *Agricultural History Review* 41 (1993): 137–54.

Ross, Robert. "The Cape of Good Hope and the World Economy, 1652–1835." In *The Shaping of South African Society, 1652–1840*, edited by Richard Elphick and Hermann Giliomee. Middletown, Conn.: Wesleyan University Press, 1989.

Roulet, M., M. Lucotte, N. Farella, G. Serique, H. Coelho, C. J. Sousa Passos, E. de Jesus da Silva, P. Scavone de Andrade, D. Mergler, J.-R. D. Guimarães, and M. Amorim. "Effects of Recent Human Colonization on the Presence of Mercury in Amazonian Ecosystems." *Water, Air, and Soil Pollution* 112 (1999): 297–313.

Rouse, Irving. *The Tainos: Rise and Decline of the People Who Greeted Columbus*. New Haven: Yale University Press, 1992.

Russell, Carl Parcher. *Guns on the Early Frontiers: A History of Firearms from Colonial Time through the Years of the Western Fur Trade*. Berkeley and Los Angeles: University of California Press, 1957.

Russell-Wood, A. J. R. *A World on the Move: The Portuguese in Africa, Asia, and America, 1415–1808*. New York: St. Martin's Press, 1993.

Sack, Robert David. *Human Territoriality: Its Theory and History*. Cambridge: Cambridge University Press, 1986.

Sakai, Robert K. "The Satsuma-Ryukyu Trade and the Tokugawa Seclusion Policy." *Journal of Asian Studies* 23 (1964): 391–403.

Sale, Kirkpatrick. *The Conquest of Paradise: Christopher Columbus and the Columbian Legacy.* 1st ed. New York: Knopf, distributed by Random House, 1990.

Salisbury, Neal. *Manitou and Providence: Indians, Europeans, and the Making of New England, 1500–1643.* New York: Oxford University Press, 1982.

Sanchez-Albornoz, Nicholas. "The Population of Colonial Spanish America." In *The Cambridge History of Latin America,* vol. 2, edited by Leslie Bethell. Cambridge: Cambridge University Press, 1984.

Sanderson, Stephen K. *Social Evolutionism: A Critical History.* Studies in Social Discontinuity. Cambridge, Mass.: Blackwell, 1990.

———. *Social Transformations: A General Theory of Historical Development.* Cambridge, Mass.: Blackwell, 1995.

Sato, Tsuneo. "Tokugawa Villages and Agriculture." In *Tokugawa Japan: The Social and Economic Antecedents of Modern Japan,* edited by Chie Nakane, Shinzabur Oishi, and Conrad D. Totman. Tokyo: University of Tokyo Press, 1990.

Schilder, Gunter. "Development and Achievements of Dutch Northern and Arctic Cartography in the Sixteenth and Seventeenth Centuries." *Arctic* 37, no. 4 (1984): 493–514.

Schlosser, I. J. "Dispersal, Boundary Processes, and Trophic-Level Interactions in Streams Adjacent to Beaver Ponds." *Ecology* 76, no. 3 (1995): 908–25.

Schopka, Sigfus A. "Fluctuations in the Cod Stock off Iceland during the Twentieth Century in Relation to Changes in the Fisheries and Environment." In *Cod and Climate Change: Proceedings of a Symposium Held in Reykjavík, 23–27 August 1993,* edited by Jakob Jakobsson and the International Council for the Exploration of the Sea, 175–93. ICES Marine Science Symposia, v. 198. Copenhagen: International Council for the Exploration of the Sea, 1994.

Schrire, Carmel. "Excavating Archives at Oudepost I, Cape." *Social Dynamics* 16, no. 1 (1990): 11–21.

Schwartz, Stuart B. "Colonial Brazil, c. 1580–c. 1750: Plantations and Peripheries." In *The Cambridge History of Latin America,* vol. 2, edited by Leslie Bethell. Cambridge: Cambridge University Press, 1984.

———. *Sugar Plantations in the Formation of Brazilian Society: Bahia, 1550–1835.* Cambridge: Cambridge University Press, 1985.

Scoresby, William. *An Account of the Arctic Regions, with a History and Description of the Northern Whale-Fishery.* Reprint of the 1st ed. Newton Abbot: David and Charles, 1969.

Seaton, Albert. *The Horsemen of the Steppes: The Story of the Cossacks.* New York: Hippocrene Books, 1985.

Seed, Patricia. " 'Are These Also Not Men?': The Indians' Humanity and Capacity for Spanish Civilisation." *Journal of Latin American Studies,* 25, no. 3 (1993): 629–53.

Serchuk, Fredric M., Marvin D. Grosslein, R. Gregory Lough, David G. Mountain, and Loretta O'Brien. "Fishery and Environmental Factors Affecting Trends and Fluctuations in the Georges Bank and Gulf of Main Atlantic Cod Stocks: An Overview." In *Cod and Climate Change: Proceedings of a Symposium Held in Reykjavík, 23–27 August 1993,* edited by Jakob Jakobsson and the International Council for the Exploration of the Sea, 77–109. ICES Marine Science Symposia, v. 198. Copenhagen: International Council for the Exploration of the Sea, 1994.

Seymour, Susanne, Stephen Daniels, and Charles Watkins. "Estate and Empire: Sir George Cornewall's Management of Moccas, Herefordshire, and La Taste, Grenada, 1771–1819." *Journal of Historical Geography* 24 (1998): 313–51.

Shammas, Carole. *The Pre-industrial Consumer in England and America.* Oxford: Clarendon Press; New York: Oxford University Press, 1990.

Sharp, Buchanan. *In Contempt of All Authority: Rural Artisans and Riot in the West of England, 1586–1660.* Berkeley and Los Angeles: University of California Press, 1980.

Shaw, D. J. B. "Southern Frontiers of Muscovy, 1550–1700." In *Studies in Russian Historical Geography,* edited by James H. Bater and R. A. French. London: Academic Press, 1983.

———. *Russia in the Modern World: A New Geography.* Oxford: Blackwell, 1999.

Sheehan, Gene W. "Whaling Surplus, Trade, War, and the Integration of Prehistoric Northern and Northwestern Alaskan Economies, A.D. 1200–1826." In *Hunting the Largest Animals: Native Whaling in the Western Arctic and Subarctic,* edited by Allen P. McCartney and the Canadian Circumpolar Institute, 185–206. Alberta: Canadian Circumpolar Institute University of Alberta, 1995.

Shelden, Kim E. W., and David J. Rugh. *The Bowhead Whale, Balaena mysticetus: Its Historic and Current Status.* Seattle: National Marine Mammal Laboratory, National Marine Fisheries Service, National Oceanic and Atmospheric Administration, 1997.

Shepherd, John Robert. *Statecraft and Political Economy on the Taiwan Frontier, 1600–1800.* Stanford, Calif.: Stanford University Press, 1993.

Shepherd, Verene A. "Livestock and Sugar: Aspects of Jamaica's Agricultural Development from the Late Seventeenth to the Early Nineteenth Century." *The Historical Journal* 34, no. 3 (1991): 627–43.

Sheridan, Richard B. *Sugar and Slavery: An Economic History of the British West Indies, 1623–1775.* Baltimore: Johns Hopkins University Press, 1974.

Silver, Timothy. *A New Face on the Countryside: Indians, Colonists, and Slaves in South Atlantic Forests, 1500–1800.* Cambridge: Cambridge University Press, 1990.

Simpson, Lesley Byrd. *Exploitation of Land in Central Mexico in the Sixteenth Century.* Berkeley and Los Angeles: University of California Press, 1952.

Sinclair, A. R. E. "Serengeti Past and Present." In *Serengeti II: Dynamics, Management, and Conservation of an Ecosystem,* edited by A. R. E. Sinclair and Peter Arcese, xii, 665. Chicago: University of Chicago Press, 1995.

Sippel, Patricia. "Abandoned Fields: Negotiating Taxes in the Bakafu Domain." *Monumenta Nipponica* 53, no. 2 (1998): 197–223.

Slezkine, Yuri. *Arctic Mirrors: Russia and the Small Peoples of the North.* Ithaca, N.Y.: Cornell University Press, 1994.

Sluyter, Andrew. "Changes in the Landscape: Natives, Spaniards, and the Ecological Restructuration of Central Veracruz, Mexico, during the Sixteenth Century." Ph.D. diss., University of Texas at Austin. Ann Arbor: University Microfilms, 1995.

———. "The Ecological Origins and Consequences of Cattle Ranching in Sixteenth Century Spain." *Geographical Review* 86 (1996): 161–77.

———. "From Archive to Map to Pastoral Landscape: A Spatial Perspective on the

Livestock Ecology of Sixteenth-Century New Spain." *Environmental History* 3, no. 4 (1998): 508–28.

———. "The Making of the Myth in Postcolonial Development: Material Conceptual Landscape Transformation in Sixteenth-Century Veracruz." *Annals of the Association of American Geographers* 89, no. 3 (1999): 377–403.

Smil, Vaclav. *Energy in World History.* Boulder, Colo.: Westview Press, 1994.

Smith, R. E. F. *Peasant Farming in Muscovy.* Cambridge: Cambridge University Press, 1977.

Smith, Thomas C., Robert Y. Eng, and Robert T. Lundy. *Nakahara: Family Farming and Population in a Japanese Village, 1717–1830.* Stanford, Calif.: Stanford University Press, 1977.

Smithers, Reay H. N., and Clare Abbott. *Land Mammals of Southern Africa: A Field Guide.* 1st ed. Braamfontein, Johannesburg: Macmillan South Africa, 1986.

Smout, T. C. *Nature Contested: Environmental History in Scotland and Northern England since 1600.* Edinburgh: Edinburgh University Press, 2000.

Snodgrass, J. W. "Temporal and Spatial Dynamics of Beaver-Created Patches as Influenced by Management Practices in a South-Eastern North America Landscape." *Journal of Applied Ecology* 34, no. 4 (1997): 1043–1156.

Snow, Dean R., and Kim M. Lanphear. "European Contact and Indian Depopulation in the Northeast: The Timing of the First Epidemics." *Ethnohistory* 35, no. 1 (1988): 15–33.

Song, Jie. "Changes in Dryness/Wetness in China during the Last 529 Years." *International Journal of Climatology* 20 (2000): 1003–15.

Sparrman, Anders, and Vernon S. Forbes. *A Voyage to the Cape of Good Hope, towards the Antarctic Polar Circle, Round the World, and to the Country of the Hottentots and the Caffres, from the year 1772–1776, based on the English Editions of 1785–1786 Published by Robinson, London.* Cape Town: Van Riebeeck Society, 1975.

Spores, Ronald. *The Mixtecs in Ancient and Colonial Times.* Norman: University of Oklahoma Press, 1984.

Stannard, David E. "Disease and Infertility: A New Look at the Demographic Collapse of Native Populations in the Wake of Western Contact." *Journal of American Studies* 24, no. 3 (1990): 510–28.

Stebelsky, I. "Agriculture and Soil Erosion in the European Forest-Steppe." In *Studies in Russian Historical Geography,* edited by James H. Bater and R. A. French, 45–63. London: Academic Press, 1983.

Steele, Ian Kenneth. *Warpaths: Invasions of North America.* New York: Oxford University Press, 1994.

Stevens, Carol Belkin. *Soldiers on the Steppe: Army Reform and Social Change in Early Modern Russia.* DeKalb: Northern Illinois University Press, 1995.

Stoker, Sam W., and Igor I. Krupnik. "Subsistence Whaling." In *The Bowhead Whale,* edited by John J. Burns, J. Jerome Montague, Cleveland J. Cowles, and the Society for Marine Mammalogy, 579–629. Lawrence, Kans.: Society for Marine Mammalogy, 1993.

Stora, Nils. "Russian Walrus Hunting in Spitsbergen." *Etudes/Inuit/Studies* 11, no. 2 (1987): 117–38.

Strickland, Marjorie A. "Harvest Management of Fishers and American Martens." In

Martens, Sables, and Fishers: Biology and Conservation, edited by Steven Buskirk, 149–64. Ithaca, N.Y.: Cornell University Press, 1994.

Stroganov, S. U. *Carnivorous Mammals of Siberia.* Jerusalem: Israel Program for Scientific Translations, 1969, available from the U.S. Department of Commerce Clearinghouse for Federal Scientific and Technical Information, Springfield, Va.

Swan, Susan L. "Mexico in the Little Ice Age." *Journal of Interdisciplinary History* 11 (1981): 633–48.

Taggert, C. T., J. Anderson, C. Biship, E. Colbourne, J. Hutchings, G. Lilly, J. Morgan, E. Murphy, R. Myers, G. Rose, and P. Shelton. "Overview of Cod Stocks, Biology, and Environment in the Northwest Atlantic Region of Newfoundland, with Emphasis on Northern Cod." In *Cod and Climate Change: Proceedings of a Symposium Held in Reykjavík, 23–27 August 1993,* edited by Jakob Jakobsson and the International Council for the Exploration of the Sea, 140–57. ICES Marine Science Symposia, v. 198. Copenhagen: International Council for the Exploration of the Sea, 1994.

Tarussov, A. "The Arctic from Svalbard to Severnaya Zemlya: Climatic Reconstructions from Ice Cores." In *Climate since A.D. 1500,* edited by Raymond S. Bradley and Philip D. Jones, 505–16. Rev. ed. London: Routledge, 1995.

Taylor, S. A. G. *The Western Design: An Account of Cromwell's Expedition to the Caribbean.* 2d ed. London: Solstice Productions, 1969.

Taylor, William B. *Landlord and Peasant in Colonial Oaxaca.* Stanford, Calif.: Stanford University Press, 1972.

Teng, T'o. "Les mines de charbon de Men-t'ou k'ou." *Annales, Economies, Sociétés, Civilization* 22 (1967): 50–87.

Thirsk, Joan. *English Peasant Farming: The Agrarian History of Lincolnshire from Tudor to Recent Times.* London: Routledge and Kegan Paul, 1957.

———, ed. *The Agrarian History of England and Wales.* Vol. 4: *1500–1640.* Cambridge: Cambridge University Press, 1967.

Thomas, Brinley. "Escaping from Constraints: The Industrial Revolution in a Malthusian Context." *Journal of Interdisciplinary History* 15, no. 4 (1985): 729–53.

———. "Was There an Energy Crisis in Great Britain in the Seventeenth Century?" *Explorations in Economic History* 23 (1986): 124–52.

Thomas, Peter A. *In the Maelstrom of Change: The Indian Trade and Cultural Process in the Middle Connecticut River Valley, 1635–1665.* New York: Garland, 1990.

Thompson, Laurence G. "The Earliest Chinese Eyewitness Accounts of the Formosan Aborigines." *Monumenta Serica: Journal of Oriental Studies of the Catholic University of Peking* 23 (1964).

Thunberg, Carl Peter, and Vernon S. Forbes. *Travels at the Cape of Good Hope, 1772–1775: Based on the English Edition, London, 1793–1795.* Cape Town: Van Riebeeck Society, 1986.

Thwaites, Reuben Gold, ed. *The Jesuit Relations and Allied Documents: Travels and Explorations of the Jesuit Missionaries in New France, 1610–1791.* Cleveland: Burrows Brothers, 1896–1901.

Toby, Ronald P. *State and Diplomacy in Early Modern Japan: Asia in the Development of the Tokugawa Bakufu.* Princeton, N.J.: Princeton University Press, 1984.

Totman, Conrad D. *Early Modern Japan*. Berkeley and Los Angeles: University of California Press, 1993.

———. *The Green Archipelago: Forestry in Preindustrial Japan*. Berkeley and Los Angeles: University of California Press, 1989.

———. *The Lumber Industry in Early Modern Japan*. Honolulu: University of Hawaii Press, 1995.

———. "Preindustrial River Conservancy: Causes and Consequences," *Monumenta Nipponica* 47 (1992).

Trautman, Wolfgang. "Geographical Aspects of Hispanic Colonization on the Northern Frontier of New Spain." *Erdkunde* 40, no. 4 (1986): 241–50.

Trelease, Allen W. *Indian Affairs in Colonial New York: The Seventeenth Century*. Ithaca, N.Y.: Cornell University Press, 1960.

Trewartha, Glenn Thomas. *Japan, a Physical, Cultural, and Regional Geography*. Madison: University of Wisconsin, 1945.

Trigger, Bruce G. *The Children of Aataentsic I: A History of the Huron People to 1660*. Montreal: McGill-Queen's University Press, 1976.

———. "Early Native North American Responses to European Contact: Romantic versus Rationalistic Interpretations." *Journal of American History* 77, no. 4 (1991): 1195–1215.

Ts'ui-jung, Liu. "Han Migration and the Settlement of Taiwan." In *Sediments of Time: Environment and Society in Chinese History*, edited by Mark Elvin and Liu Ts'ui-jung, 165–202. Cambridge: Cambridge University Press, 1998.

Tuck, J. A. "Basque Whalers in Southern Labrador, Canada." In *Proceedings of the International Symposium, Early European Exploitation of the Northern Atlantic, 800–1700*, edited by Rijksuniversiteit te Groningen, Noordelijk Centrum, 69–77. Groningen, Netherlands: Arctic Centre, University of Groningen, 1981.

Tuck, James A., and Robert Grenier. *Red Bay, Labrador: World Whaling Capital, A.D. 1550–1600*. St. John's, Newfoundland: Atlantic Archaeology, 1989.

Turgeon, Laurier. "Bordeaux and the Newfoundland Trade during the Sixteenth Century." *International Journal of Maritime History* 9, no. 2 (1997): 1–28.

———. "Fluctuations in Cod and Whale Stocks in the North Atlantic during the Eighteenth Century." In *Papers Presented at the Conference Entitled "Marine Resources and Human Societies in the North Atlantic since 1500," October 20–22, 1995*. St. John's, Newfoundland: Institute of Social and Economic Research, Memorial University of Newfoundland, 1997.

———. "French Fishers, Fur Traders, and Amerindians during the Sixteenth Century: History and Archaeology." *William and Mary Quarterly*, 3d ser., 55, no. 4 (1998): 585–610.

Unger, Richard W. "Energy Sources for the Dutch Golden Age: Peat, Wind, and Coal." *Research in Economic History* 9 (1984): 221–53.

U.S. Department of Agriculture, Agricultural Research Service, Nutrient Data Laboratory Home Page. *USDA Nutrient Database for Standard Reference* (Release 13), 1999.

Usner, Daniel H., and Institute of Early American History and Culture. *Indians, Settlers, and Slaves in a Frontier Exchange Economy: The Lower Mississippi Valley before*

1783. Chapel Hill: University of North Carolina Press, for the Institute of Early American History and Culture, Williamsburg, Va., 1992.

Utterstrom, Gustaf. "Climatic Fluctuations and Population Problems in Early Modern History." In *The Ends of the Earth,* edited by Donald Worster. Cambridge: Cambridge University Press, 1988.

van der Knaap, W. O. "De invloed van de landstations op hun directe omgeving; klimaatsverandering in de zeventiende eeuw." In *Walvisvaart in de gouden eeuw: Opgravingen op Spitsbergen,* edited by Louwrens Hacquebord and Wim Vroom, 140–45. Amsterdam: De Bataafsche Leeuw, 1988.

Van der Merwe, P. J., and Roger B. Beck. *The Migrant Farmer in the History of the Cape Colony, 1657–1842.* Athens: Ohio University Press, 1995.

van Dyke, Paul A. "How and Why the Dutch East India Company Became Competitive in Intra-Asian Trade in East Asia in the 1630's." *Itinerario* 21, no. 3 (1997): 41–56.

van Riebeeck, Jan, and Nederlandsche Oost-Indische Compagnie. *Journal.* Cape Town: A. A. Balkema, for the Van Riebeeck Society, 1952.

van Wijngaarden-Bakker, L. H., and J. P. Pals. "Life and Work in Smeerenberg: The Bio-Archaeological Aspects." In *Proceedings of the International Symposium, Early European Exploitation of the Northern Atlantic, 800–1700,* edited by Rijksuniversiteit te Groningen, Noordelijk Centrum, 133–52. Groningen, Netherlands: Arctic Centre, University of Groningen, 1981.

van Zanden, Jan Luiten. "Economic Growth in the Golden Age: The Development of the Economy of Holland, 1500–1650." In *The Dutch Economy in the Golden Age,* edited by Karel Davids and L. Noordegraaf, 5–26. Amsterdam: Nederlandsch Economisch-Historisch Archief, 1993.

Vaporis, Constantine Nomikos. *Breaking Barriers: Travel and the State in Early Modern Japan.* Cambridge: Council on East Asian Studies, Harvard University, 1994.

Varner, John Grier, and Jeannette Johnson Varner. *Dogs of the Conquest.* 1st ed. Norman: University of Oklahoma Press, 1983.

Vaughan, Richard. *The Arctic: A History.* Dover, N.H.: A. Sutton, 1994.

Veale, Elspeth M. *The English Fur Trade in the Later Middle Ages.* Oxford: Clarendon Press, 1966.

Veer, Gerrit de, Charles T. Beke, and Laurens Reinhart Koolemans Beijnen. *The Three Voyages of William Barents to the Arctic Regions (1594, 1595, and 1596).* New York: B. Franklin, 1964.

Vermeer, Eduard B. "Ch'ing Government Concerns with the Exploitation of New Farmland." In *Études thématiques,* edited by Léon Vandermeersch, 3:203–48. Paris: École française d'Extrême-Orient, 1994.

Vermeer, Edward B. "The Mountain Frontier in Late Imperial China: Economic and Social Developments in the Dabashan." *T'oung Pao* 77 (1991): 306–35.

Vibe, Chr. "Animals, Climate, Hunters, and Whalers." In *Proceedings of the International Symposium, Early European Exploitation of the Northern Atlantic, 800–1700,* edited by Rijksuniversiteit te Groningen, Noordelijk Centrum, 203–18. Groningen, Netherlands: Arctic Centre, University of Groningen, 1981.

Vickers, Daniel. "The Price of Fish: A Price Index for Cod, 1505–1892." *Acadiensis* 25, no. 2 (1996): 92–104.

Vickers, Daniel, and the Institute of Early American History and Culture. *Farmers and Fishermen: Two Centuries of Work in Essex County, Massachusetts, 1630–1850.* Chapel Hill: University of North Carolina Press, for the Institute of Early American History and Culture, Williamsburg, Va., 1994.

Viljoen, Russel S. "Disease and Society: VOC Cape Town, Its People, and the Small-pox Epidemics of 1713, 1755, and 1767." *Kleio* 27 (1995): 22–45.

Vincent, Thierry, and Nicolas-Victor Fromentin. *Le "Groënlandais": Trois-mats baleinier des mers polaires: Journal de bord du Capitaine Fromentin.* Luneray: Editions Bertout, 1994.

Voigt, Harald. *Die Nordfriesen auf den Hamburger Wal- und Robbenfängern, 1669–1839, Studien zur Wirtschafts- und Sozialgeschichte Schleswig-Holsteins, Band 11.* Neumünster: K. Wachholtz, 1987.

von Glahn, Richard. *Fountain of Fortune: Money and Monetary Policy in China, 100–1700.* Berkeley and Los Angeles: University of California Press, 1996.

Walker, Brett L. "Matsumae Domain and the Conquest of Ainu Lands: Ecology and Culture in Tokugawa Expansionism, 1593–1799." Ph.D. diss., University of Oregon, 1997.

———. "Reappraising the *Sakoku* Paradigm: The Ezo Trade and the Extension of Tokugawa Political Space into Hokkaido." *Journal of Asian History* 30 (1996): 170–92.

Wang, Risheng, Shaowu Wang, and K. Fraedrich. "An Approach to Reconstruction of Temperature on a Seasonal Basis Using Historical Documents from China." *International Journal of Climatology* 11 (1991): 381–92.

Wang, Shaowu. "Reconstruction of Palaeo-Temperature Series in China from the 1380's to the 1980's." *Warzburger Geographische Arbeiten* 80 (1991): 1–19.

———. "Reconstruction of Temperature Series of North China from 1380's to the 1980's." *Science in China,* ser. B, 34 (1991): 751–59.

Wang, Shaowu, and Risheng Wang. "Seasonal and Annual Temperature Variations since 1470 A.D. in East China." *Acta Meteorological Sinica* 4 (1990): 428–39.

Ward, J. R. "The Profitability of Sugar Planting in the British West Indies, 1650–1834." *Economic History Review* 31, no. 2 (1978): 197–213.

Watanabe, Hitoshi. *The Ainu Ecosystem: Environment and Group Structure.* Edited by the American Ethnological Society. Rev. ed. Seattle: University of Washington Press, 1973.

Watts, David. *The West Indies: Patterns of Development, Culture, and Environmental Change since 1492.* Cambridge: Cambridge University Press, 1987.

Webb, James L. A. *Desert Frontier: Ecological and Economic Change along the Western Sahel, 1600–1850.* Madison: University of Wisconsin Press, 1995.

Wellington, John H. *Southern Africa: A Geographical Study.* Cambridge: Cambridge University Press, 1955.

Wells, Roger A. E. *Wretched Faces: Famine in Wartime England, 1793–1801.* New York: St. Martin's Press, 1988.

Werger, M. J. A. "Tropical Grasslands, Savannas, Woodlands: Natural and Manmade." In *Man's Impact on Vegetation,* edited by W. Holzner, M. J. A. Werger, and Isao Ikushima. Vol. 5 of *Geobotany.* The Hague: Kluwer, 1983.

West, Robert C. "Early Silver Mining in New Spain, 1531–1555." In *In Quest of Mineral*

Wealth: Aboriginal and Colonial Mining and Metallurgy in Spanish America, edited by Alan K. Craig and Robert Cooper West, 119–35. Vol. 33 of *Geoscience and Man.* Baton Rouge: Geoscience Publications, Department of Geography and Anthropology, Louisiana State University, 1994.

Wheatley, Margaret A. "Social and Cultural Impacts of Mercury Pollution on Aboriginal Peoples in Canada." *Water, Air, and Soil Pollution* 97 (1997): 85–90.

White, Adam, Friedrich Martens, Isaac de La Peyrère, and Edward Pellham. *A Collection of Documents on Spitzbergen [sic] and Greenland.* London: Hakluyt Society, 1855.

White, Bruce M. "The Woman Who Married a Beaver: Trade Patterns and Gender Roles in the Ojibwa Fur Trade." *Ethnohistory* 46, no. 1 (1999): 109–47.

White, D. H. "Stocking Rate." In *Managed Grasslands,* edited by R. W. Snaydon, 227–38. Amsterdam: Elsevier, 1987.

White, Richard. *The Roots of Dependency: Subsistence, Environment, and Social Change among the Choctaws, Pawnees, and Navajos.* Lincoln: University of Nebraska Press, 1983.

Whitmore, Thomas M., and B. L. Turner II. "Landscapes of Cultivation in Mesoamerica on the Eve of the Conquest." *Annals of the Association of American Geographers* 82 (1992).

Whitney, Gordon Graham. *From Coastal Wilderness to Fruited Plain: A History of Environmental Change in Temperate North America, 1500 to the Present.* Cambridge: Cambridge University Press, 1994.

Wien, Thomas. "Castor, peaux, et pelleteries dans le commerce canadien des fourrures, 1720–1790." In *"Le Castor Fait Tout": Selected Papers of the Fifth North American Fur Trade Conference, 1985,* edited by Bruce G. Trigger, Toby Morantz, and Louise Dechene, 72–92. Montreal: Lake St. Louis Historical Society, 1987.

Wigley, T. M. L., M. J. Ingram, and G. Farmer. *Climate and History: Studies in Past Climates and Their Impact on Man.* Cambridge: Cambridge University Press, 1981.

Willmoth, Francis. "Dugdale's *History of Imbanking and Drayning:* A 'Royalist' Antiquarian in the Sixteen-Fifties." *Historical Research* 71, no. 176 (1998): 281–306.

Wills, John E., Jr. "The Seventeenth-Century Transformation: Taiwan under the Dutch and the Cheng Regime." In *Taiwan: A New History,* edited by Murray A. Rubinstein, 84–106. Armonk, N.Y.: M. E. Sharpe, 1999.

Wilson, Alexander T. "Isotope Evidence for Past Climatic and Environmental Change." In *Climate and History: Studies in Interdisciplinary History,* edited by Robert I. Rotberg and Theodore K. Rabb, 215–32. Princeton, N.J.: Princeton University Press, 1981.

Wilson, Monica, and Leonard Monteath Thompson. *The Oxford History of South Africa.* Oxford: Clarendon Press, 1969.

Wimmer, Linda. "African Producers, European Merchants, Indigenous Consumers: Brazilian Tobacco in the Canadian Fur Trade, 1550–1821." Ph.D. diss., University of Minnesota, 1996.

Wolf, Eric R. *Europe and the People without History.* Berkeley and Los Angeles: University of California Press, 1982.

Wong, Roy Bin. *China Transformed: Historical Change and the Limits of European Experience.* Ithaca, N.Y.: Cornell University Press, 1997.

Wood, Peter H. "The Changing Population of the Colonial South: An Overview by

Race and Region, 1685–1790." In *Powhatan's Mantle: Indians in the Colonial Southeast*, edited by Gregory A. Waselkov, M. Thomas Hatley, and Peter H. Wood. Lincoln: University of Nebraska Press, 1989.

Woodby, Douglas A., and Daniel B. Botkin. "Stock Sizes Prior to Commercial Whaling." In *The Bowhead Whale*, edited by John J. Burns, J. Jerome Montague, Cleveland J. Cowles, and the Society for Marine Mammalogy, 387–407. Lawrence, Kans.: Society for Marine Mammalogy, 1993.

Woodward, Donald. "Straw, Bracken, and the Wicklow Whale: The Exploitation of Natural Resources in England since 1500." *Past and Present*, no. 159 (1998): 43–76.

Wu, Yu. "Jamaican Trade, 1688–1769: A Quantitative Study." Ph.D. diss., Johns Hopkins University. Ann Arbor: University Microfilms, 1995.

Wursig, Bernd, and Christopher Clark. "Behavior." In *The Bowhead Whale*, edited by John J. Burns, J. Jerome Montague, Cleveland J. Cowles, and the Society for Marine Mammalogy, 157–99. Lawrence, Kans.: Society for Marine Mammalogy, 1993.

Yerbury, J. C. *The Subarctic Indians and the Fur Trade, 1680–1860.* Vancouver: University of British Columbia Press, 1986.

Zahedieh, Nuala. "London and the Colonial Consumer in the Late Seventeenth Century." *Economic History Review* 47, no. 2 (1994): 230–61.

Zantkil, H. J. "Reconstructie van de behuizing op Smeerenburg." In *Walvisvaart in de gouden eeuw: Opgravingen op Spitsbergen*, edited by Louwrens Hacquebord and Wim Vroom, 67–79. Amsterdam: De Bataafsche Leeuw, 1988.

Zeitlin, Judith. "Ranchers and Indians on the Southern Isthmus of Tehuantepec: Economic Change and Indigenous Survival in Colonial Mexico." *Hispanic American Historical Review* 69, no. 1 (1989): 23–60.

Zolitschka, B. "High Resolution Lacustrine Sediments and Their Potential for Palaeoclimatic Reconstruction." In *Climatic Variations and Forcing Mechanisms of the Last 2000 Years*, edited by Philip D. Jones, Raymond S. Bradley, Jean Jouzel, and the North Atlantic Treaty Organization, Scientific Affairs Division, 453–78. Berlin: Springer, 1996.

Zorgdrager, Cornelis Gijsbertsz, and Georg Peter Monath. *Beschreibung des groenlaendischen Wallfischfangs und Fischerey, nebst einer gründlichen Nachricht von dem Bakkeljau- und Stockfischfang bey Terreneuf und einer kurzen Abhandlung von Groenland, Island, Spitsbergen, Nova Zembla, Jan Mayen Eiland, der Strasse Davids u. a.* Nuernberg: G. P. Monath, 1750.

INDEX

Indexer: Ruth Elwell
Cartographer: Bill Nelson
Compositor: Binghamton Valley Composition, LLC
Text: 10/12 Baskerville
Display: Baskerville
Printer and binder: Sheridan Books, Inc.

DATE DUE
